Picasso and Portraiture: Representation and Transformation

Picasso and Portraiture

REPRESENTATION AND TRANSFORMATION

Edited by William Rubin

With essays by

Anne Baldassari, Pierre Daix,

Michael C. FitzGerald, Brigitte Léal,

Marilyn McCully, Robert Rosenblum,

William Rubin, Hélène Seckel, and Kirk Varnedoe

THAMES AND HUDSON

Published on the occasion of the exhibition *Picasso and Portraiture: Representation and Transformation*, organized by William Rubin, Director Emeritus, Department of Painting and Sculpture, The Museum of Modern Art, New York, in collaboration with the Musée Picasso, Paris.

The Museum of Modern Art, New York: April 28–September 17, 1996
Grand Palais, Paris: October 1996–January 1997

This exhibition is sponsored in part by Philip Morris Companies Inc.

An indemnity for the exhibition has been granted by the Federal Council on the Arts and the Humanities.

This publication is made possible by generous grants from the William S. Paley Foundation, Inc., and the Blanchette Hooker Rockefeller Fund, with additional support from Agnes Gund and Daniel Shapiro, and Mrs. Donald B. Straus.

The Luxury Collection of ITT Sheraton is the exclusive hotel sponsor.

EXHIBITION ADVISORY COMMITTEE: Pierre Daix, Claude Picasso, John Richardson

Produced by the Department of Publications
The Museum of Modern Art, New York

British Library Cataloguing-in-Publication Data
A catalogue record of this book is available from the British Library.
ISBN: 0-500-23724-7
Printed and bound in Italy

FRONTISPIECE: Picasso at Golfe-Juan, August or September 1948. Photograph by Ervin Marton. Musée Picasso, Paris. Gift of Sydney and Claude Picasso

* See credits at page 490 for additional notices.

DEDICATION

With great respect and affection, the Trustees of The Museum of Modern Art dedicate this book to their beloved friend and colleague, Elizabeth Bliss Parkinson Cobb. She has served this institution with extraordinary wisdom and imagination for more than six decades, first as a member of its Advisory Committee, then as a Trustee, as its President and Vice Chairman, and now as a Life Trustee. As a founding member and leader of the Museum's International Council, she has actively fostered international cooperation and exchange in the arts. In all of these roles, by eloquent word and example, with wit and spirit, she has encouraged the Museum to think innovatively and courageously about its future while valuing and preserving its outstanding legacy. This distinctive legacy owes much to Eliza Cobb's guidance and devotion over the years, and we are very warmly grateful for her continuing involvement.

Contents

Foreword

Picasso and Portraiture is the fourth exhibition of the artist's work organized by William Rubin, Director Emeritus of The Museum of Modern Art's Department of Painting and Sculpture. Though smaller in scale than the seminal Pablo Picasso: A Retrospective and Picasso and Braque: Pioneering Cubism, it continues Mr. Rubin's study of the myriad aspects of Picasso's protean oeuvre.

Few museums have had as sustained an interest in the study and display of the works of Picasso as The Museum of Modern Art. Alfred H. Barr, Jr., the Museum's founding director, was among the artist's earliest and most prominent supporters, and through his extensive exhibitions and writings helped to establish him as one of this century's most important artists. Barr's interest in Picasso also led to The Museum of Modern Art acquiring over time an astonishing number of the artist's finest works, a collection that now stands at more than 61 paintings, 20 sculptures, 49 drawings, and 329 prints.

Within this context one can only admire the wisdom and cultural perspicacity of the French government, whose treasury sacrificed substantial revenues by accepting from Picasso's heirs, in lieu of death duties, a large and choice part of the artist's enormous collection (including remarkable works by other artists). Prior to the housing of this prize collection in the splendid Hôtel Salé, now home of the Musée Picasso, that museum's founding director, the late Dominique Bozo, collaborated in 1980 with William Rubin on Pablo Picasso: A Retrospective, which remains the most integral and exhaustive exhibition of Picasso's work ever held.

The 1980 retrospective could not have succeeded without a very large number of loans from the holdings of the soon-to-be installed Musée Picasso. The same is also true, at least proportionately, of Picasso and Portraiture. Like the 1980 exhibition, this is a collaborative effort. I want there-fore, first and foremost, to thank the Musée Picasso's present director, the scholar and critic Gérard Regnier, for making this undertaking possible. To Hélène Seckel, chief curator at the Musée Picasso, goes our gratitude for the enormous effort she has put into this renewal of our museums' collaboration. A version of the exhibition will subsequently be displayed in Paris at the Grand Palais, under the auspices of the Musée Picasso.

The cooperation of the Musée Picasso alone would not have made this exhibition possible. Therefore I want to acknowledge and express our gratitude for the support given to us by numerous lenders, public and private. Fore-most among these have been members of Picasso's family and the daughter of his second wife, Jacqueline Roque, all of whom made many major loans. They and the other lenders to the exhibition are listed separately in this vol-ume and thanked individually by Mr. Rubin in his acknowl-edgments. I want, however, to highlight here the cooper-ation and support we received from Mikhail Piotrovski, Director, The State Hermitage Museum, St. Petersburg, and Irina Antonova, Director, The Pushkin State Museum of Fine Arts, Moscow. The important loans they made to the exhibition contributed immensely to the quality of the show and reflect the increasing cooperation that the chang-ing political climate of recent years has made possible.

Finally, I want to thank William Rubin, who served both as curator of the exhibition and editor of this publi-cation, for his extraordinary dedication and commitment to the study of Picasso. His scholarship and insights have contributed greatly to an increased knowledge and appre-ciation of Picasso's work, which continues the scholarly tradition established by Barr over sixty years ago.

GLENN D. LOWRY
Director
The Museum of Modern Art

Preface

In this "century of abstraction," no genre of painting might have been expected to fare worse than the portrait. At first glance, the pictorial requirements for portraying particular individuals would seem more alien to abstractness than are the more generalized pictorial signs needed for landscape or still life. By the first years of the century, the public was finally ready to accept the landscapes of the Impressionists as important art. Some could even tolerate the relatively more abstract landscapes of the Fauve painters. But *portraits* by the latter—though no more radical or daring than other Fauve works—became special targets of anger and scorn.

Ninety years have made a considerable difference. Even as such prominent nineteenth-century genres as history painting and religious art virtually disappeared, the portrait found a new lease on life as the multitudinous styles of modern painting were marshaled to its purposes. To be sure, many of these modernist portrayals did not correspond to received ideas about portraiture. But, as had been the case in the Renaissance and Baroque periods, the genius of painters had redefined the genre.

Leaving largely to photography the role of naturalistic representation, modern painters enlarged upon those aspects of portraiture that had always been present but had been less obviously exploited: the communication of psychological and poetic values, and the ways in which purely pictorial values might be mobilized to support them. These qualities, rather than verisimilitude or resemblance, had always, in fact, distinguished great portraiture; modern painters were destined to make more explicit those subjective aspects of representation that had formerly been implied.

The identity of concerns between the pictorialism of twentieth-century painting and the possibilities of portraiture is reflected in the fact that the two greatest artists of our era, Picasso and Matisse, have been responsible for its greatest portraits. It would be fair to say, however, that the human figure, especially in the guise of a specific individual, played an even greater role in the art of Picasso than in that of Matisse. More than any other artist, Picasso explored the openings for such imagery inherent in modernism.

This exhibition and book are the first that propose to study Picasso's career from the perspective of portraiture. As in past exhibitions I have organized—even those nominally titled retrospectives—I have tried to formulate the project in terms of an aesthetic or historical "problem." Sometimes there are no solutions to such problems, but scholars cannot even begin to try solving them until they can study the actual works. *Picasso and Portraiture* should, therefore, be seen as opening the door—raising the issue, if you will—to a relatively unstudied aspect of Picasso criticism. As fuller studies can only be possible *after* the works are seen in concert, we can only hope that the suggestions we have proffered in this volume will ring true.

Those familiar with Picasso's work—and thus with the central role of the human image within it—will realize that adequate justice to this aspect of his enormous oeuvre could only be done in an exhibition at least twice as large as the one we have been able to undertake (for reasons both of space and expense). Regrettably, it has been necessary, for example, to sacrifice virtually all Picasso's portrait sculpture; impressive as this sculpture is, it is not as crucial to portraiture as are his painting and drawing (and, in purely practical terms, one sculpture absorbs the gallery space of about three pictures). But very hard choices were also necessary with regard to the paintings. If one elected to do full justice to the portraits of individuals whom Picasso painted just once or twice, one would not have been able to show any depth among the portraits of those he painted and drew frequently—in many cases, hundreds of times. Faced with this dilemma, we have chosen to emphasize the multiple portrayals of persons central to his life, with the thought that the very range of these representations would best reveal Picasso's inventiveness and qualities.

WILLIAM RUBIN
Director Emeritus, Department of Painting and Sculpture
The Museum of Modern Art

Notes on Titles and References

Picasso never gave formal titles to his pictures. In exhibitions of his work arranged with his participation, the titles used, like the overwhelming majority of those he provided to the cataloguer of his oeuvre, Christian Zervos, were generic descriptions (*Seated Woman*, *Man Leaning on a Table*, etc.). This was true even in most cases where his pictures were inspired by actual individuals well known to his intimates. For only a small minority of catalogue entries did Picasso communicate a proper name to Zervos. Even less frequently did he describe the portrayal of an identified individual as a "portrait," a term he used very inconsistently. Picasso occasionally improvised (or accepted from friends) studio "handles" to differentiate among his pictures. Some of these hardened into formal titles as they were used in exhibitions and publications.

Since the 1920s, critics, biographers, museum curators, and even collectors have had a hand in inventing or reinventing titles for Picasso's pictures. Some of these have survived; many have not. It is not unusual to find half a dozen variant titles for the same well-known picture in different publications. No attempt has been made to impose a wholly consistent system of titles for the works in this book and exhibition, especially given the preference of many museums for retaining their traditional, often generic, designations.

Many of Picasso's single-figure pictures, busts, and heads were inspired by specific persons whose names did not appear—sometimes for reasons of personal privacy—in Zervos's *catalogue général*. Some of these were identified in Pierre Daix's entries for the *catalogues raisonnés* of 1966 and 1979, which covered Picasso's work through 1916. Most of the titles containing proper names used in this book—especially those in which the name is prefaced by the words "Portrait of"—can be found in similar form in prior publications. They are here given in italics. Where the identity of the subject who inspired a given picture is known but not referred to in the title, we have placed his or her name in roman type in parentheses after the title,

omitting family names, as is common in the Picasso literature, for such figures as Fernande Olivier, Olga Khokhlova, Marie-Thérèse Walter, Dora Maar, Françoise Gilot, and Jacqueline Roque. This parenthetical addition has been omitted for a few highly transformed images where the source of inspiration for Picasso's picture is not clearly demonstrable. On the other hand, the presence of a name in parentheses does not always mean that the picture can automatically be said to portray the person designated, especially in instances where the image is much transformed. It only suggests that documentary evidence, preparatory drawings, or the artist himself have indicated that person as the primary subject.

In the captions, the following abbreviations are given for frequently cited references:

Bloch: Georges Bloch. *Pablo Picasso: Catalogue de l'oeuvre gravé et lithographie, 1904–1969*. 2 vols. Bern: Kornfeld & Klipstein, 1968–71.

D.B.: Pierre Daix and Georges Boudaille, with Joan Rosselet. *Picasso: The Blue and Rose Periods—A Catalogue Raisonné of the Paintings*. Boston: New York Graphic Society, 1966.

Daix: Pierre Daix and Joan Rosselet. *Picasso: The Cubist Years 1907–1916—A Catalogue Raisonné of the Paintings and Related Works*. Boston: New York Graphic Society, 1979.

Geiser/Baer: *Picasso, peintre-graveur*. Vol. 1, by Bernard Geiser (Bern: B. Geiser, 1933). Vol. 2, by Geiser, in collaboration with Alfred Schneidegger (Bern: Kornfeld & Klipstein, 1968). Vols. 3–6, by Brigitte Baer (Bern: Editions Kornfeld, 1985–94). Vol. 7, forthcoming.

Spies: Werner Spies. *Das plastische Werk*. Stuttgart: Verlag Gerd Hatje, 1983.

Zervos: Christian Zervos. *Pablo Picasso*. 33 vols. Paris: Cahiers d'Art, 1932–78.

Picasso mixing paints for *Guernica* in his studio at 7, rue des Grands-Augustins, Paris, spring 1937. Photograph by Dora Maar

Reflections on Picasso and Portraiture

WILLIAM RUBIN

It was as an undergraduate auditing Meyer Schapiro's lectures at Columbia University that I first heard the word "transformation" used as the key to Picasso's way of working; it is the central theme of this exhibition. I want particularly to underline my debt to Schapiro's teachings, since many of his extraordinary insights have not yet found a place in the nonetheless considerable measure of his published writings and will likely survive only through the memories and publications of his friends and students.

In my exhibitions and texts for The Museum of Modern Art, I have had frequent recourse to Schapiro's ideas; and thinking about Picasso's portraiture during the last few years, I have been particularly conscious of the views of this great polymath. It is a subject that, perhaps more than any other I have confronted, demands the multiplicity of approaches, the art-historical inclusiveness, and the deep human sympathy that characterize Schapiro's work. With his teachings as a model, I have tried in the following pages—aided by a number of distinguished colleagues— to provide some insight into the work of the artist who, more than any other twentieth-century painter, has expanded the possibilities and parameters of portraiture.

At the beginning of the twentieth century, the word "portrait" still presupposed a visual parallelism between a thing seen and its image. Viewers presumed that a painted portrait, or at least its preliminary studies, were made "from life." It was assumed that the *raison d'être* of a portrait was to communicate the appearance and personality of the sitter. By redefining the portrait as a record of *the artist's personal responses* to the subject, Picasso transformed it from a purportedly objective document into a frankly subjective one.

Picasso's portraiture casts the very concept of identity into doubt; it is no longer fixed, but mutable. Caught in the flux of the artist's passion for metamorphosis, the images and identities of his real-life subjects continuously dissolve and re-form. Many of these transitory conceptions are not, of course, "portraits" in the received genre sense of the word, though they are clearly portrayals. Is there a difference? Here it is worth reflecting on the etymology of the word "portrait."[1] It was originally a simple synonym for portrayal, so broad as to cover the image of *any* object. Only slowly did its usage narrow to focus primarily on the human body and face. The more it became associated with a particular genre of painting, the more it became overlaid with assumptions and pulled away from the broader sense of "portrayal."

The work of great artists, however, recasts the meaning of terminology by its own force and inventiveness. Already in the nineteenth century, the Post-Impressionists had undermined some traditional assumptions about the portrait. By breaking decisively in his work with the conventional implications of the genre, Picasso reopened the word portrait to something of its original breadth— and then some. Painted mostly from memory, Picasso's portrait subjects were largely imaged not as seen, but as conceptualized, in a variety of figural modes. Picasso invented or reinvented the abstract, surreal, classical, and expressionist portrait types as we know them in twentieth-century art. He did not wholly abandon realism, but ceased to give it a privileged role in the portrait's definition. And he dissociated it from any ineluctable relationship to direct perception. Some of the most abstract of Picasso's portraits were, in fact, made from life and involved repeated sittings by the subject (pp. 17, 285); conversely, others, among his most realistic, were made from memory (p. 16).

Picasso could quite literally draw a variety of contrasting emotions and pictorial inspirations out of a single individual. He did not try to sum up his experience of people he knew well in single portraits. Exploiting the resources of his accumulated language of figuration, he would distribute differing aspects of their personalities— and his own changing feelings toward them—through a whole series of portrayals that often altered dramatically from one image to the next. This exhibition has therefore been constructed primarily around groups of portraits rather than single images, and around images of the persons closest to Picasso.

Even so, Picasso's penchant for transformation sometimes makes it difficult, if not impossible, to draw a clear line between his portrayals of real people and his more generic depictions of the human face and figure. Defining what constitutes a "portrait" in Picasso's work is not a simple matter. One might logically wish to start with the artist's own use of the term. The problem is that he used the word "portrait" only casually in identifying his pictures, often omitting it even where it was obviously applicable. For more than four decades, Picasso cooperated intermittently with the publisher Christian Zervos on the *catalogue général* of his oeuvre, providing identifications for thousands of works ranging from major canvases and sculptures to tiny sketches.[2] There are numerous recognizable portrayals of actual persons in the thirty-three volumes of Zervos's catalogue, but remarkably few of these subjects were identified by name and far fewer were called "portraits." For instance, of the almost two thousand images in the volumes of Zervos covering the years 1904 through 1912 (including supplements), only three canvases and sixteen works on paper were identified as representing Fernande Olivier, the artist's companion of those eight years, and some of those were not called "portraits," despite the fact that we can recognize Fernande's features in more than a hundred other images. One might imagine that formal, seemingly posed portrayals of Fernande would be labeled as portraits, while the more casual sketches might not. But that would be

Portrait of Fernande. 1906. Lead pencil on paper. Zervos VI, 745. Private collection

expecting a consistency alien to Picasso. Thus a sketch of Fernande asleep, from the winter of 1904–05 (opposite, left), is identified as a "portrait," while a large, formally posed brush drawing on canvas of a few months later (opposite, right) is labeled simply "Fernande."[3]

Sometimes Picasso's silence about his subjects' identities was motivated by discretion. From the mid-1920s onward, for example, many of his pictures reflected the features and physiognomy of the young girl Marie-Thérèse Walter, with whom he was conducting a clandestine affair. However, her existence remained a secret from even his closest friends until 1932, when she appeared as an unmistakable presence in a number of works exhibited at the Galerie Georges Petit. Even then she remained a face without a name. Many in the artist's immediate circle discovered her actual identity only after World War II. Not until the 1960s did Picasso confide, primarily to his friends and biographers Pierre Daix and John Richardson, most of the identities missing in Zervos's catalogue. And, even today, some remain a mystery.

When Picasso did employ the term "portrait" to describe his work, he was hopelessly inconsistent. The contradictions and confusions in the *catalogue général* stem, in part, from the fact that the artist hated all titles (as he did all genre terms and art terminology), largely for the same reason that he disliked talking about specific

Fernande Asleep. 1904–05. Lead pencil on paper, 14⅝ × 10⅝″
(37 × 27 cm). Zervos VI, 649, where it is titled *Portrait of Fernande.*
Private collection

Portrait of Fernande. 1906. Oil on canvas, 39⅜ × 31⅞″
(100 × 81 cm). Zervos I, 254, where it is titled *Fernande.*
D.B. XV, 41. Private collection, Boston, Mass.

works: he did not want anything to direct, deflect, or
delimit the viewers' reactions to his pictures, preferring to
let the latter speak for themselves. And though he was, in
fact, responsible for a few titles that had been generated
as studio "handles," his claim never to have titled a work
was substantially true. The determination as to whether
Picasso's images are (or are not) pictures of actual people
thus becomes largely the responsibility of the biographer,
art historian, or curator. In some cases, fortunately, Picasso
named a particular subject; in others, photographic or
written documentation exists, making it possible to identify them. Even where formal transformations have virtually eliminated verisimilitude, it is sometimes possible to
identify Picasso's models by the characteristic signs associated with them, or by a chain of preparatory drawings
leading from a "realistic" to an "abstract" or "distorted"
image.

It may emerge that, after this exhibition, it will be even
harder than before to define what Picasso meant by a
portrait. If so, the artist's ghost will be chuckling, for he
thought of himself very much as a challenger of definitions. To be sure, there are a number of portraits in his
work that would satisfy even the most conventional interpretation of the term. But these represent only a minority
of his images inspired by recognizable individuals. For
such pictures as transcend conventional conceptions of

portraiture, I will use the terms "transformed" or "conceptual" portrait. To be sure, all portraits are transformations insofar as they are, by definition, schematic
representations. But within the world of images themselves, I will reserve "transformed" for those that break
radically with the notion of verisimilitude.

Even within the realm of the "transformed" or "conceptual" portrait there is a considerable range of objectivity and subjectivity. Portraits in Picasso's various Cubist
and classicist modes tend toward objectivity—even in the
case of very abstract works—while the more surreal and
expressionist images are more subjective. From the later
1920s onward, these alternative modes of representation
were often chosen more as a function of Picasso's feeling
at the time he embarked on a picture than of his overall
attitude toward the subject. (However, as we shall see,
some stylistic morphologies tended to be associated with
images of certain individuals.) Just as Picasso might execute a still life in a Neoclassical mode one morning and
return to that same motif in an edgy, pronged, and acidu-
lously colored expressionist mode that afternoon, so too
the style in which he depicted an individual—Marie-
Thérèse Walter or Dora Maar—would vary to a considerable extent with his mood.[4] To that degree, it would not
be far from the truth to consider these pictures "autobiographical" portraits.

Portrait of Jacqueline. 1955. India ink and pencil on paper, 25⅝ × 19¾″ (65 × 50 cm). Zervos XVI, 485. Private collection

Picasso's images of his second wife, Jacqueline Roque, which dominate the last twenty years of his art, constitute the largest single group of his portraits. Throughout Picasso's years with Jacqueline, he executed many fairly realistic pictures of her. A few of these were drawn or painted as she sat for him, mostly during the first year of their relationship. But such posed pictures were rare. The overwhelming majority of Jacqueline's portraits, including some of the most realistic (above), were made from memory. This is true of all the nude Jacquelines (p. 479), none of which were "life studies," as Jacqueline—like Olga Khokhlova before her—never posed nude. She was so much a part of Picasso's daily life, and the painter's visual memory was so acute, that there was no need for her to pose, nude or otherwise.

Some of the Jacquelines are expressionistically distorted, and even more of them are rendered abstractly (and many are both). Those that were pushed furthest will be recognized as images inspired by Jacqueline only by viewers familiar with Picasso's art and with the various artistic conventions he developed to represent her face and impressive carriage (the latter being a feature the painter liked enormously). The most radically transformed of these images shade off into generalized sign structures for "woman" and, hence, become generic.

Can one draw a clear line separating Jacqueline's portrayals from other pictures that may incorporate a few signs or conventions associated with her? When does Picasso's portrayal of any actual person cease to be a portrait? Such questions are, in a sense, unanswerable. Among Picasso's hundreds of portrayals of Jacqueline, ranging along a continuum from extreme realism to extreme transformation, there is no simple divide, no fixed or single point at which an image inspired by her can securely be said to cease being her portrait. The *Seated Woman* of November 1960 (opposite), for example, is one of the most dramatically transformed images of Jacqueline in our exhibition. It might well be argued that such a painting should not be called a portrait. Yet Jacqueline herself recognized it as one, and said of this very picture: *"Ça, c'est moi."*[5]

Such an approach to portraiture implies a fundamental revolution in the idea of likeness. From 1906 onward, Picasso increasingly understood "resemblance" in broad and ultimately almost poetic terms, closer to the wide range of metaphorical possibilities in the French verb *ressembler* (even when used in the vernacular) than to the limits of the English "resemble." Charles Baudelaire, one of the first poets Picasso learned to read in French, could say *"au pays qui te ressemble,"* and the twentieth-century poet Jacques Prévert (a friend of Picasso's) *"une chanson qui nous ressemble"*[6]—usages which cannot be directly rendered in English.

Nor was this broadened sense of "resemblance" limited to poetry. The Symbolist tradition deriving from Baudelaire by way of Stéphane Mallarmé was also influential in freeing French artists from the belief that painting required the literal reproduction of appearances. Daniel-Henry Kahnweiler, Picasso's longtime dealer, cited an 1864 letter in which Mallarmé stated his poetic goal as being "to describe not the thing itself but the effect it produces." Impressionism, as it emerged in the following years, was often seen as a visual counterpart to Mallarmé's poetry: the critic Jules Antoine Castagnary, for instance, defended the Impressionists by explaining that they rendered "not the landscape but the sensation produced by the landscape."[7]

Kahnweiler himself rightly rejected the latter comparison, pointing out that the emotional "sensation" of Mallarmé's poetry was not the same thing as the visual, fundamentally empirical sensation of Impressionist painting.[8] Mallarmé's incantatory poetry was meant to create a new reality, not to reproduce an existing one. Its true pictorial counterpart, Kahnweiler insisted, was Cubism. Indeed, he argued, the Cubists were able "to re-invent conceptual painting" only because of their discovery of Mallarmé's later poems.[9]

Whether or not Picasso was familiar with these particular poems, it is clear that he had absorbed the Symbolist

Seated Woman (Jacqueline). November 27, 1960. Oil on canvas, 39⅜ × 31¾″ (100 × 80.5 cm). Zervos XIX, 403. Museum of Modern Art, Toyama, Japan emphasis on expression rather than representation. Summarizing a fall 1910 interview with the artist, the critic Marius de Zayas wrote that "Picasso tries to produce with his work an impression, not with the subject but the manner in which he expresses it . . . [He believes] that the picture should be the pictorial equivalent of the emotion produced by [the subject]."[10]

This Symbolist ideal of nonliteral, expressive representation was more acceptable when applied to subjects such as landscapes and still lifes, however, than to the representation of the human figure. By 1905, Monet's once rejected, highly colored landscapes were widely acclaimed as masterpieces, but Matisse's *Portrait of Madame Matisse/ The Green Line* (p. 140, top left) could still cause a scandal at that year's Salon d'Automne. In portraiture, above all, realistic likeness was still considered a *sine qua non*. One year later, in the summer of 1906, Picasso's portraits moved into uncharted post-Symbolist territory.

The modernist revolution in the nature of portraiture required a fundamental shift in what some historians have called the "portrait situation," which had remained fairly stable from the Renaissance up to modern times. Most Old Master portraits were ordered, paid for, and possessed by their subjects or their families; the others were largely institutional commissions. As the purchasers were usually people of considerable wealth and high social status, there existed from the outset a psychosocial as well as literal distance between most portraitists and their sitters. (Because of their own renown, Leonardo, Titian, Rubens, Velázquez, and a few other great masters constituted exceptions—though only partial ones—to this rule.) This distance tended to diminish dialogue and intimacy and encouraged the painter to concentrate on externals: facial features, costumes, and accessories symbolizing the sitter's formal place in the world. Generally, the portraitist was expected to strive for verisimilitude, tempered only by the need to make the sitter look as attractive as possible.

Nonetheless, the finest portrait painters managed to make great paintings. But these omnipresent preconditions no doubt contributed to the fact that portraiture, in anything less than outstanding hands, was usually the most boring of Old Master genres (as art-sensitive visitors to the "stately homes" will readily attest). The invention of photography had set the stage for unshackling portraiture. By the second half of the nineteenth century, most of the strictly memorializing purposes to which portraitists had formerly bent themselves could be satisfied by photographers. As Picasso (who loved photographs and was himself an avid photographer) argued, the rapid spread of this medium should be considered an important liberating factor for modern art.[11]

The rise of photographic portraiture coincided with other major changes in the nature of patronage—at least, for modern artists—particularly the loss of institutional patrons such as church and state. In their place arose a new art-dealer system, simultaneously liberating and perilous, that largely displaced direct dealings between the executors of portraits and their commissioners, whether private or institutional. As a result of the existence of this relatively new personage, situated between the artist and the final purchaser, the portrait became—except for painters lacking dealers, or for hacks—rather more a matter of choice than of command. And, despite the increasing abstractness of modern painting, portraiture took on an unexpected new kind of life by the dawn of the twentieth century—even as such major genres as history painting and religious art faded from the scene.

In the work of the first generations of modernists, sitters were drawn almost exclusively from among the friends and families of the painters. The artist was now the social equal of his or her subject. Furthermore, the two were linked by personal, often complex psychological relations and sometimes sexual ones. Not surprisingly, this led to significant change in the nature of portraiture. Psychological content became more evident, more intense, and sometimes—by the first decades of the twentieth century—manifestly invasive.

Psychological interests also led vanguard artists toward alternative conventions for the imaging of the human figure. Gauguin had borrowed conceptual elements from the art of other cultures; van Gogh, who, like his French colleague used color in an affective, antinaturalistic Symbolist manner, had introduced expressionism into portraiture (though he carefully balanced its effects through his gift for decorative drawing and coloring). This broad tendency toward a conceptual type of image was further reinforced by the Douanier Rousseau, whose portraits fed as directly into Picasso's 1908 primitivist Cubism as Cézanne's did to the Cubism of the succeeding years.

Gauguin's, van Gogh's, and Rousseau's tentative explorations of what might be called the conceptual portrait never broke, however, with nineteenth-century definitions of modern painting. Even these great pioneers remained faithful to the traditional assumption that the portrait image should be made "from" or "before" a sitter (or, at least, based on drawings made from life). Despite their addition of conceptual motifs, they remained committed to a fundamentally perceptual transcription of their sitters' appearance.

As we shall see, Picasso broke decisively with this perceptual mode of portraiture in summer 1906, initiating, during the following year's long preparation for *Les Demoiselles d'Avignon,* what I have called the transformed or conceptual portrait. This eventually took many forms: the highly abstract primitivist and Cubist portraits, the more realistic Neoclassical portrait, the fantastical, Surrealist portrait, and the unnaturally "distorted" Expressionist portrait. Picasso's work, as well as that of the countless painters he influenced, offers a host of extrapolations, conflations, and spin-offs from each of these transformative modes. It would be absurd to suggest that Picasso was the initiator of *all* the modes of twentieth-century portraiture. But Matisse apart, the most significant alternatives to his example—such as the Expressionist portraits of Oskar Kokoschka and Chaim Soutine—were extensions of such nineteenth-century models as the portraits of Vincent van Gogh and Edvard Munch and were much less radical in their transformations than those Picasso introduced in 1907. However important their place in the history of portraiture, those painters stand somewhat apart from the decisive innovations of twentieth-century art.

The emergence of the transformed portrait subverted almost all of the assumptions on which the traditional portrait commission had been based. Even if a patron found the artist willing to undertake such a commission, there was no longer any assumption that the resulting portrait would reflect the self-image desired by the sitter. Despite this risk, the wish to have their features recorded by vanguard artists of their time led a certain number of twentieth-century patrons to press forward with portrait commissions. Often, they were met with simple refusals, as many of those artists still interested in portraiture preferred to choose their own subjects. Nevertheless, even the most advanced of modern artists were sometimes pressured by their dealers (or by others with some kind of leverage) to paint portraits of people they did not know or care for.

While this happened only rarely to Picasso and Matisse, the results of such commissions illuminate the changed conditions of twentieth-century portraiture. In both cases, the artist found himself almost constitutionally unable to carry out the task. Matisse's projected oil portrait of Dorothy Paley went unexecuted after sittings that produced numerous drawings.[12] Picasso's portrait of Helena Rubinstein shared the same fate, and the struggle between sitter and artist, in this instance, reveals a good deal about the psychological dynamics of Picasso's approach to portraiture.

"I cannot make a portrait of just any person," Picasso remarked.[13] His choice of subjects, over the years, defies rational attempts at analysis. Some people who knew Picasso very well—such as his friend and biographer Roland Penrose—were never drawn, let alone painted, by him. On the other hand, he did numerous portrait drawings and a small number of painted portraits (mostly early) of individuals who knew him only slightly. The motivations for the making of these portraits varied, but the impetus almost always came from Picasso.

Helena Rubinstein—cosmetics magnate, collector of tribal art, and *grande dame*—was not a member of Picasso's circle and would not in the normal course of events have been a candidate for one of his portraits. However, she deeply wanted to be painted by him and campaigned for years to this end (p. 99, bottom left). In the summer of 1955, she thought she had succeeded, telling her confidential clerk and (later) biographer, "Picasso has finally agreed to paint me."[14] Having done an important favor for Marie Cuttoli, a friend of the artist and an important collector of his work, Rubinstein persuaded Cuttoli to plead her case. Picasso grudgingly consented. (Madame Rubinstein believed wrongly that Picasso "owed" a favor to Cuttoli because "they were once sweethearts": hence her apparent success in persuading him.[15])

It is not clear whether Picasso's agreement to paint Madame Rubinstein was entirely in bad faith. He clearly was not eager to paint "that Rubinstein woman."[16] Nonetheless, he may have reflected, stranger things had happened. Her willful intrusion would, at least, be used to generate a bit of entertainment. This began with Picasso's Kafkaesque game of letting her cool her heels in Cannes for days on end. When she and her amanuensis telephoned the villa, they got through only to anonymous intermediaries saying that the artist was "at work," "sleeping," or "absent." (These intermediaries often identified themselves as gardeners; actually, Madame Rubinstein claimed, they were Picasso himself.) Picasso may well have been busy with another project, and when he was pursuing an idea in his work, he stopped to see no one. But his handling of Rubinstein was more likely a variation of his occasional (mis)treatment of visitors who needed, in his opinion, to be taken down a peg. Those subjected to this treatment were usually over-eager or importunate acquaintances, art professionals, *collectionneurs* (pronounced with an extra-heavy rolling of the "*r*"), or—worse yet—art dealers. Exploiters all, Picasso sometimes felt.

Madame Rubinstein finally showed up, unannounced, on August 15, 1955, and was admitted for an early evening sitting; she was invited back for another sitting the following night. The first night, Picasso began by making a serious effort. A few of the seven drawings he did of her the first evening are among his better ones of that year. The artist started with a not unsympathetic profile sketch (p. 20, top center). By the third drawing he had warmed up and secured a good fix on Madame's features. By the fifth, he was convincingly communicating something of her face's character. The seventh and last drawing of the evening showed Picasso's attitude toward Madame Rubinstein hardening, as he found what looks almost like a man's profile within her full face (p. 21, top right).

By the following day, Picasso could see nothing but

Helena Rubinstein. c. 1930s. Photographer unknown. Musée Picasso, Paris, Picasso Archives

Study for a Portrait of Helena Rubinstein (I). August 15, 1955. Lead pencil on paper, 10⅝ × 8¼″ (27 × 21 cm). Zervos XVI, 405. Private collection

Study for a Portrait of Helena Rubinstein (II). August 15, 1955. Lead pencil on paper, 10⅝ × 8¼″ (27 × 21 cm). Zervos XVI, 406. Private collection

Study for a Portrait of Helena Rubinstein (I). August 16, 1955. Lead pencil on paper, 17⁵⁄₁₆ × 12⅝″ (44 × 32 cm). Zervos XVI, 413. Himeji City Museum of Art, Japan

Study for a Portrait of Helena Rubinstein (II). August 16, 1955. Lead pencil on paper, 17⁵⁄₁₆ × 12⅝″ (44 × 32 cm). Zervos XVI, 412. Himeji City Museum of Art, Japan

Study for a Portrait of Helena Rubinstein (V). August 16, 1955. Lead pencil on paper, 17⁵⁄₁₆ × 12⅝″ (44 × 32 cm). Zervos XVI, 416. Himeji City Museum of Art, Japan

Rubinstein's elaborate costume and imposing jewels[17] ("under an opera cloak quilted in shades of orange and lemon with calla lilies and sprigs of mimosa, Madame wore a medieval tunic of acid green velvet"[18]). The first drawing that evening, a half-length "portrait," omitted her head; the next closed in on her bracelets and ring. From then on it was all downhill as Picasso's anger at this "portrait situation" was increasingly projected into his conception of the subject's visage. That night's sitting ended with a fine but furious conté-crayon drawing (above, right).

Rubinstein's final sitting took place more than three months later, on November 27, and the nineteen drawings Picasso made of her that day need no commentary, though they give a clue as to what he meant when he told Roland Penrose that all good portraitists were something of caricaturists. The thirteenth of the series (opposite) shows Picasso half-consciously assimilating Rubinstein to a portrait type familiar in Japanese prints of grimacing actors.[19] The next shows him paying homage to Matisse's featureless portraits of Father Couturier.[20] (If the inspira-

Study for a Portrait of Helena Rubinstein (III).
August 15, 1955. Lead pencil on paper,
10⅝ × 8¼″ (27 × 21 cm). Zervos XVI, 407.
Private collection

Study for a Portrait of Helena Rubinstein (V).
August 15, 1955. Lead pencil on paper,
10⅝ × 8¼″ (27 × 21 cm). Zervos XVI, 409.
Private collection

Study for a Portrait of Helena Rubinstein (VII).
August 15, 1955. Lead pencil on paper,
10⅝ × 8¼″ (27 × 21 cm). Zervos XVI, 410.
Private collection

Study for a Portrait of Helena Rubinstein (XIII).
November 27, 1955. Conté crayon on paper,
17⁵⁄₁₆ × 12⅝″ (44 × 32 cm). Zervos XVI, 516.
Himeji City Museum of Art, Japan

Study for a Portrait of Helena Rubinstein (XIV).
November 27, 1955. Conté crayon on paper,
17⁵⁄₁₆ × 12⅝″ (44 × 32 cm). Zervos XVI, 517.
Himeji City Museum of Art, Japan

Study for a Portrait of Helena Rubinstein (XVIII).
November 27, 1955. Conté crayon on paper,
17⁵⁄₁₆ × 12⅝″ (44 × 32 cm). Zervos XVI, 521.
Himeji City Museum of Art, Japan

tion for Matisse was the ineffable, that of Picasso was
closer to the unspeakable, but the result, in both cases,
was the effacement of the subject's facial features.) The
much reworked penultimate sketch is very revealing: by
adding an inner contour, which had nothing to do with
Madame Rubinstein's actual chin, and slightly reworking
the hair and the eyes, Picasso found himself staring at
nothing less than a suggestion of his own angry countenance (immediately above, right).[21]

"The painter always paints himself," Picasso said to me

once, citing Leonardo da Vinci. In the case of Picasso's
Helena Rubinstein portrait, this was literally the case:
he had transformed her face into an image of his own
features. But Picasso clearly meant Leonardo's remark
in a broader, less literal way, as if to say, "whatever a
painter's subject, he is painting his own feelings and experience." And since Picasso's portrayals of people he knew
were virtually all made for his own personal understanding and satisfaction rather than for that of his subjects or
for any collective "public," it little mattered if an image of

Bust of a Sailor (study for *Les Demoiselles d'Avignon*). Early 1907. Oil on canvas, 15¾ × 16½″ (40 × 41.9 cm). Zervos II¹, 6. Daix 13. Galerie Jan Krugier, Geneva

one person began looking like someone else, or both, or several people.

The figures in Picasso's pictures were often extensions of his own persona, or were invested with literal and/or symbolic references to members of his different entourages. These fluctuant identities were not usually conceived in advance, but emerged by association, as it were, in the process of painting. It was as if Picasso's hand revealed to him the protagonists of his pictures. Such

identities were precarious, sometimes investing his figures only fleetingly, and in narrative scenes they could be iconographically contradictory. The telling visual resemblance or symbolic attribute might disappear; the figure could metamorphose into someone else or be conflated with other identities. Such iconographic inconstancy was not limited to the figures in Picasso's narrative compositions but could pervade even projects begun deliberately as portraits. Alternatively, single figures undertaken with

WILLIAM RUBIN

Portrait of Max Jacob. Early 1907. Gouache on paper mounted on cardboard, 24⅜ × 18⅝″ (62 × 47.5 cm). Zervos II¹, 9. Daix 48. Museum Ludwig, Collection Ludwig, Cologne

generic intentions might be transformed into likenesses of particular individuals as work on them progressed.

The transient and uncertain manner in which images of particular individuals inhabit Picasso's work is most evident in studies for large "narrative" pictures such as *Les Demoiselles d'Avignon,* and in prints that passed through many states. For example, about halfway through the preparatory studies for the *Demoiselles,* the Sailor begins to resemble Max Jacob. Like his counterpart, the Medical

Student, the Sailor had begun as a fairly recognizable self-image of the painter. But Picasso was led radically to change the character of the Sailor into a more passive, timid figure (opposite). This happened at about the time (early 1907) that he executed the most important of his portraits of Jacob, who was shown wearing a sailor's jacket (above). While the new personality of the Sailor cannot simply be equated with that of Picasso's then closest friend, the affinities between the studies of the Sailor's

Raphael and La Fornarina II. September 8, 1968. Etching, 5¹³⁄₁₆ × 8¼″ (14.8 × 20.9 cm). Geiser/Baer VI, 1814. Private collection

head and the *Portrait of Max Jacob* oblige our consideration of the poet as a protagonist in the changing drama of the picture's iconography.[22]

Six decades later, Picasso conscripted his friend the printmaker Piero Crommelynck to play a not unrelated stand-in role in a series of drawings and etchings devoted to the theme of Raphael and La Fornarina (above). Picasso had humorously revised Ingres' composition to equate painting and lovemaking. In a September 1968 etching, Piero is seen entering from a door on our left, drawing back a curtain to reveal the scene to the viewer—a gesture closely resembling that of the voyeuristic Medical Student in the studies for *Les Demoiselles d'Avignon*. The Student, in these early studies, had derived directly from a 1907 self-portrait by Picasso.[23] Piero, in the 1968 print, is thus an alter ego for the artist. Picasso, who was eighty-seven in 1968, represents himself a second time (disguised as "Michelangelo") as a hairy and jealous-looking monster peeking out from under the bed, in impotent rage.

As a portrait subject for Picasso (pp. 26, 27), Piero, who with his brother, Aldo, pulled Picasso's prints during the last decade of his life,[24] was at the opposite end of the spectrum from Helena Rubinstein. Picasso was particularly drawn to him as a subject; the portraits of Piero on canvas and paper (many uncatalogued, some unpublished)

together outnumber those of such very close friends as Guillaume Apollinaire, Max Jacob, and Jaime Sabartés. Indeed, they outnumber those of anyone outside the artist's various family circles. This is probably because Piero reminded Picasso of his own father, don José, who frequently sat for his son's portraits and of whom the young Picasso had been extremely fond.[25] To be sure, Picasso has been cited as saying that, when he worked, "[every] man is don José, and will be all my life."[26] But it is clear that some men were more don José than others and, by extension, were symbols of Picasso himself. In Piero's case there was a certain resemblance: both he and don José were very tall and thin, with long faces terminating in short beards (though Piero's was and is a goatee, which gives him a touch of the satyr absent in don José[27]). While Piero did not have don José's red hair, Picasso on occasion endowed him with it. Like don José, Piero was an artist and a professional—and devoted to Picasso's art.

In a 1971 etching of Piero arriving *chez* Picasso (opposite), he serves again as the artist's stand-in. Once more the substitute protagonist arrives through a door on the left, carrying a print portfolio, which replaces the book held by the Medical Student. Piero is greeted by his beautiful wife and attractive young daughter in a scene that probably recalled Picasso's memories of the spring of

Piero Crommelynck Arrives at Picasso's Studio, Greeted by His Wife, Daughter, and Kabul. March 7, 1971. Etching, 5⅞ × 8¼″ (15 × 21 cm). Baer VII, 1932. Private collection

Piero as Painter Drawing His Model at the Maison Tellier. 1970. Etching, 20⅟₁₆ × 25³⁄₁₆″ (51 × 64 cm). Baer VII, 1876. Private collection

Portrait of Piero Crommelynck. September 21, 1966. Charcoal on paper, 23¹³⁄₁₆ × 19½″ (60.5 × 49.5 cm). Not in Zervos. Private collection

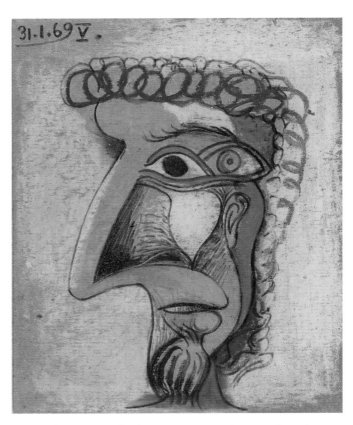

Portrait of Piero Crommelynck. January 31, 1969. Crayon and pastel on cardboard, 6¹⁄₁₆ × 4⅞″ (15.4 × 12.4 cm). Not in Zervos. Private collection

Piero Crommelynck, Nôtre-Dame-de-Vie, Mougins, September 25, 1966. Detail of a photograph by Jacqueline Picasso

1907, when the *Demoiselles* was being developed.[28] In those days he was being greeted in the Bateau-Lavoir by Fernande and their pretty adopted daughter Raymonde, who, like Piero's daughter, had blond bangs and was about thirteen—on the verge of puberty.[29] In the 1971 etching, Kabul leaps up to Piero just as Picasso's dog Fricka leaped toward the Medical Student in an early study for the *Demoiselles*.[30] Finally we note that although Piero's wife, Landa, is shown in a dress she actually wore, the attention given to her nipples, her open mouth, long eyelashes, and exaggerated coiffure endow her here with something of the air of a whorehouse madam, which tends to thrust the image, by dint of association, back into the bordello world of the *Demoiselles,* indeed, the setting of choice for Picasso's late prints (p. 25, bottom).

It was rare for Picasso simply to paint the image of the person in front of him: his view of his subjects was almost invariably filtered through a rich web of personal and artistic associations which found visual expression in the transformations of his subject. Throughout his life, Picasso chose as muses women who coincided to some extent with preexisting mental images. Sometimes these were images he had carried about since childhood; just as often, they were images he had formed from his experi-

Portrait of Piero Crommelynck. September 21, 1966. Engraving on linoleum, 25³⁄₁₆ × 20⁷⁄₈″ (64 × 53 cm). Geiser/Baer VI, 1849. Private collection

Portrait of Piero Crommelynck. September 23, 1966. Aquatint, 22¹⁄₄ × 15¹⁄₂″ (56.4 × 39.2 cm). Geiser/Baer VI, 1400. Private collection

Portrait of Piero Crommelynck. September 28, 1968. Pastel and ink on cardboard, 11⁵⁄₈ × 8¹¹⁄₁₆″ (29.5 × 22 cm). Not in Zervos. Private collection

ence of other artists' paintings. If Olga was the "inspiration" for many of his paintings of 1917–19, she often had to share that role then with Ingres, just as Jacqueline would later share her star billing with female figures in the paintings of Delacroix (p. 456) and Velázquez (p. 459, bottom). These women's images, furthermore, were occasionally "contaminated" with Picasso's fleeting recollections of other women (or even men).

To be sure, this phenomenon of psychological projection is an essential element in all human and artistic experience. But it had not hitherto found expression as such in the visual arts. Picasso's transformed portraits open up a realm of psychological experience which had always been foreclosed by traditional portraiture's insistence on fidelity to perceptual experience. This shift from perceptual to conceptual image-making is usually identified with the invention of Cubism in 1908–14. However, the evidence of Picasso's portrait studies indicates that the real breakthrough (for once this tired word is warranted) occurred in the Spanish village of Gosol, in the summer of 1906. It was a function, in effect, of Picasso's search for a schematic type of sculptural drawing. Surprisingly, he seems to have been more strongly influenced, at this juncture, by the masklike simplifications of features in certain ancient Iberian sculptures than by any of his modernist forerunners.

Josep Fontdevila. 1906. India ink on paper, 18⅞ × 12⅜"
(48 × 31.5 cm). Not in Zervos. Private collection

imagine him both forward and backward in time: as he would be and would have been. One drawing proposes something close to a "death mask" of Fontdevila's face after his demise (below, right); another sketch shows him as a man perhaps thirty years younger (below, left). This is the first of many drawn portraits, done throughout his career, in which Picasso envisioned his subject's appearance at different ages (p. 100). Picasso may have seen drawings by Leonardo in which the Florentine master played with similar transformations (p. 94, left), but this practice probably had its roots in Picasso's obsession with mortality.[32]

Along with recollections of the abstract and effigy-like faces of many of the ancient Iberian sculptures Picasso had seen at the Louvre in the spring of 1906,[33] Fontdevila's "death mask" provided a crucial model for the increasingly masklike faces the artist executed that summer, such as that of Fernande in the full-figure standing nude with clasped hands (p. 261). When Picasso returned to Paris, he used the twin models of Iberian sculpture and the Fontdevila "mask" as inspirations for the heads in two pictures that he had begun earlier: a stunningly beautiful portrayal of Fernande as a *Woman Plaiting Her Hair* (p. 265) —summing up in one canvas Picasso's transition from lyrical softness to a harder, more sculptural precision of form—and the celebrated *Portrait of Gertrude Stein* (p. 267).

Picasso had labored over Stein's portrait for many months before departing for Gosol in May 1906. In the course of eighty or ninety sittings, he arrived at a satisfactory rendering of her hands and body, but he remained dissatisfied with the depiction of her face, and painted it out before leaving Paris. Shortly after his return from Gosol, he repainted Stein's face, without asking for any

At Gosol, Picasso became fascinated—not to say obsessed—with the figure of Josep Fontdevila, a retired smuggler, some ninety years old, whose family kept the inn at this remote mountain village where Picasso and Fernande spent most of the summer. Fontdevila, whom Fernande described as "a fearsome old man of a strange and savage beauty,"[31] was very taken with Picasso and delighted in regaling him with tales of his adventures. Fernande mentions that Picasso had made a drawing of Fontdevila that was *"très ressemblant."* Actually, he made quite a number of them, as well as a moving oil portrait (opposite). In all of these we see Fontdevila's strongly etched features, characterized by his high and accentuated cheekbones. Some drawings, which show Picasso impressed by Fontdevila's body, still lean and strong despite his age (above), seem like presentiments of the aged Picasso.

Picasso was so fascinated with this old man's personality and appearance that he was led to

Josep Fontdevila. 1906. Pencil on lined paper, 8¼ × 5⅛" (21 × 13 cm). Zervos XXII, 453. Musée Picasso, Paris

"Death-Mask" of Josep Fontdevila. 1906. India ink on paper, 12⅜ × 9⅝" (31.5 × 24.3 cm). Zervos VI, 765. Musée Picasso, Paris

Head of a Catalan Peasant (Josep Fontdevila). 1906. Oil on canvas, 17¾ × 15⅞″
(45.1 × 40.3 cm). Zervos VI, 769. D.B. XV, 53. The Metropolitan Museum of Art,
New York. Anonymous gift, 1992

sittings. His new, conceptual understanding of resemblance had made further perceptual "input" superfluous.

The *Portrait of Gertrude Stein* raises another critical question: to what extent does our response to Picasso's portraits depend on our knowledge of the sitters' identities? It could well be argued that the quality and character of the *Portrait of Gertrude Stein* would be the same even if Miss Stein had never existed and the picture at the Metropolitan Museum of Art were merely a generic portrait. But in practice one's experience of the Stein portrait is colored by numerous historical, literary, and biographical associations inseparable from its subject. Even if formal structure is the primary stimulus shaping our response to a picture, additional knowledge inevitably conditions—and, with luck, enriches—our experience of it.

Picasso's Gosol breakthrough, the completion of the portrait of Fernande braiding her hair, and the contemporaneous reworking of the Stein portrait opened the door, methodologically speaking, to the more radical inventions that were to follow. Had Picasso died in 1905, he would be remembered today as a fine late Symbolist painter (author of *The Family of Saltimbanques*) who drew the curtain on the nineteenth century at the very time that Matisse and the Fauves seemed to be opening it on the twentieth.[34] It was the revolutionary equation between representation and transformation first glimpsed in these 1906 portraits—a transformation made possible through conceptualization—that took Picasso beyond Symbolism and established him, ultimately, as the dominant historical figure of twentieth-century art.

The transformation of Gertrude Stein's and Fernande's faces remained, as it were, latent in the portraits of them that Picasso finished in autumn 1906. In contrast, the theme of transformation becomes explicit in his summer 1907 studies for a portrait of André Salmon, the poet, novelist, and critic who, with Max Jacob and Guillaume Apollinaire, formed the nucleus of what Fernande called *"la bande Picasso."* Insofar as Salmon—more than any other of Picasso's close friends—was both a connoisseur of Oceanic and African art and one of the (rare) admirers of *Les Demoiselles d'Avignon,* he steps to the forefront of the painter's world at that moment. Picasso's portrait was intended to take the form, not of a painting, but of a wooden sculpture, acknowledging Salmon's role as a champion of the *"enchanteurs Océaniens et Africains"* whom Salmon would later evoke in his publications on the artist.

Portrait of André Salmon. 1907. Charcoal on paper, 23⅝ × 15¾″ (60 × 40 cm). Not in Zervos. Private collection, Paris

Studies for Portrait of André Salmon (detail). 1907. Ink on paper, 12⅞ × 15¾″ (32.5 × 40 cm). Zervos XXVI, 180 (detail of verso, Zervos XXVI, 179). Private collection

Studies for Portrait of André Salmon. 1907. Ink on paper, 12¾ × 15¾″ (32.5 × 40 cm). Zervos XXVI, 179. Private collection

Study for Wood Sculpture of André Salmon. 1907. Charcoal on paper, 24¾ × 18¾″ (63 × 47.5 cm). Zervos VI, 967. Musée Picasso, Paris

Study for Wood Sculpture of André Salmon (final state). 1907. Charcoal and India ink on paper, 24¾ × 18⅞″ (63 × 48 cm). Zervos XXVI, 284. Private collection

The large, somewhat caricatural portrait drawing of Salmon (opposite, top left) shows him holding a book as well as a pipe (to which extent, he too becomes a kind of distanced stand-in for the Medical Student in the *Demoiselles*); his head is turned in three-quarter view, better to expose his long nose and prominent jaw. The next sheet of studies (opposite, bottom), inscribed *nota bene* very unusually in Picasso's own hand as *Portrai[t]s d'André Salmon*, subjects the poet's head to a series of fantastical transformations. Some of these, in which the hatched shading of the first drawing becomes a fishbone pattern reminiscent of "primitive" scarification marks, show Picasso looking at tribal sculpture out of the corner of his eye. The wave in Salmon's hair is simplified into a jutting crest which, given the elongation of both the cranium and the face, suggests Egyptian Pharaonic sculpture of the Akhenaton era. This crest would drop down, as Picasso proceeded, to become a jutting brow.

Adam Gopnik has aptly described these particular studies as "the art-historical equivalent of the intermediate fossil, which is the dream and despair of the paleontologist," wherein Salmon's likeness is "caught forever in transition from caricature to primitivised image, caught in transit between *Charivari* and the Congo."[35] The stylistic transformation of Salmon's effigy complements the medium—wooden sculpture—as an explicit reference to his role as a champion of tribal sculpture. Transformation no longer plays a hidden role but has been explicitly mobilized for its metaphorical potential.

André Salmon (detail). 1922 or earlier. Photographer unknown

The penultimate and final studies for the projected wood carving (above, left and right) suggest that Picasso's mind had again begun to dwell on the old outlaw Fontdevila, whose protruding cheekbones and aged body have been melded in these to Salmon's lantern jaw and generous nose. The sculpture (never finally executed)[36] would have represented, had it followed its definitive study, a conflation of Picasso's two friends, and, in effect, is a summary of the conceptual revolution which had taken place in Picasso's work between summer 1906 and summer 1907.[37]

Paul Cézanne. *Portrait of Ambroise Vollard* (detail). 1899. Oil on canvas, 39½ × 32″ (100.3 × 81.3 cm).
Venturi 696. Musées de la Ville de Paris, Petit Palais

Picasso's work of the period 1907–14 is characterized by a shift from a narrative to an iconic mode of presentation, a shift which tended to result in the suppression of individual identities. As I have discussed elsewhere,[38] in the winter of 1908–09, Picasso was elaborating a large allegorical canvas (on the model of his 1905 *Saltimbanques*) called *Carnival at the Bistro,* which included representations of himself (as Harlequin) and Fernande, along with symbolic portraits of Cézanne and the Douanier Rousseau; but the final form of this canvas was the still life, *Bread and Fruit-dish on a Table,* in which Picasso had reworked the shapes of the *Bistro* figures, directly adopting their contours to those of the still-life objects. Not only individual identity, but human form itself, was suppressed in the transformed composition, save for the provocative vestiges of legs under the table.

While there are numerous portrayals of Fernande in the period 1909 through early 1911, she is treated in these pictures more as an impersonal object or "motif" than as a portrait subject, as Pierre Daix argues (p. 276). It is thus doubly surprising to find that the advent of high Analytic Cubism is marked by the execution of three of Picasso's greatest portraits: those of Wilhelm Uhde (p. 281), Ambroise Vollard (p. 283), and Daniel-Henry Kahnweiler (p. 285). We are surprised, first of all, that Picasso should turn to portraiture at a moment when his style seemed, at least superficially, to be approaching pure abstraction. It is also surprising that Picasso's portrait subjects of this period should all be men.

In the earliest stages of his career, Picasso's portraiture was, in fact, dominated by men rather than women. He drew his father far more frequently than his mother, and his formative years in Barcelona yielded a rich crop of drawings of his artistic and literary compatriots. However, throughout the rest of his career, portraits of the women in his life (and of his children) considerably out-number his portraits of men. His Cubist portraits—the three 1910 pictures, along with the 1909 portraits of the

Portrait of Ambroise Vollard (detail). 1910. Oil on canvas, 36¼ × 25⅝″ (92 × 65 cm). Zervos II², 214. Daix 337. Pushkin State Museum of Fine Arts, Moscow. (Colorplate of whole, p. 283)

dealer Clovis Sagot and the painter Manuel Pallarés (pp. 254, 273)—are thus something of an anomaly.

Picasso's emphasis on the male portrait may have been a function of the relatively impersonal, conceptual, and speculative character of Cubist painting itself—qualities which Picasso, given his late-nineteenth-century Spanish upbringing, probably associated with maleness. It may also be significant that his primary artistic dialogue during those years was with a male painter, Georges Braque (although he never painted an actual portrait of Braque).[39] In contrast, the artists with whom he was most closely involved later in his career were both women: his companions Dora Maar and Françoise Gilot.

That the sitters for all three 1910 portraits (and one of the two from 1909) were Picasso's art dealers has not, I believe, been sufficiently discussed. The motivations here seem to have had a particular significance beyond that of simply pleasing individuals who were important to Picasso's financial well-being.[40] The 1910 portraits coin-

cided with a moment in the artist's career when, as a result of the radicality of his thinking, the thread connecting his pictures to the visual world seems nearest to breaking. In order to test just how abstract he could be and still communicate an individualized subject, Picasso needed sharply etched, salient models, who would not disappear into types and generalized symbols in the manner of "passive" still-life and landscape motifs. Inasmuch as Picasso had always been essentially a painter of the human figure, these experimental pictures were almost predestined to be portraits, and only if he thought of them as portraits in an almost conventional way would the experiment be valid.

Picasso's problem here was that he needed portrait subjects who, like Gertrude Stein before them, would sit for hours and hours, day after day, while the artist pondered the problem of the nature and limits of representation. As his art dealers, at least Uhde and Kahnweiler, were themselves caught up in these artistic problems and

Eva Gouel (Marcelle Humbert; detail).
Avignon, summer 1914. Photograph by
Picasso. Yale Collection of American
Literature, Beinecke Rare Book and
Manuscript Library, Yale University

Head of Eva Gouel. 1916. Engraving with
roulette; plate: 3⅛ × 2″ (8 × 5.1 cm).
Geiser/Baer I, 52. The Museum of
Modern Art, New York. Mrs. Bertram
Smith Fund

Study for Woman in an Armchair (Eva Gouel).
1913. Pencil and wax crayon on paper, 9⅛ × 7⅞″
(23 × 20 cm). Zervos XXIX, 2. Daix 638 (verso).
Private collection

understood better what Picasso was about than anyone
besides Braque, and as, moreover, they were beholden to
him, Picasso could make huge demands on their time and
energy. Then, too, they could be counted on not to complain that the portraits did not look like them.

The only picture within the group of high Cubist portraits that seems at all inconsistent with Picasso's development in 1910—it is, indeed, a bit of a sport—is the portrait
of Ambroise Vollard (p. 283). It is also the only one for
which there were probably not multiple or extended sittings. Pierre Daix believes that Vollard did not sit for
Picasso at that time, and that the portrait was based on a
photograph, now presumabably lost.[41] The Vollard portrait, in any case, uniquely blends Cubism with an almost
illusionistic realism. What explains its particular character?

We should start by reminding ourselves of certain differences between these three picture sellers. Vollard had
been a highly successful dealer during the 1890s (when,
aside from being Cézanne's unique representative, he
showed works by various major Impressionists and Post-
Impressionists). All this happened while Picasso was still a
boy. By 1910 Vollard was enormously rich and powerful,
an almost mythical art-world figure who clearly had the
upper hand in his relations with Picasso. Conversely, Uhde
and Kahnweiler were relatively impecunious, as yet more
amateurs than seasoned dealers, and clearly dependent
on Picasso for favors. Unlike Vollard, they were Picasso's
creatures. He could demand from both of them the
extended time he needed and such dialogue as he might
want to have—unthinkable given his rapport with
Vollard. This explains, I believe, why the Uhde and

Kahnweiler portraits became purer models of Picasso's
new elliptical conception of the portrait, while that of
Vollard, which has a strong dollop of very seductive realism, remains somewhat apart.

Exquisite as it is, the Vollard portrait represented a certain accommodation of high Cubism and illusionism: by
using his grasp of psychological characterization and by
cleverly eliding Cubist signs and shaded flesh tones (found
uniquely in the head), Picasso produced an image that
Vollard would (and did) appreciate as a likeness.[42] The
picture was thus a cunningly versatile exercise in craft—
a counterpart in Cubist terms of the sheer laureate virtuosity characteristic of winter 1905–06 (for example, *Boy
Leading a Horse*), which Vollard liked most in Picasso's
work. Somewhat paradoxically, Picasso's rendering of
Vollard's face is in many ways more realistic, as well as
psychologically penetrating, than Cézanne's portrait of
Vollard, painted eleven years earlier, for which the dealer
had repeatedly posed (pp. 32, 33).

The abstractness of high Cubism was certainly not
in itself at all conducive to the practice of portraiture.
Braque, for his part, never tried his hand at the genre.
Picasso's talent as a caricaturist, however, allowed him to
isolate and emphasize a series of telling details that would
remain legible amid the pictorial flux of Analytic Cubism:
Uhde's pinched upper lip, Vollard's heavy eyelids, and
Kahnweiler's features, which Picasso himself summarized
as "the wave in the hair, an earlobe [and] the clasped
hands."[43] Such traits endowed these portraits, despite the
latter's considerable abstractness, with an evocative
ressemblance to their subjects.

The portraits of Uhde, Vollard, and Kahnweiler have no sequels in the years 1911–14. During the height of Cubism's Analytic phase—from 1911 through the spring of 1912—Picasso seems to have felt that identity should (or only could) be characterized typologically, being implied primarily through props or textual inscriptions with a personal significance. The figures in his paintings now became schematic types, identifiable as male or female only because of the addition of conventional markers: moustaches for men, stylized breasts for women. The emergence of Synthetic Cubism in 1912, under the impetus of collage, *papier collé,* and construction, made possible a mode of figuration that was less "abstract" and more legible than its Analytic forerunner, but even more schematic and typological. Meyer Schapiro called it the "Cubism of Rehabilitation": the figures and objects that had been diced, fragmented, and increasingly displaced in Analytic Cubism were now reincorporated as shaped flat planes forming coherent signs. But if Synthetic Cubism was more legible than Analytic Cubism, it was also less illusionistic. The shallow space of Picasso's 1910–11 pictures—the last vestige of "real," three-dimensional space—was now pressed completely flat.

Under these circumstances, it was perhaps inevitable that Picasso's 1911–14 "portraits" of his new love, Marcelle Humbert (later known as Eva Gouel), only rarely attempted to reproduce her facial features (opposite), but grafted elliptical identificatory phrases—*"Ma Jolie"* or *"J'aime Eva"* (p. 289)—onto the stock types of Cubist figuration; Eva was "very sweet," Picasso had told Kahnweiler in a spring 1912 letter sent from the south of France: "I love her very much and I will write this in my paintings."[44] The *Woman in an Armchair* of 1913 began with stylized sketches in which Eva was recognizable (p. 290, top), but the final painting lacked even the familiar allusive inscriptions addressed to her (p. 291).

Out of the complex circumstances of Picasso's art in 1912–13—a combination of purely formal considerations and intimate personal experience—emerged a new type of symbolic "portrait," dense with visual associations and ambiguities. The evocative fragments of words and phrases painted and stenciled on his Cubist paintings and glued to his *papiers collés,* and the freewheeling fantasy of his 1913 figures, would establish Picasso a decade later as the prototype of the modernist *peintre-poète.* After Joan Miró and Paul Klee had created brilliant oeuvres based in part on Picasso's model, André Breton would proclaim the painter the embodiment of the Surrealist hero, the *peintre-poète,* declaring that Surrealism "has only to pass where Picasso has passed and where he will pass in the future."[45] It should be said that Picasso would become not only a painter-poet in the general sense of the term

Female Nude: "J'aime Eva" (detail). 1912. Columbus Museum of Art, Columbus, Ohio. Gift of Ferdinand Howald. (Colorplate of whole, p. 289)

The Artist and His Model (detail). 1914. Musée Picasso, Paris. (Colorplate of whole, p. 298)

Seated Man. 1901. Conté crayon on paper. Zervos VI, 339. Private collection

Young Man Sitting, Leaning on the Chair Back. 1914. Pencil on paper, 12⅛ × 9½″ (30.8 × 24 cm). Zervos VI, 1206. Private collection

but in a quite literal one, having written a considerable volume of poetry and plays.[46] Although his reading was otherwise quite limited, Picasso throughout his life found himself deeply moved by poetry and enjoyed close and intense relationships with poets—Jacob, Apollinaire, Cocteau, Breton, and Eluard, to name just a few. On the door of his Bateau-Lavoir studio he tacked the sign *"Au rendez-vous des poètes."*

Essential to Picasso's type of poetic, free-associational imagery was an extreme rapidity—which should not be equated with rapid drawing—in the decision-making process. Picasso almost always drew at a quite deliberate speed, and never, or at least very rarely, with anything like the velocity of "automatists" such as Masson or Pollock (who themselves never painted as quickly as is supposed). He worked really quickly only on occasion, with the brush, not drawing but "brushing-in." Delacroix had described a good draftsman as one who could draw a body falling from a building before it hit the ground, requiring not only a virtually instantaneous coordination of eye and hand,[47] but a mind that determines the *crucial aesthetic choices* swiftly. This is where Picasso's enormous gifts came into play, for most draftsmen would never have been able to respond so agilely to the chain of associations. Picasso's deliberate speed is much less reflected in

an appearance of rapid execution than in the staggering *number* of his drawings. Some measure of his obsession with image-making can be gauged by the fact that he surely made far more drawings (and paintings) than any other serious artist in history. Cézanne, for example, who enjoyed a long career, executed somewhere in the neighborhood of nineteen hundred sheets (including watercolors). Picasso made almost nineteen thousand.[48] Only if van Gogh had maintained the level of production of his final years to a ripe old age would the world have witnessed an oeuvre of comparable numbers, though with less range in mediums.

Cubism thus yielded two completely distinct forms of portraiture. If I stress this point, it is because critics and scholars (myself included) have often tended to present Cubism—or at least Analytic Cubism—as a kind of monolithic entity. Clement Greenberg, for example, used to argue that Cubism was Picasso's greatest accomplishment in part because for four or five years he allowed himself to be "enclosed" or "set" within a style. In this regard, Greenberg liked to equate Picasso's Cubism of 1908–12 with Pollock's "allover" style of 1947–50. During these respective periods, he remarked, the artists could

Smoker in a Top Hat Leaning on a Table. 1914. Lead pencil on paper, 12¾ × 9⅝″ (32.5 × 24.5 cm). Zervos XXIX, 61. Private collection

Man Leaning on a Table. 1916. Oil on canvas, 78¾ × 52″ (200 × 132 cm). Zervos II², 550. Daix 889. Private collection

"relax in their style" and seemingly "do no wrong."[49]

If The Museum of Modern Art's 1989 exhibition *Picasso and Braque: Pioneering Cubism* made one thing clear to me it was that Picasso could not possibly be described as having been "enclosed" within a single style during the years 1908 to 1912, or even for the period (summer 1909 to early 1912) of Analytic Cubism alone. While admiring Greenberg's brilliant insight that Analytic Cubism provided the infrastructure for Pollock's allover poured style, I cannot help feeling that Greenberg was overlooking (or ignorant of)[50] the many remarkable changes in Picasso's work between 1908 and early 1912. "Cubism" may be useful as an historical label, but there is no one pictorial style that can be intrinsically defined as Cubist. On the contrary, Picasso's notorious tendency toward stylistic multiplicity—usually associated with his work only after World War I—actually emerges fully after Gosol, when he first takes on his real identity as an artist.

Other painters—Mondrian and Malevich, for instance—saw Analytic Cubism as evolving toward abstraction and drew the conclusion that nonfigurative painting was the logical and inevitable end point of this process. However, neither Picasso nor Braque had the slightest intention of going over into a wholly abstract art. Both were, and would remain for the rest of their lives, committed to the notion that painting was an inherently figurative and representational art: what interested them was precisely the tension between the abstract elements of painting and the contours of an actual motif. It is significant, in this respect, that the most elliptical phase of Analytic Cubism occurs nearer its beginnings, in the bare scaffoldings of Picasso's summer 1910 canvases, than its terminus, in comparatively legible pictures such as *Man with a Violin* and *The Aficionado*.[51] After he had arrived at a virtually abstract style, Picasso's first impulse was to complicate it by reintroducing legible aspects of reality.

Picasso's ambivalence with regard to abstraction was, in part, a function of his abiding instinct for contradiction. Whatever the thesis or proposition mooted, he inevitably turned it around in his mind and delighted in such paradoxical truth as he could find in its contrary. To some extent his forward motion depended on this dialectic. Picasso disliked all rational, consistent, and closed systems, both in life and in art. Even in his most tightly structured Cubist paintings, there is usually something that doesn't quite "work" visually, someplace where a monkey wrench has been thrown into the gears. Yet, it is precisely such passages that, on extended looking, often come to seem to us the very guarantors of the pictures' "lifelikeness" (in the deepest sense of the word).

Eva Dying. 1915. Pencil on paper, 12⅝ × 9⅞" (32 × 25 cm). Zervos II², 842. Private collection

Eva on Her Death Bed. 1915. Pencil on paper, 6¼ × 9⅝" (16 × 24.5 cm). Zervos XXIX, 186. Galerie Jan Krugier, Geneva

Picasso's instinct for contradiction is also visible in his lifelong battle against virtuosity. His repeated turns to one variety or another of "primitivism" were essentially means of escaping from his own talent. The most obvious cases are those in which he turned to models outside the mainstream of European painting: Romanesque manuscript illuminations, ancient Iberian carvings, "tribal" sculptures from Africa and Oceania, or the canvases of the Douanier Rousseau. In other instances, he sought a formal or methodological primitivism determined by a reaction against his own painterly achievements. Thus, the supremely nuanced light and brushwork of Picasso's 1911–12 Analytic Cubism— Rembrandtesque in its profundity, Mallarméan in its subtlety—were followed by the deliberately raw and simple expedients of collage and *papier collé.* Picasso now sacrificed painterly mastery in favor of a kind of *art brut.* His 1912–13 collages, in their crudeness and (seeming) simplicity, compare to *"Ma Jolie"* in much the same way as the *Demoiselles* does to the paintings of the Rose period. What, for example, could have been more homely, simple, raw, and unprepossessing than the sheet-metal *Guitar,* conceived in the late summer of 1912?[52] Yet the "primitive" execution and "constructed" character of this work constituted a fundamentally new approach to sculpture, transcending the alternatives— carving vs. modeling—that had dominated Western sculpture from the ancient Greeks through Rodin.

In a 1919 letter to Kahnweiler, Braque condemned Picasso's adoption, during the years of World War I, of a new classical and representational style, commenting that "what is really constant in this artist is his temperament. Picasso remains for me what he has always been,

a virtuoso full of talent."[53] Picasso himself was equally scornful of mere virtuosity. However, he identified it with the facility that resulted from working continuously in a single style, as Braque now did. "Style," he told one writer, "is often something which locks the painter in the same vision, the same technique, the same formula during many years, sometimes for a lifetime."[54] For Picasso, style was a *"camisole de force"*—a straightjacket.[55]

The artist had made a series of drawings in 1914–15 that combined, in various ways, elements of both Cubist and "classical" representational figuration (p. 37 and above). Many of these depicted the Cézannesque figure of a seated man: one version of this figure—showing the man seated at a table, head resting pensively on his hand (p. 36, right)—was explored in a series of summer 1914 sketches and then transferred to a large canvas, which Picasso labored over from 1915 through 1916, transforming it from a representational to a Cubist (but still-legible) image, and then into an almost totally abstract *trompe l'oeil* of *papier collé,* suggesting vertical strips of material covered with gridded dots (p. 37, right).[56]

Back in the spring of 1914, Picasso had shown Kahnweiler several of the first realistic figures from this series, commenting: "Still, they're better than before."[57] It was true. As remarkable a draftsman as Picasso had been from the turn of the century through the Rose period, his long pilgrimage through the "primitivism" of 1906–08 and the multiple Cubisms of 1909–14 had mysteriously informed and thus transformed the quality of his representational drawing. Picasso's line was now much more taut, more wiry, and yet more implicitly sculptural than it had been before, while the infrastructure of his compositions continued to profit from the implicit grid of Cubism.

The disparity between the fragmentation of Picasso's

1910–14 Cubist personages and the massive solidity of his new, realistic, and somewhat classicizing figures makes it difficult to see the extent to which his representational drawings after 1914 remained indebted to Cubism. The continuity of his work is more evident in certain still lifes and landscapes in which the subdivided nature of the motif allowed it to be more obviously aligned with the picture's infrastructure.

Comparing Picasso's 1921 drawing of vine leaves (right) with any of Matisse's line drawings of similar motifs, one is astonished by how much Cubism could be subsumed in Picasso's Neoclassicism. Matisse's more lyric, decorative line characteristically "sits" on the picture surface, reconfirming its flatness; Picasso's line "bites" sculpturally into the surface. Even without the aid of shading, the leaves seem to bow outward toward the spectator in a shallow frontal space deriving from Cézanne. Within the rectangle of the drawing paper, the leaves are "set" in a Cubist manner, their accented forms piling up toward the center and dissolving toward the edges. The "architecture" of the branches echoes the vertical and horizontal axes of the field, locking the curved and diagonal accents into its scaffolding. Even the little cluster of grapes near the top serves as a "button" for the composition in a manner analogous to the nails, knobs, and clusters of green that often "anchor" Cubist compositions at top or bottom.

The Vine. July 4, 1921. Charcoal on paper, 25¼ × 20¼″ (64 × 51.4 cm). Zervos IV, 292. Private collection

Seven Dancers (including Olga Khokhlova in foreground). 1919. Pencil and traces of charcoal on paper, 24⅝ × 19¾″ (62.6 × 50 cm). Zervos III, 353. Musée Picasso, Paris

Olga Khokhlova (foreground) in *Les Sylphides*, taken during the first New York tour of Diaghilev's Ballets Russes, April 1916. Photograph by White Studio, New York

Standing Bather. 1921. Grease pencil on paper, 13 × 6¹¹/₁₆″ (33 × 17 cm). Zervos XXX, 152. Private collection

Three Bathers. 1920. Oil on canvas, 21¼ × 31⅞″ (54 × 81 cm). Zervos IV, 208. Private collection

The Cézannesque figure of a seated man of 1914 had been immediately incorporated into a realistic, proto-Neoclassical painting, *The Artist and His Model* (p. 298), on which Picasso was working when World War I began in August 1914.[58] These and other representational figures of 1914 also led directly to the 1915 pencil portraits of Ambroise Vollard and Max Jacob (p. 299), drawings whose unmistakably Ingresque facture mark the emergence of a first full-fledged Neoclassical style, which would continue as a part of Picasso's work into the next decade.

During the 1920s, Neoclassical styles would become commonplace among Parisian vanguardists, as a feature of a general "recall to order" provoked by the upheavals, displacements, and horrors of the war.[59] Recent studies on this subject invariably describe Neoclassicism as a strictly conservative movement. In this context, Picasso's return to a representational style and his supposed abandonment of Cubism have often been considered a simple retreat. A not untypical response is one scholar's description of Picasso's Neoclassical style as a "peculiar and momentously reactionary alternative to Cubism . . . a deep conundrum for historians of modernism."[60] Furthermore, this opinion was shared by many of Picasso's avant-garde contemporaries, who viewed his Neoclassicism as a desertion of modernism.

For artists such as Mondrian and Malevich, committed to a formal, teleological view of modernism, there could be no question of a turning back from abstraction to representation. Braque, who virtually equated Cubism and modern painting, considered Picasso's "Ingresque"

drawings of 1915–19 (pp. 39, 308, 310) an abandonment of modernity. The palpable sense of betrayal in the comments of Picasso's contemporaries is a response not only to his additional style but also to the content of his new portraits, many of whose subjects were drawn from the world of the ballet and the *"beau monde."*

Picasso, needless to say, did not share this teleological view of the history of art. As he said in an interview that Marius de Zayas re-edited in English in 1923, "The several manners I have used in my art must not be considered as an evolution. . . . If the subjects I have wanted to express have suggested different ways of expression I have never hesitated to adopt them."[61] For him there was no such thing as a privileged style inherently either better or more modern than other styles. There were only inspired pictures and bad ones. Picasso's lack of interest in modernity, as such, was evident in the way he lived, in the extraordinary hodge-podge of the furnishings with which he surrounded himself. On one occasion, discussing his passion for chairs, tablecloths, and curtain pulls with old fashioned tassels and fringes—constant motifs in his high Cubist pictures—the artist asked almost angrily why he should be expected to admire modern furniture (which he disliked) or modern architecture (much of which he hated).[62] Contrarily, Picasso loved objects, people, and behavior that were not only outside the pale of "good taste" but somehow beyond any definable taste at all—as exemplified by the indescribable breakfront that appears in photographs of his various lodgings over the years.[63]

Furthermore, the scholarly analysis of Neoclassicism

as an element in the postwar "recall to order" fails to take into account the fact that the seeds of Picasso's Neoclassicism (as well as his Surrealism and Expressionism) were already present in his drawing and painting *before* World War I.[64] Whatever the significance of Neoclassicism in the work of the artists who turned to it in the 1920s, Picasso's initial adoption of this style seems to have taken place for artistic reasons particular to himself. It is equally important to bear in mind that the emergence of Neoclassicism in Picasso's work did not put a dent in his exploration of Synthetic Cubism. On the contrary, his largest and boldest statements in that style—the *Harlequin* (1915; p. 301), *Man Leaning on a Table* (1916), the two versions of *Three Musicians* (1921), and *The Birdcage* (1923; below)—were executed over exactly the same period that saw the emergence and refinement of his Neoclassical style.

Of these two styles, Cubism and Neoclassicism, critics almost invariably view the former as the more serious and the latter as the more superficial. But unbiased examination of the years in question might suggest that the opposite was often true. During the years 1918 through 1923, the flattened, fragmented forms of Synthetic Cubism are often arranged into exceedingly decorative, quite lighthearted compositions, while Picasso's Neoclassical Bather compositions of 1920 to 1923 came to subsume all that was solid and weighty (both literally and figuratively) in his art.

Somewhat paradoxically, Picasso's Neoclassical style became heir to those aspects of Cézanne's style that had played an important role in the monumental and sculpturally modeled Cubism of 1908–09 (*Three Women*; *Woman with Pears*, p. 277), but had been undercut, so to say, by the increasing dissolution of forms in Analytic Cubism and then by the flatness of its Synthetic successor. While recent scholarship has often focused on the form-dissolving qualities of Cézanne's late style, artists and critics in the early years of this century were far more aware of the solidity, the compelling *gravitas* of his figures, still lifes, and landscapes of the years 1875 to 1900. Picasso's renewed attention to Cézanne is evident in a series of 1921 drawings and canvases reprising the earlier artist's depictions of a standing male bather (opposite). His Neoclassical figures share the psychological inwardness and self-absorption of Cézanne's bathers; their appearance of "primitive" massiveness—the figures' circumscribed gestures are literally wrung from them—is intensified by the shallow, often claustrophobic spaces they occupy. The projecting, front-modeled forms (and reciprocal "bas-relief" space) of early Cubism are recaptured in these Neoclassical Picassos of the early 1920s, but are handled with vast reserve and tautness (below, left).

The Pipes of Pan. 1923. Oil on canvas, 80¹¹⁄₁₆ × 68½″ (205 × 174 cm). Zervos V, 141. Musée Picasso, Paris

The Birdcage. 1923. Oil and charcoal on canvas, 79⅛ × 55¼″ (200.7 × 140.4 cm). Zervos V, 84. Private collection

Portrait of Olga. July 26, 1920. Charcoal on canvas, 51 × 38¼″ (130 × 97 cm). Zervos IV, 99. Private collection

Transmitted Infrared Vidicon image of *Woman in an Armchair* (Olga) (detail)

Transmitted Infrared Vidicon image of *Woman in an Armchair* (Olga)

The virtual interchange between Synthetic Cubism and Neoclassicism is unexpectedly revealed in a 1920 Curvilinear Cubist representation of a *Woman in an Armchair* (opposite). An infrared scan of this image performed in The Museum of Modern Art's conservation laboratory reveals that the painting actually began as a Neoclassical figure in which the face and figure of Picasso's wife Olga were perfectly legible. Picasso's drawings and prints provide many examples of motifs translated in a similar fashion from one style to another. But this is one of only two instances in which we can securely demonstrate, on a single canvas, the oscillation between Neoclassicism and Cubism.[65] The image of Olga visible in the underpainting is reprised in a charcoal sketch on another canvas of somewhat similar size (above), suggesting that Picasso may originally have planned to make two portraits of Olga in precisely the same pose, one Cubist, the other Neoclassical.

Comparison between the infrared prints and the finished version of *Woman in an Armchair* makes it clear that some of the contours of the Cubist version of *Woman in an Armchair* were carried over directly from the original Neoclassical image: the curve of Olga's chin, her right shoulder and arm, her left upper arm, a part of that lower arm and hand, as well as virtually the entire outline of the chair, right down to the pinched oval of the armrest. The vertical supports of the chair's back remained in the same place, while their silhouette was selectively altered. The remaining contours of the Cubist composition were invented, in effect, out of whole cloth.

Perhaps the most puzzling of these is the vertically divided blue rectangle at the lower center. At first glance this seems to be a purely abstract shape. Neither the underpainting visible in the infrared photograph nor the painting's charcoal-on-canvas "twin" (above, left) reveal a "realistic" motif at this location, suggesting that the two-paneled rectangle was a late (and not altogether felicitous) addition to the composition. The shape derives, I believe, from still another depiction of Olga (below, left), an oil on canvas, showing her as a seated figure reading a book with opened covers, one lit and one in shadow. The motif of a book opened in a woman's lap can be traced back in Picasso's work at least as far as 1913;[66] its potential for sexual symbolism becomes explicit in an etching of 1933 (p. 66, bottom), where the intersecting planes corresponding to the covers of a book, accompanied by a pair of spheres, represent the contours of both female and male sex organs.[67]

Olga Reading. 1920. Oil on canvas, 39⅜ × 28¾″ (100 × 73 cm). Not in Zervos. Musée Picasso, Paris

Beginning in 1920, Picasso's vision of the classical largely takes leave of Ingres in favor of a variety of "Greek" and Mediterranean models whose chiton-draped figures, sometimes inflated to massive proportions, reflect a wide variety of influences: Pompeian and Ostian frescoes and

Woman in an Armchair (Olga). July 29, 1920. Oil on canvas, 45¾ × 33˝ (116 × 89 cm). Zervos IV, 127. Private collection

Head of a Woman. 1921. Pastel on paper, 25 × 18⅞″ (63.5 × 48 cm). Zervos IV, 349. Beyeler Collection, Basel

mosaics, Renaissance paintings and reliefs, Renoir's late paintings, and Maillol's early canvases. The influence of the early Italian Renaissance is particularly evident in what remain, for me, the greatest of Picasso's Neoclassical pictures: the generic pastel "portrait" heads of 1921 (above), rather than the major paintings of that year, such as *Three Women at the Spring*. These pastels really must be seen in person, as the magical quality of their modeling rarely comes through adequately in reproductions.

Picasso seems to have been inspired, in these images, by Giotto and his fifteenth-century successors, painters whose works reflected the study of both high Gothic and classical sculpture. Of course, Picasso himself, as a student, had drawn studies after plaster replicas of antique sculptures (p. 58, bottom left). The heads in his greatest 1921 pastels, such as his portrait of Olga (opposite), seem,

close-up, almost to be carved from tinted stone. In these, Picasso realizes an illusion of sculptural plasticity as compressed and intense as that of Masaccio or Piero della Francesca. He had clearly intuited the fact that the great fifteenth-century Florentine masters did not build their images by transcribing them directly from nature, but by first abstracting from nature a limited number of fundamental qualities—volume, mass, light, and space—and then constructing their pictures out of these isolated, already conceptualized, building blocks.

Unlike many of the Neoclassicizing painters of the 1920s "recall to order," Picasso continued to reject deep perspectival space. Nor did he accept, as they did, the notion of a single and consistent source of light, which had been one of the major discoveries of fifteenth-century painting. Picasso's 1909 experiments with painted

Portrait of Olga (detail). 1921. Pastel and charcoal on paper. Musée Picasso, Paris, on extended loan to the Musée des Beaux-Arts, Grenoble. (Colorplate of whole, p. 315)

and sculpted versions of the same faceted head of Fernande (pp. 276, 277) had revealed to him how much more plastically vivid he could make an imagined play of light and shadow relative to the modeling evoked by the same head lit by an actual consistent light source. His 1921 pastels retain this "autonomous" lighting, even as the rough facet planes of the 1909 heads are replaced by smooth, unbroken contours, modeled with infinitely subtle gradations, but nevertheless preserving much of the sculptural energy of early Cubism.

In 1922–23 Picasso's classical figures become freer and more fluid in posture, costume, and coiffure. His drawing is more lyrical, his modeling softer and looser. It is tempting to ascribe this shift to a more atmospheric, more

veiled pictorial fabric—reenacting the evolution of Cubism from 1909 through 1911—in Wölfflinian terms, as a shift from a linear/tactile to a painterly/optical style. But the painterliness of Picasso's 1922–23 work does not transcribe visual sensations in the manner of Rembrandt, Rubens, and the other Baroque masters in Wölfflin's artistic taxonomy. It is closer, rather, to the more tactile, "abstract" painterliness found in Leonardo's unfinished works and Titian's late paintings. This stylistic change provides the vehicle for a new sense of ineffable tenderness in Picasso's Neoclassical works of 1922–23, but the shift in emotional tenor also seems to correspond to changes in the artist's life.

According to a famous half-truth proposed by Dora Maar, Picasso's styles, homes, friends, favorite poets, and even dogs changed with each new mistress. Similarly,

Olga in a Robe. 1920. Pencil on paper, 15¼ × 12⅝″ (38.5 × 32 cm). Zervos IV, 90. Private collection

Seated Woman (Sara Murphy). 1923. Ink on cardboard, 5½ × 4⅛″ (14 × 10.5 cm). Zervos V, 261. Private collection

Picasso's longtime friend and secretary Jaime Sabartés claimed that "with each new amorous experience, we see [Picasso's] art progress, new forms, another language, a particular expression to which one could give the name of a woman."[68] That Picasso's homes and friends should alter with serious new loves is hardly surprising. But Picasso's artistic language was clearly *not* determined by the entries and exits of different lovers. On the contrary, it might well be argued that these entries and exits were themselves determined by Picasso's desire to explore differing realms of artistic and emotional experience.

Picasso remarked that he was sometimes introduced to people whose images he had seemingly painted years earlier.[69] At a less-mystical level, Picasso's tendency, from Cubism onward, to represent men and women as generic types only intermittently particularized by the addition of individual traits might be taken to reflect more general psychological attitudes. To some extent, he may have seen actual men and women as actors who could be cast in one role or another of his private psychodrama. There is, in effect, a Pygmalion quality to Picasso's treatment of the human figure, aptly symbolized by a pair of drawings done during his student years in Spain, one of them offering a realistic description of a plaster bust of an antique figure, the other depicting the same figure as if she had come to life (p. 58, bottom).

Between 1918 and 1938, we find at least four different women—Olga Picasso, Sara Murphy, Marie-Thérèse Walter, and Dora Maar—associated with Picasso's shifting classical ideal. As each woman is assimilated to this ideal, her individual features are transformed and, on some occasions, merged with those of her rivals. Similarly, the characteristic costume of one woman may also be found in a portrait of another. For example, there are portraits of Sara Murphy wearing Olga's costume.[70] By the same token, Marie-Thérèse, the reigning ideal of the *Vollard Suite* of etchings, is represented in one of them with the turban worn by Sara (p. 103) in her photograph with Picasso (p. 52) and the portrait drawing of her taken from it. Thus, Picasso's exquisite pencil portrait of Olga from 1920 (above) draws on a typically Ingresque typology whose vocabulary was first secured (in a three-dimensionally modeled version) in his portraits of Max Jacob and Ambroise Vollard (p. 299) executed in 1915—a year before Picasso met Olga. Other drawings in this vein such as those based on a promotional photograph for Diaghilev's troupe (p. 39), are so generalized that Olga herself is scarcely recognizable. Nonetheless, it is clear that Olga hovers as a muse over Picasso's pictures of 1918–21.

In a similar fashion, it is an American woman, Sara Murphy, whose image reverberates through his work of 1922–23. Sara was the wife of the painter Gerald Murphy (whose small but original oeuvre, prophetic of Pop art, was exhibited at The Museum of Modern Art in 1974).

Marie-Thérèse Looking at a Sculpture of Herself (4th state). 1933. Etching on copperplate, 10½ × 7⅝″ (26.7 × 19.4 cm). Geiser/Baer II, 345 (B). The Museum of Modern Art, New York. Abby Aldrich Rockefeller Fund

Dora with a Wreath of Flowers. February 13, 1937. Lead pencil and pastel on paper, 11⁷⁄₁₆ × 9¹⁄₁₆″ (29 × 23 cm). Zervos VIII, 347. Private collection

The couple, wealthy expatriates, were attractive personalities, and their unconventional lifestyle drew a wide circle of writers and artists. F. Scott Fitzgerald modeled Dick and Nicole Diver, the protagonists of *Tender is the Night,* on the Murphys; indeed, both Fitzgerald and Hemingway fell in love at one time or another with Sara—attracted by both her beauty and her combination of intelligence, sensitivity, and maternal warmth. Picasso and Olga probably met the Murphys in the fall of 1921, when the painter Natalia Goncharova, with whom they were studying, encouraged them to do volunteer work repainting damaged scenery for the Ballets Russes.

As Sara's countenance has something in common with generic types of female faces found in Picasso's art in the years immediately preceding, his paintings of her were long thought to be images of a generic Neoclassical beauty; a few critics have even mistaken them for representations of Olga. The first intimations of Sara Murphy's image appear in Picasso's work in such Neoclassical pictures as *Seated Woman* of the winter of 1921–22[71] and *Bust of a Woman,* of early 1922 (p. 104, right). Comparing these with confirmed portraits of Sara (pp. 53, 55), we note the similarities in her delicate chiseled features, her demure pose (head and eyes tilted downward), and her characteristic luxuriant coiffure (long wavy hair drawn or tied back and then cascading down her neck). These cascading waves

of hair, in particular, differentiate the pictures inspired by Sara from those inspired by Olga, who is almost invariably shown with her hair pinned tightly to her head. (On the other hand, there are heads somewhat similar to Sara's that appear in a few charcoal and sanguine "postludes" [p. 104, left] to *Three Women at the Spring,* which may have been drawn before Picasso and Sara met.)

By the summer of 1922, the two families had become good friends. Picasso, Olga, and their son, Paulo, spent that summer at Dinard, in Brittany, while the Murphys were staying in Normandy, a little more than an hour away by automobile. It seems safe to assume that they visited each other at least occasionally, and if Picasso did not sketch Sara from life he would at least have had the opportunity to refresh his visual image of her. A series of notebook drawings, followed by a pastel and four paintings made in the latter half of 1922, reveal that the two women had clearly become linked in Picasso's mind: both of them maternal figures, but Sara warm and relaxed while Olga was tense and fastidious.

Picasso did curiously few drawings of Olga with Paulo, then one and a half years old. However, there are several sketches devoted to this subject in his Dinard notebooks (p. 48); these lead to studies for a more formal *maternité.*[72] In the definitive watercolor of the series, the mother resembles Sara more than Olga, and the same can be said

Woman and Child (Olga and Paulo). 1922. Pencil on paper, 16½ × 12″ (42 × 30.5 cm). Zervos XXX, 343. Musée Picasso, Paris

Woman and Child (Olga and Paulo). 1922. Pencil and watercolor on paper, 6⅛ × 4½″ (15.5 × 11.5 cm). Not in Zervos. Musée Picasso, Paris

Mother and Child. 1922. Pencil and watercolor on paper, 6⅛ × 4½″ (15.5 × 11.5 cm). Not in Zervos. Musée Picasso, Paris

Mother and Child. 1922. Pencil and watercolor on paper, 6⅛ × 4½″ (15.5 × 11.5 cm). Not in Zervos. Musée Picasso, Paris

Mother and Child. c. 1922. Pencil on paper, 16½ × 12″ (42 × 30.5 cm). Zervos XXX, 360. Private collection

of the oil paintings, especially that in the Baltimore Museum of Art (p. 51), which is closest to the watercolor. But can we say that these oils are portraits of Sara? Certainly Sara was celebrated for her qualities as a mother—her understanding of and intimacy with children, the games she played with them, and the costumes she made. In contrast, Olga left Paulo largely in the hands of governesses. Watching Paulo play with the Murphy children under Sara's supervision, Picasso would probably have been charmed by the maternal qualities not frequently noted, or imaged, in relation to his wife.[73] But it would seem more accurate to describe the mother in the oil paintings as a kind of wish-fulfillment, subsuming echoes of both Olga and Sara into a classical apotheosis of the ideal mother/wife. In this sense, the image also antedates both women to the extent that its roots can be found in Picasso's youthful sketches made after antique busts of Greek goddesses (p. 58).

Mother and Child Before a Red Curtain. 1922. Oil on canvas, 51¼ × 38⅝″ (130 × 98 cm). Not in Zervos. Private collection

Mother and Child. 1922. Oil on canvas, 39⅜ × 31⅞″ (100 × 81 cm). Zervos IV, 371. The Baltimore Museum of Art. The Cone Collection, formed by Dr. Claribel Cone and Miss Etta Cone of Baltimore, Maryland

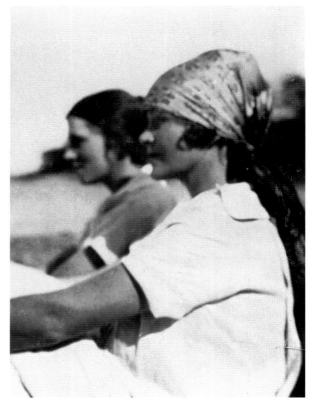

Head of Sara Murphy. 1923. Pen and India ink on paper, 14⅜ × 10½″ (36.5 × 26.5 cm). Not in Zervos. Collection Marina Picasso, courtesy Galerie Jan Krugier, Geneva

Olga Picasso and Sara Murphy, La Garoupe beach, Antibes, summer 1923. Photographer unknown. Collection Honoria Murphy Donnelly

Head of Sara Murphy. 1923. Pen and India ink on paper, 14⅜ × 10½″ (36.5 × 26.5 cm). Not in Zervos. Collection Marina Picasso, courtesy Galerie Jan Krugier, Geneva

Sara Murphy and Picasso, La Garoupe beach, Antibes, summer 1923. Photograph by Gerald Murphy. Collection Honoria Murphy Donnelly

Portrait of Sara Murphy. 1923. Bistre ink on paper, 42³/₈ × 28¹/₄″ (107.7 × 71.6 cm). Zervos V, 369. Private collection, Switzerland

Picasso, Olga, and their young son, Paulo, spent much of the summer of 1923 with the Murphys at the Hôtel du Cap in Antibes. As a special favor to the two families, the proprietor had kept the hotel open during the summer (then the off-season), and they, together with a Chinese family who had decided to stay on, were the sole guests. During the course of the summer of 1923, Picasso painted three portraits of Sara on canvases covered with layers of sand (no doubt from the beach at La Garoupe, where the

Picasso family spent almost every day with the Murphys and their children). Only one of these oils, the largest, most stylized, and probably the last of the three, found its way into Zervos's catalogue, under the title *Seated Woman in Blue and Pink* (p. 56). Much smaller, and almost certainly the first (p. 54, bottom), was a picture that, according to Jacqueline Picasso, the artist had kept apart with other paintings and objects that were clearly memorabilia. When I discussed this canvas with her in 1982, Jacqueline could

Head of Sara Murphy. 1924. Pen and ink on paper, 12¼ ×
9¼″ (31 × 23.5 cm). Zervos V, 295. Private collection

Portrait of Sara Murphy. 1923. Oil and sand on canvas, 21½ × 18″ (54.6 × 45.8 cm). Not in Zervos.
Private collection

Portrait of Sara Murphy. 1923. Oil and sand on canvas, 21⅝ × 17¾″ (55 × 45 cm). Not in Zervos. Private collection

identify it only as "a portrait of a beautiful American woman." It seemed at the time likely that this was a portrait of Sara Murphy, but I was unable to confirm this until some time later. First, I came upon an outsize portrait drawing of the same person (p. 53), shown wearing a turban; this was obviously based on the image of Sara in a photograph showing her arm in arm with Picasso on the beach (p. 52, bottom right). Picasso, not surprisingly, had

kept a print of this image. Later, I learned from Pierre Daix that Picasso himself had, in confidence, identified the very pictures in question as being portraits of Sara Murphy.

From the three sand portraits and a large number of sketches and variants was to come, somewhat later in the summer, the masterpiece among the portraits inspired by Sara, the *Woman in White* (p. 57). Picasso's fragile, dreamlike vision of Neoclassical perfection is expressed here via

Portrait of Sara Murphy. 1923. Oil and sand on canvas, 39⅜ × 31¾″ (100 × 80.5 cm). Zervos V, 2. Kunstmuseum, Bern, on long-term loan from the Estate of Hilde Thannhauser

transparent white washes and delicate, superimposed contours. In a little sketch, fixing the pose and framing line of the canvas (right), Sara is shown wearing pearls, which were one of her trademarks. She believed that sun and sea air were good for them and wore the pearls to the beach every day. Like Fitzgerald, Picasso was fascinated by Sara's pearls; indeed, he had himself photographed wearing them.[74]

Picasso had told Sara that he would picture her with her pearls,

Woman in White (Sara Murphy). 1923. Oil on canvas, 39 × 31½″ (99.1 × 80 cm). Zervos V, 1. The Metropolitan Museum of Art, New York. Purchase, Rogers Fund, acquired from The Museum of of Modern Art, New York. Lillie P. Bliss Collection, 1951

OPPOSITE, BOTTOM: Notebook page, detail of sketch for *Woman in White*. Carnet 067, p. 11. Musée Picasso, Paris and they are indeed visible in many of his portrait and beach studies of summer 1923. They also appear in most of the preparatory drawings and pastels for a very large projected painting, *The Pipes of Pan* (p. 41).[75] Here, Sara was depicted as a nude Venus, while Picasso himself, in the form of a handsome young alter ego, was represented as Mars. In several studies, he holds a mirror shaped like a picture frame up to Venus, as if to recall his earlier portraits of Sara.[76]

Note that his first version of the sketch for *Pipes of Pan* was not dedicated to Sara. On the contrary, it grew from a ballet commission: Diaghilev had asked Picasso to design new sets for a production of his Mallarmé, Debussy, and Nijinsky ballet *Afternoon of a Faun,* a project which ultimately came to nought. The earliest known sketch for the composition, dated February 4, 1923,[77] did not yet show Sara in the role of Venus. The following summer, when Picasso decided to use *The Pipes of Pan* as a vehicle for his infatuation with her, he assimilated Sara to Venus rather than Venus to her.[78]

Picasso submitted all his Neoclassical heroines — indeed, most of his portrait subjects of 1916–23 — to this sort of idealization, correcting any facial or bodily imperfections they might possess. Olga's weak, somewhat reces-

Portrait of Madame Errazuriz. c. 1920. Graphite on white paper, 11¾ × 9¼″ (29.8 × 23.5 cm). Not in Zervos. The Art Institute of Chicago. Bequest of Grant J. Pick

Drawing of an Antique Bust, in Profile. 1895. Lead pencil on paper, 4⅝ × 3¼″ (12 × 8.2 cm). Not in Zervos. Museu Picasso, Barcelona

Bust of a Woman in Profile. 1895. Lead pencil on paper, 4⅝ × 3⅛″ (12 × 8 cm). Not in Zervos. Museu Picasso, Barcelona

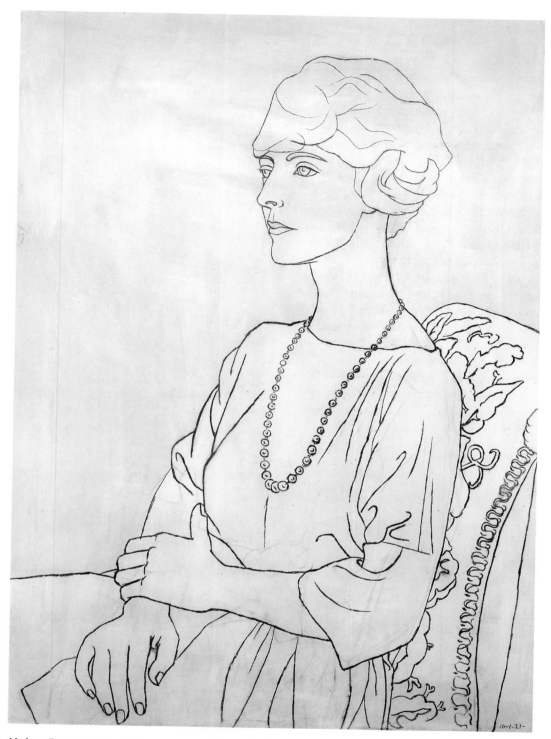

Madame Eugenia Errazuriz. January 10, 1921. Charcoal and gesso on prepared paper, 41⅜ × 29⅛" (105 × 74 cm). Zervos IV, 222. Private collection

sive chin (p. 325) is disguised in all of Picasso's pictures prior to 1923; similarly, Sara's slightly turned-up nose is eliminated from his paintings and drawings, even the one based directly on a photograph (p. 53). In a like manner, the large, idealized, and exquisitely limned profile portrait of the aging Chilean-born society beauty Eugenia Errazuriz was also cleansed of imperfections (above), as comparison with Picasso's other images of her confirm

(opposite, top). Her friend Igor Stravinsky, who had lauded Eugenia's "subtle and unrivaled understanding of an art which was not that of her generation," said that "she had preserved almost intact marks of great beauty and perfect distinction."[79] Picasso's large Neoclassical portrait deletes Stravinsky's qualifying term "almost," showing Madame Errazuriz looking some years younger than the artist's other, less idealized images of her.

Since the 1950s, scholars have recognized Marie-Thérèse Walter as a crucial muse for Picasso's work of the 1930s. But the precise date of her entry into the artist's life and work long remained a mystery. As the first canvases in which her presence seemed obvious dated from 1932, it initially appeared reasonable to assume that their relationship had begun the previous year. However, in 1974 Pierre Cabanne published an interview with Marie-Thérèse Walter in which she told him that she had met Picasso on Saturday, January 8, 1927, while shopping on the Boulevard Haussmann.[80]

This information led to a new conundrum, since—as several scholars subsequently pointed out—Marie-Thérèse's image seemed to be latently visible in Picasso's work at least a year earlier.[81] The mystery was resolved in the minds of some specialists by describing such pictures as "premonitory," or by relying on the idea that Picasso had been drawn to Marie-Thérèse herself because of her resemblance to a model generated from his own imagination.[82] This Gordian knot was sliced by Dr. Herbert T. Schwarz, a professional physician and Marie-Thérèse aficionado, who has argued that Picasso and Marie-Thérèse had indeed met outside the Galeries Lafayette—but in 1925 or 1926 rather than 1927. Picasso's long silence about her, and his subsequent misleading statements,

Passport photograph of Marie-Thérèse Walter (detail). Paris, 1930. Photograph by Photomaton. Collection Maya Picasso

Seated Girl (Marie-Thérèse?). 1926. Ink on paper. Zervos VII, 24. Private collection

Standing Girl (Marie-Thérèse?). 1926. Ink on paper, 18½ × 12⅝″ (47 × 32 cm). Zervos VII, 25. Private collection

WILLIAM RUBIN

Bust of a Girl (Marie-Thérèse). 1926. Charcoal and oil on canvas, 31⅞ × 25½″ (81 × 64.7 cm). Not in Zervos. Musée Picasso, Paris, on extended loan to the Musée d'Art Moderne, Strasbourg

could thus be explained by the fact that their acquaintanceship, though probably *not* their love affair, had begun when she was fifteen or sixteen. From this it would follow that, if their liaison was carried on with obsessive secrecy, it was not only because he feared Olga's wrath but because the relationship's history carried with it the potential for criticism of Picasso's discretion.

Dr. Schwarz's imaginative but unscholarly book proposes that Picasso quickly became a welcome visitor at the home in which Marie-Thérèse lived with her mother and sisters in Maisons d'Alfort, near the Marne. Indeed, the monumental canvas called *The Milliner's Workshop* (p. 62),[83] long believed to represent an atelier across the street from the artist's studio on rue La Boétie (following

The Milliner's Workshop. January 1926. Oil on canvas, 67¾ × 100⅞″ (172 × 256 cm). Zervos VII, 2. Musée National d'Art Moderne, Centre National d'Art et de Culture Georges Pompidou, Paris

Picasso's own misleading indications), turns out more logically to represent Marie-Thérèse, her mother, and her sister sewing in their home.[84] It is a strangely Intimist subject for such a monumental canvas. The uncanny, almost dreamlike, and strangely cinematic quality of the composition is accentuated by its striking Curvilinear Cubist style, combining sensual, interlacing arabesques with austere tones of black, gray, and white. Picasso himself appears as a mysterious black silhouette entering through the glass-paneled door at right: the door's oversize knob functions as an unmistakable sexual metaphor, which would reappear in Picasso's pictures of Marie-Thérèse for more than a decade (opposite and p. 336).[85]

There are a number of sketches and several oil paintings of Marie-Thérèse dating from winter 1925–26, when *The Milliner's Workshop* was nearing completion. In the most important of these, an oil portrait that Picasso never showed nor provided information about to Zervos, we

see this schoolgirl in the striped dress (and square bib collar) that would be characteristic for her image (p. 61).[86]

But if Dr. Schwarz's theory makes possible the identification of the highly personal motif in this 1926 canvas, it simultaneously complicates our sense of the relationship of subject to style in the work that Picasso would do five years later. From 1917 onward, Jean Arp and Surrealist artists such as Miró, Tanguy, and Masson had elaborated a biomorphic form language indirectly alluding to the internality of the human body.[87] It was, in a sense, a reaction against the Cubist grid, with its tacit reference to the inorganic, impersonal forms of architectural structure (beginning with the frame of the picture field itself). But their work was also an extension of Cubism insofar as it drew on Picasso and Braque's discovery of the poetic, evocative power of ambiguous shapes. In the later 1920s, Picasso himself experimented with biomorphic forms, both flat and modeled. His monumental

1927–28 figure drawings of concupiscent Bathers brought him close to the Surrealist imagery of Miró and Tanguy (pp. 66, top).

In 1931 Picasso suddenly adopted a new biomorphic style of painting characterized by organic forms in brilliant, unmodeled colors surrounded by heavy black contours (often compared to the "leading" used in making stained glass). It was, in effect, a surreal counterpart to his Curvilinear Cubism of the 1920s. Since the emergence of this style coincided with the date at which Marie-Thérèse was long believed to have entered his life, and since he used it for so many important images of her, it has come to be widely known as the "Marie-Thérèse" style. However, the fact that this style emerged six years after the commencement of their liaison suggests that Marie-Thérèse can hardly have constituted its sole and sufficient cause.[88]

At the same time, it cannot be doubted that Picasso's long, intense, and sexually passionate liaison with Marie-Thérèse helped inspire what is, after all, the most erotic style in the whole of modern painting. The link between style and biography in Picasso's work of the 1930s is too important to be ignored or dismissed. Certain paintings, such as the coldly monochromatic "bone" *Seated Bather* of 1930 (p. 64), were "inspired" by Olga (as Picasso himself indicated in this case[89]); while others, such as the colorful 1932 *Bather with Beach Ball* (p. 65), were clearly prompted by Marie-Thérèse—however much the finished images emerged as types rather than as individuals. Although one leading scholar has characterized these two pictures, stylistically, as "nearly twins,"[90] they seem to me remarkably different and not only in their morphologies.

By the later 1920s, Olga had been profoundly wounded by the failure of her marriage. While unaware of Marie-Thérèse's identity, she was probably conscious of the fact that Picasso was deceiving her. Olga reacted to this situation with frequent bouts of anger and with constant attempts to rein in her increasingly absent husband, to whom she would not grant a divorce.[91] A decade earlier, Picasso had treated her "like a goddess." He now began to treat her "like a doormat."[92] Later, she would chase after him everywhere, especially at the beach. Picasso, in turn, reacted with rage at Olga's attempts to control his private life and, by extension, his art. Having myself been an inadvertent witness to a momentary but volcanic outburst by the *monstre sacré* directed toward Jacqueline, I can feel only sympathy for Olga. Picasso's *terribilità*—the galvanic rage against inhumanity and death that generated *Guernica*—could also be aroused by personal friction.

Picasso's angry vision of Olga is unforgettably evoked in the 1930 *Seated Bather,* a darkling image of a woman as an aggressive ogress. She is made up of largely angular, hard, and unyielding forms, has a head with a sawtooth, steel-trap mouth and a back as impenetrable as a tortoise's carapace. Her mouth is a *vagina dentata,* a nightmarish symbol of castration that fascinated the Surrealists. (Indeed, the Bather's head also recalls another Surrealist

Woman with Sculpture. 1925. Oil on canvas, 51⅝ × 38⅛″ (131 × 97 cm). Zervos V, 451. Private collection

Woman in Front of a Window. 1937. Colored pencil on paper, 11⁷/₁₆ × 9³/₁₆″ (29 × 23.3 cm). Zervos IX, 79. Private collection

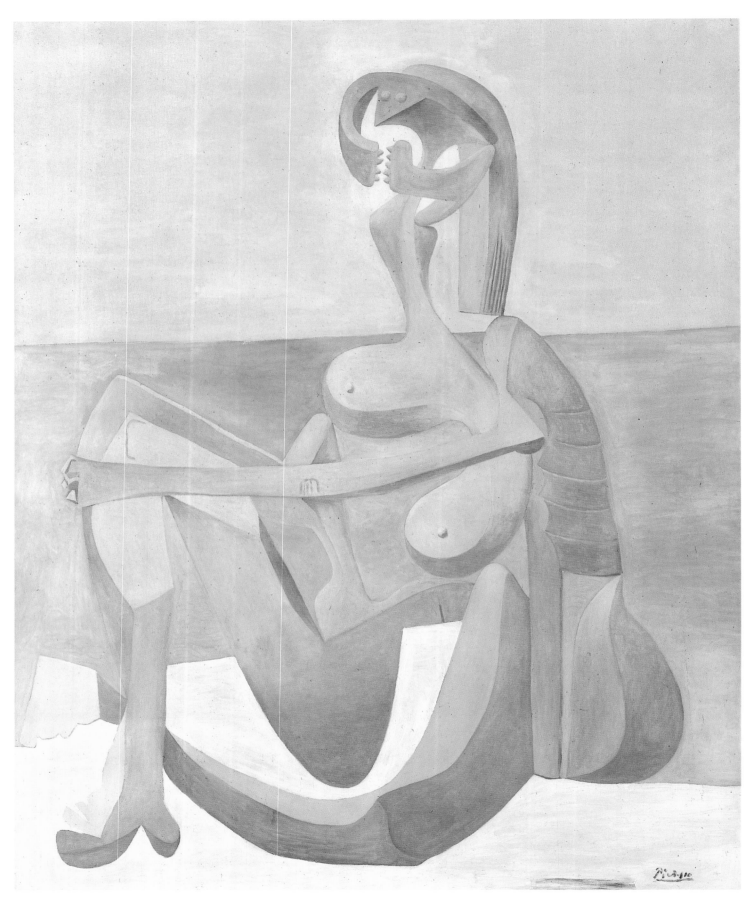

Seated Bather (Olga). 1930. Oil on canvas, 64¼ × 51″ (163.2 × 129.5 cm). Zervos VII, 306. The Museum of Modern Art, New York. Mrs. Simon Guggenheim Fund

Bather with Beach Ball (Marie-Thérèse). August 30, 1932. Oil on canvas, 57⅝ × 45⅛″ (146.2 × 114.6 cm). Zervos VIII, 147. The Museum of Modern Art, New York. Partial gift of an anonymous donor and promised gift of Ronald S. Lauder

"Bather." 1927. Pencil on paper, 12 × 9⅛″ (30.5 × 23 cm). Not in Zervos. Private collection

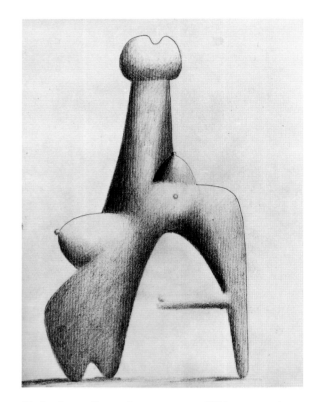

"Bather." 1927. Charcoal on paper, 12 × 9⅛″ (30.5 × 23 cm). Zervos VII, 109. Private collection

icon, the praying mantis, which devours its mate in the act of sex.)

The *Seated Bather* embodies the devouring woman, threatening and repellent; in contrast, the *Bather with Beach Ball* conceives Marie-Thérèse as a kind of squishy sexual toy—gay, decorative, squeezable, and playful.[93] The complementary violet and yellow of her bathing suit are like a banner, heraldically trumpeting Marie-Thérèse's "personal" colors in Picasso's paintings of that time, as Linda Nochlin has observed.[94] The morphologies of her body parts, in contrast to those of the seated Bather's, are rounded and soft rather than hard and bony. Marie-Thérèse plays with an inflated beach ball, or *ballon;* her whole figure has, in fact, become a kind of weightless Thanksgiving Day parade balloon, her mouth serving as the balloon's *embouchure,* the oval of which simultaneously evokes her genitals. She is, literally, the "pneumatic woman." The formal inventions which made possible the metaphoric languages of these two canvases cannot be attributed to the "influence" of either Olga or Marie-Thérèse; however, the differing formal vocabularies of the paintings clearly reflect Picasso's responses to the characters of their "models."

It might be objected that, even if the *Bather with Beach Ball* is clearly a portrayal of Marie-Thérèse, the so-called Marie-Thérèse style, with its "stained-glass" combination of dark contours and bright colors, is still only contin-

Marie-Thérèse Considering Her Sculpted Surrealist Effigy. May 4, 1933. Etching, 10⁹∕₁₆ × 7⁹∕₁₆″ (26.8 × 19.3 cm). Geiser/Baer II, 346. The Museum of Modern Art, New York. Abby Aldrich Rockefeller Fund gently linked to her—that she happened to be Picasso's chief model at the moment when he evolved this style but was not in any significant sense its inspiration. In support of this position, one might adduce the fact that Picasso's earliest essays in this style are not figure paintings, but such pictures as *Still Life on a Pedestal Table* (p. 69).

Is Marie-Thérèse really absent, however, from such a painting? A quarter of a century ago, discussing the "insistent anthropomorphism" of this picture, I described it as alive with "a pneumatic expansion and contraction . . . as if the components of the human body had been redistributed and transformed into fruit and objects." I also hazarded, with what now seems like surprising reticence, that it was "perhaps not too far-fetched to consider this picture a metaphoric tribute" to Marie-Thérèse.[95]

With the passage of time, this interpretation no longer appears farfetched; on the contrary, it has seemed—and not to me alone—almost inescapable. It is apparent that Picasso's tendency to exchange animate and inanimate forms was a fundamental element of his artistic personality, predating by many years the rise of Surrealism, with which it is frequently associated. It is evident in his 1908–09 canvas *Bread and Fruitdish on a Table,* in which the arrangement of the still-life motifs derives directly from an earlier figure composition.[96] The equation between the

guitar and the female figure in Picasso's Cubist pictures is by now virtually a critical cliché.[97] Indeed, this equation reappears in *Still Life with Guitar* (p. 71, top), a still-life composition painted on February 13, 1932, in which the instrument's fingerboard curves around its sound box in a formal configuration virtually identical to that of Marie-Thérèse's nose and head, as we see it in many painted and sculpted images of the early 1930s (p. 70, top).

Picasso's use of the anthropomorphic still life to "portray" a particular person links it to earlier symbolic portraits such as *"Ma Jolie"* and *"J'aime Eva"* of 1912–13. Here, individual identity was conveyed by poetic fragments—a bit of a refrain from a popular song, a declaration of love—containing private biographical allusions. However, it seems to me that the most richly poetic of Picasso's symbolic portraits are those that utilize nonliterary, purely visual symbols. More than any other painter (with the possible exception of Leonardo da Vinci), Picasso was able to perceive analogies between the shapes of different objects, assembling a formal lexicon that constituted a veritable "pan-physiognomic" of the visual world.

The analogies and transformations in Picasso's work might be compared to Dali's Surrealist double images, in which a single set of contours can be read as representing two different motifs. But Dali's double images are achieved

Seated Woman (Marie-Thérèse). 1932. India ink on paper, 14⁹⁄₁₆ × 9⅝" (37 × 24.5 cm). Zervos VIII, 2. Private collection

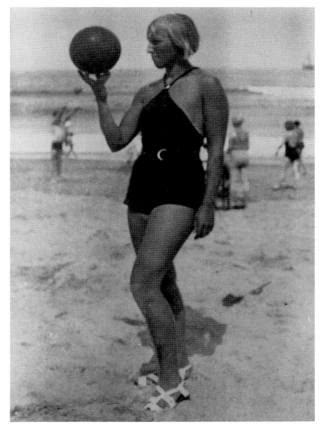

Marie-Thérèse Walter at age twenty, on the beach at Dinard, summer 1929. Photograph by Picasso. Collection Maya Picasso

The Studio. 1926. Ink on paper, 18½ × 12⅝″ (47 × 32 cm). Zervos VII, 32. Private collection

by a kind of brilliant trickery, a visual sleight of hand; stylistically, his pictures remain firmly within the realm of conventional illusionism. In contrast, Picasso—drawing on the biomorphism of Arp and Miró—abstracts and transforms his motifs to the point where their configuration leads the viewer to associate them, consciously or unconsciously, with other things. These open-ended images set off a series of associational reverberations, enhanced by the viewer's own imagination and experience and also by his or her familiarity with Picasso's other works. It is an animated, phantasmagorical, and erotic world in which the lips of pitchers and bowls approach each other, plants converse, and teapots kiss their *faïence* neighbors.[98]

Still Life on a Pedestal Table (opposite) is the greatest of Picasso's essays in this form of visual poetry. There is a surpassing ease and musicality in its drawing, and its metaphoric density reflects the accumulation of many years of associated motifs. The picture's nucleus can be traced, I believe, to a 1926 study (above) depicting a pitcher and an unrolled bolt of cloth, set atop the legs of a dressmaker's dummy (identifiable by its stitched seams). In itself, the motif of a dummy would seem to recall the

work of Giorgio de Chirico, with whom Picasso had had a fruitful period of exchange during World War I.[99] At first glance, there is no obvious reason why Picasso should have returned to this motif in 1926. However, Dr. Schwartz's thesis that *The Milliner's Workshop* probably depicts Marie-Thérèse and her family sewing in the living room of their Maisons d'Alfort villa, and his further observation that Picasso had set up a small working area there suggest that the drawing reflects an actual dressmaker's dummy belonging to Marie-Thérèse's family.[100] One suspects that Picasso himself set the pitcher and bolt of cloth atop the dummy's semicircular waist, thus confecting an anthropomorphic *assemblage* of real materials, of a type not unrelated to photographs of lost constructions in Picasso's studios and from such representations as the etching on page 66, bottom.

Five years later, in the 1931 *Still life on a Pedestal Table*, virtually the same kind of pitcher we see in the 1926 drawing reappears on the semicircular tabletop in conjunction with a tablecloth. Picasso seems primarily to have associated the curved contour of this kind of pitcher with Marie-Thérèse's breasts and torso, as in a 1932 drawing (p. 67, left) which offers, as it were, an interpretive sequel to the 1931 canvas. The pitcher's curved, rising spout seems to echo the "rising spill" of Marie-Thérèse's breasts in several drawings in which she is shown offering her body to a series of antique warriors. In a related drawing of such warriors, one figure is given Picasso's features; we might say that they are all his alter egos (p. 70, bottom).

Picasso's deliberately ambiguous figuration encourages alternative readings: the pitcher's hue and particularly its elegant golden handle may also be read as an intimation of Marie-Thérèse's blond hair, while the nearby green apples on the red tablecloth cry out to be read as breasts. The lavender "womb" shape to the left of the pitcher— which we will see again the following year in Marie-Thérèse's reflected image in *Girl Before a Mirror* (p. 357)— encloses red and green circles with a prominent black button, which may be read literally as an apple in a bowl, but seems also intended to evoke the image of his paramour's sex. The "womb"-shape's association to the vessel at its right is embodied in the yin-yang reciprocity of their organic forms and in their pairing of complementary colors—the yellow and lavender associated, as we have seen, with Marie-Thérèse. The striped pattern of the table's wooden slats may be a private allusion to the striped dress in which Picasso had drawn and painted Marie-Thérèse (pp. 60, 61) in 1926, not long after they met; it also anticipates the pattern of the bathing suit she wears in *Girl Before a Mirror*. In the same manner, the allusive biomorphism of the stemmed fruit bowl and its contents in the upper right has implicit physiognomic characteristics spelled out more explicitly in some of Picasso's other still lifes.[101]

Still Life on a Pedestal Table. March 2, 1931. Oil on canvas, 76¾ × 51¼″ (194 × 130 cm). Zervos VII, 317. Musée Picasso, Paris

Bust of Marie-Thérèse. 1931. Plaster, 28⅛ × 16⅛ × 13″ (71.5 × 41 × 33 cm). Spies 110, I. Musée Picasso, Paris

Bust of Marie-Thérèse (detail). 1931. Bronze, 30¾ × 17½ × 21⅛″ (78 × 44.5 × 54 cm). Spies 131, II. Musée Picasso, Paris

Soldier and Nude. April 30, 1930. Charcoal on paper, 11 × 10⅝″ (28 × 27 cm). Zervos VIII, 200. Private collection

The Peace between Athenians and Spartans (detail). December 31, 1933. India ink on paper, 13⁹⁄₁₆ × 19⅞″ (34.5 × 50.5 cm). Zervos VIII, 155. Private collection

Still Life with Guitar. 1932. Oil on canvas, 40¼ × 51¼″ (97 × 130 cm). Zervos VII, 375. Private collection

Sleeping Nude (Marie-Thérèse). April 4, 1932. Oil on canvas, 51¼ × 63¾″ (130 × 161.7 cm). Zervos VII, 332. Musée Picasso, Paris

Sheet of sketches. May 1, 1936. India ink on paper, 10¼ × 6¾ ″ (26 × 17.3 cm). Not in Zervos. Musée Picasso, Paris

These ambiguous significations were not limited to Picasso's still lifes; they could equally well appear in the representation of one body part by another. A 1936 drawing (above) provides a kind of "Rosetta Stone" to Picasso's metamorphic language of this period, showing how the image of a recumbent woman (Marie-Thérèse) was transformed into two radically new figurations of the human head. The relatively realistic drawing at the top of this sheet depicts the woman from above, sleeping (or perhaps merely resting) in a narrow bed with striped sheets and a blanket drawn up below her spreading breasts. (Comparison to a 1915 Cubist drawing of a woman in bed [p. 38] suggests that Picasso had long ago been struck by the way that a woman's breasts, normally pulled in the same direction by the force of gravity, might incline in different directions when she is lying down.[102]) The overhead per-

spective of the "realistic" drawing also yields an unusual view of the face, with the nostrils, seen from below, seeming to merge with the outer contour of the woman's face.

In the second drawing on this sheet, marked with a Roman "II," the head as a whole has been reconfigured as a pair of rounded, breastlike forms. The wildly divergent eyes echo the woman's everted nipples in the first drawing, but the juxtaposition of the two somewhat conical shapes also seems to owe something to the earlier configuration of chin and nose.

In sketches II and III, Picasso experimented with what look like different forms of sculptural bases and supports for what might have become a surreal construction.[103] But this head was almost immediately realized instead as an oil painting of moderate dimensions, the *Woman in a Straw Hat* (opposite), of May 1, 1936.[104] Picasso retained

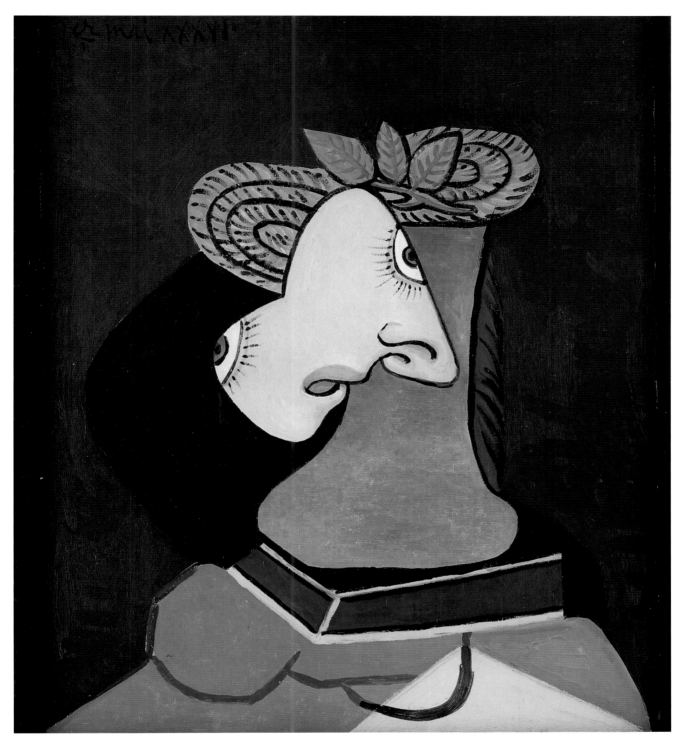

Woman in a Straw Hat (Marie-Thérèse). May 1, 1936. Oil on canvas, 24 × 19¾″ (61 × 50 cm). Not in Zervos. Musée Picasso, Paris

this startling work in his own collection. Acquired after the artist's death by the Musée Picasso in Paris, it was included in The Museum of Modern Art's Picasso retrospective of 1980, where it caught the attention of Jasper Johns, inspiring a new set of variations in his subsequent work.

It is, in a sense, easier to elucidate the formal evolution of this head than it is to define its biographical references.

The continuity between nose and forehead is typical of Picasso's Neoclassical portraits of Marie-Thérèse and of the biomorphic sculptural busts inspired by her. However, the sense of anguish evident in the revised head is hardly characteristic of Marie-Thérèse—or at least of Marie-Thérèse as Picasso depicted her. I had originally felt that it might possibly be among the earliest paintings influenced

Nusch in a Hat by the Sea (2nd state). 1936. Sugar-lift aquatint, 6¼ × 4¼″ (15.9 × 10.8 cm). Geiser/Baer III, 607 (2). Musée Picasso, Paris

Portrait of Nusch Eluard (2nd state). 1936. Sugar-lift aquatint, 6¼ × 4¼″ (15.9 × 10.8 cm). Geiser/Baer III, 607 (1). Musée Picasso, Paris

by Dora Maar. Picasso had met her some months before the date of the picture's execution, and its sense of apprehension and foreboding—particularly the feeling of conflict and cross-purposes expressed in the bipolarized glance—was to become a commonplace in pictures of Dora made several years later (p. 384).[105] However, it seems more likely that Picasso was primarily imaging through Marie-Thérèse his own inner turmoil at a moment when he was caught between conflicting demands from her (she had recently given birth to their daughter, Maya), and Olga, who was rendered nearly hysterical by the not unrelated formalization of her separation from Picasso.

The painter would later recall this period as "the worst time of my life."[106] Of course it cannot have been very enjoyable for Olga or Marie-Thérèse, either; but it seems safe to assume that the anguish evoked in Picasso's pictures of this period is essentially his own, even if it is projected onto a female subject. (Similarly, it might be questioned whether the most agonized of the 1936–43 Dora portraits [p. 400, bottom] necessarily "have their roots in [her] chronic distress"[107]—as opposed to serving as a vehicle for Picasso's own anxieties.[108])

In any case, the distressed visage of the *Woman in a Straw Hat* soon became a transposable element, which reappeared a month later in an aquatint done as an illustration for Paul Eluard's *La Barre d'appui* (above, left). The head and the adjacent jar might be regarded as signs for

Marie-Thérèse, but the cloche hat and the mass of frizzy hair emerging from it mark the image also as a symbolic portrayal of the poet's wife, Nusch, subject of another, more realistic aquatint in the same volume (above, right).

In the fourth sketch on the "Rosetta" sheet, Marie-Thérèse's head has been imagined as something resembling a Jerusalem artichoke or a mandrake root covered with "contour lines" found on many roots and tubers—the first instance of what would become a favorite morphology in Picasso's work of the following years. The tips of the tuber's extrusions identify themselves as eyes and nose, but these surreal elements cohabit with the relatively realistic shock of hair to the left, recognizable from photographs of Marie-Thérèse and from other portraits of her. The oil painting based upon this sketch (p. 76, top left) was executed later on the same busy day as the drawings and canvas of the *Woman in a Straw Hat*. As in the previous case, the associations with Marie-Thérèse appear to vanish as soon as the morphology is redeployed. In 1937 it would do service in a series of studies inspired by Dora Maar, culminating in the superb transformed portrait, *Seated Woman with a Hat* (p. 394).

More surprisingly, this tuber morphology would serve, in the interim, as the nucleus of the monstrous and effeminate cavalier/dragon symbolizing evil, Fascism, and Franco in the *Dream and Lie of Franco* (p. 76). In the third scene (in order of execution) of this nightmare fantasy,

"Franco" is shown attempting to destroy an allegorical statue of Truth, based precisely on Marie-Thérèse in her Neoclassical form, which suggests that for Picasso the forces of destruction issue from the same nucleus as those of creation. But it also attests to the contingent character of such morphologies in the artist's work. They have an independent expressive life which allows them very differ-

ent meanings depending on the contexts of the drama into which they are inserted—essentially political in the *Dream and Lie of Franco*. A psychoanalytic interpretation might relate the tuber morphology elliptically to Marie-Thérèse, or, more generally, to the profound ambivalence that invariably tended, for Picasso, to insinuate itself into love or passion. It was as if the artist's very attraction to a

Grand Air, from *Les Yeux fertiles*, by Paul Eluard (Paris: G.L.M., 1936). June 3–4, 1936. Etching, 16⅞ × 12½″ (41.7 × 31.8 cm). The Museum of Modern Art, New York. A. Conger Goodyear Fund

Head of a Woman (Marie-Thérèse). May 1, 1936. Oil on canvas, 24 × 19¾″ (61 × 50 cm). Not in Zervos. Musée Picasso, Paris

Seated Woman with a Hat (Dora). September 10, 1938. Oil and sand on wood panel, 21⅝ × 18⅛″ (55 × 46 cm). Zervos IX, 228. The Menil Collection, Houston. Gift of Dominique de Menil. (Colorplate, p. 394)

Dream and Lie of Franco, I (detail, upper left; detail, center right). January 8, 1937. Etching and aquatint, 12⅜ × 16⁹⁄₁₆″ (31.4 × 42.1 cm). Geiser / Baer III, 615. The Museum of Modern Art, New York. The Louis E. Stern Collection

Dream and Lie of Franco, II (detail, center; detail, center right). January 8–9, June 7, 1937. Etching and aquatint, 12⅜ × 16⁹⁄₁₆″ (31.4 × 42.1 cm). Geiser / Baer III, 616. The Museum of Modern Art, New York. The Louis E. Stern Collection

L'Arlésienne (Lee Miller). 1937. Oil on canvas, 31⅞ × 25⁹⁄₁₆″ (81 × 65 cm). Zervos VIII, 370. Musée Réattu, Arles

woman—especially if she risked becoming a "muse"—endowed her with a threatening power over him, which could then find itself extrapolated into wholly unrelated (to her) dramas of risk and danger.

Insofar as Picasso's art sprang from the deepest well-springs of his private experience, it is not surprising that the great majority of his portraits are devoted to the women with whom he was intimately involved. However, I want to examine the portraits of at least one masculine subject of this period—the poet Paul Eluard—precisely because of the light they cast on the interaction between portraiture as public statement and portraiture as private expression.

Eluard had known Picasso since the pioneer days of Surrealism and had formed a significant collection of his work.[109] But their intimacy really began in 1933, when the two worked together on the first issue of *Minotaure*. It was publicly solemnized in 1936, when Eluard "represented" the absent artist by delivering a lecture at the opening of Picasso's first large exhibition in Spain, organized by the young Catalan architect José-Luis Sert and The Friends of New Art (ADLAN) in Barcelona. A handsome, if bland, portrait drawing of Eluard made at that time (p. 78, left) was one of the first in a series of amicable gestures on Picasso's part that included other portraits and illustrations for books of Eluard's poems. Another portrait, done in 1941, is drawn in an angular style recalling the faceted planes of 1909 Cubism, but remaining fundamentally within the realm of conventional illusionism (p. 78, right). Picasso evidently considered some form of

Portrait of Paul Eluard (frontispiece for *Les Yeux fertiles*). January 8, 1936. Lead pencil on paper, 9¹³⁄₁₆ × 6³⁄₈″ (25 × 16.2 cm). Zervos VIII, 273. Musée d'Art et d'Histoire, Saint-Denis. Gift of Dominique Eluard, 1955

Portrait of Paul Eluard. October 5, 1941. Ink on paper, 10⅝ × 8¹⁄₁₆″ (27 × 20.5 cm). Not in Zervos. Private collection

"realism" to be the appropriate style for such images, done as gestures and meant for public consumption.

The artist permitted himself far greater liberties in other works, such as his illustrations for Eluard's texts. In the 1936 etching decorating the poem *Grand Air,* which Eluard was able to write out on the zinc plate in his own hand through a new technique developed by Picasso's printer Lacourière (p. 75), the artist surrounded Eluard's text with symbolic figures representing his associations to it. On the right, a beautiful feminine nude with satyr's horns holds a mirror that blinds the eyes of Sol, in the sky on the left. Only the figure of a recumbent woman at the bottom—a synthesis of "abstract," surreal, and expressionist constituents—is as conceptually challenging an image as Picasso's contemporary representations of Marie-Thérèse or Dora.

None of these images, however, prepare the viewer for the profound strangeness of Picasso's 1937 oil portrait of Eluard (opposite). In contrast to the public portraits we have just examined, this is a distinctly private image. When it was painted, Picasso and Dora were vacationing in Mougins with Paul and Nusch Eluard. Picasso emerged from his studio in the small hotel where they were staying and announced that he had just completed a portrait of Paul. The friends present on this occasion—a group

including Roland Penrose, Lee Miller, and probably also Man Ray, as well as the Eluards—were first excited and then shocked, for the portrait was not only a transvestite but a transsexual image. "It was," Penrose recalled, "a problem for all of us. One could distinguish in the strong features and sparkling eyes a certain resemblance to the profile of Eluard, but one was disconcerted to see this head topped with a little hat in the manner of the women of Arles and to note that the poet had changed sex. Jutting out beneath the bright green shawl were generous breasts at which a striped cat was suckling."[110]

The *Portrait of Paul Eluard* seemed a puzzling and disturbing image to Picasso's friends and such it has remained. Indeed, this portrait obviously so flustered Penrose (who was himself a Surrealist artist) that he remembered the colors wrongly. The shawl was at most a kind of olive green; the bright green was Eluard's skin. Picasso's friends were not the only ones left speechless; although an entire book was later dedicated to the subject of Eluard, Picasso, and painting, its author, Jean-Charles Gateau, made no direct reference to the portrait.[111] To be sure, one finds oneself torn between admiration for the painting—the sureness of its drawing and the daring of its palette—and confusion produced by its image.

Some light may be cast on it, however, by examining

Portrait of Paul Eluard. 1937. Oil on canvas, 31⅞ × 25¾″ (81 × 65.5 cm). Zervos VIII, 373. Private collection

Picnic at Mougins, summer 1937. From left to right: Paul and Nusch Eluard, Lee Miller, Man Ray, and Adrienne Fidelin. Photograph by Roland Penrose. Lee Miller Archives

Picasso's portraits of Eluard's wife, Nusch. Several of Picasso's biographers—some of them no doubt simply following Françoise Gilot—suggest that he and Nusch had had a "carnal adventure," most likely in 1937.[112] Indeed, Françoise cites Picasso as saying that Eluard himself had urged the two to be lovers, as a way of symbolizing his own love for both of them.[113] This is not quite as improbable as it may sound: Eluard's first wife, Gala, had, with his consent, entered into an affair with Max Ernst and then divorced Eluard (without, however, ending their sexual liaison) in order to marry Salvador Dali. In true Surrealist fashion, Eluard insisted that he was "above" possessiveness when it came to love and that he considered sexual jealousy contemptible. Whatever actually happened between Picasso and Nusch, the assumption that they had been lovers became, in the event, so widespread that—in what I believe is a unique instance—the painter actually denied it.[114]

Picasso's more conventional portraits of Nusch seem intended to depict her in a public role as the poet's consort. The most "presentable" of these shows her in a decorative palette as an elegant, smiling *parisienne* (p. 82, top). Executed in late summer 1937, this picture subsequently served as an "illustration" to the publication of a poem that her husband dedicated to her, *"Je veux qu'elle*

Portrait of Man Ray. January 3, 1934. India ink on paper, $13^{5}/_{8} \times 9^{3}/_{4}$" (34.5 × 24.8 cm). Zervos VIII, 165. Private collection

L'Arlésienne (Lee Miller). 1937. Oil and ripolin on canvas, 28½ × 23½″ (72.5 × 60 cm). Not in Zervos. Private collection

Portrait of Nusch Eluard. 1937. Oil on canvas, 36¼ × 25¾″ (92 × 65.2 cm). Zervos VIII, 377. Musée Picasso, Paris

Nusch Eluard. [Paris 1936]. Photograph by Man Ray. Man Ray Trust / ADAGP, Paris, 1996. Collection Lucien Treillard

soit reine!"[115] There is some formal invention in this double-profile oil portrait, but Nusch's elegantly double-breasted coat and chic hat establish an air of public decorum, countered only by the provocation of the horseshoe in the Schiaparelli-like hat. Another, very casual sketch from the same moment—tinted with plant sap and lipstick—shows Nusch in a movie-star pose, adjusting her sunglasses (p. 108).

In contrast to such public images, a small contemporaneous oil portrait of Nusch that Picasso kept for himself testifies to the intensity of the artist's private feelings toward her (opposite). The pure profile on the right side of the image and the decorative palette of blue, yellow, green, and magenta—which form a color chord in descending quantities—seem to evoke Nusch's "public" persona. But within this impersonal silhouette and deco-

Portrait of Nusch Eluard. 1937. Oil on canvas, 21½ × 18″ (54.6 × 45.7 cm). Zervos VIII, 369. Private collection

rative underpinning, Picasso's surreal/expressionist hand exposes a private, frontal image drawn and modeled in somber blacks and grays. Virtually every facial feature has been altered or displaced; Nusch's right eye faces the "wrong" direction and her tear-shaped nostrils recall the numerous "Weeping Women" Picasso painted that same year. The highlight of her hair has been transformed into a bony vertebral carapace—an allusion, perhaps, to the "bone" Olgas, which pictures the latter as a "destroying woman." Nusch is presented here as a woman simultaneously beautiful and terrifying, a duality intensified on every level by the tension between the picture's decorative and expressive constituents.

This "private" Nusch directly recalls the feline *femme fatale* in some of Man Ray's photographs (right). The bland, guarded smile of Nusch in the "public" portrait

Nusch Eluard. [Montlignon, 1935]. Photograph by Man Ray. Man Ray Trust/ADAGP, Paris, 1996. Collection Lucien Treillard

Portrait of Nusch Eluard. 1938. Charcoal and pencil on canvas, 36¼ × 28⅜″ (92 × 72 cm). Not in Zervos. Private collection

is transformed in this small oil into a toothy rictus, somewhere between the smiles in *Les Demoiselles d'Avignon* and the smile of Willem de Kooning's *Woman I*. Nusch's gleaming but menacing teeth seem ready to bite off a limb of the unwary viewer; their ominous (not to say castratory) associations are underscored by the fact that Nusch's own neck and head are presented on what looks like a yellow tabletop, as though they had been severed from her body. It is possible, of course, that the "tabletop" is nothing more sinister than the wide collar of a yellow summer dress; but, if so, Picasso's cropping of it has imbued it with aggressive implications never dreamed of by its designer. The sadistic undertones of the painting inescapably recall Françoise Gilot's description of Picasso

Portrait of Nusch Eluard. 1941. Oil on canvas, 28¾ × 23⅝″ (73 × 60 cm). Zervos XI, 274. Musée National d'Art Moderne, Centre National d'Art et de Culture Georges Pompidou, Paris. Gift of Paul Eluard, 1947

as having "a kind of Bluebeard complex that made him want to cut off the heads of all the women he had collected in his little private museum."[116]

Four years later, in 1941, Picasso would paint a tender and fragile—almost disincarnate—portrayal of a waiflike Nusch (above), whose echo of the Blue period may well be a reference to Nusch's early years as a performer with a traveling circus. This picture—in which, as Brassaï said, Picasso "wanted to put aside the terrible and rest in the gracious"—the artist gave to Eluard.[117]

There may also be an allusion to Nusch in the frizzy hair, decorative hat, elegant dress, and high heels of the recumbent woman at the bottom of Picasso's 1936 illustration to Eluard's poem *Grand Air.* Her somewhat

Portrait of Nusch Eluard. 1941. Ink on paper, 10⅝ × 8¼″
(27 × 21 cm). Not in Zervos. Private collection

tuberlike head relates to the fourth sketch in the
"Rosetta Stone" drawing we have already examined (p. 72); at her breast is curled a cat that suck-
les three tiny fish. This image is sister to the print
we have mentioned from the poet's *Barre d'appui,*
which fused aspects of Nusch and Marie-Thérèse
in a feminine Surrealist "construction."

Returning, with these works in mind, to
Picasso's 1937 *Portrait of Paul Eluard,* we may formulate an extremely provisional hypothesis
about its meaning. Whatever actually transpired
between Nusch and Picasso, the artist may well
have interpreted Eluard's willingness to "offer"
his wife as an expression of the poet's own
unconscious desires. Crudely put, Picasso may
have seen Eluard as a repressed homosexual,
employing his wife as a means of entering vicari-
ously into a sexual relationship with the artist.
The painting would thus offer a visual expression
of the cliché—now outmoded—that a male
homosexual is "really" a woman in a man's body.
Such a popular theory might, at least, explain
some of the confusion and embarrassment with
which Eluard's friends greeted the canvas.[118]

I remain puzzled by the Arlésienne costume in
which the poet is dressed. There are no references to Arlésiennes in Eluard's poetry.[119] It may
have to do with the painting's brilliant, high-
keyed "meridional" color, recalling somewhat the
paintings of van Gogh, who would return increas-

ingly over the next decades as a point of reference in
Picasso's work. Indeed, Eluard's portrait was immediately
followed by some highly colored, abstract "Arlésiennes"
that Picasso identified as portraits of Lee Miller (p. 77).[120]
As for the cat suckling at Eluard's breast, it seems possible,
at least, that it is linked to the woman with a cat at the
bottom of the *Grand Air* etching. Considering the two
images together, one might read the cat as representing
Nusch herself, receiving love and sustenance from Eluard
(in the painting) while herself offering them to other men
(in the etching).

Paul Eluard in his apartment at 35, rue de la Chapelle, Paris, 1944. Photograph by Brassaï

Minotaur and Woman (Marie-Thérèse). June 24, 1933. India ink on blue paper, 18½ × 24½″ (47 × 62 cm). Zervos VIII, 112. The Art Institute of Chicago. Gift of Margaret Blake

Minotaur and Woman (Dora). September 1, 1936. India ink and colored pencil on paper, 16⁹⁄₁₆ × 27⁹⁄₁₆″ (42 × 70 cm). Zervos VIII, 296. Private collection

Reclining Woman with a Book (Marie-Thérèse). January 21, 1939. Oil on canvas, 38 × 51⅜″ (96.5 × 130.5 cm). Zervos IX, 253. Musée Picasso, Paris

Although Nusch and Paul Eluard remained Picasso's portrait subjects into the early 1940s, neither's image would again reflect the signs of intimacy with the artist that we see in 1937. As the 1930s drew to a close, the Spaniard's art was dominated by imagery of Marie-Thérèse and Dora, the two women between whom he was now dividing his life. It is sometimes said that pictures of Marie-Thérèse during this period are drier than they had been before, reflecting Dora's ascendancy as Picasso's primary companion. This, I think, may be unfair to both Marie-Thérèse and Picasso himself, for it implies that the artist could love only one woman at a time. Moreover, some portraits of Marie-Thérèse from the later 1930s are among the most lyrical of his career (above and p. 381).

It would hardly be surprising if, following the birth of Maya, and after more than a decade with Marie-Thérèse, the purely sexual aspect of Picasso's love for her might somewhat have diminished—especially in the face of the relative novelty of his sexual life with Dora (though the purely sensual side of the Dora imagery is much less impassioned or abandoned than the comparable imagery of Marie-Thérèse; p. 87). That Picasso was now spending

more of his time with Dora than with Marie-Thérèse had, I believe, less to do with passion for Dora than the fact that, as an artist and an intellectually absorbing woman, she fit easily into the painter's circle of friends, and, moreover, challenged the artist in psychological and political ways. Meanwhile, Marie-Thérèse (and Maya, to whom Picasso was deeply attached) remained the center of that secret private world she had always embodied for him.

On a single day in January 1939 Picasso took stock of his emotional life by painting both Marie-Thérèse and Dora in a similar reclining position, in the same setting, on canvases of the same shape and size. This unusual *paragone,* or comparison, was clearly as much an investigation into, as a statement about, his feelings toward the two women and, as such, revealed two very different kinds of love and fascination. The two pictures also stand as excellent examples of the way different "subjects," as Picasso had observed, tended in his art to elicit differing styles, or at least characteristically different morphologies. Both women are pictured in front of the triple windows of the studio that Vollard had put at the artist's disposal at Le-Tremblay-sur-Mauldre, though it is improb-

Reclining Woman with a Book (Dora). January 21, 1939. Oil on canvas, 38½ × 51″ (97.8 × 130 cm). Zervos IX, 252. Private collection

able that either woman was there that day, at least while Picasso was working. Something of the confrontation in this *paragone* had been anticipated three years earlier, just after Picasso met Dora, in a drawing of a voluptuous Marie-Thérèse reclining in that same studio; a mysterious woman (doubtless Dora) is seen through the window (p. 109, left). Such images are not infrequent in the work of Picasso, who had a tendency to dramatize his thoughts and sentiments as a form of private theater.

The deeply felt if not very flattering portrait of a reclining Dora (above) shows her wearing the hat familiar from many earlier portraits. The orange / red and yellow of the couch and dress, combined with the pale green of her skin, remind us of the overheated palette of Dora's portrait as the "Weeping Woman" (p. 390). But here these expressionist hues are softened by the less-acid, more-languid lavender, purple, and magenta of the costume and hat. Nevertheless, the overall effect, if more decorative than most of Picasso's portraits of Dora, seems characteristically tense and discomforted; the forms are predominantly angular and seem sliced into the surface. The anachronistic budding trees seen through the windows

provide an out-of-season note of optimism, though at some cost in terms of the continuity of the surface patterning—a type of decision characteristic for Picasso, especially in these years, in that he sacrifices formal values in favor of expressive and poetic effects.

The opaque green panels that form the windows of the Marie-Thérèse portrait symbolically suggest a verdant world outside, but at the same time emphasize the model's enclosure within the wholly private world of Picasso's studio. Marie-Thérèse herself is realized in sympathetic terms, her large blue eyes dominating the soft curves of her handsome, naturalistically colored face and golden hair. The same lyrical, curvilinear morphology extends through the breasts and torso, establishing a bold contrast between the organic shapes of the figure and the geometrically rigorous ones of the windows. Dora's portrait is marked by its splayed arms and clawlike fingers and by the nervous articulation of her surroundings—the wallpaper pattern, trees, pillow, and bolster. In contrast, the image of Marie-Thérèse is characterized by an unencumbered decorative simplicity, her relaxed, clasped hands reflecting her inner ease.

Leonardo da Vinci. *Mona Lisa*. Oil on wood panel, 30¼ × 20⅞″ (76.8 × 53 cm). The Louvre, Paris

The portraits from the remaining thirty-three years of Picasso's career offer a rich panorama of formal invention, visual symbolism, and biographical incident. However, aside from those of Jacqueline, about which I have written in the closing essay of this volume, I will leave them entirely in the capable hands of other scholars in order to conclude by addressing certain unexpected parallels between Picasso and the painter of what is certainly the most famous portrait in the history of Western art, the Mona Lisa.

The comparison between Picasso and Leonardo may, at first glance, seem farfetched or irrelevant. As a young art historian, I myself would probably have rejected any connection between their work as mere coincidence. However, in the course of a series of extended visits with Picasso during the last three years of his life, I found myself surprised by the relative frequency with which the name of Leonardo passed the artist's lips—a greater frequency than is apparent in the various conversations with Picasso published by his intimates and friends. Alas, of Picasso's various references to the Renaissance master, the only one which appears verbatim in my notes is his

citation of Leonardo's celebrated remark: "the painter always paints himself."

Over the decades since then, as I have returned repeatedly to Picasso's work in a series of exhibitions and scholarly studies, his curious affinities with the Florentine master have become increasingly apparent to me. Both were primarily draftsmen, gifted with an instantaneous wiring of eye and hand. And both used their gift for drawing more to seize, record, and, above all, comprehend their respective worlds of experience than to make paintings. To be sure, Leonardo's comprehension of the world was far more scientific than Picasso's. But then Leonardo lived at a time when it was still possible to be an *uomo universale,* simultaneously in the vanguard not only of art and literature, but of subjects such as geology, physics, anatomy, and mathematics.[121] (As Meyer Schapiro observed, this was, in part, because fifteenth-century science dealt only with visible phenomena.) Picasso's relative lack of interest in science reflects not only the vicissitudes of his education, but also the almost unbridgeable gap between art and science in the modern world.

In Picasso's work as in Leonardo's, the realms of the real and the imaginary overlap because it is through the imagination that both artists grasp the real. Beyond this, there is a certain similarity to the emotional tenor of their work: a strange combination of passion and remoteness, longing and revulsion, idealism and perversity. Walter Pater, in a famous passage in his book *The Renaissance,* described the Mona Lisa as a kind of "vampire," whose beauty was "wrought out from within upon the flesh, the deposit . . . of strange thoughts and fantastic reveries," a figure "into which the soul with all its maladies has passed."[122] Surely this description could be applied with equal if not greater justice to Picasso's 1937 portrait of Nusch Eluard (p. 83) and to countless other portraits by him from the Blue period through the 1960s.

Of course, Pater's purple prose itself offers a "strange" and "fantastic" vision of the Mona Lisa. Arguably, it tells us more about the origins of the Decadent movement in England than it does about Leonardo. But this is hardly irrelevant to Picasso, whose Barcelona compatriots were fervent admirers of Oscar Wilde and *The Yellow Book*.[123] Picasso would surely have endorsed the notoriously amoral conclusion of Pater's *Renaissance:* that the goal of life was to experience the broadest possible range of passions and insights, "to burn always with [a] hard, gem-like flame," to seek out "ecstasy" wherever it might be found.[124] And he might have found philosophical justification for the liberties of his portraiture in Pater's insistence that the "clear, perpetual outline of face and limb" was in fact an optical illusion, an arbitrary image disguising the endless combination and recombination of the elements composing the human frame.[125]

Yet Pater's comments, however exaggerated, respond

Leonardo da Vinci. *Head of a Woman Three Quarters to the Left* (study for Saint Anne). Red and black chalk with touches of white, 9⅝ × 7⅜″ (24.4 × 18.7 cm). Royal Library, Windsor, No. 12,534

Leonardo da Vinci. *The Madonna of the Rocks* (detail). Panel, 74⅝ × 47¼″ (189.55 × 120.2 cm). National Gallery, London

to a genuine strangeness in Leonardo's portrait. The fame of the painting is not due to its realism: we probably wouldn't recognize Mona Lisa if we bumped into her on the subway. What we recall is not the details of her face (how many people have noticed that she has no eyebrows?) but the intimate and enigmatic quality of her expression. The *Mona Lisa* is so much the prototype for subsequent portraiture that it is hard for us to remember that the more usual pose for *quattrocento* portraits had been a profile view such as we find in Pollaiuolo and Uccello. The profile was felt to capture the true and timeless character of the subject's face, disengaged from the accidentality of everyday perception; it was almost invariably used for emblematic images of rank or power, as in the official portraits stamped on coins. The profile deliberately distanced the viewer from the person portrayed.

Mona Lisa's pose is ambiguous—somewhere between a frontal and a three-quarter view. Together with the dimly lit setting and the muted light playing over her features, it creates a sensation of unusual intimacy between subject and viewer. To this intimacy is added a sense of enigma, generated in part by the mysterious landscape in the background—which Richard Offner described as "winding around the figure like a wreath of smoke"[126]— and in part by Mona Lisa's famously peculiar smile.

Ludwig Goldscheider linked the latter to a Renaissance manual advising young women that they could acquire a special allure by smiling on only one side of the face, keeping the lips on the other side pressed together in a horizontal line.[127] When my wife tried this, it seemed more laughable than alluring. That the source of the smile is Leonardo's unconscious store of imagery, and not the face of Signora del Giocondo, is seemingly confirmed by the similarity of her smile to those of Leonardo's earlier, more generic figures, such as Saint Anne (above, left) in the *Madonna and Child with Saint Anne and Saint John,* and the angel (above, right) in *The Madonna of the Rocks.* But whatever the source of Mona Lisa's asymmetrical smile, Leonardo made out of it a magnificent poem about the duality of the human soul.

Works such as Picasso's 1937 oil portrait of Nusch Eluard (p. 83)—and also the closely associated charcoal-on-canvas drawing of the following year (p. 84)—seem to me descendants not only of Walter Pater's Mona Lisa but also of Leonardo's. The seated pose and the sense of intimacy between artist and subject are, in a sense, common properties of the Western portrait tradition deriving from Leonardo. The more profound affinity has to do with both artists' ability to mobilize formal details for expressive purposes: for instance, to evoke psychological tension

Mother and Child. c. 1922. Pencil on paper, 16½ × 12″ (42 × 30.5 cm). Zervos XXX, 360. Private collection. (Colorplate, p. 49)

Leonardo da Vinci. *The Madonna and Child with Saint Anne and Saint John*. Charcoal heightened with white, on brown paper, 54¾″ × 39⅜″ (139.7 × 100.1 cm). National Gallery, London

by emphasizing the asymmetries of the human visage.

Picasso's conceptual (rather than perceptual) approach to representation allows him to explore such asymmetries in the face as a whole, not just in individual features. Thus Nusch's outlined profile on the right (p. 83) recalls the heraldic conventions of public portraiture, while the more frontal presentation of her eyes and mouth permits the viewer to glimpse the "private" self hidden within the public image. The contrast between profile and frontal views seems to parallel the tension between the seductiveness of Nusch's partly closed, heavy-lidded eyes and the threat in her toothy smile and reflects, in turn, the polarization between decorative and expressive components of the image. Here, as in so many of his images, Picasso uses painting to exorcise his own profound ambivalence toward women. Elsewhere, as in his portraits of Marie-Thérèse Walter, he employs similar reconfigurations to evoke the combination of masculine and feminine qualities within the same human being.

Picasso's work sometimes also displays surprising affinities with the formal rather than the psychological aspects of Leonardo's style. This is most apparent in certain of his Neoclassical drawings, such as the 1922 sketch

of a *Mother and Child* (above, left; p. 49), in which the interlocked figures form a "pyramidal" composition of the type originated by Leonardo and reproduced in countless canvases by Raphael and his followers. The benign, half-smiling expression on the mother's face, the shy tilt of her head, and the bulk of her figure, are—save for some "mannerist" elongation—extraordinarily similar to those of the figures in Leonardo's cartoon for the unfinished *Saint Anne, the Virgin, the Infant Christ, and the Young Saint John* in London's National Gallery (above). The gentle and delicate pencil shading, here and in numerous other Neoclassical works, is also remarkably reminiscent of Leonardo. Yet the indefinable classic beauty of certain of Picasso's and Leonardo's figures is, in both cases, the other side of the coin of their fascination with monsters, both "human" and otherwise (opposite)—unlikely subjects from the hand of a Matisse.

It might also be argued that, even where there is no superficial resemblance to Leonardo, Picasso's approach to color and shading remains basically within the model defined for the first time by the Renaissance master. In a brilliant 1962 essay, John Shearman pointed out that Leonardo's handling of *chiaroscuro* entailed a fundamental

Winged Bull Observed by Four Children. 1934. Etching, 9⁵⁄₁₆ × 11⁵⁄₈″ (23.7 × 29.5 cm). Geiser/Baer II, 444. The Museum of Modern Art, New York. Purchase Fund

Leonardo da Vinci. *A Dragon.* Black chalk and pen and ink on paper, 7³⁄₈ × 10⁵⁄₈″ (18.8 × 27 cm). Royal Library, Windsor, No. 12,369

Leonardo da Vinci. *Profiles of Men and Half-length of a Girl* (detail). Pen and ink on paper, 15¹⁵⁄₁₆ × 11⁷⁄₁₆″ (40.5 × 29 cm). Royal Library, Windsor, No. 12,276 (verso)

Leonardo da Vinci. *Five Grotesque Heads*. Pen and ink on paper, 10¼ × 8¹⁄₁₆″ (26 × 20.5 cm). Royal Library, Windsor, No. 12,495 (recto)

revision in the role of color within Western art.[128] While the masters of the Early Renaissance, from Giotto through Fra Angelico, had refined the use of shading to model three-dimensional form, their approach to color had remained fundamentally Gothic in the sense that they tended to use each of the colors available to them—typically blue, red, green, and yellow—in its purest, most characteristic hue. Shading was imposed locally—for instance, to model a piece of colored drapery. However, as Shearman points out, they made little attempt to compensate for the fact that different *hues* had inherently different *values:* red, for instance, being darker than yellow. The sharp shift in value from one colored area to the next created a disjunction between neighboring forms, undoing the consistency of the three-dimensional illusion.

Leonardo's conceptual breakthrough, Shearman argues, was to define his overall composition *a priori* through a consistent system of light-dark shading, to which the *colors were strictly subordinated*. Adjacent red and yellow draperies, for example, might be brought together in overall value by lightening the red with white tints and darkening the yellow with black shading. Leonardo's illusionistically consistent example quickly carried the day, and color remained subordinate to drawing and shading in Western art from the High Renaissance to the late nineteenth century. Leonardo's model begins to lose its stranglehold only with the rise of Impressionism; indeed, the story of modern art is in large part the story of color's progressive liberation from line and shading, in the

work of artists from Claude Monet to Henri Matisse to Mark Rothko.

In this sense, Picasso remains closer to Leonardo's essentially draftsmanly and tonal model than to the coloristic tradition in twentieth-century modernism; in many pictures, Picasso deliberately lets the tonal underdrawing show through or remain uncovered (p. 326), as if to remind us that the color—however beautiful or poetic—is an "add-on" to the determining light-dark matrix. A black-and-white photograph of a canvas by Picasso gives us a fairly clear understanding of the painting's construction, since it is primarily the rightness of the light-dark values which accounts for the coherence of the pictorial scaffolding. In contrast, a black-and-white photograph of a Matisse often communicates little sense of the picture's real aesthetic arrangement, since his compositional structures depend primarily on the rapports of hues.

"Colors," Picasso said to Apollinaire, "are only symbols. Reality is to be found in light [and dark] alone."[129] Not only is the visual scaffolding of a Picasso painting determined by its linear structure and accompanying distribution of lights and darks, but the color choices within this scaffolding—no longer dependent upon visual reality—become virtually interchangeable structurally *as long as the color at any given point in the composition has the appropriate value.* Hence, the artist's much-repeated but insufficiently understood *mot,* "When I run out of blue, I use red."[130]

To say this is not, however, to accept the conventional

bromide according to which Picasso is "not a colorist." On the contrary, in works such as the 1931 *Still Life on a Pedestal Table* and the 1932 *Girl Before a Mirror*, Picasso established himself as one of the great colorists of the century. But he employed color to psychological and poetic, rather than structural, ends. There are a handful of drawings, such as sketch III of the 1936 "Rosetta Stone" drawing examined above (p. 72), in which Picasso jotted down his notations of the colors he planned to use in his painting. Virtually all of the indications that can be determined in this example, such as "burnt sienna" for the ground, "blue" for the hat's sprig of leaves and "light gray" for its brim, "light yellow" for the edges of the collar/sculpture base, and "black" for the dark mass of hair at the left and bottom right, are precisely those of the finished picture.

What this notational procedure tells us is that Picasso, at least in this instance, chose his hues conceptually, out of feeling for—and in association with—the forms they inhabited. For him, color's primary purpose was its *affective* function. Once he had made a drawing to establish the compositional matrix of light and dark, he could visualize the colors clearly enough to finish the picture without further modification. He apparently did not feel any need to test colors, to "see what they looked like," though we can be sure that if he had been disappointed by the result he would have changed his picture, as he sometimes did.

Finally, it seems to me that the most significant antecedent for the protean quality of what I called Picasso's "pan-physiognomic" imagination is to be found in the drawings of Leonardo. Both artists had an extraordinary ability to imagine common denominators of form between different things, to find analogies in the patterns and shapes of alien objects. Just as Picasso could discover canine features inhabiting the faces of Dora and Jacqueline (pp. 400, 475),[131] and an owl's in that of Françoise, so too Leonardo could pass uninterrupted from the jaw of a roaring lion (itself compared with the heads of nearby horses) to the brow of a shouting soldier, leveling the distinction between man and beast (below). Similarly, Picasso's 1906 sketches exploring Josep Fontdevila as both a younger and an older man (p. 28, bottom) are matched by a sheet in which Leonardo juxtaposes the profiled head of a youth with the profile of the same man, grown to maturity (opposite). Such "associational" enchainments of mental images are common in the drawings of both artists. Perhaps I should not

Leonardo da Vinci. *Studies of Horses' Heads and of a Rearing Horse*. Pen and ink on paper, 7¾ × 12⅛″ (19.6 × 30.8 cm). Royal Library, Windsor, No. 12,326 (recto)

Leonardo da Vinci. *A Deluge*. c. 1514. Pen and ink and brown wash over black chalk on paper, 6¼ × 8″ (15.7 × 20.3 cm). Royal Library, Windsor, No. 12,379

Leonardo da Vinci. *A Cloudburst*. After 1513. Black chalk on paper, 6¼ × 8″ (15.8 × 20.3 cm). Royal Library, Windsor, No. 12,377

Leonardo da Vinci. *Studies of a Woman's Head and Coiffure*. Pen and ink over black chalk on paper, 7⅞ × 6⅜″ (20 × 16.2 cm). Royal Library, Windsor, No. 12,516

Leonardo da Vinci. *Study of Swirling Water* (detail of a sheet of drawings). Pen and ink on paper, 6 × 8⅜″ (15.2 × 21.3 cm). Royal Library, Windsor, No. 12,579 (recto)

Leonardo da Vinci. *Deluge*. After 1513. Black chalk on paper, 6⅜ × 8¼″ (16.3 × 21 cm). Royal Library, Windsor, No. 12,378

have been surprised when Picasso mentioned the affinity he felt with Leonardo as a draftsman.[132]

For both artists, the drive toward metamorphosis seems to have been impelled by a profound anxiety linked ultimately to intimations of mortality. Leonardo, famous as a young man for his own beauty and for that of the generic youths and maidens he conjured on canvas, was obsessed by the images of grotesque old men and women (p. 94). Picasso's private demons, on the contrary, were projected almost exclusively onto images of women.[133] We do not need to posit anything so banal as "influence" at work here; rather, we can simply observe that Leonardo's grotesques lie at the origin of the caricatural tradition adapted and transfigured in Picasso's work.

Art served both Leonardo and Picasso as a means of exorcising anxiety—first by confronting the images of danger and disorder associated with it and then by endowing those images with an aesthetic order. In Leonardo's

drawings of an apocalyptic deluge, terror is ultimately overcome by transforming the uncontrollable waves and winds into a kind of virtual architecture (above). The entwining curves of water patterns of the deluge (and of his scientific studies of flowing water) reappear in the girl's braided locks, turning and twisting like serpents (opposite, bottom): not unlike Nusch, the girl is simultaneously "virgin" and "monster," Leda and Medusa. The twinelike coils and "basket-weave" surfaces in many of Picasso's 1938 portraits (p. 394) offer another kind of parallel to Leonardo's drawing. But even without these examples, one would sense the affinity between these two artists, who traveled into the heart of darkness and returned with an image of the human figure at once beautiful and terrifying, personal and impersonal, human and inhuman. "If we give a form to [threatening] spirits, we become free." Picasso's declaration to André Malraux might equally well have been made by Leonardo.

NOTES

My friend and colleague Pepe Karmel has given liberally of his time and energy to maintain, for me, a most fruitful dialogue about this text, for which he has offered numerous helpful suggestions. Moreover, his acute editorial instincts have been of profound help in shaping this manuscript. As in the past, Judith Cousins, Curator of Research for the Department of Painting and Sculpture, has been of enormous assistance in all matters bibliographic, and has taken on the extra responsibility in our search for documentary photographs. I owe her more than I can say.

1. See Jean Clair's illuminating remarks on the history of the word "portrait," including its transmission from one language to another, in his essay "Trait pour trait, oeil pour oeil, dent pour dent," in *A Visage découvert* (Paris and Jouys-en-Josas: Flammarion and Fondation Cartier pour l'art contemporain, 1992), pp. 124–34.

2. Christian Zervos was born on January 1, 1889, in Argostoli, on the Greek island of Cephalonia, and grew up in Alexandria. After living for several years in Marseille, he came to Paris to finish his studies at the Sorbonne, where, during the war years 1914–18, he completed his doctorate in letters on Plotinus. By 1924 he was sufficiently involved with contemporary art to be taken on as managing editor of *L'Art d'aujourd'hui*, published by Albert Morancé. The aim of this influential review was to acquaint a wide public with the work of leading masters of contemporary art such as Picasso, Matisse, Braque, Gris, and Léger, among others. Zervos probably met Picasso during 1924 (the earliest letter from Zervos to Picasso is dated November 22, 1924; my thanks to Sylvie Fresnault for checking the Picasso Archives, where a substantial correspondence from Zervos to Picasso is preserved). The 1924 issue of *L'Art d'aujourd'hui* contained an article by Maurice Raynal on Picasso; several subsequent issues had articles on Picasso by Zervos. In 1926 Zervos started his own art magazine *Cahiers d'art*, which in the late 1920s and 1930s was to be "one of the strongest and most original voices of School of Paris modern art, which Zervos widened to include not only Picasso and the Cubists, the Surrealists and older fantastic art, but also the culture of the entire Mediterranean basin, to which, as a Greek, he was particularly attracted, supervising major publications on Cycladic, Sardinian and Cretan Arts" ("Art News International. Obituaries: Christian Zervos," *Art News* 69, no. 6 [October 1970], p. 32). Jean Cassou described *Cahiers d'art* as the embodiment of modern art and said of Zervos that he "was a smiling, prudent, discreet man, the one best suited to give to this triumph [of 'l'art *moderne*'] an atmosphere of tranquil dignity" ("Christian Zervos . . . était un homme souriant, mesuré, discret, le plus propre à donner à ce triomphe [de l'art *moderne*] un air de tranquille dignité"). The excerpt is from Jean Cassou's "Hommage," statement in the exhibition catalogue *Hommage à Christian et Yvonne Zervos* (Paris: Galeries Nationales d'Exposition du Grand Palais, 1970–71), n.p.

In 1926 Zervos published his first compilation of Picasso's work, which was called *Picasso: Oeuvres 1920–1926*, and in the first volume of *Cahiers d'art* he printed an extensive extract of its text (Christian Zervos, "Oeuvres récentes de Picasso," *Cahiers d'art* I [June 1926], pp. 89–93). This information is found in Eunice Lipton, *Picasso Criticism 1901–1939: The Making of an Artist-Hero* (New York: Garland Publishing, 1976), pp. 148–51. In 1928, at Dinard, Zervos met Yvonne Marion, whom he was to marry in 1932. As early as 1928 she had run the gallery "Cahiers d'Art" and would become an indefatigable collaborator in Zervos's publishing ventures.

According to Christian Derouet (who, in collaboration with Yves de Fontbrune, present owner of *Cahiers d'art*, is preparing an exhibition on Zervos and Picasso), the idea for a *catalogue général* of Picasso's oeuvre (Derouet prefers the term *catalogue général,* which more accurately describes the series of volumes comprising photographs of the work than does *catalogue raisonné,* which the volumes are not), occurred in the late 1920s and announcement of its publication appeared in *Cahiers d'Art*, no. 3 (1930) and no. 3/5 (1932). In the latter it was listed as the first volume of a projected five-volume series. Volume I, published on June 15, 1932, went on sale at a Picasso exhibition at the Galerie Georges Petit (June 16–July 30, 1932). It was issued in an edition of 537, of which 225, with an English text, were sold in advance to Weyhe Bookstore, New York. Picasso was greatly flattered by the idea, since this type of publication devoted to work being produced by a living artist was quite unprecedented. A second edition of this first volume was published, with a few corrections, in 1942, at the same time as two supplements to the second volume. According to Zervos, the Picasso catalogue, far from being a commercial failure, was always self-sustaining.

The project was carried out by means of photographs, Zervos indicating questions on photographs, which he would submit to Picasso, with an ensuing "dialogue autour des photos." Work was facilitated during the 1930s due to the fact that Picasso still lived in and around Paris. During World War II and subsequently, communication was considerably more difficult: Zervos usually managed to spend one or two months during the summer in the south of France, living nearby, but often had to wait until such time as the artist consented to see him. In 1950, for example, Zervos complained that he had not seen Picasso in two years. From 1964 onward, Zervos's letters are usually addressed to Jacqueline (the last letters are from 1970, the year Zervos died).

Design and layout were always submitted to Picasso for his approval (at least in the 1950s). The quality and availability of photographic documentation often determined the layout; the discrepancy in scale and quality of the reproductions was a direct function of the uneven quality of the photographs. The source of Zervos's information about works, titles, etc., was invariably Picasso.

In his letters, Zervos gives the impression of being invested with a mission. The realization of each volume was excruciating; he worked eighteen hours a day. His constant worry was that he might betray the artist; he needed explanations in order to avoid making blunders. Many letters describe the progress of the "book," as he referred to it, page by page. It was not an easy project. Zervos was often in competition with others for Picasso's attention and for information about the latest works, so that he had to flatter the artist and induce his collaboration by means of special issues of *Cahiers d'art* devoted to his work. Zervos would send packets of photographs on which Picasso was supposed to scribble dates, or whatever information was requested. At times Picasso worked seriously and closely with Zervos; at others he refused to pay attention and months would go by without his returning photographs with the needed information. When Zervos died in Paris on September 12, 1970, the *catalogue général* was incomplete, having only reached volume 22, with works from 1962–63. This volume was published in April of 1963. The catalogue was still incomplete at the time of Picasso's death in 1973, by which time volumes 23, 24, and 25 had appeared. It would only be completed following the publication of volumes 26 through 33, in the years 1973 to 1978, respectively. The Picasso catalogue project was described by Marc de Fontbrune as Zervos's "oeuvre-fleuve," which, more than any of his other considerable number of publications, contributed to his renown (Marc de Fontbrune, "Biographie," in *Hommage à Christian et Yvonne Zervos*, n.p.).

In the preparation of this note I am indebted to Sylvie Fresnault, Documentalist, Musée Picasso; Christian Derouet; and especially to Yves de Fontbrune for their invaluable help with information on the collaboration of Zervos and Picasso.

3. Zervos I, 254, listed as "Fernande. Oil. 1905. Paris." As Zervos mistakenly listed a large group of 1906 pictures (especially those from Gosol) as dating from 1905, it is probable, as Daix insists in his catalogue of the early work (*Picasso: The Blue and Rose Periods* [Neuchâtel, Switzerland: Editions Ides et Calendes], 1966), that this portrait dates from the following year.

4. This point was made by Meyer Schapiro in his lectures at Columbia University in 1949–50.

5. Jacqueline Picasso in conversation with the author, June 1983. It was in the course of this same conversation about Picasso's portraits of Jacqueline that she identified the extraordinary drawing of her illustrated on page 16 as, in fact, having been made from memory.

6. Charles Baudelaire, "L'Invitation au voyage," from *Les Fleurs du mal*, in *Oeuvres complètes* (Paris: Editions Gallimard, 1961), p. 51; Prévert reference from his poem "Feuilles mortes" ("Autumn Leaves").

7. Daniel-Henry Kahnweiler, *Juan Gris: His Life and Work*, translated by Douglas Cooper

(New York: Harry N. Abrams, 1969), p. 98. Jules Antoine Castagnary, "L'Exposition du boulevard des Capucines: Les Impressionistes," *Le Siècle*, April 29, 1874, translated in Richard Schiff, *Cézanne and the End of Impressionism* (Chicago: University of Chicago Press, 1984), p. 2. I would like to thank Pepe Karmel for suggesting the citations from Castagnary.

8. Kahnweiler, *Juan Gris*, p. 98.

9. Ibid., pp. 100 and 127.

10. Marius de Zayas, "Pablo Picasso," 1911, reprinted in Gert Schiff, ed., *Picasso in Perspective* (Englewood Cliffs, N.J.: Prentice-Hall, 1976), p. 47. De Zayas's essay was originally published in a pamphlet accompanying Picasso's first American exhibition, at Alfred Stieglitz's Photo-Secession Gallery; the essay was also published in Stieglitz's magazine *Camera Work*, no. 35 (1911), pp. 65–67. Pepe Karmel, who drew this passage to my attention, suggests that Picasso's phrase "pictorial equivalent" may have provided the title "Equivalents," which Stieglitz later employed for his semiabstract, photographic compositions.

11. In a conversation with Brassaï in September 1939, Picasso told the photographer, "When you see what you [can] express through photography, you realize all the things that can no longer be the objective of painting. Why should the artist persist in treating subjects that can be established so clearly with the lens of a camera? It would be absurd, wouldn't it? Photography has arrived at a point where it is capable of liberating painting from all literature, from the anecdote, and even from the subject" (Brassaï, *Picasso and Company*, translated by Francis Price [Garden City, N.Y.: Doubleday, 1966], pp. 46–47); originally published as *Conversations avec Picasso* (Paris: Editions Gallimard, 1964).

12. In his memoirs, William Paley recalled the commission as follows: "This same period [around 1935], I came to know Matisse, who agreed to do a painting of my wife Dorothy.

Every day I accompanied her to his studio for the sketches—he must have done fifty sketches of her—but when he was about to start to paint, he fell ill, and said, 'I can't finish it this year, but next year we'll do it.' He never did do the painting. Later he sent one of the sketches to Dorothy for Christmas" (William S. Paley, *As It Happened: A Memoir* [Garden City, N.Y.: Doubleday, 1979], pp. 99–100).

According to Dominique Szymusiak (*Dessins de la donation Matisse* [Le Cateau Cambrésis: Musée Matisse, 1988], p. 74, no. 30), eight charcoal drawings of Mrs. Paley by Matisse are known to exist, three of which are dated September 10, 12, and 13, 1936, respectively. Mrs. Szymusiak also indicates, on the basis of the account given by Lydia Delectorskaya, that it was Mrs. Paley who commissioned Matisse to do her portrait and that he did only a few drawings of her. Xavier Girard (*Henri Matisse Dessins: Collection du Musée Matisse* [Nantes, Nîmes, and Saint-Etienne, 1989, p. 108, no. 39) refers to the portrait drawings as a "série de huit essais."

13. As reported by Geneviève Laporte, in "*Si tard le soir, le soleil brille . . .*" (Paris: Librairie Plon, 1973), p. 140, Picasso told her, "D'ailleurs, je ne peux pas faire le portrait de n'importe qui." Jaime Sabartés remarked: "[Picasso] does not like to be bound by the exigencies of a commission. It is well known how little interested he is in doing commissioned portraits" (Jaime Sabartés, *Portraits et Souvenirs* [Paris: Louis Carré and Maximilien Vox, 1946], p. 132), and Brassaï noted "Basically Picasso has a horror of all 'commissions'" (Brassaï, *Picasso and Company*, p. 170).

14. Patrick O'Higgins, *Madame: An Intimate Biography of Helena Rubinstein* (New York: Viking Press, 1971), p. 218. I am indebted to John Richardson for bringing this book to my attention.

15. Ibid., p. 219.

16. This expression was used by the artist in

conversation with the present author. An article titled "A Beautician's Booty" in *Time*, April 29, 1966, noted that "As befits a beautician, Helena [Rubinstein] found one subject irresistible—herself. Over the years she was painted 30 times. . . . The portrait she most coveted escaped her. It was by Picasso" (pp. 82, 85). Accompanying the article was a fascinating photograph of Madame posing in front of ten portraits of herself—among which were those by Marie Laurencin, Pavel Tchelitchew, Cândido Portinari, Graham Sutherland, and Salvador Dali (see below, left).

17. Observed by Werner Spies, "Picasso und seine Zeit," in *Pablo Picasso: Eine Austellung zum hundertsten Geburtstag. Werke aus der Sammlung Marina Picasso* (Munich: Prestel-Verlag, 1981), p. 20: "Als [Picasso] von Helena Rubinstein aufgefordert wird, ein Porträt zu machen, wandert sein Blick zunächst auf die Kleidung, den Schmuck . . . dann kommt es zu der geradezu obszönen Inventarisierung des Schmucks"; reprinted as "Picasso: L'Histoire dans l'atelier," *Cahiers du Musée National d'Art Moderne* (Paris: Centre Georges Pompidou), no. 9–10 (1982), p. 60f.

18. O'Higgins, *Madame*, p. 221.

19. I had seen an example of this kind of actor's portrait in an album of original prints in Picasso's studio. Regrettably, the present inaccessibility of the materials from Picasso's library and studio makes it impossible for me to identify accurately the print I had seen. The portrait by Utagawa Toyokuni, a bust of the actor Ichikawa Komazo II, dated 1797, in the collection of the Brooklyn Museum, which I reproduce here, is surely close to the one owned by Picasso. I am extremely grateful to Colta Ives, Curator of Drawings and Prints at the Metropolitan Museum of Art, for bringing this portrait to my attention. I also want to thank Donna Welton, Assistant Curator in the Department of Asian Art, for her help in

Helena Rubinstein in her apartment at 625 Park Avenue, New York, with portraits of herself by Marie Laurencin, Salvador Dali, Graham Sutherland, and Pavel Tchelitchew, among others. 1959. Photographer unknown. Collection Helena Rubinstein Foundation

Utagawa Toyokuni. *Portrait of Ichikawa Komazo II*. 1797. Woodblock color print, 14⅝ × 10″ (37.2 × 25.4 cm). The Brooklyn Museum. Gift of Mr. Louis V. Ledoux

Henri Matisse. *Saint Dominic* (detail; posed for by Father M.A. Couturier). 1950. Glazed tile; altar decoration. Notre-Dame-de-Toute-Grâce, Assy

searching for the appropriate example of a Japanese actor portrait; and Lisa Zeitz, Intern in the Department of Painting and Sculpture of The Museum of Modern Art, for assistance with this search.

20. Matisse's featureless portraits of Father Couturier are to be seen in the altarpiece of Saint Dominic in Notre-Dame-de-Toute-Grâce at Assy (painted and glazed tiles, completed May 7, 1950); (see illustration, p. 99, right); and in the full-length mural of Saint Dominic for the Chapel of the Rosary of the Dominican Nuns of Vence (painted and glazed tiles, completed June 7, 1950). For a reproduction and history of the latter, see Xavier Girard, *Matisse: La Chapelle du Rosaire* (Nice, Cimiez: *Cahiers Henri Matisse* 8, 1992), pp. 94–101. The Assy Saint Dominic is reproduced in Alfred H. Barr, Jr., *Matisse: His Art and His Public* (New York: The Museum of Modern Art, 1951), p. 511. See also William Rubin, *Modern Sacred Art and the Church of Assy* (New York: Columbia University Press, 1961), pp. 34, 150, 156–59, and figs. 46 and 47, and plate p. 158.

21. According to Helena Rubinstein's biographer, Picasso rather meanly (or perhaps not, in view of their character) never showed Madame any of the drawings he had done of her and, as she died shortly before volume 16 of Zervos's catalogue appeared, she never did see what they were like. "The Picasso portrait, for all of Madame's ferocious persistence or maybe because of it (she bombarded him with inquiries, journeyed to Cannes repeatedly, used many intermediaries to lobby for her) was never finished. Nor did she see him again, nor ever see the drawings he did" (O'Higgins, *Madame*, p. 226).

22. See William Rubin, "The Genesis of *Les Demoiselles d'Avignon*," in *Les Desmoiselles d'Avignon*, Studies in Modern Art 3 (New York: The Museum of Modern Art, 1994), pp. 60–62.

23. For a discussion of the identity of the Medical Student, see ibid., p. 59 and nn. 180 and 181.

24. "One cannot overestimate the role," as John Richardson observed, "these young painters and their attractive wives played not just in Picasso's art, but in his daily life" (Richardson, *Pablo Picasso: Meeting in Montreal* (Montreal: Montreal Museum of Fine Arts, 1985), p. 88.

25. Picasso himself had drawn Piero's attention to his resemblance to don José during the first of two sittings with the artist. Picasso's earliest portraits of his father originated in La Coruña in 1894–95. The features and personality of don José became an ever-present subject of the work of the youthful artist in the following years in Barcelona, dominating his portraiture in the period 1895–99. Picasso's absences from Barcelona, initiated by his first visit to Paris in October 1900, signaled the corporeal disappearance of don José from his work.

In addition to Sabartés's informative remarks about don José and Picasso in *Picasso: An Intimate Portrait,* translated by Angel Flores (New York: Prentice-Hall, 1948), *passim,* there

are two important essays on the subject: Jürgen Glaesemer, "Don José Ruiz Blasco und Pablo Picasso: Der Vater als Lehrer und Modell," in *Der Junge Picasso: Frühwerk und Blaue Periode* (Bern: Kunstmuseum Bern, 1984), pp. 30–43; reprinted with slight modifications, as "Don José Ruiz Blasco et Pablo Picasso: Le père en tant que maître et modèle," in *Picasso/Miró/Dali: Evocation d'Espagne* (Charleroi: Palais des Beaux-Arts, 1985), pp. 21–37; and M. Teresa Ocaña, "José Ruiz Blasco *versus* Pablo Ruiz Picasso," in Brigitte Léal, ed., *Picasso jeunesse et genèse: Dessins 1893–1905* (Paris: Musée Picasso, 1991), pp. 32–49.

26. Picasso told Brassaï, "Every time I draw a man, it's my father I'm thinking of, involuntarily. For me, a man is Don José, and will be all my life. He wore a beard, and every man I draw I see more or less with his features" (Brassaï, *Picasso and Company*, p. 56).

27. Regarding Picasso's portraits of his father in the Barcelona period of 1896, Richardson observed that don José "had aged into a figure of patriarchal distinction, gloomily handsome as an El Greco saint. . . . Especially poignant is the contrast between the arrogant casualness of the son's virtuosity and the melancholy dignity of the old father" (John Richardson, with the collaboration of Marilyn McCully, *A Life of Picasso, Volume 1: 1881–1906* [New York: Random House, 1991], p. 82).

28. For an account of the development of the *Demoiselles'* composition, see Rubin, "The Genesis of *Les Demoiselles d'Avignon*," pp. 64–91.

29. See Rubin, "The Genesis of *Les Demoiselles d'Avignon*," pp. 14–15, for a discussion of Raymonde's complicating role in the lives of Picasso and Fernande in the spring of 1907, and for reproductions of three drawings of Raymonde by Picasso.

30. This is *Study for the Medical Student*, March 1907, reproduced in ibid., p. 52, no. 59.

31. "Vieillard farouche, d'une beauté étrange et sauvage" in Fernande Olivier, *Picasso et ses amis* (Paris: Librairie Stock, 1933), p. 116.

32. Pepe Karmel has convinced me that such drawings are more likely the fruit of Picasso's general obsession with mortality than—as I had felt at first—the example provided by Leonardo, who, to be sure, shared this obsession.

33. Spring 1906 is the date traditionally given for an installation of newly acquired Iberian sculptures in the Louvre Museum. But some of these objects may have been displayed as early as 1905, or even when they first arrived from Spain following their excavation at Cerro de los Santos, Osuna, and Córdoba in 1902, 1903, and 1904. See Richardson, *A Life of Picasso*, p. 517, n. 24; and Rubin, "The Genesis of *Les Demoiselles d'Avignon*, p. 36 and p. 129, nn. 133 and 134.

See Pierre Daix's text in the present volume (pp. 264–66) for a mention of the impact, besides that of Iberian sculpture, of Catalan sculpture on Picasso, in particular of the Virgin of Gosol (p. 262), first noted by Josep Palau i Fabre and then clarified by John Richardson. According to Richardson, "a major revelation of Gósol was the remarkable twelfth-century Madonna and Child (the Santa Maria del Castell de Gósol) that has now been removed to the Museum of Catalan Art in Barcelona. This left more of a mark on Picasso's work than is generally allowed" (Richardson, *A Life of Picasso*, pp. 451–52).

34. I say "seemed to be opening it" because, contrary to the majority opinion, I consider Fauvism, the vanguard style of 1905–06, as the final phase of the nineteenth-century Impressionist tradition, far more synthesizing late-nineteenth-century options than pointing forward to subsequent twentieth-century styles. It was only when Matisse, in 1907, emerged from Fauvism and established his truly individual style (with such paintings as *Sailor II*) that the tradition of twentieth-century color painting got under way. This took place at about the

Young Boy with Basket. 1939. Lead pencil on paper, 8⅝ × 6¼" (21.8 × 16 cm). Zervos X, 61. Private collection

Old Man. 1939. Lead pencil on paper, 8⅝ × 6¼" (21.8 × 16 cm). Zervos X, 62. Private collection

same time that Picasso made his break with the past in the "run-up" to *Les Demoiselles d'Avignon*.

35. Adam Gopnik, "High and Low: Caricature, Primitivism, and the Cubist Portrait," *Art Journal* 43, no. 4 (winter 1983), p. 375.

36. The sculpture was first mentioned by André Salmon in a review of a Metzinger exhibition held in January 1919. In this review, in which he resumed his history of the origins of Cubism (first explicated in his "Histoire anecdotique du cubisme," in *La Jeune peinture française*, 1912, pp. 42–52), Salmon stated, "Dans le même temps, Picasso exécuta, étude préparatoire à une statuette en bois, encore à tailler, un portrait de moi-même, au fusain qui, avec la grande toile en question [*Les Demoiselles d'Avignon*], est à la base du cubisme" ("La Semaine artistique. Cubisme: Exposition Metzinger [Galerie Rosenberg]," *L'Europe nouvelle* 2, no. 3 [January 18, 1919], p. 139); reprinted in English translation in Hélène Seckel, "Anthology of Early Commentary on *Les Demoiselles d'Avignon*," in Rubin, *Les Demoiselles d'Avignon*, p. 247.

Salmon's only other reference to the unrealized sculpture occurred in the final volume of his memoirs *Souvenirs sans fin: Troisième époque (1920–1940)*, vol. 3 (Paris: Gallimard, 1961), p. 185: "En 1920, quand je publiai *Peindre*, long poème qui précéda le didactisme de l'*Art vivant*, je donnai en frontispice une réduction du merveilleux fusain de Picasso: mon portrait daté de 1906, naissance du cubisme; une esquisse en vue d'une statuette à tailler dans le bois, ce qui ne serait pas réalisé."

37. A photograph taken by Picasso in 1908, showing the interior of his studio at the Bateau-Lavoir, with the sketches of the bust of Fontdevila/Salmon and a full-length nude figure of Salmon visible on the wall, is reproduced on p. 184 of this volume. For a larger and clearer reproduction made from the "tirage original," and a detailed analysis of the photograph in terms of its composition and contents, see Anne Baldassari, *Picasso photographe, 1901–1916* (Paris: Editions de la Réunion des musées nationaux, 1994), pp. 149, 152, and fig. 115. Baldassari identifies the sketches on the wall as *Buste de Josep Fontdevila* (Zervos II², 630), and as a first state of either the *Homme nu aux mains jointes* (Zervos VI, 967; M.P. 1990-59) or the *Nu debout, portrait d'André Salmon*.

38. William Rubin, "From Narrative to 'Iconic' in Picasso: The Buried Allegory in *Bread and Fruitdish on a Table* and the Role of *Les Demoiselles d'Avignon*," *The Art Bulletin* 65, no. 4 (December 1983), pp. 636–39 and *passim*.

39. Picasso has indicated more than once—including directly to this author—that the so-called *Portrait of Braque* was whimsically titled by him and Braque on the basis of the fact that the generic figure in the picture was wearing a *chapeau melon*. See Pierre Daix, with Joan Rosselet, *Picasso: The Cubist Years 1907–1916* (Neuchâtel, Switzerland: Editions Ides et Calendes, 1979), p. 252, no. 330.

40. This purely practical consideration is the only one ever advanced for the unusual group of painted Cubist portraits, and it no doubt contains much truth—though not, I believe, the entire truth of the matter. The most detailed presentation of this position may be found in Michael C. FitzGerald, *Making Modernism: Picasso and the Creation of the Market for Twentieth-Century Art* (New York: Farrar, Straus and Giroux, 1995), pp. 32–37. FitzGerald points out that Picasso's new financial stability in the fall of 1909 enabled him to move from the Bateau-Lavoir to the boulevard de Clichy around the same time that Matisse signed a very advantageous contract with the Bernheim-Jeune gallery in September 1909. Picasso lacked a regular dealer, and FitzGerald observes that "his search for a steady backer appears to be registered in the portraits he painted at this time [1909–1910]," during which he painted five portraits, four depicting dealers. "Picasso labored for months over portraits of Clovis Sagot, Ambroise Vollard, Wilhelm Uhde, and Daniel-Henry Kahnweiler" (p. 33).

41. Daix in conversation with this author. Picasso would presumably have procured this photograph, rather than have taken it himself, inasmuch as Vollard—unlike many of Picasso's close friends—had apparently not posed for a portrait photograph by the painter himself. Daix is convinced that the absence of any references in the literature to Vollard having frequented the studio during the months Picasso worked on this portrait is tantamount to the dealer's not having posed for it.

42. Reinforcing his sense of the likeness in Picasso's portrait of him, Vollard recounted the following anecdote: "Picasso did a very notable portrait of me. This painting, of the artist's Cubist period, is now in the Moscow Museum. Of course when they saw this picture, even people who considered themselves connoisseurs indulged in the facile pleasantry of asking what it was meant for. But the son of one of my friends, a boy of four, standing in front of the picture, put a finger on it and said without hesitation, 'That's *Voyard*'" (Ambroise Vollard, *Recollections of a Picture Dealer*, translated by Violet M. MacDonald [New York: Hacker Art Books, 1978], pp. 221–24; original French edition, *Souvenirs d'un marchand de tableaux* (Paris: Editions Albin Michel, 1948).

43. Speaking with Gilot about his Cubist portrait of Kahnweiler, Picasso explained, "In its original form it looked to me as though it were about to go up in smoke. But when I paint smoke, I want you to be able to drive a nail into it. So I added the attributes—a suggestion of eyes, the wave in the hair, an earlobe, the clasped hands—and now you can" (Françoise Gilot and Carlton Lake, *Life With Picasso* [New York: McGraw-Hill, 1964], p. 73). In an antecedent conversation, Picasso told John Richardson, "That's just what he looked like. . . . His ears appear to have grown a lot bigger since then" (John Richardson, "America's Tribute to Picasso," in *Picasso: An American Tribute* [New York: Chanticleer Press, 1962], n.p.).

44. Picasso's letter of June 12, 1912 written from Céret to Kahnweiler in Paris, is cited in William Rubin, ed., *Picasso and Braque: Pioneering Cubism* (New York: The Museum of Modern Art, 1989), p. 395 (documentary chronology by Judith Cousins). Until the time she entered Picasso's life in the winter of 1911–12, Eva Gouel had been known as Marcelle Humbert and had been the mistress of the painter Louis Marcoussis. Later that summer Picasso began referring to her as "Eva."

45. The complete passage reads, "Le surréalisme, s'il tient à s'assigner une ligne de conduite, n'a qu'à en passer par où Picasso en a passé et en passera encore" (André Breton, *Le Surréalisme et la peinture* [New York and Paris: Brentano's, 1945], p. 29); original edition, Paris, 1928.

46. See Marie-Laure Bernadac and Christine Piot, eds., *Picasso: Collected Writings*, translated by Carol Volk and Albert Bensoussan (New York: Abbeville Press, 1989); published as *Picasso Ecrits* (Paris: Réunion des Musées nationaux and Editions Gallimard, 1989).

47. It was in Meyer Schapiro's lectures at Columbia University that I first heard a reference to Eugène Delacroix's definition of what constitutes a good draftsman—as it was reported by Baudelaire in his essay on Delacroix in *The Mirror of Art*: "Once he [Delacroix] said to a young man of my acquaintance: 'If you have not sufficient skill to make a sketch of a man throwing himself out of a window in the time that it takes him to fall from the fourth floor to the ground, you will never be capable of producing great *machines*'" (Jonathan Mayne, ed., *The Mirror of Art: Critical Studies by Charles Baudelaire* [Garden City, N.Y.: Doubleday, 1956], p. 331; translated from the Conrad editions of *Curiosités esthétiques* (1923) and *L'Art romantique* (1925).

48. This figure is derived from a numerical study of typologies in Picasso's art according to their frequency over his career. The study was executed by Kathleen Robbins and Pascaline Maare at the author's request.

49. In conversation with the author, from my notes of interviews held in winter 1961–62 on the general subject of Jackson Pollock.

50. In fairness to Greenberg, it should be observed that his views on Cubism were set in the 1950s at a time when many important Cubist works now familiar to us were unseen and even unknown in the United States, if not in the West. The standard account of Cubism, that of Alfred H. Barr, Jr., in *Picasso: Fifty Years of His Art* (New York: The Museum of Modern Art, 1946), failed, for example, to include such major turning points of the movement as *Three Women*, 1907–08 (The State Hermitage Museum, St. Petersburg) or *Bread and Fruitdish on a Table*, 1908–09 (Kunstmuseum, Basel), neither of which had been seen by Greenberg at the time.

Greenberg saw what was shown at The Museum of Modern Art, A.E. Gallatin's Gallery of Living Art at New York University, The Museum of Non-Objective Art, and at New York galleries—where the tendency was to exhibit the same locally owned Picassos over and over again. It is very difficult today to put oneself back in the state of mind of an *amateur* living in the 1940s and 1950s because we now know so much more about Cubism than was the case fifty years ago. Because Greenberg was unfamiliar with *Three Women* and *Bread and Fruitdish on a Table*—apart from Zervos's publication of both pictures in 1942 (Zervos II¹, 108, 134), neither work resurfaced in the literature on Picasso until 1966 and 1970, respectively—and a host of Cubist works he saw for the first time only in the 1980 Picasso retrospective, he was not aware of the variety and degree of change in Cubism from the completion of the *Demoiselles* in 1907 to 1911. Moreover, Greenberg did not own Zervos's *catalogue général* of Picasso's work, and was not given to perusing it in libraries, so that his knowledge of Picasso's Cubism was based primarily on pictures he saw in New York.

51. Compare the summer 1910 paintings reproduced in *Picasso and Braque: Pioneering Cubism*, pp. 164, 168, and 169, with the spring 1912 *Man with a Violin*, p. 217, or *The Aficionado* of summer 1912, p. 239.

52. For a discussion of the sheet-metal *Guitar* and its place in the chronology of Cubist construction sculpture, see William Rubin, "Picasso and Braque: An Introduction," in Rubin, *Picasso and Braque: Pioneering Cubism*, pp. 30–41, and nn. 52–86. See also Yve-Alain Bois, "Kahnweiler's Lesson," *Representations* (Berkeley), no. 18 (spring 1987), pp. 33–68; revised text published in Yve-Alain Bois, *Painting as Model* (Cambridge, Mass.: MIT Press, 1993), pp. 65–97, 280–93; pub-

lished in French as "La Leçon de Kahnweiler," *Les Cahiers du Musée National d'Art Moderne*, no. 23 (spring 1988), pp. 29–56.

53. Braque, writing to Kahnweiler in Bern on October 8, [1919], from Sorgues on his return from the front, commented, " J'ai trouvé Gris en train de faire des tableaux patriotiques. . . . Quant à Picasso il créait un nouveau genre dit genre *Ingres*. . . . Ce qui est vraiment constant chez l'artiste, c'est son tempérament. Or Picasso reste pour moi ce qu'il a toujours été, un virtuose plein de talent. . . . C'est en partie ces impressions et d'autres qui m'ont poussé à écrire dans *Nord-Sud*" (cited in Isabelle Monod-Fontaine, et al., *Daniel-Henry Kahnweiler: Marchand, éditeur, écrivain* [Paris: Centre Georges Pompidou, Musée National d'Art Moderne, 1984], p. 126); and in English translation in Rubin, *Picasso and Braque: Pioneering Cubism*, pp. 51–52, and n. 159.

54. André Verdet, prefatory text to *Picasso* (Geneva: Musée de l'Athénée, 1963): "Le style, c'est souvent quelque chose qui enferme le peintre dans une même vision, une même technique, une même formule pendant des années et des années, pendant toute une vie parfois"; extract cited in English translation as "Style," in Dore Ashton, *Picasso on Art: A Selection of Views* (New York: Viking Press, 1972), pp. 95–96.

55. This expression was used by the artist in conversation with the author in June 1970.

56. As Pepe Karmel pointed out in his Ph.D. dissertation "Picasso's Laboratory: The Role of His Drawings in the Development of Cubism, 1910–1914," New York University, 1993, pp. 296–99, the figure of the standing man with wine-glass was translated in Picasso's drawings from a realistic to a Synthetic Cubist image, and then transferred to canvas. The resulting painting (Daix 783), completed in summer 1914, was Picasso's largest and most ambitious—though far from his most successful—work since the *Three Women* of 1908.

57. In relating this episode to Francis Crémieux, Kahnweiler was not altogether clear as to the meaning of the artist's observation. "Furthermore, I must tell you that in the spring of 1914 Picasso had shown me two drawings that were not cubist, but classicist, two drawings of a seated man. He had said, 'Still, they're better than before, aren't they?' On being asked by Crémieux what Picasso meant when he said 'They're better than before,' did Picasso mean the drawings were better than what he did before cubism, to which Kahnweiler replied, 'Precisely: Better than the classicist, or, if you will, the naturalistic drawings I did before.' That's all he meant. He never really 'abandoned' cubism; he did both things concurrently" (Daniel-Henry Kahnweiler with Francis Crémieux, *My Galleries and My Painters* [New York: Viking Press, 1971], p. 54).

X ray of *Olga in a Fur Collar*. Laboratoire de recherche des musées de France

Olga in a Fur Collar. 1923. Oil on canvas, 45⅝ × 31¾″ (116 × 80.5 cm). Not in Zervos. Musée Picasso, Paris

58. For a summary of the different dates proposed by art historians Kenneth E. Silver and Pierre Daix for the unfinished *Artist and His Model* (Musée Picasso, Paris), not catalogued by Zervos and not published until after Picasso's death, see FitzGerald, *Making Modernism,* pp. 48–51 and nn. 3, 4, and 11; FitzGerald is in agreement with Daix's suggestion that Picasso must have begun the picture during the summer of 1914 before the outbreak of war, and that its unfinished state reflected Picasso's questioning of Cubism and return to natural forms (See Daix and Rosselet, *Picasso: The Cubist Years,* pp. 164–66, no. 763). Elizabeth Cowling described it as "probably the first naturalistic painting Picasso had made since 1906, and it therefore anticipates the return to classicism of 1917 onwards." Cowling considered it to have been painted in Avignon in June 1914. (See Elizabeth Cowling and Jennifer Mundy, *On Classic Ground: Picasso, Léger, de Chirico and the New Classicism 1910–1930* [London: Tate Gallery Publications, 1990], p. 204, no. 130.)

59. Although Cocteau's phrase "Le rappel à l'ordre" dates from 1926 (in the title he chose for a volume of essays, published by Stock) and is frequently cited in the context of 1920s Neoclassicism, it should be noted that the expression "Le rappel à l'ordre" (variously translated as "the call to order," or "the return to order") was first stated in print by Roger Bissière and André Lhote in March and June 1919, respectively, in their reviews of Braque's March 1919 exhibition at Léonce Rosenberg's gallery "L'Effort moderne." The expression came to designate the postwar phenomenon of classicism in France and elsewhere—a broad range of artistic and cultural manifestations involving the gradual and steady "classicizing" of avant-garde art and Cubism, a turn toward the classical French masters of the past, *la grande tradition,* and the use of traditional techniques—generally perceived as a reaction to the war but now known to have been already in place by World War I, if not prior to it. On the subject of "Le rappel à l'ordre," see André Fermigier, ed., *Jean Cocteau entre Picasso et Radiguet* (Paris: Hermann, 1967), pp. 9–33; "Le Retour à l'ordre dans les arts plastiques et l'architecture, 1919–1925," *Actes du second colloque d'histoire de l'art contemporain,* Université de Saint-Etienne, Travaux VIII (Saint-Etienne: Musée d'Art et d'Industrie de Saint-Etienne, February 17, 1974); Kenneth E. Silver, *Esprit de Corps: The Art of the Parisian Avant-Garde and the First World War, 1914–1925* (Princeton, N. J.: Princeton University Press, 1989), pp. 186–298; Christopher Green, *Cubism and Its Enemies: Modern Movements and Reaction in French Art, 1916–1928* (New Haven and London: Yale University Press, 1987); Elizabeth Cowling, "Introduction," in Cowling and Mundy, *On Classic Ground,* pp. 11, 14; Pierre Daix, "Return to Order" in his *Picasso: Life and Art,* translated by Olivia Emmet (New York: HarperCollins, 1993), pp. 161–71; original French edition, *Picasso créateur* (Paris: Editions du Seuil, 1987).

60. This was the phrase used by Rosalind Krauss to characterize Picasso's Neoclassicism in "We Lost It at the Movies," her contribution to the forum on "The Subject in/of Art History," in *The Art Bulletin* 76, no. 4 (December 1994), p. 580.

61. From the interview Picasso gave to Marius de Zayas in Spanish, subsequently published in English translation as "Picasso Speaks," in *The Arts* 3, no. 5 (May 1923), p. 323 (reprinted in Barr, *Picasso: Fifty Years of His Art,* p. 271).

62. In conversation with the author, March 1970. Geneviève Laporte recalled Picasso looking around with admiration in a hotel room with a décor "pour voyageur de commerce," and his comment, "J'aime les choses laides et sans âge. Quelle chambre extraordinaire pour moi qui peut y voir tant de choses!" (Laporte, "Si tard le soir, le soleil brille," p. 49).

63. This breakfront, actually in an exaggerated version of the Henri II style, appears in such paintings and drawings as Zervos XVIII, 375, 379, 384, 385, 389, 394, and 395.

64. As Alfred Barr was the first to note, Surrealism was present in many of Picasso's drawings and some paintings executed between winter 1912–13 and the outbreak of war in August 1914, and Expressionism in and around the final version of *Les Desmoiselles d'Avignon* and its studies.

65. My thanks to Hélène Seckel for drawing my attention to the fact that *Olga in a Fur Collar* was painted over a more recent rectilinear Cubist version of the picture, which has been retrieved by an X ray made by the Louvre services (see illustration, p. 102). See *Picasso: Une Nouvelle Dation* (Paris: Editions de la Réunion des musées nationaux, 1990), p. 28. In this case, the image began as a Cubist painting and was transformed into a Neoclassical one—reversing the process observed in *Woman in an Armchair.*

66. See, for example, the spring 1913 paper construction depicting a guitarist with sheet music (Daix 582), reproduced in Rubin, *Picasso and Braque: Pioneering Cubism,* p. 282.

67. This is the etching *Model and Surrealist Sculpture,* dated Paris, May 4, 1933, from the Sculptor's Studio theme (no. 74 in the *Vollard Suite*). In Geiser and Baer, the print is titled *Marie-Thérèse considérant son effigie surréaliste sculptée* (p. 175, no. 364). The open book on the chair cushion corresponds to the motif of the open book in the lap that was interpreted by Leo Steinberg "as a surrogate for the female sexual organ . . . symbolizing the woman's openness" (letter from Sheila Schwartz to Judith Cousins, December 25, 1995). The idea was first broached in Steinberg's extraordinary study of *Les Demoiselles d'Avignon,* published in 1972 (see below). Discussing the motif of the docked tabletop that spears the picture from below, he declared, "Of all the ways Picasso invented to insinuate the physical availability of the image, this visual metaphor of penetration is the most erotic." In a footnote to this pas-

Two Nudes and Self-Portrait of Rembrandt from the *Vollard Suite* (detail). January 31, 1934. Engraving on copper, 10⅞ × 7¾″ (27.7 × 19.7 cm). Geiser/Baer II, 414. The Museum of Modern Art, New York. Abby Aldrich Rockefeller Fund sage, Steinberg added: "The most innocent-looking Picasso may fall into this erotic class. E.g., the Cubist *Liseuse* of 1909 (Zervos II¹ 150), a seated nude dozing, with a book held open between parted thighs" (Leo Steinberg, "The Philosophical Brothel, Part I," *Art News* 71, no. 5 [September 1972], p. 23 and p. 28, n. 12; republished with minor revisions in French translation for the exhibition catalogue *Les Demoiselles d'Avignon*, Musée Picasso, Paris, 1988; and in Spanish translation at the Museu Picasso, Barcelona, 1988; additional footnotes and a "Retrospect" in *October* (Cambridge, Mass., and London), 44 (spring 1988), p. 24, n. 12.

The subject of the open book in the lap was further developed by Steinberg in terms of three specific Picasso works, all concerning Marie-Thérèse Walter: *Woman Reading* of 1932 (Norton Simon Collection); *The Dream* (ex-Alsdorf Collection, Chicago; Zervos VII, 363); and *Reading* (Marie-Thérèse) (Musée Picasso, Paris; Zervos VII, 358); these works formed the substance of a lecture titled "The Interrupted Reading, or How Men Have Perceived Women with Books from the 14th Century to Modern Advertising." "Since 1981, Leo Steinberg has given the lecture repeatedly around the country, including: Whitney Museum of American Art, November 7, 1984; Harvard University Inaugural Levintritt Lecture, January 13, 1986" (Schwartz letter of December 25, 1995). I wish to express my thanks to Jane Necol and to Pepe Karmel for drawing these unpublished

lectures to my attention, and my indebtedness to Sheila Schwartz for specifying the subject of Steinberg's lectures on the theme of the open book in the lap and the dates they were given in New York and at Harvard.

68. "À chaque nouvelle expérience amoureuse, nous voyons son art progresser, apparaître une nouvelle forme, un autre language, un mode d'expression particulier auquel on pourrait donner un nom de femme" (Jaime Sabartés, *Picasso: Documents iconographiques*, translated by Félia Léal and Alfred Rosset [Geneva: Pierre Cailler, 1954], p. 50).

69. When Picasso first met Françoise Gilot in May 1943, he saw her together with her school friend Geneviève. Gilot quotes Picasso as saying, "I'm meeting beings I painted twenty years ago." On another occasion he observed: "You know, I've always been haunted by a certain few faces and yours is one of them" (Gilot and Lake, *Life with Picasso*, pp. 21, 49).

70. Zervos V, 29.

71. Zervos IV, 360.

72. An earlier sketchbook, however, contains a remarkable generic drawing of a *Mother and Child* (p. 49 of this volume), which comes about as close as Picasso gets to fifteenth- and early-sixteenth-century models. The benign, half-smiling expression on the mother's beautiful face and the shy tilt of the head are reinforced by the gentle and delicate shading of the pencil throughout. While this hairstyle would be characteristic of Sara's portraits, the face, which no longer resembles Olga at all, adumbrates Sara's

portraits less in its facial features than in its tender fragility and seeming state of grace. The elongation and bulk of the figures add a not wholly unexpected Mannerist note that recalls the London cartoon for Leonardo's *Madonna and Child with Saint Anne and Saint John* (see p. 92).

73. Indeed, it was precisely the *Tellus Mater* inflection of Venus / Sara in the *The Pipes of Pan*—an inflection directly connected to Venus / Sara's pairing with Cupid / Paulo in that image—which was intended to give that monumental projected "love song" its particular aura.

74. The photograph of Picasso wearing Sara Murphy's pearl necklace is reproduced in Calvin Tomkins, *Living Well Is the Best Revenge* (New York: Viking, 1971), in the section of reproductions called "An Album," between pp. 44 and 113.

75. See William Rubin, "The Pipes of Pan: Picasso's Aborted Love Song to Sara Murphy," *Art News* 93, no. 5 (May 1994), pp. 138–47.

76. Picasso's adaptation of Sara to the figure of Venus was entirely in keeping with the transformative and mythologizing nature of his imagery. Later, Marie-Thérèse would appear in a variety of classical roles, not least as Myrrhina from Aristophanes' *Lysistrata* (Geiser 389).

77. The sketch is *Cupidon et danse au son de la flûte de Pan*, February 4, 1923, Paris. Musée Picasso, Paris, M.P. 983.

78. It seems likely that Picasso intended to execute the monumental canvas of *The Pipes of Pan* in a style of white washes and linear con-

Head of a Woman. August 1921. Charcoal and sanguine on paper, 25 × 19¹¹⁄₁₆″ (63.5 × 50 cm). Zervos IV, 344. Private collection

Bust of a Woman. 1922. Oil on canvas, 13¾ × 10⅝″ (35 × 27 cm). Zervos IV, 396. Private collection

Project for The Pipes of Pan. 1923. India ink on paper, 9½ × 12″ (24.5 × 32 cm). Zervos V, 130. Private collection

(September 1983), pp. 124–29. See also Schwarz, *Picasso and Marie-Thérèse Walter,* pp. 85–86, for comments on Daix's article.

82. Rosalind E. Krauss, "Life with Picasso: Sketchbook No. 92, 1926," in Arnold Glimcher and Marc Glimcher, eds., *Je suis le cahier: The Sketchbooks of Picasso* (New York: Pace Gallery, 1986), pp. 113–39. The danger in arguing "premonitory" identifications is illustrated by Krauss's assimilation of the woman in the turban (Zervos V, 369) as an image of Marie-Thérèse executed in advance of Picasso's meeting her. In fact, it is clear from the snapshot which served as this drawing's basis that it is a portrait of Sara Murphy.

83. The painting was published in Zervos VII, 2, as *Les Modistes,* 1926. Under the title *L'Atelier de la modiste,* it was shown in the 1955 Picasso retrospective exhibition at the Musée des Arts Décoratifs, Paris, of which Maurice Jardot was the "commissaire." A note was appended to the catalogue entry for the picture specifying that "Cet atelier se trouvait effectivement de l'autre côté de la rue, en face des fenêtres de l'appartement que Picasso occupait rue de la Boétie" (*Picasso: Peintures 1900–1955* [Paris: Musée des Arts Décoratifs, 1955], no. 67). Antonina

tours similar to that of *Woman in White,* preserving the amorous iconography of the pastel studies. Instead, at the end of the summer, Picasso overpainted the original composition (already laid out on the canvas and still visible in X rays) with the painting we know by that title today (p. 57), which has a very different subject: two solipsistic men in a melancholy de Chiricoesque space. Its facture too changed, returning to the firmer, more monumental Neoclassicism of 1920–21. There is no way of knowing whether this was primarily a formal decision or a reaction to a romantic disappointment—or a combination of both.

79. Quoted in Igor Stravinsky, *An Autobiography* (New York: W. W. Norton, 1962), p. 63; translated from *Chroniques de ma vie* and quoted with slight variants in Philippe Jullian, "The Lady from Chile," *Apollo* 89, no. 86 (April 1969), p. 266.

80. Pierre Cabanne, "Picasso et les joies de la paternité," *L'Oeil,* no. 226 (May 1974), p. 2. Herbert T. Schwarz, *Picasso and Marie-Thérèse Walter, 1925–1927* (Montmagny, Quebec: Editions Isabeau, 1988), p. 14, mistakenly attributed the date of the meeting to have been imparted by Françoise Gilot: "[Picasso] finally revealed to Françoise Gilot that 'this meeting took place on the 8th of January 1927 in front of the Lafayette store in Paris.'" Gilot, in fact, while she made numerous references to Marie-Thérèse, specified only that "[Picasso] had met Marie-Thérèse on the street one day near the Galeries Lafayette when she was seventeen, he told me" (Gilot and Lake, *Life with Picasso,* p. 234). The date January 8, 1927, has often been cited in the literature on Picasso and Marie-Thérèse without a reference to its original source.

81. See Pierre Daix, "On a Hidden Portrait of Marie-Thérèse," *Art in America* 71, no. 8

Project for The Pipes of Pan. 1923 (subsequently misdated, upper right, by artist). Pastel and India ink on paper, 8⅞ × 7⅞″ (22.5 × 20 cm). Zervos V, 122. Private collection

Valentin repeated this identification in her book about Picasso, published two years later: "D'un monde crépusculaire émergent les courbes fantomatiques de l'Atelier de la modiste (Musée national d'art moderne, Paris. . . . Mais si insaisissable et difficile à déchifrer que paraisse ce nocturne il est un reflet d'une chose vue. L'étrange choix du sujet s'explique par le fait que, de son appartement de la rue La Boétie, Picasso pouvait en effet plonger le regard dans cet atelier situé en face et voir clientes et modistes y évoluer dans cette ambience étrange, inattendue dans un cadre banal" (Antonina Valentin, *Pablo Picasso* [Paris: Editions Albin Michel, 1957], p. 268).

Relevant to this and other misinformation communicated by Picasso is his following observation: "You must not always believe what I say. Questions tempt one to tell lies, particularly when there is no answer." This remark was made to Jacques Prévert, who reported it to André Villers. It is cited in Schwartz, *Picasso and Marie-Thérèse Walter,* p. 117. Picasso certainly resented questions about his private life, especially as regards Marie-Thérèse, for obvious reasons.

84. In the course of researching Picasso's early relationship with Marie-Thérèse, Herbert T. Schwarz set out to find what he called Picasso's "mysterious Atelier de la Modiste," in which the young Marie-Thérèse seemed to figure. The search for the atelier on rue La Boétie proved fruitless; it was, according to Schwarz, nonexistent. But Schwarz subsequently decided that the painting, in fact, represented the setting of the Maisons d'Alfort at 6, Cité d'Alfort—where Marie-Thérèse lived with her mother, Emilie Marguerite, and a sister. Dr Schwartz proposes that on one of his first visits, Picasso had probably observed the mother with her two daughters busy making the broad-brimmed felt hats they were so fond of. Their presence, in addition to Picasso himself at the door of the atelier, constitutes the subject of the composition. Schwarz believes Picasso's first visit to 6, Cité d'Alfort took place in October or November 1925, that he got the inspiration for *Les Modistes* possibly in December when Marie-Thérèse's sister, a student, was there for Christmas holidays, and that he finished the picture early in January 1926. (See Schwarz, *Picasso and Marie-Thérèse Walter,* pp. 101–05, 123–24, 152.) Schwarz's research includes a photograph of the actual glass-panel door that appears to the right in the *Atelier des Modistes.*

85. That such a large canvas should have been devoted to this subject at that moment in Picasso's life has been a conundrum for Picasso students. Schwartz's thesis not only makes the subject and mysterious aura of the picture understandable, but rationalizes the presence in it of Picasso himself on the right.

86. See John Richardson, *Through the Eye of Picasso, 1928–1934: The Dinard Sketchbook and Related Paintings and Sculpture* (New York: William Beadleston, 1985), n.p., and Richardson, "Picasso and l'Amour Fou," *New York Review of Books* 32, no. 20 (December 19, 1985), pp. 59–68; Schwartz, *Picasso and Marie-Thérèse Walter,*

pp. 11–14. Schwarz seems not to have been aware of the oil portrait of Marie-Thérèse (p. 61; not in Zervos), which Picasso had kept for himself and which descended to Jacqueline and, later, to her daughter, Catherine Hutin-Blay, who gave it to the Musée Picasso (see *Picasso: Une Nouvelle Dation,* p. 36).

87. For a discussion of the origin and development of Surrealist biomorphism, see William Rubin, "Toward a Critical Framework," *Artforum,* special issue (September 1966), pp. 36–55; and William Rubin, *Dada and Surrealist Art* (New York: Harry N. Abrams, 1968), pp. 18–22, and *passim.*

88. For one of the earliest critiques of the origin of this style see Adam Gopnik, "P loves MT: A Note on the First Appearance of Marie-Thérèse Walter in the Picasso Theater," *Marsyas* (Institute of Fine Arts, New York University) 21 (1981–82), pp. 57–60.

89. I had talked about the Museum's *Seated Bather* briefly on two different occasions with Picasso, once in June 1971 and then in July of the following year. On the second of these occasions, he had identified the painting's hard and aggressive, somewhat surreal anatomy as having been "inspired" by his wife, Olga Khokhlova, from whom he was estranged though not yet separated at the time of its execution. As the word "inspired" is in French in my notes, I can vouch for its having been the precise word used by the artist. My notes of conversations with Picasso were set down after about an hour's drive from his villa or, at the latest, the following morning. They recorded in English the general substance of what he said; if I remembered a particular word he used, I put it in the original French.

90. "But in all those conditions that we would call style the paintings are nearly twins" (Rosalind E. Krauss, "In the Name of Picasso," in *The Originality of the Avant-Garde* [Cambridge, Mass.: MIT Press, 1985], p. 23).

My distinguishing between the two styles of these paintings was originally presented as a lecture on October 12, 1980, at a symposium on the Cubist legacy in twentieth-century sculpture. My comparison of *Seated Bather* with *Bather with Beach Ball,* from which Krauss launched her critique, had been (and remains) in part based on a comparison between the *Seated Bather* and *Nude in an Armchair* (1929; Zervos VII, 263) that Meyer Schapiro had made in his 1949–50 lectures at Columbia University.

91. Picasso married Olga Khokhlova on July 12, 1918. Not long after the birth of their son, Paulo, in February 1921, and notably in the summer of 1923, the marriage began to founder, and it worsened into growing estrangement during the later 1920s and early 1930s. Its disintegration ensued upon the revelation of Marie-Thérèse's pregnancy in early 1935. Olga finally agreed to grant Picasso a divorce, but on terms that were impossible for the artist to accept, as they entailed Picasso's parting with a large part of those paintings and sculptures of his that he had kept, and which he felt were absolutely necessary for the continuity of his work. In the end, Picasso was able to retain access to these

works in the framework of a legal separation agreement rather than a divorce.

92. This expression was used by Françoise Gilot in recalling that Picasso "was rather fond . . . of saying, 'For me, there are only two kinds of women—goddesses and doormats.' And whenever he thought I might be feeling too much like a goddess, he did his best to turn me into a doormat" (Gilot and Lake, *Life with Picasso,* p. 84).

93. I am aware that this anodyne view of *Bather with Beach Ball* is not universally shared. Some critics insist on reading this picture as a monstrous or sinister image. But I believe that reading is wrong and misses what Picasso intended as whimsy. John Golding, for example, viewed the figure as a "giant squid and her limbs . . . sinister and tentacular" ("Picasso and Surrealism," in Roland Penrose and John Golding, eds., *Picasso 1881–1973* [London: Paul Elek, 1973], p. 103). Robert Rosenblum's reading in this volume (see pp. 360–61) tends also in this direction. While the association of Marie-Thérèse's body in this picture to some kind of sea creature (though hardly to a "tentacular" squid) seems logical to me, since I believe Picasso wanted to think of the female torso here as squishy—in the sense of soft, wet, and slippery—I cannot square the aggressive assumptions of these readings with the decor of the costume and the playfulness of the motif.

94. Linda Nochlin, "Picasso's Color Schemes and Gambits," *Art in America* 68, no. 10 (December 1980), pp. 120–23, 177–80.

95. William Rubin, catalogue entry for *Girl Before a Mirror* in *Picasso in the Collection of The Museum of Modern Art* (New York: The Museum of Modern Art, 1972), p. 140, and p. 226, n. 1.

96. See Rubin, "From Narrative to 'Iconic' in Picasso."

97. For Picasso's association of the guitar to both female and male anatomies, see Rubin, *Picasso in the Collection of The Museum of Modern Art,* pp. 82–83, 211.

98. See *Still Life with Cherries* (opposite]). Also, *Still Life with Pitcher and Apple* (1938; not in Zervos; see *Picasso intime* [Tokyo: Seibu Museum of Art, 1981], p. 101]; *Plantes Tropicales* (Zervos XV, 83–86).

99. For Picasso's borrowings from de Chirico associated with a period of cross-fertilization during World War I, see William Rubin, "De Chirico and Modernism," in *De Chirico* (New York: The Museum of Modern Art, 1982), pp. 66–70, 78–79 and nn. 31–34.

100. It should be kept in mind that Maya Picasso unconditionally rejects Dr. Schwartz's thesis. She considers pictures which to Schwartz and other critics might resemble or allude to Marie-Thérèse either generic images or inspired by other individuals.

101. Zervos VII, 82, 354.

102. Observed by Pepe Karmel in conversation with me.

103. Marie-Thérèse's face in sketch III is largely unchanged, except that her lips are once again shown parted, now in apprehensiveness, by carrying over into her mouth the same kind

of *S*-curve that defines the nostril and the pattern of the hat. In its unstable and ambiguous implications, the *S*-curve may be said to be the leitmotif of the sketch.

104. Hélène Seckel has kindly drawn my attention to the fact that in 1989 Marie-Laure Bernadac (then a curator at the Musée Picasso) organized an exhibition entitled *Picasso poète: "Le Crayon qui parle"* (Musée Picasso, Paris, 1989–90), in which the series of drawings executed by Picasso from April 2 to May 1, 1936, were shown in conjunction with several of the paintings (none of them recorded by Zervos) to which they relate. The pairings included M.P. 155, *Woman in a Straw Hat*, May 1, 1936 (see p. 73), and M.P. 1162, *Sketches for "Woman in a Straw Hat,"* May 1, 1936 (see p. 72)—in which the notations for the color scheme correspond very precisely to the colors of the painting.

105. See also, for example, pp. 399 and 400.

106. David Douglas Duncan appears to have been the first to record the often-cited phrase Picasso used to describe this period (*Picasso's Picassos* [New York: Harper & Brothers, 1961], p. 111).

107. "Many of the cruel distortions of the late Thirties and early Forties have their roots in Dora's chronic distress" (John Richardson, "Introduction," in *Homage to Picasso for his 90th Birthday: Exhibition of Paintings and Works on Paper* [New York: Saidenberg Gallery and Marlborough Gallery, 1971], p. 9).

108. "For months [Picasso] was plagued by these abortive proceedings [legal procedures for divorcing Olga], so much so that for a while he could not bear to go upstairs to his studio [at rue La Boétie] . . . the solitude of Picasso had become more than the inevitable solitude of genius," wrote Roland Penrose in *Picasso: His Life and Work* (London: Victor Gollancz, 1958), pp. 250, 253. Brassaï described Picasso during this period: "Bruised and battered in the conjugal wars, disgusted even with painting, living alone in his two apartments, he had sent out a call for help to the great friend of his childhood, Jaime Sabartés. . . . It was a cry of real distress; he was going through the gravest crisis of his life" (Brassaï, *Picasso and Company*, p. 41). Sabartés also portrayed Picasso's troubled frame of mind in 1935–36: "Procés, visites aux avocats, aux notaires. . . . En un mot tout ce qui peut contribuer à l'empêcher de travailler. . . . En 1936, tracassé par son divorce, il ne veut plus peindre. Il ne monte plus à son atelier, et la seule vue de tableaux et de dessins l'exaspère" (Sabartés, *Picasso: Documents iconographiques*, pp. 67–69). "At the beginning of March . . . [1936], he told me that he wanted to go away. He was sick and tired of people, of exhibitions, of hearing the same things from the same persons, and he had no desire to work, or, even if he did, he was bereft of incentive. . . . 'I can't stand it any longer,' he would tell me day after day. . . . 'I can't stand it any longer. You know that this is no life'" (Sabartés, *Picasso: An Intimate Portrait*, p. 124).

109. Between 1919 and 1924 Gala and Paul Eluard had managed to acquire a fairly substantial collection of paintings so that by the time the collection was partially sold at auction on July 7, 1924, it numbered six works on paper and five paintings by Picasso purchased at the auctions of Wilhelm Uhde's collection (May 30, 1921) and those of Daniel-Henry Kahnweiler's collection (June 13–14, 1921; November 17–18, 1921; July 4, 1922; and May 7–8, 1923). When Eluard sold his collection to Roland Penrose on June 27, 1938, it included ten Picassos. (See Jean-Charles Gateau, *Paul Eluard et la peinture surréaliste* [Geneva: Librairie Droz, 1982], pp. 357–60, annex 1 and 2.)

110. From Roland Penrose, "Un Oeil de liberté," in *Paul Eluard et ses amis peintres 1895–1952* (Paris: Centre Georges Pompidou, Musée National d'Art Moderne, 1982–83), p. 20. By way of conclusion to his description of the portrait (cited above) Penrose added, "La blague n'était pas sans rappeler la forme féminine au bas de la planche qui illustre *Grand air* où l'on voit un chat allaitant trois petits poissons." In his biography of Picasso published in 1958, Penrose had specified that Picasso first portrayed Eluard as an Arlesienne: "As a reaction to his recent preoccupations with tragedy [i.e., *Guernica*], [Picasso] was seized with a diabolical playfulness. The 'portraits' were most frequently of Dora Maar, but at other times he would announce that his model was Eluard or Nusch or Lee Miller. The paintings were strangely like their models but distorted and disguised by surprising inventions. Eluard first appeared in the traditional costume of an Arlésienne, and a few days later, in a second painting, he was dressed as a peasant woman suckling a cat" (Penrose, *Picasso: His Life and Work*, p. 279).

111. In *Eluard, Picasso et la peinture (1936–1952)* (Geneva: Librairie Droz, 1983), pp. 28, 31,

Still Life with Cherries. June 10, 1939. Oil on canvas. Zervos IX, 315. Private collection

Gateau, on the basis of a conversation with Penrose in summer 1969, claimed that the portrait in question was that of Paul "habillé en femme" (Zervos VIII, 368, where it is identified as *Femme assise*, 1937–38). Gateau reproduced it as "*Portrait (Paul Eluard en femme?)*." He either was unaware of or—more likely—chose to overlook the existence of *La femme au chat*, August 30, 1937 (Zervos VIII, 373), generally identified as the portrait of Eluard mentioned by Penrose in 1958, and in the text cited above. In his biography of Eluard published in 1988, Gateau merely referred to the portraits Picasso made of Nusch and Paul Eluard during the summer of 1937: "Dès le 3 août, Picasso dessine un portrait de Nusch. Il en fera plusieurs cet été-là, et peindra même Eluard en costume féminin" (Jean-Charles Gateau, *Paul Eluard ou le frère voyant 1895–1952* [Paris: Editions Robert Laffont, 1988], p. 245).

112. Indeed, it should be noted that there is no suggestion of any "carnal" adventure between Picasso and Nusch in the recollections by Penrose, Sabartés, or Brassaï.

113. Gilot recalled that "Paul and Nusch had 'discovered' Mougins in the thirties and induced Pablo, he told me, to spend a part of his vacation there in 1936, 1937, and 1938. From that period date Pablo's studies of Nusch. Pablo had had a vague affair with Nusch at that period, he told me, and Paul—he was certain—had turned a blind eye to it: the ultimate test of friendship." Gilot added that Picasso told her, "But it was a gesture of friendship on my part too. . . . I only did it to make him happy. I didn't want him to think I didn't like his wife" (Gilot and Lake, *Life with Picasso*, 1964, p. 137).

Taking his cue from Gilot, Pierre Cabanne proceeded to situate the "affair" between Nusch and Picasso in the summer of 1936: "Paul et Nusch Eluard sont les compagnons les plus proches de ces mois d'été, et le poète, dont le comportement en amour le pousse à ne bien posséder que ce qu'il offre à autrui, et aimer ce qu'il donne à aimer, se fait l'amical intercesseur entre Nusch et Picasso. Ce n'était pas la première fois que la jeune femme se prêtait aux expérimentations amoureuses provoquées par son mari, à la grande indignation de Breton dont le rigorisme s'accommodait mal de ce procédés qu'il réprouvait. Nusch y mettait une grande gentillesse. . . . Le don qu'[Eluard] faisait à Picasso de celle à l'égard de qui il éprouvait une grande passion sublimera l'amitié entre les deux hommes" (Pierre Cabanne, *Le Siècle de Picasso: I. 1881–1937* [Paris: Editions Denoël, 1975], p. 491).

114. According to Geneviève Laporte, Picasso told her he had refused to sleep with Nusch: "Nusch était admirable. Juste comme il fallait à Paul. Tu sais que Paul aurait voulu que je couche avec elle . . . et moi je ne voulais pas. J'aimais beaucoup Nusch . . . mais pas pour ça. Paul était furieux. Il me disait que je n'étais pas vraiment son ami pour refuser . . . Parfois il allait à l'hôtel avec une prostituée. Nusch et moi on l'attendait, au café en bas, en bavardant" (Laporte, "Si tard le soir, le soleil brille," p. 39).

115. The poem and portrait were reproduced two years later in *Cahiers d'art* 14 (1939), pp. 138–

39. About this portrait Penrose wrote, "As proof of friendship [Picasso] frequently drew or painted the exquisite charm of Nusch. . . . With her usual taste for originality and elegance, Nusch one day appeared at the rue des Grands Augustins in a new black dress and hat. On the lapels were two gilt cherubs and the top of the hat was ornamented by a horseshoe. The pale fragile face of Nusch, with her combination of ethereal charm and simple candid high spirits, looked all the more enchanting in the severity of these clothes. Picasso remarked that the hat was shaped like an anvil with the horseshoe in position to be hammered into shape. In the portrait he painted as soon as she had gone he traced the base of the anvil in transparent shadows vertically across the oval shape of her face. The gilt cherubs appeared on the lapels and her dark hair surrounded her head with the movement of clouds" (Penrose, *Picasso: His Life and Work*, pp. 283–84).

116. See Gilot and Lake, *Life with Picasso*, p. 242.

117. In May 1945 Brassaï paid a visit to Paul and Nusch Eluard's apartment in the quarter named La Chapelle. "Since my last visit here, however, it is the Picassos that now dominate the walls. Among them, is a portrait of Nusch dated August 1941; a masterpiece. Picasso has painted this ethereal creature with all the gentleness, all the delicacy of which his brush is capable, as if he had wanted to put aside the terrible and rest in the gracious" (Brassaï, *Picasso and Company*, p. 154).

118. This interpretation—a more convincing variant of a line of thinking argued in Mary Mathews Gedo, *Picasso: Art as Autobiography* (Chicago: University of Chicago Press, 1980), pp. 184–85—was suggested to me in conversation with Pepe Karmel.

119. At least up to the date of the "Arlésienne"; see volume I of Paul Eluard's *Oeuvres complètes*, edited by Marcelle Dumas and Lucien Scheler (Paris: Editions Gallimard, 1968).

120. In his biography of Picasso, Penrose described the summer of 1937 which he spent at Mougins at the Hôtel Vaste Horizon in the company of Picasso and Dora Maar, Nusch and Paul Eluard, and Lee Miller. "[Picasso] installed himself in the only room with a balcony in the hotel. When he emerged on to the terrace for meals he would tell his friends, who were then occupying the entire hotel, what he had been doing . . . but more often he would announce that he had made a portrait. As a reaction to his recent preoccupation with tragedy [*Guernica*, completed in June 1937], he was seized with a diabolical playfulness. The 'portraits' were most frequently of Dora Maar, but at other times he would announce that his model was Eluard or Nusch or Lee Miller. The paintings were strangely like their models but distorted and disguised by surprising inventions. . . . The profile of Lee Miller seemed all the more recognizable when combined with large liquid eyes that had been allowed to run with wet paint and an enormous smile from a pair of bright green lips. It was by a combination of characteristics set out in hieroglyphic shorthand that the person in question became ludicrously

recognizable" (Penrose, *Picasso: His Life and Work*, p. 279).

121. From an unpublished lecture titled "Leonardo as Artist and Scientist," given by Meyer Schapiro at the Y.M.H.A. in New York City c. 1952.

122. Walter Pater, *The Renaissance: Studies in Art and Poetry* (Oxford: Oxford University Press, 1986), p. 80.

123. See Richardson, *A Life of Picasso*, p. 121.

124. Pater, *The Renaissance*, p. 152.

125. Ibid., p. 150.

126. Richard Offner, unpublished lectures on High Renaissance painting at New York University, Institute of Fine Arts, 1950–51.

127. According to Ludwig Goldscheider in *Da Vinci: Paintings and Drawings* (London: Phaidon Press, 1964), p. 157, "A Frenchman (Robert de Sizeranne, 1986) had observed that Gioconda smiles with only the left part of her mouth—but this is in accordance with the advice given to women in Renaissance times as how to look most graceful: we read in Agnolo Firenzuola's *Della perfetta bellezza d'una donna*, 1541: 'From time to time to close the mouth at the right corner with suave and nimble movement, and to open it at the left side, as if you were smiling secretly . . . not in an artificial manner, but as though unconsciously—this is not affectation, if it is done in moderation and in a restrained and graceful manner and accompanied by innocent coquetry and by certain movements of the eyes.'"

128. John Shearman, "Leonardo's Colour and Chiaroscuro," *Zeitschrift für Kunstgeschichte* 25 (1962), pp. 13–47.

129. "Les couleurs ne sont que des symboles et la réalité n'est que dans la lumière." From two typewritten pages titled "Guillaume

Portrait of Nusch Eluard. 1937. Drawing on paper tablecloth, 9 7/16 × 5 11/16″ (24 × 14.5 cm). Private collection, England, on loan to the Scottish National Gallery of Modern Art, Edinburgh. (See p. 82)

Apollinaire, 'Propos de Pablo Picasso'" preserved in the Fonds Apollinaire of the Bibliothèque littéraire Jacques Doucet (7540, B'II-2), first published in Pierre Caizergues, ed., *Apollinaire Journaliste* (Paris: Minard, Lettres Modernes, 1981, pp. 596–98); reprinted in Pierre Caizergues and Hélène Seckel, eds., *Picasso/Apollinaire Correspondance* (Paris: Editions Gallimard/Réunion des Musées nationaux, 1992), pp. 201, 204, and 152. I am indebted to Hélène Seckel for information as to the origin of this statement by Picasso.

130. "How often haven't I found that, wanting to use a blue, I didn't have it. So I used a red instead of the blue" (Tériade, "En causant avec Picasso," *L'Intransigeant,* June 15, 1932); reprinted as "Propos de Picasso à Tériade," in *Verve* 5 nos. 19–20 (1948); reprinted in English translation in Ashton, *Picasso on Art: A Selection of Views*, p. 89. "Combien de fois au moment de mettre du bleu j'ai constaté que j'en manquais. Alors j'ai pris du rouge et l'ai mis à la place du bleu. Vanité des choses de l'esprit" (from "Couleur de Picasso. Peintures et dessins. Textes de Picasso et Sabartés," *Verve* 5, nos. 19–20 [1948], n.p.). This remark of Picasso has been published on a number of occasions, sometimes with other pairs of colors.

131. Penrose wrote that soon after the completion of *Guernica*, June 4, 1937, Picasso closed his studio and set off to join Nusch and Paul Eluard at the Hôtel Vaste Horizon at Mougins, taking Dora Maar with him. "A third passenger in the Hispano was Kasbec, an Afghan hound Picasso had acquired not long before. The drowsy oriental dignity or sudden alertness of this slender animal earned him a considerable amount of attention. He never left his master's side, and his profile with its sharp inquisitive

nose became traceable for several years among the human heads that Picasso invented. In fact Picasso has told me jokingly that his two most important models in these years before and during the Second World War were Kasbec and Dora Maar" (Penrose, *Picasso: His Life and Work*, p. 278). Kasbec's elegant snout would be associated with many of the portraits Picasso did of Dora Maar in this period. Penrose tells us also that at the time of Paloma's birth in 1949, a new dog named Yan, a boxer puppy, replaced Kasbec, and took his place in paintings of the children at play with their mother. "The shape of the children's faces in the new pictures reflected rather the round snub-nosed head of Yan" (ibid., p. 330).

In June 1961, Picasso and Jacqueline moved into the house called Notre-Dame-de-Vie at Mougins. Part of their ménage was the Afghan hound Kabul, who from now on would appear in many portraits of Jacqueline, his muzzle incorporated in her features, as in *Nude Woman Seated on Grass*, Mougins, December 11, 1961 (Collection Marina Picasso), which was preceded on the same day by another composition showing a nude with Jacqueline's eyes and Kabul's muzzle in the attitude of a baby on its dressing table; or he is shown standing at Jacqueline's side, as in *Woman in an Armchair*, Mougins, December 13, 1961–January 10, 1962, The Museum of Modern Art, New York.

The acquisition of the château of Boisgeloup, which followed upon the maturing of Picasso's liaison with Marie-Thérèse, was marked by the acquisition of a huge Saint Bernard whose "ghostly bark," according to John Richardson, "can occasionally be detected in paintings of the period, for instance, when its vast head and distinctive markings—dark

smudges of eyes and ears which fit, neatly, as pieces of a puzzle, into the sides of the white snout—suggest an ingenious new pattern for Marie-Thérèse's features. . . . No. 74 [*Baigneuse sur la plage*, January 8, 1931, charcoal on primed canvas, Collection Marina Picasso] is especially interesting in that it combines both the canine and the sexual elements. The double profile can be seen in terms of the Saint Bernard also as a pair of meshing genitalia" (John Richardson, "Picasso and Marie-Thérèse Walter," in *Through the Eye of Picasso 1928–1934*, n.p.).

132. In conversation with the author, July 1971.

133. One of the most familiar of Picasso's symbols of death was either the distorted head or menacing sex of the prostitute. This image was already indelibly established by 1907 in the head of the crouching whore of *Les Demoiselles d'Avignon*. Picasso returned to this theme at intervals throughout his career, especially in his late years (see below).

Reclining Couple. July 29, 1936. India ink on paper, 13⁹⁄₁₆ × 20¹⁄₁₆″ (34.5 × 51 cm). Not in Zervos. Private collection

Old Prostitute. June 3, 1972. India ink on paper, 11⁵⁄₈ × 8¹⁄₄″ (29.6 × 21 cm). Zervos XXXIII, 406. Private collection

Picasso at age fifteen. Barcelona, 1896. Photographer unknown. Musée Picasso, Paris, Picasso Archives

Picasso's Self-Portraits

KIRK VARNEDOE

Picasso's ego was so vast and his art so rooted in personal experience, we might assume his field of self-depictions would be similarly broad and deep. Yet he made only a few unequivocal paintings of his own likeness, all before he was thirty. For the rest, we find specific renderings of his face only in a smattering of drawings or prints, mostly early and usually minor. This anomaly disappears and the field expands exponentially, of course, if we admit the teeming horde of surrogates—the carnival of harlequins, minotaurs, and musketeers—into which Picasso continually projected self-references. Then the dearth becomes a virtually uncontainable surfeit: the entire oeuvre can, after all, be read, by one tactic or another, as autobiographical. The trick is to find some useful path between the two alternatives—neither to constrict self-portraiture into a narrow literalism, nor to inflate it by including a host of guesswork identifications. The middle ground is large but slippery.

As with his portraits in general, simple criteria of resemblance founder. Elements of Picasso's appearance—past, present, future, or mixes thereof—may meld in his art with features of other people real or imagined, contemporary or historical. Such seemingly telltale markers as large dark eyes, a striped sailor's tunic, a shock of hair, or a domed pate turn out to be poor gauges of any serious self-examination, since these clues are often fragmentary, scrambled, or, within a series of closely variant personages, unstably evanescent. The absence of such bits of likeness is, alas, equally inconclusive. Picasso often "inhabited" his creations without any reference to his physiognomy, vesting himself in a bestiary of natural and fanciful creatures, in objects like pipes or doorknobs, and even in patterns (such as the varicolored diamonds of the Harlequin's costume) or other abstract signs. He also found countless ways to reflect his own interests and desires in his portrayals of others; for example, his companion Marie-Thérèse Walter was metamorphosed in a 1935 sculpture into a part of him (p. 153, right).

Many of these sublimated selves may embody Picasso's private myths and superstitions or self-directed varieties of the animisms and fetishisms that constituted his own personal voodoo.[1] As with so much in his art, though, his troupe of alter egos is also, for all its exoticism, the extrapolation of a basic, shared human experience. Each of us is inherently various; each develops as a community of conflicting potentials. These assemblies, moreover, are never mustered solely from within but are largely conscripted along the way. In our public and also in our intimate lives, we may cobble together ways to present our selves by appropriating bits and pieces from other people, often adapting attributes or behaviors that correspond to our fantasies of being (at least a little) of another age or nationality or class. With insight we may come to recognize, among these parts that make up our personas, which of them represent the parents, teachers, lovers, rivals, or fictional characters we have known or imagined. Picasso's

Self-Portrait side by side with a Relative. 1895. Oil on canvas, 23⅝ × 17 q̃ (60 × 45 cm). Zervos XXI, 45. Collection Marina Picasso

Self-Portrait. 1896. Oil on canvas, 18⅜ × 12⅜″ (46.5 × 31.5 cm). Not in Zervos. Museu Picasso, Barcelona

polymorphous self-projection offers a lifelong, evolving catalogue of such insights.

It would be trite to say that the variety of these avatars is only an "expression" of his multilayered personality. Between the worlds he created and the life he lived, the traffic ran both ways; each shaped his understanding of the other, as his art allowed him not simply to express, but to construct and to discover, the complexities in himself. The companions of Picasso's later life described games in which personalities were ascribed, by group discussion, to personages in completed paintings,[2] and Françoise Gilot witnessed the way Picasso would first create a figure and only later—over a period of weeks or months, by continuing to work on it or its variants—decide who it was.[3] He was also a devotee of tarot, a card game of divination based on the notion that unplanned combinations of conventional figures can, if "read" attentively, reveal a unique personal destiny.[4] Doubtless, then, Picasso let tumble from his brush, pen, and stylus many a stock faun or artist, carouser or codger whom he recognized, during the working process or later, as a likely carrier for some aspect of his own identity. He encouraged or suppressed these "self-portraits" according to his whim, as he by turns followed the characters of his imaginings and led them in whatever directions he desired. As one upshot of his overall fusion of truth-seeking and myth-making, this process involved discovery, disclosure, and disguise in varying dialogue.

What is at issue, however, is not self-analysis in the abstract but visual art, and Picasso's manipulation of

the markers of identity has an essential formal aspect as well. There are constant, central tensions between abstraction and reference or between deformation and description in Picasso's work, and they gain another dimension when, in the almost infinitely variable domain of the face, the marks he makes are caught in an oscillation between anonymity and resemblance. An interchange between extreme stylization and the pointed evocation of character begins in the comedy of Picasso's early caricatures, with their exorbitant exaggerations and pithy economies (p. 116, bottom; p. 119, bottom). It gains in drama when, in the *Portrait of Gertrude Stein* (p. 267), he begins to confound the distinction between reductive marks that summarize an identity and autonomous masks that impose one. Variations on this tension remain key to his redefinitions of portraiture throughout his life.[5] As his art always shows and as he occasionally said, Picasso wanted to use the signs he created not to encode specific messages or meanings but to produce disruptively fertile ambiguities and confusions, which often allowed contradictions to cohabit.[6] Applied to the imaging of personalities—and certainly not least the portrayal of his own—this opened up an exceptional range of possibilities.

Perhaps this preference for disorientation and double entendres may help explain why the mature Picasso made so few specific, look-in-the-mirror self-images: his sense of his own being was so protean and volatile that a simple recording of his appearance likely seemed an impoverished premise for art. But the paucity of direct self-portraits after 1907 may also reflect a more complex

Self-Portrait in a Wig. c. 1897. Oil on canvas, 22 × 18⅛″ (55.8 × 46 cm). Zervos XXI, 48. Museu Picasso, Barcelona

form of egotism. His prime desire in art, with his identity as with everything else in the world, was to control and reinvent rather than merely observe and record. However much it amused and informed him to use his art to look into himself, he grew warier of having his aging mortal self—the outer shell whose changing forms time, not he, commanded—look back at him undisguised.

It has been suggested that Picasso turned to self-portrayal in times of crisis, when he felt threatened or aggrieved,[7] but the episodic production is actually grouped around a motley variety of moments in his life, hardly consistent in tone or importance. By far the most productive of these periods were his adolescence and early manhood, when he experimented with his appear-

ance as, in John Richardson's words, "a romantic vagabond, a glamorous jeune premier, a decadent poet, a top-hatted dandy and much else besides."[8]

The mature Picasso was given to denouncing the whole idea of an artist having *a* style. (He cited God to justify painting in multiple manners, arguing that the cosmos demonstrated its maker's disdain for consistency of design.[9]) Nonetheless, a restless, posturing search for a personal style marks his juvenile self-images, in modes of depiction as well as in costume and carriage. The adoption of an eighteenth-century gentleman's powdered wig, with its overtones of a Beaux-Arts ball and its premonition of the masquerades of Picasso's later period, is only the most obvious of these wishful fancies (see above). By contrast, the so-called "bewildered" self-image of 1896 (left) has a writhing Art Nouveau curvilinearity that starts

Picasso Bewildered. 1897. Conté crayon on paper, 12⅝ × 9¾″ (32 × 24.7 cm). Zervos VI, 114. Private collection

in the flame-lick lapels and rises like smoke through the chin, cheek, and jaw structure, into the snaking white midline of the wavy hair. Both the *modernista* manner and this slicked-down coiffure, seen again in a contemporary self-image at the easel (below), assert a faux-adult dandiness, in contrast to the less-kempt look of a slightly earlier oil portrait (opposite, top). Ironically, though, it is the latter, unruly mane that seems, in conjunction with the pouting expression and sullenly lowered gaze, not just more truculently youthful but also more premonitory.

Picasso's hair, a malleable public signboard of self-discipline or its absence, was a recurrent focus of his youthful efforts to style himself; yet the closest model for the look he eventually adopted—a shaggy, boyish bang spilling down from a part on the side—is already seen in the novice self-descriptions of his early teens (opposite). Thus, when this combing arrangement was codified around 1908, it may have been a conscious throwback (p. 138, top right; the side on which the hair is parted has changed from left to right). Even in these early variations, the eye looking in the mirror seems to have spotted the way in which such a large forelock could allow a renderer to pin the eyebrow to the ear and flatten the curve of the cranium at the temple (p. 116, bottom left and right).

In several other early self-images, by contrast, center-parted hair served Picasso's interest in marking his own physical and psychic symmetry, or lack thereof. Almost all

Self-Portrait. 1899. Charcoal on paper, 17¾ × 20⅛″ (45.2 × 51.3 cm). Zervos I, 14. Daix, p. 22. Private collection

Self-Portrait with Unkempt Hair. 1896. Oil on canvas, 12⅞ × 9⅜″ (32.7 × 23.6 cm). Not in Zervos. Museu Picasso, Barcelona

Self-Portrait. 1896. Pencil on paper, 5⅜ × 4⅛″ (13.5 × 10.5 cm). Zervos VI, 50. Private collection

Self-Portrait. 1897. Charcoal and brown crayon on paper, 8⅝ × 5⅛″ (22 × 13 cm). Not in Zervos. Private collection

Self-Portrait. 1900. Charcoal on gray paper, 8⅞ × 6½″ (22.5 × 16.5 cm). Not in Zervos. Museu Picasso, Barcelona

Self-Portrait. 1899. Pencil on paper, 15⅝ × 10⅞″ (39.5 × 27.5 cm). Not in Zervos. Private collection

Self-Portrait and Sketches of Fuentes, Marti, Pompeu Gener, and Others. 1899–1900. Pen and ink on paper, 12⅝ × 8¾″ (32 × 22 cm). Not in Zervos. Museu Picasso, Barcelona

Self-Portrait. 1899. Conté crayon on paper, 13¼ × 9¼″ (33.6 × 23.5 cm). Zervos VI, 107. Private collection

Self-Portrait. c. 1902. Black crayon with color washes on paper, 12 × 9⅜″ (30.4 × 23.8 cm). Zervos XXI, 336. D.B. V, 81. National Gallery of Art, Washington, D.C. Ailsa Mellon Bruce Collection

his full-face, frontal self-portraits appear in this period (above; opposite, top, and bottom left and right), but they are accompanied by a concern to establish a midline that differentiates the two sides of the physiognomy, usually by the standard formula of bisecting the face into areas of light and shadow to intimate a darker interior mood coexisting with the illuminated outward gaze (opposite, bottom center and right; p. 120, top left). Also in three-quarter views, and sometimes with partly hooded eyes or a downcast gaze, this *sol y sombra* division added seriousness to the young man's mien.

While all such teen-age self-portraits by Picasso are to one degree or another recognizable likenesses, they lack any evidence of their author's consistent certainty about his own face. Early photographs, however, are unmistakable in this regard. Picasso was already Picasso by the age of fifteen (p. 110), but his adolescent search for a "look"

seems to have precluded his forming a ready scheme to encode that appearance. If the "bewildered" drawing, for example, is prescient in its peculiarly unfocused gaze and prominent dark eyes, the skull still seems elongated and the emphasis on the bulb of the nose does not allow the relative breadth in the forehead and nostril wings that will later become canonical. Of course, Picasso saw himself far less often in photographs in these years, and he also may have resisted codifying his features because his interest lay precisely in charting a series of rapid-fire changes not just in dress and manner (p. 118) but equally in his physical being and in his idea of it. Richardson has convincingly proposed, for instance, that two unusual self-portraits with bared torsos (p. 119, top) record Picasso's chunky body momentarily emaciated—and hence for once fashionably long of line—after a bout of illness.[10]

His delay in grasping any consistent sense of his own

Self-Portrait. 1901. Conté crayon on paper, 18⅛ × 6½″ (46 × 16.5 cm). Zervos I, 45. Galerie Schmit, Paris

Self-Portrait. 1901. Conté crayon on paper, 13½ × 6″ (34.3 × 15.3 cm). Zervos I, 49. D.B. III, 14. Private collection

Self-Portrait. 1901. Conté crayon on paper, 12 × 6⅛″ (30.5 × 15.5 cm). Zervos XXI, 416. Private collection

features is especially surprising in light of Picasso's precocious skills as a caricaturist. In this same period, the overbrimming swarms on his sketchbook pages show his glee in the power of caricature to remake, attack, ridicule, and gain power over the world around him—to exaggerate people's characters, to age them, to transform them into oddities, and to spawn whole new societies of grotesques (opposite, bottom). A fusion of observation and invention, caricature was a marvelous tool for dealing with the world, but it was not, apparently, one Picasso was prepared as yet to turn effectively on himself. In the series of little *modernista* portraits he showed at Els Quatre Gats café in Barcelona in 1900, his caricaturist's wit and economy were very much in play, but the one with a tenebristically divided face inscribed *"Yo"* is proportioned more like Beethoven than its author, and ignores the power of his eyes (p. 120, top left). In group scenes, too, he often wound up being vague about his own presence, resorting to devices such as burying his features behind high coat collars (p. 120, top right). Any young artist who could inscribe a self-portrait, as Picasso did, *"Yo, el rey"* ("I, the

Notas de Arte, "Madrid." 1901. Charcoal on paper. Advertisement in *Arte Joven* for new publication planned by Picasso and Francisco de Asis Soler. Zervos VI, 357. Daix, p. 130. Private collection

Picasso Stripped to the Waist (Self-Portrait). 1898. Charcoal on paper, 13 × 9¼″ (33 × 23.4 cm). Zervos VI, 63. Musée Picasso, Paris

king") three times over could hardly be accused of simple bashfulness;[11] and it may be overreaching to speculate that these anomalies suggest an adolescent inability or reluctance to step outside himself and see himself as a player like others in the world. Still, it is clear that the pace and pungency of Picasso's self-codification in caricature increased when he experienced himself as an anonymous stranger adrift in a new world of possibilities, with his first trips to Paris in 1900 and 1901.

Picasso produced his most elaborate self-caricature to date when he posed himself before the Moulin Rouge as the newly arrived *artiste-peintre par excellence* (p. 121). Even if the overemphasized eyebrows and disproportionate neck still seem slightly off target, the essential features of the broad, fleshy nose, large, dark orbs, and flyaway coif are now succinctly pegged. This tiny head sits, however, atop an outsized physique, as if Picasso had stuck his face through a pasteboard photographer's prop at a fair. From his favorite "turkey-breeder's" hat to his collar, he is still a Barcelona boy; below he becomes the very model of a modern painter, bedecked with every possible attribute of the trade and sporting a remarkable outfit that we would hardly believe true were it not documented as his in contemporary photographs (p. 120, bottom). The slightly rueful incongruity between familiar and newly donned personas in this send-up is evidence that a capacity for self-satire had expanded, not a moment too soon, to leaven the formerly earnest task of self-presentation.

Caricatures and Portraits: Guillaume Apollinaire, Paul Fort, Jean Moréas, Fernande Olivier, André Salmon, Henri Delormel. . . . 1905. Pen, brown ink, and lead pencil on paper, 10 × 12⅞″ (25.5 × 32.7 cm). Zervos XXII, 200. Musée Picasso, Paris

Sketches with Pierrot Figures. 1900. Ink, conté crayon, and colored pencil on paper, 8⅝ × 12½″ (22 × 31.8 cm). Not in Zervos. Museu Picasso, Barcelona

Self-Portrait. 1900. Pen, ink, and watercolor on paper, 3¾ × 3⅜″ (9.5 × 8.6 cm). Zervos XXI, 109. The Metropolitan Museum of Art, New York. Gift of Raymonde Paul, in memory of her brother, C. Michael Paul, 1982

Picasso and Casagemas. 1899–1900. Ink and watercolor on paper, 7⅛ × 3⅛″ (18 × 8 cm). Zervos VI, 219. D.B. I, 7. Museu Picasso, Barcelona

the phantom photograph and this painting's aura of hypnotism. The discoverer of the photograph, Anne Baldassari, has argued for such a connection.[14]

The best-known and most ambitious of these related self-images from the first part of 1901, called *Yo, Picasso* after the prideful inscription he set on the painting (p. 126), uses the theatrical lighting of the "hallucination" picture without its heavy-handed intimations of salon diabolism. While the latter painting and the *Self-Portrait in a Top Hat* seem to have been private essays, *Yo, Picasso* was clearly conceived as a presentation piece; it is the first work listed in the catalogue of the Picasso exhibition held that summer at Ambroise Vollard's Paris gallery. In the vein of the *Portrait of Gustave Coquiot* in the same show, the picture is determinedly flashy in every sense. The blinding white shirt against the darkened ground offsets lurid notes of gaslit color, including, in the flesh of the face, an adventurous green that Picasso later promoted as having stolen an

Picasso went on to paint four self-portraits in Paris in 1901, and the first three, most likely created during the spring and summer, show a profound surge in self-confidence and self-consciousness. One of these, the sketchy little *Self-Portrait in a Top Hat* (p. 123), connects suggestively to a newly discovered photograph of the same general period that shows Picasso, similarly top-hatted, as a ghostly, transparent presence (p. 122).[12] The latter was inscribed by Picasso on its verso: "This picture could be entitled 'the strongest walls open at my passing—behold'" (or perhaps more accurately, "Watch out!").[13] In the very material world of the painting, the artist is a rich man amid women for sale, coolly detached from the panderings of hot flesh around him, the sinecure of every soliciting eye, whose own gaze is outward and beyond. In the spirit world of the photograph—whose double exposure is common to countless turn-of-the-century capturings of "ghosts" on film—he is a transparent wraith who can pass through walls. The common denominator of these fantasies, beyond the affectation of the attire, is Picasso's new wish to see himself as aloof, a man apart—the powerful observer, present but untouchable.

The "spirit photograph" may connect as well to the unusual head-and-shoulders image in which the artist appears in mug-shot frontality, with a Frankenstein forehead and exaggeratedly wide-eyed expression, stagily underlit as if by a flash of lightning (p. 124). As has often been remarked, Picasso here seems in the grip of some trance or hallucination, his visionary gaze fixed on matters beyond the mundane. Given our knowledge of his superstitious nature and of the circles in which he moved, it seems highly likely that some vein of Symbolist fancy for the occult, pandemic in European bohemias at the turn of the century, informed both the séance theater of

Picasso, Pedro Mañach, and Torres Fuster in the studio at 130*ter,* boulevard de Clichy, Paris, 1901. At left is Picasso's portrait of Iturrino; beneath the flower piece on the back wall (Zervos I, 59) are pages from *Arte Joven* and a lost sketch for the *Moulin de la Galette* (Zervos I, 41). Photograph by Picasso. Musée Picasso, Paris, Picasso Archives

Self-Portrait in Front of the Moulin Rouge. 1901. Ink and colored pencil on paper, 7⅛ × 4½″ (18 × 11.5 cm). Zervos XXI, 250. D.B. IV, 23. Private collection

advance on Matisse's more celebrated liberties with hues.[15] Picasso originally thought to present himself at work (p. 125), but then omitted the easel and the lower body to enhance a pure show of charisma—conveyed most evidently in the intense, dark dots of his widened eyes, which, isolated by the flattening light, fix their laser power on the viewer.

The color and expressionist brushwork of *Yo, Picasso* doubtless owe something to the example of van Gogh, but—in conjunction with the two smaller self-portraits that preceded it—the painting also sheds a more complex light on Picasso's development at the time. These nocturnal pictures, like Coquiot's portrait, belong to the seedy world of Parisian libertinism that Toulouse-Lautrec had captured with cynical affection; however, that world

appeared more provocative to young outsiders from repressive countries, such as Picasso and Edvard Munch. Both these painters caught a whiff of sulfurous menace in the raunchy atmosphere of stale perfume and beer. When Picasso first learned how to breathe these fumes as he entered his twenties, they (and the opium he began to sample) had an intoxicating force that fueled his emerging sense of himself as someone with a destiny, set apart from others by exceptional, even magic, powers. The pyrotechnic blend of stagey virtuosity and prestidigitation in *Yo, Picasso* evokes the mix of the decadent and the youthful, the sensual rush and psychic electricity, that accompanied his new fantasy of exploding on the Paris scene as a demiurge sprung from the humus of the fleshpits.

In the Paris studio, c. 1901–02. On the wall are works from 1901, including *Yo, Picasso* (p. 126), *The Absinth Drinker* (Zervos I, 100), and *Portrait of Gustave Coquiot* (Zervos I, 84). Photograph by Picasso. Musée Picasso, Paris, Picasso Archives. (Colorplate, p. 205)

Still, there is arguably something too eager to please about the mugging, cabaret *espagnolismo* of *Yo, Picasso,* and we might dismiss it and the other 1901 self-portraits as juvenilia were it not for the two telling self-discoveries they embody. First, it is not unusual for an artist to study his own face in exaggerated expressions—Rembrandt and Courbet are among the countless precedents—but

Picasso's decision to limit the mime to the eyes, within otherwise frozen features, unbottles an original and personal genie of lifelong consequence. Second to this augurlike gaze, though, and of equal importance, is the figurative intimation of a wink. In the cocksure bravado of *Yo, Picasso* and the "hallucination" image, a certain element of pleasurable charade and entertaining excess

Self-Portrait in a Top Hat. 1901. Oil on paper, 19¾ × 13″ (50 × 33 cm). Zervos XXI, 251. D.B. V, 41. Private collection

insinuates a grace note of complicitous wit and irony.[16] Picasso's future achievement, the breadth of his appeal and his ability to sustain and renew himself, would ultimately depend not just on the piercing power of vision conjured here, but also on the correcting force of such spirits and on this other, ironical way of looking at himself. These twin elements of his real "magic" announced

themselves here, before he found the formal means to empower his swelling sense of originality.

At the end of 1901, following the failure of the Vollard show to launch his career as he had hoped, Picasso began the long detour of the Blue period, striving to make his

Self-Portrait. 1901. Oil on cardboard (cradled), 21¼ × 12½″ (54 × 31.8 cm). Zervos
I, 113. D.B. V, 1. Collection Mrs. John Hay Whitney

art weightier by taking on the monochrome hairshirt of a poet of misery and pathos. His *Self-Portrait* (p. 127), painted near the close of the year, is one of the first announcements of this drastic shift. The footlights have now gone out, and a morgue pallor sits on this huddled figure, which tentatively intrudes from the right edge of the canvas. As in some distant echo of Rodin's *Monument to Balzac* (which Picasso had seen the year before), a heavily maned head sits high on the pedestal of a cloaked and armless body. Irony and farce are extinguished in this grimly serious self-scrutiny. Pity, which replaces them, takes on luxuriant subtleties when it is self-directed, and this face is appropriately rendered with a ghoulish delicacy that offsets the brooding mass of the body below it.

Surrounded by the fine wisps of a drooping moustache and a beard, the febrile pink of the lips against a porcelain skin offers a frail note of sensibility leeched of sensuality.

Under the influence of El Greco's soulfully mannered distensions, Picasso also adjusted his features to suit the mood of spiritual anorexia: the nostril wings and eyebrows are narrowed and subsumed into a verticality that leads to a broadened forehead, capped by a massive helmet of hair. The signature dark eyes still turn toward us, but now with a hooded and less focused world-weariness. Their inner searchlight seems dimmed and their avidity muffled: we almost feel, for once, that we look into Picasso as much as he looks into us. Finally, the picture as a whole achieves a sullen, wintry integrity that eludes the

Sketch for *Yo, Picasso.* 1901. Pastel and charcoal on paper, 26⅜ × 16⅝″ (67 × 42 cm). Zervos XXI, 190. D.B. V, 3. Private collection

bathos often afflicting the work of the succeeding two years. Picasso felt the work marked an important transition for him, and kept it for life.

The Blue period saw no more independent self-portraits. Several study drawings of 1902 and 1903, however, show that Picasso's drive toward graver themes included an ambition to cast himself as a player within an allegorical drama. Three self-portrait drawings in the nude (p. 128, bottom) replace earlier sartorial experiments with a new notion of moving his identity out of time and into the realm of ideals; the hieratic gestures of command or oath-taking (p. 128, bottom left and center) and an Egyptoid posture (p. 128, bottom right) aim to show the young painter as no longer merely urbane but tarot-

like—an emissary of the timeless and the embodiment of a principle.[17] While it is unclear what abandoned project these studies may have served, they seem connected with the early ideas for the elaborate, still obscure painting of the following year, *La Vie* (p. 129, right). It was first conceived as an allegory of an artist and his female companion in a studio, and the initial studies show that Picasso thought to depict himself, falsely smooth-shaven and with gestures that recall the 1902 nude drawings, as the artist (p. 129, left). In the end, his dead friend, the poet Carles Casagemas, who had shot himself in 1901, occupied this position. Especially given that change, it is difficult to say whether the allegory was initially drawn, as later ones would be, from events in Picasso's life, or whether it

Yo, Picasso. 1901. Oil on canvas, 29 × 23⅞″ (73.5 × 60.5 cm). Zervos XXI, 192. D.B. V, 2. Private collection

Self-Portrait. 1901. Oil on canvas, 31½ × 23⅝″ (80 × 60 cm). Zervos I, 91. D.B. VI, 35. Musée Picasso, Paris

Self-Portrait. 1902–03. India ink on paper, 5½ × 4⅜″ (14 × 11 cm). Zervos XXII, 38. Daix, p. 55. Private collection

was always a more universal morality play in which he thought to act; it was likely a little of both.[18] In any event, his apparent sense of the incompatibility of a specific self-image and a willfully mysterious symbolism might be seen as an initial step toward later allegories such as the *Minotauromachy* of 1935 (p. 155), in which his personal involvement can be discerned only by interpreting more oblique disguises.

There is another harbinger of the Minotaur, too, in a very different place. *La Vie* seemingly occupied Picasso during much of the spring of 1903; but on New Year's Day of that year, he had jotted a quick caricature of himself as a grinning monkey-man (p. 130). This wicked little gibe seems miles apart from the serious ambition to make an allegory of life itself, but in fact it is the merger of the two that would later yield some of his most characteristic works. The monkey raises, lightheartedly, the issue of Picasso's sense of his animal nature—here mostly just mischievous, but also, without too much a stretch of implication, a creature of unruly instincts unashamedly demonstrative about all his appetites. Preceding by decades the parade of fauns and bulls and griffins and minotaurs, this first self-image as a "monster" reminds us that in modern art—and in this artist's work especially—the expressive means of gravity can start out light.[19] The juxtaposition of the simian self and the ideal nude of the studies for *La Vie* further cautions us how, even before he developed the means to express this condition, Picasso

Self-Portrait with Arm Raised. 1902–03. Pencil on paper, 10⅞ × 8½″ (27.5 × 20 cm). Zervos VI, 456. Private collection

Self-Portrait with Arm Raised. 1902–03. Pencil on paper, 7³⁄₁₆ × 3⅞″ (18.5 × 10 cm). Zervos VI, 507. Marina Picasso Collection, courtesy Galerie Jan Krugier, Geneva

Self-Portrait Standing. 1903–04. Ink on paper. 13⅜ × 10½″ (33.8 × 26.7 cm). Zervos XXII, 117. D.B. D.XI, 24. Fogg Art Museum, Harvard University Art Museums, Cambridge, Mass. Bequest of Meta and Paul J. Sachs

Sketch for *La Vie*. 1903. Pencil on paper, 10½ × 7¾″ (26.7 × 19.7 cm). Zervos XXII, 44. D.B. D.IX, 5. Private collection

La Vie. 1903. Oil on canvas, 77⅜ × 50⅞″ (196.5 × 129.5 cm). Zervos I, 179. D.B. IX, 13. The Cleveland Museum of Art. Gift of the Hanna Fund

Sketch for *La Vie*. 1903. Pencil on paper, 6¼ × 4⅜″ (15.9 × 11 cm). Zervos VI, 534. D.B. D.IX, 4. Musée Picasso, Paris

(like most humans) simultaneously harbored self-images of opposing temperament. Paralleling the blunter instrumentation of *La Vie,* the sketchbooks carried on the notion of an incorrigibly scurrilous artist who looked on art as a naughty, barbed weapon. Aspirations to take on big, noble subjects like Life with a capital *L* were, of course, central to Picasso's art; those ambitions often returned, albeit later shorn of some of this solemn, youthful piety. But it was the monkey in his makeup—his malefic "animal" nature, wit, and talent for caricature—that would be the source of some of his most original, world-conquering achievements. To echo the earlier photograph inscription, when Picasso brings these two selves together—when the monkey makes peace with the magus and the beast teams up with the bard—"Watch out!"

The painting *At the Lapin Agile,* made in late 1904 and early 1905 when Picasso was emerging from the depressive colors and themes of the preceding three years, was something of a "sport," executed quickly and thinly to adorn a wall in a low-rent bar on the Butte de Montmartre.[20] Picasso had done such decorations before, usually directly on studio walls and typically in a mock-grandiose vein of allegory.[21] Here, however, we find an unfamiliar blend of realism and metaphor that looks back to Lautrec with one eye and forward to the world of the *Saltimbanques* with the other. Tempered by the experiences of the intervening years, the picture replaces the sardonic glamour of

Self-Portrait as a Monkey. 1903. Pen on paper, 4⅝ × 4¼″ (11.8 × 10.7 cm). Not in Zervos. Museu Picasso, Barcelona

Picasso's early nightlife scenes with a more downbeat, noncommunicative ennui—more like the world of Edgar Degas's *Absinthe,* which also centered on the seminarcotic and notably unconvivial liqueur the Harlequin is nursing here. This disaffected soul, far from the swaggering *boulevardier* of the 1901 *Self-Portrait in a Top Hat,* now identifies himself (more accurately, given Picasso's straitened circumstances) with outcasts in dives rather than revelers in the high life.

Harlequin had earlier appeared as a moody café thinker, alone or with a female companion, in Blue period paintings that established the trope of the gaily clad performer with a melancholy inner life;[22] *At the Lapin Agile* is the first instance in which Picasso specifically and unmistakably assumed this guise. Several months later, in the final transformative stages of the more important and substantial *Bateleurs* (p. 132), he would rework the figure of an itinerant acrobat to insert another self-image, more idealized and responsible—a *paterfamilias*—in the same costumed role.[23] From then on, Harlequin (or even just his costume) would recur as one of the artist's most important avatars (see pp. 145, 146). The nature of Picasso's identification with this figure from the *commedia dell'arte*—and precedents in the works of artists from Watteau through Daumier to Cézanne—have been amply examined.[24] *At the Lapin Agile* seems at least as notable, though, for the first promotion of the caricatural self-notation of Picasso's sketchbooks—the shock of hair linking eyebrow to ear, the narrowed chin and broad nose—into an oil painting. It is the combination of this pithy specificity with the emergent role-playing and disguise—a marriage of slang's economy and poetry's ellipsis—that constitutes the particular interest here.

Such elisions and inversions seem to have been of the moment. This bar scene inflates a caricatural slice of life to painting scale, while a watercolor of the same period (late 1904) confers an uncommon, resonant depth on a smaller drawing of a private moment (p. 133). *Meditation* shows Picasso (looking younger by having shaven his Blue-period beard) gazing down on the radiant figure of a sleeping woman. The motif is thought to stem from the onset of the artist's relationship with Fernande Olivier; a related work showing a haggard figure glaring at this same sleeper is thought to picture Picasso's rival, Fernande's estranged husband.[25] The image, however, has wider implications. Like many of Picasso's mature compositions, it involves two opposing figures in a static relationship, with the gaze as a key element; more particularly, it belongs to what Leo Steinberg has analyzed as a long line of "sleepwatcher" scenes in Picasso's oeuvre, where wakeful consciousness is juxtaposed in wondering speculation to the vulnerable figure of a dozer absorbed in dreams.[26] The watercolor all but eclipses its minor sketchbook precedent, a caricature of Picasso with a

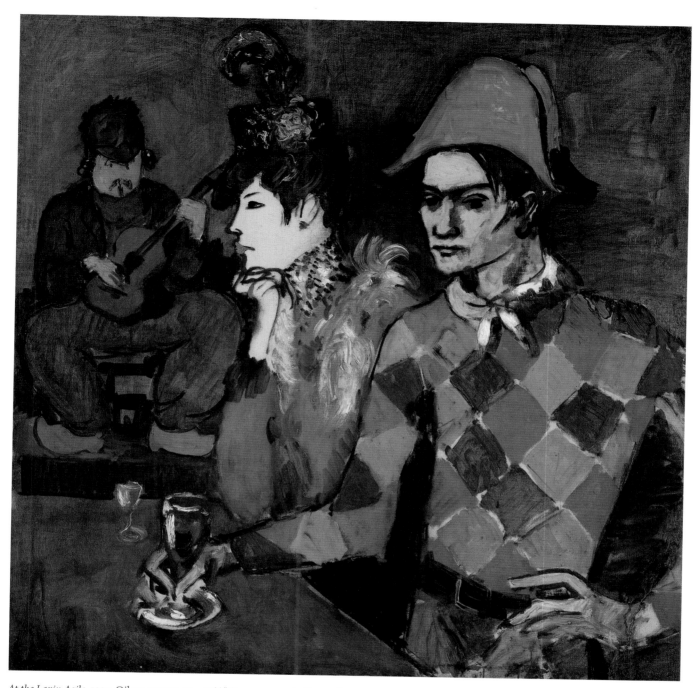

At the Lapin Agile. 1905. Oil on canvas, 39 × 39½″ (99 × 100.3 cm). Zervos I, 275. D.B. XII, 23. The Metropolitan Museum of Art, New York. The Walter H. and Leonore Annenberg Collection, Partial Gift of Walter H. and Leonore Annenberg, 1992

whore (p. 348), apparently mimicking the composition of Gauguin's *Spirit of the Dead Watching* (p. 348). However, the two pictures have in common exactly what the trick "ghost" photograph also embodied: Picasso's wish to imagine himself as the unseen seer, a "spirit" (whether figuratively or literally) who, though present, cannot be perceived. This is his position in *At the Lapin Agile* as well, turned away in more soulful three-quarter view from the schematic profile and frontal figures behind him, standing outside and looking beyond; his companions are eccentrics of the moment's fashion, but he, in dress and solitary character, is a performer on a larger, more timeless stage.

Between the autumn of 1904 and his summer 1906 visit to Gosol in the Spanish Pyrenees, Picasso's private life and public position each shifted radically. His amorous arrangements were regularized, as Fernande moved into his quarters in Montmartre; but his position in the Parisian art world was thrown into new question by the *succès de scandale* of the Fauve painters, led by Matisse, at

Les Bateleurs (The Family of Saltimbanques). 1905. Oil on canvas, 83¾ × 90⅜″ (212.8 × 229.6 cm). Zervos I, 285. D.B. XII, 31. National Gallery of Art, Washington, D.C. Chester Dale Collection

the Salon d'Automne in 1905 and again at the Salon des Indépendants in the spring of 1906. The face that stares at us from the self-portrait drawing done at Gosol (p. 134) is thus also staring down a challenge.

The drawing offers a rare throwback to early sketch-book studies in its frontal symmetry but attacks matters of fashion and style from a sharply different angle. Fore-locks, for example, have become a nonissue. In childhood Picasso's head was shaven for the summer months, as a strategy against lice (see p. 110),[27] and he may have shaved it again at Gosol;[28] in any event, he showed himself as a skinhead, with a smoothed pate that matched the bald-ness of the aged Gosol innkeeper Josep Fontdevila (see p. 29). Picasso was taken with the skull-like cranium and weathered face of this venerable part-time smuggler; Fontdevila prompted many drawings in the course of the summer, and as an emblem of old age was to haunt Picasso's imagination far longer (see p. 173).[29]

As Picasso presents his own face here, however, it has less of the old fox of the hills than of the young one at home; the feline, almond eyes, thin, arcing eyebrows, and full lips echo those of Fernande (compare the portrait head on p. 135, top). Spurred by his experiences of early Iberian sculpture, the artist was searching throughout

this summer for simplified ways of drawing old men and youths, males and females, which in their "primitive" reductiveness moved toward similarity or even uniformity. It was an enterprise that stood caricature on its head: salient differences in age, gender, physical type, and phys-iognomy were generalized or suppressed rather than heightened, in a search both for a primal sculptural solid-ity and for a graphic language of depersonalization. In this study of his own face Picasso intentionally resisted allowing a likeness built on the easy and familiar markers of eyes, nose, and hair, and perhaps just as knowingly moved to adapt for himself some of the stylizations he had been devising for the portraits of his beloved.

In Gosol or in the immediate wake of his sojourn there, we find several paintings of men or boys, and one of a family group, which traditionally have been desig-nated self-portraits (p. 135, bottom). Yet, while they share certain features with Picasso—the hairline, the ear— these bull-necked drones and fresh youths typically have the kind of generic "personality" one finds in archaic Greek *kouroi*, and there is a high level of generalization in their features. In retrospect, they seem relatively imper-sonal and unrevealing exercises in self-rejuvenation when compared to the more aggressively specific self-examina-

Meditation (Contemplation). 1904. Watercolor and pen on paper, 13⅝ × 10⅛″ (34.6 × 25.7 cm). Zervos I, 235. D.B. XI, 12. The Museum of Modern Art, New York. Gift of Louise Reinhardt Smith

tion they lead toward, the *Self-Portrait with Palette* (p. 137).

Picasso began this picture when he returned to Paris in the autumn, at the same time that he painted a masklike face onto the *Portrait of Gertrude Stein* (p. 267); it would become his most important self-portrait since the blue painting of 1901, and one of the most carefully considered of his life. For the first time, leaving aside the initial

notion for *Yo, Picasso* (p. 126), he determined to show himself as a working painter—or more exactly, in contrast to the overequipped, farcical *artiste-peintre* of early days (p. 120, bottom), as a worker-painter, stripped down to a laborer's tunic and alone in the studio.

In this rawboned self-portrait (in contrast to the prematurely aged Picasso in the *Self-Portrait* of 1901; see

Self-Portrait. 1906. Charcoal on paper, 9⅞ × 9⅛″ (25 × 23 cm). Zervos XXII, 450. Private collection

p. 127), any former echoes of Rodin's *Balzac* are supplanted by anticipations of Brancusi. Painterly modeling of the features is suppressed in favor of sharp, isolated strokes that evoke direct carving; instead of the shaggy capstone atop the dark columnar body, here the head is a smooth ovoid poised atop a block. Gone, too, is El Greco. Picasso now accepts and plays to advantage his own

stocky proportions; the increased ratio of skull to torso imparts a sense of both youthfulness and compressed power. The unusually heavy line where the chin seems to rest on the clavicles simultaneously insists on the four-square chunkiness of the body and the masklike quality of the face; anchoring the jaw, like pinning the arms to the sides, uses physical rigidity to imply inner rigor.

Head of a Woman (Fernande). 1905. Bronze, 14¼ × 9¼ × 9⅛″ (36.1 × 23.5 × 23.1 cm). Zervos I, 232. Spies 6. Hirshhorn Museum and Sculpture Garden, Smithsonian Institution, Washington, D.C. Gift of Joseph H. Hirshhorn

By diminishing the chin and lower face and proportionally enlarging the ear, nose, and eyes, Picasso simultaneously pushes his physiognomy back toward that of his youth (compare p. 110) and suggests a more exotic, Polynesian or Negroid cast—an overlap of childhood and tribal allusions then credible, along with the archaic stiffness and the reduced, cement-and-sandstone palette, as

appropriate attributes of a "primitive" spirit. (Gauguin's posthumous retrospective was being shown at the Salon d'Automne in these same months, but the coloration and modeling here signal a rejection of Gauguin's painterly exoticism in favor of a tougher, more sculptural look.) For the all-important eyes, some initial studies show them downcast, and the artist thereby absorbed in paint preparation (p. 136, top); even thinking about this step—eliminating his most distinctive trademark and shutting down the black beacons of *Yo, Picasso*—confirms how heightened impersonality and intensified interior vision had become linked in importance for him.

In the end, the stare he settled on is as impenetrable in its own way as the closed lids. Both eyes are shown essentially frontal despite the three-quarter turn of the head; only size—diminution and compression of his right side—residually signals perspectival foreshortening. The broad, shadowless separation of the eyes adds to the eeriness of the gaze, which is directed neither at the viewer nor, apparently, at work being done on an unseen easel; the absence of a brush in the right hand further stresses that virtuosity of touch is not the point, just as the fist negates the long-fingered gestures of self-address or delicately mimed communication often found in the Blue and early Rose periods. The fixated gaze may recall the "hallucination" picture of five years before, but it is now utterly earnest and unsettling in its unfocused blankness. In this presentation, freeze replaces fervor and alienated sensitivity turns to stony implacability.

No matter how strong his inner conviction and sense of his own singularity, however, there were many points in his career at which Picasso wanted to see himself through, or even as, another artist he admired;[30] this is the

Self-Portrait as a Child. 1906. Oil on canvas, 15⅜ × 11⅞″ (39 × 30 cm). Zervos II², 592. Private collection

Self-Portrait. 1906. Oil on canvas, 25⅝ × 21¼″ (65 × 54 cm). Zervos II¹, 1. D.B. XVI, 26. Musée Picasso, Paris

Man, Woman, and Child. 1906. Oil on canvas, 45¼ × 34⅝″ (115 × 88 cm). Zervos II², 587. D.B. XVI, 30. Öffentliche Kunstsammlung Basel, Kunstmuseum. Gift of the artist, 1967

Studies for Self-Portraits. 1906. Lead pencil on paper, 12⅜ × 18⅞˝ (31.5 × 47.5 cm). Zervos XXVI, 5. D.B. A, 22. Musée Picasso, Paris

Studies for Self-Portraits. 1906. Lead pencil on paper, 12⅞ × 18⅞˝ (32.5 × 48 cm). Zervos XXVI, 3. Musée Picasso, Paris

first self-portrait to evidence that desire. He modeled the image on a Cézanne self-portrait—the one that Meyer Schapiro called the most impersonal of all Cézanne's self-portraits,[31] and the only one that explicitly shows him as an artist (p. 136, bottom). Picasso clearly appreciated the locked-in alignments of edges and shapes, which Schapiro analyzes in the Cézanne, even to the point of bending his left sleeve outward to join the edge of the palette, although the willful tilting of that slab injects a rebellious note of imbalance. The palette was, in any event, a false prop, as many witnesses testified that Picasso did not typi-

cally hold one;[32] but he almost always included it as an attribute of the painters he depicted, and this one may serve another function. While Cézanne holds his at waist height, Picasso, by straightening his left arm, brings the prominent detail of the protruding thumb down to crotch level. With another artist, the idea that this yields a displaced surrogate phallus might seem inadmissable; with Picasso, whose later images so often conflated the acts of sex and painting, it seems unavoidable.

While the *Self-Portrait with Palette* of 1906 has the solid heft of a planned statement, the following year's *Self-Portrait* (p. 139) looks like an impetuous, explosive revelation. On first impression it may seem just an aggressive caricatural sketch, exploiting crude cartoon features in sensational, over-the-top exaggeration: a colossal nose, for instance, and eyes that have become as salient a signature as Mickey Mouse's ears, with about the same relation to anatomical reality. The force of the shock is, happily, long-lasting; among all Picasso's self-portraits, this small canvas embodies the fullest expression of his creative powers. It actually derives its strength, though, not just from radical simplifications but from a more complex collision of manners. Structured on bold geometries and harsh formal rhythms, it nonetheless retains the life of something based on visual experience rather than formula, and rewards extended examination.

Picasso conjures his likeness here from a scaffolding of essentially flat, unmodulated, and evenly weighted angular slashes and rhythmical arcs, potently locked together by insistent parallelisms, repetitions, and alignments. The strictness and coherence of these marks make the reductive contours of the 1906 *Self-Portrait with Palette* seem, by contrast, weakly indecisive: compare the two areas of the hairline and forehead to judge the change. Here, the outer edge of the ear exactly joins the sweep of the skull's

Paul Cezanne. *Self-Portrait with Palette.* 1885–87. Oil on canvas, 36¼ × 28¾˝ (92 × 73 cm). Foundation E. G. Bührle Collection, Zurich

Self-Portrait with Palette. 1906. Oil on canvas, 36¼ × 28¾″ (92 × 73 cm). Zervos I, 375. D.B. XVI, 28. Philadelphia Museum of Art. A. E. Gallatin Collection contour, and its top arch—aided by the forelock, which stands for the whole head of hair—rebounds directly into the eyebrow. With this, and with the slashing cheekbone line that simultaneously extends into the curve of the ear, the rear of the head is collapsed into the front; what seems the back of the skull is pulled around to profile flatness, and the face subsumes the head.[33]

The angled forelock also drastically reduces and reshapes the forehead, which had been a broad dome of thought in previous self-portraits, into an almost equilateral, spear-point triangle—a shape that harmonizes with several other, more acute triangles and V-forms, from the cheek areas to the points of the collar and lapels, and even into the herringbone pattern of the coat fabric. The upward-pointing wedge of the nose area then locks in with the two downward-pointing daggers of the cheeks to create an implicit W configuration that, beginning in the jaw contour at the right and ending in the mirror stroke of the cheekbone on the left, structures the face between the eyes and the lips.

Such bold strokes and acute angles would become

Self-Portrait (Bonjour, Mlle. Cone). 1907. Pen and ink on paper, 8⁵⁄₁₆ × 5p″ (21 × 14 cm). Not in Zervos. The Baltimore Museum of Art. The Cone Collection, formed by Dr. Claribel Cone and Miss Etta Cone of Balitmore, Maryland

At the Bateau-Lavoir, 13, rue Ravignan, Paris, c. 1908–09. Photograph by Picasso. Musée Picasso, Paris, Picasso Archives

typical of Picasso's Africanizing work following *Les Demoiselles d'Avignon,* but their order here is so exceptionally lean, clear, and consistent that it also anticipates the economies of later Cubism's linear constructions, as in the syncopated arcs that make up the *Man with a Hat* of 1912–13. A signal difference, however, is that neither the *Demoiselles* nor any of the other Iberian-influenced or Africanized figures of this period were based on the presence of a model, whereas observation seems implicit in this *Self-Portrait*. Picasso parted his hair on the right in 1908 (see above, right); the left-side part here would be a classic index of study from a mirror. Also, the herringbone coat is apparently not mere formal invention but a record of one he wore at the time (above, left). More important, though, we find clues to the input of observation in the numerous enlivening idiosyncrasies that flesh out the graphic skeleton: the one stray hair in the forelock that keeps it loose and flyaway, the slender tongue of the neck that sets the jaw forward below the ear, and all the soft passages initially sketched in slightly shifted skin tones—the ridge of the ear, for example, or the bulb of the nose, or the channel above the upper lip.

The interchanges between this subtle level of description and the harsher, more autonomous schemas of abstraction are especially clear in the nose. The dark diagonal stroke that designates its left side (from our vantage) is balanced by another on the right, establishing what seems a flat handle for the brow's spear point or axe head; but the relative faintness of that parallel line still seems residually to point up, in this three-quarter frontal pose, a difference between near (left) and far (right) edges, just as the paler paint between the lines suggests a highlight on

Man with a Hat. 1912–13. Pasted paper, charcoal, and ink on paper, 24½ × 18⁵⁄₈″ (62.2 × 47.3 cm). Zervos II², 398. Daix 532. The Museum of Modern Art, New York. Purchase

Self-Portrait. 1907. Oil on canvas, 19¾ × 18⅛″ (50 × 46 cm). Zervos II¹, 8. Daix 25. Národní Galerie, Prague

Henri Matisse. *Portrait of Madame Matisse/The Green Line*. 1905. Oil on canvas, 16 × 12⁷⁄₈″ (40.5 × 32.5 cm). Statens Museum for Kunst, Copenhagen

the shelflike ridge of this extraordinary proboscis. In this way, as in the disproportion of the two nostril wings and in the triangular plane of subtly altered flesh tone that "shades" the left side, a flat, sharply unnaturalistic graphic structure that deals only in edges is joined to painterly codes for planar volume and spatial position. We need only compare the more typical *quart de brie* or "pie-wedge" nose of Picasso's Africanizing stylizations (see below) to dramatize the greater complexities here. More than confounding painterly cues for flatness and three-dimensionality, such junctures between the subtle and the crude—between the soft codes of illusion and the hard lattice of linear pattern—help give the face the compelling life it has. Picasso's *Self-Portrait* of 1907 stands with Matisse's *Portrait of Madame Matisse/The Green Line* of 1905, with which it is a competitive alternative, as one of early modern art's most radical renegotiations of the terms of collaboration between abstract invention and physiognomic description.

The most riveting aspects of the image, of course, are the eyes; and they might seem the most formulaic signs of all. The compression and miniaturization that differentiated the offside eye in the three-quarter pose of 1906 have now been eliminated; these giants stand side by side like twin die-cut logos, in wholly unnatural proximity. As the rear arc of the cranium seems to rotate frontward on the left, so here the right side of the face seems stretched sideways and pulled around to accommodate the full-size frontal-

Head of a Woman. 1907. Oil on canvas, 18¹⁄₈ × 13″ (46 × 33 cm). Zervos II¹, 12. Daix 34. The Barnes Foundation, Merion, Penn.

ity of the eye. Despite such insistent symmetry, however, there are willful distinctions between the two halves of this gaze, and they determine its impact. The little diagonal stroke of declivity below Picasso's right eye, for example, establishes depth in what is the "near" socket, while the blank "far," or left, side seems paradoxically flattened, inverting its spatial recession. At the same time, Picasso's more solidly dark and centered right pupil attaches itself firmly to the top of the eye, while his left pupil, marked by a touch of light in its center, rolls more freely across the bottom lid toward a cross-eyed asymmetry. If we cover one half of the face and then the other, we see the emotive results of all this: his darker, more sunken right eye, anchored at almost the exact midline of the canvas—and the one typically covered in shadow in early self-images (see p. 116, bottom; p. 118, top right; p. 120, top left)—is calmer and more passive in its stare, while his left eye, with highlights above and below, has a more startling, aggressively pop-eyed expression. In this gaze, as in the whole of this remarkable picture, Picasso found the means to give several of his earlier identities—the facile caricaturist and the ambitious painter, the theatrical self-projector and the man of inner magic—a single face.

Yet there may be a still more profound and original synthesis here, for something subliminally familiar, and chilling, lurks in this visage: the uninterrupted, acute curve of the back of the head, the huge eye sockets, and the decisive jaw with its narrowed chin combine to evoke the latent image of a skull. As if in compression of the tension between eros and thanatos that later would inform *Les Demoiselles d'Avignon,* the exaggerated signs of intense life here—the wide windows of the soul and the broad, fleshy protrusion of the nose—compete for ascendancy with the configuration of a death's-head.

Picasso revived the Harlequin in 1908–09, at least once with covert personal reference,[34] but he never brought the language of early Cubism to bear any more directly on self-representation; it was only after the breakup of his sustained dialogue with Georges Braque, at the time of World War I, that he resumed contending with his own image. In the summer of 1914, the year the war broke out, he started, in a revivified naturalistic mode, a large *Artist and His Model* canvas that likely referred to himself (though the male figure hardly resembles him) and his current companion, Eva Gouel (p. 298); when Eva died the following year, in a hospital overcrowded and understaffed because of the war, the canvas was still unfinished, and the artist decided to leave it so. But this was only one of the ways in which the 1914–18 period brought death, figuratively and literally, to the milieu in which Picasso had been at home since his arrival in Paris. With Eva's passing and with key cohorts such as Braque and

In the studio at 5*bis*, rue Schoelcher, Paris, c. 1915–16. At left is *Guitar, Clarinet, and Bottle on a Pedestal Table* (Zervos II², 538; Daix 886); at rear, *Man Leaning on a Table* (Zervos II², 550; Daix 889). Photograph by Picasso. Private collection

In the rue Schoelcher studio, wearing fine-art-mover's felt (or flannel) smock and patched work trousers, c. 1915–16. Photograph by Picasso. Private collection

In the rue Schoelcher studio, wearing shorts and zinc worker's jacket, c. 1915–16. At rear is *Seated Man with Glass*, in progress (Zervos II², 845; Daix 783). Photograph by Picasso. Musée Picasso, Paris. Gift of Sir Roland Penrose

In the rue Schoelcher studio, in "boxer" pose, c. 1915–16. Photograph by Picasso. Musée Picasso, Paris. Gift of Sir Roland Penrose

Self-Portrait. 1918. Lead pencil on paper, 13⅜ × 9¼″ (34 × 23.5 cm). Zervos III, 76. Private collection

Guillaume Apollinaire in the army, he found himself drawn into very different circles by his association with a new dealer, Paul Rosenberg, the poet Jean Cocteau, and a new romantic interest, the Russian ballerina Olga Khokhlova. Picasso, solidly prosperous in his middle and later thirties, let this new coterie lead him away from the ruder life he had lived in Montmartre toward more elegant comforts and a smarter look.

As Anne Baldassari has described, a series of photographs taken around 1915–16 seems to show the painter in this period of transition, literally stripping away the tailoring of his new *boulevardier* identity to reassert for the camera first the guise of a blue-collar worker—a self-image of the Cubist years, now increasingly untenable—and then the bare-chested swagger of youth (p. 141); run this photographic sequence in reverse and one has a truer "film" of

Picasso's history of the previous decade.[35] Perhaps partly from similar concern for the mutations in his physical condition, or because in courtship he was freshly conscious of his looks, or simply because his new style of classicizing naturalism once again allowed it, Picasso also returned around 1917 to the youthful practice he had abandoned for more than a decade, of drawing his own likeness. Three of these renderings seem obvious homages to the drawings of Ingres: two images of the artist at work (above; opposite, bottom), including one where a linear body supports a fully tonal and representational, if unprepossessing, facial portrait; and a tautly incised overworking of a mirror study (opposite, top right) in which Picasso's romantic, over-the-shoulder stare recalls Ingres's *Self-Portrait at the Age of Twenty-four*.[36] A similar three-quarter pose appears in reverse in a fourth,

Jean-Auguste-Dominique Ingres. *Self-Portrait at the Age of Twenty-four.* 1804. Oil on canvas, 30⅜ × 24⅞″ (77 × 63 cm). Musée Condé, Chantilly

Self-Portrait. 1917. Pencil on paper, 25¼ × 19½″ (64 × 49.5 cm). Zervos XXIX, 309. Musée Picasso, Paris

Self-Portrait. 1917. Pencil on paper, 12⅝ × 8½″ (32 × 21.5 cm). Not in Zervos. Private collection

related drawing that was for many years held to be Picasso's final direct self-portrait, and that ostensibly presents his face as he saw it in a mirror at the Hôtel Lutetia on the eve of the armistice in 1918, at the moment he received the news of Apollinaire's death (p. 144, top left).[37]

The plump and smoothly groomed composure of all these images seems notably at odds, however, with the more intimate, shaggily agitated, and intense sketchbook study Picasso made of himself near the same time (p. 144, top right); and there is equally contradictory import in the indirect, caricatural image that closed out this flurry of self-portrayals (p. 144, bottom). As Michael FitzGerald has analyzed, this 1919 sketch shows Picasso conjugally ensconced in the elaborate trappings of a grand new apartment he and Olga had rented on the elite rue La Boétie; however, his face-off with the caged songbird— perhaps partially a metaphor for the ballerina he had pursued and now possessed—clearly prompts us to question who is the real captive.[38]

None of these renderings is of great substance, though; the truly telling self-representations of the period are less evident. In contrast to *The Artist and His Model* of 1914 (p. 298), for instance, the element of self-identification and the connection to Eva are much deeper in the abstract *Harlequin* of the following year (p. 145, top). Preparatory drawings show that the image was first conceived as a dancing couple, and only at the last became a solitary

Self-Portrait. 1918. Pencil on paper, 13⅜ × 10¼″ (34 × 26 cm). Zervos III, 75. Private collection

Self-Portrait. 1918. Pencil on paper, 5½ × 3¾″ (14 × 9.5 cm). Not in Zervos. Private collection

Self-Portrait in Front of the Window, rue la Boétie. 1919. Watercolor on paper, 6¾ × 5⅞″ (17 × 15 cm). Zervos XXIX, 340. Private collection

The 1915 *Harlequin* includes a rectangular area apparently left "unfinished," possibly representing either a painting or a palette held in the figure's left hand (p. 147); it has been noted that the brushy passages of paint here hold in reserve the suggestion of a silhouetted profile.[43] If this reading is correct, Picasso would have insinuated into the scene a disembodied "second self," seemingly latent or emergent in the painting process itself (both Picasso's and his avatar's). James Scarborough has proposed that a similar silhouette of Picasso's opposite profile is created in negative (light against dark) along the edges of the brushy shadow area to the left of the head of Olga in her 1917 portrait (p. 147, top right, bottom).[44] In either instance, Picasso may have had partly in mind the venerable legend that art began when a woman traced her lover's features from his cast shadow, to preserve a sign of him when he went off to war.[45] Resulting connotations of the projected profile as a primal marker of love, absence, and the menace of mortality thus would have overlain his wartime adoption of this means to "haunt" one picture made under the threat of loss, and another enthroning a new mistress. The device took on still other associations, though, when he used it more explicitly and more frequently in the next decade.

Harlequin. 1915. Oil on canvas, 72¼ × 41⅜″ (183.5 × 105.1 cm). Zervos II², 555. Daix 844. The Museum of Modern Art, New York. Acquired through the Lillie P. Bliss Bequest. (Colorplate, p. 147)

painter/jester by his easel in a blackened studio. The dark mood—extending, as William Rubin has remarked, to a sober palette as foil for the diamond-paned costume[39]—connects both to the general wartime experience and to Picasso's anguish over the terminal illness that was daily pulling Eva closer to her death while he painted.[40] In its troubling ambiguity, the emotional resonance of this toothily grinning *Harlequin* is far more profound than the sentimental sad-clown aura of its predecessors; it connects more tellingly to the grave concert of the 1921 *Three Musicians* (p. 146), in which Picasso's self-representation as Harlequin anchors a threnody for lost friends and a bygone bohemian life.[41] In between, in 1919, a less somber Harlequin musician had proffered a music sheet, the title of which seems Picasso's message of concession to the woman who in part had fostered the change, and who wanted to marry: *"Si tu veux"*—"If you wish."[42]

Harlequin with Violin ("Si Tu Veux"). 1918. Oil on canvas, 56 × 39½″ (142 × 100.3 cm). Zervos III, 160. The Cleveland Museum of Art. Purchase, Leonard C. Hanna, Jr. Bequest

Three Musicians. 1921. Oil on canvas, 79 × 87¾″ (200.7 × 222.9 cm). Zervos IV, 331. The Museum of Modern Art, New York. Mrs. Simon Guggenheim Fund

For years biographers reiterated the story that Picasso decided to abandon self-portraiture after the fateful drawing done in the mirror on the day of Apollinaire's death in 1918 (p. 144, top left). We now know that this drawing was not, in fact, the last of its kind, and there also may be reason to question the legend of its morbid conception.[46] Whatever the truth of the matter, however, Picasso clearly licensed the story, and allowed the related inference that this cessation—as well as his well-publicized dislike for mirrors—was involved with a superstition about death.[47] It may not be coincidental that his self-representation in the 1920s centered on the idea of *not* looking himself in the eye, and even entailed an implication of his not being physically present. For Picasso

the preferred vehicle for all this was the profile view.

Picasso had drawn casual side views of himself from very early on, in comic-strip narratives but also as independent sketches (p. 148, top left and center); in 1921 he made two more formal, medallion-like versions, probably from photographs (p. 148, top right, bottom left; compare p. 148, bottom right). The evocative profiles of the later 1920s are, however, more idealized, almost generic, likenesses, in the form of blank silhouettes or line renderings (pp. 150, 151; p. 152, top). These may connect, as Baldassari has suggested, to the cabaret shadow-puppet performances of Picasso's early years in Barcelona. Baldassari also has published an intriguing undated photograph from Picasso's papers that shows a profile shadow

Harlequin (detail). 1915

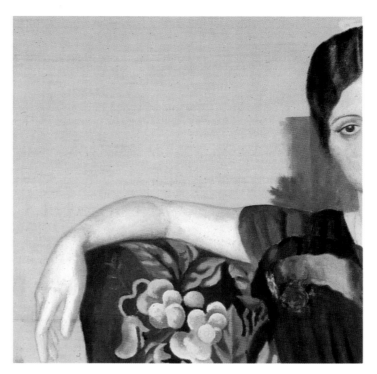

Olga in an Armchair (detail). 1917

(perhaps the artist's own) cast across a framed drawing (p. 149, top); she persuasively argues for a connection between this photographic experiment and the paintings of 1927–29 in which a shadowy Picassoid face confronts a grotesque, usually female presence (pp. 150, 151; p. 152, top).[48]

In what has become a canonic interpretive linkage between Picasso's art and his life, these latter paintings are commonly read as expressions of the mounting discord between the artist and his ever-more-shrewish wife, Olga. The idea seems highly plausible in select instances where, as if in oneiric transformation of the little living-room scene of the marriage as a face-off between songbird and husband (p. 144, bottom), these domestic interiors become chambers of horror in which a shrieking, spiky monster affronts a phantom head (p. 150, top, second from right and right). Returning to the idea already latent in the "spirit photograph" of his youth, Picasso wishfully imagines himself as an *ombre* in the multiple senses of the French term, denoting both a cast shadow and the spirit form of a person released from the mortal encumbrance of the body. The disembodied head inserts Picasso in the scene of strife (of which he is, of course, the maker, perhaps in more senses than one) as a blameless bystander, intangible, impassive, and even eyeless; and given the interest in unconscious or "automatic" creativity in the Surrealist circles around Picasso, we might derive still another level of meaning from this mixed imagery of presence and absence. "Projecting" his shadow into these pictures as a sidewise, silhouetted bust with no hands

Olga in an Armchair. 1917. Oil on canvas, 51¼ × 34⅝″ (130 × 88 cm). Zervos III, 83. Musée Picasso, Paris. (Colorplate, p. 307)

Self-Portrait in Profile. 1903. Watercolor on paper, 8¼ × 5⅛″ (21 × 13 cm). Zervos VI, 601. Private collection

Self-Portrait with A. F. de Soto and Sebastià Junyer Vidal. 1902. Ink on paper, 5¼ × 3⅝″ (13.2 × 9 cm). Zervos XXI, 332. Museu Picasso, Barcelona

Self-Portrait in Profile. 1921. Crayon on paper, 10⅝ × 8¼″ (27 × 21 cm). Zervos XXX, 141. Private collection

seems a way to position himself as an objective outsider beside the strange configurations that arise from his imagination; denying the frontality and hands-on agency of the conscious painter, he literally does not "face up" to his role as inventor of the image.

Along these lines, we would also do well to examine the seemingly specific "Olga" scenes in the context of the broader set of artistic "marriages" from which they emerged—Picasso's concurrent experiments with oppositions and overlays of linear structures and transparent planes both dark and light, and with confrontations between sharply divergent forms of stylization. The "shadow vs. monster" conflict entails a face-off between a vestige of Picasso's Neoclassical style of the early 1920s

Self-Portrait in Profile. 1921. Pencil on paper, 10⅝ × 8¼″ (27 × 21 cm). Zervos XXX, 149. Private collection

Picasso in 1917. Photographer unknown

and the surrealizing manner that increasingly dominated his art after 1924—a juxtaposition that also appears, without the connotations of domestic strife, in other paintings of the date. *Painter and Model* of 1928 (p. 152), for example, features the smoothly idealized silhouette on the easel as a creation of the artist at work, and also as his emblem: an island of classical serenity, standing apart from the potent transformations that structure the surrounding world. In a 1927 illustration for Balzac's *Le Chef d'oeuvre inconnu* (p. 152), Picasso celebrated the painter's obsession to pull apart and retangle into an obscure private language the tidy knit of the visible world. In the later work he shows the reverse: the artist distilling from the jumbled codes of the world a pure, even styleless sign that may connote the primal origins of art and that is, not surprisingly, the vehicle of his own persona.

With this in mind, we can reconsider the earlier, hidden profiles as possible counterpoints—in their simplicity and in their "natural" or emergent origins within "unfinished" areas of paint—both to the Cubism of the *Harlequin* and to the sophisticated realism of Olga's portrait. Similarly revisiting the oppositional grotesques and shadow silhouettes of 1927–29, we see how often one or the other personage is not, in fact, a live presence but a work of art, nailed to the wall or set in a frame (p. 150, top, second from right and right). The shadow profile confronts the abstracted bone head *as art*, or vice versa, setting up a dialogue between the "natural" or indexical sign of the projected silhouette and the invented deformations of the other being. The constant is that the male presence, Picasso's face, is always figured as a natural trace or styleless sign—whether transparent, when a cast shadow, or opaque, when a silhouette in a frame[49]—while the other personage, not always of determined sex but most often female, is the bizarre or monstrous enigma.

Even though particular pictures may have been slanted toward their marital discontent, the spats of Olga and Pablo are only one possible overlay on this broader psychic struggle and stylistic battleground—a field on which the artist, as prime mover, wins either way. As in the *Painter and Model,* we might say that he wants literally to keep his head as he paints: always able to stand outside the confounding distortions and reformulations, an untouchable presence, to witness the power his art has over the world; and conversely, always able to use that art to resolve for himself, within the refuge of the canvas, a more ideal, and exempt, identity. Profile views are intrinsically more objectified and distanced, but we must reckon with all these added fantasies of absence, dematerialization, and primal autonomy to begin to measure the force of Picasso's evident impulse, as he approached fifty, only to show himself outside his own regard.

Picasso shown in left profile, Paris, 1927. Photograph by Picasso. Musée Picasso, Paris, Picasso Archives

The Studio. 1928–29. Oil on canvas, 63¾ × 51¼″ (162 × 130 cm). Not in Zervos. Musée Picasso, Paris

Woman in an Armchair (Composition). 1927. Oil on canvas, 28¾ × 25⅝″ (73 × 65 cm). Zervos VII, 78. The Minneapolis Institute of Arts. Gift of Mr. and Mrs. John Cowles

Harlequin. 1927. Oil on canvas, 31¾ × 25½″ (80.6 × 64.8 cm). Zervos VII, 80. Private collection

Bust of a Woman with Self-Portrait. 1929. Oil on canvas, 28 × 23⅞″ (71 × 60.5 cm). Zervos VII, 248. Private collection. (Colorplate, p. 329)

Figure and Profile. 1927–28. Oil on canvas, 25⅝ × 21¼″ (65 × 54 cm). Zervos VII, 144. Private collection. (Colorplate, p. 328)

Head. 1928. Oil on canvas, 18⅛ × 21⅝″ (46 × 55 cm). Zervos VII, 126. Private collection

Head of a Woman. 1928. Oil on canvas, 18⅛ × 18⅛″ (46 × 46 cm). Zervos VII, 125. Private collection

The silhouette shapes in the 1927 paintings, with their long, straight lines from rounded forehead to nose tip, were ideograms Picasso adapted to stand for himself rather than strict descriptions of his profile; with minor adjustment, they also could be adapted to the representation of Marie-Thérèse Walter when she began to appear in his sculptures and paintings of the early 1930s (p. 153, left). (Or, conversely, since Picasso had already met Marie-Thérèse by 1927, we might speculate that his sign for himself at that earlier date already subsumed—as in the case of the Fernande-like self-portrait completed at Gosol, p. 134—some element of the image he was beginning to encode for her; it would be logical, after all, that Marie-Thérèse, as well as he, would be implicated in the *agon* against the "Olga" forms.⁵⁰) The device of combining profile and frontal views in a face—most famously associated with Marie-Thérèse's sun-and-moon head in the 1932 *Girl*

Before a Mirror (p. 357)—also allowed Picasso the opportunity to continue to inhabit or haunt, in this covert fashion, the images of others he created for years to come.

Yet if this provides an element of continuity between the 1920s and the 1930s in Picasso's work, it is only in the context of a massive change—from wiry line and transparent plane to *zaftig* volume, from claustrophobic interiors or stark metaphysical beachscapes to fruit- and eros-filled chambers and breeze-caressed loggias on the Mediterranean, from carping wife to pliant young lover. Nothing could stand in sharper contrast to the disembodied shadow heads, for example, than the robustly physical artist figures of the *Vollard Suite* of etchings done in 1933 (p. 154, top, center left, and bottom left). Although there are no explicit self-portraits in this series, few observers would dispute Picasso's wish to identify himself with these men, who consort with models umistakably based

Figure and Profile. 1928. Oil on canvas, 28¾ × 23⅝″ (73 × 60 cm). Zervos VII, 129. Musée Picasso, Paris

Painter and Model. 1928. Oil on canvas, 51⅛ × 64¼″ (129.8 × 163 cm). Zervos VII, 143. The Museum of Modern Art, New York. The Sidney and Harriet Janis Collection

Painter and Model Knitting. 1927. Plate IV from *Le Chef-d'oeuvre inconnu* by Honoré de Balzac (Paris: Ambroise Vollard, Editeur, 1931). Etching, 7⁹⁄₁₆ × 10⅞″ (19.2 × 27.7 cm). Geiser/Baer I, 126. The Museum of Modern Art, New York. The Louis E. Stern Collection

Head of a Woman. 1931. Bronze, 50⅝ × 21½ × 24⅝″ (128.5 × 54.5 × 62.5 cm). Not in Zervos. Spies 133. Musée Picasso, Paris

Bust of a Woman. 1931. Bronze, 24⅝ × 11 × 16⅜″ (62.5 × 28 × 41.5 cm). Not in Zervos. Spies 111. Musée Picasso, Paris

on the placid moods and youthful physique of Marie-Thérèse. That new presence in his life had prompted Picasso to pursue a fulsome series of modeled sculptures around 1933 (see above), and the artists in the *Vollard Suite* are predominantly sculptors—not thinkers who configure the world into two dimensions but physically laboring creators in constant, palpable touch with the sensual realities of life—cradling "warm flesh in one hand," as he described them later, "and cool champagne in the other."[51]

The typical atelier scene in this series features not the cerebral labor by which the world is remade in art but a postcoital air of relaxation that sets artist and model together in contemplation of the finished object (p. 154, top right). Once again there are oppositions between a classicizing naturalism and surrealist invention (p. 154, center right), but the dominant spirit seems a dream of *luxe, calme et volupté* that rejects the stark, oneiric fantasies of the late 1920s and rebuts the intellectualized nightmares of canonical Surrealism. The Mediterranean order here evokes a sensual, arcadian classicism, immune to the spartan purism of other Neoclassical manners and antipodal to the chilly melancholy that, in the period

between the wars, attended many of the attempts to imagine ancient culture.

This world of instinct, however, also harbors fates and punishments that may attend the indulgence of animal pleasures; these come to center on the figure of the Minotaur, a hybrid monster of virile power and unbridled appetite who had first begun appearing in Picasso's art in 1928. This cruel beast of ancient legend bore the body of a man, but his head, the seat of reason, had been displaced by that of a bull; incapable of being civilized, he lived in a labyrinth on Crete, and was propitiated by having maidens sacrificed to his appetites, until the hero Theseus slew him. In the *Vollard Suite,* the Minotaur is sometimes a hearty *convive* at the studio revels (p. 154, bottom left), but in the later plates it is clear that Picasso saw this creature both as an aspect of himself and as an ultimately tragic figure (p. 154, bottom right). At this point in his life, if not well before, he had come to think of himself as a "monster" in a complex way—not simply as a beast of marauding instincts but as a freak of nature in a higher sense. He gave friends to understand that he lacked complete comprehension of his own special creative

Sculptor Working on the Design with Marie-Thérèse Posing.
1933, printed 1939. Etching, 7⅝ × 10½″ (19.4 × 26.7 cm).
Geiser/Baer II, 321. The Museum of Modern Art, New
York. Abby Aldrich Rockefeller Fund

Sculptor at Rest with His Model, Anemones, and Small Torso.
1933, printed 1939. Etching, 7⅝ × 10½″ (19.4 × 26.7 cm).
Geiser/Baer II, 315. The Museum of Modern Art, New
York. Abby Aldrich Rockefeller Fund

Model and Sculptor with His Sculpture. 1933, printed 1939.
Etching, 10½ × 7⁹⁄₁₆″ (26.7 × 19.3 cm). Geiser/Baer II, 300.
The Museum of Modern Art, New York. Abby Aldrich
Rockefeller Fund

Marie-Thérèse Considering Her Sculpted Surrealist Effigy. May 4,
1933, printed 1939. Etching printed in black, 10⁹⁄₁₆ × 7⁹⁄₁₆″
(26.8 × 19.3 cm). Geiser/Baer II, 346. The Museum of
Modern Art, New York. Abby Aldrich Rockefeller Fund

Bacchanal with Minotaur. 1933, printed 1939. Etching, 11¹¹⁄₁₆ ×
14⅜″ (29.7 × 36.6 cm). Geiser/Baer II, 351. The Museum of
Modern Art, New York. Abby Aldrich Rockefeller Fund

Dying Minotaur. 1933, printed 1939. Etching, 7⁹⁄₁₆ × 10⁹⁄₁₆″
(19.3 × 26.8 cm). Geiser/Baer II, 366. The Museum of
Modern Art, New York. Abby Aldrich Rockefeller Fund

Minotauromachy (7th state). 1935. Etching, 19½ × 27⅜″ (49.6 × 69.6 cm). Geiser/Baer III, 573. The Museum of Modern Art, New York. Abby Aldrich Rockefeller Fund

powers; he said he felt commanded by, rather than only in possession of, his gifts. It is this imagining of himself simultaneously as a *sacré monstre* and a *monstre sacré,* set apart by his special power and isolated by inner forces fated to drive him according to their demands, which finds form in the part-man, part-animal who is both blessed and cursed by his transcendence of the conventions of human society. Speaking later to Gilot of another scene from the *Vollard Suite* (see p. 161, top), Picasso said that the horned intruder is wondering whether the sleeping woman he observes "loves him *because* he is a monster."[52] The element of self-pity in this self-aggrandizing myth comes sharply to the fore in the *Vollard Suite*'s later visions of an afflicted Minotaur, and in the brilliant *Minotauromachy* etching of 1935: at a time when Marie-Thérèse's pregnancy had precipitated a crisis in his already troubled marriage to Olga, Picasso adopted the image of the wounded monster much as he previously had adopted that of the sad clown, showing the hulking beast as an object of pity, led by an innocent child with the features of his young mistress.[53] No longer the disembodied and untouchable presence he was in 1927, Picasso

becomes an all-too-physical creature of instinct, touch, and smell, not bystander but agent and victim of disorder.

On simpler terms, though, the Vollard etchings are notable for the acknowledged, if idealized, discrepancy between the hirsute maturity of the men (Picasso was past fifty) and the youth of the women (Marie-Thérèse was barely in her twenties). Picasso found this issue of age increasingly unavoidable as he approached sixty. In 1938 he could show himself as still boyish, in a sailor's tunic (p. 157), but the two self-portrait drawings done from a mirror in 1940—apparently his first such studies since 1918—tell another tale (p. 156, top). One of these images is bolder and more familiarly wide-eyed, the other more recessive and seemingly withdrawn, but both remove his haggard visage from the center of the field of view toward the margin. In this regard they echo a remarkable self-portrait photograph of Picasso's small, fragmentary face spying at us from the corner of a mirror (p. 156, bottom).[54] Drawings and photograph were all done in Royan, in the summer of 1940, when the Germans invaded and occupied France. Picasso, who had arranged to have his current companion, Dora Maar, with him but

Self-Portrait. 1940. Pencil on paper, 6¼ × 4⅜″ (16 × 11 cm). Zervos XI, 82. Private collection

Self-Portrait. 1940. Pencil on paper, 6¼ × 4⅜″ (16 × 11 cm). Zervos XI, 81. Museum Ludwig, Collection Ludwig, Cologne

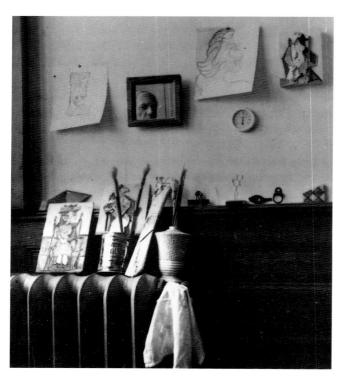

In the studio at Villa les Voiliers, Royan, 1940. The artist's face is visible in the small mirror hanging between sketches of Dora Maar. Photograph by Picasso. Musée Picasso, Paris. Gift of Sir Roland Penrose

also to have Marie-Thérèse and their daughter in residence in Royan, was living in acute uncertainty under pressures both political and domestic. His life's work had been reviewed at The Museum of Modern Art's retrospective the previous year, and he had been forced to undertake another, more literal sorting and packing of his career when the outbreak of war and the invasion of France obliged him to gather and store all his art and belongings in Paris. With reflection on the past thus forced upon him, questions that clouded the future would have been all the more trying.

On one of his hectic visits to Paris before the Germans arrived, Picasso allowed the photographer Brassaï to shoot a series of candid portraits of him in the cafés and restaurants he frequented.[55] The evidence of these photographs may have helped seal the artist's recognition of the changes time had worked on his face—and most especially on the top of his head (p. 158, top). By their close cropping, the Royan drawings neatly obfuscate the fact that Picasso by then had lost a great deal of his hair. By 1941, when he drew the amusing little overhead "portrait of the author" that is the frontispiece for his play *Le Désir attrapé par la queue* (p. 158), he was more candid; in what seems a paraphrase of one of Brassaï's photographs (p. 158, top left), he caricatures not only the wispy sparse-

The Artist Before His Canvas. 1938. Charcoal on canvas, 51¼ × 37″ (130 × 94 cm). Not in Zervos. Musée Picasso, Paris

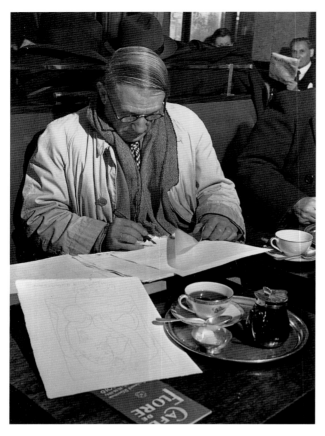

At the Café de Flore, Saint-Germain-des-Prés, Paris, September 18 or 19, 1939. Photograph by Brassaï

In the studio at 7, rue des Grands-Augustins, Paris, September 18 or 19, 1939. Photograph by Brassaï

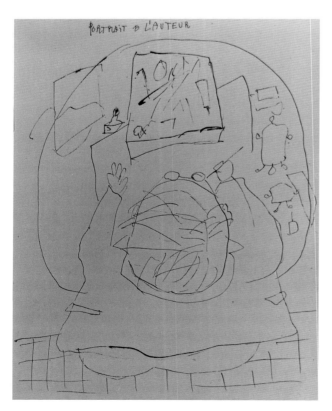

Le Désir attrapé par la queue. 1941. Pen on paper. Published in *Messages*, no. 2 (1944). Not in Zervos. Musée Picasso, Paris

ness of his scalp, but also the addition of reading glasses to his fabled gaze.

Picasso could continue, of course, to imagine himself, and portray his surrogates, in youthful form; but with the war years he stopped denying, on some crucial levels, that he was actually advancing through his sixties. In May 1945 he took the decisive step of cutting off the forelock that had been a signature trait throughout his adult life, and that had served more recently to camouflage his baldness.[56] We know from Gilot that Picasso was deeply superstitious about having his hair clipped,[57] and this particular cut was without question a significant ceremonial gesture; he may well have been aware of the rite of passage in other cultures, where cutting one's topknot marked the entry into old age.[58] The symbolism here, however, was not involved so much with forsaking the world as with clearing the decks for another phase. Picasso called the change to the attention of friends who failed to note it,[59] and he remarked simply to Brassaï after showing him the newly exposed pate, *"On ne peut être et avoir été,"* which might translate loosely as "You can't live in the present and also in the past"; then he asked, "So when are you going to photograph me without my forelock?"[60]

The Shadow. December 29, 1953. Oil and charcoal on canvas, 51 × 38″ (129.5 × 96.5 cm). Zervos XVI, 100. Musée Picasso, Paris

Committed to a new look in life, Picasso was still long in finding his new face in art after World War II. One identity with which he was familiar, but which he perhaps found newly problematic in his sixties, was that of parent to young offspring. With Françoise Gilot, who replaced Dora Maar in his affections in the late 1940s, he fathered a boy and a girl—Claude and Paloma—who brought a fresh surge of interest in infantile delights. In the 1920s he had painted Paulo, his son by Olga, more as a little adult, even showing him in a Harlequin's costume as a junior edition of his father. (Some writers also have seen, almost certainly erroneously, a self-portrait in the 1938 *Maya in a Sailor Suit,* with its cap identifying Marie-Thérèse's daughter as a swabby on the good ship *Picasso* [see p. 377]).[61]

The Shadow on the Woman. 1953. Oil on canvas, 51½ × 38½″ (130.8 × 97.8 cm). Zervos XVI, 99. Art Gallery of Ontario, Toronto. Gift of Sam and Ayala Zacks, 1970

However, whether in recognition of a new age of permissive thinking about early childhood or out of a greater concern to absorb for himself some of the budding vitality of their youth, Picasso in the early 1950s doted on the childishness of Paloma and Claude; rather than imposing premature adulthoood on them in his work, he often let their games, their toys, their own creations—as

well as the mercurial intensity of their emotional life—inform his art.[62] Aside from one or two ambiguous examples,[63] however, he never opted to show himself as the head of this new family; the image doubtless would have underlined with unwanted clarity the gap in years that separated him from these sprouts and their young mother.

It was the breakup of that family that occasioned

Faun Unveiling a Sleeping Girl. 1936, printed 1939. Etching, 12p × 16p″ (31.6 × 41.7 cm). Geiser/Baer III, 609. The Museum of Modern Art, New York. Abby Aldrich Rockefeller Fund

the revival of a former self-image: on December 29 and 30, 1953, after a Christmas during which Picasso and Françoise remained separated, the artist painted two canvases showing the shadow of a figure falling into a room where a woman lies naked (p. 159; opposite). It is unclear whether the recumbent woman represents Françoise (he had never shown her as a nude during their years together), but there is less doubt, since Picasso later said so to a visitor, that this is the artist's own shadow, in the bedroom they had shared.[64] The device recalls Picasso's previous imaginations of himself as an intruding silhouette (see pp. 150, 151), as well as the plate from the *Vollard Suite* in which a minotaur-like faun steals in

through a flood of raking light to unveil a sleeping woman (left). Now he confirms his position in front of, yet outside, the scene, and—as if in two different photographic exposures—alternately projects his shadow as something solid and opaque, from which the female body seems to arch away, and as an all-covering transparent veil. In either case, the notion of the *ombre,* which previously had carried connotations of untouchable power, now seems to assume more poignant overtones of an inability to touch; the towering shadow could signal either an advancing entry or a departure, and the lover within is seen, whether in anticipation or retrospect, by the light of a declining sun.

From the 1950s onward Picasso was the subject of innumerable photographs, but as vanity can provide conflicting goads he often encouraged the photographers who lionized him and then deflected the candor of their recording lenses by literally making a fool of himself, in what became a familiar parade of impromptu masks, fake moustaches, and other forms of posing buffoonery. For those disposed to think so, this stream of mugging self-presentations could, when paired with the costumed caprices of the late paintings, confirm the image of a self-indulgent old man concerned principally to amuse himself. Seen through a different optic, the clowning masquerades might be aligned with the later art to suggest a more complex attitude of often sardonic, partly defensive gamesmanship in the face of age's inexorable encroachments and an increasing awareness of death. Toward the end, Picasso took an even more active role with regard to this string of photographs, drawing on some of them to

In the Studio. 1954. India ink on paper, 9⅝ × 12½″ (23.8 × 31.8 cm). Zervos XVI, 183. Private collection

The Painter. 1965. Oil on canvas, 39⅜ × 31⅞″ (100 × 81 cm). Zervos XXV, 25. Private collection

alter his appearance and to produce antic scenes of himself and his friends as players in little costume dramas.[65]

Amid all these camouflages, however, the one avatar Picasso embraced most consistently in his final decades was the one with the least disguised self-reference: the figure of the artist. Near the breakup with Gilot, he undertook a series of drawings, often lightly satirical, of the artist in his studio (p. 161, bottom), some of which were published in *Verve* in late 1953; after that, one or another variant of this theme recurred at intervals, especially among his drawings and prints. The focus was not on his own circumstances. Neither live models nor traditional palettes, which are constant attributes of these late studio scenes, had anything to do with his practice, and the artists in question almost never display his features in more than allusive fashion; they tend to be stock types, typically bearded, which Picasso never was. Here, as in

the case of countless male busts or figures (above; opposite; p. 165), Picassoesque combinations of traits can come and go within a series (p. 164) in a way that suggests we may risk a certain arbitrariness in singling out one or another as an authentic self-examination. There is, however, a strong consistency in the basic opposition between young female models and older male painters, which does mark the particular and personal framework through which Picasso saw this idea of artmaking as a broadly metaphoric subject.

As he dwelled on the image of the older artist, Picasso in his last twenty years also sought to fraternize and contend with a pantheon of painters of the past. The major steps are well-known and well-studied: a reprise of Courbet's *Demoiselles au bord de la Seine;* a series based on Delacroix's *Femmes d'Alger,* stimulated in part by the legacy of Matisse's *odalisques* and in part by the look of

Seated Man (Self-Portrait). April 3, 1965. Oil on canvas, 39¼ × 31¾″ (95 × 80.5 cm). Zervos XXV, 95. Private collection

Picasso's new wife, Jacqueline Roque; an extended remak-ing of Manet's *Déjeuner sur l'herbe;* and a lengthy reimag-ining of the elements of Velázquez's *Las Meninas.* As this latter series melded with the more generic studio scenes, so in reverse certain of the generic busts and images of artists took on costumes or features that associated them with particular painters from history. The first intimation of this seems to have come as early as 1950, when Picasso paraphrased an El Greco *Portrait of an Artist,* which, as Susan Galassi has noted, was then often taken to be a self-portrait by the master of Toledo.[66] The practice began in greater earnest, however, after Picasso's illness and surgery in 1963, and seems to have centered most tellingly on the disparate figures of Rembrandt and van Gogh.

As Richardson has pointed out, these two artists may have been special cases for Picasso precisely because they are so strongly identified with self-portraiture.[67]

Rembrandt, particularly, had set the standard for charting each rise and fall of his fortunes in a self-image, continu-ing through the most unflinching confrontations with his flabby features and ebbing vitality in old age. The aging Picasso apparently felt a strengthening bond with the great Dutchman's secular materialism, which fostered an earthy realism about all the body's functions and its weaknesses; but he also found an affinity in Rembrandt's contrary penchant for lavish costumes and theatrical mas-querade.[68] Not least, he realized that Rembrandt, like Titian, was admired for the achievements of his late style. Gilot recounted that Picasso told her all painters think of themselves as Rembrandt, and described how a spiteful Olga would send a picture of Rembrandt to her former husband inscribed "If you were like him, you would be a great artist."[69] Jacqueline felt that all the swashbuckling "musketeer" types that frequent Picasso's later work ulti-

Head of a Man. 1969. Ink on paper, 12 × 9½″
(30.5 × 24 cm). Zervos XXXI, 209. Private
collection

Head of a Man. 1969. Ink on paper, 12 × 9½″
(30.5 × 24 cm). Zervos XXXI, 210. Private
collection

Head of a Man. 1969. Ink on paper, 12 × 9½″
(30.5 × 24 cm). Zervos XXXI, 211. Private
collection

Head of a Man. 1969. Ink on paper, 12 × 9½″
(30.5 × 24 cm). Zervos XXXI, 212. Private
collection

Head of a Man. 1969. Ink on paper, 12 ×
9½″ (30.5 × 24 cm). Zervos XXXI, 213.
Private collection

Head of a Man. 1969. Ink on paper, 12 × 9½″
(30.5 × 24 cm). Zervos XXXI, 214. Private
collection

Seated Man (Self-Portrait). December 26, 1966. Pencil on paper, 21⅝ × 18⅛″ (55 × 46 cm). Zervos XXV, 249. The Hakone Open-Air Museum, Tokyo

mately began in his fascination for the seventeenth-century world of *The Night Watch* (p. 166; p. 167, top left), and Richardson also has noted how often Picasso would add a swift little "portrait" of a Rembrandt-like face to his signature when dedicating a book to a friend (p. 167, top right).[70]

If Rembrandt in his velvet beret seemed the quintessential painter of the North, of material pleasures, and of old age, then his fellow Dutchman, van Gogh, in his straw hat provided for Picasso the perfect counterpoint: an adept of Southern sunlight, never compromised in his bohemian ardor by either wealth or senescence. Even though Picasso spent part of his later years quite close to Aix-en-Provence and Mont Sainte-Victoire, he did not retain the powerful attraction for Cézanne he had felt in his youth (see p. 136, bottom; p. 137). The image of the bald old painter living ascetically in isolated concentration amid the skulls in his studio, and painting by patiently cumulative increments, evidently held no appeal. More stimulating were van Gogh's "physiognomic" brushwork, with its reminiscences of Daumier in the expressive caricature of things, and the passionate intensity for life Vincent had always portrayed in his own eyes.[71]

Since traits of these artists could mingle with Picasso's own or with those of other familiars such as Balzac,[72] few specific or "dedicated" portraits of them exist, yet they still seem paired touchstones in the transfer of Picasso's sense of his own life into the fictions of his art. Years before, he had told his dealer, Daniel-Henry Kahnweiler, that he wanted to "live like a poor man with a lot of money,"[73] and his final decades fulfilled some of that paradox. He was a beach bum in a castle, spending his days T-shirted or bare-chested in sandals and shorts, in the

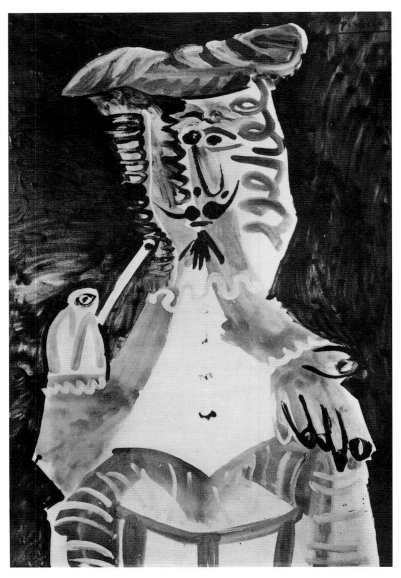

Man with a Pipe. 1968. Oil on canvas, 57½ × 38¼″ (146 × 97 cm). Zervos XXVII, 383.
Private collection

salons of his châteaux from centuries past, which had
become makeshift studios or cluttered, pleasurably dusty
bins for the accumulation of his art. He obviously loved
this straw-hat existence in the remnants of a plumed-hat
age, combining the disparate privileges of palace and
plage. Fantasies of courtly manners cohabited with the
casual informality of a sun-soaked Mediterranean routine, in this waning life lived in and through art, at once in
the shady groves of history and in the invigorating sun of
Provence. Amsterdam and Arles, Rembrandt and van
Gogh, became complementary coins in this exchange.

Very close to the end of his life, in 1971, Picasso added
another figure to this pantheon, when he undertook a
short series of etched variations on several monotypes by
Degas that he owned, showing scenes of bordello life
(opposite, bottom). There is bittersweet irony in this
late return to the brothel, which had been the site of the

eruption of his most complex artistic energies in *Les
Demoiselles d'Avignon*. In that earlier work, he at first had
thought to show an opposition between a male figure
engaged in sensual pleasure (a sailor amid the prostitutes)
and a complementary one whose detached observation
was associated with reminders of mortality (a medical
student holding a skull and standing to the side). Both
males were banished in 1907, but one, the dispassionate
observer, returns in these etchings in the role of Degas
(whose ambiguous, apparently chaste behavior in the
brothels was a point of curiosity for Picasso), standing
aside as the whores display themselves or traffic with their
clients.[74] With its urbane clothes and long, bearded physiognomy, this Degas-like figure also may connote associations with Picasso's father, don José, thus mingling an
Oedipal specter of artistic failure with the suggestion of
neutered sexuality.[75] Earlier in life, when Picasso had

Head of a Man. 1969. Wash on paper, 10½ × 8½″ (26.5 × 21.5 cm).
Zervos XXXI, 58. Private collection

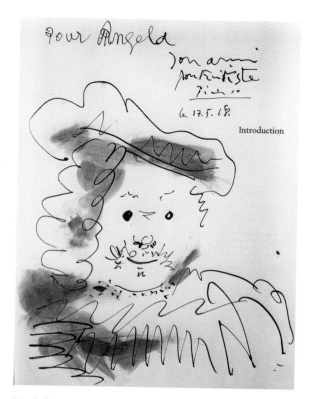

Head of Rembrandt. 1968. Pen, India ink, and wash on paper,
12⅞ × 9⅞″ (32.8 × 25 cm). Zervos XXVII, 267. Collection
Angela Rosengart, Lucerne

shown himself as immune to whorish solicitation (p. 123) or as a profiled presence in a scene (pp. 150, 151), he did so to promote fantasies of visionary power; casting the artist in this new, "uninvolved" role has more problematic overtones of voyeuristic impotence.

It is axiomatic that strong art can be made from personal weakness or affliction, and Rembrandt and van Gogh prove the premise. Their way of dealing with straitened circumstances, infirmity, and desperate disappointment was to show themselves with brutal directness. By adopting their attributes, however, Picasso scanted this crux of their achievement, and wound up for many years referring to his own dilemmas— old age, impotence, or just increasing insulation from the daily variety of life that had given his early art sustenance— only in more oblique and inferential ways. Though the graphic works of the 1950s and 1960s are often brilliant in their virtuosity and impressive in the energy of

their fantasy, the countless paintings with Picassoesque attributes or other artists' guises need a devotedly friendly interpretation to be seen, in regard to self-portraiture, as something more than a talented but indulgent spinning of

Bordello Scene. 1971. Etching, 14⅝ × 19½″ (37 × 49.5 cm). Private collection

Picasso, His Work, and His Public. 1968. Plate 1 from *Suite 347*, state VII. Etching, 15⁵⁄₁₆ × 22⁵⁄₁₆″ (39.5 × 56.7 cm). Geiser/Baer VI, 1496. The Museum of Modern Art, New York. Gift of the Bibliothèque Nationale (by exchange)

the wheels, without traction in deeper substance and thereby gaining little new ground. Rembrandt and van Gogh left us images of themselves that have surpassed their circumstances and added something central to human understanding. Picasso's invocations of them seem by contrast only to add something marginal to his legend.

For all the masking and charades, however, Picasso in old age did remain capable of seeing himself—and occasionally showing himself—with candor and even painful mockery; this is evident in the scattering of more direct, caricatural self-portraits that began to appear when he entered his late eighties. The very practice of caricature, from its prehistory in Leonardo's drawings of grotesque heads, has always been associated with cruelty, and specifically with the power to impose the ravages of age on a face.[76] Picasso had indulged this penchant early, with results that came to have disturbingly personal predictive force (right); at the end of his life, he turned the device against himself with far more savage power. The first intimations come early in the outpouring of etchings that became known as *Suite 347*, from 1968. Two plates contain direct likenesses of Picasso, profiles so precise that one suspects they may reflect photographs (above; opposite); both show him as a dwarfish sideline spectator

Homunculus Attacks Formally Attired Old Man. 1902 or 1903. Pen and ink on paper. Zervos I, 150. Private collection

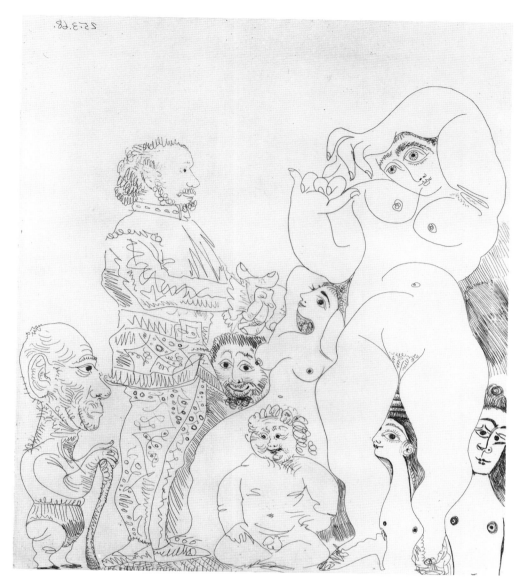

Self-Portrait with a Cane, with Actor in Costume, Sated Love, and Women. 1968. Plate 8 from *Suite 347.*
Etching, 16⅝ × 13½″ (42.3 × 34.2 cm). Geiser/Baer VI, 1503. Galerie Louise Leiris, Paris

in theaters—the circus and the bordello—where formerly he had seen himself as a performer in more active roles. The suite then goes on to feature other such dwarfs or giant infants (p. 170, top left) that, as credibly as the hairy old Silenuses in other scenes (p. 170, center left), seem plausibly to embody Picasso's commentary on his own diminished condition as a bystander in the orgies of female sexual display and male voyeurism, and in the conflations of painting and lovemaking, that dominate the 347 etchings.[77]

One of the prices exacted for the gift of a long life is an incessantly deepening consciousness of loss; one by one, increment by increment, many of the people and the pleasures that have given the world its savor depart.

Somewhere behind what Gert Schiff called the *theatrum mundi* of Picasso's art in his last years—behind the tumbling troupes of voluminous spread-legged women, gay swordsmen, and antically leering faces—and beneath the consolations of Jacqueline and new young friends lay a life of increasing isolation. The draining hourglass steadily enfeebled the artist's senses, sapped his sexuality, took away the dependable reference points of his universe—rivals and colleagues such as Matisse and Braque, lifelong friends like Jaime Sabartés, dependables such as Cocteau—and left him more and more alone in a world of commercial television, Cuban missile crises, and Pop art that seemed already to have discounted him as passé and left him for dead. One of the visitors who saw Picasso regularly in these late years was Pierre Daix, and it was to him, during a visit on the last day of June in 1972, that the

Venus and Love, in the Style of the Sixteenth Century. 1968. Plate 159 from *Suite 347.* Etching, 16⅜ × 19½″ (41.5 × 49.6 cm). Geiser/Baer VI, 1655. Galerie Louise Leiris, Paris

Old Man Sitting with a Woman, and Dancer. 1968. Plate 239 from *Suite 347.* Etching, 6¾ × 10⅜″ (17.2 × 26.3 cm). Geiser/Baer VI, 1736. Galerie Louise Leiris, Paris

like the shoulders below it, by furrows of folds and wrinkles; everything that should protrude—nose, ears, lips—is instead flattened or pulled inward. This puckering has accelerated in the definitive version of June 28–July 4, in which the lips have been reversed, the nose has become a snout with upraised nostrils, and the ear has withered into a shrunken cavity.[79] Here, too, the wrinkling has proliferated with psychedelic intensity into a calligraphic web of linear patterning that overwhelms the few rounded features it snags as they drift, unmoored. These holes and orbs and spots rhyme in equivalency; the eyes, each of which seems to have a blind twin in the darkened, socket-like form below it, are no more prominent than the spidery black spot on the left cheek—a blemish of age that helps peg this as a specific account of the artist's own face.[80] The asymmetries of expression that mark the 1907 self-portrait (p. 139) seem exaggerated into a dementia of incoherence here, where the targetlike left eyeball is enlarged, pulled to the vertical, and anchored into an enigmatic trapezoidal chunk appended to the side of the head. The descent down the head's left side—from that fixated monocular gaze to the dark, pupil-less "blind eye" below it, to the insectlike spot, and then to the nostril—is an amazing concatenation of cognate signs for surface and depth, or psyche and physiognomy, the leveled simi-

Head. June 27, 1972. Watercolor and colored pencil on paper, 25⅞ × 18⅞″ (65.7 × 50.5 cm). Zervos XXXIII, 432. The Hakone Open-Air Museum, Tokyo

artist showed something special. Daix had come to work on a book about the Cubist years, but Picasso was concerned with focusing on present explorations. "I did a drawing yesterday," he said as he led Daix into a semi-darkened studio, "and I think maybe I touched on something. It's not like anything I've done before." When Picasso opened the shutters partially and presented the work, it was a riveting, unforgettable self-portrait head in a peculiar palette of green, blue, and mauve crayon (p. 173).[78]

This June 30 drawing is in many ways a singular work, "not like anything . . . done before," but it also has compelling connections both to its immediate neighbors in Picasso's work and to the early epoch of his first self-examinations. Shortly before, on June 27, Picasso had made a study for a head (right) that he then completed, between June 28 and July 4, in a highly finished drawing (opposite). The June 27 study sets the image of a plaintively dislocated gaze in a turtlelike head defined largely,

Self-Portrait. June 28–July 4, 1972. Colored crayon, gouache, India ink, and ink wash on paper, 25⅞ × 19⅞″ (65.7 × 50.5 cm). Zervos XXXIII, 448. Private collection larity of which has unnerving implications for our sense of the relation between spirit and flesh.

Still, this remarkable drawing is less harrowingly confrontational than the one Picasso showed Daix (opposite), which demands comparison in every aspect of its impact as well as its configuration with the great self-portrait of 1907. Like that piece, this one is caricatural yet also seems made, exceptionally, from the scrutiny of the mirror; the spidery age spot on the left side of the artist's face, remade in a burst of vectors that link it to the jawline, now marks the opposite cheek—incorrectly, but true to mirror reversal. This drawing differs drastically in conception from the one begun just before it and completed soon after (p. 171); bristling calligraphy has given way to a willfully slow handling, with patiently burnished modeling in the face and grassy hatching in the chin and shoulder areas. Sculptural concerns dominate, and the graphic structure has a brutish reductiveness. The twin ice-tong curves that link the apex of the nose to the lip and chin area combine with the enlarged eyes, for example, to give a dominant facial structure as simple as a pear with two leaves at its stem. The combination of such coarsely blunt lines with the evident *pentimenti* and scumbling thickets of pencilwork communicates a sense of labor and even clumsiness that, no matter how consciously selected, adds pathos to the power of this emblem of life's terminal ravages.

As Adam Gopnik has noted, the bald, bone-and-jowl schemas for old age in this self-excoriation look directly back to the 1906 drawings of Josep Fontdevila in Gosol[81] —drawings that Richardson has said Picasso kept near at hand in his studio even in the 1970s.[82] We have to reach back that far, too, for a self-examination so squarely frontal (p. 134). But nothing, early or late, prepares us for the intensely uncomfortable fixity of this gaping stare. The mug-shot rigidity of the head, with its dome flat-tened against the top of the page and its sides grazing the edges, is undermined by the disconcertingly weak juncture below the chin, which makes the cranial mass into a perilously balanced boulder on the uncertain rolling terrain of shoulders and chest (a comparison with the confidently firm balance of the 1906 self-portrait, on p. 137, will emphasize the point). Monumentality is paired with instability, just as the basic symmetry is countered by the scrubbed-out effacement and jagged, massively illogical reconstruction of the head's right side.

Capped with stubble and cleaved by an inexplicable vertical from crown to eye, the forehead is as vague and lumpy a terrain as the torso below; lines of worry have supplanted the eyebrows as the most prominent features. Below, the signature X-ray eyes have been replaced by a mismatched pair of scumbled, dimmed, and irregularly dilated pupils, one of which seems to roll in a twisting spiral. In 1907 the facial structure flexed to accommodate such a wide-eyed gaze (p. 139), but here that taut stenography of marks has dissolved into a hobo's code of arrows, crescents, and disconnected vectors from which the dominant eyes seem disengaged. In 1907, too, the mouth was a decisive slash augmented above and below by full lips; in 1972 an inversion occurs, with two hard, firm lines clamping between them a murkily pink, uncertain softness. Finally, the nose structure that was such a key to Picasso's face in 1907—that wedge with a bold, sharp thrust that ends in a fleshy knob and wide wings—now appears as a soft, bulbous sack, flattened to expose prominent nostrils. With this, and the heavy pockmarks of the upper lip, the impression of an animal muzzle—and perhaps the muzzle of a specific animal—intrudes.

The skull qualities that were latent in 1907 are here overt, and become even more evident in the ghostly, rock-like afterimage Picasso made of this earless head on July 2 (p. 174). Less obvious, though, but perhaps equally telling,

Seated Woman with a Monkey. 1954. Ink on paper, 9⅞ × 13⅜″ (25 × 34 cm). Zervos XVI, 176. Private collection

In the Studio. 1954. Ink on paper, 9½ × 12⅝″ (24 × 32 cm). Zervos XVI, 175. Galerie Louise Leiris, Paris

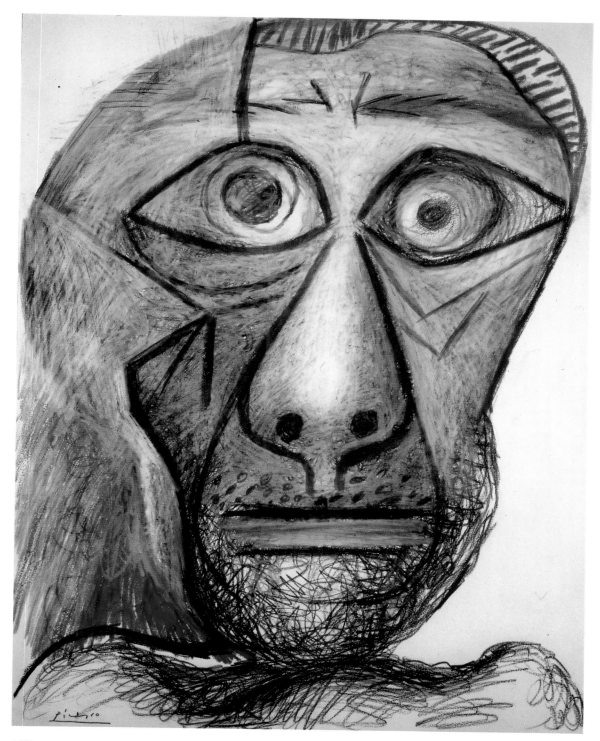

Self-Portrait. 1972. Wax crayon on paper, 25⅞ × 20″ (65.7 × 50.5 cm). Zervos XXXIII, 435. Courtesy Fuji Television Gallery, Tokyo

is the suggestion of the monkey that fleshes out these bones.[83] Picasso's features always had a slightly simian aspect, and we know that early on he identified himself as a monkey-man in a playful way (p. 130). Later, in scenes of the 1950s, he put the monkey in the place of the artist, in satirical fulfillment of the old notion of art as the ape of nature (opposite). The ape has a more profound place, however, not simply in man's evolutionary origins, but in symbolic imaginations of the baser qualities in human nature; he often has appeared in Western European art as the dark, physical, and mortal antonym to the higher aspirations of the spirit.[84] As the early means of comedic caricature seem repitched in this image to the most complex level of tragic expression, it would not seem impossible that, even subliminally, the mischievous monkey has returned through blackest humor to supplant the

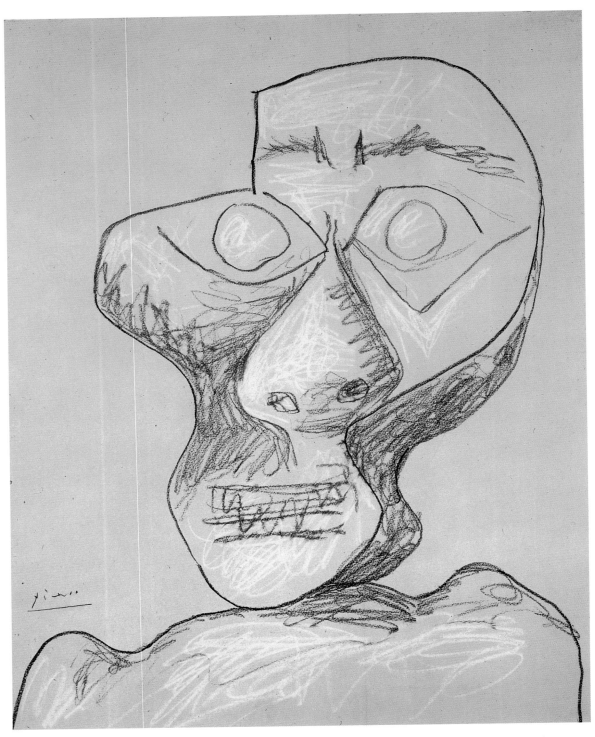

Self-Portrait. 1972. Crayon on paper, 26 × 19⅝″ (66 × 49.8 cm). Not in Zervos. Collection Gilbert de Botton, St. Moritz

Minotaur as the unspeakably self-mocking avatar of Picasso's eleventh hour.

Make no mistake: the issue here is death. Daix sensed this when he recognized the recurrence in this drawing of the morbid purple-and-green color scheme Picasso had used in a still life of a cow's skull done shortly after the demise of his friend, the sculptor Julio Gonzalez, in 1942.[85]

Even without such expertise, we feel we can see it in the eyes. Cross-eyed or dislocated gazes had become a formula, in countless other Picasso faces of the later years, for a kind of loopily deranged, usually antic spirit; here they convey a volatile combination of quizzical vulnerability and sheer terror. And yet Picasso talked to Daix about the singular qualities of this image in an easy and

At Notre-Dame-de-Vie, Mougins, July 1967. Photograph by Henri Cartier-Bresson

impersonal way, and did not flinch at the suggestion of a connection with the Gonzalez death's-head painting. When he first showed the drawing, the day after it was made, he in fact made a point of holding it up directly beside his own face, "to establish that the fear on the portrait's face was an invention."[86] In a matter of a few months, he died. This self-portrait stands, then, as the final fiction by which he chose to portray his ultimate truth. He once told André Malraux that *Les Demoiselles d'Avignon,* worked over after he inferred from tribal art the power of images to intercede with and alter life, was

his first "exorcism" picture.[87] This was his last. Into its mask he projected emotions that he did not want to have contained in himself, so that he, and now we, could contend with them as representations. When Picasso looked in the mirror on that summer day in his ninety-first year, he was navigating in territory where few of us will ever go, and where little art has ever been produced. On the verge of an exploration from which no travelers return, he looked forward and left us, before pushing on, this final encryption in the ciphers of physical resemblance.

NOTES

This essay is dedicated to Albert Elsen, *in memoriam*. I would like to thank Judith Cousins, Kathleen Robbins, and Jodi Hauptman for invaluable research assistance. Photographs by Picasso reproduced on pages 120, 122, 138, 141, 149, and 156 were very generously made available by Anne Baldassari, author of the two-volume study *Picasso photographe, 1901–1916* (Paris: Editions de la Réunion des musée s nationaux, 1994) and *"A plus grande vitesse que les images…": Picasso et la photographie* (Paris: Editions de la Réunion des musées nationaux, 1995).

1. For a remarkable consideration of the superstitions Picasso held and of the forms of "magic thinking" that seem to have informed much of his work, see Lydia Gasman, "Mystery, Magic, and Love in Picasso, 1925–1938: Picasso and the Surrealist Poets," 6 vols., Ph.D. diss., Columbia University, 1981.

2. Hélène Parmelin recounts this game in her memoir *Voyage en Picasso*: "Nous regardions tous les toiles droit dans les yeux. On jouait à donner nos versions de l'homme en face qui ne nous quittait pas de l'oeil. . . . Celui-là est à ne pas rencontrer. Celui-là se moque de nous. Celui-là a une énorme satisfaction de sa personne. Celui-là est un intellectuel lourd. Et celui-là, disait Picasso, regarde comme il est triste, le pauvre! 'C'est surement un peintre quelque part'" (Parmelin, *Voyage en Picasso* [Paris: Editions Robert Laffont, 1980], p. 87). The passage appears in English translation in Gert Schiff's "The Musketeer and His *Theatrum Mundi*," in *Picasso: The Last Years, 1963–1973* (New York: George Braziller in association with the Grey Art Gallery and Study Center, New York University, 1983), p. 31: "Picasso and the Pignon-Parmelin couple met again and engaged in a new game, ascribing a character to every musketeer. 'With this one, you'd better watch out. That one makes fun of us. That one is enormously self-satisfied. This one is a grave intellectual. And that one, Picasso said, look how sad he is, the poor guy. He must be a painter, somewhere.'"

3. Françoise Gilot observed Picasso working through successive states of a lithograph, and only gradually arriving at the certainty that the figure he was working on represented Dora Maar. See Gilot and Carlton Lake, *Life with Picasso* (New York/Toronto/London: McGraw-Hill, 1964), p. 92. Also, when showing Françoise other etchings, Picasso said: "You see this truculent character here, with the curly hair and mustache? That's Rembrandt. . . . Or maybe it's Balzac; I'm not sure. It's a compromise, I suppose. It doesn't really matter. They're only two of the people who haunt me. Every human being is a colony, you know" (p. 44).

4. John Richardson, in *A Life of Picasso, Volume 1: 1881–1906* (New York: Random House, 1991), pp. 269–70, 274–75, discusses how Picasso was introduced to tarot by the poet Max Jacob, and possibly used it as a model for certain of his early works.

5. On the relation between caricature and portraiture in Picasso's work, see Adam Gopnik, "High and Low: Caricature, Primitivism, and the Cubist Portrait," *Art Journal* 43, no. 4 (winter 1983), pp. 371–76; see also his further considerations on the same subject in "Caricature," in Kirk Varnedoe and Adam Gopnik, *High and Low: Modern Art and Popular Culture* (New York: The Museum of Modern Art, 1990), pp. 101–51.

6. On Picasso's wish that his art always be subversive in this fashion, see Gilot and Lake, *Life with Picasso*, p. 72.

7. Pierre Daix has stated that Picasso "always painted self-portraits at critical junctures of his life: at the time of Apollinaire's death or of the disaster in 1940." See Daix, *Picasso: Life and Art*, translated by Olivia Emmett (New York: HarperCollins, 1993), p. 369; originally published as *Picasso créateur* (Paris: Editions du Seuil, 1987).

8. John Richardson, "The Significance of Picasso's Self-Portraits," in John Herbert, ed., *Christie's Review of the Year 1969/1970* (London: Hutchinson of London, 1970), p. 124.

9. See Gilot and Lake, *Life with Picasso*, p. 50, for Picasso's affirmation that "God is really only another artist. . . . He has no real style. He just keeps trying other things."

10. Richardson discusses Picasso's bout with scarlet fever in Madrid, and the subsequent stay in Horta de Ebro, where these self-portrait drawings were made, in *A Life of Picasso*, pp. 98, 99–107.

11. Richardson cites two instances of the inscription *"Yo, el rey"* on Picasso's early drawings, including one self-portrait formerly in the Junyer Vidal collection but now lost, on which the inscription had been repeated three times; see *A Life of Picasso*, pp. 156–57.

12. The photograph was first published by Anne Baldassari in the exhibition catalogue *Picasso photographe, 1901–1916* (Paris: Editions de la Réunion des musées nationaux, 1994), fig. 23, p. 47.

13. Discussed in Baldassari, *Picasso photographe*, pp. 43, 48. The original inscription, written on the back of the photograph, is reproduced on the back cover of Baldassari's book: "Esta fotografia puede titularse 'Los muros mas fuertes se abren a mi paso. Mira!'" Baldassari's French translation is: "Cette photographie peut s'intituler 'Les murailles les plus fortes s'ouvrent sur mon passage. Regarde!'"

14. Ibid., pp. 43, 48.

15. See Richardson, *A Life of Picasso*, p. 228.

16. We forget that potent originality and amused, self-assessing irony can coexist in the same instant; for a not entirely fatuous comparison with another emergent revolutionary showing off an incandescent combination of electric joy and casually self-satirizing irony while rewriting the rules, revisit film of Elvis Presley's appearance on *The Milton Berle Show* on June 5, 1956. (For a description of his performance, see Peter Guralnik, *Last Train to Memphis: The Rise of Elvis Presley* [Boston: Little Brown and Co., 1994], pp. 284–85).

17. Richardson, in *A Life of Picasso*, pp. 274–75, discusses specifically the relation of Picasso's art to tarot in this period.

18. For a thorough discussion of the meaning of *La Vie*, see Theodore Reff, "Themes of Love and Death in Picasso's Early Work," in Roland Penrose and John Golding, eds., *Picasso in Retrospect* (New York: Praeger, 1973), pp. 10–47.

19. See the discussion by Adam Gopnik on the roots in comics of tragic expression in Philip Guston's late work, in his chapter "Comics," in Varnedoe and Gopnik, *High and Low*, pp. 153–229. It was one of the general premises of the investigations in that book that the loop of creativity in twentieth-century art, by which material from popular culture was taken up by artists, involved the inversion of Marx's dictum that history repeated itself acording to the rule "first time tragedy, second time farce"; in the translations of modern art, on the contrary, material first taken lightly, as farce, more often winds up being adapted as the form of tragedy. Samuel Beckett's use of slapstick is only one of many examples. In discussing caricature and its reinterpretation in Picasso's late work, Gopnik quotes Kenneth Tynan's remark that the central story of modern expression is "the steady annexation by comedy of territories that once belonged to the empire of tragedy" (p. 150).

20. On the origins of *At the Lapin Agile*, its personas, and its setting, see Richardson, *A Life of Picasso*, pp. 371–72.

21. For descriptions of Picasso's paintings on studio walls, see Richardson, *A Life of Picasso*, pp. 151, 242.

22. See *Harlequin* (1901), The Metropolitan Museum of Art, New York (Zervos I, 79); and *Two Saltimbanques* (1901), Pushkin State Museum of Fine Arts, Moscow (Zervos I, 92).

23. On the development of this painting, see E. A. Carmean, *Picasso: The Saltimbanques* (Washington, D.C.: National Gallery of Art, 1980).

24. See Theodore Reff, "Harlequins, Saltimbanques, Clowns, and Fools," *Artforum* 10, no. 2 (October 1971), pp. 30–43.

25. Richardson, *A Life of Picasso*, pp. 315–17.

26. See Leo Steinberg, "Picasso's Sleepwatchers" (1968), in *Other Criteria* (New York: Oxford University Press, 1972), pp. 92–114.

27. On the practice of cutting one's hair close as a protection against lice, see Richardson, *A Life of Picasso*, p. 61.

28. The photograph of Picasso and Fernande taken just before their departure for Gosol shows him still with a full head of hair; see Richardson, *A Life of Picasso*, p. 435. On Picasso's general sensitivity to having his hair cut, see Gilot and Lake, *Life with Picasso*, p. 231. Gilot wrote that "Pablo always had a great distaste for having his hair cut. He would go for months needing a haircut but unable to bring himself to walk into a barbershop. If anyone mentioned the subject, it was high drama. I'm sure that mixed in with his other fears on this subject was the old notion of hair as a symbol of male vigor, as in the Biblical story of Samson and Delilah." This paragraph on Picasso and haircuts begins with Gilot's discussion of the "prim-

itive belief that one person can assume power over another through the possession of his fingernail or hair trimmings; hence they should never be allowed to fall into the hands of someone else. But if they were burned to remove them from an enemy's reach, the person himself might die. The true believers often carried the trimmings in little bags until they found a place secret enough to dispose of them with complete assurance."

29. See Richardson, *A Life of Picasso,* p. 438.

30. Richardson, in *A Life of Picasso,* pp. 290–91, notes how, in an early sketchbook, Picasso inscribed *"Yo El Greco"* and *"Yo Greco."* Daix, in *Picasso: Life and Art,* also notes that in December 1903, learning of Paul Gauguin's death, he signed a nude in the style of his great elder "Paul Picasso" (p. 34). This drawing is reproduced as *Homage to Gauguin* (no. 937) in Josep Palau i Fabre, *Picasso: The Early Years 1881–1907* (New York: Rizzoli, 1981), p. 360; originally published as *Picasso vivent 1881–1907: Infantesa i primera joventut d'un demiürg* (Barcelona: Ediciones Polégrafa, 1980).

31. Meyer Schapiro, *Paul Cézanne* (New York: Harry N. Abrams, 1988), p. 34.

32. Jaime Sabartés, *Picasso: An Intimate Portrait* (London: W. H. Allen, 1948), p. 79; originally published as *Picasso: Portraits et souvenirs* (Paris: Louis Carré et Maximilien Vox, 1946). "As a rule the palette was on the floor. . . . I do not recall ever having seen Picasso holding the palette in his hand. He assures me that sometimes he does, just like everyone else. It may be so, but I have always seen him preparing his colors by leaning over a table, a chair or the floor."

33. For a thorough discussion of Picasso's will to combine the frontal and the back views of bodies in his representations, see Leo Steinberg, "The Algerian Women and Picasso at Large" (1972), in *Other Criteria,* pp. 125–234, as well as Steinberg's "The Philosophical Brothel," *October,* no. 44 (spring 1988), pp. 55–57. For a specific discussion of Picasso's rethinking of the face's spatial structure, particularly the positions of ear and eye, see Steinberg's "Algerian Women," pp. 162–64.

34. See Carmean, "Harlequins," in *Picasso: The Saltimbanques,* pp. 56ff.; see also William Rubin, "From Narrative to 'Iconic' in Picasso: The Buried Allegory in *Bread and Fruitdish on a Table* and the Role of *Les Demoiselles d'Avignon,*" *The Art Bulletin* 65, no. 4 (December 1983), pp. 615–49.

35. See Baldassari's discussion in *Picasso photographe,* p. 71. These photographs are reproduced as figs. 47–51, and 73–77.

36. Gary Tinterow has dated this drawing to 1919; see Tinterow, *Master Drawings by Picasso* (Cambridge, Mass.: Fogg Art Museum, 1981), no. 60, p. 152. On the broader dialogue of Picasso with Ingres's work, Robert Rosenblum presented his findings in a lecture, "Picasso and Ingres," presented at the International Foundation for Art Research, January 19, 1983. See also Rosenblum's brief discussion of Ingres in the present volume, pp. 359–60.

37. Illustration no. 122, dated 1918, in Jaime Sabartés, *Picasso: Documents iconographiques* (Geneva: Pierre Cailler, 1954), shows a later print based on this drawing, accompanied by the following caption: "C'est ainsi que Picasso se vit dans la glace d'une salle de bain, a l'Hôtel Lutetia, en 1918, au moment que l'on venait lui communiquer, par téléphone, la nouvelle de la mort de son ami Guillaume Apollinaire." For a consideration of the ambiguities lurking in this statement, see n. 46, below.

38. See Michael C. FitzGerald, *Making Modernism: Picasso and the Creation of the Market for Twentieth-Century Art* (New York: Farrar, Straus and Giroux, 1995), pp. 131–32, as well as FitzGerald's "Picasso: In the Beaux Quartiers," *Art in America* 80, no. 12 (December 1992), p. 61. On the larger issue of birdcages in art as metaphors of imprisonment, see Lorenz Eitner, "Cages, Prisons, and Captives in Eighteenth-Century Art," in Karl Kroeber and William Walling, eds., *Images of Romanticism: Verbal and Visual Affinities* (New Haven, Conn.: Yale University Press, 1978), pp. 13–38.

39. See William Rubin, *Picasso in the Collection of The Museum of Modern Art* (New York: The Museum of Modern Art, 1972), p. 98.

40. On the circumstances of Eva's death, and on Picasso's citation of his anguish over her loss in a letter in which he also mentions having just completed the 1915 *Harlequin,* see Daix, *Picasso: Life and Art,* pp. 146–47.

41. See Theodore Reff, "Picasso's *Three Musicians*: Maskers, Artists and Friends," *Art in America* 68, no. 10 (December 1980), pp. 124–42.

42. For a discussion of this *Harlequin with Violin* in terms of its particular hybrid costume, see Carmean, "Harlequins," in *Picasso: The Saltimbanques,* p. 57.

43. The possible existence of this profile in the area of unfinished paint in the 1915 *Harlequin* has long been a matter of curiosity among those who have worked with the painting at The Museum of Modern Art. I also believe it was pointed out by Theodore Reff in lectures given at Columbia University in the early 1970s. Recently, John Richardson has focused special attention on this latent image. Richardson has stated in lectures that he believes this profile is a hidden self-portrait, made by Picasso in response to the covert self-portrait Matisse had included in his *Goldfish and Palette* (1914, The Museum of Modern Art). Richardson will examine this issue in greater depth in the forthcoming second volume of his biography of Picasso.

44. Scarborough will advance his argument regarding this concealed self-portrait in a forthcoming article in *Apollo* magazine; I am grateful to him for providing me in advance with a copy of the research paper on which the article will be based.

45. On this motif, see Robert Rosenblum, "The Origin of Painting: A Problem in the Iconography of Romantic Classicism," *The Art Bulletin* 39, no. 4 (December 1957), pp. 279–90.

46. Sabartés was the first to present the story in his discussion of *Picasso par lui-même,* reproduced as no. 122 in *Picasso: Documents iconographiques.* His wording, cited in n. 37, above, holds some ambiguities. Did Sabartés mean to say that this drawing shows us how Picasso looked at that time, or did he mean specifically to say that Picasso was executing this self-portrait when the news came? Seven later texts tell some version of the tale. While Sabartés never actually wrote that Picasso was sketching himself in the mirror at the time the message came that Apollinaire had died, subsequent authors have described Picasso drawing a portrait of himself in the mirror at that moment. Roland Penrose, for example, in *Picasso: His Life and Work* (London: Victor Gollancz, 1958), defined the drawing done then as "a portrait which marks the end of an epoch for two reasons. A great friend had gone, and Picasso, with this drawing, abandoned his habit of making frequent lifelike portraits" (pp. 205–06). Brassaï first presented the notion that Picasso was shaving when he received the news, in *Picasso and Company,* translated by Francis Price (Garden City, N.Y.: Doubleday, 1966), pp. 43–45; originally published as *Conversations avec Picasso* (Paris: Editions Gallimard, 1964). This version was reiterated by Jean-Paul Crespelle in *Picasso, les femmes, les amis, l'oeuvre* (Paris: Presses de la Cité, 1967), but neither author had a word to explain why the artist would have been shaving in the late afternoon, which is when he received the news. More recently, Daix has explained that Picasso responded "reflexively" to the news of Apollinaire's death by making a "drawing, the image the mirror sent back to him when the telephone gave him the news he had been dreading" (Daix, *Picasso: Life and Art,* p. 34). Ariana Huffington, in *Picasso: Creator and Destroyer* (New York: Simon and Schuster, 1988), blames Picasso for the story's perpetuation: "For the next twenty years, Picasso kept all his self-portraits secret and even spread the false story that the one he painted the moment the news of Apollinaire's death reached him was his last" (p. 159). Sabartés, in *Picasso par lui-même* and Daix in *La Vie de peintre de Pablo Picasso* (Paris: Editions du Seuil, 1977), made serious attempts to identify or associate a particular portrait with Apollinaire's death. Both refer to the self-portrait, Zervos III, 75.

However, Peter Read has identified another of the four principal self-portrait drawings from this period—the Ingresque rendering with a more fully modeled head reproduced on p. 143, top right—as being the one done on the evening of the poet's demise. In *Picasso et Apollinaire: Les métamorphoses de la mémoire 1905/1973* (Paris: Jean Nichel Place, 1995), p. 143, Read (relying on testimony in David Douglas Duncan, *The Silent Studio* [New York: W. W. Norton & Company, 1976], pp. 3, 19) notes that when Picasso later dedicated this latter drawing to Jacqueline Roque, he told her that it was the self-portrait he had drawn on the evening of November 9, 1918. Read also notes that, according to John Golding (in "Guillaume Apollinaire and the Art of the Twentieth Century," *The Baltimore Museum of Art News* 26–27, nos. 4–1 [summer–autumn 1963], p. 30), Picasso affirmed that he had executed two self-portraits on that evening, leading to the presumption that the one identified by Sabartés was the second.

Read, on pp. 142–43, further undertakes an informative discussion of the special importance to Picasso of Apollinaire's death within the general framework of Picasso's superstitious nature and fear of death; in this discussion he cites Michel Décaudin's article "Apollinaire et Picasso," *Esprit*, no. 61 (January 1982), p. 82, where Décaudin remarks: "Or, apprendre une mort quand on se regarde dans un miroir, c'est, dit-on, voir sa propre mort." Décaudin also notes that in describing the atelier of the "oiseau du Bénin [Picasso]" in *Le Poète assassiné*, Apollinaire had noted a huge broken mirror hung on the wall as a "chose fatale . . . une insondable mer morte." Read in turn cites the following line from Cocteau's *Orphée*: "Regardez-vous toute votre vie dans une glace et vous verrez la Mort travailler comme des abeilles dans une ruche de verre."

47. Brassaï explained that Picasso began to hate mirrors and ceased making self-portraits because he learned of Apollinaire's death as he was shaving: "It was after this that he developed his hatred of mirrors. . . . Having seen the shadow of death pass across his own face that morning he ceased completely to paint or draw it" (Brassaï, *Picasso and Company*, p. 119). Sabartés also described Picasso's fear of mirrors: "Je sais d'ailleurs que Picasso—je le lui ai entendu dire bien souvent—a la phobie des miroirs et ne peur supporter l'image qu'ils lui peut renvoient lorsque le hasard l'amène devant une glace" (Sabartés, *Picasso: Documents iconographiques*, pp. 10–11). Hélène Seckel, in *Max Jacob et Picasso* (Paris: Editions de la Réunion des musées nationaux, 1994), quotes Jacob as saying, shortly before he was arrested, "Picasso disait: les miroirs mentent, les photographies mentent . . . et ce n'était pas un paradoxe. Picasso n'était pas un homme de paradoxe" (p. 274).

48. For Baldassari's discussion of shadow-theater, see her essay, "Heads Faces and Bodies": Picasso's Uses of Portrait Photographs," in this volume, pp. 206–08. The photograph is reproduced in Baldassari, *Picasso photographe*, figs. 57 and 58, p. 83.

49. Another possible reading of the picture titled *Bust of a Woman with Self-Portrait* (p. 150) is that the framed silhouette on the wall represents a mirror reflection—another form, like a shadow, of "projection" into the picture from outside.

50. In his work on the life of Marie-Thérèse, Herbert T. Schwarz has uncovered evidence which indicates that Picasso may well have met Marie-Thérèse as early as 1925, although strong evidence suggests that their sexual liaison did not begin until the summer of 1927. See Schwarz, *Picasso and Marie-Thérèse Walter, 1925–1927* (Montmagny, Quebec: Editions Isabeau, 1988), and Robert Rosenblum's discussion of the relationship in this volume, pp. 339–40.

51. Gilot and Lake, *Life with Picasso*, p. 50.

52. Ibid., see the broader discussion here of the nature of the Minotaur, pp. 49–50.

53. For an overview of the many interpretations of the Minotaur in Picasso and especially of this important print, see Sebastian Goeppert and H. Corinna Goeppert, *Minotauromachy by Pablo Picasso* (Geneva: Patrick Cramer, 1987).

54. Photograph published in Baldassari, *Picasso photographe*, fig. 67, p. 89.

55. See Brassaï's description of shooting the candid photographs at the Café Flore, the Brasserie Lipp, and elsewhere in Paris in October 1939, in *Picasso and Company*, pp. 43–45.

56. Brassaï, in *Picasso and Company*, p. 150, described his visit to Picasso's studio on May 12, 1945, after a one-year absence. Picasso talked of the great influx of visitors since the liberation, then showed Brassaï a volume of Mallarmé in which he had drawn a portrait of the poet:

"It seems, however, that he had another reason for showing me the Mallarmé. Beneath the portrait he has scrawled three words, in his spasmodic, unpredictable handwriting. Three words that mark a historic event in his life:

"'NO MORE FORELOCK! Paris, May 12, 1945'

"The famous black lock of hair that escaped from beneath Picasso's broad-brimmed hat and frightened his family; the raven's wing that was so often drawn, caricatured, even sculpted, departing abruptly from the extreme right of his forehead and sweeping across it until its point brushed his left eyebrow. . . . In reality it had been gone for a long time. There was nothing left of it but a few sparse symbolic hairs, powerless to mask his baldness, but he continued to groom and nurture them carefully, as emblems of his youth. . . . It was only this morning that he had had the courage to break at last with the past and solemnly inter the dead forelock on this volume of poetry.

"'PICASSO: One cannot both be and have been. So . . . when are you going to photograph me without my forelock?'"

57. See n. 28, above.

58. Henry Smith describes the Japanese ritual of shaving one's head and taking ceremonial monk's vows at the age of sixty in *Hiroshige: One Hundred Famous Views of Edo* (New York: George Braziller, in association with The Brooklyn Museum, 1986), p. 10.

59. André Malraux recounted that when he visited Picasso after the war, in his studio on the rue des Grands-Augustins, Picasso asked, "Haven't you noticed anything?" When Malraux replied, "No," Picasso pointed out: "I cut off my forelock!" See Malraux, *Picasso's Mask*, translated by June and Jacques Guicharnaud (New York: Holt, Rinehart and Winston, 1976), p. 102; originally published as *La Tête d'obsidienne* (Paris: Editions Gallimard, 1974).

60. See n. 56, above.

61. In a conversation with Picasso, an American soldier, Pfc. Jerome Seckler, offered his interpretation of the portrait of Maya in a sailor suit. To Seckler, it was a "self-portrait—the sailor's suit, the net, the red butterfly showing Picasso as a person seeking a solution to the problems of the times . . . the sailor's garb being an indication of an active participation in this effort." While Picasso agreed that the painting was a self-portrait, he denied that it had any political meaning, telling Seckler he chose the sailor suit not for its military allusions but because it was his habit to wear a sailor's striped jersey as an undershirt. For excerpts from this interview, see Alfred H. Barr, Jr., *Picasso: Fifty Years of His Art* (New York: The Museum of Modern Art, 1946), pp. 247, 268. A transcript of the entire interview can be found in The Museum of Modern Art Archives. Anyone who reads the full interview will see that Picasso seems hardly to have taken seriously the fanciful interpretations Seckler posed, and there is every reason to assume that, regardless of whatever covert self-projection may have been involved, the painting was predominantly conceived as a portrait of Maya.

62. See Werner Spies, *Picasso's World of Children*, translated by John William Gabriel (Munich: Prestel-Verlag, 1994), as well as his exhibition catalogue prepared for the Kunstsammlung Nordrhein-Westfalen, Düsseldorf, and the Staatsgalerie, Stuttgart, *Picasso's Welt der Kinder* (Munich: Prestel-Verlag, 1995). See also Helen Kay, *Picasso's World of Children* (Garden City, N.Y.: Doubleday and Co., n.d.).

Gilot, in *Life with Picasso*, noted Picasso's predilection for taking articles of clothing from Claude, and concluded that "Pablo hoped by this method that some of Claude's youth would enter into his own body. It was a metaphorical way of appropriating someone else's substance, and in that way, I believe, he hoped to prolong his own life" (p. 232).

63. See p. 441 of the present volume for Michael FitzGerald's discussion of the drawing that apparently shows Picasso with Françoise, Claude, and Paloma. According to FitzGerald, this drawing was begun on the last day of the year, 1953, and then picked up again on the first day of the next year. Much doubt surrounds the authorship of the profile of Picasso, manifestly rendered in a different (more Cocteau-like) style and scale than the other figures. Werner Spies has also brought to my attention two groups of cutout shadow silhouettes or *ombres chinoises* from 1952, now in the collection of Paloma Picasso, which apparently represent Picasso with Françoise and the children; these were shown recently in Berlin in the exhibition *Picasso: Die Zeit nach Guernica, 1937–1973* (Stuttgart: Verlag Gerd Hatje, 1993), cat. nos. 100 and 101A.

64. Picasso told David Douglas Duncan in 1961: "It was our bedroom. See my shadow? I'd just turned from the window—*now* do you see my shadow and the sunlight falling onto the bed and across the floor? See the toy cart on the dresser and the little vase over the fireplace? They're from Sicily and still around the house" (Duncan, *Picasso's Picassos* [New York: Harper and Row, 1961], p. 183). The French version of this text is cited by Denis Hollier in the context of his discussion of these paintings in "Portrait de l'artiste en son absence," *Cahiers du Musée national d'art moderne* 30 (winter 1989), pp. 9–10.

65. On Picasso's practice of drawing on photographs, see Anne Baldassari, *"A plus grande vitesse que les images"* (Paris: Editions de la Réunion des musées nationaux, 1995), pp. 86–171. On p. 158 Baldassari cites a particularly interesting inscription written on one such

altered image: "En 1972 un an avant sa mort, il adressait à Lucien-René Durbach, lissier à Saint Rémy de Provence, un portrait de lui, pris par Lucien Clergue, qu'il avait vivement surchargé à l'encre, parant son crâne de veillard d'une chevelure et d'un barbe de jais ainsi qu'un monocle. Avec ce commentaire: 'J'ai fait cela pour vous, pour comprendre la différence entre ce que l'on perçoit de nous-même ou de l'autre qui n'est souvent que la caricature de nous-même ou de l'autre'" (this quote was taken from Lucien Clergue, *Picasso, mon ami* [Paris: Editions Plume, 1993], p. 170).

66. Susan Galassi discusses Picasso's 1950 painting of a variation after El Greco's *Portrait of a Painter* in her Ph.D. dissertation for the Institute of Fine Arts, New York University, "Games of Wit: Picasso's Variations on the Old Masters," 1991. She notes that the El Greco painting had been exhibited and discussed in the literature as a self-portrait of El Greco in the nineteenth century, but that twentieth-century scholarship has tended to see the work as a portrait of El Greco's son. Galassi's findings on this and other Picasso variations will be included in a book to be published by Harry N. Abrams, as yet untitled, on Picasso's variations after old-master paintings; my thanks to her for bringing this material to my attention.

67. See John Richardson, "Picasso's Last Years: Notre-Dame-de-Vie," in *Pablo Picasso: Meeting in Montreal* (Montreal: Montreal Museum of Fine Arts, 1985), especially pp. 91–95. See also Janie Cohen, "Picasso's Exploration of Rembrandt's Art, 1967–1972," *Arts* 58, no. 2 (October 1983), pp. 119–26, including her suggestion that Picasso took interest in Rembrandt's documentation of his own aging process, p. 119.

68. See Schiff's remarks on Picasso and Rembrandt in "The Musketeer and His *Theatrum Mundi*," in *Picasso: The Last Years, 1963–1973,* especially pp. 31–40.

69. On Picasso's dictum "All painters take themselves for Rembrandt," see Gilot and Lake, *Life with Picasso,* p. 51; on Olga and the pictures, p. 154.

70. In *Picasso's Mask,* Malraux recounted a conversation with Jacqueline in which he asked about Picasso's *Man with a Sword* (published on a poster for the artist's 1920 show in Avignon): "Where do the musketeers come from? *Las Meninas?*" Jacqueline replied, "No; they came to Pablo when he'd gone back to studying Rembrandt" (p. 4). Later in the book, Malraux wrote about this conversation again: "As Jacqueline explained, Picasso had discovered those musketeers in an album on Rembrandt during his last illness" (p. 86). Richardson also links Picasso's musketeers to Rembrandt: "For Picasso's ubiquitous musketeers could not have a more Rembrandtian provenance; they had stepped straight out of *The Night Watch,* which the artist used a slide machine to project in all its vastness on his studio wall" (Richardson, "Picasso's Last Years," in *Pablo Picasso: Meeting in Montreal,* p. 94).

71. On Picasso's earlier expression of van Gogh's importance, see Gilot and Lake, *Life with Picasso,* pp. 74–75: "Beginning with Van Gogh, however great we may be, we are all, in a measure, autodidacts." On p. 75 he is further cited as saying that the individual adventure in art "always goes back to the one which is the archetype of our times: that is, Van Gogh's—an essentially tragic and solitary adventure."

72. See n. 3, above.

73. Describing Picasso's desire for financial stability, Daniel-Henry Kahnweiler wrote in his book *My Galleries and Painters:* "A long time ago Picasso told me, 'I'd like to live like a poor man with a lot of money.' This is really the secret. Picasso wanted to live like a poor man, to continue to live like a poor man, but not to have to worry about tomorrow. That is really what he meant—to be free of financial worry." See Kahnweiler with Francis Crémieux, *My Galleries and Painters,* translated by Helen Weaver, introduction by John Russell (New York: Viking Press, 1971), p. 91; originally published as *Mes Galleries et mes peintres: Entretiens avec Francis Crémieux* (Paris: Editions Gallimard, 1961).

74. When Picasso brought out his Degas monotypes to show to William Rubin, in 1971, he expressed to Rubin his curiosity as to what Degas ever did, aside from looking, in his visits to these *maisons closes* (author's conversation with William Rubin). See also Daix, *Picasso: Life and Art,* p. 366.

75. In his essay "Picasso's Last Years: Notre-Dame-de-Vie" for the catalogue *Pablo Picasso: Meeting in Montreal,* Richardson describes the "significant trick" Picasso plays on "the father-like figure of Degas": "On occasion he adds a network of wrinkles to his face so that he looks even older than the ninety-year-old artist who is portraying him. And why not? As Picasso said to Brassaï, 'Everytime I draw a man, automatically I think of my father. . . . I see all the men . . . with his features.' Indeed, so striking is the resemblance between Degas and Picasso's father that one of the artist's recent biographers, Patrick O'Brian, has mistaken the former for the latter in references to these prints. O'Brian's confusion is welcome for the Oedipal light it sheds on the earliest and the latest periods of Picasso's art and life" (p. 99). The text from O'Brian is as follows: "Many of the same subjects had appeared in the 1968 etchings, a series into which he introduced his father on occasion, sometimes as a voyeur, sometimes as a more active participant" (O'Brian, *Pablo Ruiz Picasso: A Biography* [New York: G. P. Putnam's Sons, 1976], p. 475). The Brassaï reference is from *Picasso and Company,* p. 56.

76. See Gopnik, "Caricature," in Varnedoe and Gopnik, *High and Low,* pp. 101–51.

77. See Gert Schiff, "Picasso's *Suite 347,* or Painting as an Act of Love," in Gert Schiff, ed., *Picasso in Perspective* (Englewood Cliffs, N.J.: Prentice-Hall, 1976), pp. 163–67.

78. Daix, *Picasso: Life and Art,* pp. 368–69.

79. According to both Rubin and Richardson, Picasso had become hard of hearing in one ear in old age; especially as he had made an issue of his ears in youthful self-portraits (see p. 135, bottom center; p. 139), the diminished opening here may connote the dulling of that sense.

80. Spies referred to this age spot on the left cheek as a "cyclopean third eye" in "The Painter of the Century Is Dead: Pablo Picasso, 1881–1973," in *Focus on Art* (New York: Rizzoli, 1982), p. 51. According to Rubin, who was shown this June 28–July 4 drawing by Picasso, the artist further confirmed that it was a self-image, in pointing out the little marks that suggest a matching stubble on the chin and on the top of the head; apparently Picasso frequently used such stubble-signs to refer to his own physiognomy, even though in life he rarely showed any sign of a beard (author's conversation with William Rubin).

81. See Gopnik, "Caricature," in Varnedoe and Gopnik, *High and Low,* p. 50, on the connection between the Josep Fontdevila drawings at Gosol and the June 30, 1972, head.

82. See n. 29, above.

83. Gopnik refers to this drawing's "weak monkey jaw" in "Caricature," in Varnedoe and Gopnik, *High and Low,* p. 150.

84. See H. W. Janson, *Apes and Ape Lore in the Middle Ages and the Renaissance,* Studies of the Warburg Institute, vol. 20 (London: Warburg Institute, University of London, 1952).

85. Daix, *Picasso: Life and Art,* p. 368.

86. Ibid., p. 369.

87. See Malraux's description of Picasso's experience of tribal art at the Trocadéro Museum in 1907, and his reference to the *Demoiselles* as his first "exorcism-painting," in *Picasso's Mask,* p. 11.

Portrait of Guillaume Apollinaire. 1913. Pencil, India ink, and wash on paper, 8¼ × 5⅞″ (21 × 15 cm). Zervos XXVIII, 214. Daix 579. Private collection; formerly collection Guillaume Apollinaire

Three Portrait-Manifestoes of Poets: André Salmon, Guillaume Apollinaire, and Max Jacob

HÉLÈNE SECKEL

Portraits of poets are not a category in themselves. For a viewer who cannot identify the sitter, they might seem to belong to the most indeterminate group of portraits. Yet a connoisseur asked to name some of Picasso's famous portraits would quickly call to mind those of Guillaume Apollinaire or Max Jacob. A scholar would cite Jean Cocteau, Pierre Reverdy, or André Breton. This is not surprising considering that, in his youth in Barcelona, the painter frequented literary circles and that a poet, Max Jacob, first served as his mentor upon his arrival in Paris. We know that at the Bateau-Lavoir on place Ravignan, where he moved in 1904, Picasso "wrote in blue chalk on the door of his studio: *Au rendez-vous des poètes,* in imitation of bistro signs. . . . Poets familiar with the studio had no doubt: Picasso appreciated their work."[1] That "Picasso had a very keen sense of French poetry" was confirmed by Daniel-Henry Kahnweiler, citing Apollinaire, who said: "Even several years ago, when he could hardly speak French, he was completely able to judge, to appreciate immediately the beauty of a poem."[2] Gertrude Stein justified Picasso's preference for writers in her own way: "Why have painters for friends when he could paint as he could paint. . . . He had to know those who were interested in ideas, but as to knowing how to paint he was born knowing all of that."[3] André Salmon spoke of elective affinities: "We were a generation of poets linked to a generation of painters,"[4] whereas Apollinaire spoke of

being chosen: "Picasso . . . lived only among poets, one of whom I am honored to be."[5]

Poets frequently dipped their pens in the inkwells of criticism—some, including Apollinaire and Salmon, made it a profession—fortified by their often daily encounters with painters. Well aware of the new life poets were bringing to a practice that was academic by nature, Salmon had proclaimed in the March 1914 issue of *Montjoie!* the rebirth of criticism: "We have killed the old criticism. It is dead forever. Criticism placed in the hands of poets renders that of critics—makeshift magistrates who condemn or acquit—impossible. It is the criticism of poets that has delivered the public from the strongest prejudices."[6] So Picasso committed himself to art in this century, and, following Apollinaire's and Salmon's example (Max Jacob was *persona muta* for a long time), Reverdy, Cocteau, Leiris, Aragon, Breton, and Eluard sang his praises.

One might think it appropriate, then, that Picasso created portraits of his poet friends. Although generally reticent to do commissioned works,[7] he gladly agreed to the sometimes urgent requests of one or another poet who wanted a portrait to accompany his writings.[8] Whether these portraits were drawn and reproduced as the frontispiece of a book or engraved by Picasso for a deluxe edition does not seem to have been quite as important for the authors as for the publishers, who relied on these deluxe editions to attract an audience of bibliophiles.[9] Thus, Cocteau, though he scarcely knew Picasso

André Salmon in Picasso's studio at the Bateau-Lavoir, 13, rue Ravignan, Paris, spring–summer 1908. Photograph by Picasso. Musée Picasso, Paris, Picasso Archives

Guillaume Apollinaire in Picasso's studio at 11, boulevard de Clichy, Paris, autumn 1910. Photograph by Picasso. Musée Picasso, Paris, Picasso Archives

in 1915, was eager to have a portrait done; he was obliged in 1916, and was delighted to see it published in 1918, reproduced as the frontispiece of *Le Coq et l'arlequin*.[10] Reverdy, who had countless difficulties getting *Cravates de chanvre* published, asked Picasso straight out for a contribution to his book: "Would you help me make this an object of value? I'm asking you for an etching and, if you would be so inclined, for a few deluxe editions extra, my portrait by you."[11] The painter did an engraved portrait[12] and generously offered two etchings for the deluxe edition.

André Breton also solicited Picasso for his engraved portrait for *Clair de terre*. In a somewhat grandiloquent manner but one that revealed the anxious hope of a young author aware of the "inestimable price" of what he was requesting, Breton wrote: "I would do my utmost were you to consent to having the volume open with a portrait of me by you, something I have dreamed about for a long time and have never had the audacity to approach you with."[13] And so the engraved portrait of Breton in imperious profile eventually "illustrated"—this much-used term is obviously inappropriate—the first copies of the book (it was reproduced in the others).[14] As for the engraved portrait of Paul Eluard, dated April 21, 1942, it was two years before it appeared as the frontispiece of the first edition of *Au Rendez-vous allemand*, published in December 1944. There again the first twenty copies included the engraving,[15] while the others had a reproduction—"after an etching by Picasso," the caption specified.

Picasso also did portraits of Salmon, Apollinaire, and Jacob for the frontispieces of their books. But some of these portraits seem to us, in a very specific way, to be valuable as manifestoes in regard to Cubism, insofar as Cubism was, to varying degrees, for the triad of poets also, something of a rite of passage. For if the poets were obviously witnesses to this movement, they were also truly "implicated" in it, more so than is revealed by the usual citations in the footnotes of Cubism's history—the discovery of primitive art and the first title given to *Les Demoiselles d'Avignon*: *Le Bordel philosophique*.[16] This would endure in the years that followed.[17] The focus on this trio of poets, so often singled out by historians, critics, exegetes, and hagiographers, was legitimized early on by Picasso himself. He cited all three when comparing the renewal of the plastic arts with that of literature, saying to Florent Fels in 1923: "In turn, inspirers of cubism and inspired by it, Max Jacob, Apollinaire, and Salmon wanted that precision of form that springs from clear thought, that attaches a new attitude to language."[18]

Picasso happened to have taken portrait photographs of our three poets[19] at the very moment of Cubism's first development. This is not insignificant. Need we detail what these images tell us about the "situation" of the poets photographed in relation to the decor that the painter-photographer chose for them? Must we reiterate that in 1908 Salmon, at the Bateau-Lavoir studio, is camped in front of *Three Women*, in the course of execution, and near

Max Jacob in Picasso's studio at 11, boulevard de Clichy, Paris, autumn–winter 1910. Photograph by Picasso. Musée Picasso, Paris, Picasso Archives

Les Demoiselles d'Avignon,[20] analysis of which he was the first to attempt (opposite, left)? Must we point out that Apollinaire, seated in the little salon of the apartment on the boulevard de Clichy (where Picasso moved in 1909), is posed in a *mise-en-scène* that emphasizes the presence of the Tiki of the Marquesas Islands placed on the floor next to him (opposite, right)? This designated him as friend and defender of primitive art, as the famous lines of "Zone," the first poem in *Alcools,* would recall: "You walk toward Auteuil you want to walk home and sleep / Among your fetishes from Guinea and the South Seas."[21] But Jacob turns away from the lens (above), thereby indicating that what is essential is not the abandoned mandolin next to him, which appears so often in Picasso's Cubist still lifes. What is important is the very existence of these photographs, conserved by Picasso despite the extreme fragility of the glass plates that fixed them.[22] They tell us that the painter-photographer and his poet-sitters were there, the former calling the latter to witness the revolution he was in the midst of making, the latter accepting the challenge. These photographs offer a testimony that echoes Goethe's famous remark at the Battle of Valmy: "From this time and place a new epoch is beginning, and you will be able to say that you were there."[23]

ANDRÉ SALMON. *PEINDRE.* PARIS: EDITIONS DE LA SIRÈNE, 1921

On January 9, 1919, Salmon wrote to Picasso to invite himself to lunch: "I will read to you, over dessert, a long didactic poem: *Peindre,* written, I would like to believe, to please you." At the very bottom of the page he added: "And my portrait? When?"[24] Was Salmon waiting for Picasso to do his portrait for this soon-to-be-published book? The fact remains that *Peindre,* a small book, attempting to be *engagé,* was published two years later with the reproduction of a much older portrait of the author, in charcoal, as the frontispiece (below, right). But the choice of this drawing, according to Salmon, was far from trivial, as he recalled in *Souvenirs sans fin:* "In 1920, when I published *Peindre,* a long poem that preceded the didacticism of *L'Art vivant,* I used as the frontispiece a reduction of Picasso's marvelous charcoal portrait of me, dating from 1906, the birth of Cubism; it was a sketch for a statuette that was to be carved in boxwood but which would never be executed."[25] He spoke elsewhere in *Souvenirs* of this "magnificent drawing, half-realist, half-cubist."[26] Thus Salmon was indeed referring to this drawing when he wrote an article for *L'Europe nouvelle* in January 1919 about a Metzinger exhibition, in which Cubism was more generally discussed. Citing Picasso as the source of this movement, Salmon evoked, without naming, *Les Demoiselles d'Avignon,* and established the link between the painter's "discoveries" and the "negro statuettes" in which he was greatly interested. He stated: "At the same time, Picasso executed as a preliminary study for a wood statue, yet to be carved, a portrait of me in charcoal which, along with the large canvas in question, is at the root of Cubism."[27]

André Salmon. 1922 or earlier. Photographer unknown

Portrait of André Salmon. 1907. Charcoal on paper, 23⅝ × 15¾" (60 × 40 cm). Not in Zervos. Private collection, Paris; formerly collection André Salmon

Studies for Portrait of André Salmon. 1907. Ink on paper, 12¾ × 15¾″ (32.5 × 40 cm). Zervos XXVI, 179. Private collection

It is surprising that Salmon would describe this drawing as "half-realist, half-cubist," which is instead a caricature and which corresponds rather well to Max Jacob's description of the poet. Recounting his first meeting at the beginning of 1905 with this "tall gentleman," Jacob

wrote: "He bowed in sarcastic benevolence in a raglan coat the color of ocher. His face had the shape of a crescent moon above his upturned collar. His white jaw held a pipe that went opposite his nose."[28] At the very most, the schematization of the face, by evoking the style that characterizes the studies for *Les Demoiselles d'Avignon* of winter 1906–07, brings the portrait closer to the working drawing, giving the quintessence of it, but to excess. But Salmon clearly thought of this drawing in relation to others, which he must have been familiar with, as they were assembled on the same sheet (left), and later titled "Portrai[t]s d'André Salmon" by Picasso. There one observes the poet's long, serpentine silhouette—which recalls that of the Medical Student in the preliminary studies of *Les Demoiselles*—next to the sketches of his head. Here Picasso pushed stylization to the point of making Salmon look Egyptian; views of the figure are also seen from behind, showing a fishbone pattern, like scarifications, instead of a spinal column. Salmon's invocation of Cubism concerning this portrait and the possibility of it as a plan for a sculpture are illuminated in a more satisfying manner by this sheet of sketches. And Salmon's remarks are all the more meaningful when one examines other studies (below, left, and p. 31, top left)

Study for Wood Sculpture of André Salmon (final state). 1907. Charcoal and India ink on paper, 24¾ × 18⅞″ (63 × 48 cm). Zervos XXVI, 284. Private collection

Picasso's studio at the Bateau-Lavoir, 13, rue Ravignan, Paris, spring 1908. On the wall are two drawings that derive from Picasso's portrait of André Salmon (*Study for Wood Sculpture of André Salmon* [Zervos VI, 967] and *Bust of a Man*, 1907 [Zervos II², 630]). Photograph by Picasso. Private collection

Portrait of André Salmon. 1905. Pencil on cardboard, 4⅛ × 2⅝″ (10.4 × 7.2 cm). Not in Zervos. Private collection; formerly collection Guillaume Apollinaire

Portrait of André Salmon. [1905]. Ink wash on paper (from a sketchbook), 7⅛ × 5″ (18 × 12.6 cm). Not in Zervos. Musée Picasso, Paris

Portrait of André Salmon. 1905. Ink on paper, 7¼ × 4½″ (18.5 × 11.5 cm). Illustration on a page of Salmon's *Poèmes* (1905). Not in Zervos. Bibliothèque Historique de la Ville de Paris, Bibliothèque Apollinaire

Portrait of André Salmon. [1905]. Ink on paper, 11¾ × 9″ (30 × 23 cm). Not in Zervos. Private collection; formerly collection André Salmon

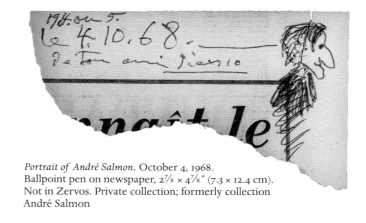

Portrait of André Salmon. October 4, 1968. Ballpoint pen on newspaper, 2⅞ × 4⅞″ (7.3 × 12.4 cm). Not in Zervos. Private collection; formerly collection André Salmon

showing a standing figure whose body seems to be carved with a billhook, a "savage" working drawing derived from preceding sketches.[29]

Clearly, this series of drawings assumed great importance for Picasso at the time in relation to the painting *Les Demoiselles d'Avignon* and the wood carvings more or less contemporaneous with these drawings. This is indicated by a photograph the painter took in the spring of 1908 (opposite, bottom right): one of the clever arrangements Picasso was so fond of when taking photographs of his studios—and which are always illustrative—unites *Les Demoiselles d'Avignon* (we see only the left edge), two wood carvings (one, a head fringed with hair, contemporary with the genesis of the large painting) and two of the large drawings (a full-length figure and a bust) that most likely are derived from Salmon's portrait.

There is another series of portraits of the poet which always presents him in the same position: seated, in left profile, his chin jutting severely, his straggling lock of hair, a stiff collar and hastily tied lavaliere, rounded back, and hands crossed on his knees holding a pipe. The latter gesture must have been rather characteristic of Salmon, for Fernande Olivier, ever observant, wrote: "His fine hands held the wooden pipe, which he always smoked, in a way which was typically his. His gestures were a little gauche and clumsy: a mark of his shyness."[30] To obtain Picasso's authorization to reproduce one of these drawings (p. 185, bottom left) in the first volume of *Souvenirs sans fin*, Salmon wrote to the painter on December 14, 1954: "I would like for the frontispiece the reproduction of the drawing, in pen, that you did of me in the winter . . . 1903–04: it is quite a beautiful drawing, never yet reproduced and seen only by my visitors."[31] His visitors had, in fact, mentioned it. Frédéric Lefèvre, who called on Salmon to conduct one of the interviews he published regularly in *Les Nouvelles littéraires* under the heading "One hour with . . . ," described the drawing: "It is dated 1904: this is perhaps the only portrait of Salmon sporting a beard, for this whim would scarcely last."[32]

It is remarkable that once again the poet does not use the word "caricature" in regard to this portrait, which he considers "quite a beautiful drawing." Yet, the exaggerated representation of the figure and the model's clearly pronounced (and peculiarly aged) features—a strong nose, a smile that has been called Mephistophelian or Voltairean, which is actually more of a grin, the prognathism, a light beard that most often gives the model a "poorly shaven" and somewhat down-and-out look, and the excessive posture with its hunched back and shoulders—bring this image closer to caricature, as does its repetition, because it is a sort of generic image, a type, which on numerous occasions sprang from Picasso's pen or pencil and was repeated, unchanged. One such sketch was done on a page of a notebook that the painter took with him to Holland at the beginning of the summer of 1905 (p. 185, top center).[33] There is also a drawing, dated "1905" in pen in one of the copies of Salmon's *Poèmes* published that year (p. 185, top right),[34] which Apollinaire owned.[35]

On a final portrait (p. 185, center right)—the poet was to die five months later—commemorating their past youth and their meeting, at the approximate date of "1904 or 5," Picasso scribbled "4.10.68" in honor of Salmon's eighty-seventh birthday (the artist himself would reach the same age three months later). Picasso wrote the accompanying dedication, "from your friend," on this corner of torn newspaper[36] and drew the tousled locks of a young man, in a harsh profile with an undeniably toothless mouth this time. It is almost a mortuary mask of the friend with whom Picasso was reunited.[37]

Portrait of Guillaume Apollinaire. [1908]. Reconstruction through montage of the versos of Zervos II¹, 39, and Zervos XXVI, 355; charcoal on paper, 19⅜ × 12⅝″ (49.1 × 31.9 cm). Musée Picasso and private collection, Paris

GUILLAUME APOLLINAIRE. *ALCOOLS*. PARIS: LE MERCURE DE FRANCE, 1913

Apollinaire's *Méditations esthétiques* was published in March 1913. This work dealt with "new painters" broadly grouped under the label of Cubism,[38] with Picasso presented as its "founder." One month later, Apollinaire published *Alcools*, a collection of poems comprising almost fifteen years of creative work; it opened with "Zone," a text written in the fall of 1912 and added at the last minute, which begins with the words: "In the end you are weary of this ancient world."[39] It is this volume, the sum of his poetic art, and not, as one might have expected, the theoretical and possibly polemical work of *Méditations esthétiques*, which bears as its frontispiece a reproduction of the Cubist portrait of Apollinaire (p. 180). We have not been able to establish how this decision was made— discussed with Picasso?—or even if the portrait was done with the prospect of its reproduction in *Alcools*.[40] Nonetheless, Apollinaire chose this portrait as the frontispiece for his book, and in 1912, a portrait by Picasso was a Cubist portrait.[41] There was no harm in the fact that it happened to tally with the aesthetic choices of the author of *Méditations*, and there is no doubt that it was important to the poet to publish his collection with the ensign of an innovative drawing. In any case, it was not meant to establish some sort of parallel between Cubism and literature.[42]

Commentaries that appeared in the press[43] often made an amalgam of what seemed newest and most shocking in Apollinaire's poems—the elimination of all punctuation (yet, in doing this, the poet had not imagined he was playing Alcibiades)[44]—and the portrait's Cubism. Even before the publication of the book, *Le Courrier français* announced in a gossip column: "Great news. Mr. Guillaume Apollinaire is to publish poetry with no punctuation. . . . And cu-cubism is back in the spotlight, under the auspices of Picasso. Do you know him? He did the portrait of Mr. Guillaume Apollinaire, and this portrait is to serve as the frontispiece for the volume of poetry . . . with no punctuation. . . . Isn't that enough to revolutionize the Left Bank?"[45] Others wanted to see Apollinaire's choice of the Cubist portrait as a promotional device thought up by the poet, "an unbridled apologist for the cubists whom he defends with a devotion worthy of a better cause":[46] "Well! He's 'launching' the cubists; he has decorated his poetry collection with his portrait by Picasso, a masterpiece of indecipherable trigonometry."[47] The Cubist image was disturbing; yet, it is amusing to note that the negative descriptions of it are rather just perceptions. It is not incorrect to describe the portrait as "a number of stovepipes behind which a tousled lock of hair can be seen."[48] To speak of the breaking down of the figure by planes—in scarcely flattering terms, of course —or the persistence of realist detail ultimately suggests a sound appreciation of Cubist representation.

One obviously prefers the "enlightened" remarks of Marc Brésil and Louis de Gonzague Frick—supporters of the criticism of poets that we mentioned earlier: "Lovers of modern art will find at the threshold of this volume an unequaled portrait of Mr. Apollinaire by Mr. Picasso. The great Spanish painter has developed a synthesis of metaphysical decoration and has succeeded in showing us Mr. Guillaume Apollinaire at once frontally, in profile, and from the back; this work is more surprising than we can say, and Mr. Apollinaire's admirers will appreciate this portrait of our new Amphion, rendered in its entelechy."[49] There is a certain pride in Apollinaire's account of how, on his way to the publisher Le Mercure de France to deliver "this beautiful drawing by Picasso, my portrait which figures at the beginning of my collection of poems," he ran into Rémy de Gourmont, who was seized with admiration for the portrait and conceived the vain hope of also having "a cubist portrait of his person": "I spoke to Picasso about it, but he had something else

to do and since he did not, so to speak, know Rémy de Gourmont, this portrait would have been too much work for him."[50] Picasso's response is interesting here for what it tells us of the necessary relationship between the painter's knowing the sitter and the latter's representation, for it was important that the portrait be a likeness. Apollinaire was convinced of this: "The portrait is a likeness in the immediate sense of the word."[51]

It is little known that there exists a portrait of Apollinaire that one could call proto-Cubist, drawn in charcoal on two sheets that are separated today: the top of the face is found on the back of a drawing in gouache, *Standing Nude* of 1908, and the bottom on the back of *Head,* in India ink of the same period.[52] Placing the two versos edge to edge has allowed us to see a man's head; it is undoubtedly that of Apollinaire (opposite), constructed in great geometric masses, as are the figures painted at La Rue des Bois during the summer of 1908. Apollinaire spent several days there, invited by Picasso and Fernande Olivier. Was it then that Picasso drew this massive face, whose natural morphology led to the stylization applied to it?

Apollinaire is portrayed by Picasso once again in his book *Calligrammes,* the last collection published before his death in 1918, which bears the subtitle *Poèmes de la paix et de la guerre.* The poet, who enlisted in December 1914, was

Portrait of Guillaume Apollinaire Wounded. 1916. Graphite on paper, 11⅝ × 8⅞″ (29.7 × 22.5 cm). Zervos VI, 1324. Musée Picasso, Paris; formerly collection Guillaume Apollinaire

Portrait of Guillaume Apollinaire. 1905. India ink on paper, 12¼ × 9⅛″ (31 × 23 cm). Zervos XXII, 294. Collection of the Family of Henry Brandon

Guillaume Apollinaire in the Fields. [1905]. Lead and colored pencil on cardboard (reverse of Bénédictine liqueur advertisement), 6⅛ × 4¼″ (16 × 10.7 cm). Not in Zervos. Private collection; formerly collection Guillaume Apollinaire

Portrait of Guillaume Apollinaire. [1905]. Violet ink on paper, 5⅛ × 4⅛″ (13 × 10.5 cm). Not in Zervos. Private collection

Guillaume Apollinaire as a Bank Employee. December 6, 1905. Ink on paper (letter-card to Apollinaire), 5½ × 4¾″ (14 × 12 cm). Not in Zervos. Private collection; formerly collection Guillaume Apollinaire

Guillaume Apollinaire as an Academician. [1905]. Ink and wash on paper, 8¾ × 4⅜″ (22 × 12 cm). Not in Zervos. Musée Picasso, Paris; formerly collection Guillaume Apollinaire

The Duel, or *Guillaume Apollinaire as a Fencer.* 1907. Graphite and colored pencil on paper, 7⅛ × 5⅜″ (18 × 13.6 cm). Not in Zervos. Private collection; formerly collection Guillaume Apollinaire

wounded in the head in a shell explosion in the trenches on March 17, 1916. Picasso possessed several of the photographs taken while the poet was convalescing at l'Hôpital italien after his trephination. In one of these photos, he is seen with his head bandaged, almost in profile but nevertheless looking at the lens.[53] Did Picasso draw, from the photograph, the famous portrait of the wounded Apollinaire in profile (p. 187), the one the poet is probably speaking of in a letter to André Breton on August 27, 1916: "I will publish my war poetry at Le Mercure, with a portrait of me by Picasso"?[54] The rather serene profile,[55] as though beyond pain, finely drawn in graphite in a very realistic manner, was reworked, its essential features simplified by a stronger line. This technique and the pose

La Culture Physique, or *Guillaume Apollinaire as an Athlete.* 1907. Ink on paper, 12¼ × 9¼″ (31 × 23.5 cm). Zervos XXII, 286. Private collection; formerly collection Gertrude Stein

Guillaume Apollinaire as a Sailor. [1910]. Ink on paper, 8½ × 5⅛″ (21.5 × 13 cm). Not in Zervos. Private collection; formerly collection Guillaume Apollinaire

Guillaume Apollinaire as an Artilleryman. December 22, 1914. Ink and watercolor on paper (letter to Apollinaire), 9 × 4⅞″ (23 × 12.5 cm). Zervos XXIX, 116. Private collection; formerly collection Guillaume Apollinaire

Guillaume Apollinaire at Nîmes, between December 7 and 15, 1914, when he was with his unit in the Thirty-eighth Artillery regiment of the French army. Photograph by G. Meunier

Guillaume Apollinaire as Pope. Page from André Billy's 1923 monograph *Apollinaire vivant* (Paris: Éditions de la Sirène, 1923). The original drawing was in the collection of Guillaume Apollinaire

Portrait of Guillaume Apollinaire. 1918. Violet ink on paper, 5⅜ × 3⅜″ (13.5 × 8.7 cm). Not in Zervos. Musée Picasso, Paris

give the poet the appearance of a bas-relief effigy on a marble funerary monument: Apollinaire—"When into himself eternity changes him."[56] This image of a wounded man was in keeping with the theme of the war poems published in *Calligrammes*. If the critics railed against what they considered typographical extravagance, artifice, and the out-and-out novelty of these poems, where text created

image, they remained indifferent to the portrait, the classicism of which did not seem to have a particular connection to the innovations of the writing it accompanied.[57]

In addition to the thirty-five copies on vellum "with a drawing by Pablo Picasso," the subscription notice announced four extremely rare copies on old Japanese paper "with two drawings by Pablo Picasso signed by the

Portrait of Guillaume Apollinaire. 1916. Graphite on paper, 19¼ × 12″ (48.8 × 30.5 cm). Zervos XXIX, 200. Private collection; formerly collection Guillaume Apollinaire

Portrait of Guillaume Apollinaire. 1916. Pencil on paper, 12¼ × 9⅛″ (31 × 23 cm). Zervos II², 923. Private collection, courtesy Galerie Cazeau-de La Béraudière, Paris

artist."[58] The second drawing is the haughty portrait of Apollinaire seated, in full military uniform (left), his cap hiding the bandage that is still wrapped around his head. In all likelihood, it is a posed portrait, in the tradition of those initiated by the *Portrait of Max Jacob* of 1915 (opposite), where the meticulous realism of the figure is confronted with a representation of space that bears the mark of Cubism.[59] There is another portrait, almost identical to this second drawing, which is its ghostly double (bottom, left). Drawn with a less incisive line, shaded and incomplete, even in areas as essential as the bottom of the face, this portrait gives the wounded poet, with his anxious gaze, an image that seems to be erasing itself, as though life were already slipping away.[60]

Aside from several other portraits of Apollinaire, a young man who still had a moustache[61] when he met Picasso, there exist numerous caricatures of the poet. Max Jacob no doubt thought of these when he wrote in his "Souvenirs sur Picasso": "The figure of Apollinaire is often repeated in [Picasso's] works."[62] From descriptions of the poet found in literature, we understand that Apollinaire had a physique and a demeanor that lent themselves to caricature. He had a "pear-shaped" head (p. 188, top left)—"Guillaume did not at all like it when people spoke of his resemblance to Louis-Philippe; he preferred Louis XIV or Racine" notes André Billy[63]—and a rather astonishing stoutness,[64] which certainly gave him presence. Habits such as stuffing his pockets with books made his hips even rounder, and he always carried a pipe, which he "suckled with greedy lips."[65]

One of the loveliest descriptions of Apollinaire is given by Jacob, evoking their meeting in early 1905. Apollinaire was wearing "a very small straw hat placed on top of his famous pear-shaped head. He had hazelnut eyes, terrible and brilliant. A tiny tuft of blond, curly hair, a small mouth like a pimiento, very strong limbs, a vast chest traversed by a platinum watch chain, a ruby on his finger."[66] Cocteau, who would meet him in 1916, still described with emotion, thirty years later, his "gawky look of a captive balloon."[67] His close relations thought he had the air of a prelate, of a Roman emperor. From these physical characteristics, Picasso extracted character traits and even personal ethics, an archetypal image of Apollinaire that he repeated tirelessly:[68] a strapping fellow with a head in the shape of a pear, a worried brow, and a somewhat breathless air about him, outfitted with his everyday accessories—a watch, a pipe, a hat that is a bit too small—or imaginary ones, such as a papal tiara or an academician's suit.

The caricatures mock him, certainly, but one senses above all that they are charged with tenderness and with that complicity born of a real intimacy. Evidence of this are the few saucy drawings, such as the one where we see Apollinaire in the fields "relieving himself" (p. 188,

Portrait of Max Jacob. 1915. Pencil on paper, 13 × 9¾″ (33 × 24.8 cm). Zervos VI, 1284. Private collection

Portrait of Max Jacob. 1916. Graphite on paper, 12⅞ × 10″ (32.6 × 25.3 cm). Zervos III, 73. Musée Picasso, Paris

top center), his inordinately large anus "represented" by a hole in the paper, while in the distance Diana chases a stag; or the one of the poet sitting, masturbating, a scatological detail that Picasso hides with a bowler hat (p. 188, top right).[69] The caricatures often refer to episodes in the sitter's life, which could not have failed to sustain the conversations of the little *"bande Picasso."* Indeed, they enliven them; Apollinaire, his arms laden with books, passing in front of the Bourse, is shown to us as Picasso knew him in 1905, when the poet was a bank employee (p. 188, bottom left); *Apollinaire as an Academician* (p. 188, bottom center) may evoke his hope of one day being crowned with the Prix Goncourt (he was to be an unhappy candidate in 1910 with *L'Hérésiarque et Cie*); *Apollinaire as a Fencer* (p. 188, bottom right) refers to the duel he almost had in March 1907, for which he had asked Max Jacob— in black clothes in the drawing—to be his second;[70] *Apollinaire as an Athlete* (p. 189, top left) reminds us that in March 1907 he contributed an article entitled "Guy de Maupassant athlète" to the review *La Culture physique;*[71] *Apollinaire as a Sailor* (p. 189, top center) perhaps alludes to the news items he published in *Paris-Journal* on the winter floods in Paris in 1910;[72] *Apollinaire as an Artilleryman* (p. 189, top right), which Picasso drew on the back of a letter he sent to the poet, stationed in Nîmes, on December 22, 1914: "Don't think this is a shell exploding in the

sky of your portrait; it's the most beautiful sun appearing through the clouds."[73] Was it inspired by a photograph taken in Nîmes of a cocksure Apollinaire in his military outfit (p. 189, bottom left)?[74]

It is evident that Apollinaire was fond of these comical, warm images, a good number of which he owned.[75] In his friends' eyes as well, these caricatured representations had the noble stature of portraiture. Proof of this was the widespread success of these drawings. When he published the first monograph on Apollinaire in 1923, André Billy specifically chose to reproduce two caricatures: *Apollinaire as an Academician* (p. 188, bottom center) and *Apollinaire as Pope* (p. 189, bottom center).[76] Wasn't this a sort of homage?

MAX JACOB. *LE CORNET À DÉS.* PARIS: CHEZ L'AUTEUR, 1917.

"I am posing for Pablo at his studio. He is doing a portrait of me in pencil that is very beautiful; it resembles at once my grandfather, an old Catalan peasant, and my mother."[77] So wrote Max Jacob to Guillaume Apollinaire on January 7, 1915. The extreme detail of the drawing gave the portrait (above, left)—which, we may note, Max Jacob does not say resembles him[78]—a realism that prompted many questions. Was Picasso renouncing Cubism? So worried was *le Tout-Paris* frequenting the ateliers that

Portrait of Max Jacob with Laurels. 1928. Graphite pencil and charcoal on paper, 11 × 8¼″ (28 × 21 cm). Not in Zervos. Musée des Beaux-Arts, Orléans

Portrait of Max Jacob. 1921. Drypoint, 4¾ × 3⅞″ (11.9 × 10 cm). Geiser/Baer I, 62. Musée Picasso, Paris

Beatrice Hastings made it a "scoop" for *The New Age,* where she regularly had a column: "By the way, Monsieur Picasso is painting a portrait of M. Max Jacob in a style the mere rumour of which is causing all the little men to begin to say that of course Cubism was very well in its way, but was never more than an experiment. The style is rumoured to be almost photographic, in any case very simple and severe. I can say nothing as I haven't seen it, but I can testify to the state of soul among the cubists."[79]

Picasso regally reassured those around him who were worried, and the naïveté of his responses matched that of his interlocutors. He replied to Henri Mahaut that he wanted "to see if he could still draw like everyone else."[80] He was probably already playing the same game in 1914 when, showing Kahnweiler the first "non cubist . . . drawings of a seated man," he asked: "It's better than before, isn't it?"[81] This portrait would even be discussed in the Swedish press, in an article written by the painter Arvid Fougstedt for *Svenska Dagbladet,* recounting a visit to Picasso's studio in the company of Jacob in December 1915. There Fougstedt encountered at once a large Cubist painting in progress, *Man Leaning on a Table,* and the two portraits of Jacob and Ambroise Vollard. He marveled at the "miniaturist detail" Picasso was able to demonstrate, drawing "with a pencil as thin as a needle." Though he felt this might be a wager on Picasso's part, speaking of the

Portrait of Max Jacob, he subtly concluded: "He is sitting there, in flesh and blood, and yet we are a thousand leagues away from a banal naturalism such as that of Memling."[82]

In December 1916, when Ozenfant reproduced the drawing of Jacob on the first page of his review *L'Elan,* the debate became even more heated. An anonymous article in *Le Bonnet rouge* of January 13, 1917, sarcastically asked: "Which is the real Picasso," the one of "indecipherable cubism" or the one who draws like "old Ingres"?[83] As for Picabia, he proclaimed in *391* that he "doesn't hesitate for a minute" to adhere to the new school of photographic realism founded by a "repentant Picasso."[84] And at the end of the year, Salmon gave a turbulent talk on "La Jeune Peinture" at the meeting place of "Lyre et Palette," which he described this way to Picasso: "[For] . . . Metzinger and Co. . . . the school of Metzinger is the only way out, and he does not admit that one can make the portrait of Vollard or Max after what has preceded."[85]

Jacob was indifferent to this commotion. He knew that it was absurd to contrast Cubism and realism, and that this portrait was not a return or regression of art to the style of Ingres or Memling, which would not have been progress. On the contrary, it bore witness to the essential lesson that Cubism brought to painting—a new definition of space. And so Jacob specifically chose to have this drawing, more avant-garde than it would seem at first glance, reproduced as the frontispiece of his book of prose poems, *Le Cornet à dés*, the "great work" he spent more than ten years shaping and that he finally published in 1917, accompanied with a "theoretical preface," as the subscription notice announced. A similar subtle and secret divergence from classical form united the painter and the poet. The first copies—published very late, at the beginning of 1918—would include an engraving in the purest Cubist tradition.[86] Eager theoreticians of literary cubism would not need this pretext to start the debate.[87]

Picasso beside Max Jacob. [1904]. Ink on paper (letter to Suzanne Bloch). Not in Zervos. Whereabouts unknown

In the fall of 1916, at Montrouge, Max Jacob had once again posed for Picasso. The portrait (p. 191, right), a more linear and reductive drawing, like *Portrait of Apollinaire as a Soldier,* done slightly earlier, bears the dedication, "To my friend Max Jacob," leading one to think the poet owned it for a while.[88] It is certain, in any case, that he owned the portrait he requested from Picasso in 1928 for reproduction in the small catalogue accompanying his

Dessin de Picasso

MAX JACOB

Portrait of Max Jacob. [1904]. Frontispiece for *Le Cornet à dés* by Max Jacob (1923 edition), with handwritten note from 1936 by Jacob. Original drawing not in Zervos. Private collection

exhibition at the Galerie Théophile Briand. It is a stark portrait (opposite, left), in the manner of a Roman bust, crowned with laurels,[89] which can be seen as the farcical counterpart to the austere 1916 effigy of Apollinaire with his head bandaged. Jacob would reciprocate with this ironic quatrain: "Of the laurels adorning my head / You more than I are deserving / Picasso, my master, my friend / King of painters and painter of kings."[90]

What neither Salmon nor Apollinaire would receive, an engraved portrait as the frontispiece of a book, Jacob hoped for, and almost obtained, during his lifetime. A portrait for which the poet probably sat in 1921, before his retreat to Saint-Benoît-sur-Loire, had been engraved to illustrate *Visions infernales* (opposite, right). Though two years later, in December 1923, Jacob reminded Picasso of the existence of this plate and told him that the book's publication had already been announced with the engraving, the insistent letters that Gaston Gallimard sent to the painter remained unanswered, and the book eventually appeared in 1924 with the author's self-portrait engraved by Aubert. Thus, the only portrait of Jacob engraved for a book upon request of the author was not included in the work for which it was intended.[91] But in 1953, when the art publisher Louis Broder undertook the publication of *Chronique des temps héroïques*, a book Jacob had written in 1935–36, he asked Picasso for a lithograph for the frontispiece. From memory, the painter did a three-quarter portrait of a young and bald Jacob, a faint smile on his lips, the diamond-shaped pattern around his neck giving him the look of a harlequin.[92] The book was ultimately published in 1956, with an additional three etchings by Picasso: a nude man seen from behind,[93] a portrait in profile that was not a very good likeness, and a depiction of the poet, his forehead enormous, writing in the glow of his oil lamp,[94] recalling the first images Picasso made of his friend.

The story the poet tells of meeting the very young painter, who was showing at Vollard's gallery in June 1901, is by now legendary. He recounts how they were immedi-

L'Histoire claire et simple de Max Jacob (The Plain and Simple Story of Max Jacob). January 13, 1903. Ink on paper, 7½ × 11″ (19 × 28 cm). Zervos VI, 606. Musée Picasso, Paris

Portrait of Max Jacob. Early 1907. Gouache on paper mounted on cardboard, 24⅜ × 18⅝″ (62 × 47.5 cm). Zervos II¹, 9. Daix 48. Museum Ludwig, Collection Ludwig, Cologne. (Colorplate, p. 23)

Max Jacob. c. 1905–10. Photographer unknown. Universités de Paris, Bibliothèque Littéraire Jacques Doucet

ately fascinated by each other and how the day after Jacob's visit, Picasso in turn went to see the poet at his house. Jacob read him his poems "all night long" while Picasso "painted on a large canvas, since lost or painted over, a portrait [of him] sitting on the ground, amid [his] books and before a great fire."[95] This first portrait and the only one painted on canvas, which X rays now reveal, shows us the poet's large, already bald head, and the beard, moustache, and pince-nez he wore at the time. There are two known portraits in profile, which probably date from 1904,[96] showing him as young and beardless with a five-o'clock shadow. One of them would be reproduced as the frontispiece of two small editions of *Le Cornet à dés*, in 1922 and 1923. On a copy of the latter (p. 193, bottom), in a dedication to someone who is not identified, Jacob, embittered and spiteful, wrote in 1936: "This portrait has never resembled me either up close or from afar. It's a café drawing I don't know who picked up."[97]

Jacob's nature was that of a tormented soul, who thought his portraits were always caricatures, for he eventually had disparaging remarks for almost all of them. Picasso no doubt did more caricatures of him than we know about, freely accentuating the appearance that Fernande Olivier describes thus: "His head was possibly too large and set on a badly proportioned body with narrow shoulders. There was something slightly provincial about his appearance, and this was emphasized by the cut of his too-new clothes."[98] A small touching drawing at the top of a letter sent to the singer Suzanne Bloch shows the painter and poet shoulder to shoulder in the studio at the Bateau-Lavoir (p. 193, top). But the most comical of the caricatures of Jacob is the one presented in the form of a comic strip, "The plain and simple story of Max Jacob and his glory, or the rewards of virtue" (opposite, top), where we see first the down-and-out poet, writing by the light of an oil lamp; he brings his manuscript to an editor, who agrees to publish it: Joy! The poet celebrates with a feast, fame crowns him with laurels, and Rodin erects a monument to him. No doubt the mockery here is mixed with Picasso's early admiration for, and unshakable confidence in, the poet's talent in January of 1903.

Finally, if the portrait of 1915 proved, by its economy, that there was no longer any question of abandoning Cubism, another essential portrait of 1907 (opposite, bottom left) revealed its beginnings. This was a painted head in gouache on a large sheet of Ingres paper showing characteristic elements of the preliminary studies for *Les Demoiselles d'Avignon*.[99] Max Jacob best described these studies, all showing the same reductive stylization: a very long nose, "attached to the eyes," and drawn in continuity with the arch of the eyebrow and touching the mouth. Of these figures, which Jacob called "staggering," the poet said without hesitation: "Cubism was born." At the same time, he had the great humility to recognize that he did not comprehend it. In a categorical statement implicating his two friends, he said: "I did not understand cubism. Guillaume praised it without penetrating it. Salmon was its enemy." He concluded, "Picasso is the sole creator of this painting."[100]

It is likely that the painter and the poets were the only ones truly aware of the subtle web being woven between the former's drawings and the latters' texts. The reader, when not simply unaware of the private aspects of this relationship, has been led to erroneous interpretations, as we have seen in the case of *Alcools*. But this was of little importance. Apollinaire had chosen a drawing that he considered a "masterpiece" to accompany the publication of a veritable "poetic summation" (most of the texts in *Alcools* had already been published in journals). As for *Le Cornet à dés*, the discrepancy between the apparent classicism of the 1915 *Portrait of Max Jacob* and the disconcerting writing, fairly unknown by the public until then (the poet had published very little), concealed the fact, for the uninitiated, that the portrait was no less innovative than the text. And, opening Salmon's small book in 1921, who could have guessed the importance of the portrait that illustrated it and known that it was part of the origins of Cubism? Yet each time the graphic work placed the stamp of modernity on the written work.

With the exception of the single painted portrait of Jacob, which was immediately covered over, the poets' portraits were all graphic works. One might think that this technical choice was dictated by the fact that the sitters were men of letters and that the painter joined the poets through pencil, pen, and paper, tools with which they all expressed their talent. Years later, the idea of this working community was still present in Picasso's thoughts when he said to Hélène Parmelin: "At that time, we had no other preoccupation but what we were doing. And all the people who were doing it saw nobody but each other. Apollinaire, Max Jacob, Salmon. . . . Think of it, what an aristocracy!"[101]

NOTES

I would like to thank Jacqueline and Jacques Gojard for all that I have learned about Salmon; Pierre-Marcel Adéma, Gilbert Boudar, and Pierre Caizergues for all that I have learned about Apollinaire; and Judith Cousins, who, as usual, gave generously of her knowledge. Pierre Bergé, Elisa Breton, Maurice Déchery, Gaston Diehl, Aube Elléouët, Claude Picasso, Maya Picasso, and François Valéry should also be warmly thanked. This essay was translated from the French by Jeanine Herman.

1. André Salmon, *Souvenirs sans fin* (Paris: Gallimard, 1961), vol. 3, p. 182.

2. Daniel-Henry Kahnweiler with Francis Crémieux, *My Galleries and Painters* (New York: Viking Press, 1971), p. 49.

3. Gertrude Stein, *Picasso* (London: B. T. Batsford, 1938), p. 3. She specifies: "So in the beginning he knew intimately Max Jacob and at once afterwards Guillaume Apollinaire and André Salmon, and later he knew me and much later Jean Cocteau and still later the Surréalistes."

4. Salmon, *Souvenirs*, vol. 2, 1956, p. 252.

5. Guillaume Apollinaire, "La Vie anecdotique," November 16, 1912, reprinted in *Oeuvres en prose complètes* (Paris: Gallimard, 1993), vol. 3, p. 131.

6. André Salmon, "Le Salon," *Montjoie!*, no. 3 (March 1914), p. 1. For his part, Apollinaire subscribed to "the liberty and sincerity" of Salmon's remarks, which he used in turn to defend his own criticism in an article entitled "La Critique des poètes" (*Paris-Journal*, May 5 1914, reprinted in *Oeuvres en prose complètes*, vol. 2, 1991, p. 671f.).

7. "We already know that [Picasso] took no pleasure in doing a portrait he was asked to do, and the same went for the illustration of a text," Jaime Sabartés wrote in 1946. He added disdainfully: "If books are published with his engravings, it is because the abundance of his oeuvre always allows one to find something to insert if one is not very demanding; his work has such merit and gives such value to the book that nothing else counts" (*Portraits et souvenirs* [Paris: Louis Carré and Maximilien Vox, 1946], p. 140). These are excessive remarks, as we know.

8. The counter example is the lithographed portrait of Paul Valéry that Picasso agreed to do, after much effort on the part of the publisher, for the new edition in 1921, of *La Jeune Parque,* which was published by La Nouvelle Revue Française. The two men do not seem to have known each other previously. Valéry nevertheless came to Picasso's studio on the rue La Boétie to pose, as shown by two letters addressed to the painter. Valéry wrote to Picasso on April 17, 1921, to let him know that only at the beginning of the afternoon, and not in the morning, was he free for sittings: "I shall be happy to go to see you and bring you my head," he added. Two months later, on June 16, he proposed to call on Picasso "on the off-chance": "If you are at home, and if you feel like having me pose a little more, I shall try to be very well-behaved" ("Je serai heureux d'aller vous voir et de vous apporter ma tête"; "Si vous y êtes, et si vous avez envie de me faire poser encore un peu, je tâcherai d'être bien sage"; Picasso Archives, Paris). This perhaps pushes back the date of execution for the portrait proposed in Geiser/Baer, vol. I, no. 224. Regarding Valéry's portrait, Brigitte Baer noted that "Valéry and Picasso were not made to fraternize, as Picasso, much later, would give François Valéry to understand."

9. One of the perverse effects of this indisputably discriminatory distinction is that only works bearing an original print attain the rank of "illustrated book." This explains why one does not find *Alcools* by Apollinaire, for example, or *Le Coq et l'arlequin* by Cocteau (the list would be long) in *Pablo Picasso, les livres illustrés,* the *catalogue raisonné* compiled by Sebastian Goeppert, Herma Goeppert-Frank, and Patrick Cramer (Geneva: Patrick Cramer, 1983). Apollinaire's *Calligrammes* does not appear there either, because the portraits of the poet by Picasso were engraved for the publication by René Jaudon, after drawings by Picasso.

10. Cocteau wrote to Picasso on September 1, 1918: "I have finished correcting the proofs of *Le Coq et l'arlequin* with my portrait (head) and the two monograms" ("Je finis de corriger les épreuves du 'Coq et l'arlequin' avec mon portrait [tête] et les deux monogrammes"; these are two single-line drawings reproduced in the text; letter in the Picasso Archives). Cocteau had posed at Picasso's studio on May 1, 1916, as he wrote to Valentine Gross: "This morning, pose for Picasso in his studio." The portrait is a drawing in graphite on notebook paper (Zervos XXIX, 199) that Cocteau pronounced "an 'Ingres' head," which he envisioned would be "very suitable for portrait of young author to accompany posthumous works after premature death" (letter quoted in Francis Steegmuller, *Cocteau: A Biography* [Boston: Little, Brown, 1970], p. 147). He took pleasure in the role of the young *poète maudit* whom death would strike down before his time, since in September 1915 he had already written to Picasso: "You must paint my portrait quickly because I am going to die" ("Il faut vite peindre mon portrait parce que je vais mourir"; letter in the Picasso Archives). Perhaps they had not even met each other yet (see Pierre Caizergues, "Poèmes à Picasso," *Revue des deux mondes* [July–August 1993], p. 13).

11. Pierre Reverdy to Picasso, June 27, 1921. "Voulez-vous m'aider à en faire un objet de valeur? Je vous demande une eau-forte et si vous vouliez bien pour quelques luxes en plus mon portrait par vous" (letter in the Picasso Archives). Reproduced in Geiser/Baer, vol. I, p. 129, where the Reverdy–Picasso correspondence, in correct order, allows one to retrace the history of the book's publication.

12. Geiser/Baer, vol. I, no. 63. Baer suggests that this engraving could be dated the same day as a little portrait drawn in graphite dated November 15, 1921, and inscribed: "For Pierre Reverdy his friend Picasso" (Zervos XXX, 266). This drawing, engraved by Aubert, would accompany the publication of *Ecumes de la mer* in 1925. That Picasso had contributed with pleasure to Reverdy's project is suggested by the freedom of the model's pose for his engraved portrait. The poet is seated, absorbed in a book, so much in profile that he is almost turning his back to us.

13. André Breton to Picasso, September 18, 1923. "Je ferais l'impossible auprès de vous pour que vous consentiez à ce que le volume s'ouvre sur un portrait de moi par vous, rêve que je forme depuis longtemps et dont je n'ai jamais eu l'audace de vous entretenir" (letter in the Picasso Archives). Moreover, in this letter the poet stated that he was ready to reduce his demands and content himself, if Picasso had it on hand, with "something that could pass for my portrait, without eyes, nose, mouth or ears" ("quelque chose qui puisse passer pour mon portrait, sans yeux, sans nez, sans bouche et sans oreilles") or any unpublished drawings that he could reproduce.

14. Geiser/Baer, vol. I, no. 110. Baer dates the engraving October 30, 1923. The book was printed soon thereafter, on November 15, so the engraving was completed just in time for its publication in the book. Picasso had abandoned the first plate—in which the sitter was seated facing forward—because the likeness could not be captured in the drypoint (no. 111).

15. Baer, vol. 3, 1986, no. 681. In our opinion, this portrait "resembles" Dora Maar at least as much as it does Eluard, an example of "contamination" so frequent in Picasso. In the second edition of *Au rendez-vous allemand*, published in 1945, another portrait of Eluard appears in reproduction. It was one of eighteen in the famous series of portraits of 1941, in which Eluard's profile is seen evolving from a realistic representation toward a geometric schematization (no. 17 in the series, which was published for the first time in 1941 in Eluard's small book *Sur les pentes inférieures*). The portrait, drawn on January 8, 1936 (Zervos VIII, 273), had been reproduced in *Les Yeux fertiles* in 1936. On Picasso's taste for series, where swift, repetitive execution allows for a deepening of representation and brings out certain characteristic features of the sitter, see the series of portraits of Prévert in 1956 (Zervos XVII, 221–54) and that of portraits of Leiris in 1963 (Zervos XXIII, 228–38), all dated April 28.

16. It was Salmon who evoked the Trocadéro Museum of Anthropology where he said, "Picasso, Apollinaire, Max Jacob and myself discovered *l'Art nègre*" (*Souvenirs*, vol. 3, 1961, p. 253). It was Salmon again who revealed the first title of *Les Demoiselles*, "suggested, reviewed and adopted by Picasso's friends: Guillaume Apollinaire, Max Jacob and myself" (*Propos d'atelier* [Paris: Crès, 1922], p. 16).

17. One might think, for example, of the debates surrounding "literary cubism," which first concerned Max Jacob, or the attack on *Les Mamelles de Tirésias,* which greatly affected Apollinaire.

18. Florent Fels, "Propos d'artistes: Picasso," *Les Nouvelles littéraires*, no. 42 (August 4, 1923), p. 2.

19. See Anne Baldassari's analysis of these photographic portraits in *Picasso photographe, 1901–1916* (Paris: Editions de la Réunion des musées nationaux, 1994), p. 93f., in which she suggests their relation to the plastic oeuvre as "a veritable strategy." She precisely dates and describes the three photographs.

20. *Intelligenti pauca*: One would indeed have to know *Les Demoiselles* well in order to recognize the work, on the left in the photograph and partly covered by a flowered cloth. This confirms that these photographs concern a small number of initiates.

21. Guillaume Apollinaire, *Zone*, translated by Samuel Beckett (Dublin: The Dolmen Press, and London: Calder and Boyars, 1972), p. 23.

22. The glass negatives are conserved in the Picasso Archives.

23. "Von hier und heute geht eine neue Epoche der Weltgeschichte aus, und ihr könnet sagen, ihr seid dabei gewesen" (Johann Wolfgang von Goethe, *Kampagne in Frankreich*, September 19, 1792, *Sämtliche Werke*, Jubiläumsausgabe, vol. 28, 1903, p. 60).

24. André Salmon to Picasso, January 9, 1919. "Je te lirai, au dessert, un long poème didactique: *Peindre*, fait, je veux croire, pour te plaire." "Et mon portrait? Quand?" (letter in the Picasso Archives).

25. Salmon, *Souvenirs*, vol. 3, 1961, p. 185. The exact date of this drawing remains to be determined based on Salmon's absences from Paris in 1906–07; he was away due to theatrical touring engagements with the Baret company (*Souvenirs*, vol. 1, 1955, pp. 354–55).

26. Salmon, *Souvenirs*, vol. 2, 1956, p. 333. He added that the book was dedicated to Derain, a "French painter" (which designation made Picasso "grumble"); "I wanted to show myself surrounded by two friends, the two greatest artists of my time: Picasso and Derain." The didacticism of this little book of poetry is relative (and, moreover, Salmon himself amended his initial idea). We read in his book, for example: "To paint is to imitate imitation / The only secret if you must re-create nature / And to imitate nothing / But the limitless / In order and measure" (p. 16; the poem then evokes faux marble and the use of letters in painting, which were to be eminent Cubist materials and techniques). Picasso is mentioned several times in the book, and Léger, Braque, and Gris also appear; one of the poems begins thus: "I compare Picasso's limitless work with Nungesser's terrible flight" (p. 22).

27. Salmon, "La Semaine artistique. Cubisme: Exposition Metzinger (Galerie Rosenberg)," *L'Europe nouvelle*, 2nd ser., no. 3 (January 18, 1919), p. 139.

28. Max Jacob, "Naissance du cubisme et autres," *Les Nouvelles littéraires*, April 30, 1932, p. 7, reprinted in Hélène Seckel, *Max Jacob et Picasso* (Paris: Editions de la Réunion des musées nationaux, 1994), p. 224.

29. For analysis of this series of drawings, the study of the caricature in relation to primitive art, the effect of "contamination" between the portrait of Salmon and that of an old farmer, Josep Fontdevila, whose image obsessed Picasso during and after his stay in Gosol in the summer of 1906, and the question of the sculptures carved directly in wood by Picasso in 1907–08, see William Rubin, ed., *"Primitivism" in 20th Century Art* (New York: The Museum of Modern Art, 1984), vol. 1, p. 282f. and p. 31 of this book. It may be amusing to note that Picasso possessed an African Yaka sculpture, a figure of a standing man with a carved protruding chin, which Maya Picasso remembers the painter would call Salmon (below, left).

30. Fernande Olivier, *Picasso and His Friends* (London: Heinemann, 1964), p. 75.

31. André Salmon to Picasso, December 14, 1954. "Je voudrais pour frontispice la reproduction du dessin, à la plume, que tu fis de moi en l'hiver . . . 1903–1904: c'est un bien beau dessin, jamais reproduit encore et vu seulement par mes visiteurs" (letter in the Picasso Archives). Writing to Picasso, Salmon forgot that the drawing had already appeared in an article he had written for *Les Nouvelles littéraires* on "La Jeunesse de Picasso," July 11, 1931, p. 8, and that Fernande Olivier reproduced it in turn in 1933 in *Picasso et ses amis* (Paris: Librairie Stock, 1933), p. 193. In Salmon's *Souvenirs*, the drawing appears with its title, "André Salmon," handwritten on top and the date 1904 in the printed caption. Picasso and Salmon probably met each other in early 1905.

32. Frédéric Lefèvre, "Une heure avec André Salmon," *Les Nouvelles littéraires*, May 5, 1928, p. 1. Describing the poet, Lefèvre wrote: "Salmon smiles that strange smile his friends know well and in which there still remains a bit of sadness and sometimes a bitter sarcasm." A later photograph of Salmon (below, right) in his apartment, 73, rue Notre-Dame-des-Champs, taken by Pablo Volta in January 1956, shows the portrait by Picasso mentioned by Lefèvre attached to a bookcase.

33. On page 14 of this same notebook (M.P. 1856) there is a seated figure, facing front and rather corpulent, who may possibly be Apollinaire.

34. There are other drawings (we will not enumerate them here), particularly one in pencil which also belonged to Apollinaire (p. 185, top left). Salmon also appears on sheets of sketches in the company of his literary consorts of the time, Paul Fort, Jean Moréas, and, of course, Apollinaire (Zervos XXII, 200). We find the poet again, disguised as a Napoleonic general in battle, drawn by Picasso in a letter he wrote on May 6, 1915, to his friend, who had voluntarily enlisted (p. 199, right). This drawing is enhanced with watercolor.

35. This copy does not have the engraving. Apollinaire also owned a copy which included Picasso's drypoint of *Two Saltimbanques*. This was the extremely rare, first "illustrated book" by Picasso (Geiser/Baer, vol. 1, no. 6).

36. The newspaper, no doubt published in Cannes, is dated, on the back, Saturday, October 5, 1968. Did Picasso and Salmon see each other that day? In any case, this drawing was preserved in the Salmon archives.

37. We know that for political reasons, during the Spanish Civil War, Picasso carried on a long, stubborn feud with Salmon. They were reconciled at the beginning of the 1950s.

38. *Méditations esthétiques: Les Peintres cubistes* (Paris: Figuière, 1913), p. 24. The subtitle, *Les Peintres cubistes*, was added by the publisher in boldface on the title page of the work Apollinaire had chosen to call *Méditations esthétiques*, which was more in keeping with his intentions.

39. Apollinaire, *Zone*, p. 9.

40. Correspondence between Picasso and Apollinaire shows only the painter's uneasiness concerning the quality of the reproduction, as he wrote to Apollinaire from Céret on Febru-

Yaka figure. Wood, 24³⁄₈ × 5½ × 6¼"
(62 × 14 × 16 cm). Private collection

André Salmon (detail) reading in his apartment at 73, rue Notre-Dame-des-Champs, Paris, January 1956. Attached to the bookcase is Picasso's caricature of Salmon done in 1904 (p. 185). Photograph by Pablo Volta. Archives of the Foundation Erik Satie ary 27, 1913: "Max [Jacob] who was with you the other day at Le Mercure de France tells me that he saw a proof of your portrait for your book of verse printed in blue. I want it to be printed in black, not otherwise, and all printing in another color should be prevented" (*Picasso–Apollinaire, Correspondance* [Paris: Gallimard, 1991], pp. 100–102). In March, still worried, Picasso wrote: "If you have proofs of your portrait for Le Mercure send them to me" (p. 102). The phrase "your portrait for your book of verse" does not necessarily mean that the portrait was done for *Alcools*.

41. That friendship—and not solely aesthetic preoccupations—guided this project is evident. This hardly needs repeating. Let us merely point out that in this collection of poems, a long one entitled "Les Fiançailles" is dedicated to Picasso, of whom Apollinaire says in a letter of July 30, 1915, to Madeleine Pagès: "The newest and most lyrical, the most profound is *Les Fiançailles* dedicated to Picasso whose sublime art I admire" (Guillaume Apollinaire, *Oeuvres complètes* [Paris: Balland, 1966], vol. 4, p. 495).

42. This is perhaps what Frédéric Lefèvre wanted to suggest in his work *La Jeune Poésie française* (Paris and Fribourg: Rouart, 1917), a chapter of which bears the unfortunate title "Literary Cubism." In it is a remark whose conciseness could lead to confusion: "Guillaume Apollinaire is the official, so to speak, representative, advocate, interpreter of cubism. One of his poetry collections, *Alcools*, contains his portrait by Picasso" (p. 202).

43. The file of press clips on *Alcools* was published in several issues of the Apollinairean journal *Que vol-ve?*, 2nd ser., no. 18 (April–June 1986); no. 22 (April–June 1987); no. 29 (January–

March 1989); no. 30 (April–June 1989); and 3rd ser., no. 4 (October–December 1991). See also Michel Décaudin's study, *Le Dossier d'* "Alcools" (Geneva and Paris: Droz and Minard, 1960), p. 38f.

44. To Apollinaire's way of thinking, eliminating punctuation was not avant-garde: "As far as punctuation is concerned, I eliminated it because it seemed useless to me and, in fact, it is. The rhythm and the line breaks are the true punctuation, and there is no need for another" (letter to Henri Martineau, July 19, 1913, in Apollinaire, *Oeuvres complètes,* vol. 4, p. 768).

45. Le Masque bleu, "Echos," *Le Courrier français*, February 22, 1913, p. 8. A similar connection is made by Graville in *La Gazette de France* of June 27, 1913, p. 2, concerning the absence of punctuation and an "aesthetic of the futurist school": "These are a lot of attempts at strangeness." Henri Hoppenot, in *Rivista d'Italia* of December 1913 (reprinted in *Que vol-ve?*, no. 30), wonders: "Wouldn't Mr. Guillaume Apollinaire's poetry reveal all its mystery just by being transposed as cubist paintings? . . . The cubist portrait exists only to shock the bourgeois and to play an excellent joke on the public, the sense of which I have not yet fully understood but which at the very most can only reflect poorly on its author."

46. Henriette Charasson, "Chronique du mois: Les poèmes," *Le Temps présent*, July 2, 1913, p. 61.

47. Henri Ghéon, "La Poésie . . . *Alcools* par Guillaume Apollinaire," *Nouvelle Revue française*, August 1, 1913, p. 286.

48. See Graville, n. 45, above.

49. Marc Brésil and Louis de Gonzague Frick, "Le Mois du littérateur," *La Phalange*, July 20, 1913, p. 96.

50. Guillaume Apollinaire, "A propos des croquis de Raoul Dufy d'après Rémy de Gourmont," reprinted in *Oeuvres en prose complètes*, vol. 2, 1991, pp. 1046–47.

51. Guillaume Apollinaire, letter to Madeleine Pagès, July 30, 1915, in *Oeuvres complètes*, vol. 4, p. 491. The young girl had read *Alcools* and must have shown either reticence or incomprehension in the face of the portrait. Apollinaire refused to explain it: "The course in aesthetics on this subject that I could send you would be inappropriate. And all that remains is your disappointment, my love, before a drawing that is a masterpiece. It is a quite natural disappointment for one uninformed of a highly legitimate art which one appreciates as soon as one has discovered its sense and its logic."

52. *Standing Nude* is in the Musée Picasso, Paris (Zervos II[1], 39; M.P. 575); *Head* in the Picasso estate (Zervos XXVI, 355; succ. no. 986). One day the conservators of the Musée Picasso were given the opportunity to see the second drawing and to discover its verso, which had never been reproduced. The entire sheet of paper, which now measures approximately 19⅜ by 12⅝ in. (49.1 by 31.9 cm), was roughly cut through the middle by Picasso no doubt even before the execution of the drawings on the recto side. This reconstituted portrait was recently published in Peter Read, *Picasso et Apollinaire: Les Métamorphoses de la mémoire* (Paris: J.-M. Place, 1995).

53. Picasso Archives. Reproduced in the *Album Apollinaire* (Paris: Gallimard, 1971), pp. 240–41. There are other known photos of Apollinaire with his head bandaged and his body squeezed into his military uniform. In particular those taken at Paul Guillaume's house (ibid., p. 247), and the one reproduced in André Billy,

Guillaume Apollinaire bandaged after his trephination and in uniform in Paul Guillaume's apartment/gallery at 16, avenue de Villiers, Paris, summer 1916. Photograph by Paul Guillaume

Guillaume Apollinaire as a Coffeepot. [1905]. Ink and watercolor on paper. Not in Zervos. Whereabouts unknown; formerly collection Guillaume Apollinaire

Apollinaire (Paris: Seghers, 1967), opposite p. 33, and here, opposite, left. *L'Esprit nouveau* published a photograph of Apollinaire in his hospital bed (no. 26 [October 1924]).

54. Apollinaire to André Breton, August 27, 1916, in *Oeuvres complètes*, vol. 4, p. 877. (The poet here is wearing the *croix de guerre* awarded to him on June 17.) There is nothing in the correspondence between Picasso and Apollinaire that mentions an appointment for a sitting that year. The wounded Apollinaire also inspired André Rouveyre, whose tragic portrait of him, done in May 1916, was reproduced as the frontispiece of *Le Poète assassiné*, published in 1917. It was first reproduced in *Le Mercure de France*, July 1, 1916, p. 46.

55. André Billy finds that in this portrait "pain dominates." He notes that the poet "wears a small goatee and a military cross, as we saw him walk around town then, proud of his new tunic, his boots and his baldric" (*Apollinaire vivant* [Paris: Editions de la Sirène, 1923], p. 89). There is a good chance Picasso had this portrait in mind when, in 1940, he began drawing profiles that are generally identified as showing Apollinaire. One, with tousled hair and an anxious look, was done at Royan on March 17, 1940 (Zervos X, 519; reproduced in the exhibition catalogue *Présence d'Apollinaire* at the Galerie Breteau in 1943 [below, left]). There is also a series of portraits of 1945 in which Apollinaire is crowned with laurels (one dedicated to the Baron Mollet, "in memory," July 5, 1945, Blache sale, Versailles, June 17, 1971, no. 151; another dedicated to Georges Hugnet, in his copy of *Calligrammes*, August 3, 1945, reproduced in Billy, *Apollinaire*, opposite p. 128), and a series of 1948 (one, of December 23, 1948, added on the half-title page of a copy of *Alcools*,

the binding of which is also decorated by Picasso, no. 5 of catalogue no. 53, *Livres romantiques et modernes*, of the Librairie Berès; another at the Musée Picasso, M.P. 1990–89; yet another, dedicated to Aragon, auctioned at Hervé-Chayette-Laurence-Calmels at Drouot on December 10, 1987, no. 142; and several in the artist's estate). Picasso would also do memorial portraits of Max Jacob.

56. Guy Michaud, "Le Tombeau d'Edgar Poe," *Mallarmé* (New York: New York University Press, 1965), p. 93.

57. See the press file of *Calligrammes* published in *Que vol-ve?*, 2nd ser., no. 13 (January–March 1985), and no. 14 (April–June 1985). Victor Snell, in *Le Canard enchaîné* of August 21, 1918, speaks of the "wretched portrait that decorates this curious volume."

58. Reproduced in *Picasso–Apollinaire, Correspondance*, p. 156. In a letter dated March 22, 1917, and sent to the painter, who was in Rome, Apollinaire encouraged him to publicize the book about to be published: "If you would tell people around you that there are a few deluxe editions with the two drawings by you and semi-deluxe editions with one drawing, that would be good" (p. 150). What neither the subscription notice nor Apollinaire point out is that the two drawings by Picasso would be engraved by René Jaudon, one on wood, the second on copper. Apollinaire would not obtain from Picasso what he so wished, original engravings, for either one of his books. It was Dufy who did the woodcuts for *Le Bestiaire*, which was published in 1911; *Vitam impendere amori*, "a little book of verse" for which he wanted "an etching or two" from Picasso, was published with illustrations by André Rouveyre in 1917. Picasso did not respond to a request for engraved

illustrations for *Odes*, the project Apollinaire worked on in the summer of 1918 (see Pierre Caizergues, "Sur deux apothéoses," in *Picasso–Apollinaire, Correspondance*, pp. 11–16).

59. The space is vaguely defined by the diagonal of the paneling, but the chair seat has no depth. Why does this portrait, dedicated to Apollinaire to whom it belonged (as did the other drawing published in *Calligrammes* and the Cubist portrait that is reproduced in *Alcools*), appear in issue no. 26 of *L'Esprit nouveau* in October 1924 with the note "Paul Rosenberg collection"? On the series of "military" portraits of 1916, see Kenneth E. Silver, *Esprit de Corps: The Art of the Parisian Avant-Garde and the First World War, 1914–1925* (Princeton, N.J.: Princeton University Press, 1989), p. 111f.

60. This drawing was dedicated and given by Picasso to Jacques Guérin in 1942. The serrations on the left edge tell us that this is a page from a sketchbook.

61. Zervos VI, 728, and Zervos XXII, 287 and 288.

62. Jacob added: "So is mine." This is not quite as obvious. See Max Jacob, "Souvenirs sur Picasso," *Cahiers d'art* 2, no. 6 (1927), pp. 199–202, reprinted in Seckel, *Max Jacob et Picasso*, p. 208. Baron Mollet recalled that "Picasso, who spent his evenings drawing, did heaps of caricatures [of Apollinaire]" (*Les Mémoires du Baron Mollet* [Paris: Gallimard, 1963], p. 57).

63. Billy, *Apollinaire vivant*, p. 88. The caricatures, aided by his corpulence, sometimes make him resemble Jarry's Père Ubu.

64. Apollinaire's enjoyment of food, which had become legendary, is not irrelevant to this portliness. Carco described him while eating: "Excessively fond of eating and drinking, enor-

Portrait of a Man (Guillaume Apollinaire). March 17, 1940. Pencil on paper, 9½″ (24.2 cm) high. Zervos X, 519. Whereabouts unknown

Letter to André Salmon with a portrait of the poet. May 6, 1915. India ink, gouache, and watercolor on paper, 6⅞ × 8¾″ (17.5 × 22.2 cm). Not in Zervos. Musée Picasso, Paris. Gift of Mr. and Mrs. Alain Mazo, 1980

ANDRÉ SALMON, GUILLAUME APOLLINAIRE, AND MAX JACOB

mous, delectable to watch, he broke the bones he was served between his jaws, sucked them, covered himself in grease" (*De Montmartre au Quartier Latin* (Paris: Albin Michel, 1927, p. 183). Apollinaire's hearty love of food explains how Picasso got the idea for an ex libris for the poet showing an obese monarch at table, a new "king drinks" (Zervos I, 225; this is not, strictly speaking, a caricature of Apollinaire), but also how he depicted Apollinaire as a coffeepot with a steaming spout instead of his usual pipe (p. 198, right). Billy notes that "this portliness admirably suited his moral nature, made for radiance and pleasure" (exhibition catalogue, *Présence d'Apollinaire*, 1943). This corpulence prompted Salmon to say that Tio Pepe, one of the figures in *Bateleurs*, had the "look of Apollinaire" (*Souvenirs*, vol. 2, 1956, p. 260). This has led to sometimes questionable interpretations of Picasso's large canvas of 1905. Apollinaire does not always seem to have been very fond of himself. He wrote to Madeleine Pagès on August 5, 1915: "Take me as I am: not ugly but certainly no longer handsome, oh! no. . . . Not at all deformed, lots of hair, but I very often find myself almost ugly" (Apollinaire, *Oeuvres complètes*, vol. 4, p. 501).

65. Salmon, *Souvenirs*, vol. 3, 1961, p. 133. Salmon's descriptions of Apollinaire's pipes cannot be outdone (ibid., vol. 1, 1955, pp. 53 and 110). Fernande Olivier speaks of Apollinaire's laugh, "which seemed to filter through the pipe stuck permanently between his teeth" (*Picasso and His Friends*, p. 141).

66. Max Jacob, text from a lecture given in Nantes in 1937, published in Seckel, *Picasso et Max Jacob*, p. 244.

67. Jean Cocteau, *La Difficulté d'être* (Paris: Morihien, 1947), p. 173. He described Apollinaire after his injury wearing his small leather helmet (a sartorial detail that allows one to date the last caricatures; p. 189, bottom right): "I saw him in a pale blue uniform, his head shaved, one temple marked by a scar, just like a starfish. An arrangement of bandages and leather made him a sort of turban or little helmet. It seemed this little helmet hid a microphone through which he heard what others could not hear, and he secretly surveyed an exquisite world. He transcribed its messages" (pp. 169–70).

68. These drawings appear to be spontaneous, as though a graphic habit with Picasso. This explains, for example, what we find in the so-called "Catalan" notebook which Picasso had with him at Gosol during the summer of 1906. Next to the typically Gosol drawings are two caricatures of "Don Guillermo" (*Carnet Catalan* [Paris: Berggruen, 1958], pp. 40 and 55).

69. Most likely Picasso is representing Apollinaire in this same activity, one hand in his pants pocket, the other on his fly, in a caricature in which he is seen wearing a papal tiara, a pipe in his mouth. At his side, a naked woman in a lascivious pose encourages one to consider this a scabrous subject (Zervos XXII, 290). André Salmon wondered "where Guillaume had gotten . . . that gift of joyous scatological fury" he was known to possess (*Souvenirs*, vol. 1, 1955, p. 114). Another drawing, which is not a caricature, shows Apollinaire masturbating (right).

This was, no doubt, a topic of conversation between Picasso and the author of *Les Onze Milles Verges* and *Les Exploits d'un jeune Don Juan*; it was certainly a topic with Louise de Chatillon-Coligny, to whom Apollinaire wrote on January 13, 1915: "When we were in school, we made a hole in our right pocket, put our hand through it and we did this during the whole class" (*Lettres à Lou* [Paris: Gallimard, 1970], p. 103). Apollinaire and his mistress called this "giving yourself a little hand."

70. See Seckel, *Max Jacob et Picasso*, pp. 59–60.

71. Might not this athletic representation mean that Picasso considered Apollinaire a strapping figure, a "muscle man" of poetry?

72. The "P. J." on his beret may signify *Paris-Journal*, as Pierre Caizergues, whom we consulted, has suggested. Several comical news items, which evoke the rising of the Seine in January 1910 (see *Oeuvres en prose complètes*, vol. 2, 1991, p. 1270f.), corroborate this. Apollinaire lived at 15, rue Gros at the time, a location that provided him with a ringside seat during the flood.

73. *Picasso-Apollinaire, Correspondance*, p. 122.

74. The text of a letter dated January 14, 1915, that Apollinaire sent to Rouveyre (now in the Bibliothèque Littéraire Jacques Doucet), is generally reproduced with this photograph in which, Apollinaire says, "I look like Mars waiting for Venus." The photograph is not included in the letter (see the reproduction with the five verses by Apollinaire in André Rouveyre, *Apollinaire* [Paris: Editions Gallimard, 1945], as the frontispiece). It was printed on a postcard to be sent to friends. Pierre-Marcel Adéma, who dates it more precisely between December 7 and December 15, 1914, has confirmed this information, telling us that the photographer was "G. Meunier, 16 rue des Marchands, Nîmes." Did Picasso receive one of these postcards? It seems likely, given how much the drawing is inspired by it. The Picasso Archives does not have any information on this subject. In another photograph, taken at the same time, the pose is less directly related to Picasso's drawing (see the catalogue of the Apollinaire exhibition at the Bibliothèque Nationale, Paris, 1969, no. 362, opposite p. 136). Apollinaire was proud of his martial allure. On December 26, 1914, he wrote to Eugène Montfort: "I am rather well-dressed, I have beautiful spurs, I walk around town proudly, my revolver strapped across my chest in a beautiful case" (*Oeuvres complètes*, vol. 4, p. 797).

75. Years later Apollinaire's widow, who had preserved the poet's collection with great care, wrote to Sabartés: "Picasso drew on anything. I have some small portraits of Guillaume on café

stationery, even on metro tickets" ("[Picasso] dessinait sur n'importe quoi. J'ai de[s] petits portraits de Guillaume sur du papier de café même dur des tickets de métro" [Jacqueline Apollinaire to Jaime Sabartés, November 28, 1944, letter in the Picasso Archives]). Apollinaire noted without displeasure that Salmon compared him to "a troika coachman," and Elémir Bourges to "Fabrice del Dongo" or to "a young Roman prelate." "I've even been seen as Emperor Napoleon, Nick Carter and as far as antiquity is concerned, a young painter did a picture where I am Nero" (letter to "Les Treize," September 5, 1910, in *Oeuvres complètes*, vol. 4, pp. 739–40). Apollinaire, however, was far from insensitive, as was demonstrated by an episode Léautaud recounts in his *Journal littéraire* (dated November 17, 1908; [Paris: Le Mercure de France, 1955], vol. 2, pp. 333–34): During a literary gathering, he whispered mockingly about "Apollinaire's pouting face." Apollinaire was unable to conceal his distress, and Léautaud, cruelly, replied: "You know, caricatures of people are not only done with lines. They're done with words, too."

76. André Billy had borrowed these drawings from Jacqueline Apollinaire. He wrote to Picasso on April 7, 1922, to let him know that he was counting on reproducing them and to verify that they were indeed by him (Picasso Archives). Let us note that *Apollinaire as an Academician* is reproduced reversed and without

Portrait of Guillaume Apollinaire. [1905]. India ink on paper, 9⅛ × 5⅛″ (23 × 13 cm). Zervos XXII, 287. Private collection; formerly collection Guillaume Apollinaire

the caricatures that surround it (we are reproducing the original drawing). There is every reason to believe that the same goes for *Apollinaire as Pope*, the original of which we have not seen. These two drawings appeared again in the issue of *L'Esprit nouveau* devoted to Apollinaire (no. 26, October 1924). To cite only one or two of the oldest publications that feature these caricatures, we should mention the book by Apollinaire, *Contemporains pittoresques*, published in 1929, which reproduces one of Apollinaire's pear-shaped heads with pipe and bow tie (p. 188, top left), a large series of which exists (Zervos XXII, 291–94), or the 1946 edition of *Les Mamelles de Tirésias*, which contains six reproductions of caricatures. There is also a small caricature of Apollinaire among the drawings used to illustrate André Salmon's 1920 *Le Manuscrit trouvé dans un chapeau* (p. 108), along with one of a hydrocephalic Delormel.

77. Max Jacob to Guillaume Apollinaire, January 7, 1915 (Seckel, *Max Jacob et Picasso*, p. 16). Regarding Max Jacob, we will refer to our research published in the above catalogue.

78. This is at once praise—Picasso captures not only the model's likeness but that of his ancestors—and disapproval (having to do with the complex relationship Max Jacob had with Picasso, in which admiration existed alongside jealousy). Of the *Portrait of Ambroise Vollard* (p. 299) drawn by Picasso in an identical style in August 1915, however, Max Jacob would say that it is "a very good likeness in the manner of Ingres" (Seckel, *Max Jacob et Picasso*, p. 120). In 1933 the poet wrote a verse for his friend Conrad Moricand as a dedication in a copy of *Le Cornet à dés*, giving this scarcely laudatory assessment of the portrait: "I dedicate this portrait of myself to you / as Picasso depicted it in this place / the stupid peasant's ruddy face / the pallid brow and awkwardness" (ibid., p. 124).

79. Beatrice Hastings (under the pseudonym of Alice Morning), "Impressions of Paris," *The New Age* 16 (January 28, 1915), p. 343. It is because she had not seen the portrait that she speaks of a painting (Picasso barred her from his studio because they had fought about Henri Rousseau).

80. Henri Mahaut, *Picasso* (Paris: Crès, 1930). Mahaut concluded that Picasso continued "to draw and paint, both in the cubist mode and 'like everyone else'" (p. 12).

81. Daniel-Henry Kahnweiler, introduction to the catalogue for an exhibition of Picasso's engraved works at the Musée des Beaux-Arts in Mulhouse, June 25–August 30, 1960.

82. Arvid Fougstedt, "En visit hos Pablo Picasso," *Svenska Dagbladet*, January 9, 1916, p. 10. Quoting Picasso: "People say I've abandoned cubism to do this sort of thing; it's not true, you can see for yourself."

83. "Les Deux Picasso," in *Le Bonnet rouge*, January 13, 1917, p. 2.

84. Francis Picabia, "Odeurs de partout," *391*, no. 1 (January 1917), p. 4.

85. André Salmon to Picasso, December 14, 1917. "[Pour] . . . Metzinger et Cⁱᵉ . . . l'école Metzinger est l'unique issue et il n'admet pas qu'on puisse faire le portrait de Vollard ou de Max après le reste" (Picasso Archives).

86. The book, published by the author, was paid for by subscription of the fourteen copies on Japanese paper with the engraving, and the thirty copies on Holland paper, with the reproduction of the portrait. Since March of 1917, Max Jacob had asked Picasso to do an engraving, but he was not particularly concerned whether it was Cubist. He even wrote to the painter, who was in Barcelona, on August 12, 1917: "Don't do something cubist so as not to scare the inspectors" (they were in the middle of war) and added: "Do whatever you like, it will always be beautiful enough coming from your hand" (Seckel, *Max Jacob et Picasso*, p. 146). The portrait was kept by Picasso until 1944. A few days after Max Jacob's death at Drancy, the play Picasso had written in 1941, *Le Désir attrapé par la queue*, was read in Louise and Michel Leiris's apartment. The painter had the 1915 drawing brought there so that this reading could be done in homage to the deceased poet, and, in a way, in his "presence."

87. On the history of "literary cubism," see Michel Décaudin and Etienne-Alain Hubert's article, "Petit historique d'une appellation: 'Cubisme littéraire'" in *Europe*, no. 638–39 (June–July 1982), pp. 7–25. Max Jacob was not entirely innocent in this matter, writing: "While all poetic prose renounces being for pleasing, the prose poem has renounced pleasing for being. It is something like a cubist painting" ("La Vie artistique," *291*, no. 10–11 [December 1915–January 1916]). This statement would delight Frédéric Lefèvre (see n. 42, above).

88. This drawing was found in Picasso's estate. Did the painter buy it back from the poet, who was in financial straits? See Seckel, *Max Jacob et Picasso*, p. 139, n. 48. As soon as it was finished, the portrait was reproduced in several copies and accompanied by a short poem taken from *Le Cornet à dés*—"L'archange foudroyé n'eut que le temps de desserrer sa cravate" ("The archangel struck down, only had time to loosen his tie"). Those reproductions of the portraits were sold in early December 1916, to benefit Max Jacob, at a lecture that Dermée devoted to the poet under the auspices of the "Lyre et Palette" association.

89. "Picasso once drew me as Lucullus with a wreath and blossoming cheeks," Max Jacob wrote to Jean Rousselot on June 2, 1942 (Seckel, *Max Jacob et Picasso*, p. 214). He did not keep this drawing, since on the back, written in his hand, we read: "Drawing done by Picasso in a quarter of an hour for the exhibition of his old friend Max Jacob. This exhibition took place December 28 at Th. Briand 32, rue de Berri. Jacob sold this drawing to his friend André Lefèvre in order to go on vacation because he is very tired. April 10, 1929. Max Jacob." This portrait would become very popular and be widely reproduced (notably in *Le Domaine* in May 1929 and on the cover of *L'Année poétique* in January 1934). Maurice Sachs described Max Jacob around this time in this way: "His face is gentle and serious, but his eyes are filled with mischief. His upper lip is thin, the lower one pleasant and sensuous. He looks like a Roman emperor, sometimes a prophet of Israel, and sometimes, too, a faun from La Fontaine" (*La*

Décade de l'illusion [Paris: Gallimard, 1950], p. 200).

90. "Ce laurier qui pare ma tête / Tu le mérites mieux que moi / Picasso mon ami, mon maître / Roi des peintres et peintre des rois." See Seckel, *Max Jacob et Picasso*, pp. 214 and 215, n. 21.

91. Ibid.

92. Fernand Mourlot, *Picasso Lithographs* (Boston: Boston Book and Art Publisher, 1970), no. 271. Of this characteristic smile, Max Jacob had said: "I have the kind of smile which would long be taken for an amiable smile and which is the smile of madness" (Seckel, *Max Jacob et Picasso*, p. 215).

93. Was this an allusion to Max Jacob's homosexuality, as John Richardson surmises? See *A Life of Picasso, Volume 1: 1881–1906* (New York: Random House, 1991), p. 260.

94. Respectively, Baer, vol. 4, 1988, nos. 959–60 and 958.

95. See Seckel, *Max Jacob et Picasso*, p. 1f. This portrait was covered over by *Woman Crouching and a Child* (Zervos I, 115).

96. We know that in 1904, following Picasso's example, Max Jacob shaved his moustache and beard (ibid., pp. 30–31).

97. On the subject of the portrait reproduced in *Le Cornet à dés* in 1922–23, Max Jacob's bad faith is evident, since it could not have been published at the time without him at least being aware of it. A drawing similar to this one is Zervos XXII, 124. Max Jacob was at that time as Pierre Abraham described him: "His columnar forehead, his premature baldness emphasized by his jet-black hair, his thick, sensual nose, his elastic jowls like those of old ham actors on tour, all this seemed to have been covered in a sort of transparent lacquer: it was the first face that entirely conjured for me the word *hairless*" (*Les Trois Frères* [Paris: Les Editeurs français réunis, 1971], p. 46).

98. Olivier, *Picasso and His Friends*, p. 33. She nevertheless thought that "all his features were beautiful": "A pretty, elegantly curved mouth, which gave a suggestion of delicacy and wit and malice as well."

99. Let us say in passing—for it has been too abundantly developed to return to it in detail (see, in particular, the exhibition catalogue *Les Demoiselles d'Avignon* [Paris: Editions de la Réunion des musées nationaux, 1988])—that stylistic reasons alone do not place the drawing in the realm of this painting. The fact that Max Jacob is wearing a sailor's pea coat here has prompted critics to consider that he was one of the figures, the Sailor, in the preliminary studies for the great painting (see Seckel, *Max Jacob et Picasso*, p. 57f.).

100. Max Jacob, "Naissance du cubisme et autres," reprinted in Seckel, *Max Jacob et Picasso*, p. 57. See also pp. 53–57 and pp. 206–09.

101. Hélène Parmelin, *Picasso says . . .* (London: George Allen and Unwin, 1969), p. 106.

Portrait of Dora Maar. c. 1936–37. Photogram by Picasso. Gelatin-silver print from *cliché-verre*, 11¾ × 9⅜″ (29.8 × 23.9 cm). Musée Picasso, Paris, Picasso Archives

"Heads Faces and Bodies": Picasso's Uses of Portrait Photographs

ANNE BALDASSARI

"And so Picasso commenced his long struggle to express heads faces and bodies of men and of women in the composition which is his composition. The beginning of this struggle was hard and his struggle is still a hard struggle, the souls of people do not interest him, that is to say for him the reality of life is in the head, the face and the body and this is for him so important, so persistent, so complete that it is not at all necessary to think of any other thing and the soul is another thing."[1]

With this remarkable assessment, Gertrude Stein takes us to the very heart of the portrait's meaning within Picasso's research. We ought, therefore, to focus on the head, face, and body and above all refrain from seeking some subjective essence of the model. If, in the course of his pictorial work, Picasso began to practice photography,[2] it was no doubt due to the inherent objective nature of this "vision."[3] The camera's mechanical, monocular eye enabled both the cutting out of reality, by the use of framing, and the cutting off from reality. Confronted with the ductility of the living being, the technical distancing of the camera offered a way to capture its bodily form alone.

We now know that Picasso began taking photographs in the first decade of the century and that he printed them himself.[4] In the years of Cubism's invention, it was one of the ways he strove to *analyze* his vision and to define other modes of representation.[5] Some of these experiments can be directly related to the elaboration of *papiers collés* and Cubist constructions.[6] Later, rayographs[7] were to develop "cameraless" photography in which darkroom work was substituted for camera work and combined with drawing or engraving. Parallel to these experiments and throughout his life, Picasso collected a vast number of photographic documents of the most diverse nature, many of which, through chance visual encounters, were to become a direct source of his work.[8]

Three aspects of this constant interchange between painting and photography are dealt with here. A series of photographs will be used to establish what the profile— omnipresent motif in Picasso's approach to the human figure—owes to the processes involved in shadow-theater as well as to those of photography's precursors: silhouette, shadow, and blockout. Some Cubist portraits from the years 1910–12 will then be compared with line drawings from the period 1917–20; despite their stylistic disparity, both were, in fact, elaborated in close relation to a photographic referent: photographs taken by the artist or studio portraits. Finally, the juxtaposition of the 1917 painting *Olga in an Armchair* and its photographic precedent will be considered. An attempt will thus be made to suggest the complexity of Picasso's uses of photography. Self-portraits or portraits: all are enigmas whose raw material is composed of bodies, faces, and heads.

In the artist's archives there is a small, full-length silhouette of a man cut out from an old photograph (left).[10] It is a portrait of Picasso dating back to the beginning of the century. The figure can be compared to a drawing bearing the title *Picasso in Spain,* which accompanied a letter sent by the artist to his friend Max Jacob in July 1902 (below).[11] Although the two documents leave contrasting impressions, the self-portrait in pen and ink clearly derives from the photograph, recapturing its overall configuration. The cutout shows a young bourgeois in a suit and Panama hat; the drawing is of an "artist," whose studied outfit is described by Jaime Sabartés: "Trousers slightly tied at the ankles, a rather broad-brimmed hat and bow tie. . . . In 1902, the walking stick was an indispensable accessory. Everyone carried one, and Picasso more regularly than anyone else. It kept him company and served him as entertainment; with it he would fence with the trees and poles he found on his way."[12]

The edges of the photographic silhouette *Self-Portrait with a Cane* bear traces of black ink. These traces may correspond to a drawing that served to guide the action of the scissors. In general, *line* is foreign to the photographic image, which expresses a play of values created by the uneven darkening of the silver salts. Here the cutout of the snapshot operates as a drawing that demarcates and as an engraving that incises. But this ring of ink also suggests the use of the silhouette as a template for the sketch. The comparable scale of the two works allows us to hypothesize that the photograph was at least partially transferred. *Picasso in Spain* presents an angular line quite unlike the artist's usual drawing style, possibly due to the

Self-Portrait with a Cane. [Barcelona, 1902]. Photographic cutout by Picasso. Gelatin-silver print and black ink, 2¾ × 1¾" (7 × 4.3 cm). Musée Picasso, Paris, Picasso Archives

Picasso in Spain. 1902. Ink on paper (letter to Max Jacob), 8⅛ × 10¼" (20.5 × 26 cm). Not in Zervos. Private collection

Self-Portrait in the Studio. Paris, [1901–02]. Photograph by Picasso. Gelatin-silver print, 4¾ × 3⅝″ (12 × 9 cm). Musée Picasso, Paris, Picasso Archives

adjustment of the pen to the edge of the photographic paper. It is also possible to notice a number of similarities between the cutout and the drawing: to the right, the slope of the shoulder, the bend of the arm, and the inexplicable bump on the side of the thigh, which corresponds to the contour of the jacket worn by the artist in the snapshot; to the left, the relative positioning of arm, leg, and cane. Finally, if, in the drawing, the outline of the legs and their shadows is modified or reversed, the most

significant elements from the photograph are retained.

Picasso's first forays into photography appear to date specifically from the years 1901–02. Two original prints bear witness to this: the overprinted photograph Self-Portrait in the Studio (above) and the "assemblage" Blue Studio.[13] Both show a remarkable command of photographic framing as well as printing. They stand out among other contemporaneous work for their vigorous principle of construction: an allover flat composition and a figure superimposed on a wall of paintings. Executed in a similar spirit, the cutout[14] Self-Portrait with a Cane appears to have been inspired by the procedure for making *sombras,* shadow-theater figures, which were featured at the cabaret Els Quatre Gats in Barcelona,[15] following the example of Le Chat Noir in Paris.[16] Picasso was no doubt aware of the experiments of Miquel Utrillo,[17] the creator of these shows, and drew on their principles. Furthermore, recently found in the Picasso archives was a page from *L'Illustration*[18] devoted to *"l'ombromanie,"* a *fin-de-siècle* parlor game in which the players, using their hands and a few accessories, tried to re-create pictograms of characters or animals (below). As for the *sombras,* they were drawn on cardboard or sheet metal and then incised piece by piece. During projection, they were placed in front of a translucent set lit from behind. Similarly, the cutout of the photograph isolates the subject by extracting it from its context. The drawing's rendering of the cutout then "situates" the model in a symbolic landscape: in this instance, the facade of a church and a bullfighting arena.

An idea of portraiture was being elaborated here, which would assert itself from the years 1898–99 and during the Blue period. The model, wrested from its familiar environment, which is blocked out by a plain color, is singled out. Of his portrait dating from 1901 (p. 239), Sabartés wrote: "Here is the specter of my soli-

"L'Ombromanie" from *L'Illustration*, December 20, 1890. Musée Picasso, Paris, Picasso Archives

tude seen from without."[19] This exteriority indeed distances the artist from his subject, who is seen as the bodily ideogram of an unfathomable psychological entity. Such an approach inspired a series of sketches of his Catalan friends, which Picasso exhibited in February 1900 at Els Quatre Gats. As Josep Palau i Fabre has pointed out, the first of these figures is depicted in descriptive surroundings. Next, the artist "gradually simplified this background to such a degree that in the last ones of all he eliminated it entirely, concentrating the interest of the drawing exclusively on the sitter."[20]

Similar to the figures in shadow-theater, such portraits also evoke the profiles "à la Silhouette," one of the historical sources of photography.[21] These summary figures were thus named, in derision, due to their economy of means:[22] taken from life, they were limited to expressing the model's distinctive contours through a black cutout on a white backdrop. The simplicity of such a stamp of identity remained a sort of phantasm for Picasso, who, as late as 1960, wondered aloud to the photographer André Villers about an impossible project: "We could make a life-size figure from a photograph, I'll make it naked and we'll cover it in vermicelli, that would be funnier, don't you think?"[23] On the scale of the palm of a hand, the self-portrait *Picasso in Spain* combines, "from a photograph," the silhouetting of the model, its outline delineation, and an imaginary environment. It was to set up, at the start of the century, the founding paradigm linking photography, cutouts, and drawing in Picasso's oeuvre.

The physical arrangement that gave depth to the theatrical space of shadow-theater can also be compared to the processes Picasso was to use in his darkroom experiments to confer thickness on the photographic medium. *Sombras* were manipulated in front of backdrops painted on glass that could comprise up to twenty plates bearing distinct elements, a device that allowed changes of scenes and a great variety of values and color shadings. In the most sophisticated forms of shadow-theater, wire figures bore layers of tight gauze that introduced nuances and semitransparent patterns. From 1911–12, Picasso affixed cardboard masks to the glass of photograph negatives in order to modify the structure and the meaning of the image.[24] Similarly, in the works on half-tone plates carried out in 1913–14,[25] and again in 1937,[26] he was to make use of the thickness of the copperplate, this time by incising it. The result was an image of photographic origin completely revised by engraving.

In 1936–37 Picasso executed a series of rayographs which would be published in the review *Cahiers d'art* in a portfolio prefaced by Man Ray's essay "Picasso, photographe."[27] Dora Maar, who assisted the artist in this research, explained that he "spread a thick layer of oil paint on glass and drew in the paint with the blade of a pocket knife in order to create the lines, a process that

Portrait of Dora Maar. c. 1936–37. Photogram by Picasso. Gelatin-silver print from *cliché-verre,* 11¾ × 9⅜″ (29.8 × 23.9 cm). Musée Picasso, Paris, Picasso Archives. (Colorplate, p. 202)

Dora Maar. Paris, 1936–37. Photograph by Picasso. Gelatin-silver print, 9½ × 7¼″ (24 × 18.2 cm). Musée Picasso, Paris, Picasso Archives

recalled engraving, and he obtained a negative."[28] She points out that for some of these portraits "lace was placed directly on the paper."[29] Thus, with Portrait of Dora Maar (above), the modernist practice of the photogram—here a netting placed between the light source and sensitized paper—was combined with the earlier technique of the *cliché-verre,* which involved painting on glass subsequently printed in a photographic manner.[30]

The production of such a work was similar to that of the *sombras,* but seen from the other direction, from behind the scenes. The light projected onto the surface of the glass in the darkroom outlined the contour of the face at the same time that its beam, softened by the muslin screen, superimposed a grid pattern on it.[31] The grid evokes the process recommended by Alberti in order to facilitate the squaring of the perspective line: "A veil loosely woven of fine thread . . . [is] divided up by thicker threads into as many parallel square sections as you like, and stretched on a frame."[32] The work thus becomes as much a metaphor for the artist's gaze as a portrait of his model. The rayographs, moreover, may be compared to three photographs taken by Picasso, which, in a sort of descriptive puzzle, present Dora Maar in three-quarter view, frontally, and in profile (above). This last image may well have served as a reference for the creation of the Portrait of Dora. The negative indeed seems to have been reversed in order to guide, by transparency, the drawing

Self-Portrait in Profile. [Paris, 1927]. Photograph by Picasso. Modern print, 4¾ × 2¾″ (12 × 7 cm). Musée Picasso, Paris, Picasso Archives

Mask. Cannes, Vallauris, [1954–61]. Photogram by Picasso and André Villers. Gelatin-silver print, 12 × 9½″ (30.5 × 24 cm). Musée Picasso, Paris, Picasso Archives

Head of a Woman. Cannes, Vallauris, [1954–61]. Photogram by Picasso and André Villers. Gelatin-silver print, 12 × 9½″ (30.5 × 24 cm). Musée Picasso, Paris, Picasso Archives

executed on the glass negative. Viewed in this way, the photograph plays a dual role: the picture the artist takes of his model is as much a source as a pattern for engraving on glass; the subsequent arrangement of the printing gives it a radical interpretation.

As in the Freudian game of Fort-Da,[33] the process involves the artist photographically parting with reality, retrieving it with the scratch of a pocket knife, and then letting it spin off into the distance again. The painter would then seize it in turn. In fact, the series of rayographs is among the very first group of works using Dora Maar as a model. It would have thus contributed to the inventory of physiognomic elements that the painter then condensed into a new schema characterized by the brutal combination of two eyes facing forward and a nose jutting out at a three-quarter angle. This exploration was to culminate in 1940–41 with the canvases that, taking such a principle to the extreme, appear as icons of "ugliness."[34]

The photo-pictorial investigations of 1937 exploit the motif of the profile in all its specificity. In what would be a historiography of portraiture, the profile emerges as one of the earliest forms of representation of a subject. On cave walls, large animal profiles have been found alongside prints of open hands dipped in pigment. According to ancient tradition, the first portrait arose from the drawing "in outline on the wall the contours

Woman with a Cat. Cannes, Vallauris, [1954–61]. Photograph by André Villers of a cutout by Picasso. Gelatin-silver print from the original negative, 12 × 9½″ (30.5 × 23.8 cm). Collection André Villers, Mougins

of [a man's] profile"[35] so as to retain his features before he departed. The profile would therefore be the image arrested by the gaze of another; an image offered by the body turning away and leaving. This is not the frontal figure of the subject who looks at, recognizes, and represents himself or herself: the symmetrical effigy, like the divine image in its *mandorla,* inscribed at the center of the world in order to dominate it. Rather, the profile stands out *against* the world. It is the mark of alterity: the sharp, cutout, antagonistic figure of a human traversing space as well as time. Within the primitive community, the profile thus offered the first recording of dissimilarity, reviewing the variants of the species before the individual had definitively constituted his or her "self-image."

Like this original form of representation, a photographic negative taken by Picasso shows his own profile as a shadow standing out against the drawing of a head seen from a three-quarter angle (p. 207).[36] Interposed between the light source and the projection surface, the artist's body photographically outlines its contours in the imaginary space of the drawing. Of great complexity, such an image may be read, in the context of Picasso's photographical experiments, as an equivalent of Self-Portrait with a Cane of 1902 and the Portrait of Dora of 1936–37. The cogency of the profile motif in the canvases of the years 1925–30 has also been emphasized.[37] However, this shadow recurs throughout all the artist's work. Profiles proliferate[38] in an exploration of the multiple possibilities of their noncentrality.[39] Linked to the frontal or three-quarter view of the Cubist portraits, they participate in the systematic dislocation of a self-centralized figure. In the course of the 1920s, unilinear profiles would give way to infinite combinations.

With the photograms Picasso made between 1954 and 1961 in collaboration with André Villers,[40] cutout profiles and masks became the matrix of a series of portraits or self-portraits. With increasingly sophisticated experimentation, work with the negative was then to unite preexisting photographs, cutouts, photograms of objects or of fabric, and photographic *mise-en-scènes.* Among the several hundred works created in this way, the series of Fauns and Masks has its origin in four cutout pictograms— a sunlike head, a bird, a man with one arm raised, and a small bull—that combine to draw a face which is none other than that of the artist (opposite, top left). This rebus thereby condenses the symbols and keys through which Picasso projected his own portrait. Reproduced by contact prints, distorted by the inlaying of plants or other objects, these materials were cut out again so as to form a new mask. Picasso, obliterating the initial face while at the same time accentuating it, superimposed a mouth on the mouth, a ridge on the nose, a hole on the eye. Fused together by the photogram, these different photographic *tailles*[41] form a palimpsest of identity in which features,

like Narcissus' reflection in the water's troubled mirror, link and become blurred in an incessant vibration of the image. If Masks and Fauns grimace frontally, the profiles of female figures—Portrait of Jacqueline, Head of a Woman (opposite), and Woman with a Cat (opposite)— are drawn in an ambiguous game of simultaneous surfaces; dual motifs in which cutout figures and their outlines endlessly conjugate the interior and the exterior, the full and the empty, the positive and the negative.

EVERYBODY'S PORTRAIT

In 1910–11, when Picasso photographed his closest friends one after the other in the small sitting room of his studio on the boulevard de Clichy, it was with the likely intention of using this iconographic material for his painting. He had, in fact, recently begun the series of portraits that was to *embody* Analytic Cubism. The photographs show their models sitting in front of a wall where, juxtaposed, there hang a Spanish shawl, the charcoal drawing *Nude Woman,* the canvas *Mountain of Santa Bárbara,*[42] a pipe holder, and a Punu mask, whose enigmatic smile echoes Matisse's *Portrait of Marguerite.*[43] Like wax figures at a shooting gallery, the dark silhouettes go past: Ramón Pichot, Max Jacob, Guillaume Apollinaire, Frank Burty Haviland, Daniel-Henry Kahnweiler (p. 211), or Picasso himself, appearing in a self-portrait with a Siamese cat (p. 210). Among these photographs, that of Kahnweiler is to be placed in direct relation to the portrait painted by Picasso (p. 211, center right), which can be considered its transcription.[44] Moreover, playing on both the similarities and dissimilarities of the photographs, the entire sequence can be seen as the source of the paintings *The Poet*[45] and *Man with a Pipe*[46] (p. 211), which combine, in a composite manner, their singular details and recurrent elements.[47] Devoted, in theory, to picking out a model's specific characteristics, the portrait here becomes a collective stock of signs that painting redistributes and reorganizes with no further concern for realism. Thus from the photographs taken on the boulevard de Clichy arose synonymous montages that, like the *papiers collés,* incorporated disparate elements into new plastic unities. The process started with the familiar, the intimate, the known, in order to elaborate a generic system of representation that transcended strict individuality.[48]

The reverse course was to be taken in the years 1917–20, when Picasso, on several occasions, took to drawing after images borrowed from a stock of photographic portraits dating from the previous century. The documents presented here, until now unpublished, are all *carte-de-visite* prints. This inexpensive format, invented by Adolphe-Eugène Disdéri in 1854, was commonly used by commercial studios until World War I. As Gisèle Freund has pointed out, it was to assure photography an unprece-

Picasso in his studio at 11, boulevard de Clichy, Paris, December 1910. Photograph by Picasso. Gelatin-silver print, 5¾ × 4½″ (14.7 × 11.6 cm). Musée Picasso, Paris, Picasso Archives

dented social success: "From this time on, the debonair, smiling bourgeois himself appeared on mantelpieces, pedestals, sideboards, and apartment walls, along with photographs of his favorite statesmen, scholars, and actresses."[49] Picasso was to draw on these two types of subjects, making equal use of effigies of unknown men, such as Man at a Stand (p. 212, top left)[50] and Family Portrait (p. 213, top left),[51] or of famous figures, like The Family of Napoléon III (p. 213, bottom left).[52]

These diverse examples indicate the strict codification to which photography was subjected: "Members of all professions and all social classes parade before the viewer's eyes, but real personalities are almost entirely obscured, buried beneath conventional social types."[53] The sovereign's family is arranged in the same triangular configuration as that of the anonymous bourgeois, and the male figure is so strangely similar in Family Portrait and in Man at a Stand that it is difficult to say whether these are two photographs of the same individual or two different men converted by the camera to the same "type."

The portrait has indeed become a simulacrum that allows the subject to be reduced to a model, to a form that has internalized the necessities of legitimate representation. Alone or in a group, the man places himself standing or sitting amid the studio's toneless decor. The body interacts with some piece of furniture or false architecture, which delineates the space and upholds the pose. Most often this is a pedestal, a half-pilaster, or a balustrade whose curved supports parallel the legs. These anthropomorphic markers suffice to suggest a terrace, a point of view, a panorama. Into the space of a classical "landscape," nature is ordered by and for the gaze. But in the

Ramón Pichot in Picasso's studio at 11, boulevard de Clichy, Paris, autumn–winter 1910. Photograph by Picasso. Gelatin-silver print, 11¾ × 9½″ (29.9 × 24 cm). Musée Picasso, Paris, Picasso Archives

Max Jacob in Picasso's studio at 11, boulevard de Clichy, Paris, autumn–winter 1910. Photograph by Picasso. Modern print from the original glass negative, 4¾ × 3½″ (12 × 9 cm). Musée Picasso, Paris, Picasso Archives

Guillaume Apollinaire in Picasso's studio at 11, boulevard de Clichy, Paris, autumn 1910. Photograph by Picasso. Gelatin-silver print, 8⅝ × 6⅞″ (21.9 × 17.4 cm). Musée Picasso, Paris, Picasso Archives

Frank Burty Haviland in Picasso's studio at 11, boulevard de Clichy, Paris, early 1912. Photograph by Picasso. Modern print from the original glass negative, 4¾ × 3½″ (12 × 9 cm). Musée Picasso, Paris, Picasso Archives

Daniel-Henry Kahnweiler in Picasso's studio at 11, boulevard de Clichy, Paris, autumn–winter 1910. Photograph by Picasso. Modern print from the original glass negative, 4¾ × 3½″ (12 × 9 cm). Musée Picasso, Paris, Picasso Archives

Portrait of Daniel-Henry Kahnweiler. 1910. Oil on canvas, 39⅝ × 28⅝″ (100.6 × 72.8 cm). Zervos II¹, 227. Daix 368. The Art Institute of Chicago. Gift of Mrs. Gilbert W. Chapman in memory of Charles B. Goodspeed. (Colorplate, p. 285)

The Poet. 1911. Oil on canvas, 51⅝ × 35¼″ (131.2 × 89.5 cm). Zervos II¹, 285. Daix 423. The Solomon R. Guggenheim Foundation, New York. Peggy Guggenheim Collection, Venice

Man with a Pipe. 1911. Oil on canvas (oval), 35¾ × 27⅞″ (90.7 × 71 cm). Zervos II², 738. Daix 422. Kimbell Art Museum, Fort Worth, Texas

Man at a Stand. Paris. Photograph by Studio Antonin. Albumen-silver print (*carte de visite*), 4 × 2⅜″ (10.2 × 6 cm). Musée Picasso, Paris, Picasso Archives

Man at a Stand. 1920. Lead pencil and charcoal on gray paper, 18⅞ × 15⅜″ (48.1 × 39.1 cm). Zervos IV, 61. Musée Picasso, Paris

studio, the camera takes the place of the absent landscape and the model's erratic gaze rests on the lens as on nature itself. In the overlapping of roles, technique seems to enter the order of "arranged nature." Picture-taking presents itself as a natural-science experiment, regulated by physicochemical laws, of which art would be solely an exact recording.

From these images, Picasso seems to "draw" his "subjects," as one does at a lottery. He attempts to reconstruct them, scrupulously. In his own way, he creates faithful portraits of them. For *The Family of Napoléon III* as for *Family Portrait* (opposite, bottom right and top right), Picasso tightens the framing on the torsos of the figures and the circle formed by their glances and hands. The empress looks lovingly at the heir to the throne, who is absorbed in contemplation of his father. In the photograph, the latter seems to be facing the camera as though looking at his people. The drawing style that literally translates the pose of the woman and child nevertheless alters the image of the familiar state leader, whose ornamental chair is the only prop that suggests a noble occupant. The slightly rumpled self-satisfaction to which the photograph attests gives way in the drawing to a figure whose barely sketched body appears to be perched on his fingers and whose absent gaze becomes lost outside the focal field. The drawing is highlighted with pastel, in a

manner similar to that used for the *Portrait of Olga,* dating from 1921 (p. 315). Cerulean or lilaceous blues are similarly juxtaposed to the pinkish-white flat tints of the faces and hands. Equally noticeable is the identical treatment of the busts of the two women and their Leonardesque smiles. The graphic translation, however, is doubly paradoxical for a work based on a photograph, an image whose expressive register ignores line as well as color.

Evoking the earlier practice of tinting daguerreotypes by hand, Roland Barthes described his impression of color in photographs as "a coating applied *later on* to the original truth of the black-and-white."[54] Similarly, here, the addition of chromatic flat tints, instead of conferring an added "realism," seems to propose a transcription of the photograph that evokes the naïve illumination of the *images d'Epinal.*[55] But far from wishing to restore "lifelike colors" to these photographic phantoms, Picasso seems to have deliberately played on the political connotations of such a vocabulary. The blue and red of the clothes, lightened by the white of the flesh tones, offer a tricolor scale which the artist used in several works dating from World War I.[56] He was to use this scale again in 1922 in the canvas *The Village Dance,* in which the relationship to the patriotic iconography of the time has been noted.[57] Lent to this idyllic familial and dynastic image, the same chromaticism sums up, in blue, white, and red, the tremendous historical

Family Portrait. Photograph by Feulard. Albumen-silver print (*carte de visite*), 4¹⁄₈ × 2³⁄₈″ (10.5 × 6.1 cm). Musée Picasso, Paris, Picasso Archives

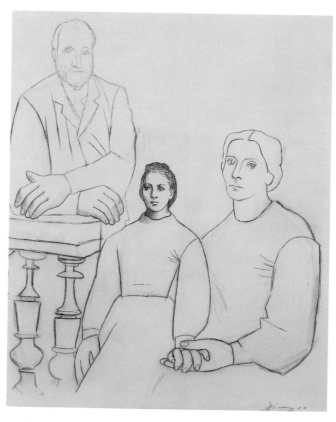

Family Portrait. 1919. Pastel on paper. Not in Zervos. Private collection

The Family of Napoléon III. Photograph by Studio Levitzky. Albumen-silver print (*carte de visite*), 7¹⁄₁₆ × 4¹⁄₈″ (10.5 × 6.2 cm). Musée Picasso, Paris, Picasso Archives

The Family of Napoléon III. 1919. Pastel on paper, 24½ × 18⁷⁄₈″ (62 × 48 cm). Zervos III, 412. Private collection

farce that, in less than four years, would turn the president of the Republic, cloaked in the colors of 1848, into the second hereditary emperor of the French people.[58]

Picasso seems to take a more innocuous subject when he decides to transpose *Man at a Stand* (p. 212, top right). The technique used is common to numerous drawings of this same period, also executed with reference to photographs; notably, the portraits of Sergei Diaghilev and Alfred Seligsberg (below, right), Olga Khokhlova, Lydia Lopokova, and Loubov Chernicheva (right), or Auguste Renoir.[59] The graphite line is superimposed on the initial softened line drawn in charcoal. This blurring of the contour would scarcely seem justified were it a matter of consigning an immobilized figure to the spatial coordinates of the photographic framing and *mise-en-scène*. This reworking of the drawing aims, instead, to suggest the density of an image in which one can read, in a single glance, the instant of the shot as well as the duration that separates us from it. The light shading of charcoal has the uncertainty of that "very subtle moment" when every model can say: "I am neither subject nor object but a subject who feels he is becoming an object: I then experience a micro-version of death (of parenthesis): I am truly becoming a specter."[60] But Picasso also chose warm gray paper for his drawing in order to reproduce the chromatic affinities that the aging of the print creates between the

Three Dancers: Olga Khokhlova, Lydia Lopokova, and Loubov Chernicheva. 1919. Lead pencil and charcoal on paper, 24³⁄₄ × 18¹⁄₂″ (62.7 × 47 cm). Zervos III, 352. Musée Picasso, Paris

Sergei Diaghilev, director of the Ballets Russes, and Alfred F. Seligsberg, counsel to the Metropolitan Opera Company of New York, New York, [April] 1916. Photograph by Count Jean de Strelecki. Gelatin-silver print, 9¹⁄₄ × 7″ (23.5 × 17.8 cm). Musée Picasso, Paris, Picasso Archives

Sergei Diaghilev and Alfred Seligsberg. 1919. Charcoal and black pencil on paper, 25¹⁄₂ × 19⁵⁄₈″ (65 × 50 cm). Zervos III, 301. Musée Picasso, Paris

ANNE BALDASSARI

Bather with Beach Ball. September 1, 1929. Oil on canvas, 8⅝ × 5½″ (21.9 × 14 cm). Not in Zervos. Musée Picasso, Paris

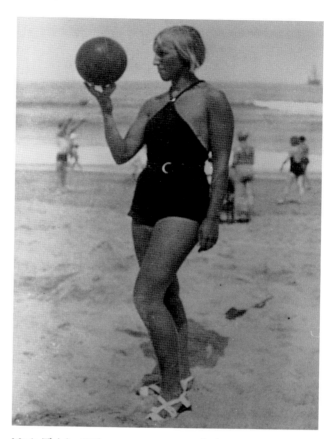

Marie-Thérèse Walter at age twenty, on the beach at Dinard, summer 1929. Photograph by Picasso. Collection Maya Picasso

model and the background. Graphite, charcoal, and the coarse paper all work toward establishing a system of material equivalence with the sepia photograph and with the passage of time doubly inscribed in it. The stand, the man, and the wall of spotted collodion against which he is leaning form an inseparable entity, occupying a hidden recess, a temporal hollow, of which the drawing offers a muted resonance.

An "anonymous" portrait is thus elaborated, whereby ignorance of the model is so great that the drawing is set up as the body's sole truth. This meticulous survey of appearances simultaneously registers the banality of the image and that which, through its interstices, escapes ordinary codes of representation. For no matter how mediocre a photograph might be, it retains from its very origin the distinctive feature of being the real *index*[61] of an existential experience and of preserving its trace. With his body leaning against the balustrade, the poser observes the photographic act as it happens. This fixedness, this consent, this focused attention are necessary in order for the portrait to take shape. In this way the subject participates entirely in "his" shot. He is its author as much as its object.

Photography requires such an encounter, at the center of its lens, between the model's gaze and that of his image. There is a dialogue "in the mirror" in which the subject surrenders to the medium a moment of his head, face, and body. It is this initial experience that the examination of any photographic portrait re-creates: "From a real body, which was there, proceed radiations which ultimately touch me, who am here; the duration of the transmission is insignificant; the photograph of the missing being will touch me like the delayed rays of a star. A sort of umbilical cord links the body of the photographed thing to my gaze: light, though impalpable, is here a carnal medium, a skin I share with anyone who has been photographed."[62]

Leaning on the anthropomorphic balustrade, the subject poses. "Don't move!" The model stiffens: it is time for the "pose" required by the emulsion's low sensitivity. The image will reveal the spectacle of this straining to become the image. The body is exposed, hindered as much as supported by the complications of the console table, the suit, the accessories, sometimes the "headrest," which, Barthes says, "was the pedestal of the statue I would become, the corset of my imaginary essence."[63] Indeed, like works in progress in a sculptor's studio, the body is erected here, an amalgam of flesh and bone, an ossuary wrought by the death drive as depicted by Picasso in the canvas *Bather with Beach Ball* (above, left), a tubular totem possibly inspired by a photograph of Marie-Thérèse Walter on the beach at Dinard in 1929 (above, right).

A similar tension can be seen in the drawings presented here. *Family Portrait* (p. 213), for example, incorporates—in the most disquieting "layering"—a gigantic mother, the man's elongated bust, which appears as a vertical extension of the balustrade, and the microcephalic head of the disproportioned girl. Although this is mainly a line drawing, the girl's miniature face is rendered by a network of fine hatchings that reproduces the photographic model in a manner similar to that of engravings in nineteenth-century illustrated journals. Its denser graphic matter is inscribed, like a collage, at the exact intersection of the diagonals.[64] Here, as in other drawings, the figures, through a reverse effect of dilatation, are endowed with enormous hands, heavy links of a chain surrounding the image. In this case, such visual distortion of ordinary representation does not appear to be the result of real proximity, as the studio's arrangement ensured the model was kept at a sufficient distance from the lens.[65] On the contrary, the hands in such photographs, as much as the face emptied of expression, formed part of the necessary vocabulary of appearance: "Some subjects placed their right hand across their breast; others held it nonchalantly at their belts or let the hand drop to their thighs. One man plays with his watch-chain, while another plunges his right hand into his waistcoat in the manner of a great parliamentary orator."[66] Such visual rhetoric nevertheless revealed itself to the eye—"even in the more natural poses, these figures appear inflated with pride and comically naive in their sense of self-importance"[67]—while also revealing the constraint imposed on the subject.

In the hands, particularly in their "knotted" gesture, is concentrated the almost painful energy of this action, which is inaction: the pose. They are securely fastened to their prop, and their enlargement betrays a life that would become autonomous. In the hands surges all of the power of the stationary figure. Constricted by the shot, they are monstrously alive and almost animal-like. They squeeze, grip, superpose, and intertwine one another. They are sensual rhizomes of a body immured in propriety.

As *Family Portrait* symptomatically illustrates, hands take on a growing importance in Picasso's drawings and paintings of the 1917–23 period. The wholly physical approach distinguishes itself from the emblematic gestures of the paintings of the Blue and Rose periods. It evokes the Surrealist fetishization of objects of desire, the autonomous life of each member that, according to Jean-Paul Sartre, arouses the existential malaise,[68] or the strategies of symbolic dismemberment used by the fictional characters of Witold Gombrowicz.[69] The model appears cut off from himself, dissociated in a swarm of partial representations. With the weight of his body leaning on the Neoclassical balustrade, he is called to the stand to testify to his enigmatic presence in the world.

Playing with Fans

At Montrouge, in the studio where Picasso retreated in the last years of the Great War,[70] Olga poses. The artist has truly positioned her for a photograph (opposite, upper left): her arm is across the back of the chair, her legs crossed, with the right foot propped up on a thick, leather-bound volume to maintain a precarious balance.[71] The subject of the photograph appears to be the rococo armchair as much as the model herself; or, rather, it is their concordance, the interplay of their motifs, their "embrace," in a literal sense. A pencil sketch dating from 1917 similarly unites the chair, the studies tacked to the wall, and Olga in an almost identical attitude (opposite, top right). But the framing still accentuates the bias of the composition: here, the interlace of corollas and foliage covering the low-slung chair occupies the center of the image, and the model's body is cut off by the edge of the paper.[72]

In two other studies (opposite, bottom left and right), Olga, seated on the tapestry-covered chair, is undressed, her hair down. The universe of the studio is summed up in a superimposition of frames and stretchers that form a geometric background for the nude. The model seems to be searching for her position, her hand successively supporting her head, placed against the back of the chair, or in the hollow of her neck—unless the artist invented this unclothed Olga, as the unlikely posture of the body would suggest. The two, three, or four pencil lines brought together create the resonance of a Cézannesque volume. These contours, the falseness of the pose, and the elongated limbs evoke the nudes that, for lack of living models,[73] the master of Aix sometimes painted from photographs.[74]

But let us return to the photograph. Olga, resting on the edge of the chair, drapes her white arm across its back and holds a half-open, richly colored fan in her other hand. Her evening attire contrasts with the studio's disarray. The floor is strewn with rubbish, miscellaneous objects, and crumpled papers. On the wall, the painting *Nude with Raised Arms* of 1908 hangs beside still lifes in pencil, and a Cubist canvas leans on an easel. The model sports a brocade dress with a transparent yoke, silk stockings, and shoes trimmed with ribbons. She is adorned like an icon, her flesh seemingly set in the leafy design of the garment and tapestry. A living idol, she sits beside two Baga statues[75] placed on the ground. One frontal, the other in profile, they look like keepers of the code of figuration. Each of these heads is divided by a median line, a structure that seems to echo the rigorous symmetry of Olga's face and hairstyle. The setting also evokes the double photographic image of Clovis Sagot (p. 218), which, in 1909, had been the basis for one of Picasso's first "Cézannesque" Cubist portraits (p. 219, top).[76] Model for a painting, the

Olga Picasso in the studio at 22, avenue Victor-Hugo, Montrouge,
November 1917. Photograph by Picasso. Gelatin-silver print, 9¼ ×
6¾″ (23.5 × 16.4 cm). Musée Picasso, Paris, Picasso Archives

Olga Picasso. 1917. Lead pencil on paper, 10⅝ × 7¾″ (27 ×
19.5 cm). Zervos III, 82. Private collection

Studies. 1917. Lead pencil on paper, 15½ × 10⅝″ (39.3 × 27 cm).
Zervos III, 2. Private collection

Woman in an Armchair. 1917. Conté crayon on paper, 10¼ × 7½″
(26 × 19 cm). Zervos III, 3. Private collection

Clovis Sagot shown full-face, in Picasso's studio at the Bateau-Lavoir, 13, rue Ravignan, Paris, spring 1909. Photograph by Picasso. Modern print from the original glass negative, 4¾ × 3½" (12 × 9 cm). Musée Picasso, Paris, Picasso Archives

Clovis Sagot shown in profile, in Picasso's studio at the Bateau-Lavoir, 13, rue Ravignan, Paris, spring 1909. Photograph by Picasso. Modern print from the original glass negative, 4¾ × 3½" (12 × 9 cm). Musée Picasso, Paris, Picasso Archives

photograph of Olga with fetishes can equally be read as an allegory of the system of representation itself.

Using the image as a starting point, Picasso undertook to execute a life-size oil portrait of the young woman he was to marry the following year, and to do so in a deliberately "classical" manner, restituting the delicacy of her complexion and the shimmer of the materials (opposite, bottom left). The canvas is often interpreted as a symbol of his new "Ingresque" manner. There is, nevertheless, reason to emphasize that Picasso chose to leave it "unfinished"[77] and that the passage from photograph to painting, far from being a mere copy, follows an entirely dialectic course.[78] Picasso blocked out the background of the image and isolated the woman/chair entity revealed by the examination of the pose. This dual element is as if pasted onto the raw canvas, where the composition is limited to a few slashes or smears of paint. Similarly, whereas the chair in the photograph was trimmed with wide fringe, in the painting it is reduced to the tapestry alone, a simplification already effected by the studies in pencil.

Picasso frequently used this type of visual cutting in his treatment of photographic images.[79] Here the process emphasizes the subject's outline while fusing the elements into a new formal unity. This painting, classical in appearance, thus juxtaposes a flat, unperspectival background, literally designated as a piece of the canvas and

a motif that affirms itself as pattern. The almost punctilious description of the tapestry is spread, through proximity, to the fabric and pleats of Olga's dress, then to her face. The effect is similar to that of the fragment of wallpaper, canework, or fake wood decorating Picasso's *papiers collés,* where ironic, excessive imitation contributed a little more to the undoing of the codes of illusionism. Here, *trompe l'oeil*—pictorial facsimile—leads definitively to emptying the "likeness" attested to in the photograph. The painting scrupulously, stubbornly, transcodes what the lens has established: the delineation of contour, the system of chromatic equivalence, the arrangement of space. Whether they are transcribed exactly or somewhat "corrected" by the drawing, the distortions born of a monocular vision—such as the extreme foreshortening of the arm or the disproportion of the foregrounds—lose their own expressive value and lead to a flattened representation reduced to a single plane.

Furthermore, in the initial photograph, Olga's dark hair stands out against the still life hanging on the wall parallel to the oblique axis of her body. The pencil drawing of Olga emphasizes the imbrication of the oval of her head and the sheet of white paper. In the painting, the canvas, left untouched, against which the figure of the model detaches itself, seems the metonymic transposition of this framing device. Olga, the armchair, and the white rectangle reassume the places assigned by the photo-

Portrait of Clovis Sagot. 1909. Oil on canvas, 32¼ × 26″ (82 × 66 cm). Zervos II¹, 129. Daix 270. Hamburger Kunsthalle, Hamburg. (Colorplate, p. 254)

graph, but in a different hierarchy: the rectangle, the armchair, Olga. The rough sketch on paper is echoed on the canvas by the zigzag of a line of paint. One of the studies of Olga naked in the studio at Montrouge bears opposite it an anthropomorphic diagram. One could likewise read the canvas *Olga in an Armchair* as the collage of a figure—a woman pinned down like a butterfly—and of a monochromatic geometry—the expanse of the canvas.

In this case, the photograph is therefore neither a source nor a guarantee of the "truth" of the model or of its representation. Instead, it is used as a tool of subtle, formal dislocation. Gertrude Stein said of Picasso: "He analyzed his vision, he did not wish to paint the things that he himself did not see, the other painters satisfied themselves with the appearance, and always the appearance, which was not at all what they could see but what they knew was there."[80] Elsewhere she was to write: "A child sees the face of its mother . . . it knows one feature and not another, one side and not the other, and in his way Picasso knows faces as a child knows them and the head and the body."[81] These remarks apply to the upheaval of vision introduced by the Cubist experience. They could equally apply to the year 1917, when a new mode of representation was developed, marked by an

Olga in an Armchair. 1917. Oil on canvas, 51¼ × 34⅝″ (130 × 88 cm). Zervos III, 83. Musée Picasso, Paris. (Colorplate, p. 307)

Woman with a Fan (Fernande). 1908. Oil on canvas, 59⅞ × 39¾″ (152 × 101 cm). Zervos II¹, 67. Daix 168. The State Hermitage Museum, St. Petersburg. (Colorplate, p. 271)

ostensible return to tradition. For Picasso, at least, such a "neoacademicism" was intentionally ambiguous.

Of this portrait of Olga, Kenneth Silver wrote: "The brilliant incorporation of the unpainted ground which, with the pencil lines and slashes of gray-green paint on both sides, brackets the figure (literally making a quotation of the central form), establishes Picasso's distance from Ingres by way of Cézanne's unfinished canvases."[82] Similarly, if the photograph serves here as a "model," it is not only as a method of *mise-en-scène* or as a guide to illusionist perfection. Through the connection he establishes point by point between the print and the painting, Picasso attempted to introduce, into the very heart of pictorial effusion, automatism, technical distancing, the "inhuman" quality peculiar to the photographic gaze. As a consequence, the figure's formal elegance ultimately emerges to the detriment of its aura. No longer is there either the living presence of the model, of which the photograph preserves traces, or the complete pictorial illusion of what would have been a truly "Ingresque" painting. Rather, one should see this denatured painting as the didactic expression of a new pictorial conception in which the modern aesthetic borrows from the lessons of classicism, just as painting and photography interact.

One of the major canvases that marked the beginning of the Cubist revolution was *Woman with a Fan,* today in the Hermitage (p. 219). Though separated by a decade and despite stylistic disparities, this painting shares with *Olga in an Armchair* a structure in which the model's assymetrical pose stands out against a flat rectangle, its epicenter a half-opened fan.[83] In 1908 this object captured the eye as an inaugural sign, introducing the Cubist aesthetic.[84] It announced the decomposition of the visual pyramid into a multilayering of superimposed, semitransparent planes, sliding over one another, revealing and obscuring their subject beneath a variety of angles and focal distances. Like the fan, the space of painting was thus to become compressed by the rapid flattening of successive planes. At the end of the pictorial adventure of Cubism, a fan, the symbol of a folded and unfolded surface, will be, in the same way, the focal point of Olga's photograph and then of her painted portrait. This time, representation in a new form of antiperspective ambiguity makes use of a broad deployment of planes, like so many strips delicately brought edge to edge to form a single, unified surface.

In a final comparison of the print and the painting one notes that Picasso raised his angle of vision. He placed himself at a point of focal disequilibrium from which the eye lowers the fan to a plane almost parallel to that of the panel, while extending the motif of the tapestry and the garment. The resultant pattern effect definitively erases the temptation of volumetric rendering. While the canvas presents the appearance of Olga—she is undoubtedly identifiable: that is indeed her "head," her "face," her "body"—at the same time the work dissuades from any adhesion to her image. It is not a portrait: it is a *painting*.

"And here the essential question first appeared: did I *recognize* her ? . . . sometimes I recognized a region of her face, a certain relation of nose and forehead, the movement of her arms, her hands. I never recognized her except in fragments, which is to say that I missed her *being,* and that therefore I missed her altogether. It was not she, and yet it was no one else. I would have recognized her among thousands of other women, yet I did not 'find' her. I recognized her differentially, not essentially."[85]

NOTES

This essay was translated from the French by Jeanine Herman and Suzanne Cotter.

1. Gertrude Stein, *Picasso* (London: B. T. Batsford, 1938), pp. 13–14.

2. From 1994 the Musée Picasso in Paris organized a series of exhibitions devoted to Picasso's use of photography at various stages of his work. The first two of these exhibitions were *Picasso photographe, 1901–1916*, June 1–July 31, 1994, and *"A plus grande vitesse que les images . . ."*: *Picasso et la photographie*, October 4–December 31, 1995. Catalogues of these exhibitions are by Anne Baldassari and were published by the Réunion des musées nationaux.

3. Since 1839 the term *objectif* in French, used as a noun, has designated the optical system of the camera. It derives from the term *verre objectif*, which, starting in 1611, was applied to optical lenses in reference to the object observed.

4. Anne Baldassari, *Picasso photographe, 1901–1916* (Paris: Editions de la Réunion des musées nationaux, 1994), pp. 25–34.

5. Gertrude Stein was the first to point out the photographs of the countryside taken at Horta de Ebro in 1909 and the photographic compositions of objects dating from 1910–11. See Gertrude Stein, *The Autobiography of Alice B. Toklas* (New York: Harcourt, Brace and Company, 1933), pp. 110 and 135, and Stein, *Picasso*, pp. 8–9 and 18.

6. See Baldassari, *Picasso photographe*, pp. 213–43, and Anne Baldassari, *"A plus grande vitesse que les images . . ."*: *Picasso et la photographie* (Paris: Editions de la Réunion des musées nationaux, 1995), pp. 24–35.

7. The first photograms made by Picasso were the subject of Man Ray's essay "Picasso, photographe," *Cahiers d'art*, no. 6–7 (1937), p. 165: "A man comes and puts himself in the place of the eye, with all the risks this gesture involves. Haven't you ever seen a living camera?" ("Vient un homme qui se met à la place de l'oeil, avec tous les risques que ce geste comporte. N'avez-vous jamais vu une caméra vivante?")

8. In early 1997 the Musée Picasso in Paris will devote a third exhibition to this aspect of the relationship between Picasso and photography. During the artist's lifetime, and upon his instructions, Christian Zervos's catalogue identified several drawings of the 1917–20 period as having been based on photographs. Research conducted in the artist's archives has led to the rediscovery of most of the reference documents. These documents show that cases in which photography can be considered an image source prove much more numerous and varied than the examples most often cited. For example, in *The Painter and the Photograph, from Delacroix to Warhol* (Albuquerque: University of New Mexico Press, 1972), p. 64, Van Deren Coke pointed out only four cases of Picasso's works based on photographs, two of which are oils from 1923 depicting the artist's son, Paulo,

the first limited to the face (see p. 322), the second showing the child seated on a little donkey (see p. 323). A more in-depth study of the photography/painting relationship is offered by Carsten-Peter Warncke in the chapter "Kamera und Klassizismus, 1916–1924" in his book *Pablo Picasso 1881–1973* (Cologne: Benedikt Taschen Verlag, 1992), vol. 1, pp. 245–304.

9. These are Spanish terms meaning shadow/sun. They designate the two semicircles of tiers where audiences sit at bullfights. The letters SOL SOMB appear in the painting *Spanish Still Life*, Céret, spring 1912, oil on canvas, 18⅛ x 13 in. (46 x 33 cm); Zervos II, 301; Daix 476.

10. Probably cut out of a photograph taken by a street photographer, this portrait was rediscovered in an envelope bearing the words "Laurgraff, Fotografia Electrica Automatica, Calle Bailen (Bilbaina) Bilbao" and the number 766.

11. Hélène Seckel, *Max Jacob et Picasso* (Paris: Editions de la Réunion des musées nationaux, 1994), pp. 9–10. This letter was sent from Barcelona. The double page measures 8⅛ x 10¼ in. (20.5 x 26 cm).

12. Jaime Sabartés, *Picasso: An Intimate Portrait* (New York: Prentice-Hall, 1948), p. 87.

13. Baldassari, *Picasso photographe*, figs. 23 and 106 and pp. 43 and 143.

14. As a child, Picasso had shown remarkable skill in cutting out, with embroidery scissors, "little men" as well as "animals, flowers, strange garlands, and combinations of figures" ("bonshommes . . . animaux, fleurs, étranges guirlandes, combinaisons de figures"; Jaime Sabartés, *Picasso: Documents iconographiques* [Geneva: Pierre Cailler, 1954], p. 305).

15. John Richardson, *A Life of Picasso, Volume 1: 1881–1906* (New York: Random House, 1991), pp. 129–30, and Josep Palau i Fabre, *Picasso: The Early Years 1881–1907* (New York: Rizzoli, 1981), pp. 156–57.

16. Mariel Oberthür, *Le Chat Noir*, Musée d'Orsay (Paris: Editions de la Réunion des musées nationaux, 1992).

17. Pere Romeu, future manager of Els Quatre Gats, and Miquel Utrillo had frequented Le Chat Noir and had joined Léon-Charles Mârot's shadow-theater troupe, Les Ombres Parisiennes, which in 1893 was one of the attractions at the Chicago World's Fair.

18. Issue dated December 20, 1890.

19. Sabartés, *Picasso: An Intimate Portrait*, p. 63.

20. Palau i Fabre, *Picasso: The Early Years*, p. 184.

21. In addition to the profiles drawn at the end of the eighteenth century with the help of the physionotrace, one might also point out the experiments of J. A. C. Charles, who, as early as 1780, projected profiles on a screen by using a "solar megascope," and the experiments of Thomas Wedgwood, who attempted to use the photosensitive qualities of silver nitrate to the same ends.

22. Etienne de Silhouette was a controller of finances in France around 1757–59, whose austere policies made him particularly unpopular.

23. André Villers, *Photobiographie* (Belfort: Dôle, 1986), unpaginated.

24. These printing experiments with masks had as their basis a negative of a Photographic Composition of a Guitar Player, which represented a complex arrangement of works and objects in the studio on the boulevard Raspail. Cf. Baldassari, *Picasso photographe*, figs. 166, 167, 177, and 178, and pp. 229–43.

25. The reference is to seven states of an engraving (Baer, vol. 1, no. 40), executed on a half-tone plate, the basis of which was a photograph by Daniel-Henry Kahnweiler depicting the construction *Guitar and Bottle of Bass*, in its early stages. Picasso's work was reproduced in *Les Soirées de Paris* on November 15, 1913. Cf. Baldassari, *Picasso et la photographie*, figs. 9 and 12–23, and pp. 24–35.

26. This is notably the series Nude in the Studio of 1936–37 (Baer, vol. 3, pp. 103–05), engraved on a half-tone plate that has been used to print a photograph depicting the studio on rue La Boétie and published in *Cahiers d'art*, no. 7–10 (1935). Cf. Baldassari, *Picasso et la photographie*, figs. 32–35 and pp. 36–48.

27. Four of the rayographs then made were reproduced in *Cahiers d'art*, no. 5–6 (1937). Portrait of Dora Maar (p. 207), which was not published then, was executed during the same work session; it is currently in the Musée Picasso in Paris. The two photograms—one of Dora Maar, the other of a Woman in a Mantilla —were printed by contact from the same glass negative. Cf. Baldassari, *Picasso et la photographie*, figs. 42–46 and pp. 49–69.

28. "[Il] a étalé la peinture à l'huile en couche épaisse sur un verre et a dessiné avec une lame de canif dans la peinture pour obtenir les traits, procédé rappelant la gravure, et il a obtenu un négatif" (Dora Maar, unpublished letter of February 15, 1989, to Pierre Georgel, then director of the Musée Picasso, Paris).

29. Ibid.

30. Discovered by experiment in England as early as 1839 by the engravers Frederick James Havell and James Tibitt Willmore, the technique of *cliché-verre* was developed in France by Adalbert Cuvelier, who suggested its use to Jean-Baptiste Corot, to the Barbizon School painters, and to Eugène Delacroix. On this subject, see Adalbert Cuvelier, "Sur plusieurs méthodes de dessin héliographique," *Bulletin de la Société Française de Photographie* (Paris), 1856, pp. 23–24. Cf. also Elisabeth Glassman and Marilyn F. Symmes, *Cliché-Verre: Hand-Drawn, Light-Printed, A Survey of the Medium, from 1839 to the Present* (Detroit: The Detroit Institute of Arts, 1980), and Alain Paviot, *Corot, Delacroix, Millet, Rousseau, Daubigny: Le Cliché-Verre* (Paris: Paris Musées/Paris Audiovisuel, 1994).

31. The fabric used for the printing of the Portrait of Dora Maar is a checkered scarf bearing a regularly spaced pattern of an ace of spades.

32. Leon Battista Alberti, *On Painting* (London: Penguin Books, 1972), p. 65.

33. Cf. Sigmund Freud, *Beyond the Pleasure Principle* (1920), trans. James Strachey (London: Hogarth Press, 1971), p. 9. The author describes a game his own eighteen-month-old son plays, making a wooden spool with a string tied

around it disappear (Fort, "gone" in German) then reappear (Da, "there"). The way the child mimes the departure, then the return, of his mother can be understood as the first symbolic apprenticeship of the "reality principle."

34. Leo Steinberg, "Who Knows the Meaning of Ugliness?" (1972), reprinted in Gert Schiff, ed., *Picasso in Perspective* (Englewood Cliffs, N.J.: Prentice-Hall, 1976), pp. 137–39. Cf. Baldassari, *Picasso et la photographie*, pp. 113–14.

35. The myth of Dibutade's daughter drawing the shadow of her lover is told by Pliny the Elder in *Histoire naturelle de Pline*, trans. Ajasson de Grandsagne (Paris: C. L. F. Panckoucke, 1833), vol. 20, book 35, pp. 61 and 63.

36. Baldassari, *Picasso photographe*, figs. 57–58 and pp. 82–87.

37. Ibid.

38. Yvon Taillandier, "Les Profils proliférants," in *XXe siècle*, special issue, Paris, 1971, pp. 87–92.

39. Aaron Scharf has pointed out how Cubism's interpenetration of forms, transparent superimpositions, and ambiguity of spatial relations are indebted to chronophotography and to the practice of instantaneous photography. Cf. *Art and Photography* (New York: Penguin Books, 1994), pp. 268–71.

40. A part of these investigations was published under the title *Diurnes*, text by Jacques Prévert (Paris: Berggruen, 1962). On this experiment, cf. Baldassari, *Picasso et la photographie*, pp. 219–55.

41. This word should be understood in its technical sense as it applies to sculpture or intaglio engraving.

42. This is a painting by Manuel Pallarès dating from 1899.

43. The canvas dates from 1907.

44. On this subject, see William Rubin's analysis, "Picasso," in *"Primitivism" in 20th Century Art* (New York: The Museum of Modern Art, 1984), vol. 1, p. 310, as well as Baldassari, *Picasso photographe*, pp. 115–19.

45. Céret, summer 1911, oil on canvas, 51⅝ x 35¼ in. (131.2 x 89.5 cm); Zervos II¹, 285; Daix 423.

46. Céret, summer 1911, oil on canvas, 35¾ x 27⅞ in. (90.7 x 71 cm); Zervos II², 738; Daix 422.

47. Baldassari, *Picasso photographe*, pp. 123–25.

48. The Cubist painters' use of illusionist materials stemming from photography can be compared to that of the native described by Fernande Olivier in "Africans and Photography," in *Picasso and His Friends* (New York: Appleton-Century, 1965), p. 175. To do the portrait of a naval officer, he first drew "the head, the body, the legs and the arms, as he saw them, in the traditional style of tribal figures"; then, wishing to depict the uniform, "he saw no reason to put the buttons in their proper place. Instead, he surrounded the face with buttons! He did the same thing with the stripes, putting them at the side of the arms and over the head."

49. Gisèle Freund, *Photography and Society* (Boston: David R. Godine, 1980), p. 68.

50. The photograph is from the Antonin studio, 47, boulevard de Sébastopol, Paris.

51. The photograph is signed "Feulard, peintre et photographe." The corresponding draw-ing, from a private collection, is unpublished.

52. The photographic portrait of Napoléon III, Empress Eugénie, and the imperial prince is from the Levitzky studio, 22, rue de Choiseul, Paris.

53. Freund, *Photography and Society*, p. 61.

54. Roland Barthes, *Camera Lucida* (New York: Hill and Wang, 1981), p. 81.

55. These were popular engravings, generally with a political subject, painted with a stencil. On this subject, see the article by Meyer Schapiro, "Courbet and Popular Imagery: An Essay on Realism and Naïveté" (1941), reprinted in *Modern Art, 19th and 20th Centuries: Selected Papers* (New York: George Braziller, 1982), pp. 47–85.

56. See especially the canvas of 1914–15 *Still Life with Cards, Glass, and Bottle of Rum ("Vive la France")* (Avignon, summer 1914–Paris, 1915, oil and sand on canvas, 21¼ x 25⅝ in. [54 x 65 cm]; Zervos II², 523; D. B. 782); a drawing sent to Guillaume Apollinaire in a letter of December 22, 1914 (see p. 189), in Pierre Caizergues and Hélène Seckel, eds., *Picasso/Apollinaire, Correspondance* (Paris: Gallimard/Editions de la Réunion des musées nationaux, 1992), no. 98, pp. 122–24; a letter of December 31, 1914, sent to Apollinaire (pen, ink, and colored pencil, 10½ x 8⅜ in. [26.7 x 21.3 cm]; M. P. 1985–72); and a drawing sent to André Salmon in a letter of May 6, 1915 ("Vive la France," gouache, watercolor, and India ink, 6⅞ x 4⅜ in. [17.5 x 11.1 cm]; M. P. 1980–108). On these works and their political interpretation, cf. Kenneth E. Silver, *Esprit de Corps: The Art of the Parisian Avant-Garde and the First World War, 1914–1925* (Princeton, N.J.: Princeton University Press, 1989), pp. 36–39.

57. Fixed pastel and oil on canvas, 54¾ x 33⅝ in. (139.5 x 85.5 cm); Zervos XXX, 270; M. P. 73. Cf. Silver, *Esprit de Corps*, p. 287.

58. Louis-Napoléon Bonaparte, the nephew of Napoléon I, was elected president of the Republic by universal suffrage on December 10, 1848. He would proclaim himself emperor following the *coup d'état* of December 2, 1852, and would remain emperor until the military defeat of Sedan in September 1870. During the revolutionary days of February 1848, the poet Lamartine had helped to preserve the tricolor flag inherited from 1789, defeating the proposal of a red flag.

59. Paris, 1919–20, graphite and charcoal, 24 x 19⅜ in. (61 x 49.3 cm); Zervos III, 413; M. P. 913.

60. Barthes, *Camera Lucida*, p. 14.

61. In the semiology of Charles S. Peirce, the index is a sign that refers to the object it denotes by a relation of physical connection. The author suggested that photographs, luminous imprints of their objects, come under this category, at least when they have been "produced under such circumstances that they were physically forced to correspond point by point to nature" (Justus Buchler, ed., *Philosophical Writings of Peirce* [New York: Dover Publications, 1955], p. 106). Cf. on an application to the analysis of photography and certain aspects of contemporary art, Rosalind E. Krauss, "Notes on the Index," in *The Originality of the Avant-Garde and Other Modernist Myths* (Cambridge, Mass.: MIT Press, 1985), pp. 196–219.

62. Barthes, *Camera Lucida*, pp. 80–81.

63. Ibid., p. 13.

64. This effect is strangely similar to the one produced by a collage by Francis Picabia (*Portrait of Max Goth*, 1917; reproduced in the first issue of the review *391*, February 1, 1917). Combining a line drawing and a cutout face in a photographic portrait, this collage, which Picabia called a "kodak," was an explicit parody of the "classical" manner adopted two years earlier by Picasso in his *Portrait of Max Jacob* (see p. 299), which was published on the first page of *L'Elan*, no. 10 (December 1, 1916).

65. Aaron Scharf, following Van Deren Coke, has compared the disproportions characteristic of some of Picasso's paintings from the 1920s with the distortion to which photographic perspective in amateur photographs subjects body parts in the foreground. Cf. *Art and Photography*, pp. 272–73. Scharf (p. 369, n. 63) takes up the analysis already developed by Alfred H. Barr, Jr.: "The grotesque foreshortening of the running figure in the background of *By the Sea* suggests the snapshots of reclining picnickers whose feet are comically magnified by the camera" (*Picasso: Fifty Years of His Art* [New York: The Museum of Modern Art, 1946], p. 130).

66. Freund, *Photography and Society*, p. 64.

67. Ibid.

68. "I see my hand spread out on the table. It lives—it is me. It opens, the fingers open and point. It is lying on its back. It shows me its fat belly. It looks like an animal turned upside down. The fingers are the paws. I amuse myself by moving them very rapidly, like the claws of a crab which has fallen on its back . . . It becomes intolerable . . . I draw back my hand and put it in my pocket; but immediately I feel the warmth of my thigh through the stuff. I pull my hand out of my pocket and let it hang against the back of the chair. Now I feel a weight at the end of my arm. It pulls a little, softly, insinuatingly it exists. I don't insist: no matter where I put it, it will go on existing; I can't suppress it" (Jean-Paul Sartre, *Nausea* [New York: New Directions, 1964], pp. 98–99).

69. One character's "speciality was breaking down individuals into their constituent parts, with the aid of calculation": "The master of analysis said with intense mental concentration: 'Fingers, the five fingers of each hand.' Mrs. Philifor's resistance, unfortunately, was insufficient to conceal a reality which disclosed itself to the eyes of those present in all its stark nakedness, i.e. the five fingers of each of her two hands. There they were, five on each side. Mrs. Philifor, utterly profaned, gathered her last strength to try to put on her gloves" (Witold Gombrowicz, *Ferdydurke* [New York: Penguin Books, 1986], pp. 88 and 90).

70. As Kenneth Silver suggests, Picasso's position as foreigner and noncombatant in a city filled with uniformed soldiers could not have been without its difficulties (*Esprit de Corps*, p. 5).

71. A drawing depicting the same chair (p. 15R in Carnet 7, December 1919–February 1920, M. P. 1990–1999; *Picasso: Une nouvelle dation* [Paris: Editions de la Réunion des musées

nationaux, 1990], p. 199) confirms that, in the portrait of 1917, Olga is seated on the far edge of the narrow, low, armless chair embroidered with tapestry. The environment of this drawing is that of the studio on rue La Boétie, where Picasso and Olga moved at the end of 1918.

72. A vast, padded sofa, a low, armless, tapestry-covered chair, and a fringed pedestal table play a comparable role to that of this chair—that of graphic signs and anthropomorphic equivalents—in the series of portraits, self-portraits, or still lifes made in 1910–11 in the studio on the boulevard de Clichy. Cf. Baldassari, *Picasso photographe*, pp. 112–39.

73. Cf. Gustave Coquiot, *Paul Cézanne* (Paris: Librairie Ollendorff, n. d.), pp. 219–20.

74. The Museum of Modern Art in New York has a photograph that served as a point of departure for Cézanne's painting *The Bather* (1885–90). Cf. Coke, *The Painter and the Photograph*, pp. 82–83.

75. According to William Rubin, Picasso had already acquired these statues, originating from Guinea, by 1907. The author connects them in particular with two drawings titled *Head* (one frontal, one in profile), which are representative of the "primitive" style of this same year. See Rubin, "Picasso," in *"Primitivism" in 20th Century Art*, vol. 1, pp. 275–80.

76. Baldassari, *Picasso photographe*, pp. 98–103.

77. According to Carsten-Peter Warncke, this "incompletion" is related to the difficulty of continuing to transcribe the photograph's visual material without submerging the portrait "in a conglomeration of forms" (*Pablo Picasso 1881–1973*, vol. 1, pp. 288–89).

78. The portrait of Olga that ends the Cubist period echoes one of the last portraits Picasso painted in a traditional manner—that of Benedetta Canals, dating from 1905—before embarking on the research that would lead to *Les Demoiselles d'Avignon*. Cf. Baldassari, *Picasso photographe*, fig. 26, p. 51. As we have already noted, it is significant that this last portrait was also quite likely painted from a photograph. Separated by more than ten years, the two paintings reveal a similar treatment of the background, scarcely painted or left untouched, a similar outline of the model against the background, and a comparable pattern motif.

79. An example of this, dating back to 1903, is offered by *The Soler Family*. We know now that this painting was inspired by a studio photograph from which the painter chose to eliminate the conventional decor of rustic furniture and potted palms. Cf. Baldassari, *Picasso photographe*, figs. 5 and 6, and pp. 17–18.

80. Stein, *Picasso*, p. 19.

81. Ibid., pp. 14–15.

82. Silver, *Esprit de Corps*, p. 143.

83. Another canvas, dating from the Rose period (*Woman with a Fan*, Paris, 1905, 39 x 32 in. [99 x 81.3 cm]; Zervos I, 308; Daix XIII, 14), already showed a woman holding an upside-down fan in front of her; the model appears in profile, her right arm raised. Cf., on this painting, Meyer Schapiro, "Picasso's *Woman with a Fan*: On Transformation and Self-Transformation" (1976), reprinted in *Modern Art: 19th and 20th Centuries*, pp. 111–20.

84. The fan is a recurring motif during the years 1909–10. Cf., in particular, *The Fan*, Paris, fall 1909, oil on canvas, 12 x 26 in. (30.5 x 66 cm); Zervos II, 229; Daix 168; and *Woman with a Fan*, Cadaqués, summer 1910 (completed in 1918), 72⅞ x 28½ in. (185 x 72.5 cm); Zervos II, 944; Daix 364.

85. Barthes, *Camera Lucida*, pp. 65–66.

Pedro Mañach. 1901. Oil on canvas, 41½ × 27½″ (100.5 × 67 cm). Zervos VI, 1495. D.B. V, 4. National Gallery of Art, Washington, D.C. Chester Dale Collection

To Fall "Like a Fly Into the Trap of Picasso's Stare": Portraiture in the Early Work

MARILYN McCULLY

Picasso's lifelong ability to dramatize, enhance, and manipulate the identities of his sitters and models—many of them members of his most intimate circle—distinguishes his approach to portraiture from that of any other twentieth-century artist. From the very earliest period of his artistic apprenticeship, his personal response to his models (whether they actually sat for him or not) was always reflected in the final work.

Many later developments in Picasso's oeuvre have their roots in his formative years. A principal feature of the artist's working method was his obsessive practice of drawing. This can be traced back to his childhood habit of sketching everyone and everything around him. The technical virtuosity he quickly but painstakingly mastered, and his incisive observation of every physical or emotional detail in the people he portrayed, allowed him to invent and elaborate a whole repertory of approaches to the figure, approaches which he transformed into a personal and exceptionally wide-ranging artistic language. This practice carried through to Picasso's very last paintings and drawings—the portraits he painted of his second wife, Jacqueline, and the elaborate suites of theatrical prints and drawings in which he employed a cast of characters taken from history, drama, and fiction as well as from his own life.

What always comes as something of a surprise in Picasso is that for all his experimentation in form,

medium, and technique, he remained, in certain respects, a traditional painter. He took his subjects from life and memory—they were never "abstract"—and he preferred to work within the most basic given categories of art-historical tradition: still life, landscape, and, principally, the figure. While he was stimulated by the work of contemporary artists, he also responded to older masters, including El Greco, Velázquez, Ribera, and Goya, whose work he encountered as a student. The portraits of his early period (1895–1905) bear this out. In addition to painting conventional portraits (some of which were commissioned and purchased by the sitters), he used recognizable models for other types of figure painting, including genre subjects. He also made character sketches for publication in literary and art magazines. Once he left his native country for France, he embarked on his lifelong preoccupation with painting the female nude. Even Picasso's nudes are hardly ever done from anonymous models; they turn out to be portraits of the women in his life.

As an art student in La Coruña (1891–95), Picasso attended drawing classes, where he worked more often from casts than from life;[1] outside the classroom he painted and drew his family and himself and also worked from other models, which were arranged for him by his father. Picasso's father, don José Ruiz Blasco, a modest and unsuccessful painter principally of pigeons, was his son's first art master. Don José fervently hoped that the young Pablo would win the prestige he himself had failed

The Artist's Father (José Ruiz Blasco). 1895–96. Pen and ink and aquatint on paper, 6½ × 5⅞″ (16.5 × 15 cm). Zervos XXI, 39. Museu Picasso, Barcelona

José Ruiz Blasco, Picasso's father (detail). Málaga, 1870. Photographer unknown. Musée Picasso, Paris, Documents section. Gift of Sir Roland Penrose

José Ruiz Blasco. c. 1900. Photographer unknown

The Artist's Father (José Ruiz Blasco). 1895. Oil on canvas, 20½ × 12⅝″ (52 × 32 cm). Zervos XXI, 32. Private collection

to achieve as an academic artist, and, for this reason, he set up a rigorous program for his son's preparation. In addition to teaching him drawing at the art school, don José instructed him at home by giving him his first lessons in oils. He taught him to employ a generally monochromatic palette—so typical of Spanish painting—and to emphasize the sculptural aspects of forms by setting them against shallow, tapestry-like space.

Don José was himself a patient and willing model, and Picasso drew and painted him over and over again, beginning in La Coruña and continuing until the end of the 1890s in Barcelona (above). The image of him that emerges from his son's work is that of a man of elegance and distinction rather than a disappointed, failed artist (p. 228). Don José had been known among his friends in Málaga as "the Englishman" because he was tall, slim, and fair—so

different from the shorter and darker Andalusian looks of his wife and son—and that is how Picasso preferred to portray him. As don José grew older, his reputation as a man about town had been hard to maintain, especially since he had had to take a job away from his hometown and rely upon the meager resources of an art teacher, his own painting having become a sideline. This defeated spirit is reflected in a number of Picasso's drawings, in which an air of melancholy pervades the most intimate portrayals (opposite). Some seventy years later, at the end of his life, Picasso "corrected" his own family history, elevating his father's status as a small-time Spanish art teacher to that of a modern master by presenting him in the guise of Degas. In certain late prints (p. 228), a tall, bearded, and fine-featured don José/Degas can be seen peering from the margins of compositions as a voyeur watching

Don José with an Umbrella. 1898. Charcoal on paper, 23⅝ × 18⅛″ (60 × 46 cm). Zervos XXI, 86. Private collection

the exchanges in a brothel. These prints were inspired by Degas monotypes that Picasso himself had begun to collect.

Picasso's sister Lola served as his other principal model up to the time of his first visit to Paris in late 1900. The fact that he drew and painted her so often allowed him to experiment with his approach to the female figure, in this case always clothed. (The models at art school were generally male, and it was not until he reached Paris that he had ready access to female nude models.) Lola sometimes appears as a distant and enigmatic young girl with her doll, sometimes as a typically Andalusian *maja*. Other portraits of her reflect Picasso's response to the contemporary Catalan *modernista* movement: in some paintings she appears in diaphanous whites, while in others she is seated in the vague light of Symbolist-inspired *modernista* interiors. His personal adaptation of a fashionable, *fin-de-siècle* graphic style also gives Lola an air of modern sophistication in his portraits of her (opposite and p. 231). Picasso painted his mother less, no doubt because she was too busy to pose, unlike her daughter or husband. Nevertheless, the portrait of her done in Barcelona in 1896 is an affectionate and convincing likeness (p. 233). While the use of pastels allows him to focus on subtle textures— especially in the areas of the white blouse and warm skin tones and in the glowing quality of the light—there is no attempt to embellish or enhance his mother's features.

The Bordello. May 16, 1971. Drypoint, 14⁹⁄₁₆ × 19¹¹⁄₁₆″ (37 × 50 cm). Galerie Louise Leiris, Paris

Portrait of a Young Woman (Lola?). 1901. Oil on panel, 14 × 8¾″ (35.6 × 22.4 cm).
Zervos XXI, 230. D.B. V, 56. Private collection

From an early age Picasso was well aware of the rich portrait tradition that existed in Spanish art from the seventeenth century onward. His father had first taken him to the Prado on a visit in 1895, and the boy's response to his artistic forebears—among them Velázquez (p. 252) and Goya—played an important role in the earliest of his portraits, just as some of the same painters would represent an artistic challenge to him in his later years. Picasso's remarkably mature portrait of his Aunt Pepa (p. 235), painted in Málaga in the summer of 1896, combines the somber palette of traditional Spanish art, especially that associated with religious portraiture, with a typically late-nineteenth-century bravura manner of painting. Picasso's

cantankerous maiden aunt apparently was at first reluctant to sit for the fourteen-year-old boy, and he was equally reluctant to carry out the commission.[2] Nevertheless, a photograph shows that Picasso achieved a high degree of resemblance (p. 235). That the young artist allowed her face—modeled in paint almost as if it were clay—to emerge into light from the dark background and from the surrounds of her black lace cap and cloak results in an intensity that reveals the stern character of his pious old aunt.

A further influence on Picasso was the particular brand of Spanish realism, that, in the hands of Zurbarán, Velázquez, or Ribera, could infuse everyday objects or the

Picasso and his sister, Lola (Maria de los Dolores). Málaga, 1888. Photographer unknown. Musée Picasso, Paris, Picasso Archives

Lola Ruiz Picasso, Picasso's sister (detail). Barcelona, c. 1906–09. Photograph by Picasso. Musée Picasso, Paris, Picasso Archives

commonest of models with loftier intellectual or religious ideas and meanings. In this way Velázquez's *Aesop*— evidently a portrait of a real person—is transformed into a "beggar-philosopher" (p. 253). Picasso draws on this genre in *Beggar in a Cap* (p. 253), a painting which had a special significance for the artist, who kept the canvas in his studio until the end of his life. This work was first exhibited when Picasso was only thirteen (March 1895), in the windows of a shop on calle Real, a fashionable commercial street in La Coruña.[3] Local critics singled out the "young Ruiz Blasco" for his impressive handling of paint and truthful recording, particularly in the portrait of "a well known beggar in La Coruña," as one of them pointed out.[4]

Throughout his life, Picasso would return to Spanish art and literature for inspiration. His Blue period portrait, later known as *Celestina* (p. 243), is based on the principal character of one of the most celebrated works of Spanish fiction, Fernando de Rojas's novel *La Tragicomédia de Calisto y Melibea,* first published in 1499. While acknowledging the character in the earlier work, Picasso used a contemporary sitter, Carlota Valdivia, whose name and address he wrote on the stretcher; he later confirmed that she was, in fact, a procuress in Barcelona. Sketches show her both modeling for the artist (p. 242) and also lurking in the shadows of a café, presumably looking for prospective customers.[5] Drawings confirm that Valdivia was blind in one eye (p. 242), and this aspect of her face also quite dramatically evokes the scarred face of the legendary go-between. Comparison of the painting with the sketch shows that Picasso certainly improved, if not ennobled, his model's real appearance: the scruffy, tanned, and thin face of a gypsy is turned into that of a strong-featured, smooth-complexioned *grande dame* with "an air of timeless dignity, more in keeping with a seventeenth-century prioress than a twentieth-century procuress."[6] Rojas's Celestina was a traditional subject in Spanish painting, and she appears in the work of Murillo and Goya (Picasso had actually copied a print by Goya of this subject in the Prado in 1898). When she reappears in Picasso's late work, notably in the *Suite 347* (1968), her role is to arrange the sexual encounters of the artist's voyeuristic imagination.

Portrait of the Artist's Sister, Lola. 1900. Charcoal and colored pencil on paper, 17⅜ × 11½″ (44 × 29 cm). Zervos I, 29. D.B. I, 14. Museu Picasso, Barcelona

Maria Picasso López, Picasso's mother (detail). Barcelona, c. 1900 or 1910. Photographer unknown. Musée Picasso, Paris, Documents section

Portrait of the Artist's Mother in Profile. June 9, 1896. Watercolor, pen, and pencil on paper, 7⅛ × 4⅞″ (18 × 12.5 cm). Not in Zervos. Museu Picasso, Barcelona

Portrait of the Artist's Mother. April 22, 1896. Watercolor and pencil on paper, 7⅛ × 4⅞″ (18 × 12.5 cm). Not in Zervos. Museu Picasso, Barcelona

MARILYN McCULLY

The Artist's Mother (María Picasso López). 1896. Pastel on paper, 19⅝ × 15⅜″ (49.8 × 39 cm). Zervos XIII, 40. Museu Picasso, Barcelona

This same process of transforming portraits of specific people into subjects taken from literature as well as art is found in Picasso's Rose period painting *Boy with a Pipe* (p. 250), which began as a study of a Montmartre youth, probably something of a delinquent, who was known affectionately in Picasso's circle as "P'tit Louis."[7] The artist set the unfinished canvas aside and only returned to it several weeks later, after an evening of conversation about poetry with his writer friends. Back in his studio he painted a wreath of flowers on the boy's head and added the poetic counterpoint of Redon-like patterns on the wallpaper behind, so as to transform the young artisan into a dreamy character of Symbolist inspiration, who seems to come from the pages of Verlaine.

Alongside these portraits in which the subject has become more important than the sitter, Picasso had also been painting conventional portraits. These were usually commissions or done as favors. The first of them was a portrait of the prominent physician and politician Ramón Pérez Costales (p. 234). This is another La Coruña work Picasso never parted with.[8] The doctor, who was a close friend of Picasso's father, was the young artist's first real patron. Picasso later recalled that it was don Ramón and not his father who had backed and supported his first individual exhibition in La Coruña in February 1895.[9] Picasso was only thirteen when he painted Pérez Costales, but a comparison with portraits of the doctor by local artists shows that the boy was already capable of accomplishing more than just a good physical likeness.[10] Picasso's direct and confident treatment of the face conveys the forceful personality of the celebrated liberal politician. The painting of Pérez Costales initiated a series of portraits of

Portrait of Ramón Pérez Costales. 1895. Oil on canvas, 20½ × 14½″ (52 × 37 cm). Zervos XXI, 36. Private collection

The Artist's Aunt Pepa. 1896. Oil on canvas, 22⅝ × 19⅞″ (57.5 × 50.5 cm). Zervos XXI, 38. Museu Picasso, Barcelona

Josefa Ruiz Blasco, Picasso's Aunt Pepa (detail). Málaga, c. 1870. Photographer unknown. Collection Ricardo Huelin

patrons and supporters, who included the Barcelona tailor Soler, the critic Gustave Coquiot, and later the writer Gertrude Stein and others. Likewise, the 1901 posterlike painting of the Catalan Pedro Mañach (p. 224), Picasso's first art dealer, can be seen as the earliest of a series of dealer portraits; it looks ahead to the Cubist portraits of Wilhelm Uhde, Ambroise Vollard, and Daniel-Henry Kahnweiler.

At this period Picasso was willing to undertake portraits commissioned by friends, such as his Blue period *Portrait of Sebastià Junyer Vidal,*[11] a comrade from Barcelona who with his brother Carles promoted Picasso in the press; that of the opera singer Suzanne Bloch; and the striking portrait of Benedetta Canals (p. 249). Benedetta, a professional model and the wife of another painter-friend of Picasso's, was also one of Degas's models. Indeed, there is in the character and handling of paint in

Casagemas in His Coffin. 1901. Oil on wood panel, 28½ × 22⅞″ (72.5 × 58 cm). Zervos XXI, 179. D.B. VI, 6. Private collection

Carles Casagemas. 1900. Pen and ink and watercolor on paper, 4⅛ × 3⅛″ (10.5 × 7.9 cm). Zervos XXI, 116. The Metropolitan Museum of Art, New York. Gift of Raymonde Paul, in memory of her brother, C. Michael Paul, 1982

Portrait of the Dead Casagemas. 1901. Oil on cardboard, 20½ × 13⅜″ (52 × 34 cm). Zervos XXI, 177. D.B. A.6. Private collection

The Death of Casagemas. 1901. Oil on wood, 10⅝ × 13¾″ (27 × 35 cm). Zervos XXI, 178. D.B. VI, 5. Musée Picasso, Paris

this portrait a flavor of Degas that inflects its Spanish traditionalism. What is particularly noteworthy in all of these paintings is the way in which Picasso combines the conventional demands of portraiture with his artistic language of the moment, so that he enhances his sitters' appearance and at the same time identifies them with his overall artistic concerns.

Picasso used a very different style and technique for the character sketches he did for publication or advertisement. Editors of artistic and literary journals that proliferated in turn-of-the-century Barcelona illustrated their articles with portrait drawings or photographs of the artists, intellectuals, and politicians of the progressive Catalan cultural movement who were featured in their pages. The most celebrated drawings were those by Ramon Casas that appeared in the journals *Quatre Gats* and *Pèl & Ploma*. Casas was one of the older generation of Barcelona artists who had been to Paris in the 1890s, and he enjoyed great success as a graphic artist, especially of posters. His stylish drawings, such as the portrait of the

art dealer J. B. Parés (p. 252), were excellent likenesses and followed a fairly standard formula: Casas set his subject, generally standing or seated, against the empty space of the white paper; the drawings were done in charcoal, with the occasional addition of watercolor, touches of pastel, or powdered pigments. When, in 1899, Casas exhibited more than 130 of these portraits of well-known Catalans at the Sala Parés, Barcelona's leading gallery, he provoked a challenge among the younger generation of artists. They urged Picasso to show a group of portraits at the tavern Els Quatre Gats: "Out of a spirit of rebellion, of defiance, as well as out of a desire, perhaps, to cause a commotion, we planned an exhibition of [Picasso's] portraits. Did not Ramon Casas have one-man exhibitions of his portraits? We knew, of course, that to Casas every door was open; that everyone bowed down before him; . . . If Casas had a monopoly of the distinguished people of the city, Picasso could attend to the rejects: us, for example."[12]

Picasso worked with fury, drawing everyone who appeared at the tavern and many more in the studio on riera de Sant Joan, which he shared with the melancholy

Portrait of Jaime Sabartés, Seated. 1900. Watercolor and charcoal on paper, 19⅞ × 13″
(50.5 × 33 cm). Zervos VI, 247. D.B. I, 5. Museu Picasso, Barcelona

Carles Casagemas. In general he drew the portraits from the model but invented backgrounds, often to complement the sitter's occupation or avocation. His seated *Portrait of Jaime Sabartés*—undoubtedly done in the studio—is set against a distant landscape. Working principally in charcoal, Picasso also experimented with color and employed various mediums, such as oil washes and even coffee in his *Portrait of Joan Vidal Ventosa* (p. 240). "Before long his studio was crammed with portraits," Sabartés wrote, "If he found no room for them on the table, he affixed them to the wall with one drawing-pin if he could not find two. At any rate, rather that way than on the floor."[13]

For the Quatre Gats exhibition, which opened in February 1900, Picasso tacked up more than one hundred unframed drawings (reports vary as to the exact number)

onto the tavern wall, one row above another. Although the "grand public" reportedly did not come, the show did attract reviews, some of which noted the rivalry with Casas.[14] In comparison to a certain sameness in Casas's portraits, Picasso's drawings have a far greater impact. In each case he arrives at a vivid and succinct characterization. His ability so early in his professional career to draw out the distinguishing features of each individual in this assembly of pipe-smoking bohemians was astonishing, but he had no intention of limiting himself to journalism. After he had settled in France, he turned down opportunities to work regularly as a graphic artist so as not to be distracted from his career as a painter. Nevertheless, Picasso retained a graphic style of portraiture in his repertoire, which he used for drawings of public figures, from Sergei Diaghilev, Igor Stravinsky, and the

Portrait of Jaime Sabartés. 1901. Oil on canvas, 32¼ × 26″ (82 × 66 cm). Zervos I, 97. D.B. VI, 19. Pushkin State Museum of Fine Arts, Moscow fashionable world he met in the early years of his marriage to Olga Khokhlova, to writers who wanted frontispieces for their books.

In Picasso's most unconventional portraits, he allowed free rein to the processes of dramatization and manipulation, while still retaining the identity of the model. In February 1901 Picasso's great friend Casagemas committed suicide, and he responded by painting three death's-heads some six months later. Picasso had not been present at the event, but friends who were there would have reported such gruesome details as the fact that the fatal bullet had entered the skull above the right temple. Nonetheless, both the physical features and the psychological state of his companion were well known to the artist, for they had spent almost every day in each other's company the previous year. Thus Picasso's images of the ill-fated Casagemas, while close to his friend's actual appearance (comparison can be made with a Quatre Gats

Jaime Sabartés. [Barcelona, 1904]. Photographer unknown. Musée Picasso, Paris, Picasso Archives

Portrait of Joan Vidal Ventosa. 1900. Charcoal and watercolor mixed with coffee on paper, 18¾ × 10⅞″ (47.6 × 27.6 cm). Zervos VI, 252. Museu Picasso, Barcelona

character sketch, p. 236), draw emotional strength from the way in which they are painted and to some extent distorted. Picasso turned to a non-Spanish source, in this case van Gogh, who also had shot himself, for the palette of the smallest of the three paintings (p. 237). The use of complementary colors to heighten the sense of Picasso's horror at his friend's violent death intensifies the contrast between the heat-ray-like strokes of paint emanating from the candle and the greenish face of the dead man. The closeup view of the head, emphasized by the small scale of the canvas and the device of cutting the head off from the body by the thickly painted, diagonal, yellowish-white lines of the shroud, eerily turns this moving portrait of his friend into a modern-day head of Saint John the Baptist.

In the second of these *memento mori* (p. 236), the dead man is painted disturbingly in the familiar upright portrait format. A heavy impasto of strokes of white paint beneath the head suggests a shirt rather than a shroud, while the purplish-red of the bullet wound seems to penetrate the canvas just as it had Casagemas's head. The third and largest painting shows Casagemas in his coffin and is dominated by an icy blue (p. 236).

His friend's suicide left a deep impression on Picasso,

Portrait of Jaime Sabartés. 1904. Oil on canvas, 19½ × 15″ (49.5 × 38.1 cm). Zervos VI, 653. D.B. X, 11. Berggruen Collection

Picasso Painting Carlota Valdivia. 1904. Conté pencil and colored pencil on paper. Zervos XXII, 56. Private collection

Study of Carlota Valdivia (Celestina). 1903. Colored pencil on paper, 10⅝ × 9¼″ (27 × 23.5 cm). Zervos I, 191. D.B. IX, 25. Private collection, Geneva

who later claimed that contemplating the event had triggered his Blue period. He even went so far as to merge the dead Casagemas's profile with that of his poet-friend Jaime Sabartés (who liked to see himself as "the progenitor of Blue period blueness"[15]) in the *Portrait of Jaime Sabartés,* which was done in Paris in 1901 (p. 239). Sabartés has left a description of how this painting came about. He was sitting alone and bored at the Café La Lorraine when Picasso appeared with their friends. "Unwittingly, I was serving as the model for a picture, a portrait about which I retain two distinct memories: the memory of my unpremeditated pose, in the café, . . . (when thinking I was alone, I fell like a fly into the trap of Picasso's stare), and the other is the impression I received a few days later in [his studio]. . . . When Picasso put it up on the easel, I was astonished to see myself . . . [and] the spectre of my solitude"[16]—as Picasso saw it.

This portrait is distinguished, as Sabartés noted, not only for its blue tonality but also for its sobriety and the use of an enclosing line, which in its simplicity fixes an idea: the artist's compassion upon surprising his friend in his solitude.[17] The center of the painting is occupied by the tankard of beer, the surface of which is animated with brushwork, and the three fingers of the hand positioned stiffly in front of it, as if in a symbolic gesture. This placement has the effect of distancing the figure

psychologically from his surroundings rather than emphasizing the café setting; in this way Picasso conveys a sense of Sabartés's perceived alienation. It is precisely this process—finding expressive means of distortion, color, and evocative line to convey an emotional state—which departs from, and ultimately transcends, conventional portraiture. It is a process that the artist used again and again, most notably in his great portraits of Marie-Thérèse Walter and Dora Maar in the 1930s.

The last of the early oil portraits Picasso did in Barcelona of his friend Sabartés, just before the young writer departed for South America (where he remained until he rejoined Picasso as his secretary in the late 1930s), is typical of the end of the Blue period (p. 241). The palette dominates everything from space and form to the spirit of the work. According to Sabartés, the moody atmosphere of this portrait was a reflection of the artist's state of mind rather than the sitter's. Evidently Picasso was in a particularly bad mood when he suggested painting Sabartés: "Suddenly, as if it were fated that only his ill humour or mine would stimulate him to do my portrait, he began to observe me from different angles. He took a piece of canvas, put it on the easel and got ready to paint. . . . I was standing motionless at a certain distance from his easel. His eyes went from the canvas to me and from me to the canvas; when it was

Portrait of Carlota Valdivia (later called *Celestina*). 1903. Oil on canvas, 31⅞ × 23⅝″ (81 × 60 cm). Zervos I, 183. D.B. IX, 26. Musée Picasso, Paris

Portrait of Madeleine. 1904. Pastel and gouache on cardboard, 26⅜ × 20¼″ (67 × 51.5 cm). Zervos XXII, 74. Musée Picasso, Paris

Madeleine. 1905. Pencil and charcoal on canvas, 39⅜ × 32⅛″ (100 × 81.5 cm). Not in Zervos. Musée Picasso, Paris

covered he addressed me again: 'Say something, man! There's no reason for keeping so quiet. Anybody would think you were in a bad mood.' After saying this he put away his brushes, because by now he felt relieved."[18] The work was finished later without Sabartés there, possibly using a photograph as an *aide-mémoire* (p. 240).

This story reveals how Picasso managed to rid himself of his negative state of mind by transferring his feelings to his sitter, in this case to the "blue" mood of the painting. The artist would frequently bring to the surface and dramatize psychological tensions that he himself felt, as well as those he observed or even stimulated in his sitters. This is especially evident when he portrayed those closest to him.

By far the largest proportion of Picasso's work has to do with the women in his life, and even still lifes, landscapes, and mythological subjects turn out to be portraits. Portraiture enabled Picasso to manipulate the images of these women and to exploit their innermost feelings through formal and technical experimentation. The greatest portraits of a woman during the early period are certainly those of Fernande Olivier, beginning in 1906

(pp. 257, 259); but there were others who preceded her and who can be identified in the artist's work.

After Picasso settled in Paris in 1904, one of his first girl friends was a model called Madeleine (above), about whom we know little except her name. Her thin body and delicate "birdlike" features[19] were the inspiration for a number of paintings and works on paper or board done in the winter of 1904–05, such as *Woman with Helmet of Hair* (opposite) and *Woman in a Chemise* (p. 246). The function of these paintings was not so much to probe Madeleine's likeness and personality as it was to provide a vehicle for artistic experimentation—as in the exquisite layering of gouache in the essentially monochromatic *Woman with Helmet of Hair,* or the transition from a blue to a pink tonality in *Woman in a Chemise.*

The female nude in Picasso's work is almost always inspired by the presence of a specific woman. The *Seated Nude* of 1905 (p. 247) is clearly based on Madeleine, but here again the artist's predominant concern is pictorial rather than narrative. The whole composition matters more to him than the individual character of the sitter or her relationship to the painter. The highlights on her face and upper body are echoed by the light touching the long, thin fingers of the hand resting on her leg. This use of

Woman with Helmet of Hair (Madeleine). 1904. Gouache on illustration board, 16⅜ × 11¾″ (41.6 × 29.9 cm). Zervos I, 233. D.B. XI, 7. The Art Institute of Chicago. Bequest of Kate L. Brewster

Woman in a Chemise (Madeleine). 1905. Oil on canvas, 28⅝ × 23⅝″ (72.7 × 60 cm). Zervos I, 307. D.B. XII, 5. Tate Gallery, London

light serves to accentuate the way in which the other hand and the rest of the figure dissolve into the red background and the area beneath her.

The last of these early works in the Museum's exhibition, the portrait of a Dutch girl (p. 251), done in the summer of 1905, looks ahead to the monumentality of the next few years. Although the identity of the model is not known for certain, she was likely Diewertje de Geus, the unmarried daughter of the postman at Schoorl, where Picasso spent several weeks painting in an attic above the room he had rented from her in a small bargeman's pension alongside the canal. The artist had convinced the young woman to pose naked for him, which apparently scandalized the local residents of this tiny village. By

Seated Nude (Madeleine). 1905. Oil on cardboard, 41¾ × 30″ (106 × 76 cm). Zervos I, 257. D.B. XII, 3. Musée National d'Art Moderne, Centre National d'Art et de Culture Georges Pompidou, Paris

Portrait of Gaby Baur. 1904. Tempera on cardboard, 40 × 29¾″ (101.6 × 75.5 cm). Zervos I, 215. D.B. XI, 17. Private collection, Paris

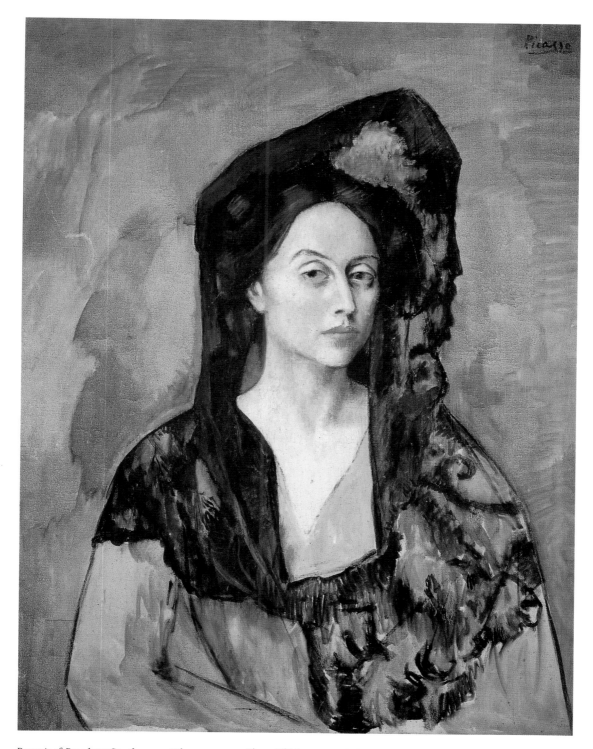

Portrait of Benedetta Canals. 1905. Oil on canvas, 34⅝ × 26¾″ (88 × 68 cm). Zervos I, 263. D.B. XIII, 9. Museu Picasso, Barcelona

painting a typically North Holland bonnet on her head, Picasso transformed the portrait into a local type, just as Gauguin used headdresses to identify his girls as Bretonnes or Arlésiennes. Picasso was also preoccupied with the sculptural possibilities of his medium, using thick gouache to give real substance to this compelling portrayal of a healthy Dutch girl—so different from the model Madeleine and the denizens of Montmartre.

The lessons Picasso had learned working from life during the early period provided him with enormous artistic resources. Later, when he set out to do a Cubist portrait of his dealer Kahnweiler or an Ingresque drawing of the musician Erik Satie, for example, all the inventive and technical diversity of his approaches to portraiture

Boy with a Pipe (P'tit Louis). 1905. Oil on canvas, 39⅜ × 32″ (100 × 81.3 cm). Zervos I, 274. D.B. XIII, 13. Collection Mrs. John Hay Whitney

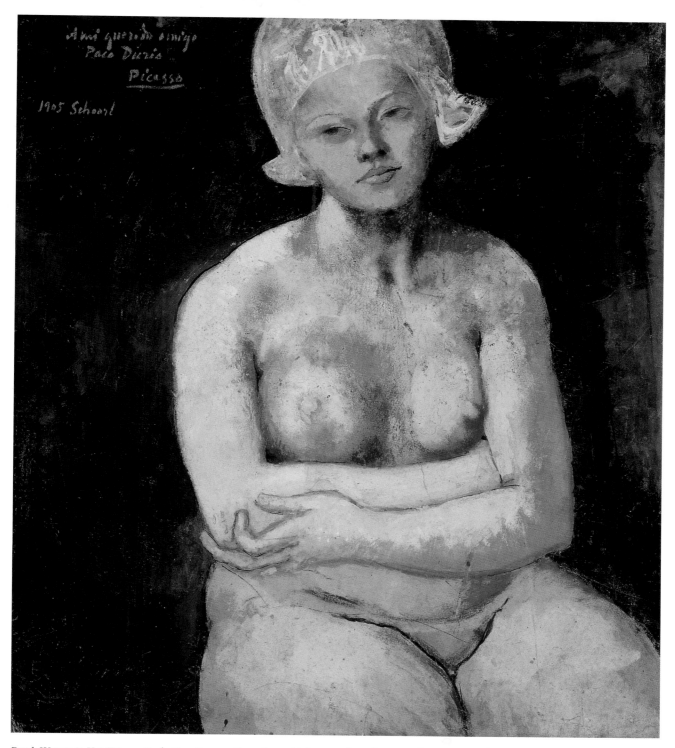

Dutch Woman in Hat (Diewertje de Geus?). 1905. Gouache and ink on cardboard mounted on panel, 30¼ × 26⅛″ (77 × 66.3 cm). Zervos I, 260. D.B. XIII, 1. Queensland Art Gallery, Brisbane. Purchased 1959 with funds donated by Major Harold de Vahl Rubin

fell into place. In contrast to those of most twentieth-century figure painters, Picasso's models were almost always personal, even when they made appearances (as his father did) as invented characters. The Minotaurs, Spanish grandees, *majas*, weeping women, circus bareback riders,[20] and *odalisques* who figure in the artist's later compositions are all, in a sense, portraits. His portraits usually have a "subject," like their distant Spanish forebears in the seventeenth century. When in 1906 Picasso returned to Spain in the company of Fernande Olivier, the image he would devise for her looked back to his own archaic, Iberian roots, but also ahead to a new, monumental plastic energy.

NOTES

1. Picasso's examination results at the School of Fine Arts in La Coruña indicate that he studied ornamental drawing (1892–93); figure drawing from plaster casts (1893–94); copying and drawing from plaster casts (1894–95); and that he took one course in painting and drawing from life (1894–95).

2. The circumstances surrounding this painting are told in Jaime Sabartés, *Picasso: Documents iconographiques* (Geneva: Pierre Cailler, 1954), pp. 295–96.

3. Picasso's painting was shown with works by another boy called Blanca Villareal. Ten days earlier Picasso had exhibited a few works in a different shop on the same street.

4. Unidentified reviewer, "De Sol a sol," *La Voz de Galicia*, March 3, 1895. Picasso is here referred to by his father's surname.

5. See, for example, Zervos VI, 480.

6. John Richardson, *A Life of Picasso, Volume 1: 1881–1906* (New York: Random House, 1991), p. 290.

7. André Salmon's account of the repainting of *Boy with a Pipe* is given in Marilyn McCully, ed., *A Picasso Anthology: Documents, Criticism, Reminiscences* (London: Arts Council of Great Britain, 1981), pp. 55, 57.

8. Richardson, *A Life of Picasso*, p. 54, recalls that Picasso would proudly show off these portraits and claim that "they still smell of Corunna."

9. Antonio Marino, "Los Cuatro años de Picasso en la Coruña," in *Picasso e a Coruna* (La Coruña: Gráficas Coruñesas, 1982), p. 6.

10. José Luis Bugallal, *Cuatro retratos y cuatro retratistas de D. Ramón Pérez Costales: Meléndez, Pardo Reguera, Picasso y Vaamonde* (La Coruña: Moret, 1956), pp. 6, 10, 28.

11. This painting is in the Los Angeles County Museum of Art; Zervos I, 174; note that Junyer Vidal appears to the right of Celestina in the drawing reproduced on p. 242.

12. Jaime Sabartés, *Picasso: An Intimate Portrait* (London: W. H. Allen, 1948), p. 53.

13. Ibid., p. 54.

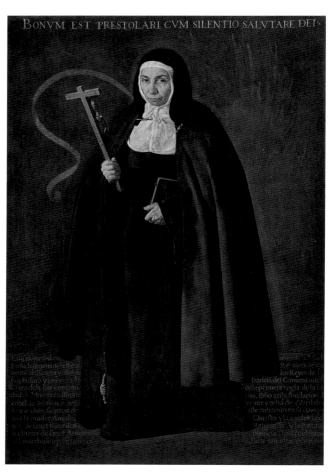

Diego Velázquez. *Mother Jerónima de la Fuente.* 1620. Oil on canvas, 63 × 43⅜″ (160 × 110 cm). Museo del Prado, Madrid

Ramon Casas. *Portrait of J. B. Parés.* 1899. Charcoal and pastel on paper, 24½ × 11¼″ (62 × 28.5 cm). Museu d'Art Modern, Barcelona

14. See, for example, Manuel Rodríguez Codolà, who alludes to Casas in his attributed review, "Els IV Gats: Exposición Ruiz Picazzo," *La Vanguardia*, February 3, 1900, in McCully, *A Picasso Anthology*, p. 22.

15. Richardson, *A Life of Picasso*, p. 216.

16. Sabartés, Picasso: *An Intimate Portrait*, p. 63.

17. Anatoli Podoksik, in *Picasso: The Eternal Quest* (Leningrad: Aurora, 1989), p. 27, believes that while Sabartés saw the portrait as his own reflection in the blue waters of a mystical lake and that within it he recognized the specter of his solitude, Picasso saw it primarily as the image of a poet.

18. Sabartés, *Picasso: An Intimate Portrait*, p. 97.

19. Richardson, *A Life of Picasso*, p. 304, describes Madeleine as "pretty, in a delicate, birdlike way (her nose and forehead formed a straight line)."

20. Richardson, *A Life of Picasso*, pp. 68–69, notes that Picasso's first Barcelona girl friend, a circus equestrienne called Rosita del Oro, reappears at the end of his life in Picasso's work and cites in particular an etching of 1970 in which the artist appears alongside her in disguise.

Diego Velázquez. *Aesop*. 1639–40. Oil on canvas, 70½ × 37″ (179 × 94 cm). Museo del Prado, Madrid

Beggar in a Cap. 1895. Oil on canvas, 28⅜ × 19⅝″ (72 × 50 cm). Zervos I, 4. Musée Picasso, Paris

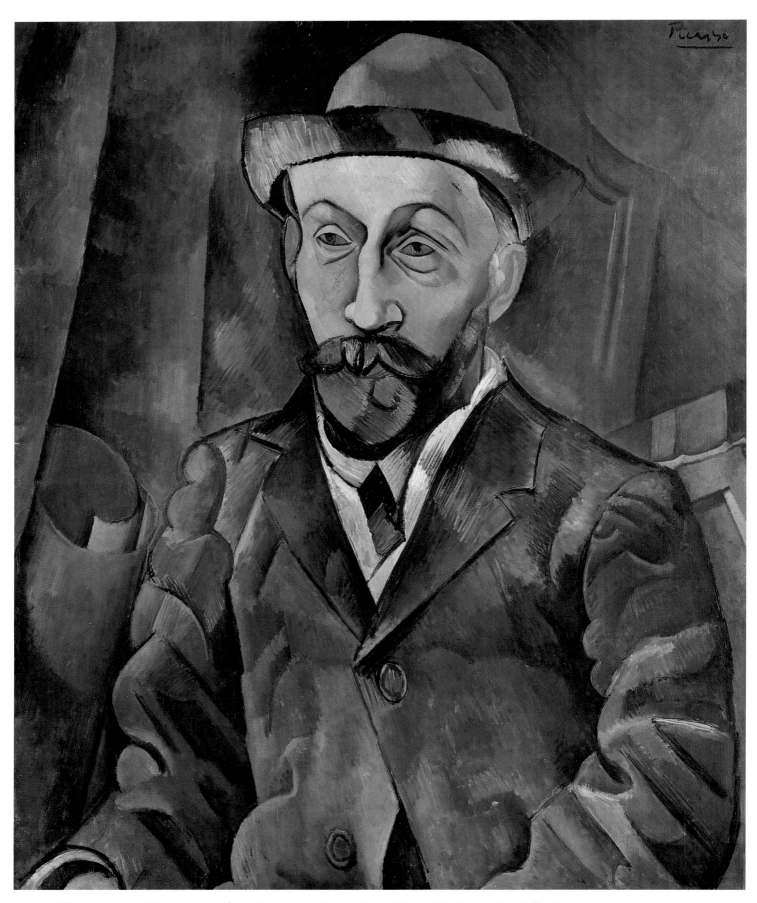

Portrait of Clovis Sagot. 1909. Oil on canvas, 32¼ × 26″ (82 × 66 cm). Zervos II¹, 129. Daix 270. Hamburger Kunsthalle, Hamburg

Portraiture in Picasso's Primitivism and Cubism

PIERRE DAIX

FROM FERNANDE TO GERTRUDE STEIN

Ever since his adolescence, Picasso had a gift for creating a good likeness. He also felt a need to grasp every possible aspect of his own face, as well as those of his most familiar models—his father and his younger sister—as if to explore the limits of resemblance. Later, his friends also served as models: Carles Casagemas, Jaime Sabartés, and then Guillaume Apollinaire; as did his mistresses, Germaine[1] and Madeleine,[2] for example. Picasso's psychological studies, his sense of caricature, his diary, his memories, or simply commissions together enabled him to produce a rich catalogue of drawn and painted portraits. In addition to traditional methods of representation, he had, from the outset, used a variety of innovations more or less removed from natural appearances; for example, lengthening faces in the style of El Greco (c. 1899), painting green shadows in his faces, such as in his self-portrait *Yo, Picasso* (spring 1901, p. 126), or creating his many well-known portraits in blue monochrome.

During the months following the paintings of Saltimbanques, and after Picasso had created *Woman in a Chemise* and *Seated Nude* (pp. 246, 247), both still inspired by Madeleine, and the *Portrait of Benedetta Canals* (p. 249; its workmanship and the fact that Canals returned to Barcelona enable us to date it prior to the spring of 1905),[3] the portrait—except symbolically or by implication—disappears from Picasso's oeuvre. He returns to it only during his summer stay in Schoorl, with the *Dutch Woman in Hat* (p. 251), the subject of which, rather remarkably, has almond-shaped eyes much like Fernande's. Contrary to what was formerly believed, Fernande moved into Picasso's studio at the Bateau-Lavoir only at the beginning of September 1905; yet she appears in several earlier works on paper (*Sleeping Nude,*[4] for example), and her profile, with her chignon and abundant hair, can be seen in a sketch for *The Actor* from the winter of 1904–05.

It seems probable, nevertheless, that the actual portraits of Fernande—which include an etching and drypoint (p. 256) and a small oil painting in a private collection (p. 257)—cannot be from the period of early acquaintanceship but were executed after her arrival at the Bateau-Lavoir. Picasso's emphasis in these two portraits on the powerful sculptural quality of Fernande's head seems to be a result of work done on his trip to Holland in the summer of 1905, whereas during the Saltimbanques period he was interested only in the frailty of Harlequin's companions.

Nevertheless, from this moment on, by her presence alone, Fernande played a decisive role in the ongoing problems of portraiture in Picasso's work. She is present continuously, under different guises, until the beginning of 1907, whereas the self-portraits no longer appear at the end of 1906 and return only in two isolated works, one

Fernande Olivier (detail). Bateau-Lavoir, 13, rue Ravignan, Paris, c. 1908–09. Photograph by Picasso. Musée Picasso, Paris, Documents section. Gift of Sir Roland Penrose

Portrait of Fernande. 1906. Etching and drypoint, 6⅜ × 4⅝″ (16.2 × 11.8 cm). Zervos XXII, 332. Geiser/Baer I, 18 bis. Worcester Art Museum, Worcester, Mass. The Sarah C. Garver Fund and anonymous gift

from summer 1907 and the other from the spring of 1908. For Picasso, unlike Braque, the face was the ultimate test of the validity of pictorial experimentation, and the portrait would become the ultimate stake.

Fernande's "type" is immediately well-defined: very long almond-shaped eyes that are heavy-lidded, at times almost completely closed; thick, voluminous hair; and a sturdy neck and body (opposite). These are loving portraits, finally, in the same tradition as the *Portrait of Benedetta Canals*, even though Picasso uses extreme and unexpected simplifications that culminate in the ravishing Fernande, nude and idealized, from the beginning of his stay in Gosol, *Nude with Joined Hands* (p. 260).

It does, in fact, seem that there was an interval of at least eight or nine months between the etching (above) and this first nude portrait of Fernande. Nevertheless, fall 1905 was dominated by the portrait. After Fernande had come to live with him, Picasso clearly went through an emotional crisis expressed in a number of works we might describe as a farewell to his youth: In *At the Lapin Agile*, he paints his portrait as a disenchanted Harlequin seated beside Germaine Florentin, shown as a coquette (p. 131).[5] In *Pierrette's Marriage*,[6] Harlequin says farewell to Columbine, and in the *Death of Harlequin*—which is for Picasso a real kind of death of the self—Harlequin disappears from Picasso's painting, at least as his double or alter ego,[7] until 1915. At this time, he also painted portraits

of such Bateau-Lavoir "juvenile delinquents" as *Young Girl with a Basket of Flowers* (p. 258)—the so-called "Fleur du Pavé," later a model for Modigliani[8]—and "P'tit Louis," who became the *Boy with a Pipe* (p. 250), crowned with a wreath of roses. The latter was painted at the time Picasso had already begun to work on the *Portrait of Gertrude Stein*.[9] The *Death of Harlequin* was painted a short while later, at the beginning of 1906.

At this time Picasso experienced a crisis in his art. His portraits lack any stylistic unity or relationship to one another. The mysterious *Woman with a Fan*,[10] for example, is completely isolated. Picasso did not exhibit his *Family of Saltimbanques* (p. 132), although it had been painted in the format of a Salon work. He reworked it after his visit to the Manet retrospective at the Salon d'Automne. Until then, he had known only a few masterpieces by Manet. Seeing this retrospective greatly affected him, and at the very same Salon, he experienced the revelation of Ingres' *Turkish Bath*.[11] Given its eroticism, its fluid space (constructed by the contrasting rhythms of naked bodies), its bright colors and suppression of *chiaroscuro*, Ingres' painting led him to recognize in this artist an innovator in regard to those very problems he himself was seeking to resolve.

These intellectual jolts were amplified by the entry of Leo and Gertrude Stein into his still-small universe. Until their arrival, and despite his friendship with Max Jacob,

Portrait of Fernande. 1905. Oil on canvas, 11⅞ × 10″ (30 × 25.5 cm).
Zervos XXII, 331. Private collection

Portrait of Fernande. 1906. Oil on canvas, 39⅜ × 31⅞″
(100 × 81 cm). Zervos I, 254. D.B. XV, 41. Private collection,
Boston, Mass.

Guillaume Apollinaire, and André Salmon, his world
did not extend much beyond the Spanish community of
Montmartre and the group of Montparnasse poets known
as "Vers et prose." Moreover, by buying "paintings worth
eight hundred francs on their very first visit"[12]—Picasso's
first sale of such magnitude—the Steins virtually yanked
him out of poverty.

It was also the first time that his blue canvases—such
as *Two Women at a Bar* and *Woman in Prison* (a prostitute
from Saint-Lazare prison in her cell)—were taken seriously. Invited by the Steins to their studio on the rue de
Fleurus, Picasso saw his paintings hung next to those of
Gauguin, Lautrec, and Renoir, in addition to Cézanne,
whose work he did not then know well.[13] It was also, no
doubt, the first time that he was involved with collectors
of such stature (André Level, it seems, did not meet him
until 1906).[14]

Gertrude Stein was the first professed intellectual
whom Picasso met, and her heavily accented French
allowed him to speak freely in his Spaniard's faulty French
without feeling humiliated. Immediately a communion of
ideas was established, which led to a kind of emulation
between them, as all who saw them together remarked.
She immediately considered herself a supporter of the
same revolutionary aesthetic as Picasso. A different art
had to be created, a twentieth-century art. This was the
task that awaited both of them.[15]

Leo and Gertrude Stein "were dressed in brown cor-
duroy and sandals *à la* Raymond Duncan, who was a
friend of theirs. . . . Picasso . . . [was] attracted by the
woman's physical personality," said Fernande. "He offered
to do her portrait, before he really knew her."[16] In fact,
Gertrude's physique corresponded to the monumental
plastic and sculptural concerns that had begun to interest
him during his trip to Holland. But it is apparent that—in
the same way he remembered Degas when he painted
Benedetta Canals (she had been Degas's model)—he did
not forget America when he painted Gertrude. In making
the decision to paint a portrait of Miss Stein (p. 267), he
wanted to create a pioneering work: the first portrait
of an American incarnating the "new woman" of the
twentieth century; a different kind of woman, new in
her freedom.

Gertrude Stein remembered it this way: "Why did he
wish to have a model before him just at this time, this I
really do not know, but everything pushed him to it, he
was completely emptied of the inspiration of the harlequin period, being Spanish commenced again to be active
inside in him and I being an American, and in a kind of a
way America and Spain have something in common, perhaps for all these reasons he wished me to pose for him."[17]

In undertaking such a portrait, did Picasso intend to
compete with Henri Matisse? The latter's *Woman with the
Hat*—the portrait of Madame Matisse, which had just

Portrait of Leo Stein. 1906. Gouache on cardboard, 9¾ × 6¾″ (24.7 × 17 cm). Zervos I, 250. D.B. XIV, 1. The Baltimore Museum of Art. The Cone Collection, formed by Dr. Claribel Cone and Miss Etta Cone of Baltimore, Maryland

to be in muted colors. In short, he was reacting against both Matisse (whom he had yet to meet) and the vanguard scandal caused by the "Cage aux Fauves." We can probably get a good idea of what Picasso had been trying to express in the original version of Gertrude's face (later painted out) by referring to the small gouache portrait of

caused a scandal at the "Cage aux Fauves" (the 1905 Salon d'Automne)—was hanging at the home of the Steins, and Picasso saw it every Saturday when he visited them. Leo, who had at first been disgusted by the Matisse, had been talked into buying it by his sister-in-law, Sarah (the first in their family to become infatuated with Matisse), and, in the end, could not stop praising it. If Picasso was entering into this competition with Matisse, he was doing everything backward.

The Woman with the Hat is a portrait of a woman in formal attire in which the focus is on the hat and the elegance of the costume. Picasso, by contrast, painted Gertrude sitting in her own way and wearing her usual simple outfit à la Raymond Duncan. Her pose recalled the "monumental intimacy" and the imposing immediacy of presence of Ingres' *Monsieur Bertin*, a painting that Picasso had studied in the Louvre and obviously had in mind. The Matisse painting exploded with color and featured green shadows in the face. But as Picasso had used such colors in his self-portrait *Yo, Picasso*, the brashly colored picture of the spring of 1901, he did not feel that Matisse could teach him anything really new. He had already, he thought, used color in an expressive way. Characteristically taking the contrary artistic position, Picasso decided that the portrait of Gertrude would have

Young Girl with a Basket of Flowers. 1905. Oil on canvas, 61 × 26″ (155 × 66 cm). Zervos I, 256. D.B. XIII, 8. Private collection

Portrait of Fernande. 1906. Charcoal on ivory laid paper, 24 × 18″ (61.2 × 45.8 cm). Zervos VI, 747. The Art Institute of Chicago. Gift of Hermann Waldeck

Leo Stein (opposite) and the larger gouache portrait of their nephew, Allan;[18] those are classical portraits—elaborate, indeed, almost monochromatic.

The sittings with Gertrude were occasions for conversation between the two, and sometimes with the participation of Leo and some of his American friends. "There was a large broken armchair where Gertrude Stein posed. . . . There was a little kitchen chair upon which Picasso sat to paint . . . She took her pose, Picasso sat very tight on his chair and very close to his canvas and on a very small palette which was of a uniform brown grey colour, mixed some more brown grey and the painting began."[19]

There were some ninety sittings. This was extremely

Nude with Joined Hands (Fernande). 1906. Gouache on canvas, 38 × 29¾″ (96.5 × 75.6 cm). Zervos I, 310. D.B. XV, 28.
Art Gallery of Ontario, Toronto. Gift of Sam and Ayala Zacks, 1970

unusual for Picasso, or anyone else, and even if both model and painter clearly enjoyed their meetings, the large number of sittings indicates Picasso's growing uncertainty, either about the goal that he was trying to reach or the means of reaching it. "Spring was coming and the sittings were coming to an end. All of a sudden one day Picasso painted out the whole head. I can't see you any longer when I look, he said irritably."[20] Unfortunately, as Gertrude later would say with regret, no one thought of photographing the portrait. We are tempted to wonder whether, in this first version, Gertrude Stein wasn't looking at the viewer head on, like Ingres' *Monsieur Bertin*, whose body is also in three-quarter pose and whose "ghost . . . is revived also in the overwhelming

Standing Female Nude (Fernande). 1906. Oil on canvas, 60½ × 37⅛″ (153.7 × 94.3 cm). Zervos I, 327. D.B. XV, 27.
The Museum of Modern Art, New York. The William S. Paley Collection

The Gosol Madonna. Twelfth century. Polychrome wood, 30¼″ (77 cm) high. Museu d'Art de Catalunya, Barcelona

the *Joy of Life*, which hung in triumph at the Salon, and Matisse's large exhibition at the Druet gallery, had something to do with it. Picasso must have seen in the *Joy of Life* a kind of dialogue with the *Turkish Bath*. There was an exaltation in the rhythms of the bodies of the female nudes of the *Joy of Life* that went well beyond Ingres, because from that point on Matisse purified these rhythmic contourings of all detail and modeling so that the movement of his composition was created by arabesque outlines. At Druet's, Picasso once again found these kinds of contours—now even more exaggerated and simplified—in the three woodcuts shown there and also, very probably, in the lithographs (such as *Half-length Nude*), where the abstraction and the interruption of forms, as well as the importance placed on rhythm, broke completely with classical drawing.[22]

Matisse provoked Picasso on the latter's own ground as a draftsman and engraver, but in an entirely revolutionary way, free of everything that remained academic in Ingres' work. Their competition would become even more intense when the Steins decided to buy the *Joy of Life* and when Matisse and Picasso finally met.

Picasso must have felt surpassed by the older Matisse. We see him taking up the challenge in a new series of still lifes (he had not painted any since the *Still Life* of 1901). At Gosol, in the summer of 1906, he began to paint them again, focusing on the theme of the *porron*[23] (he had seen Matisse's *Still Life with a Purro* at Druet's). In July Picasso also made a wood engraving, *Bust of a Girl*; this type of engraving, which allows for very strong contrasts,[24] was then out of fashion, so it can only be linked to Matisse's endeavors in the same medium.

Can one speak of primitivism, in the general sense of the term, at this stage?[25] It is surely possible to do so for wood engraving and for the very theme of the *Joy of Life*. The idea of a kind of primitive pastoral was already in the air for the Fauves.[26] Picasso had met André Derain at the end of 1905 and very probably had seen his somewhat pointillist large painting *The Golden Age*; it was filled with daring innovations in its composition, and it also borrowed figures from the *Turkish Bath*. In addition, in the winter of 1905–06, he had discovered at the Louvre the Iberian sculptures that predate the Roman Empire; and, as James Johnson Sweeney suggested in 1941,[27] they offered him a primitivism from his native Andalusia. In a sense, they could be said to belong to him.

None of this means that in that spring of 1906 Picasso could already foresee the transformation of the *Portrait of Gertrude Stein* into the image we know. But we can surmise that he was discomforted by Matisse's and Derain's "anticlassical" evolution and most likely began to question the path he was following, one that was too influenced by Ingres' ideal of perfection. His stay in Spain seems not to have been planned before Ambroise

presence of Picasso's portrait of Gertrude Stein," as Robert Rosenblum would write.[21] Picasso was obviously fascinated by the way Ingres, using a dark palette, could make light appear on the face and hands, which stand out so starkly. Something of this remains in his treatment of Gertrude's hands. We must not forget that this period in which the ninety sittings took place (early 1906) was the time of his broader "rivalry" with Ingres, as in the harmonious classicism exemplified by the *Boy Leading a Horse*, a period that continues through the beginning of his stay in Gosol, as we shall see. The sudden, unexpected painting-out of Gertrude's face no doubt had to do with Picasso's decision to distance his portrait from that first illusionistic and somewhat idealizing conception of it.

Gertrude Stein connected Picasso's stopping work on her portrait with the 1906 Salon des Indépendants and in doing so offers us a clue to Picasso's decision. Perhaps the shock he experienced on seeing Matisse's large canvas

Head of a Woman with a Chignon (Fernande). 1906. Gouache on paper, 24½ × 18½″ (62 × 47 cm). Zervos I, 332. D.B. XV, 20. Collection Susan and Lewis Manilow

Vollard bought the contents of his studio—which brought in the necessary money only at the beginning of May—even though the backgrounds of *Young Acrobat on a Ball* and *The Family of Saltimbanques* as well as *The Woman of Majorca* show an obvious nostalgia for the deserts near Málaga. In any event, the choice of spending the summer in Gosol, in the Spanish Pyrenees, completely isolated atop a rugged mountain, seems to reflect Picasso's desire to return to a stark life far from all modernity, to an ancestral, if not primitive, life.

GOSOL AND THE TURN TO PRIMITIVISM

If the paintings from the beginning of Picasso's stay at Gosol—*Two Youths* and *The Adolescents*,[28] for example— display his reflections on the contours of nude bodies in a monochrome infused with the ocher of the clay from the region, the fact that they are stripped of all detail—to the point that the young girl is painted in *profil perdu*—links Ingres's influence to that of Matisse. Nonetheless, one cannot yet speak of any primitivism here. The same is true of the admirable *Nude with Joined Hands,* which is, as I have already said, a classical and even idealized portrait of Fernande. *La Toilette*[29] brought Picasso's lyricism to its apogee. The seated portrait of Fernande (p. 259) was probably painted at the same time. It shows her with an almost Ingres-like immobility (one need only turn her around to find Gertrude's pose). *Fernande with a Black Mantilla*[30] is a more psychological portrait of his companion, with a certain nostalgia in her look. After these three paintings, there was a sudden break in Picasso's work. Instead of searching for classical harmony, he used the nude and the portraits as testing grounds for primitivist simplifications in which he tried to recapture

Woman Plaiting Her Hair (Fernande). 1906. Bronze, 16½ × 10¼ × 12⅝″ (42 × 26 × 32 cm). Zervos I, 329. Spies 7. The Baltimore Museum of Art. The Cone Collection, formed by Dr. Claribel Cone and Miss Etta Cone of Baltimore, Maryland

Study for Woman Plaiting Her Hair. 1906. Crayon and charcoal on paper, 22 × 16″ (55.8 × 40.7 cm). Zervos I, 341. University of East Anglia. The Robert and Lisa Sainsbury Collection

something of the strength and the roughness of early art.

Typical is the *Standing Female Nude* (p. 261), which picks up on the half-length *Nude with Joined Hands*, now as a full-length nude portrait, the light contours of which barely emerge from the rose / ocher monochrome background. But all conventional charm has vanished. The body has lost its former triumphant femininity, the hands modestly conceal the sex. The torso has been made relatively smaller, intensified by a perspective that rises above the nude in relation to the viewer, whereas the long but heavy legs accentuate a solid monumentality. The idol-like character of Fernande in this picture is underlined by a face that has been reduced to simple volumes, with all identifying details removed. It is a sort of mask of Fernande's face.

The fact that Picasso felt the need to rupture the too-perfect harmonies that obtained in his work from the beginning of his Gosol stay is in keeping with everything we know about his temperament and the uneasiness that came over him when faced with his greatest successes, which he tended to perceive as impasses. Picasso wanted to go beyond immediate resemblance, beyond even the exaltation of beauty, in order to arrive at an image of a woman outside time, far removed from any fashion, an immemorial woman who would, in fact, hark back to the simplicity of the first attempts at artistic expression.

Did he, at that time, rely on preexisting models? A tendency to return to the origins of art, to primitivism, already existed in the *Joy of Life* and in the woodcuts from Matisse's exhibition at Druet's, with probably even an example of a face reduced to a mask.[31] No doubt it also existed in Derain's work, but because Derain was in London from the end of January to mid-March 1906, he and Picasso must not have seen much of each other. Nevertheless, Picasso probably could have seen Derain's *Golden Age* and even *The Dance*, if it had already been painted. This remains hypothetical, however. Derain's purchase of Vlaminck's Fang mask has been dated to 1906, and his enthusiasm for the Museum of Mankind of the British Museum can be seen in a letter to Vlaminck dated March 7, 1906.[32] Derain could have communicated this enthusiasm to Picasso upon his return to Paris at the time of the Salon des Indépendants.

The gouache *Head of a Woman with a Chignon* (p. 263) offers a study of this masklike face. Again we find Fernande's almond-shaped eyes, but they are expressionless. The special attention paid to her ear, which projects beneath the reduced and simplified head of hair (looking

Woman Plaiting Her Hair (Fernande). 1906. Oil on canvas, 49⅝ × 35¾″ (126 × 90.8 cm). Zervos I, 336. D.B. XVI, 7.
Estate of Florene M. Schoenborn

Gertrude Stein (detail). Fiesole, Italy, summer 1905. Photographer unknown. Yale Collection of American Literature, Beinecke Rare Book and Manuscript Library, Yale University

Saint-Lazare prison, had already assimilated the stylization of the drapery taken from Gothic sculpture. The profile of the face on the right, on the other hand, goes further in its schematic character and offers the viewer an almost frontal eye, much like that of the face of the idol in Gauguin's *The Spirit of the Dead Watching* (p. 348); Picasso would use it again in the face of the whore on the left in the final state of *Les Demoiselles d'Avignon*. (In 1902 he probably could have seen Gauguin's lithographs of that picture at the studio of Paco Durrio, a collector and friend of Gauguin's, but no doubt he was also struck by a similar kind of representation in the illuminations and in Romanesque statues in Barcelona's Museum of Catalan Art.)

Another aspect of Gosol primitivism is the break with likeness, which is a consequence of Picasso's endeavor to reduce the face to a kind of mask. In the Carnet Catalan, he made numerous sketches of the women of Gosol wearing scarves wound tightly around their heads, and he transformed Fernande in that way. But whereas the Spanish framing of the black mantilla in *Fernande with a Black Mantilla* was very becoming for the youthful grace of Fernande's nostalgic face, the Gosol scarf around Fernande's head, in *Fernande with a Kerchief* or in *Recumbent Nude* (Fernande),[36] emphasized only an abstract oval of her face. Picasso sought to render only those aspects of Fernande's face and body that could sustain this simplification and reduction to volumes. The psychological emptiness is now complete.

almost plastered to the skull), brings to mind the conventions of Iberian sculpture to such a degree that it is impossible not to see these sculptures as one of the sources for the image. But Picasso's main reference here probably lies elsewhere and comes from Gosol itself. John Richardson[33] has clarified Josep Palau i Fabre's account[34] of the role played by Picasso's discovery of the twelfth-century sculpture of the Virgin of Gosol (which had not yet been transferred to the Museum of Catalan Art in Barcelona; p. 262). He underlines "its hieratic stylizations —the Madonna's wide-open, staring eyes and eyebrows emphatically drawn in as if by a cosmetician." If the eyes in the study, like those in *Standing Female Nude*, which remained almond-shaped, do not resemble those of the Virgin, the shape of the eyebrows in raised arches and the masklike face do indeed recall her; but above all, Picasso seems to have re-created in his nude the effect produced by the disproportionate size of the head in relation to the narrowness of the torso.

The interest of these first endeavors lies in the fact that here Picasso was fabricating his own primitivism by isolating, within the "primitive objects," disparate elements which were unbalanced in their proportions. Let us recall that these were not his first reflections on archaic or (what was then called) "primitive" art, which included Western medieval styles. The large canvas *Two Sisters*,[35] painted in the spring of 1902, in the midst of the Blue period, which represents a whore and a mother beneath the arches of

Gertrude Stein (detail). 27, rue de Fleurus, Paris, c. 1909–10. Photographer unknown. Collection Edward Burns

Portrait of Gertrude Stein. 1906. Oil on canvas, 39¼ × 32″ (99.6 × 81.3 cm). Zervos I, 352. D.B. XVI, 10. The Metropolitan Museum of Art, New York. Bequest of Gertrude Stein, 1946

This is the seed of the idea that would dominate Cubism after Picasso and Georges Braque linked up—"like mountain-climbers," the latter said[37]—in the fall of 1908. Fernande had already become something of a plastic object in Picasso's mind by the middle of the summer of 1906. With these dynamics of primitivist simplification, the artist felt he was on to something both new and successful, and he must have sensed that, in terms of the avant-garde, he was catching up with Matisse and Derain, even surpassing them. A note in the Carnet Catalan expresses his intoxication: "A tenor who reaches a note higher than the one written in the score. Me!"[38]

When he returned to Paris in late summer, Picasso threw all of this accumulated experience into the mask-like face of Gertrude, completing her portrait in the form in which we know it today. No longer was this a testing ground, as had been the successive primitivizations of Fernande during the summer; it had become a way of affirming that he was painting the archetypal Gertrude Stein, beyond the circumstances of her daily life, rendered as she would look for eternity. And, as we know, he succeeded. In 1933 Gertrude wrote: "Only a few years ago when Gertrude Stein had had her hair cut short, she had always up to that time worn it as a crown on top of her head as Picasso has painted it, when she had had her hair cut, a day or so later she happened to come into a room and Picasso was several rooms away. She had a hat on but he caught sight of her through two doorways and approaching her quickly called out, Gertrude, what is it, what is it. What is what, Pablo, she said. Let me see, he said. She let him see. And my portrait, said he sternly. Then his face softening he added, *mais, quand même, tout y est,* all the same it is all there."[39] This was how he created for Gertrude Stein a face as a woman of the avant-garde. Her portrait now corresponded to the role she wanted to play in writing literature for the twentieth century.

During the same period, Picasso transformed the faces in his large canvas *La Coiffure*[40] into their respective masks. He then took up the pattern again in a series of variations that became increasingly primitivist of an image of Fernande combing her hair while kneeling, full-face, her eyebrows arched, but with blank eyes (p. 264). All of these were painted on a red background, rather than the ocher of Gosol, and they culminated in the magnificent large canvas *Woman Plaiting Her Hair* (p. 265).

PRIMITIVISM AND AFRICAN ART, LATE 1906–SPRING 1908

For Picasso, Matisse, and Derain, the fall of 1906 was dominated by various forms of primitivism. Derain had bought his African Fang mask, Matisse his first African statuette, and Gauguin's large retrospective at the Salon d'Automne brought together almost two-thirds of his entire production, including many of his previously unexhibited "Oceanic" works.

During the months that followed, Fernande was no longer recognizable in Picasso's experimental feminine figures, some of which would lay the groundwork for *Les Demoiselles d'Avignon*; significantly, the artist now used his own face as the model on which he experimented with different forms of primitivism—or at least what he considered as such. The effects culled from Iberian sculpture, such as the enlarged ears and heavy eyelids, led directly to the masklike *Self-Portrait with Palette* (p. 137). An extreme addition to this congregation of stylistic factors is the appearance, in two versions employing Iberian effects,[41] of blank eyes. It is true that Picasso had already been led to use blank eyes in his search for primitivist effects in Gosol. (He did so, for example, in the first version of *Fernande in a Mantilla*.[42]) However, the eyes in his two self-portraits closely resemble those of the first African figure bought by Matisse, a Vili object from the French Congo (below). This seated personage has large eyes that appear even more blank as the back of the sockets has been laminated with mother-of-pearl.[43] It is highly possible that this was the first African object Picasso had ever examined at leisure, and it appears that he was greatly struck by it. By the emphasis he placed on his own blank eyes, he found himself able to establish a meeting, a convergence of sorts, with the anonymous African sculptor. Hence, there

Figure. Vili. People's Republic of the Congo. Wood, 9⅜″ (24 cm) high. Private collection

Portrait of Max Jacob. Early 1907. Gouache on paper mounted on cardboard, 24³⁄₈ × 18⁵⁄₈″ (62 × 47.5 cm). Zervos II¹, 9. Daix 48. Museum Ludwig, Collection Ludwig, Cologne. (Colorplate, p. 23)

is a remarkable resemblance between the masklike face of this statuette and at least certain aspects of the two contemporaneous self-portraits,[44] in which the role of the blank eye takes on major importance. Picasso continued to explore this concern in a series of female heads with blank eyes, which culminate in the large *Seated Nude* in Prague.[45]

While this use of blank eyes is a signal of Picasso's early interest in African art, it is not yet a structural aspect of his work, remaining but one of the borrowings, references, and signatures of primitivism. He had proceeded much in the same way in the influences he had absorbed in Gosol—Roman, Iberian, or even Matissean. In early 1907 we find the same elements—including the blank eyes—in *Man, Woman, and Child* (p. 135),[46] a canvas showing a "primitivized" Picasso clearly moved by a woman in profile holding an infant (whose face is also primitivized). In all likelihood the canvas was linked to his hope of Fernande's becoming pregnant. This hope was never realized, a fact that led Fernande and Picasso to adopt a young girl named Raymonde, whose face appears in sketches in the Carnet 6 (shown in the 1988 exhibition of *Les Demoiselles d'Avignon*).[47] Though the face is sketched

in only a few lines, this image is no doubt an excellent likeness. In the meantime, Picasso had been making a number of "caricatural" portraits of both Apollinaire and Salmon and had even planned a sculpture of the latter.[48] There was also a large gouache portrait of Max Jacob from this time (above), perhaps linked to the presence of a sailor in the original idea for the brothel that became the *Demoiselles*. But these seem to have been momentary inspirations that did not together define any single answer in the direction of a primitivist approach.

The *Self-Portrait* of 1907 in the Národní Galerie, Prague (p. 139), is an entirely different matter. It dates from a time slightly later, when Picasso—under the shock of Matisse's *Blue Nude: Memory of Biskra* and Derain's *Bathers*, both of which he discovered at the spring Salon des Indépendants of 1907—moved from using bits and pieces of a primitivist vocabulary to a coherent realization of an entirely primitivist style. This formulation would reach its epitome in the repainted version of *Les Demoiselles d'Avignon*, where he replaced many of the rounded forms of the initial "Iberian" version with angular, roughhewn volumes.

In the Prague *Self-Portrait*, Picasso did not simply represent his face by means of primitivist borrowings such as

Portrait of Fernande. 1908. Pencil on paper, 7⅞ × 5¼″ (20 × 13.4 cm). Zervos II², 700. Musée Picasso, Paris

the enlarged eyes and ear. These preoccupations now became secondary in relation to his move into a primitivism that is no longer expressed mainly by the reduction of the face to a mask, but that is in a way inflicted on the very craft of painting. The Prague self-portrait flouts all the inherited assumptions of painting. The striking relief of the brushstrokes in the hair, a thickness of impasto that permits him to make grooves with the brush handle, places *within* the pictorial vocabulary of the canvas the effects of roughhewn carving found in some tribal sculptures, which probably inspired a few wood carvings made by Picasso at the same time.[49] Hence, clumsiness and violence are introduced directly into the *facture* of the painting itself. That deliberately coarse manner is virtually identical to the slashing brushwork of the masklike heads on the right in the *Demoiselles*. The *Self-Portrait* can thus be said to have served as a testing ground for Picasso's way of painting when he reworked his manifesto-like great *Demoiselles* canvas.

The question of the portrait resurfaces as Picasso rethinks African art during the spring of 1908. Tribal masks and sculpture, in their severe stylization and their frontality, were in some ways "antiportraits," in which all that is individual disappears. In Carnet 16, shown in the 1988 exhibition of *Les Demoiselles d'Avignon* at the Musée Picasso in Paris, we find a sketch of a self-portrait remarkable for the primitivism of the large eyes and ears and especially for its total frontality.[50] In the same Carnet 16 there is a *Portrait of Fernande* (above). If we assume that the order of the pages in Carnet 16 is chronological, Fernande was, in fact, the first to be used in attempts of

this kind; her portrait employs the same frontality as Picasso's *Self-Portrait*, with the exception of a slight change in the hair. Unlike the self-portrait, however, this portrait of Fernande culminates in a masterpiece, *Woman with a Fan* (opposite). The initial idea for this painting— also found in Carnet 16—was a full-face portrait of a woman standing.[51] Here we find something well beyond the "natural" Fernande: an eternal idol, the frontality of whose masklike face brings out the dynamic, powerful dissymetrical balance created by the extremely geometrized unevenness of the shoulders, reinforced by the opposition between the straight lines of the armchair or the fan and the curves of the face and the naked breast, and also by the arc of the circle that crosses the entire composition, marking the contrast of the upper limit of the white dress. Picasso probably had in mind, in addition to African frontality, a broader "archaic" frontality such as is found in Egyptian or Greek sculpture. His work moves, therefore, from the arts that he considers the most primitive, to his rapid, simplified painting, geometrized in its movement, in which he sees a workmanship for and of the twentieth century.

Here Picasso knew how to assimilate the plastic values of African statuary in order to construct from them a new contrast of his own making. He had moved from a series of African borrowings that had been, until then, local, exterior, and anecdotal, to their structural re-creation; at the same time, he went far beyond the bounds of traditional

X ray of head, *Woman with a Fan* (Fernande)

PIERRE DAIX

Woman with a Fan (Fernande). 1908. Oil on canvas, 59⅞ × 39¾″ (152 × 101 cm). Zervos II¹, 67. Daix 168. The State Hermitage Museum, St. Petersburg

Head of a Peasant Woman (Madame Putman). 1908. Charcoal on paper, 24¾ × 18⅞″ (63 × 48 cm). Zervos VI, 1008. Collection Marina Picasso. Courtesy Galerie Jan Krugier, Geneva

Bust of a Peasant Woman (Madame Putman). 1908. Oil on canvas, 31⅞ × 22″ (81 × 56 cm). Zervos II, 92. Daix 194. The State Hermitage Museum, St. Petersburg

portraiture. If Gertrude Stein's masklike face is timeless, her body, her clothing, and her attitude belong very much to the Rose period during which she actually posed. In *Woman with a Fan*, Fernande becomes a geometric abstraction, hieratic and immemorial.[52]

FROM THE *"DÉCOUPAGE"* OF VOLUMES TO THE PORTRAIT OF VOLLARD, SPRING 1909–AUTUMN 1910

Picasso's discussions with Braque about the works the latter brought back from l'Estaque, his completion of *Three Women* thereafter, and his move to the series of still lifes that marks the beginning of the Picasso / Braque dialogue took Picasso away from considerations of the portrait. At the beginning of spring the portrait reappears in *Woman in an Armchair*,[53] Picasso's first attempt at slicing the planes of the face into facets. He considered it enough of a success to send a photograph of it to the Steins on March 23, 1909.

Most significant, however, was the fact that Picasso immediately began an entirely different type of portrait with the obvious goal of bringing about a comparison of the two methods. The *Portrait of Clovis Sagot* (p. 254) is probably the most Cézannesque of Picasso's portraits, given the rippling folds in the jacket sleeves, the hat, indeed, its overall figure-from-the-nineteenth-century aspect. It is painted very delicately with faint streaks that register the reflections of the light and that are typical of the Braque-influenced workmanship of the paintings from the spring of 1909. "Organic" curves are opposed to the straight lines in the drapery—an opposition that Picasso would push even further by refining the *découpage* of his shapes in the portraits of Fernande that he made the following summer at Horta de Ebro.

The exhibition *Picasso photographe* at the Musée Picasso in 1994 included two photographs of Clovis Sagot—one frontal, the other in profile—posing in the studio at the Bateau-Lavoir (p. 218). Picasso had used them in painting this portrait.[54] Anne Baldassari noted that "this pairing of camera angles brings to mind the way photography was used for police identification. . . . The constraints of the form may be understood—and in fact were used by Picasso—as allowing for the most propitious descriptive analysis of the subject for the preparation of a rigorous synthesis of its representation."[55]

If we compare the style of the Sagot portrait to that of *Woman in an Armchair*, we can more easily comprehend Picasso's need to proceed to the most rigorous "descriptive analysis" possible and, at the same time, to remain as pictorially close as possible to Cézanne, who, among his precursors, was the one Picasso believed to have reached the utmost objectivity in this area. One could say that, in the spring of 1909, Picasso compared three models of objectivity—that of photography, and two others that

Portrait of Manuel Pallarés. 1909. Oil on canvas, 26¾ × 19½″ (68 × 49.5 cm). Zervos XXVI, 425. Daix 274. The Detroit Institute of Arts. Gift of Mr. and Mrs. Henry Ford II

Woman with Vase of Flowers. 1909. Oil on canvas, 23¾ × 20½″ (60.5 × 52 cm). Zervos II¹, 156. Daix 282.
Sprengel Museum, Hannover, on loan from Collection Bernhard Sprengel Foundation

came from his own brushes, one in the manner of
Cézanne (to whom, following Braque, he turns with
more and more intensity—the canvas *Cézanne's Hat*
dates from the same period), and finally, one that results
in the elegant geometrization of organic volumes made
possible by the cutting into facet planes.

In May 1909 Picasso left for Horta de Ebro with the
benefit of this experimentation. Very significantly, he took
advantage of a stop in Barcelona to paint a delicately
geometrized portrait of his old friend Manuel Pallarés,
executed with vibrant, broken-facet strokes (p. 273). In
this portrait Picasso is obviously seeking an objective way
to synthesize the forms, since Pallarés's portrait is mid-
way between the *découpage* of the *Woman in an Armchair*
and the Cézannism of the *Portrait of Clovis Sagot*.

On June 24, 1909, Picasso wrote to the Steins that he

had begun, at Horta, two landscapes and two figures.
As the exhibition *Picasso and Braque: Pioneering Cubism*
confirmed in 1989, he must have been talking about the
two landscapes of the Mountain of Santa Bárbara,[56] a
subject he had already painted in 1898. Now, however, he
could apply to that subject the lessons learned from
Cézanne's *Mont Sainte-Victoire*. As for the figures, since
he writes to Gertrude that it is "always the same thing,"
he must be referring to the *Bust of a Man*[57] that was made
from the photograph of a violinist, and to *The Athlete*
(destroyed in a fire at the São Paulo Museum). These two
works, in their slicing of planes, are close to the *Woman
with Vase of Flowers* (above), one of the first portraits of
Fernande at Horta in which the fragmentation of organic
shapes is still discreet.

Picasso had arrived at the point of "slicing" Fernande's

Nude in an Armchair. 1909. Oil on canvas, 36¼ × 28¾″ (92 × 73 cm). Zervos II¹, 174. Daix 302. Private collection

Head of a Woman (Fernande). 1909. Bronze, 16¼″ (41.3 cm) high. Zervos II², 573. Spies 24. The Museum of Modern Art, New York. Purchase

head into rectilinear facets, but he did this out of purely plastic motivation. To see in this either aggression or sensuality is to misread Cubism. He used this device simply because she—like the Mountain of Santa Bárbara or the bottle of Anis del Mono (Anis del Mono was a popular aperitif whose bottle offered facets of glass and on which he would base a still life)—was, so to say, there. In his first series of planarily cut portrayals (p. 295), he objectively records, in clinical detail, Fernande's plumpness, her fatigue, and the first signs of age on her face.[58]

Painting itself now reigned supreme, blossoming with renewed vitality beyond all inherited assumptions as to its limits, subject only to the geometricizing demands of his refiner's fire. In working in this manner, Picasso transferred to these portraits the monumentality acquired in his geometrization of the Horta landscapes, such as *Houses on the Hill* and *The Factory*. If Picasso exaggerated the former (far beyond what we see of these landscapes in the photographs he took) in regard to the height, proportions, and simplicity of the houses and hills rising before him (far more than what Cézanne had dared do in his "vertical perspective" of Gardanne)—and added, in *The Factory*, nonexistent palm trees in order to contrast their arabesques with the rectilinearity of the buildings[59]— he did the same thing when using Fernande as subject. She exists as little more than a "motif," a springboard to

the free improvisation of his geometric reconstruction of fragmented shapes. One can, of course, recognize Fernande's voluminous head of hair and the general contours of her face, sliced into large masses in *Woman with Pears* (opposite). But her almond-shaped eyes have become rectangles so as to harmonize with the lozenges and polygons of her diced forehead, whereas the geometrization of her torso and, above all, her neck, in an ensemble of contrasting and opposed triangles, brings to her the same exalted height, the same pyramidal "vertical perspective" as one finds in the landscapes. The only remaining fragments of curves are in her chin and hair, or in the pears in the fruit dish—also cut into rectangles—on a table to the left. But while Fernande is no longer the subject of the painting, she remains its muse or inspiration. She has become what the new painting has to say about her. This is the culmination of the creative trajectory begun in the masklike images of Fernande at Gosol and in the repainted face of Gertrude Stein, which had been carried a step further in the "African" stylization of the *Woman with a Fan*. The portrait is no longer a naturalistic representation but has become everything that painting can appropriate from the model in order to transform it into what only painting can express. The portrait becomes the sum of all that Picasso's plastic imagination can extract and transform from the model.

Clearly the stay in Horta led Picasso to another discovery. Fernande's portrait does not appear as a single canvas, but is, so to say, spread across an entire series of works, in a manner more compact in terms of theme than Cézanne's series on Mont Sainte-Victoire. This serial character is no doubt one of the motivations for Picasso's photographs of groupings of his paintings in the studio. It is also a key to the somewhat serial character of the transformations of his later companions.

After Picasso's return to Paris, the fragmentations of

Fernande Olivier and Picasso (detail). Paris, c. 1910. Photograph by Picasso. Musée Picasso, Paris, Documents section

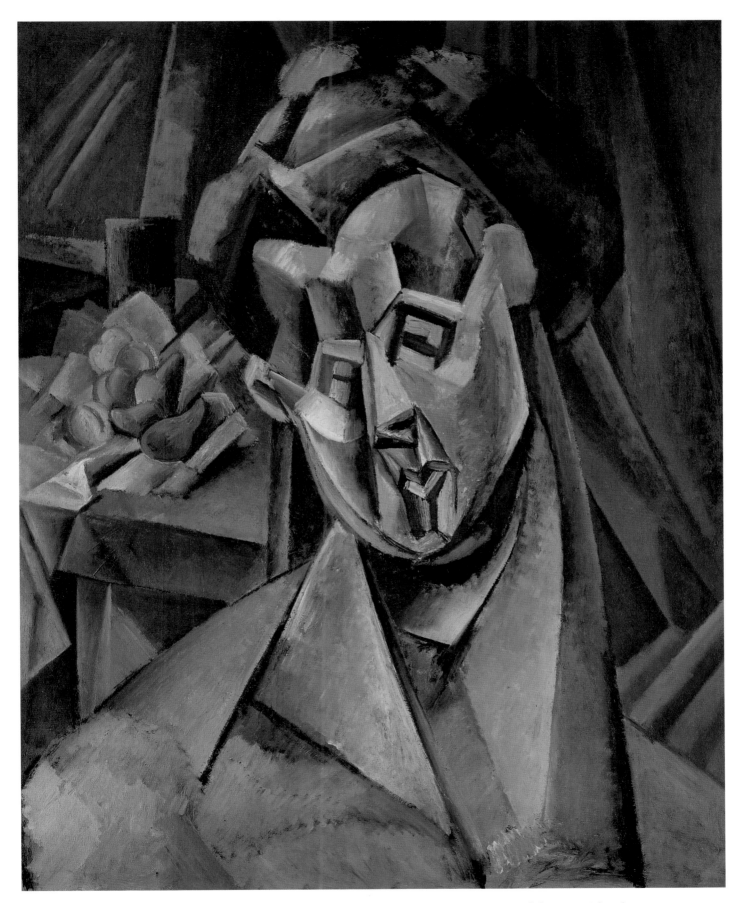

Woman with Pears (Fernande). 1909. Oil on canvas, 36¼ × 28⅞″ (92 × 73 cm). Zervos II¹, 170. Daix 290. Estate of Florene M. Schoenborn

Fernande's face are seen again in their sculptural counterpart, executed in the fall of 1909 (p. 276). From then on, Picasso had at his disposal a three-dimensional model of his *découpage* of her head. This resulted in a refinement of the painted *découpage* style, as seen in *Woman and Mustard Pot* and *Woman in Green*.[60] Although at Horta Picasso seemed to have put aside the problem of resemblance in order to concentrate on structure and monumentality, he now returned to it. If we take into account the facts that he did not come back from Horta before mid-September, and that he must have had trouble working because of the difficulties caused by his move to the boulevard de Clichy, his renewed interest in the portrait can only be related to his and Braque's response to the 1909 Salon d'Automne, which contained a large group of pictures by Corot that illustrated the artist's amazing ability to integrate his figures into their landscape settings.

At this point, Picasso changed models with *Woman in a Black Hat*—a woman who is obviously not Fernande— and with the thin figure in *Nude Woman in an Armchair*,[61] a replica of a painting he had done before leaving for Horta. He then did a painting of Mademoiselle Léonie[62] (the subject of which, according to Madame Sacher, the painting's first owner, was an acrobat from the Medrano circus), a portrait so named because Max Jacob found she resembled the heroine of his book *Saint Matorel*. At this time, taking a page from Braque, Picasso also painted his first oval format, *Woman with a Mandolin*,[63] the model for which remains unknown to us, and the remarkable *Girl with a Mandolin* (opposite), for which the professional model Fanny Tellier posed. Of course, female mandolin players had been a favorite theme of Corot's.

In the meantime, Picasso had painted two versions of a woman in an armchair, in which he abandoned the question of the portrait in favor of generic works wherein he explored the possibilities of *découpage* as a way of eliding the figure and its spatial surroundings.[64] The *Girl with a Mandolin* took up this question once again, but here Picasso seems to draw closer to the presence of his model, who was posing nude; this can be seen in the gracefulness that emanates from her pose, the delicacy of the geometrization of the chest, and especially the face, where Picasso folds back into the plane of the canvas the hidden facet of the profile, in a procedure which Kahnweiler would call, in reference to the works done in Cadaqués in the summer of 1910, "the shattering of the homogeneous shape."[65]

The *Portrait of Wilhelm Uhde* (p. 281), done in spring 1910, is painted in light tones with the same luminous vibrations, obtained by means of monochrome tonal variations, that are found in the Tellier portrait; above all, there is a fusion of the facet slices of the figure and those of the ambient space. However, the shape of the face is now shattered in a manner different from anything seen

earlier (as the left profile is interrupted near the ear), and there is more Cézannesque "passage" in the play of facet planes that the greater fracturing of the head allows. Another innovation here is that the left eye is completely in profile, while the right remains frontal. This reverses the effect produced in *Les Demoiselles d'Avignon* by the frontal eye in the profile face of the woman on the far left. Picasso would return to it again with greater vigor in the "reconstructed" faces created during World War II.

We know from a letter from Fernande to the Steins that Picasso was working on a portrait of Ambroise Vollard (p. 283) in June 1910, and that this portrait had "dragged over several months."[66] A comparison of it with works from the spring of 1910, made possible by the exhibition *Picasso and Braque: Pioneering Cubism*, has led us to shift the date of this portrait's completion to the fall, not only because the overall tonality is darker, but also because the facet planes are more delicate and more complex, the number and frequency of "passages" having increased. With Vollard's portrait, Picasso found himself in a situation similar to the one he had been in when painting that of Gertrude Stein. No doubt he wanted to prove to Vollard the validity of the progress of his "Cubism" (a word that was now already in vogue) by emphasizing its ability to characterize. Vollard would later stress the portrait's resemblance, saying: "The son of one of my friends, a four-year-old lad, finding himself in front of the painting, put his finger on it and said, without hesitating, 'That's Voyard.'"[67]

Vollard himself does not seem to have posed, nor does Picasso seem to have taken a photograph of him, as had been the case with Kahnweiler, whose portrait he began in the autumn of 1910, when he was completing the Vollard portrait.[68] This new portrait (p. 285) broke completely with the resemblance achieved in Vollard's, because Picasso takes into account the experience of painting the abstract figures in the summer at Cadaqués. He combines their structural framework with only peripheral references to his model. These references are the result of an analysis of identifying details in Kahnweiler's photograph. His eyes, nose, mouth, gloved hands, and a button of his jacket signal his character and draw attention to his fastidiousness in costume and manners, at which Picasso and his friends constantly poked fun. Except for a more luminous luster in the monochromatic gradations in the planes of the face and a kind of shadow in the torso area, however, there is nothing in the cutting of planes to mark the limit of the sitter as there was in Vollard's portrait.

Yet there is still a human presence created by the combination of the abstract scaffolding and the ensemble of coherent signs. But when we speak of Analytic Cubism in this regard, we must not forget that a process of synthesizing is already at work, though differently from the

Girl with a Mandolin (Fanny Tellier). 1910. Oil on canvas, 39½ × 29″ (100.3 × 73.6 cm). Zervos II¹, 235. Daix 346. The Museum of Modern Art, New York. Nelson A. Rockefeller Bequest

Wilhelm Uhde. c. 1906. Photographer unknown

process as it will be seen in the Synthetic Cubism of 1912–14, which will synthesize different mediums, drawings, collages, or imitations of collages. It was a synthesis within painting, a Cézannesque synthesis, produced by variations in the lighting, by gradations and *passages* between the planar facets, which transformed Kahnweiler's portrait and its peripheral analytic references into an aesthetic whole, into a unified "apparition." And as we perceive this apparition, we are able gradually to identify the model by decoding the information provided by the signs. The following summer, in Céret, Picasso would explore the possibilities offered by a tapered scaffolding, but the experimentation for such nonimitative scaffolding for a portrait dates from the autumn of 1910.

THE "LOSS" OF THE PORTRAIT AND THE ELEMENTS OF ITS SYNTHETIC RECONSTRUCTION

The *Portrait of Daniel-Henry Kahnweiler* must have seemed to Picasso a compromise between the successful illusionism of the facet slices of the portrait of Vollard and the force of the more skeletonic structural scaffoldings evident in the paintings he created at Cadaqués. In any case, the figures that follow become even more abstract compositions, almost entirely without identifiable traits other than those that can be interpreted from their titles, or

from those props that mark out space, such as the tablecloth fringe on a pedestal table, or the curtain loop with its tassel.

A careful examination of Picasso's photographs of friends in the boulevard de Clichy studio that were included in the exhibition *Picasso photographe* shows just how much "generic" paintings, such as *Man with a Pipe*, owe to them (p. 211).[69] This exploration leads Picasso, after his return to Paris in the fall of 1911, to the successful *Mandolin Player* and *Man with a Clarinet*, in which he nevertheless allows more personal attitudes to appear within his very abstract generic reconstructions.

As Pepe Karmel has pointed out, Picasso's sketches suggest that he seriously considered executing a portrait based on a photograph of Frank Haviland, a Franco-American dilettante and collector. Fernande Olivier, in her reminiscences, recalls Haviland's "magnificent dinner parties," but describes him as "stingy."[70] Though he bought only a few paintings, he seems to have been instrumental in arranging Picasso's 1909 commission to paint a series of library panels for the American painter and critic Hamilton Easter Field, who was Haviland's cousin.[71] It was also thanks to Haviland that Picasso discovered the town of Céret in southwestern France, where he spent numerous working vacations during the years 1911–14.[72]

An early 1912 photograph shows Haviland seated in Picasso's boulevard de Clichy studio (p. 286). As Karmel argues, this photograph seems to have provided a source for two series of drawings. In one, Picasso began with a caricatural sketch of Haviland's face (recalling his 1907 sketch of André Salmon, p. 183) and gradually abstracted its most salient elements: the protuberant chin, the long, "ski-slope" nose, the eyebrows, and the winglike forelocks of Haviland's center-parted hair (p. 286).[73]

In the second series noted by Karmel, Picasso transcribes and geometrizes Haviland's overall figure, emphasizing the phallic head of the cane rising between his knees and the scalloped arms of the chair in which he is seated (p. 287). In other versions of this drawing, the figure is supplemented by the little circles and crosses corresponding to the tasseled fringe of the armchair.[74]

Picasso would return to the image of a seated man with a cane in a drawing (p. 287) of summer 1912 related to the painting *The Aficionado*, but the figure here has lost the markings relating it directly to Haviland, thus entering the category of the merely generic. The figure in the painted *Aficionado* wears a moustache, which does not appear in any known photograph of Haviland. Pictures such as *Man with a Pipe*, *Mandolin Player*, and (later) *The Aficionado* are in no way portraits; they are generalized structures, hence, character types rather than individuals. When Eva Gouel enters his life, the canvas that celebrates her—*"Ma Jolie" (Woman with a Zither or Guitar)*[75]—is

Portrait of Wilhelm Uhde. 1910. Oil on canvas, 31⅞ × 23⅝″ (81 × 60 cm). Zervos II¹, 217. Daix 338. Private collection

Portrait of Ambroise Vollard I. March 4, 1937 (printed in 1939).
Aquatint, sugar lift aquatint, and engraving printed in black; plate
13¹³⁄₁₆ × 9¹⁵⁄₁₆ ″ (35.1 × 24.9 cm). Geiser/Baer III, 617. The Museum of
Modern Art, New York. Gift of Klaus G. Perls, in memory of
Frank Perls, Art Dealer (by exchange)

Ambroise Vollard. Paris, 1930s. Photograph by Thérèse Bonney.
Collection The Bancroft Library, University of California, Berkeley

Portrait of Ambroise Vollard. c. 1945. Oil on canvas, 24 × 18⅛″
(61 × 46 cm). Private collection

Ambroise Vollard. 28, rue de Martignac, Paris, 1938. Photograph by
Rose Adler. Universités de Paris, Bibliothèque Littéraire Jacques
Doucet

Portrait of Ambroise Vollard. 1910. Oil on canvas, 36¼ × 25⅝ ″ (92 × 65 cm). Zervos II¹, 214. Daix 337. Pushkin State Museum of Fine Arts, Moscow identifiable only by a single object and the inscription; indeed, the degree of abstraction is so great in this painting that Picasso hesitated for a long time between "guitare" and "cithare" for his title.

By the winter of 1911–12, Picasso's and Braque's quest for efficient associations between compositions of abstract purity (whose volumes vibrate beneath differences in the degree of illumination of the monochromatic paintings that are, for the most part, browns, beiges, grays, and whites), on the one hand, and information offered by plastic signs, on the other, exclude any and all ideas of individuality other than gesture or attitude. Thus—except in purely symbolic ways, such as in inscriptions on the surface—it excludes the portrait. This, in fact, led Pierre Reverdy, writing in the first issue of *Nord-Sud* on March 15, 1917, to state: "It will be understood that no cubist painter should execute a portrait."[76] Yet many other Cubist painters besides Picasso executed them quite well.

It is from the notion of "peripheral information" that Picasso discovers a set of possibilities that would allow him to return to a real form of portraiture without falling into illusionism. We know that after seeing the stenciled inscriptions (that is, inscriptions not made by the painter's hand) placed by Braque in his canvas *Le Portugais (The Emigrant)*, Picasso would reintroduce bright color

Daniel-Henry Kahnweiler (detail) in Picasso's studio at 11, boulevard de Clichy, Paris, autumn–winter 1910. Photograph by Picasso. Musée Picasso, Paris, Picasso Archives

Portrait of Daniel-Henry Kahnweiler, III. June 3, 1957. Transfer lithograph printed in black; comp. 25⅜ × 19⁵⁄₁₆″ (64.5 × 49 cm). The Museum of Modern Art, New York. Gift of Mr. and Mrs. Daniel Saidenberg

Daniel-Henry Kahnweiler (detail), at "Le Prieuré" of Saint-Hilaire, near Etampes, 1966. Photograph by Franco Cianetti

Portrait of Daniel-Henry Kahnweiler. 1910. Oil on canvas, 39⅝ × 28⅝″ (100.6 × 72.8 cm). Zervos II¹, 227. Daix 368. The Art Institute of Chicago. Gift of Mrs. Gilbert W. Chapman in memory of Charles B. Goodspeed

Head (Study for a Portrait of Frank Haviland). 1912. Ink on paper, 11½ × 9⅛″ (29 × 23 cm). Zervos VI, 1147. Private collection

Frank Burty Haviland (detail) in Picasso's studio at 11, boulevard de Clichy, Paris, early 1912. Photograph by Picasso. Musée Picasso, Paris, Picasso Archives

(excluded from the almost monochrome works of 1909–11) into his canvases. However, this color is not treated imitatively, but rather as an external piece of information, almost like a sign. In order to mark the rupture with earlier compositions more clearly, Picasso began to use lacquer and Ripolin, thus breaking more forcefully with the matte look of the monochromatic works (and disconcerting Braque at first).[77] But the same reasoning would lead Picasso to glue a fragment of oilcloth on a still life to represent, in illusionistic fashion, chair caning (*Still Life with Chair Caning*).[78]

Naturally there was a big step between this "information" and the realization of a nonillusionistic portrait, and Picasso was alone in taking it. The portrait did not interest Braque, whereas Picasso wanted to "sing" his love for Eva and had to content himself with merely "writing it" in his paintings. It was at Sorgues, in the summer of 1912, that he made a painting of a guitar in which there first appeared a gingerbread heart inscribed "J'aime Eva"; in another canvas, *L'Arlésienne*, the general bearing of the woman was reconstructed by the refraction of the image on several planes.[79] Picasso discovered in this way that he could return to a particular, no longer merely structural, image without recourse to illusionism. A drawing and a

famous gouache of *Girl from Arles* (from the Menil collection; p. 288) reveal his progress in capturing the rhythm of the whole, as well as his greater freedom in the choice of evocative signs.[80] Picasso continued the experiment, after his *papiers collés* at the end of the autumn of 1912, in a large canvas, *Female Nude: "J'aime Eva"* (p. 289) and in early 1913 in the *Portrait of Guillaume Apollinaire* (p. 288), which served as the frontispiece to Apollinaire's *Alcools*. These are Picasso's only portraits at the time: one of his beloved, and the other that of his poet-friend on the occasion of the latter's first great book.

Another move toward a return to the portrait is found in the studies for *Woman in an Armchair* (late 1913–early 1914; p. 291). Once again we have a "synthetic" Cubist statement, although the abstract, nonimitative composition of the woman no longer owes anything to the vertical network of *papiers collés*. The painting brings together feminine elements reconstructed in the same way as in the very abstract paintings of spring 1913, such as *Head of a Girl*,[81] in an armchair that is little modified. It is as if Picasso wanted to revive, in another way, an assemblage he had been working on in early 1913, in which a "conceptual" guitarist was holding an actual guitar.[82]

This series of studies[83] for *Woman in an Armchair* and

Man in an Armchair (Study for a Portrait of Frank Haviland). 1912. Ink (?) on paper, 12⅜ × 7⅞″ (31.5 × 20 cm). Zervos VI, 1161. Private collection

Seated Man (Frank Haviland). 1912. Ink on paper, 12⅛ × 7¾″ (30.8 × 19.7 cm). Not in Zervos. The Metropolitan Museum of Art, New York. Alfred Stieglitz Collection, 1949

the large canvas itself thus constituted another attempt at a "synthetic" portrait of Eva. The many different possibilities Picasso imagined can be seen in these studies. In one he emphasized feminine attributes, such as the waves in her long hair; in another he imagined doubling the breasts, endowing her with a European-type upper half and an African lower half, and marked out the scallops of her silk underskirt; in yet another, we see a garter, and in two others, Picasso draws a "real" face (isolated as such in larger format on the back of the second, p. 290). Here we can clearly make out Eva's features. When I asked Picasso if it could be Eva, he shrugged and replied: "The forms just came to me like that. . . . Of course, Eva was [with me] there."

In the end, Picasso abandoned the recognizable if schematic version of Eva's face and chose the most conceptual, geometrically abstract idea from among the studies. In renouncing what would have been a collage effect, or at least a quotation from Eva's face, Picasso retained in the forms, palette, and lacy details of this great canvas resonant testimony to his love for Eva, and it is surely one of his strongest figure pictures. It bristles with those poetic resonances that would later enchant André Breton.

THE PORTRAIT RECONQUERED

It was in the winter of 1913–14, at the time of a "new crusade," that of *papiers collés*, that Picasso, producing a number of lyrical, joyous canvases in which he sang the praises of "Ma Jolie," began inserting into his Cubist structures bits and pieces of quasi-illusionistic figuration. After using this figuration for objects, Picasso had, in the spring of 1914, taken on human figures. Kahnweiler recounted: "Picasso had shown me two drawings that were not cubist, but classicist, two drawings of a seated man. He had said, 'Still, they're better than before [that is, the pre-Cubist works], aren't they?'"[84]

In these drawings of men at the time, one gets the impression that Picasso was relying closely on Cézanne, once again taking up the question of portraiture that had made him paint the *Portrait of Clovis Sagot* in 1909 as a test of objectivity against the early works in which he cut the surfaces of forms into facet planes. The drawing of a bearded man with a pipe[85] thus reverses the position of the man in Cézanne's painting *Man with a Pipe*, which had been bought by Sergei Shchukin and which Picasso could have seen at Vollard's until about 1911. It is just as clear in the 1914 version of a man seated at a table (p. 36), with the

Girl from Arles. 1912. Oil on canvas, 28¾ × 21¼″ (73 × 54 cm). Zervos II¹, 356. Daix 497. Private collection. Courtesy Thomas Ammann Fine Art, Zurich

Portrait of Guillaume Apollinaire. 1913. Pencil, India ink, and wash on paper, 8¼ × 5⅞″ (21 × 15 cm). Zervos XXVIII, 214. Daix 579. Private collection. (Colorplate, p. 180)

movement of the jacket and the design of the collar closer to another painting of Cézanne's, *The Smoker*, which was bought by Ivan Morozov from Vollard. The elongation of the faces in other drawings is somewhat reminiscent of Derain's archaizing imagery of 1913–14, especially in his *Self-Portrait* and in the *Portrait of Iturrino*, which Picasso had surely seen;[86] the ties between Picasso and Derain had become much closer, leading them to spend time together in Avignon in the summer of 1914. Picasso was careful to avoid a return to real illusionism, with its perspectival space and modeling-in-the-round (as opposed to relief modeling), but was all the while feeling the need to stop fragmenting and recomposing his faces and bodies.

The experimentation that proceeds from drawing to drawing, some of which are highlighted with watercolor, is fraught with hesitation and even with repeated refusals to lapse once again into illusionism. They were only published in the posthumous volume 29 of Zervos because Picasso wanted to avoid all idle discussion of a subject that he knew was highly polemical at the time, and he continued to avoid it even in his final years. He must have retained bitter memories of Braque's reaction to his return to the figure, even if he attached less importance to the reactions of the "Salon" Cubists, who were roundly to condemn the January 1915 *Portrait of Max Jacob* (p. 299).

In addition, some of the drawings that are part of this reconquering of the portrait were no doubt later incorrectly dated 1915, due to a lack of familiarity with

Picasso's work on this problem. The canvas *The Artist and His Model* (p. 298), which issued from the drawings made in Avignon in the summer of 1914, is the prime example. Because of its highly personal significance, Picasso neither showed this picture during his lifetime nor even let it be reproduced; the female nude is the lone, realistic, painted image of Eva that he made.

But during that same stay in Avignon, Picasso had produced the most beautiful, joyous, loving, and the freest of his "synthetic" Cubist portraits of Eva, the canvas known as *Portrait of a Girl* (p. 293). Indeed, all the work from Avignon is characterized by this "dual track" simultaneity and sometimes by a combination of lyrical Synthetic Cubism (at least before World War I broke out) and a renewal of classical figuration (or with the introduction of quasi-illusionistic shapes into the synthetic works). In *The Artist and His Model* and *Portrait of a Girl*, the contrast between these two concepts of painting is pushed to the extreme.

Portrait of a Girl is above all an extraordinary compendium of the joyous and radiant Cubism that came out of the colorful *papiers collés* of 1914. Its consistent elements—some of which, such as the "light bulb," still exist in the form of paper cutouts[87]—were copied in the final picture in *trompe l'oeil*. False moldings, an electric light bulb, and the drawing of a fruit dish coexist with almost abstract pointillist passages of amazing virtuosity. The predominant saturated green—comparable to that

Female Nude: "J'aime Eva." 1912. Oil, sand, and charcoal on canvas, 39¾ × 26″ (75.6 × 66 cm). Zervos II¹, 364. Daix 541. Columbus Museum of Art, Columbus, Ohio. Gift of Ferdinand Howald

Study for Woman in an Armchair (Eva Gouel). 1913. Gouache and black pencil on paper, 12⅞ × 10⅝″ (32.7 × 27 cm). Zervos VI, 1267. Daix 637. Musée Picasso, Paris

Eva Gouel (Marcelle Humbert; detail). Villa des Clochettes, Sorgues, 1912. Photograph by Picasso. Musée Picasso, Paris, Documents section. Gift of Sir Roland Penrose

Study for Woman in an Armchair (Eva Gouel). 1913. Pencil and wax crayon on paper, 9⅛ × 7⅞″ (23 × 20 cm). Zervos XXIX, 2. Daix 638 (verso). Private collection

Woman in an Armchair. 1913. Oil on canvas, 58¼ × 39″ (148 × 99 cm). Zervos II², 522. Daix 642. Collection Sally Ganz of *Green Still Life* in The Museum of Modern Art, New York—adds to the overall joyousness.

Portrait of a Girl is a celebration of Eva, achieved by means of a compendium of all the liberties Picasso had touched upon in the vocabulary and syntax of Synthetic Cubism since Eva had entered his life. In addition, it represented the boldness that he had learned to allow himself in relation to his naturalistic representation. The slicing of the head, the hair, the fruit dish on the left, and the armchair into pointillistic planes; the room with its paneling and draperies, with dotted areas where one would expect the model's body to be, and her arms where one would least expect them: all this in the end recomposes her surprisingly young presence in the enchantment of the painting.

The Artist and His Model is the antithesis of *Portrait of a Girl*. In the former, the painter—Picasso's alter ego—is seated and thoughtful. He is very close, in his figuration, to the "classicist" drawings of seated men from the beginning of Picasso's stay in Avignon.[88] The painter is seated with his right hand resting on his thigh and the left sleeve of his jacket gathered as in some of Cézanne's male portraits (and as echoed in Picasso's *Portrait of Clovis Sagot*), with the gathers distortedly enlarged to show that they are closer to us. The delicate grace of the nude model presents Eva to us in Picasso's most realistic and direct image of her; it is the only untransformed portrait Picasso left of her, with the exception of the 1915 engraving published as the frontispiece for Max Jacob's *La Défense de Tartuffe*.[89] Unlike some parts of the picture,

Eva is entirely painted, as is a portion of the canvas of a landscape on an easel behind her and part of the back wall. There is a nail from which a drawing is hanging, while another nail supports a palette. The nail holding the drawing, as in Braque's 1910 still lifes such as *Violin and Palette* and *Violin and Pitcher*, is sufficient to suggest the orientation. Suddenly we understand that everything is not really treated as a piece of illusionistic representation, but as a graphic *sign*. In this fundamental sense, the composition still belongs to Synthetic Cubism.

The seemingly unfinished aspect of *The Artist and His Model*, I am convinced, is intentional, demonstrative, and meant to proclaim that Picasso had brought together the arts of drawing and painting, just as he had earlier assembled Cubist and perspective space and contradictory treatments of the same object in his *papiers collés* of late 1913–early 1914 from the series Glass on a Table.[90]

In *The Artist and His Model*, Picasso reconquers the portrait while not losing the freedoms of the construction of figure and space made possible by Cubism. He must have realized that he had reached a precarious balance. One might be led to believe that the war, mixed with Picasso's loneliness following Braque's and Derain's mobilizations, would have stopped cold the exploration of the "classicist" portrait, the genre of more realistic drawing that Picasso must have considered the most perilous of all. Nonetheless, he was to take it up once again, and this time very deliberately, with the *Portrait of Max Jacob* in 1915. But that is for another chapter.

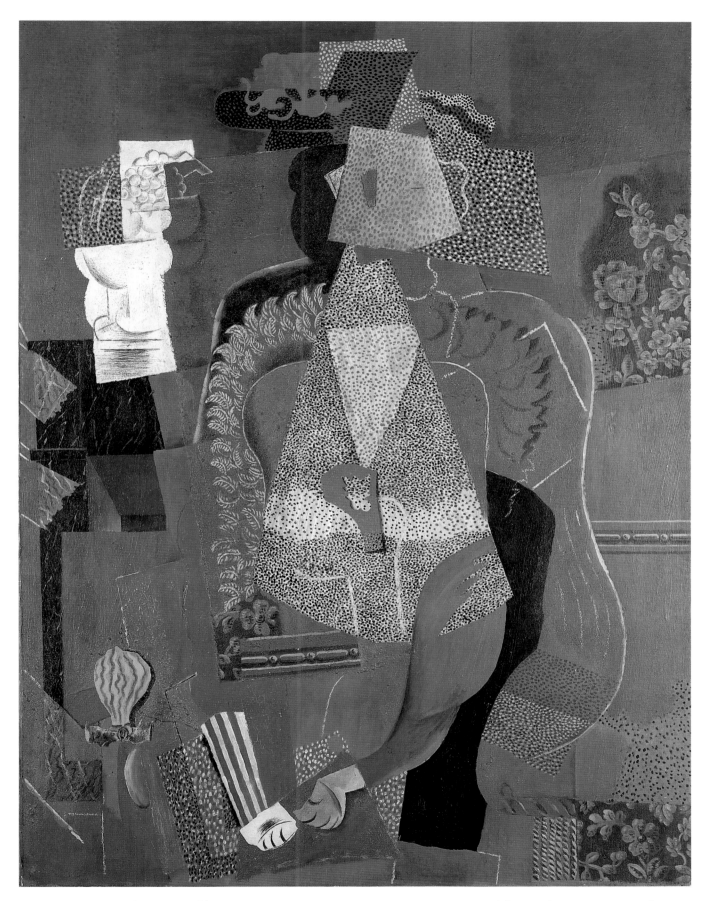

Portrait of a Girl. 1914. Oil on canvas, 51⅛ × 38″ (130 × 96.5 cm). Zervos II², 528. Daix 784. Musée National d'Art Moderne, Centre National d'Art et de Culture Georges Pompidou, Paris. Bequest of Georges Salles, 1967

Notes

This essay was translated from the French by Alyson Waters.

1. Casegemas, we must recall, committed suicide after an unhappy love affair with Germaine. Picasso painted her in *La Vie*, for example (p. 129).

2. Regarding what is known about Madeleine and portraits of her, see Pierre Daix, *Picasso: Life and Art* (New York: HarperCollins, 1993), pp. 39–41.

3. Picasso dated from 1904 the photograph that he took of Ricardo Canals in his studio, where one can see a photograph of Canals's wife, Benedetta, on the mantel.

4. In *Sleeping Nude* (D.B. XI, 11), she is shown in front of a boorish man who was probably her companion at the time, the sculptor whom she called Laurent Debienne. It is probably this couple whom we find again in *Man and Standing Female Nude* (D.B. XI, 8). In *Meditation (Contemplation)*, it is Picasso who is looking at her (p. 133). All these drawings are from late 1904–early 1905.

5. The highly colored palette of this canvas has no counterpart before Picasso's trip to Holland. The self-portrait of Picasso as a Harlequin is reminiscent of the final version of *The Family of Saltimbanques*. For many reasons I would change the date of this work, contrary to D.B. XII, 23, to autumn 1905. The identification of the flashy woman as Germaine—for whom Casagemas had committed suicide in 1901—was made by Picasso to John Richardson. See *Picasso: An American Tribute* (New York: Chanticleer Press, 1962), no. 16 (incorrectly dated 1904).

6. This painting also presents a problem in dating. Because of the overall blue tones, it had been dated 1904 (D.B. XII, 22). However, the notebook M.P. 1857 at the Musée Picasso, Paris, contains, next to studies for Harlequin, others on the theme of *La Coiffure*, which refer to autumn 1905; this was confirmed by its examination at the time the painting was up for sale in Paris in late 1989, when it broke a record, selling for more than $50 million.

7. There exists a whole sequence of Harlequin busts dating from early spring 1909 (Daix 258–61) that may be related to the watercolor *Saint Anthony and Harlequin* (Daix 257), in which the saint and Harlequin confront a nude woman (or in which Harlequin is shown with two nude women in another version). But what we have here is more an exercise in simplifications and geometric divisions of Harlequin's face or of his bust than the return of a Harlequin that might be Picasso's double. This double did not survive beyond the series of studies made in reference to the theme of *Carnival at the Bistro*. The latter was the last attempt with this subject, which became transformed, as we know, into *Bread and Fruitdish on a Table*. See William Rubin, "From Narrative to 'Iconic' in Picasso: The Buried Allegory in *Bread and Fruitdish on a Table* and the Role of *Les*

Demoiselles d'Avignon," *The Art Bulletin* 65, no. 4 (December 1983), pp. 615–49.

8. The title "Fleur de Pavé" must have been given to it by Clovis Sagot, who was announcing that the canvas was for sale at his house.

9. Picasso told Hélène Parmelin (*Picasso says . . .* [London: George Allen and Unwin, 1969], p. 71), that "P'tit Louis" used to come to the Bateau-Lavoir: "He stayed there sometimes all day. He watched me working. He loved that." P'tit Louis, with his disabused pout, had been painted many times by Picasso at the end of 1905, as *Boy with a Pipe* (D.B. XIII, 20, 21), as *Harlequin* (D.B. XIII, 15), and as *Boy with the Ruff* (D.B. XIII, 17 and 18). As for me, I have always thought that this smoker surrounded with flowers, with his absentminded air, may be the only figure alluding to Picasso's experiences with opium smoking.

10. D.B. XIII, 14.

11. See Daix, *Picasso: Life and Art*, pp. 51–52.

12. Fernande Olivier, *Picasso and His Friends* (London: Heinemann, 1964), p. 83.

13. See the photographs of the studio on the rue de Fleurus in *Four Americans in Paris* (New York: The Museum of Modern Art, 1970), pp. 90–91.

14. Michael C. FitzGerald, *Making Modernism: Picasso and the Creation of the Market for Twentieth-Century Art* (New York: Farrar, Straus and Giroux, 1995), pp. 26–31.

15. Gertrude Stein, *Picasso* (London: B. T. Batsford, 1938), passim.

16. Olivier, *Picasso and His Friends*, pp. 82, 83.

17. Stein, *Picasso*, pp. 7–8.

18. D.B. XIV, 2.

19. "The Autobiography of Alice B. Toklas," in Carl van Vechten, ed., *Selected Writings of Gertrude Stein* (New York: Vintage Books, 1990), p. 43.

20. Ibid., p. 49.

21. Robert Rosenblum, *Jean-Auguste-Dominique Ingres* (New York: Harry N. Abrams, 1967), p. 137.

22. See "Matisse's First Lithographs" and "The Three Early 'Woodcuts,'" in Alfred H. Barr, Jr., *Matisse: His Art and His Public* (New York: The Museum of Modern Art, 1951), p. 99.

23. For example, *Still Life with a Purro* and *Still Life* (D.B. XV, 13 and 14). *Purro* is a Provençal form for the Spanish *porron*.

24. The engraving, Geiser 212, was not printed until 1933. The wood block is in the Musée Picasso, Paris; M.P. 3541.

25. It must be recalled that, at the time, the word "primitive," in the sense of original, was used to denote everything that seemed archaic: Roman art as well as Assyrian or Egyptian art, and then African art.

26. See John Elderfield, "The Pastoral, the Primitive and the Ideal," in *The Wild Beasts: Fauvism and Its Affinities* (New York: The Museum of Modern Art, 1976), p. 97f.

27. James Johnson Sweeney, "Picasso and Iberian Sculpture," *The Art Bulletin* 23, no. 3 (September 1941), pp. 191–98.

28. D.B. XV, 10 and 11.

29. D.B. XV, 34.

30. D.B. XV, 43. The reproduction of this

painting, taken from Zervos, was cropped at the top and on the sides, as was realized when *Fernande with a Black Mantilla* entered the Solomon R. Guggenheim Museum in New York in 1991 as a bequest of Hilde Thannhauser.

31. I am thinking of the lithograph the *Large Nude*, whose presence at Druet's is disputed.

32. See the most recent edition of Philippe Dagen's *Lettres à Vlaminck* (Paris: Flammarion, 1994), p. 173.

33. John Richardson, *A Life of Picasso, Volume 1: 1881–1906* (New York: Random House, 1991), pp. 451–52.

34. Josep Palau i Fabre, *Picasso: The Early Years 1881–1907* (New York: Rizzoli, 1981), p. 477.

35. D.B. VII, 22.

36. D.B. XV, 45 and 47.

37. Dora Vallier, "Braque, la peinture et nous," *Cahiers d'art* 29, no. 1 (October 1954), p. 14.

38. *Picasso: Carnet Catalan*, preface and notes by Douglas Cooper (Paris: Berggruen, 1958), p. 27.

39. "The Autobiography of Alice B. Toklas," p. 53.

40. D.B. XIV, 20.

41. D.B. XVI, 27 and 29.

42. D.B. XV, 46. Picasso always kept this painting.

43. Jack Flam, "Matisse and the Fauves," in William Rubin, ed., *"Primitivism" in 20th Century Art* (New York: The Museum of Modern Art, 1984), vol. 1, p. 214.

44. See n. 41, above.

45. D.B. XVI, 22–25.

46. D.B. XVI, 30. Picasso kept this painting and later gave it to the Basel Kunstmuseum.

47. Carnet 6, 40v and 41v, in *Les Demoiselles d'Avignon* (Paris: Editions de la Réunion des musées nationaux, 1988), vol. 1, pp. 201–02. On Raymonde, see vol. 2, p. 509, n. 41.

48. See Rubin, "Primitivism," vol. 1, p. 284.

49. Especially *Figure* (Zervos II², 607).

50. Carnet 16, 51v, in *Les Demoiselles*, vol. 1, p. 307. Pepe Karmel, in a personal communication, suggests that this stylized self-portrait drawing may have been modeled on a late Roman painting from Egypt known as the "Portrait of Ammonius," which entered the Louvre's collection around 1905. See the reproduction in Christiane Desroches Noble Court and Jean Vercoutter, *Un Siècle de souilles françaises en Egypt, 1889–1980* (Cairo: Ecole du Caire and Paris: Musée du Louvre, 1981), no. 340.

51. Carnet 16, 38R, in *Les Demoiselles*, vol. 1, p. 305.

52. We also know of the contemporary geometric stylization of another face of absolute frontality (Zervos VI, 905), and its version in profile (Zervos VI, 908), which we find again in the *Figure*, sculpted in boxwood (Zervos II, 668), now in the Musée Picasso. The same problematic treatment can be seen in two other painted portraits from the same period, the *Peasant Woman*, done at La Rue des Bois, and especially the *Bust of a Peasant Woman* (p. 272), which is perfectly frontal. The latter takes up once again the stylizations of the drawing

(Zervos VI, 905). Something of this passes into the final version of *Three Women* (Daix 131). There is thus an entire period of work that addresses the issue of geometric stylization during the spring and summer of 1908. This period is, in fact, the one that should be called the "African period" ("la periode nègre"), whereas this term has been used to designate everything that was considered "savage."

53. Daix 269.

54. Anne Baldassari, *Picasso photographe, 1901–1916* (Paris: Editions de la Réunion des musées nationaux, 1994), nos. 74 and 75.

55. Ibid., p. 99.

56. Daix 275 and 276.

57. Daix 296.

58. Daix 283–88.

59. See Baldassari, *Picasso photographe*, p. 174.

60. Daix 324 and 326.

61. Daix 329 and 332.

62. Daix 340.

63. Daix 341.

64. Daix 342 and 343, in the Musée National d'Art Moderne and the Tate Gallery, respectively.

65. Daniel-Henry Kahnweiler, *Confessions esthétiques* (Paris: Gallimard, 1963), pp. 27–29.

66. Olivier, *Picasso and His Friends*, p. 144.

67. Ambroise Vollard, *Souvenirs d'un marchand de tableaux* (Paris: Editions Albin Michel, 1948), p. 273.

68. See Baldassari, *Picasso photographe*, p. 118 and fig. 90. Anne Baldassari insists that the photograph of Kahnweiler as it appears in its entirety (not the cropped version which we knew until then) makes very clear "the formal and symbolic relationship that imposes itself between the image of the dealer and the Mukuyi mask [that hung in the studio above and slightly to the right of Kahnweiler's head in the photograph]. . . . The dealer's expression of beatitude is signified, in a manner analogous to the mask, by the arc of an interior smile." It is possible that for Vollard's portrait, Picasso might have used an existing photograph not taken by himself.

69. Ibid., pp. 117, 119–22, 124–25; Daix 422.

70. For the following discussion of the Haviland drawings, see the doctoral dissertation of Pepe Karmel, "Picasso's Laboratory: The Role of His Drawings in the Development of Cubism, 1910–14," New York University, 1993, pp. 156–58. For Fernande Olivier's descriptions of Haviland, see her *Picasso and His Friends*, pp. 114–15, 143.

71. See William Rubin, "Appendix: The Library of Hamilton Easter Field," in Rubin, *Picasso and Braque: Pioneering Cubism* (New York: The Museum of Modern Art, 1989), p. 63.

72. See Jean Loize, "Frank Burty: 'né dans la peinture,'" *Reflets du Roussillon*, no. 53 (spring 1966), pp. 3–8.

73. For the more abstract versions of Haviland's head, see Zervos XXVIII, 28 (captioned "Study for the portrait of Franck [sic] Haviland") and Zervos XXVIII, 168. In addition to the compositional studies discussed below, see Zervos XXVIII, 176 and 178, both captioned "Study for a portrait of Frank Haviland."

74. For the more developed versions of this sketch, see the drawing reproduced in Zervos XXVIII, 154, and in the estate files of the Musée Picasso, negative no. 1148-322. This composition was further developed in a summer 1912 *Figure at the Piano* (Zervos XXVIII, 152; Musée Picasso). The original pencil version of this drawing represented the composer Déodat de Séverac—a mutual friend of Picasso's and Haviland's—but when Picasso redrew the composition in ink, he converted the figure into a female nude.

75. Daix 430.

76. Pierre Reverdy, "Sur le cubisme," *Nord-Sud*, March 15, 1917, p. 7.

77. I recount the entire debate in *Picasso: Life and Art*, pp. 112–13.

78. Daix 466.

79. Zervos XXVIII, 10 and 102; Daix 485 and 497.

80. Zervos XXVIII, 74.

81. Daix 590.

82. Daix 578. This assemblage, which is no longer extant, is recorded in a photograph of Picasso's studio on the boulevard Raspail.

83. Daix 635–41.

84. Daniel-Henry Kahnweiler with Francis Crémieux, *My Galleries and Painters* (New York: Viking Press, 1971), p. 54.

85. Zervos XXIX, 77.

86. The Basque painter Francesco Iturrino had been Picasso's friend since their exhibition together at Vollard's in the spring of 1901.

87. Reproduced in Zervos II, 792–803.

88. Zervos VI, 1198, 1199, and 1206.

89. Geiser 52.

90. See Daix 656–59.

Head of a Woman. 1909. Oil on canvas, 13¾ × 12⅝" (35 × 32 cm). Zervos II¹, 162 (left side). Daix 284. Private collection

Two Heads. 1909. Oil on canvas, 13¾ × 13¼" (35 × 33.5 cm). Zervos II¹, 162 (right side). Daix 285. Private collection

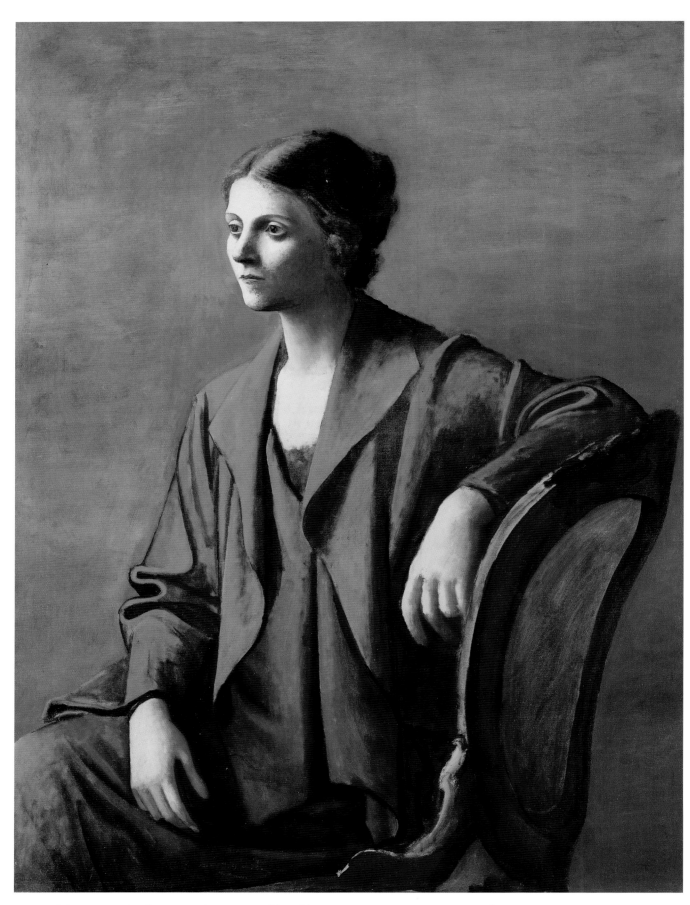

Portrait of the Artist's Wife (Olga). 1923. Oil on canvas, 51¼ × 38¼″ (130 × 97 cm). Zervos V, 53. Private collection

The Modernists' Dilemma: Neoclassicism and the Portrayal of Olga Khokhlova

MICHAEL C. FITZGERALD

In the early months of 1914, Picasso showed Daniel-Henry Kahnweiler two drawings that marked a turning point in his career. They were his first real departure from the seven-year adventure of Cubism, and they announced an engagement with Neoclassicism that would slowly grow to dominate his art during the ensuing decade.[1] Admitting that it "worried me greatly at that time," Kahnweiler recounted, "I must tell you that in the spring of 1914 Picasso had shown me two drawings that were not cubist, but classicist, two drawings of a seated man." Kahnweiler recognized these drawings as a fundamental divide, one that would soon lead to "the stage of painting."[2] During the remainder of the second decade of the twentieth century, portraiture would be the focus of Picasso's germinating Neoclassicism, until it expanded to encompass the full variety of his subjects, and Cubism temporarily abated. Among the many phases of Picasso's work, Neoclassicism is perhaps the most controversial, because its stylistic eclecticism and widespread popularity have led some writers to criticize it as a reactionary departure from modernism.[3] When placed in the context of cultural developments during World War I, however, Picasso's Neoclassicism is better understood as a renewal of the avant-garde.[4] By explicitly embracing history, Picasso escaped the strictures of an increasingly rigid modernism to define a more vital alternative. He repudiated the convention of modernism's ahistoricism in order to acknowledge its maturity, as well as his own, and reju-venate the avant-garde by immersing it in the rich humanistic traditions that many Cubist artists and theorists denied in a search for formal purity.

Picasso's interest in naturalistic description was not particularly surprising. As Kahnweiler knew, he had been salting his Cubist compositions with snippets of realistic passages since 1912, when he had begun counterpointing the near abstraction of his paintings with collage. By 1913 his canvases displayed painted versions of these devices. Even portraiture reemerged after an absence of three years; the studies for *Woman in an Armchair* contain a likeness of his companion, Eva Gouel, even though the figure in the final painting (p. 291) is blank-faced and her chemise, instead, is relatively realistic.[5]

Yet the drawings Kahnweiler saw are different. They cannot be explained by the constant ferment of Picasso's Cubism, as it fluctuated between degrees of naturalism and abstraction. These drawings are not studies that would be integrated into a Cubist composition. Quite the opposite, they were the point of departure for a composition that would subordinate Cubism to classicizing styles. Picasso worked on this composition, *The Artist and His Model*, through the summer of 1914 (p. 298).[6] Its discovery in the artist's estate was arguably the most important single addition to Picasso scholarship in recent years. Until the 1920s, when the artist became wealthy, it was rare for him to keep his paintings. Moreover, his choice never to show this picture, so far as we know, gives it special

The Artist and His Model. 1914. Oil and pencil on canvas, 22⅞ × 22″ (58 × 55.9 cm). Not in Zervos. Daix 763. Musée Picasso, Paris

status.[7] Since Picasso did not reveal his reasons for secrecy, we can only guess why he took this unusual course. But there is little doubt that many observers (in both avant-garde and academic circles) would have interpreted the retrospective style of the painting not merely as an expansive gesture by an inventor of Cubism but rather as an abrupt repudiation of modernism.

I believe that the key to *The Artist and His Model* lies in Picasso's statement to Kahnweiler that its preliminary drawings should be judged in relation to his pre-Cubist work. In describing Picasso's response to his doubts about the drawings of the seated man, Kahnweiler related that the artist had said, "Still, they're better than before, aren't they?" Kahnweiler then clarified the remark by stating that Picasso was comparing them to his work before

Cubism, and in effect was saying, "Better than the classicist, or, if you will, the naturalistic drawings I did before."[8] The direction of Picasso's Cubism, inflected by factors such as his repugnance toward the work of the salon Cubists,[9] led him to broaden his art, not narrow it, by revisiting the styles he had elaborated during the Blue and Rose periods; this opening led to his renewed involvement with a broad range of representation in Western art, which in turn spawned a reinvigorated modernism. The catalyst for this transformation may well have been his encounter with major examples of his Blue and Rose work—which he had long not seen—when they were displayed in March of 1914 for the auction of the Peau de l'Ours collection.[10]

Picasso did not simply revert to a previous style. The

Portrait of Max Jacob. 1915. Pencil on paper, 13 × 9¾″ (33 × 24.8 cm). Zervos VI, 1284. Private collection

Portrait of Ambroise Vollard. 1915. Pencil on paper, 18⅜ × 12⅝″ (46.7 × 32 cm). Zervos II², 922. The Metropolitan Museum of Art, New York. The Elisha Whittelsey Collection, The Elisha Whittelsey Fund, 1947

taut linear schema of *The Artist and His Model* recalls the manner of Ingres, as do the attenuated proportions that also link it with the work of the Blue and Rose periods, another phase of Picasso's dialogue with the nineteenth-century artist most revered by the twentieth-century avant-garde. Cézanne's seated men of the 1890s supply models for the artist's pose and his gargantuan size compared to the woman he appears to sit beside, as well as his idiosyncratic internal proportions. More surprising are indirect references to the work of Courbet. Picasso placed his artist and model before a landscape painting, thereby recalling Courbet's *Studio* (1854–55) and the allegory of representation it presents.[11] Yet *The Artist and His Model* is ultimately more concerned with the present than with the past. It turns less on questions of realism than on issues of portraiture. Although Picasso's artist is not a literal self-portrait (as is Courbet's), he is a "stand-in" persona, and the fully rendered head of the model is a stylized likeness of Eva Gouel, his companion since 1912.

Disguised portraits were, of course, common in Picasso's art of the Blue and Rose periods; the Peau de l'Ours exhibition of 1914 included several prime examples —sometimes not so disguised as all that—particularly *The Family of Saltimbanques* (in which Picasso symbolically

represented himself, Fernande, Apollinaire, Jacob, and Salmon; p. 132) and a watercolor called *Meditation* (p. 133).[12] In the latter work, the somewhat idealized portrait of Picasso musing while Fernande sleeps is especially suggestive of the couple in *The Artist and His Model.* As in the case of their predecessors, the figures in *The Artist and His Model* tie the picture's subject to the artist's self-image. At a moment of fundamental change in his art, a divergence which must have caused him considerable hesitation, Picasso portrayed the artist lost in thought. As the point of origin for Picasso's renewed Neoclassicism, *The Artist and His Model* enables us to discern that he returned to classicism through his work of the Blue and Rose periods, and it strongly suggests that his revived interest in portraiture stemmed from this process.

Certainly, Picasso's Neoclassicism became almost synonymous with portraiture during the years 1915 to 1920.[13] His first "undisguised" portrait during this eclectic revival of representational styles was a likeness of Max Jacob, which he drew in January 1915 (above). The resemblance of this portrait to the sketches from the previous spring and summer demonstrates a clear link.[14] Not only do they share the same medium (pencil on paper) and modest format of approximately thirteen by ten inches (33 by

24.8 cm), but the images correspond to a high degree. A man dressed in a baggy, nondescript suit sits on a chair in a room, the perimeter and other contents of which are only vaguely delineated. Nonetheless, there is no doubt that the latter image is a portrait in the most conventional sense, and that one of the primary purposes is to record the sitter. Picasso rendered Jacob's head with a minute precision that crawls over his collar and jacket until his figure fades into the surrounding space. Even though Picasso rarely drew portraits from life, Jacob testified that he sat for this one, and the frontal pose seems chosen to enhance the sense of confrontation between subject and artist.[15]

For both of them, this was a commemorative image. For Jacob it served an official function. It portrayed him on the eve of his baptism into the Catholic faith. With the ceremony scheduled to take place later that month and Picasso serving as godfather, both Picasso and Jacob must have intended this portrait to acknowledge the event. Yet for Picasso, too, it marked a significant moment. His life had changed drastically during the months since he had shown Kahnweiler his first sketches of a seated man. Despite Picasso's exemption from military service, guaranteed by his Spanish citizenship, the initial months of World War I had already demonstrated that he would not escape major disruptions in his life and art. One of its first effects may well be registered by the apparently unfinished state of *The Artist and His Model*,[16] but the war had an even greater impact on Picasso's Cubism, as the mobilization of Georges Braque and André Derain, followed by Guillaume Apollinaire's enlistment, left him with few like-minded artists who might vet and encourage his innovations. The most severe blow for Picasso was the loss of his devoted dealer and the isolation from his recent work that this entailed. Kahnweiler had been surprised by the war and had been caught outside France; his German citizenship precluded his return and forced the sequestration of his stock for at least the duration of hostilities. By January 1915 Picasso realized that his isolation was nearly complete. Besides the loss of contact with many of his fellow artists and his dealer, the bulk of his pictures in Kahnweiler's inventory was inaccessible, whether for his own study or for sale to collectors. The flow of ideas and money had been cut off.[17]

Max Jacob was Picasso's oldest Parisian friend. By drawing his portrait, Picasso reconfirmed contact with one of his few companions still present in the city and unthreatened by the war. The precision of the portrait seems to reflect Picasso's desire to grasp and hold his links with the past, as the style itself laps back in part to his early years in France. A similar sense of retrospection also characterizes his 1915 portrait of Ambroise Vollard (p. 299), the next in a series that would include two of Apollinaire made during 1916 (p. 190). As the presenter of Picasso's

first major exhibition in Paris, a regular buyer of his Blue and Rose work, and the purchaser of some of the most difficult Cubist work of 1910, Vollard was an important, if less intimate, member of Picasso's early community. The process of posing for this drawing confirms a revival of their relationship at a time when Picasso had severed his ties with Kahnweiler and must have been searching for a new dealer. These circumstances suggest foresight as well as reminiscence.

Despite the impression of exact description created by the meticulous detail of these drawings, they are, in fact, far from naturalistic portraits. Appropriately, the portrait of Cézanne's dealer most clearly manifests these departures. Not only is Vollard's head small for his body, but his arms and legs are made to fluctuate according to their role in the composition and their proximity to the viewer. Although Vollard's distant left arm seems almost vestigial, his right arm is elongated so that his right hand can clasp his left. Likewise, his right leg appears unusually long and thick in comparison to the nearly transparent left leg. These are the same devices Picasso had employed in his sketches of 1914, and they draw attention to the possibility that the portrait of Jacob is also less purely descriptive than it first appears. Jacob wrote to Apollinaire, "I am posing for Pablo at his studio. He is doing a portrait of me in pencil that is very beautiful; it resembles at once my grandfather, an old Catalan peasant, and my mother."[18] This characterization of Jacob does not correspond to his elegant, even dandyish, dress in contemporary photographs, but it does recall Picasso's seated man from the previous year.[19] With the portrait of Vollard, Picasso had achieved a synthesis worthy of Ingres, a style whose overarching linear armature could bend the figure to its pattern or embrace a naturalistic passage without interruption.

Picasso's friends celebrated these portraits. Jacob informed Francis Picabia that "Picasso made a pencil portrait of Vollard, genre Ingres, very recognizable and very good."[20] In March 1915 Apollinaire published André Level's recent intelligence: "Picasso . . . 'has outdone Ingres in his admirable drawings without even trying,' according to a letter I received from the anonymous author of the excellent preface to the catalogue of the *Peau de l'ours*."[21] Yet within Picasso's work, these portraits were rare anomalies; Cubism remained at that moment his primary expressive mode and was to remain a significant alternate style throughout the period we call Neoclassic. As he told a Swedish artist, Arvid Fougstedt, who saw the drawing of Vollard during a visit to Picasso's studio, "People say that I have abandoned cubism to make this sort of thing; that's not true, you can confirm it yourself."[22]

A furor had, nevertheless, erupted immediately. By late January of 1915, Beatrice Hastings reported that Picasso's portrait of Jacob had caused many people to conclude

Harlequin. 1915. Oil on canvas, 72¼ × 41⅜″
(183.5 × 105.1 cm). Zervos II², 555. Daix 844.
The Museum of Modern Art, New York.
Acquired through the Lillie P. Bliss Bequest

Portrait of Léonce Rosenberg. 1915. Pencil on paper, 18⅛ × 13¼″
(46 × 33.5 cm). Zervos XXIX, 201. Private collection

that Cubism had been only a passing experiment. Admitting that she had not seen the portrait (which she mistakenly described as a painting), Hastings wrote that she could "testify to the state of soul among the cubists," and concluded that "I can't imagine that Picasso is really doing that. I hope not."[23] When the portrait of Jacob was published in the December 1916 issue of *L'Elan*, advocates of Cubism took the offensive. Pierre Reverdy couched his rejection in theoretical terms and abstained from criticizing Picasso by name. "Cubism is an eminently plastic art; but an art of creation, not of reproduction or interpretation. . . . After the foregoing it will be understood that no cubist painter should execute a [realist] portrait."[24] In December 1917 André Salmon disrupted a conference by defending the continual ferment of Picasso's art in opposition to a Cubism that some believed immutable. Explaining his remarks to Picasso, Salmon concluded: "That [his statement that Cubism cannot be codified] cannot be agreeable to Metzinger and Co. For him, the school of Metzinger is the only way out, and he does not admit that one can make the portrait of Vollard or Max after what has preceded."[25]

As Jean Cocteau later remarked, "A [Cubist] dictatorship hung heavy over Montmartre and Montparnasse."[26] Christopher Green recently characterized the increasingly restrictive definition of Cubism that spread during the war. "Only after 1914 [that is to say, after the greatest era of Cubism had ended] did Cubism come almost exclusively to be identified with a singleminded insistence on the isolation of the art-object in a special category with its own laws and its own experiences to offer, a category considered above life." And he explained the importance of this phase of Cubist theory for conceptions of the avant-garde. "It is Cubism in this later period that has most to tell anyone concerned with the problems of Modernism and post-modernism now, because it was only then that issues emerged with real clarity in and around Cubism which are closely comparable with those that emerged in and around Anglo-American Modernism in the sixties and after."[27] Ironically, this conception, so opposed to the fluid practice of Picasso, Braque, and a few others, was not only the basis for criticism of Picasso's portraits in the second decade of the twentieth century, but it also seems to be the point of departure for those who continue to condemn Picasso's Neoclassicism as a regression from Cubism. As is often the case, theory, with its tendency to

Olga Khokhlova in the ballet *Thamar*, performed by Diaghilev's Ballets Russes during their first New York tour, [April] 1916. Photograph by Count Jean de Strelecki. Musée Picasso, Paris, Picasso Archives

reduce creativity to a set of precepts, has apparently blinded many critics.

Picasso probably dismissed the public discussion, but he could not isolate himself from this "purified" version of Cubism because he depended at that moment on one of its chief promoters for his financial well-being. The art dealer Léonce Rosenberg had quickly stepped in to fill the gap left by Kahnweiler's exile. With hardly anyone buying art, Rosenberg made major purchases from Picasso, Braque, and Léger; yet he also acquired works by Metzinger, Gleizes, and other Cubists whom Kahnweiler had refused to represent. Under the standard "L'Effort Moderne," Rosenberg's gallery and publications soon would become the preeminent forum for the presentation of Cubism as a cohesive movement.[28] Given Rosenberg's single-minded dedication to the whole of Cubism and the widespread criticism of Picasso's portraits within his camp, it may seem surprising that he posed for Picasso during the last months of 1915 (p. 301). On Picasso's part, however, the choice was predictable; the portrait of Rosenberg follows that of Vollard and confirms that Léonce had become his primary patron, thereby assuming the role Vollard had evidently declined to accept. In fact, the drawing depicts Léonce standing in Picasso's studio before a painting, *Harlequin* (1915; p. 301), which he pur-

chased in November; surely, the portrait celebrates that particular event. Apparently, Léonce put aside his dislike of realism in order to obtain tangible evidence of his importance to the artist. Picasso, for his part, probably enjoyed the irony of the situation.

Picasso's relationship with Léonce illustrates the very significant changes that took place in the artist's life during the last two years of the war. Only a few months after drawing Léonce's portrait, Picasso began to distance himself from the dealer. Léonce had reneged on one of his major purchases, and he ceased making any new ones. But the problem was not only financial. As Léonce pressed him for a commitment to the Galerie de L'Effort Moderne, Picasso grew more and more unwilling to serve as the point man of Léonce's strategy to present the Cubists as a phalanx.[29] By 1918 Picasso openly ridiculed the scheme. While visiting Rosenberg's gallery, he reportedly responded to a question about a recent burglary at his home in Montrouge with the quip that he had been "ransacked, . . . pointing to the pictures all around him" in the gallery. Perhaps most important, Léonce's conviction about party-line Cubism had led him to criticize the ballet *Parade*, the symbol of Picasso's escape from rigid conceptions of avant-gardism.[30]

Picasso's shift from a more cloistered modernism (fostered by Kahnweiler, partly codified by the "salon Cubists," and defended by Léonce) to his work with the Ballets Russes and other "worldly" activities that followed the war marks a fundamental divide in his career. Whether one chooses to say that it started with the attention of well-heeled and aristocratic buyers and museum curators at the auction of the Peau de l'Ours, or with Picasso's affection for Eugenia Errazuriz and Cocteau a year or two later, there is no question that Picasso's life and art began to take a new course during the war—well before he met Olga in the spring of 1917.[31] Kahnweiler would later say that "Cocteau was very dangerous because he saw everything in a worldly aspect."[32] During

Olga Khokhlova, Pablo Picasso, and Jean Cocteau (detail). Rome, 1917. Photographer unknown. Musée Picasso, Paris, Picasso Archives

Jean Cocteau. *Picasso and Olga*. 1917. Pencil on paper, 10⅞ × 8⅛″ (27.5 × 20.5 cm). Private collection

Olga, Left Profile. 1917. Pencil on paper, 7⅛ × 5⅜″ (18 × 13.5 cm). Not in Zervos. Collection Marina Picasso

Portrait of Olga. 1917. Pencil on paper, 9⅛ × 5⅞″ (23 × 15 cm). Not in Zervos. Private collection

the Paris debut of *Parade* in the summer of 1917, Léonce warned his artists to avoid contact with Cocteau and to refuse participation in ballets.[33]

These Parisians' skepticism of the Ballets Russes is not entirely unfair because Sergei Diaghilev had not presented a full-scale season in the French capital since 1914, and he had substantially transformed his earlier, more conventional aesthetic in the intervening years. In *Diaghilev's Ballets Russes*, Lynn Garafola characterized this change: "Ironically, *Parade* came at the end rather than the beginning of an extraordinary revolution initiated by Diaghilev in late 1914. Between that year and 1917, the *barin* yielded to the visionary radical, the bellettrist to the creative artist: as Europe warred, Diaghilev moved the Ballets Russes to the forefront of the avant-garde."[34] If most Parisians' opinion of the Ballets Russes in early 1917 was thus anachronistic, *Parade* offered a revelatory update. Contrasting with the Cubist sets and some costumes for this ballet, however, the curtain Picasso designed for the production recalls both the subjects and the styles of his pre-Cubist pictures, and one might be inclined to see it as his first major painting in a Neoclassical style. Nonetheless, its rendering fits neatly into a scenographic tradition.[35] The two important paintings he executed while working with the troupe in Rome, *Harlequin and Woman with Necklace* and *Italian Woman*,[36] are indisputably Cubist.

Picasso's exploration of Neoclassicism continued for a time to be confined almost exclusively to portraits, even though the number and stylistic variety of these works rapidly burgeoned.[37] Sketches of Diaghilev, Cocteau, Léonide Massine, and other members of the troupe fill his notebooks, but most of the pages are devoted to Olga. Their frequency reflects the romance, although hardly

any describe it. One sketch by Cocteau evokes the infectious gamesmanship that drove the exhaustive work on the ballet and spilled over smoothly into casual moments of recreation (above). In this sketch, Cocteau drew a caricature of Picasso and Olga seated at the roulette table of a Mediterranean casino. By showing Picasso holding a copy of Apollinaire's *Le Poète assassiné*, Cocteau has made the artist assume an additional guise: "the Bird of Benin," an artist who befriended the doomed protagonist of that book and shared his bohemian life.[38] In mock horror, Olga is shown throwing her hands up and turning away from her corrupter.

When Picasso met Olga in the early months of 1917, she was no neophyte in the theatrical world.[39] She had joined the Ballets Russes in 1911, at the age of twenty, to participate in Diaghilev's first independent season. The daughter of Stéphane Khokhlova, a colonel in the Imperial Russian military, and his wife, Lidia Vinchenko, she had already trained in the private St. Petersburg studio of a respected ballet master, Yevgenia Pavlovna Sokolova, but this was her first professional position. Although Olga never became a prima ballerina, she was far from neglected by Diaghilev's choreographers. In 1912 Vaslav Nijinsky chose her to join Bronislava Nijinska among the nymphs in *Afternoon of a Faun*, and she danced regularly throughout her career with the company (opposite). Massine particularly admired her talent. In 1916 he made her a principal dancer in the premiere of his ballet *The Maids of Honor*, a role she repeated the following year in Barcelona.

Among the many drawings of Olga that Picasso made in 1917 (above), one stands out (center) for its evidence of the artist's obsessive attention and the sitter's detachment.

Olga in a Mantilla. 1917. Oil on canvas, 25¼ × 20⅞″ (64 × 53 cm). Zervos III, 40. Private collection

Picasso departed from his usual practice of regarding his subjects from a distance, in full or three-quarter length.[40] He brings us close to Olga by presenting only her head and shoulders. This intimate proximity, however, is diffused by her pose in strict profile. Picasso's intense scrutiny of her features, reflected in a delicacy of nuance not seen since the portrait of Vollard, does not engage her gaze. With a wispy touch, Picasso sketched Olga's open blouse and loosely gathered, wavy hair as a frame for her deep-set eye and the crisp line of a profile that fades into a soft chin. The model for this portrait is clearly the ancient tradition of the cameo, with its formal pose enforced by a sharp outline and low relief. Not only is the drawing distinguished by its high finish, it alone among Picasso's extant portraits of Olga bears an inscription. Near the lower left corner of the sheet, Picasso wrote, *"Rome 1917 / pour Olga Khokhlova / Picasso."*

Rafael Maria Martinez Padilla. *La Mantilla.* 1909. Oil on canvas, 48⅛ × 39⅜″ (122 × 100 cm). Private collection

Woman in Spanish Costume. 1917. Oil on canvas, 45⅝ × 35⅛″ (116 × 89 cm). Zervos III, 45. Museu Picasso, Barcelona

Actually, Picasso corrected the spelling of "Khokhlova," making it difficult to distinguish the precise combination of letters he finally chose.[41] This uncertainty over the dedication, coupled with the pose and style of the portrait, suggest that Picasso made it as a formal matter, as a presentation drawing during their courtship. Despite the seductiveness of this scenario, however, artistic practice plays at least as great a role in shaping this image as does personal romance.

This drawing prepares us for Picasso's first canvas of Olga. With one or two possible exceptions,[42] all the portraits Picasso had made since 1914 were sketched on paper; the sheets were modest in size, and the medium was either pencil or ink. While in Barcelona during the

Olga Picasso in the 23, rue La Boétie apartment (detail), Paris, c. 1921. On the wall her portrait (Zervos III, 83) and some drawings for *The Three-Cornered Hat*, 1920. Photograph on a postcard by Picasso. Musée Picasso, Paris, Picasso Archives

Olga Picasso in the studio at 22, avenue Victor-Hugo, Montrouge, November 1917. Photograph by Picasso. Musée Picasso, Paris, Picasso Archives

summer and fall of 1917, Picasso transferred his pursuit of portraiture from drawing to painting and executed three canvases, the most important of which depicts Olga (p. 304). This is the portrait *"à la mantille,"* of which biographers from Penrose to Gedo have taken a sour view, as an image that evinces Olga's "apparently rigid, angry, and possessive" personality.[43] In the context of Picasso's portraiture, however, such interpretations seem dubious at best. From the beginning of his revival of the genre, Picasso had shown little interest in revealing the psychology of his sitters.[44] For all its apparent naturalism, the portrait of Jacob seemed rather fanciful to its subject, and the image of Vollard is riven with formal plays that speak more of a dialogue with art than of attention to the man. Even the cameo of Olga reflects Picasso's strategy of modulating his confrontation with the sitter through a panoply of historical styles to the point that artifice overcomes representation.

This is also the case with his first painted portraits. The canvas of Olga was paired with another picture, a portrait of a woman in Spanish costume (p. 305). In the latter painting—a bravado act in which Picasso, in effect, "repainted" a portrait by his Barcelona friend Rafael Padilla (p. 304)—Picasso fuses his native tradition with an

opposing modern style based on pointillism; in the portrait of Olga, he subjects his new Russian fiancée to that tradition. Like the "Roman portrait," this painting shows only her head and shoulders, but the delicate gradations in that previous drawing are absent. A heavy mantilla hides all but two spit curls; a searing light picks out each strand of the weave and defines Olga's features with linear precision. The edges of her lips, eyelids, and brows appear even crisper than the fringe at her forehead. Picasso's portrayal of Olga may seem unflattering, but this harshness stems from his attention to style, not personality. By adopting the idiom of Spanish realism, Picasso assimilated her into his native tradition. This is Olga playing Carmen, and Picasso beginning to evolve ideas for the ballet *The Three-Cornered Hat*.[45] Such an interpretation helps explain why he gave the portrait to his mother, who kept it throughout the remainder of her life.

With Olga's departure from the Ballets Russes at the end of June 1917 and the couple's return to Montrouge in the fall, Picasso began the painting that would be, in the view of many, his greatest portrait of his future wife and also the most controversial work of his career during the immediate postwar period, *Olga in an Armchair* (opposite). This painting is the culmination of Picasso's exploration

Olga in an Armchair. 1917. Oil on canvas, 51¼ × 34⅝″ (130 × 88 cm). Zervos III, 83. Musée Picasso, Paris

Portrait of Olga. January 27, 1918. Oil on canvas, 13¾ × 10⅝″ (35 × 27 cm).
Zervos III, 125. Private collection

Portrait of Madame Georges Wildenstein. 1918. Pencil on paper,
13¾ × 9⅝″ (35 × 24.3 cm). Not in Zervos. Private collection

of portraiture over the previous four years and his most
complex integration of classicism and modernism thus
far. Although four drawings show Picasso studying
aspects of the pose, a recently discovered photograph he
took presumably in late 1917 enables us to penetrate much
deeper (p. 306).[46] Not only does it show her seated in the
chair according to the pose in the painting, but she wears
the same dress and holds a fan. The pile of books under
her right foot proves that the pose was consciously
constructed; the photograph must have been taken to
facilitate work on the painting. The existence of the photograph, however, does not preclude the references to
Ingres that are frequently cited (or to the work of other
artists).[47] Nor, of course, does it mean that the painting
merely reproduces the photograph. Indeed, the more one
compares the two images, the more their points of con-
gruence are overwhelmed by differences, and the remarkable sophistication of Picasso's composition emerges.

Picasso chose not to reproduce the studio clutter seen
in the background of the photograph. He lightened the
shadows registered in the photograph and darkened its
brightest areas, so volumes in the painting are less heavily
modeled and seem to flatten. As a result, Olga's face
appears thinner, and her overall proportions are slimmed.
She sits more erect, her head tilts slightly to the left, and
her gaze does not engage ours. Perhaps most obviously,

Picasso left Olga hanging in midair by deleting the skirt
and legs of the chair. These steps produce an atmosphere
much like the "hermetic environment of feminine luxury" that Robert Rosenblum has ascribed to Ingres'
portraits.[48] Since at least 1914, Picasso had been deeply
interested in Ingres' ability to create portraits that overwhelm the sitter in artistic conceits without entirely dis-
patching verisimilitude. In this portrait of Olga, Picasso
equaled, if not surpassed, the master insofar as he constructed the most harmonious of his Neoclassical compositions on principles that would seem antithetical:
Picasso's *Cubist* experience drives his stylistic revivalism
far beyond its *Ingresque* roots. The portrait of Vollard, for
example, contains Cubist passages, but its structure deviates only slightly from the innovations of Cézanne and
Ingres. In the portrait of Olga, however, Picasso orchestrated a much greater and more decorative complexity
without sacrificing a classical balance. He stretched further the notorious malleability of Ingres' figures and
combined their flowing linear plasticity with an independence from strict perspective that draws on the achievements of Cézanne and Cubism.

Divergences between the painting and the photograph
cannot be explained by a slightly adjusted pose. Picasso's
pictorial manipulations of his sitter—not her shifts in posture—determine the composition and transport it beyond

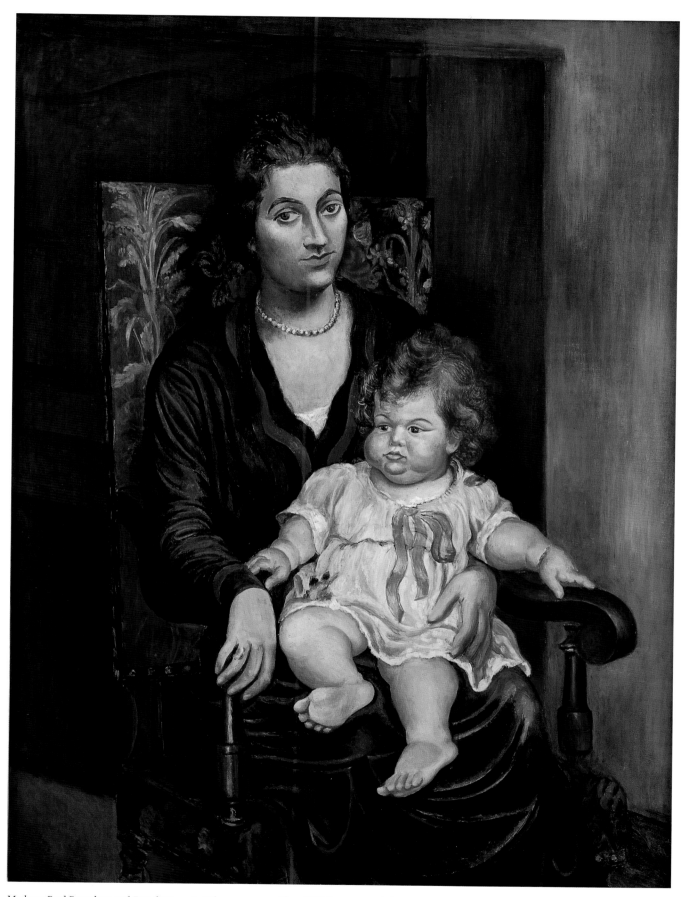

Madame Paul Rosenberg and Daughter. 1918. Oil on canvas, 51¼ × 38¼″ (130 × 97 cm). Zervos III, 242. Private collection, Paris restrictions enforced by the one-point perspective of the camera's lens. The rendering of Olga's head is an obvious departure, both from the photograph and from the preparatory sketches. Gradated with an infinite care that we expect more of Brancusi than of Picasso, this ovoid rests on a lengthened neck that betrays no evidence of the tendons necessary to support it. The face is so shallow that Olga's deep-set eyes seem only slightly indented, and her lips float on the planes of the cheeks, separated only by their color and sharp contour. The extended bonnet of Olga's somewhat reddish hair, however, introduces a distortion beyond the devices of Ingres. Although Olga's face and chest are seen from the frontal viewpoint captured by the camera, her hair disobeys perspective, not only by refusing to recede into depth but also by offering an almost aerial view. Picasso presented much of the figure as if observed from slightly above, as well as straight on. Thus we see the top of Olga's head, the full length of her left arm, and the fan from hinge to border. These variations are not the only ones Picasso wove into the image. As the effect of a higher perspective enabled him to flatten the figure along its vertical axis, another facilitated the same result laterally. Olga's body and the chair she occupies are portrayed as if viewed to the left of the scene. Not only does her right hand seem to overlap the

Igor Stravinsky. c. 1925. Photograph by Man Ray. Musée Picasso, Paris. Gift of Raoul Leven

Portrait of Lydia Lopokova. 1919. Pencil on paper, 14 × 10″ (35.7 × 25.5 cm). Zervos III, 299. Thaw Collection. The Pierpont Morgan Library, New York

Portrait of Paul Rosenberg. 1918–19. Pencil on paper, 14 × 10″ (35.6 × 25.4 cm). Zervos III, 255. Collection Rosenberg Family

Portrait of Igor Stravinsky. May 24, 1920. Pencil on gray paper, 24⅜ × 19⅛″ (62 × 48.5 cm). Zervos IV, 60. Musée Picasso, Paris

Olga in a Shawl. 1920. Lead pencil and charcoal on paper, 24¼ × 19¼″ (61.5 × 49 cm). Zervos IV, 113. Musée Picasso, Paris

Olga Reading. July 31, 1920. Lead pencil on paper, 16¾ × 10⅞″ (42.5 × 27.7 cm). Zervos XXX, 92. Musée Picasso, Paris

Studies. 1920. Oil on canvas, 39⅜ × 31⅞″ (100 × 81 cm). Zervos IV, 226. Musée Picasso, Paris

upholstery, but her arm appears foreshortened, and the surface of the upholstery flows into the glancing plane of her body.

Unlike Cézanne's portraits of his wife, Picasso's painting does not call attention to the subtle deviations from strict perspective it enfolds. Picasso maintained this visual unity by diminishing the three-dimensionality of his subject, thereby removing the depth that would bring them into conflict. He extended the illusion of shallowness across Olga's body by deleting her forward-projecting feet and by accenting her crossing knee so slightly that it appears submerged in her voluminous skirt. The patterns woven into the fabrics enhance this effect. Bright florals emerging from the black background of the upholstery are echoed in the rosettes across the bodice and skirt of Olga's gown, and the gathers at her waist extend their rhythm over her figure. Only the projecting fan creates depth in the foreground, but even here Picasso's imitation of a high viewpoint diminishes its plunge. Finally, the rarefied atmosphere of Picasso's painting is heightened by his decision to leave the surrounding canvas largely untouched. Except for the barest suggestions of the studio setting, the figure floats free of reality, mediated only by the washy strokes outlining her face and left side. Besides setting off Olga's white skin from

Woman Reading (Olga). 1920. Oil on canvas, 65⅜ × 40¼″ (166 × 102 cm). Zervos IV, 180. Musée National d'Art Moderne, Centre National d'Art et de Culture Georges Pompidou, Paris

Olga Picasso seated in the Picassos' garage at Fontainebleau, in the midst of a group of large pastel drawings (Zervos IV, 347, 356, 345, 324, 346, and 349) associated with *Three Women at the Spring* (Zervos IV, 322); a pastel landscape (Zervos IV, 279); and, tacked to the wall at the right, the *Three Musicians* (Zervos IV, 331). Summer 1921. Photographer unknown. Pushkin State Museum of Fine Arts, Moscow

the neutral canvas, this casual boundary alerts us to the artificiality of what lies within.[49]

As Pierre Daix wrote, "Picasso would get Olga into the Louvre." And Daix specified the achievements that justified this ambition. "He had reached in his painting a point of comprehension. He understood what there was in common between Poussin, Ingres, and Cézanne and the quest conducted by Braque and himself during Cubism's grand phases of discovery: the perfect rigor and order of compositions which carry the powers of painting to their peak of purity and strength."[50]

Following their marriage on July 12, 1918, the couple spent their honeymoon at Biarritz, where Picasso elaborated the Neoclassical elegance of his recent painting in a series of drawings portraying the wealthy and attractive women who increasingly surrounded them. Eugenia Errazuriz provided accommodations for the honeymooners in her villa, as she had previously shepherded Picasso through high society (p. 59). Most of the portraits were exquisite pencil sketches on paper, but the major composition was a large painting of Madame Paul Rosenberg and her young daughter, Micheline (p. 309). Adopting a pose similar to the one he had used for the 1917 Ingresque portrait of Olga, Picasso painted the mother and child in a sedate style that avoids many of the ambiguities he had just explored; its relative conventionality led him to sign a parody sketch after it "Boldini." In this way he seems to have

been poking fun at its similarity to society portraiture.[51]

Picasso's willingness to pass his honeymoon painting a formal portrait of Madame Paul Rosenberg was the direct result of his decision to join her husband's gallery; this was Picasso's first formal affiliation since the rupture with Kahnweiler in 1914, and it signaled his final rejection of his experiment with Léonce, Paul's brother. Moreover, the portrait of Madame Georges Wildenstein, which Picasso also executed that summer (p. 308), reflects Wildenstein's role as the primary silent backer of this new collaboration in commercial promotion.[52] Picasso's alliance with Paul Rosenberg would endure until the beginning of World War II (p. 310). By linking his career with this combination of world-renowned dealers, Picasso completed the migration from bohemia to the *beaux quartiers* that had begun with the move from the Bateau-Lavoir to the boulevard de Clichy in 1909, before the heyday of Cubism.

Soon after the Picassos returned to Paris in the fall of 1918, they moved into an elegant building at 23, rue La Boétie, next door to Paul Rosenberg's gallery and residence. The portrait of Madame Rosenberg had become the emblem of the new alliance. In late September, Rosenberg wrote to Picasso, "Everyone knows that Picasso painted the portrait of my wife and daughter. Léonce heard about it from Cocteau and, naturally, wishes it were Cubist, even though 'Miche' [Micheline] is 'roundist.'"[53] Léonce understood the potential effect of

Portrait of Olga. 1921. Pastel and charcoal on paper, mounted on canvas, 50 × 38″ (127 × 96.5 cm). Not in Zervos. Musée Picasso, Paris, on extended loan to the Musée des Beaux Arts, Grenobleo

Harlequin with Violin ("Si Tu Veux"). 1918. Oil on canvas, 56 × 39½″ (142 × 100.3 cm). Zervos III, 160. The Cleveland Museum of Art. Purchase, Leonard C. Hanna, Jr. Bequest

Olga Stretched Out, Knitting. 1918. Pencil on writing paper, 10⅞ × 8½″ (27.8 × 21.5 cm). Zervos III, 153. Musée Picasso, Paris

this portrait; its subject and style appeared publicly to reject the Cubist aesthetic program he championed.

In late October 1919, Paul Rosenberg opened his first exhibition of Picasso's work. It presented 167 recent drawings and watercolors, but no paintings. This selection emphasized the mediums in which Picasso had developed his Neoclassical style and demonstrated that over the preceding year it had spread far beyond the confines of portraiture. Although the exhibition included twenty-seven portraits, that group lagged behind the thirty-four studies of Open Windows at Saint Raphaël and was nearly equaled by twenty-five still lifes and twenty-three Figures. Dancers, Harlequins and Pierrots, Circus Scenes, Bull Fights, Nudes, and Landscapes were also well represented. In this abundance, portraiture took precedence by virtue of chronology: the portraits stretched back to at least 1916, while almost all of the other works dated from 1918 or 1919. Moreover, the cover of the catalogue bore a likeness of Olga.[54]

The 1919 exhibition not only had showcased Picasso's recent achievements, but also presented the roots of the current work along with a stimulus for future departures. The last three drawings listed in the catalogue were titled either "after Ingres" or "after Renoir." If Ingres had so far been Picasso's dominant inspiration for Neoclassicism,

Idyll under a Tree. 1918. Oil on canvas, 27 × 22″ (68.6 × 55.9 cm). Not in Zervos. Private collection

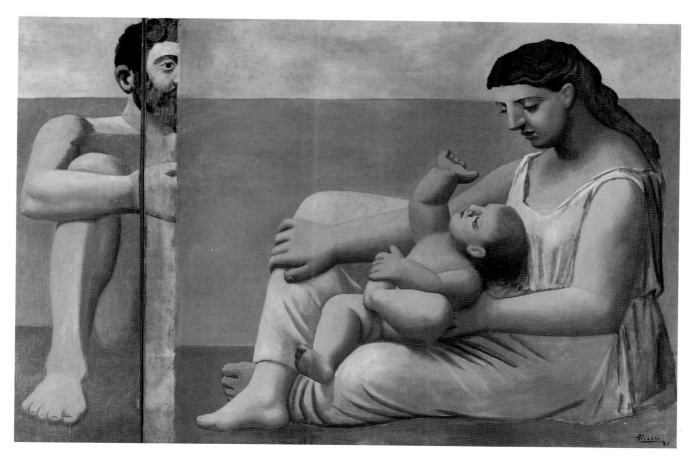

Mother and Child (before reduction cutting). 1921. Oil on canvas, 56½ × 64″ (143.5 × 162.6 cm). Zervos IV, 311. The Art Institute of Chicago. Gift of Maymar Corporation, Mrs. Maurice L. Rothschild, Mr. and Mrs. Chauncey McCormick; Mary and Leigh Block Charitable Fund; Ada Turnbull Hertle Endowment; through prior gift of Mr. and Mrs. Edwin E. Hokin

Renoir provided a model for Picasso to expand the style beyond portraiture and across the full range of his art. Even though Apollinaire had sung Renoir's praises as early as 1913 and Picasso had on occasion emulated him since at least 1918, Renoir was not to be widely respected by the twentieth-century avant-garde until after his death in December 1919.[55] Picasso's willingness to call attention to his admiration by including work "after Renoir" in the fall show underlines the Impressionist's importance for Picasso's newly emerging art. Comfortably established with Paul Rosenberg, Picasso measured his stature by addressing the artists whose work filled the gallery— primarily the Impressionists and Post-Impressionists.[56] Literally surrounded by Courbets, Manets, Monets, and Cézannes, but especially Renoirs, Picasso accelerated his dialogue with history. He expanded his Neoclassicism beyond portraiture and forged a new, inclusive modernism that played host to a variety of representational styles, including a remodeled Cubism.

Although paintings such as the *Lovers* (1919)[57] point toward his desired amalgam of Cubism and classicism, a picture of 1920 called *Studies* (p. 312) lies at its center. Across this canvas, Picasso juxtaposed his two primary styles: Cubism alternates with Neoclassicism in a confrontation

heightened by opposing subject matter—a contrast monumentalized in the summer of 1921 when Picasso painted two versions of the *Three Musicians* and *Three Women at the Spring* simultaneously in his Fontainebleau garage. Besides turning to Renoir (as well as Ingres and the Italian Renaissance) as a source for the Neoclassical figures in this painting, Picasso based its heterogeneous composition on Renoir's practice of sketching directly in oil on canvas. Like Picasso's painting, Renoir's trial canvases contain a wide diversity of styles and subjects precisely because Renoir used them to project the meditations on modernism and tradition that he had begun in the 1880s as Impressionism underwent intense scrutiny.[58]

Picasso acquired seven of Renoir's later pictures, and they clearly influenced his work of the early 1920s.[59] Hélène Parmelin long ago noted the remarkable resemblance between one of the Renoirs owned by Picasso, *Seated Bather*, and his own *Seated Nude Drying Her Foot*;[60] it provides a crucial source for the Mediterranean setting, classical poses, and—to some extent—the almost elephantine bodies of some of Picasso's figures. Yet this comparison also clarifies the differences between Picasso's Neoclassicism during the early 1920s and that of the painters of the "call to order," the broad Neoclassical

Olga Picasso with Paulo (born February 4, 1921). 23, rue La Boétie, Paris, c. 1922–23. Photograph by Man Ray. Collection Lucien Treillard

Woman and child (Olga and Paulo). 1922. Pencil and watercolor on paper, 6⅛ × 4½″ (15.5 × 11.5 cm). Not in Zervos. Musée Picasso, Paris

movement that was to gather force as the decade passed. The austerity and melancholy of Picasso's figures do not project the optimism about a paradise regained that pervades Renoir's happy scenes and those of many of his followers in the growing movement. Picasso's Neoclassicism acknowledges the difficult task of integrating Cubism and tradition, instead of seeking to minimize or dismiss it altogether. His Neoclassicism blossomed during his alliance with Paul Rosenberg and the opportunity it presented to define his position among already historical masters; his synthesis of old and new, however, speaks as much of rupture as it does of continuity.

Picasso's 1921 exhibition at Paul Rosenberg's gallery presented some works in the Cubist mode, but the majority were recent Neoclassical figures. Among these latter pictures, Picasso differentiated those he considered portraits from those that were generic figures. The 1917 portrait of Olga appeared as *Portrait of a Woman with a Fan* and the painting of Madame Rosenberg and her daughter as *Portrait of a Woman and a Child*, while unindividualized depictions of women were called *Woman in a Chemise with Crossed Arms* or *Group of Women*. The significance of this distinction is demonstrated by the largest painting Picasso included in the exhibition, *Woman in an Armchair* (now known as *Woman Reading*; p. 313). Although based on a portrait of Olga, the final painting surpasses in

its transformations any conventional definition of the genre. Its evolution reveals that Picasso detached his Neoclassicism from conventional portraiture in 1920 and that with this liberation he explored a wide range of traditional subjects, whether derived from classical mythology or Christian dogma, as well as transformed portrayals of individuals in his life.

On July 31, 1920, Picasso had sketched a portrait of Olga on holiday at Juan-les-Pins (p. 312). Reflecting the relaxed mood, this pencil drawing shows her wrapped in a long robe and seated in an armchair, reading a letter. Her wavy hair falls loosely to her shoulders, and her crossed foot dangles slipperless. This casualness corresponds to many other portraits Picasso made of her during the second decade of the twentieth century and the early 1920s (including images both of great sensuality and of extreme informality).[61] While still at Juan-les-Pins, Picasso translated the small sketch into a large painting (p. 313).[62] Although this picture retains a remarkable amount of the minutiae recorded in the drawing, Picasso altered the woman enough for her derivation from portraiture to have gone largely unnoticed. In the painting, she has become a mixture of casualness and monumentality that creates an image of classicism uneasily grafted to modernity. The clothing, hair, pose, and activity are Olga's; yet her bloated proportions overwhelm the quiescent

Mother and Child. 1922. Pencil and watercolor on paper, 6⅛ × 4½″ (15.5 × 11.5 cm). Not in Zervos. Musée Picasso, Paris

Mother and Child. 1922. Oil on canvas, 39⅜ × 31⅞″ (100 × 81 cm). Zervos IV, 371. The Baltimore Museum of Art. The Cone Collection, formed by Dr. Claribel Cone and Miss Etta Cone of Baltimore, Maryland. (Colorplate, p. 51)

original. The armchair is reproduced in meticulous detail, its mismatched legs precisely rendered, yet its proportions can no longer accommodate the massive figure. The gargantuan woman ill suits the quotidian objects surrounding her—not only the drab chair but also the cloths casually draped over its back and laid underneath, and particularly, her loose slippers.[63] In subsequent paintings, such as *Two Female Nudes*,[64] Picasso began to forgo modern dress and domestic settings in order to adopt more consistently classicizing scenes, which he painted in a style that freely mixed illusions of sculptural relief with Cubist passages.

Throughout the winter of 1920–21 and the following spring, Picasso's gradual detachment from portraiture enabled him to elaborate his exploration of classical styles across increasingly large and complex compositions. The culmination of this development is *Three Women at the Spring*, which Picasso painted during his summer residence in Fontainebleau. Although none of the figures in the painting, or in its many preparatory studies and post studies, evince an obvious reference to Olga, posterior works imply such an interplay. Probably as a postscript, Picasso drew a number of exquisite pastels, which he modeled on the head of the woman at the left in the painting. A photograph shows several of these pastels pinned to the wall of his studio (p. 314). Seated in their

midst is Olga. Even more than her proximity, her nearly profile pose suggests some relationship to the drawn figures. It is impossible to decipher if Picasso intended this juxtaposition to reveal her as a conscious source for the work, or if the photograph records a later recognition of a resemblance. Olga's image had so permeated his art over the course of the previous four years that her features habitually recur in combination with a panoply of sources and, later, other women.

By the summer of 1921, this fertilization led in many directions. In at least one case, the Neoclassicism that had grown from portraiture reversed course to shape a likeness Picasso drew of his wife. Made probably while he was executing his postscripts to *Three Women at the Spring*, this portrait could almost be part of that series (p. 315). Executed in pastel on the same size paper as that of the Neoclassical busts, it shows a three-quarter view of Olga's head, which differs in style only slightly from the generic figures: Olga, easily recognizable, is turned to the left rather than the right, and her eyes look toward the viewer. Her hair appears in heavy waves. Modeled with infinite subtlety in the soft pastel, her head swells to an imposing volume, and her nose, lips, and eyelids are thickened as if they were carved from stone. Even her deeply scalloped collar stands erect like the fluting of an antique sculpture.

Picasso's other major composition during the summer

of 1921, the two versions of the *Three Musicians*, not only involves the issue of portraiture—on a symbolic level—but also the particularly thorny question of how he pursued it in a Cubist idiom (a subject that is discussed in other essays in this volume).[65] Three Cubist paintings dating from the second decade of the twentieth century and the early 1920s, however, are tied to Picasso's portrayal of Olga. Painted in the early months of 1918, *Harlequin with Violin ("Si Tu Veux")* (p. 316) probably celebrates the couple's betrothal, as Picasso employed his frequent alter ego and the title on the sheet of music to allude to his proposal.[66] A few months later, he recorded another episode in her life, rarely mentioned by art historians. Olga broke her right leg in the late spring of 1918 and entered the clinic of Dr. Ch. Bonnet in Paris, where she apparently remained until a short time before her marriage.[67] In fine weather, she passed the time in the garden, with her encased leg elevated on a massive platform. During visits, Picasso drew the scene. After making a rough draft in one of his small notebooks,[68] he took a sheet of the doctor's stationery and charted an intricate Cubist composition, showing Olga knitting while seated on the thronelike apparatus (p. 316). In a small painting (p. 316), he dropped most of the details that had identified the subject: the border and folds of Olga's dressing gown are gone, as are the strands of her hair and the ball of yarn that is shown lying on the ground in the preceding sketch. The background is also simplified, although the painting's bright green tonality identifies the outdoor setting. Like a second painting based on a transformed likeness of Olga, *Woman in an Armchair* (1920; p. 43), which William Rubin discusses in his introductory essay, Picasso effaced almost all evidence that might identify the sitter and reveal the point of departure for the composition.

Increasingly, the elaboration of his Neoclassical paintings spun equally far from their origins in portraiture. In the summer or fall of 1921, Picasso painted another three-figure composition, which nearly equaled the size of the *Three Musicians* and *Three Women at the Spring*. No doubt stimulated by the birth of his son Paulo on February 4, 1921, he addressed a subject he had rarely treated before, the family. He showed a mother and child accompanied by a man whose gesture of handing a fish to the baby suggests his nurturing role. After painting the picture, however, Picasso soon chose to alter it fundamentally by cutting down the canvas to exclude the man's body and overpainting the long reach of his arm (p. 317). The result is *Mother and Child*, a composition of a more nearly square format, whose image of a monumental woman cradling a baby returns to the theme of maternity.[69]

Picasso's work during the summer of 1922 was dominated by studies for a suite of maternity images (pp. 318, 319), which would develop over the winter and the following year into a series of more than ten large paintings devoted

to a variety of subjects ranging from portraiture to *commedia dell'arte* characters. Beginning in 1921, Paul Rosenberg had urged Picasso to paint in series (especially harlequins), and, when complete, Rosenberg purchased the lot for the princely sum of nearly a quarter of a million francs. During the winter of 1923–24, he sent them to America as the core of the first exhibition of Picasso's paintings held in the United States (Wildenstein Gallery, New York) and the first to appear in a museum anywhere (The Art Institute of Chicago), before showing them in his Paris gallery the following spring. This international tour of Picasso's recent Neoclassical paintings did more to establish his worldwide fame than any previous event in his career; yet by its conclusion, Surrealism had displaced Neoclassicism as the primary focus of his art.

Once again it is impossible to isolate portraiture from other genres, yet Picasso's sketchbooks offer considerable insight into his process of developing compositions that stemmed from portraiture while radically transforming it. During his summer holiday in 1922, Picasso filled a sketchbook with drawings that move from the documentation of his surroundings to a sketch of Olga and Paulo at play, which immediately began to be transformed, to plans for formal compositions.[70] As if accustoming himself to his new environment, Picasso inscribed *"Dinard"* at the beginning of the sketchbook and followed this identification with a sketch of Saint-Malo (the village across the bay). On subsequent pages he drew Paulo's head and then passed on to scenes of domestic life (including Paulo seated on a chamber pot) before drawing a portrait of Olga holding their son on her lap (p. 318). Yet the images in the sketchbook are not confined to this dialogue with his immediate surroundings. Several are tentative trials for a scene of a woman at her toilette, which he would resume the next summer, but the most resolved are plans for compositions on the theme of maternity.

Interspersed with the portraits of Olga and Paulo, these drawings stand out because of their significant departure from the portraits, despite many similarities (p. 319). Although both depict a woman holding a young boy on her lap while offering him a small object, the rendering of the heads, particularly the woman's, no longer corresponds to the portraits. Instead of Olga, Picasso drew a woman with more rounded features. Most significantly, instead of Olga's tightly pinned hair, this woman's tresses fall from a loose gathering at the back of her head. In the final paintings, Picasso maintained these features, but he drew the figures more closely together so that the woman embraces the child and seems to rest her chin on his head. William Rubin has vigorously argued that the transformation of both the face and the nurturing gestures of this woman reflect Picasso's admiration for Sara Murphy, whom he had met in 1921; his admiration would blossom fully during the time they spent together

Portrait of the Artist's Son, Paulo. 1922. Pastel on paper, 24¼ × 18¾″ (61.5 × 47.5 cm). Zervos XXX, 357. Private collection

in the summer of 1923.[71] As in *Woman Reading*, Picasso developed these compositions from a wide variety of sources to create a rich amalgam that transcends individual likeness to engage broad themes. In the case of these paintings of a mother and child, we know from Picasso's handwritten receipt to Paul Rosenberg that he chose to title them *Maternity*.[72] Likewise, he called the contemporary set of paintings for which Jacinto Salvadó posed

Harlequins (pp. 326, 327). Picasso's choice of titles does not deny the fact that the origin of these pictures is portraiture; rather, the titles confirm the process of transformation through which the final image took shape, as Picasso moved into increasingly synthetic compositions.

Even though Neoclassicism would continue as one of the many styles Picasso would employ during the remaining decades of his career, its dominant role came to a

Portrait of the Artist's Son, Paulo. 1923. Oil on canvas, 10⅝ × 8⅝″ (27 × 22 cm). Zervos V, 180. Private collection

his recent compositions (but not their massive volumes), Picasso passed through portraiture to create a body of work devoted to the costumed circus performers and sentimental family groups that had been his frequent subjects before Cubism. Moreover, he adapted the saturated colors, flowing glazes, and exquisite draftsmanship he had employed to render them. In a sense, these pictures close the circle on this phase of Picasso's Neoclassicism by returning to his point of departure in the spring of 1914, when he probably responded to the exhibition of his Blue and Rose paintings at the auction of the Peau de l'Ours. By the mid-1920s, Neoclassicism had become fashionable among the Parisian avant-garde, and Picasso shed the pack, much as he had done a decade before, when Cubism had become widely imitated.

Picasso's personal and professional life changed in tandem with his art. The summer holiday in 1922 had ended abruptly when Olga fell seriously ill and had to be rushed to Paris for surgery; although she recovered, this event may have marked the end of their intimacy. Certainly by the following summer, Picasso's eye was wandering, as the recently identified group of drawings and paintings devoted to Sara Murphy reveals. The final likenesses he made of Olga are extremely detached. *Portrait of the Artist's Wife* (p. 296) of 1923 is so restrained in pose and rendering that it seems fitting it won the first prize at the conservative Carnegie International exhibition in 1930. Except for a few drawings in 1928, Olga's likeness disappeared from Picasso's art in 1923, even though the couple did not separate until twelve years later. Despite a few paintings of Paulo in festive costumes, his presence in Picasso's art also greatly diminished.

close with these paintings. In reviewing Rosenberg's exhibition of them in 1924, André Salmon wrote that "the pure harlequins . . . form a perfect unity with the Blue and Rose periods."[73] Although exaggerated, Salmon's remark captures the retrospection that pervades these works of 1922–23. While retaining the monumental proportions of

Paulo Picasso on a donkey. 1923. Photographer unknown. Musée Picasso, Paris, Documents section. Gift of Sir Roland Penrose

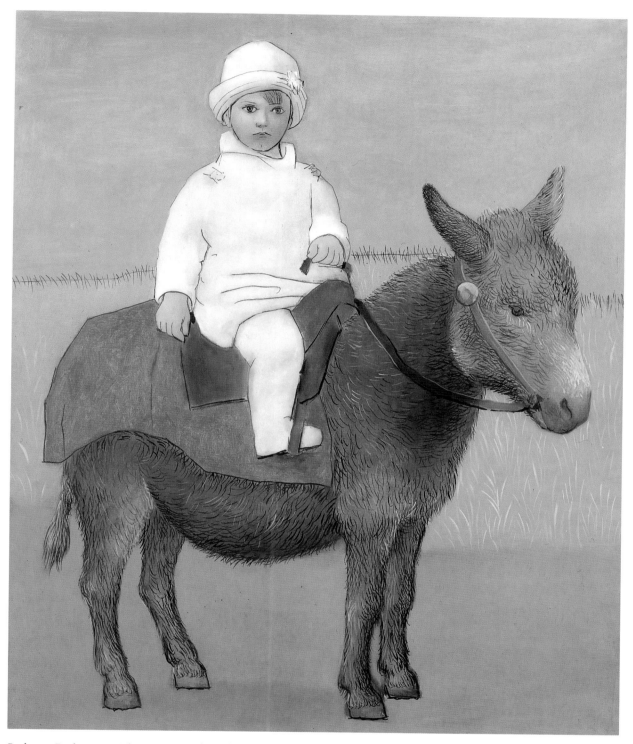

Paulo on a Donkey. 1923. Oil on canvas, 39⅜ × 31⅞″ (100 × 81 cm). Zervos VI, 1429. Private collection

Picasso's estrangement from his family was part of a profound reorientation that took place in the mid-1920s. We now know that he had formed a relationship with Marie-Thérèse Walter no later than 1926, and probably in 1925, and that his domestic situation had deteriorated to the point that heated confrontations with Olga were common.[74] Picasso was also to dismiss Cocteau and distance himself from Paul Rosenberg, thereby substantially with-

drawing from the core of people who had supported his postwar career. Instead, André Breton and the burgeoning Surrealist movement became increasingly important for him. Although Picasso's involvement with Surrealism is beyond the scope of this essay,[75] it must be mentioned in relation to paintings of the late 1920s and early 1930s that reflect his use of Olga in his art.

Among the pictures of the late 1920s, one has long

Olga Picasso with the Picassos' Saint Bernard. c. 1930–35. Photograph by "Stella Presse" photo agency. Musée Picasso, Paris, Picasso Archives

been associated with her, *Bust of a Woman with Self-Portrait* (p. 329). Roland Penrose, who once owned the painting and received this intelligence directly from Picasso, identified the framed profile in the picture as a self-portrait and stated that the female bust refers to Olga.[76] Picasso had begun to use a similar profile in paintings of 1927, and a photograph he took of his own silhouette cast over one of his framed drawings supports the conclusion that the painted profiles derive from his features (p. 207). In 1927 he also began a series of paintings, which culminated in *Figure and Profile*, in which he juxtaposed his silhouette with a highly contorted female head (p. 328). Throughout the series, certain features of the woman recur, particularly her prominent teeth and spiky strands of hair. At first she is clearly an artistic creation confined to a drawing or canvas hung on the wall, while the Picasso-like silhouette suggests the shadow of a real figure standing in space. In *Figure and Profile*, however, the relationship is reversed. Picasso's profile is framed on the wall, and the monstrous woman not only occupies the room but seems to threaten the image by sweeping across it.

Although Picasso's increasingly troubled relationship with Olga probably provided raw material for these images, their conception and sequence suggest that imaginative transformation quickly overran representation.

Rather similar to Picasso's procedure in the earlier Neoclassical pictures, his process of transformation subordinated direct experience to broader thematic concerns. The silhouettes may symbolize his emotional distance from Olga, but they also affirm a classical order that is threatened with destruction. The predatory females are obviously fantastic constructions; they derive at least as much from the Surrealists' often demonic conception of women as from any personal circumstances.[77] As if darkly mirroring the consonance of Picasso's Neoclassicism with the early years of his marriage to Olga, his immersion in Surrealism corresponded to the dissonance of their subsequent relationship.

Throughout the 1930s, Picasso absorbed the historical styles and subjects of Neoclassicism into images that evoke the violent, psychological themes of the Surrealists. The monumental figure placed in an elemental landscape of beach, sea, and sky in *Seated Bather* (p. 64) perpetuates the grandeur of his earlier Neoclassical scenes, such as *Mother and Child*, without retaining the maternal tenderness that he had originally projected into them. Isolated on the beach and stripped of the ample flesh that enfolds the Neoclassical figures, this "bone" bather's towering stature and classical equilibrium heighten the potential danger of her daggerlike nose and inverted jaws. Since Picasso told William Rubin that *Seated Bather* was "inspired by Olga," we can be confident that once again his experience with her underlies this intimidating image that, in its final form, so clearly shares the Surrealists' obsession with aggressive sexuality.[78]

At least twice during the 1930s, Picasso resurrected an historical subject to channel his themes of personal tor-

Portrait of Olga with a Fur Collar. 1923. Drypoint, 19½ × 19⅜" (49.5 × 49.2 cm). Geiser/Baer I, 109. Musée Picasso, Paris

Portrait of Olga. 1923. Pastel and black pencil on paper, 41 × 28″ (104 × 71 cm). Zervos V, 38. Musée Picasso, Paris

ment. Also associated with Olga by several authors, *Woman with Stiletto (Death of Marat)* (p. 330) casts a gorgon, resembling the previous monsters, as Charlotte Corday in the act of stabbing Marat while he lies in his bath.[79] In *The Murder* (p. 330), Picasso returned to this subject, but substituted a stylized figure of Marie-Thérèse for Marat and drew her attacker as a wizened hag, whose projecting teeth and stringy hair mirror his recent transformations of Olga. Drawn in July 1934, at the time of battles that preceded their separation the next year, this image surges from Picasso's personal life through his involvement with Neoclassicism to manifest the "convulsive beauty" admired by the Surrealists.

In contrast, Picasso's final transformed portrait of Olga

Portrait of Jacinto Salvadó as Harlequin. 1923. Oil on canvas, 51¼ × 38¼″ (130 × 97 cm). Zervos V, 17. Musée National d'Art Moderne, Centre National d'Art et de Culture Georges Pompidou, Paris. Bequest of Baronne Gourgaud, 1965

Portrait of Jacinto Salvadó as Harlequin. 1923. Tempera on canvas, 51⅜ × 38¼″ (130.5 × 97 cm). Zervos V, 23. Öffentliche Kunstsammlung Basel, Kunstmuseum

Figure and Profile. 1927–28. Oil on canvas, 25⅝ × 21¼″ (65 × 54 cm). Zervos VII, 144. Private collection

(so far as we know) is remarkably calm if deeply sad. Painted in 1935, the year in which Marie-Thérèse gave birth to Maya, and Olga left the rue La Boétie as part of a formal separation agreement, *Woman with a Hat* (p. 331) contains few of the violent distortions that characterize the other images associated with her in the late 1920s and 1930s.[80] Its pastel tonality is cool, and the woman's pinched angularity is mild compared to the twisted anatomies of some contemporaneous figures. Perhaps this moderation reflects the aftermath of Olga's departure; the dark wells of the eyes, which are recorded in contemporary photographs of her (p. 330), may bear witness to her presence and index her grief.

Given this long sequence of Picasso's images, it is

Bust of a Woman with Self-Portrait. 1929. Oil on canvas, 28 × 23⁷/₈″ (71 × 60.5 cm). Zervos VII, 248. Private collection

fitting that the final ones are by Olga. In the years follow-ing their separation she literally haunted his life, con-fronting him during regular visits to his Paris bank and interrupting his summer sojourns with Françoise Gilot, near Olga's last home at Cannes.[81] As her health failed and she became bedridden in the early 1950s, Olga resorted to photographs as one of her final means to address her hus-band. In frequent letters, she enclosed snapshots showing Picasso, herself, and Paulo during their years together.[82] These were prints from the early 1920s that she had pre-served for decades, and, tragically, she now shot back at Picasso to goad his memory. In 1949 her campaign intensi-fied; the birth of Paulo's son, Pablito, and his daughter, Marina, the following year gave her new ammunition.

Named after his grandfather, Pablito became the center of an effort to win back Picasso's affection. For her New Year's greeting in 1951 Olga constructed an intricate collage of photographs that linked the recent births with Paulo's in 1921 (p. 335). She cut, juxtaposed, and pasted images of Paulo with those of Marina and Pablito, and then surrounded them with arrays that mixed snapshots of Picasso and Paulo in the 1920s with those of Paulo's wife, Emmanuelle Lotte, and of Olga in old age. These awkward, handcrafted assemblages are a final testament to her desperate effort to maintain the family she had begun with Picasso more than thirty years before. Needless to say, he did not respond to her final pleas for reconciliation, and her death apparently left no mark on his art.[83]

The origins of Picasso's Neoclassicism signal both its distinction from the broad movement that began during World War I and its essential ties to portraiture. Rather than a revival of classical styles and subjects, his initial steps in the spring of 1914 show a return to his own early work, followed by an engagement with nineteenth-century artists who had stimulated his Blue and Rose periods. This time, however, the dialogue was very different. In the early years of the century, Picasso had largely assimilated preceding styles, before moving on to create Cubism. In 1914 he looked back from the prominence he had achieved and sought to define his contribution by separating himself from the growing Cubist movement and once again confronting his predecessors. This process would drive his Neoclassicism for a decade, though it subsided somewhat with the disruptions of the war. During those uncertain times, portraiture, which had underlain much of the Blue and Rose work, subsumed

Olga Picasso (detail of group photograph) at Château de Béthusy, Lausanne, July 1931. Photograph by Gisela Reber. Collection Christoph Pudelko, Bonn

Neoclassicism as Picasso used it to fix the diminished community that supported his continuing exploration of Cubism. With the expansion and renewal of that community through his involvement with Cocteau, Errazuriz, and the ballet, portraiture burgeoned and was transferred from small drawings to the grand paintings that reflect Picasso's growing ease outside avant-garde circles.

Woman with Stiletto (Death of Marat). December 19–25, 1931. Oil on canvas, 18³⁄₁₆ × 24³⁄₁₆″ (46.5 × 61.5 cm). Not in Zervos. Musée Picasso, Paris

The Murder. July 7, 1934. Pencil on paper, 15¾ × 19⅞″ (39.8 × 50.4 cm). Zervos VIII, 216. Musée Picasso, Paris

Woman with a Hat (Olga). 1935. Oil on canvas, 23⅝ × 19⅝″ (60 × 50 cm). Zervos VIII, 247. Musée National d'Art Moderne, Centre National d'Art et de Culture Georges Pompidou, Paris. Bequest of Georges Salles, 1967

His alliance with Paul Rosenberg in 1918 marked both his establishment in *mondaine* society and the intensification of his dialogue with old and modern masters, a process that spawned his full-blown Neoclassicism of the early 1920s. Far from a regression, Picasso's Neoclassicism both acknowledged the waning of the prewar avant-garde and defined a vital new direction that would infuse his interpretation of Surrealism both in its monumentality (*Seated Bather*, 1930) and its subject matter (*Death of Marat*, 1931), as well as contribute to his continuing examination of his position in the history of art during the years after World War II. In this process, Olga became a temporary partner, sometimes a muse, but neither a dominating force nor an original inspiration.

NOTES

1. Like most terms used to identify diverse movements in the arts, "Neoclassicism" cannot be defined with precision; however, it is generally used to refer to modern artists' practice of borrowing and adapting historical Western styles of representation. For a general discussion of this issue, see Elizabeth Cowling and Jennifer Mundy, *On Classic Ground: Picasso, Léger, de Chirico and the New Classicism 1910–1930* (London: Tate Gallery Publications, 1990). For Picasso's Neoclassicism, the basic reference is Ulrich Weisner, ed., *Picassos Klassizismus* (Bielefeld: Kunsthalle Bielefeld, 1988).

2. Daniel-Henry Kahnweiler with Francis Crémieux, *My Galleries and Painters* (New York: Viking Press, 1971), pp. 53–54. We do not know exactly which drawings Picasso showed to Kahnweiler, but the description closely corresponds to a series from the spring and summer of 1914; see, for example, Musée Picasso, Paris, M.P. 744–46.

3. This topic is too complex to deal with here, but a brief summary is necessary. Most recently, Rosalind Krauss criticized Picasso's "turn to neoclassicism," writing, "This peculiar and momentously reactionary alternative to Cubism is a deep conundrum for historians of modernism" ("We Lost It at the Movies," *The Art Bulletin* 76, no. 4 [December 1994], p. 580). Criticism of Picasso's Neoclassicism can be found in the writing of some of his pre–World War I associates, such as Maurice Raynal and Wilhelm Uhde, but it is more common in biographies and essays written by historians and journalists who began commenting on his art after the Neoclassicism of the second and third decades of the twentieth century had ended, particularly Roland Penrose, Pierre Cabanne, and John Berger. Criticism of Picasso's Neoclassicism is often linked to his relationship with Olga Khokhlova; see n. 31, below. In order to conform to the editorial guidelines of this exhibition catalogue, I will henceforth refer to Olga Khokhlova as Olga.

4. Regarding issues of modernism and avant-gardism, Jeffrey Weiss has stated the skepticism that many of us feel when comparing theories with historical evidence. "I use the terms 'modernism' and 'avant-garde' somewhat interchangeably here. . . . Theories of the avant-garde . . . require us to address the phenomenon as a unified project of shared purpose, definable goals and quantifiable success or failure. While such an argument is attractive in the abstract, and manages to comply with a handful of examples, it bears little applicable relation to the daily circumstances of . . . cultural history as they reveal themselves to students of the archive. . . . More developments at the time tend to confute the theory rather than prove it, and proscriptive definitions of convenient terms such as modernism and the avant-garde serve mostly to provide a false sense of security, dulling our intuitive grasp of predominating incongruities and conflicts" (*The Popular Culture of Modern Art: Picasso, Duchamp, and Avant-Gardism* [New Haven: Yale University Press, 1994], p. xvi).

5. From 1911 through 1913, it appears that Picasso made only one work undisputed as a portrait, a drawing of Apollinaire (p. 180) that was reproduced as the frontispiece of *Alcools*, 1913 (though there are "transformations" such as that of *Woman in an Armchair*; p. 291).

6. Picasso's partial departure from Cubism in 1914 is too broad a topic to receive full discussion here; substantial research is still needed to clarify the issues.

7. Although Picasso did not show all his paintings (he kept secret, for example, the so-called "sand" portraits of Sara Murphy), it was exceptional for him to do so with a painting of this importance.

8. See Kahnweiler, *My Galleries and Painters*, p. 54.

9. By the term "salon Cubists," I intend to refer to the Cubist artists grouped around Jean Metzinger and Albert Gleizes, who exhibited regularly in the Parisian salons beginning in 1911, in contrast to Picasso and Georges Braque, who refused to participate in these events.

10. In *Making Modernism: Picasso and the Creation of the Market for Twentieth-Century Art* (New York: Farrar, Straus and Giroux, 1995), pp. 15–46, I have discussed the Peau de l'Ours collection, as well as many other aspects of Picasso's career from 1914 to 1939 that are touched on in this essay.

11. For a discussion of Picasso's sources for this painting, see Kenneth E. Silver, *Esprit de Corps: The Art of the Parisian Avant-Garde and the First World War, 1914–1925* (Princeton, N.J.: Princeton University Press, 1989), pp. 63–68.

12. For a discussion of portraiture in relation to *The Family of Saltimbanques*, see Theodore Reff, "Harlequins, Saltimbanques, Clowns and Fools," *Artforum* 10 (October 1971), pp. 30–43. William Rubin has identified the couple in *Meditation* (Zervos I, 235) as Picasso and Fernande Olivier; see *Picasso in the Collection of The Museum of Modern Art* (New York: The Museum of Modern Art, 1972), p. 30.

13. Beginning in 1914, Picasso did make a small number of Neoclassical or realist drawings of still-life subjects. Unlike the portraits, however, they are not finished compositions and generally served as studies for details of larger compositions; see, for example, Musée Picasso, Paris, M.P. 743.

14. Hélène Seckel noted this resemblance; see *Max Jacob et Picasso* (Paris: Editions de la Réunion des musées nationaux, 1994), p. 116.

15. Most of Picasso's Neoclassical portraits, unlike those from almost every other phase of his career, appear to have been made from life and are based on sketches or on a photograph of the subject. A certain number were also surely done from memory.

16. Pierre Daix has argued that the beginning of the war interrupted Picasso's work on this painting (*Picasso: The Cubist Years 1907–1916*, with Joan Rosselet [Boston: New York Graphic Society, 1979], pp. 164–65).

17. Kahnweiler had begun buying Picasso's work in 1907 and had bought heavily from him in many of the following years. In December of 1912 they had signed a contract for Kahnweiler to purchase all of his production for a period of three years (except for a small number of works Picasso chose to keep). Thus Kahnweiler acquired, and frequently did not sell, much of Picasso's prewar Cubism. His stock was sold by the French government in a series of auctions between 1921 and 1923.

18. Cited in Seckel, *Max Jacob et Picasso*, p. 116.

19. For photographs of Jacob taken in 1915 and 1916, see ibid., pp. 121–22 and 129–30.

20. Cited in ibid., p. 120.

21. Reprinted in Leroy C. Breunig, ed., *Apollinaire on Art: Essays and Reviews, 1902–1918* (New York: Viking Press, 1972), p. 440.

22. Cited in Seckel, *Max Jacob et Picasso*, p. 125.

23. Cited in ibid., p. 116.

24. Pierre Reverdy, "Sur le cubisme," *Nord-Sud*, March 15, 1917, pp. 5–7; reprinted in Edward F. Fry, ed., *Cubism* (London: Thames and Hudson, 1966), pp. 144, 145.

25. Cited in Seckel, *Max Jacob et Picasso*, p. 137.

26. Francis Steegmuller, *Cocteau: A Biography* (Boston: Little, Brown, 1970), p. 165.

27. Christopher Green, *Cubism and Its Enemies* (New Haven: Yale University Press, 1987), p. 1.

28. For further discussion of Léonce Rosenberg's activities as a dealer, see Malcolm Gee, *Dealers, Critics and Collectors of Modern Painting: Aspects of the Parisian Art Market Between 1910 and 1930* (New York: Garland Publishing, 1981), pp. 44–58.

29. See Léonce's letters to Picasso of March 24 and November 29, 1916 (Picasso Archives, Musée Picasso, Paris).

30. This anecdote was recorded by René Gimpel, *Diary of a Picture Dealer* (New York: Universe Books, 1987), p. 71, entry of November 14, 1918. That same month, Juan Gris wrote to Léonce complaining about the high prices he was paying for "false-Picassos, false-Braques, and false-Gris" (Getty Center for the Humanities, Santa Monica). Léonce's criticism of *Parade* is recorded in a letter of September 1917 that Cocteau wrote to him (Centre Pompidou, Paris).

31. Within the Picasso literature, there is a considerable subset that seeks to place responsibility for the artist's involvement in worldly activities and even his Neoclassicism on the preferences and persistence of Olga. As with the question of criticism of Neoclassicism (see n. 3), this problem is too extensive for substantial discussion in this essay. It is worth noting, however, that the two are regularly linked by some authors. Criticism of Olga can be traced to some of Picasso's prewar friends, such as Jacob, who blamed her for their cool relations with Picasso after the war. Among writers working after World War II, Pierre Cabanne goes so far as to assert that Picasso adopted Neoclassicism or a "decorative form of Cubism because he did not wish to shock or deceive Olga" (*Le Siècle de Picasso* [Paris: Denoël, 1975], vol. 2, p. 81). In my view, Pierre Daix has offered the most cogent assessment of Olga's role in Picasso's life during the early years of their relationship: "Certainly, Olga's tastes were classic,

traditional, but the atmosphere of the Ballets Russes had corresponded to an initiation and, after all, she had not been shocked by the scandal of *Parade*. It was certainly not because of her or to please her that Picasso returned to classical portraits" (*La Vie de peintre de Pablo Picasso* [Paris: Editions du Seuil, 1977], p. 158).

This view is confirmed by interviews that I conducted in preparation for this essay. Among the many people I have questioned about Olga, two were particularly close to the Picassos during the time of their marriage: Micheline Sinclair, daughter of Paul Rosenberg, and Daniel Wildenstein, son of Georges. Although both were children during the 1920s, they grew up in close proximity to the Picassos on the rue La Boétie and saw them frequently. As adults, both maintained cordial relations with Picasso and Olga after their separation. Among those still living, they are probably the most knowledgeable about the Picassos' daily life during the 1920s and 1930s. Independently, both Sinclair and Wildenstein told me that they strongly disagree with the frequently derogatory characterizations of Olga that appear in the Picasso literature. This is also the opinion expressed by Marina Picasso (Olga's granddaughter) in *Les Enfants du bout du monde* (Paris: Ramsay/Archimbaud, 1995), pp. 59–77. The book was published after this essay was written.

32. Quoted in Cabanne, *Le Siècle de Picasso*, vol. 2, p. 94.

33. Statement for distribution, dated September 3, 1917, by Léonce Rosenberg (Centre Pompidou, Paris).

34. Lynn Garafola, *Diaghilev's Ballets Russes* (New York: Oxford University Press, 1989), p. 76.

35. See Deborah Menaker Rothschild, *Picasso's "Parade"* (London: Sotheby's Publications, 1991), pp. 209–38.

36. Zervos III, 23 and 18.

37. To my knowledge, the only painting, excluding *The Artist and His Model*, that Picasso made in a Neoclassical style before 1917 is a small oil on panel, *Head of a Young Man* (1915; Daix 813). The features of this man resemble those of the figure Picasso had drawn and painted in 1914; whether or not this painting is a portrait is unclear.

38. *Le Poète assassiné* was published in 1916. The story is loosely autobiographical, and many in the Parisian art world immediately assumed that Picasso was the model for "the Bird of Benin"; see Francis Steegmuller, *Apollinaire: Poet among the Painters* (New York: Farrar, Straus, 1963), p. 320.

39. This account of Olga's involvement with the ballet is based primarily on Garafola's *Diaghilev's Ballets Russes*. I greatly appreciate Joan Acocella's generosity in providing material about Olga, introducing me to scholars working on the ballet, and offering her own view of Olga's career and reputation.

40. Picasso had drawn bust-length portraits of Apollinaire and Cocteau in 1916.

41. There is also an inscription in Russian in another hand.

42. In 1917 Picasso also painted a series of

Harlequins in a Neoclassical style; they are generally thought to be idealized portraits of Massine (for example, *Harlequin*, Museo Picasso, Barcelona, M.P.B. 10.941).

43. The words are those of Mary Mathews Gedo (*Picasso: Art as Autobiography* [Chicago: University of Chicago Press, 1980], p. 115). For Roland Penrose's earlier interpretation of this painting, see *Picasso: His Life and Art* (New York: Harper, 1958), p. 203.

44. In a statement he made to Marius de Zayas in 1923, Picasso praised Velázquez's portraits for their subordination of the sitter to the artist's interpretation: "Velasquez left us his idea of the people of his epoch. Undoubtedly they were different from [the way in which] he painted them, but we cannot conceive a Philip IV in any other way than the one Velasquez painted. Rubens also made a portrait of the same king and in Rubens' portrait he seems to be quite another person. We believe in the one painted by Velasquez, for he convinces us by his right of might" ("Picasso Speaks," *The Arts* 3 [May 1923], p. 319).

45. Olga's direct stare is another aspect of this performance. Diaghilev first produced *The Three-Cornered Hat* in London in July 1919. Picasso designed sets, costumes, and a curtain for the ballet; according to Massine, he began to plan it while in Spain during the fall of 1917. See Musée des Beaux-Arts de Lyon, *Picasso: Le Tricorne* (Paris: Editions de la Réunion des musées nationaux, 1992), p. 11.

46. The four drawings are Zervos III, 2, 3, and 32; and estate no. 2286.

47. Anthony Blunt, "Picasso's Classical Period (1917–1925)," *The Burlington Magazine* 110 (April 1968), p. 187; Phoebe Pool, "Picasso's Neoclassicism: Second Period, 1917–1925," *Apollo* 85 (March 1967), p. 201. Despite its fame, this painting has received little analysis; for the most extensive interpretation, see Marie-Laure Besnard-Bernadac, *Le Musée Picasso, Paris* (Paris: Editions de la Réunion des musées nationaux, 1985), p. 28.

48. Robert Rosenblum, *Jean-Auguste-Dominique Ingres* (New York: Harry N. Abrams, 1990), p. 62. In reading a draft of this essay, William Rubin suggested the useful term "de-frumping" to describe Picasso's process of idealizing Olga in contrast to her appearance in this photograph.

49. At approximately the same time, Picasso painted a second portrait of Olga (Zervos VI, 1335), now in the collection of Marina Picasso. Also executed in a Neoclassical style, the picture is somewhat smaller (45 5/8 x 29 1/2 in.; 116 x 75 cm) and is rendered in a darker and heavier idiom. Neither the pose, costume, nor setting precisely correspond to the painting in the Musée Picasso.

50. Pierre Daix, *Picasso: Life and Art* (New York: HarperCollins, 1993), pp. 159–60. Despite this achievement, the painting has been attacked by several critics, both during the era in which it was painted and in recent years. Wilhelm Uhde considered the painting "pathetic" and questioned whether its retrospective style meant that Picasso had been try-

ing to please conservative ideologues in France during World War I (*Picasso et la tradition française* [Paris: Les Quatre Chemins, 1928], pp. 55–56). Yet Uhde had not been in Paris during the war, and he saw the painting under circumstances that probably colored his opinion: It hung in Paul Rosenberg's gallery at the time Uhde's own collection of Cubist pictures, which had been sequestered during the war, was auctioned by the French government in 1921—against his wishes. To cite another case, John Berger condemned the painting as "so stuffy . . . that distaste may blind us somewhat to the skill" and went on to dismiss Picasso's Neoclassicism as "caricature" (*The Success and Failure of Picasso* [Harmondsworth: Penguin Books, 1965], pp. 90, 94).

51. This drawing is reproduced in FitzGerald, *Making Modernism*, p. 86.

52. Wildenstein withdrew from the partnership in 1932.

53. Letter of September 27, 1918 (Picasso Archives, Musée Picasso, Paris).

54. Geiser/Baer 222.

55. For Apollinaire's praise of Renoir, see Breunig, ed., *Apollinaire on Art*, pp. 278–79. For Picasso's drawings of maternity images modeled after Renoir, see estate no. 2432 and Zervos III, 122. They suggest that the portrait of Madame Rosenberg and her daughter may already reflect his interest in Renoir.

56. In an interview Picasso gave at the time of this exhibition, he is quoted as having emphasized his financial and social success, particularly the patronage of Olivier Saincère (the secretary to the president of France) and Russian collectors (Georges Martin, "Dans l'air de Paris—Picasso," *L'Intransigeant*, October 27, 1919, p. 2).

57. *Lovers* is in the collection of the Musée Picasso, Paris, M.P. 62.

58. I have discussed these issues at length in "Picasso in the Beaux Quartiers," *Art in America* 80 (December 1992), pp. 86–91.

59. Picasso's acquisition of several of these works can be documented to the second decade of the twentieth century and the early 1920s, and probably all were acquired at that time. The works remained in Picasso's possession and are now in the collection of the Musée Picasso, Paris, T. 61–67.

60. Hélène Parmelin, "Picasso ou le collectionneur," *L'Oeil*, no. 230 (September 1974), pp. 6–9. Renoir's *Seated Bather* (1895–1900) is in the collection of the Musée Picasso, Paris, T. 62; Picasso's *Seated Nude Drying Her Foot* (1921) is in the Berggruen collection (Zervos IV, 330).

61. Among the most sensual are a series of drawings of 1920 (for example, Zervos IV, 90). One of the most casual is a caricature of Olga brushing her teeth (1920; estate no. 2804). In 1920 Picasso also drew the largest number of sketches of Olga in a ballet costume (for example, Zervos IV, 97 and 110). Olga's more casual appearance is recorded in a postcard the Picassos sent to Igor Stravinsky from Juan-les-Pins on July 20, 1920 (p. 335).

62. The receipt for the sale of this painting to Paul Rosenberg is dated January 18, 1921

(Pierpont Morgan Library, New York, gift of Alexandre Rosenberg). The sale is also recorded in one of the small notebooks preserved in the Picasso Archives, Musée Picasso, Paris. The entry specifies that the picture was painted at Juan-les-Pins. The entries in this notebook begin with purchases made at Biarritz in August 1918 and continue through May 1924. Another notebook includes sales made from December 1923 through January 1926. Along with other scholars who have examined these notebooks, I believe that they are in the hand of Olga. (My thanks to Anne Baldassari for advising me that this is also the opinion of Bernard Picasso, who has compared the handwriting to samples among his grandmother's papers.)

63. In 1921 Picasso gave a reduced version of this painting, *Woman Reading*, to the Musée de Grenoble. It thus became the first Picasso to enter the collection of a French museum. See *L'Art du XXᵉ siècle: La collection du Musée de Grenoble* (Paris: Editions de la Réunion des musées nationaux, 1994).

64. *Two Female Nudes* is in the collection of the Kunstsammlung, Nordrhein-Westfalen, Düsseldorf (Zervos IV, 217).

65. For an interpretation of these paintings, see Theodore Reff, "Picasso's *Three Musicians*: Maskers, Artists and Friends," *Art in America* 68 (December 1980), pp. 124–42.

66. Two previous articles that have suggested a connection between this painting and Picasso's engagement are Reff, "Picasso's *Three Musicians*," p. 131, and E. B. Henning, "Picasso: Harlequin with Violin (Si Tu Veux)," *Bulletin of the Cleveland Museum of Art* 63 (January 1976), pp. 6–7.

67. This episode is documented in Cocteau's letters; see Pierre Caizergues and Pierre Chanel, *Jean Cocteau: Lettres à sa mere, I, 1898–1918* (Paris: Gallimard, 1989), p. 370. Obviously, the accident must have limited Olga's ability to dance.

68. The rough sketch is estate Carnet 214/26.

69. Picasso had made these revisions to the composition before Paul Rosenberg sold it to John Quinn on June 12, 1922. In a letter of July 10, 1922, to Quinn, H. P. Roché mentioned having ordered a frame for "the reduction cutting of the Maternity," which Quinn apparently purchased along with the large canvas (Quinn Papers, New York Public Library). My thanks to Charles Stuckey for allowing me to examine the object files and X rays of the painting in the conservation laboratory of the Art Institute of Chicago. During 1921, Picasso painted a considerable number of maternity images, but in the summer of 1922 he returned to the subject of the family in *Family on the Seashore* (Musée Picasso, Paris, M.P. 80). A drawing for this painting (M.P. 963) shows considerable similarities with the three-figure version of *Mother and Child*.

70. The crucial sketchbook for this period is Carnet 213, especially pp. 17, 32, and 35–37. Also relevant are Carnets 1137 and 1195. Picasso used all three of these sketchbooks during his summer sojourn at Dinard. My thanks to Brigitte Léal for confirming the dating of these sketchbooks.

71. William Rubin, "The Pipes of Pan: Picasso's Aborted Love Song to Sara Murphy," *Art News* 93 (May 1994), pp. 138–47.

72. This receipt is dated October 22, 1923 (Pierpont Morgan Library, New York, gift of Alexandre Rosenberg). It is reproduced in Christian Geelhaar, *Picasso: Wegbereiter und Förderer seines Aufstiegs 1899–1939* (Zurich: Palladion, 1993), p. 148.

73. André Salmon, *La Revue de France*, May 1, 1924, p. 159. Evidence that Picasso was reconsidering his Rose period work while painting these pictures is his contemporaneous series of drawings and gouaches depicting circus performers, particularly *Traveling Circus* (December 1922; Musée Picasso, Paris, M.P. 981).

74. Regarding the breakup of Picasso's relationship with Olga (and his relations with other women), I believe that the remark attributed to his mother is most apt. Françoise Gilot relayed Picasso's own account of his mother's words: "He told me that when he went to Barcelona with Olga before their marriage and introduced her to his mother, his mother had said, 'You poor girl, you don't know what you're letting yourself in for. If I were a friend I would tell you not to do it under any conditions. I don't believe any woman could be happy with my son. He's available for himself but for no one else'" (*Life with Picasso* [New York: McGraw-Hill, 1964], p. 148).

75. See Ulrich Weisner, ed., *Picassos Surrealismus: Werke 1925–1937* (Bielefeld: Kunsthalle Bielefeld, 1991); Marie-Laure Bernadac, "André Breton et Pablo Picasso: 'tout le sang du possible vers le coeur,'" in Musée National d'Art Moderne, *André Breton: La Beauté convulsive* (Paris: Editions du Centre Pompidou, 1991), pp. 210–13; Elizabeth Cowling, "'Proudly We Claim Him as One of Us': Breton, Picasso and the Surrealist Movement," *Art History* 8 (March 1985), p. 87; and FitzGerald, *Making Modernism*, pp. 136–51.

76. Penrose wrote that the painting depicts "a profile easily recognizable as a self-portrait, set in juxtaposition to a sharp red-tongued monster," and he characterized the artist's circumstances as follows: "Picasso's reaction [to his difficult relationship with his wife] was to translate the torment that Olga caused him into new and powerful symbols, some of which can be clearly traced to his own personal feelings, whereas others became universal in their meaning. The irrational psychological cruelty that is an integral part of sexual relationships was receiving the close scrutiny of the Surrealists. . . . Both trains of thought, the personal and the universal, acted on Picasso as a stimulus" (*Picasso: His Life and Work* [London: Penguin, 1971], pp. 264–65).

77. The Surrealists' depiction of women has been the subject of wide discussion in recent years; see Mary Ann Caws, "Ladies Shot and Painted: Female Embodiment in Surrealist Art," in Susan Rubin Suleiman, ed., *The Female Body in Western Culture* (Cambridge, Mass.: Harvard University Press, 1986), pp. 262–87; Mary Ann Caws, Rudolf E. Kuenzli, and Gwen Raaberg, eds., *Surrealism and Women* (Cambridge, Mass.:

MIT Press, 1991); and Robert Rosenblum, "Picasso and the Anatomy of Eroticism," in Gert Schiff, ed., *Picasso in Perspective* (Englewood Cliffs, N.J.: Prentice-Hall, 1976), pp. 75–85.

78. See above, pp. 63, 66, and the text on this painting in Rubin, *Picasso in the Collection of The Museum of Modern Art*, p. 132.

79. See Roland Penrose, "Beauty and the Monster," in Penrose and John Golding, eds., *Picasso in Retrospect* (New York: Praeger, 1973), pp. 179–80. For the subject in late-nineteenth-through early-twentieth-century art, see Michael Marrinan, "Images and Ideas of Charlotte Corday: Texts and Contexts of an Assassination," *Arts Magazine* 54 (April 1980), pp. 158–76.

80. The identification of this painting's subject rests substantially on the statement by the eminent French curator Georges Salles, who donated the painting to the Musée National d'Art Moderne, that Picasso told him it was a portrait of Olga. (Salles relayed this information to John Richardson, whom I thank for having passed it along to me.) This painting is paired with another, *Bust of a Woman* (not in Zervos but reproduced in Weisner, ed., *Picassos Surrealismus*, p. 345), which may also be a portrait of Olga. It would be surprising if others, particularly dating from the later years, do not come to light.

81. On March 11, 1942, Cocteau met Picasso after he had encountered Olga outside his bank and described the circumstances; see Jean Touzot, ed., *Jean Cocteau: Journal 1942–1945* (Paris: Gallimard, 1989), pp. 26–27. For Olga's activities at Cannes, see Gilot, *Life with Picasso*, pp. 196–99. Picasso did pay Olga's expenses during the years after their separation.

82. For Olga's letters to Picasso, see Gilot, *Life with Picasso*, p. 149; several photographs of Picasso, Olga, and Paulo taken in the 1920s are catalogued by the Musée Picasso as coming from letters ranging from the late 1930s through the early 1950s.

83. In a forthcoming book on Picasso's variations after the work of other artists, Susan Grace Galassi will propose that the variation after Delacroix's *Women of Algiers* (p. 456), painted by Picasso on February 11, 1955, contains a reference to Olga, who died that day.

Merry Christmas, Happy New Year. 1951. Collage made by Olga Picasso, including photographs of Picasso, herself, Paulo, Paulo's wife, Emmanuelle Lotte, and their children Marina and Pablito. Musée Picasso, Paris, Picasso Archives

Photograph of Picasso and Olga on a postcard sent to Igor Stravinsky from Juan-les-Pins, July 20, 1920. Photographer unknown. Igor Stravinsky Collection at the Paul Sacher Foundation

Marie-Thérèse Seated. March 11, 1937. Oil and pastel on canvas, 51⅛ × 38⅛″ (130 × 97 cm). Not in Zervos. Musée Picasso, Paris

Picasso's Blond Muse: The Reign of Marie-Thérèse Walter

BY ROBERT ROSENBLUM

It was in 1950, at Yale University, that I heard a startling comment about Picasso from Charles Seymour, a professor not of modern, but of Italian Renaissance, art. Confronted with the recurrent problem of how to explain to undergraduates the bewildering sequence of periods and "isms" in what was then only a half-century of Picasso's art, he threw out the whimsical idea that perhaps the master's rapid succession of changing and often contradictory styles might best be defined by the names of the women who, one after another, had dominated his private life. At the time, the suggestion seemed naïvely off the mark, the uninformed comment of an outsider to the complex languages of modern art. But today, almost fifty years later, the visible connection between Picasso's art and love life is so taken for granted that when, for example, his works of the early 1930s are talked about, the growingly useful phrase "the Marie-Thérèse period" evokes something far more visually specific than, say, "the Surrealist period." In fact, in 1994, this ever more familiar approach was reflected in the very title of Judi Freeman's innovative exhibition, *Picasso and the Weeping Women: The Years of Marie-Thérèse Walter & Dora Maar*.[1]

How times have changed! It is something of a jolt to turn back to 1946, the publication date of Alfred H. Barr, Jr.'s *Picasso: Fifty Years of His Art*. In this Old Testament of the Picasso literature, a selfless masterpiece of scholarship that laid the foundation stones for the rest of us,

one discovers, for example, that Dora Maar is nowhere mentioned as the human inspiration for many of the grotesque portraits discussed at the book's conclusion, but appears only in her cameo roles as photographer of the progressive stages of *Guernica* in 1937 and, later, in 1944, as a reader in one of Picasso's plays, *Le Désir attrapé par la queue*.[2] But perhaps still more surprising today is the fact that Marie-Thérèse Walter does not even figure in Barr's name-studded index. Of course, Barr, with his always acute eye and lapidary prose, was keenly aware of a sea change in Picasso's art, noting that "in the spring of 1932 Picasso produced with amazing energy a long series of large canvases of women, usually sleeping or seated, unlike anything he had done before in their great sweeping curves, which are echoed in several paintings by philodendron leaves."[3] But this succinct truth hardly implies that these "women" might have been a particular woman. To be sure, in 1946 Marie-Thérèse's reality as a living presence in Picasso's life was still very much a secret; and even nine years later, in 1955, the catalogue of the first great Picasso retrospective held in Paris after the war tells us, in the chronology entry for 1932,[4] that some nameless woman with blond locks who appears in his paintings will be the future mother of his daughter Maya. It was only, in fact, in the 1960s, especially with the publication of Françoise Gilot's *Life with Picasso* (1964), that Marie-Thérèse lost her mysterious anonymity, a mythical blond goddess rendered mortal.

Does it matter? Perhaps Barr, relatively uninterested in the flesh-and-blood actresses who played roles in the dramas of Picasso's life, said essentially all that needed to be said about what, after all, was art and not biography. Nevertheless, what is known cannot be unknown; and in the last three decades, the welling profusion of information about Picasso's personal life has also been leavening even familiar works with new layers of meaning that may enrich, rather than adulterate, our experience of the master's art. For instance, the well-known lithograph once titled *Face* (p. 340) has slowly turned before our eyes into a portrait of the eighteen-year-old blond girl who, according to the most familiar but now challenged account, entered Picasso's life in 1927 and gradually usurped the throne then occupied by Olga Khokhlova, the artist's legal wife. With the accumulation of photographs of Marie-Thérèse to guide us (opposite and p. 341), we can now discern in the print and the related drawing (p. 340) her smooth, unblemished features coming to life, like Pygmalion's Galatea, beneath the imperturbable classical perfections of eyebrow, nose, and cheek already familiar to the teen-age Picasso in the plaster casts of Greco-Roman heads that surrounded him in the art academies of La Coruña, Barcelona, and Madrid. But as Barr put it, the face is "striking for its 'closeup' cutting,"[5] which, in biographical terms, takes on a new dimension when one realizes that this startling proximity and cropping produce unexpected effects appropriate to the artist's personal circumstances—an erotic intimacy gleaned from a lover's closeup gaze and touch, and a mood of concealment that permits us to glimpse, but perhaps not quite recognize,

Bust of a Girl (Marie-Thérèse). 1926. Pen, chalk, wash, and tempera on paper, 24⅞ × 18⅞" (63 × 48 cm). Zervos VII, 7. Staatsgalerie Stuttgart

only a fragment of the face of a newcomer still playing a clandestine role. And when we realize that this lithograph was included in the original, deluxe edition of André Level's 1928 monograph on Picasso,[6] we may be astonished by the master's temerity in half-revealing his personal secret within the public context of his art.

But this stealthy intrusion of life into art, often the equivalent of a secret diary entry, was a recurrent challenge and obvious delight for Picasso, whose ability to invent disguised allusions to his personal entourage was protean. So it was that in 1927, not only did Marie-Thérèse appear in Picasso's art as a physiognomic likeness but also as a cryptogram, disclosed in a series of variations upon that archetypal Spanish symbol, the guitar—at times, for him, almost a self-portrait—suspended on a wall over a molding (p. 343).[7] Pursuing the traditional Spanish associations between playing a guitar and making love to a woman, Picasso, in the most overt declaration of this series, animates the rectilinear patterns of the guitar so that they form, like tea leaves to be read, a mysterious message of linked initials, MT and P. (Even eight years later, in 1935, he would use this invented monogram, ꟿ, in one of his poems.[8])

Such private codes have a familiar ring, harking back to the many verbal puns in Picasso's Cubist work that might evoke, say, the spirit of his then girl friend, Eva

Head of a Woman. November 1925. Lithograph, 5 × 4½" (12.7 × 11.5 cm). Geiser/Baer I, 240. Musée Picasso, Paris

Gouel, through the phrase "Ma Jolie" (simultaneously his pet name for her and the refrain of a music-hall song)[9] or even of Max Jacob, whose tribulations were jokingly condensed in the name "Job" (at once the poet's nickname and the brand name of cigarette papers included in several still lifes).[10] And still more to the amorous point, there was the brief fling Picasso had in 1916 with Gabrielle Lespinasse, to whom he declared his love on paper by, among other things, intertwining his name with hers in a calligraphic coupling (p. 342).[11] But now, in 1927, this word play is further complicated by a mysterious human presence who seems to witness the monogrammatic marriage of MT and P. This androgynous profile of blank classical beauty, the perfect distillation of many antique heads he re-created in the early 1920s, conjures up not only the symbolic self-portrait of the artist that often appears in paintings as well as photographs (p. 207) of the late 1920s and early 1930s, but also the mythic mold of ideal serenity that would later transform Marie-Thérèse into an Olympian goddess. And in yet another cryptic way, Picasso once added to this elemental profile the far more specific features of a now seated Marie-Thérèse and incised this image on a still life of musical instruments on a table (1925–26; p. 341).[12] But to the casual eye, this linear human presence is so camouflaged beneath the fluid shapes of the mandolin overlaying her body that its existence is almost more subliminal than actual, once more a metaphorical echo of an adulterous relationship that dares not speak its name.

That Picasso, in such works, willfully secreted information about the new love in his life is irrefutable; and, given this fact, it is no surprise that there has been a strong temptation to sniff around his art for the scent of more biographical clues to these ongoing detective stories. Such a pursuit has even cast doubt on the date conventionally given for Picasso's first encounter with Marie-Thérèse. The usual story would have it that on January 8, 1927, in an almost mythical example of the Surrealist search for *l'amour fou*—an obsessive but liberating passion determined by chance rather than by middle-class constraints—Picasso picked up a living symbol of girlish ripeness and purity in front of the Galeries Lafayette.[13] But this often-repeated account of what the French call a *coup de foudre* has also been questioned on the basis of visual as well as new documentary evidence. In 1988 Dr. Herbert T. Schwarz, a professional physician, published the remarkable results of his amateur obsession with Picasso, demonstrating his belief that Picasso, in fact, had first met Marie-Thérèse at the Gare Saint-Lazare as early as January or February 1925, when she was only fifteen (she was born on July 13, 1909), that he continued to see her, and that she made frequent clandestine appearances in his art in 1925–26, an hypothesis supported by interviews with surviving members of the Walter family.[14]

Marie-Thérèse Walter at age thirteen. Studio photograph, probably taken at Weisbaden, Germany, October 20, 1922. Collection Maya Picasso

There is much to confirm this speculation. In 1926, for instance, a young, innocent girl—her fair hair parted in the middle, her face broad and rounded—seems to slip into the *dramatis personae* of his work (opposite); and at times she even wears the Peter Pan collar (what the French call a *col Claudine*) that was apparently a part of Marie-Thérèse's customary wardrobe and was also to figure in the legend of what was presumably their first encounter in January 1927, namely, that it was a *col Claudine* that Marie-Thérèse was shopping for at the Galeries Lafayette when she was first confronted by Picasso and that she would in fact keep this collar as a memento for half a century, until her death by suicide in 1977.[15] Indeed, such a teen-ager turns up throughout a sketchbook dated March 21, 1926.[16] But even going back to the previous year, there are suspicions of Marie-Thérèse's hidden presence. For instance, a pencil drawing dated November 1925 (p. 382) offers a precedent for the later appearance of the monogram MT emerging from the angular shape of a guitar;[17] and in the same month, a lithograph presents an idealized vision of a facial type (opposite) that seems to look backward not only to the sculptural clarity of Picasso's Neoclassic heads, bathed in Mediterranean

Head of Marie-Thérèse. 1927. Pencil on paper, 7⅞ × 5⅝″ (20 × 14.2 cm). Not in Zervos. Private collection

Head of Marie-Thérèse. 1928. Lithograph, printed in black; comp. 8⅛ × 5⁹⁄₁₆″ (20.6 × 14.1 cm). Geiser/Baer I, 243. The Museum of Modern Art, New York. Gift of Abby Aldrich Rockefeller

sunlight, but forward to the growing intrusion of a more secretive, inner physiognomy that Picasso would later explore so fully under the spell of an increasingly mature blond sitter.[18] Appropriate to 1925, the year of the ruptured and doubled physiognomies of *The Three Dancers* and the year in which André Breton claimed Picasso as a kindred spirit to the Surrealists, a shadowy presence emerges in this print, an alternate persona polarized not only in terms of contrasting intensities of light and darkness, but of the duality of a profile imposed upon a frontal view. By the 1930s, such an evocative coupling would become a familiar formula from which Picasso could extract endless variations on the dialogue between external and internal aspects of the human mind and body, such as wakefulness versus sleep, or conscious repression versus sexual release.

Of course, Picasso, in his art, constantly created visual and psychological fictions into which the *dramatis personae* of his life could then be fitted. In the years 1917–24, facial types re-created from Ingres and antiquity could be accommodated to the specifics of portraiture, whether of himself, his new wife, his first child, or the personages of

the well-heeled, arty milieu that transported him from prewar Bohemia to postwar high society. Yet the same types could also be abstracted to a generic ideal that might transform the domestic presence of Olga and baby Paulo into a Raphaelesque Madonna and Child. And such metamorphic fluidity kept expanding, in part under the muse of Surrealism, which demanded ever more slippery identities. The black-or-white choice of categorizing a figure as being a portrait or a nonportrait belies the infinite shades of gray with which Picasso could transform not only people into art, but even existing works of art—whether by himself, by Delacroix or Ingres, by Velázquez or Rembrandt—into contemporary people. Moreover, he could even transform one person into another, particularly in periods of emotional transition. Marie-Thérèse's surreptitious coexistence with Olga must have created the tensest of human triangles and overlappings, producing, for instance, the particularly fraught Dinard summer of 1928, when the teen-age lover, installed in a *pension de famille*,[19] was sent off to play beachside games with other minors while, nearby, the artist maintained a facade of upscale marital propriety. Describing the nature of reality

Passport photograph of Marie-Thérèse Walter (detail). Paris, 1930. Photograph by Photomaton. Collection Maya Picasso

Still Life with Musical Instruments (detail). 1925–26. Oil on canvas, 63¾ × 80½″ (161.9 × 204.5 cm). Not in Zervos. Museo Nacional Centro de Arte Reina Sofía, Madrid

in his Cubist works, Picasso once likened it to a kind of perfume, an aromatic presence that, for a moment, might coalesce and then, eluding fixed definition, evaporate;[20] and in the same way, the women in his life drifted in and out of his art, at times specific enough to be recognized and named, but as often as not, defying precise identification, re-created as mythical ideals or hybrid personae that transcend the more earthbound categories of portraiture.

So it is that the human fact of Marie-Thérèse in Picasso's life, whether from 1927 or as early as 1925 on, is subject to constant transformations that range from instantly recognizable portraits to transcendent universal symbols. In a charcoal drawing of 1928–30 (p. 345), there is no question that we are staring into the pale eyes of a young blond woman in modern clothing whose smooth, rounded face and straight hair, cropped at the neck, proclaim her identity as immediately as a snapshot. But even here, Picasso's metamorphic magic holds sway, as the pure oval of her head, reinforced by the contours of her hair and the halolike crescent of the beret, begins to evoke an almost mythical being, a nascent moon goddess. Indeed, in a painted pair of oddly cropped profile heads of

August 1928 (p. 344), we may at first intuit the same face and even sense some real-life scenario to explain the downcast eyes and the biting of a handkerchief held in a somewhat clumsy hand (a preview of the weeping women of the 1930s). However, the ideal clarity of profile, with its uninterrupted line from brow to nose, and the wreath of flowers on her pensive head waft us swiftly to an almost mythological terrain. If this is still to be considered a portrait of Marie-Thérèse (and we may well continue to recognize her altered features here), it perhaps belongs more comfortably to the domain of allegorical portraiture especially familiar to the eighteenth century, when Sir Joshua Reynolds, for example, could elevate his contemporary sitters to such varying roles as Juno, Hope, the Tragic Muse, or Saint Cecilia. But then, constantly moving between fiction and fact, Picasso, in another modest profile image, a drawing of 1930, once more locates Marie-Thérèse in the realm of portrait vignette, still preserving the incisive purity of a classical silhouette, but now adjusting it to the particularities of the twenty-year-old sitter's short-cropped hair, full chin, and high, ruffled collar (p. 345).

The delicate candor of such a portrait drawing was soon to be countered in 1931–32 by a series of painted portraits that now exalt Marie-Thérèse to a position of imperturbable grandeur and security, frequently enforced by her placement in a sturdy, upholstered armchair. The new, regal centrality of her image corresponded as well to various domestic changes, beginning in autumn 1930, when Picasso not only installed her at 44, rue La Boétie, just down the street from his and Olga's apartment at no. 23, but, at the same time, created a more complete sanctuary for himself, for his beloved, and for

Interlaced Names in Decorative Script: Gaby and Picasso (detail). 1916. Watercolor and ink on paper. Not in Zervos. Private collection

his art, by buying the seventeenth-century château of Boisgeloup, near Gisors, whose stables he converted into a sculpture studio,[21] where so much of his new work in three dimensions would also be inspired by the blond muse. Already in 1931, a plaster relief (p. 347) gives her disembodied profile a venerable pedigree, as if a Roman archaeological find of a goddess or empress were miraculously reborn, her bulbous nose, rounded cheek, fair hair, and clear, staring eye emerging from a weathered background with uncanny, quickening life.[22]

Soon after, Marie-Thérèse's visual and psychological presence became so potent that even in the early 1970s, many Picasso scholars, myself and William Rubin included,[23] tended to overlook the then known biographical information that she had already been very much part of Picasso's life in 1927 and, on the evidence of the quantum leap in his work in 1931, tacitly assumed that this date corresponded to her arrival on the scene. Yet if she had, in fact, been with Picasso for perhaps even as long as six years, it was really only in 1931 that Marie-Thérèse, now firmly entrenched in both the city and country life of a lover twenty-eight years her senior, could at last emerge from the wings to center stage, where she could preside as a radiant deity, in new roles that changed from Madonna to sphinx, from *odalisque* to earth mother. At times her master seems to worship humbly at her shrine, capturing a fixed, confrontational stare of almost supernatural power; but more often, he becomes an ecstatic voyeur, who quietly captures his beloved reading, meditating, catnapping, or surrendering to the deepest abandon of sleep.

In one of the earliest paintings in this series, *The Red Armchair*, dated December 16, 1931, an unusual anxiety marks the face and posture of Marie-Thérèse, whose crescent-shaped halo of yellow hair now becomes a telltale symbol of her charismatic presence (p. 346). Her face weds the frontal and profile views that defined her more tentatively in the late 1920s, but also alters them in a more probing and disquieting psychological direction. The mouth and pale eyes, for example, reduce the partly purified shapes of the Ingresque portrait drawing of 1927–28 to a new kind of hieroglyphic mystery; and the serene profile familiar to other work of the late 1920s has regressed to something simpler and cruder, moving rapidly away from the classical beauty already challenged in the plaster relief of 1931 and toward the kind of invisible demon Gauguin had depicted with frontal eye on flattened head in his *The Spirit of the Dead Watching* of 1892 (p. 348). Picasso must have first seen Gauguin's rendering of a primitive spirit at Vollard's in 1901,[24] and would find in it continuing inspiration, not only in 1907, in the mesmerizing gaze of the curtain puller at the left in *Les Demoiselles d'Avignon*, and in 1925 in *The Three Dancers* and its progeny, but again in 1931–32, when he newly explored the occult potential of a staring eye on a profiled head, as Gauguin himself had done in many of his would-be primitive sculptures. Moreover, Gauguin's painting may have been freshly topical for Picasso in other ways. For one, its luxurious and mysterious vibrations of complementary colors, especially yellow and violet, would be reinvented by Picasso. This particular pairing, as Linda Nochlin has shown in a path-breaking analysis of Picasso's color,[25] became virtually a chromatic symbol of Marie-Thérèse. (In *The Red Armchair*, there are, in fact, three different yellows coupled with three different violets.) And for another, Gauguin's motif of a voluptuous,

Hanging Guitar with Profile. 1927. Oil on canvas, 10¾ × 13¾″ (27.1 × 34.9 cm). Zervos VII, 54. Alsdorf Collection, Chicago

the profiled head above, whose shape distills that of the 1931 plaster relief. These sexual rumblings continue below the belt, where the sweeping arcs of the dark brown sleeves end, like a pair of calipers, in the sharp points of two white hands that look more like furry paws than human fingers. Such a subliminal canine presence may reflect the dogs in the Picasso house-hold,[26] an Airedale and a Saint Bernard whose conspicuous dark-on-white patches had earlier that year worked their way into drawings of Marie-Thérèse, much as later the snout of a pet Afghan hound would be fused with the features of Dora Maar.[27] And in the area enclosed by these protective, feral arms is the delta of love, so that here, too, what at first appears to be a human fortress of rectilinear chastity begins to curve with the animal pulsations of desire.

Some five weeks later, these sexual constraints were partly released in a painting made, according to the inscription on the stretcher, during the afternoon of Sunday, January 24, 1932, and exhibited the following June with the title *The Dream* (p. 352).[28] The taut and anxious wakefulness of the earlier Marie-Thérèse, like the red armchair that cushions her, has begun to melt, as Picasso captures the fragile moment of transition between consciousness and sleep. Now the controlling perpendicular grid of *The Red Armchair* has been banished to the upper left-hand corner, where the stripes of the dado magically split the twinned face, dividing it into an upper frontal and a lower profile view that pinpoints the passage from drowsiness to a slumber so deep that it falls below the horizon line. And the shift from the awareness of an external world to the liberation of subconscious desires is further underlined by the lipstick smudge on the upper lip that vanishes in its sleeping counterpart, as if the visible display of modern female lure had moved to a more timeless domain of feminine mystery. This sense of release even pertains to the wallpaper background found in many paintings of 1932; for here, the diamond-shaped pattern (recalling Picasso's familiar identification with the harlequin costume) as well as the three- and four-leaved florets (recalling the ace of clubs, whose traditional symbolism

supine nude being quietly observed could also be absorbed into the sexually charged voyeurism of these years. (Indeed, already in 1902–03, Picasso made a rapid drawing after Gauguin's painting in which he transformed the head of the Polynesian evil spirit into a self-portrait [p. 348], a figure who both watches and touches not an exotic, but a contemporary, Western nude.)

In *The Red Armchair*, the fusion of frontal and profile physiognomy that may find its modern roots in Gauguin's revival of an Egyptian convention now yields a conflicting duality of repression and desire that informs the entire work. The incisive vertical line that marks the length of the nose skewers the figure into rigid place, intersecting a pair of crossed arcs that read as a stressfully furrowed brow. This plumb line is enforced above by the sharp vertical that visibly marks the juncture of the two wall planes behind her and, to her left, by the four stripes on the chairback. And as a further bolt in this imprisoning grid, the perpendicular of the molding and the belt, as well as the diagonal stripes of the chair arm, immobilize her head and body in a frontal posture of iconic stillness that prompts awe and veneration. But within this stiff, heraldic pattern, reminiscent of medieval Madonnas and sixteenth-century Northern court portraiture, organic juices begin to flow. The square of the constraining belt buckle is echoed by the irregular circle of a frontal breast discerned beneath a dress of total concealment; and to its left, a profiled breast matches the swelling protrusions of

Profile of a Woman. August 12, 1928. Oil on canvas. Zervos VII, 228.
Private collection

Profile of a Woman. August 13, 1928. Oil on canvas . Zervos VII, 229.
Private collection

of good fortune made it the favorite playing card in
Picasso's Cubist still lifes)[29] begin to wobble with ever-
growing freedom from geometry as they yield to the
breathing pulse of Marie-Thérèse. And the armchair,
glowing with the Spanish national colors, red and yellow,
swells, too, embracing, like an imaginary lover, the sitter's
transport to an erotic reverie. This sexual unveiling is
almost literal. As her blouse falls from her rounded shoulders, caressed by a red-and-yellow necklace that matches
the chair's colors, her left breast and nipple, discreetly
covered in *The Red Armchair*, now half emerge into view.
And the pincer claws that met at her groin in *The Red
Armchair* have now become fleshy and pliant, defining a
pubic triangle that even includes a sixth finger on her

right hand, perhaps a sexual pun evoked as well in the
phallic shape of the upper half of her head that rises
above the dado, snaking over her lunar profile.

In contrast to this mood of silent inwardness, the
colors are ablaze with every hue in the rainbow, often
ordered in complementary pairings that clash and merge
with magnetic force. Here once again, Picasso may have
been competing with his eternal rival in life as in death,
Henri Matisse,[30] whose 1931 retrospective at the Galerie
Georges Petit (June 16–July 25) was to be followed, exactly one year later (June 16–July 30), by Picasso's own
retrospective at the same Paris gallery. Of the 145 paintings in the Matisse exhibition, about two-thirds were from
the Nice period, which meant a particularly strong display

Marie-Thérèse at Twenty. 1930. Lead pencil on paper, 24¾ × 18¾″ (62.7 × 47.5 cm). Not in Zervos. Private collection

Marie-Thérèse in a Beret. 1928–30. Charcoal on paper, 24⅞ × 18⅞″ (63 × 48 cm). Not in Zervos. Private collection

of variations on a traditional French theme, a domestic harem populated by seated, standing, and reclining women, some nude, some dressed in contemporary or exotic clothing. But Matisse had also rejuvenated this familiar and commercially viable territory with a chromatic dazzle that, in one painting of 1929, *The Yellow Hat*,[31] even focused on the same complementary hues, yellow and violet, that Picasso would soon favor in his treatment of Marie-Thérèse's hair and flesh. Freshly challenged by the Frenchman's genius, Picasso embarked on his own version of a cloistered female paradise where the highest-pitched colors could yield an *Arabian Nights* enchantment; and by the time of the opening of his retrospective in June 1932, he was able to bring to a climax this grand summary of his career with a group of new paintings inspired by Marie-Thérèse, including *The Dream*.

Characteristically, Picasso's vision of an erotic Eden carried a far denser symbolic and literary weight than Matisse's bourgeois hothouse of the 1920s, recalling more closely the youthful Matisse of the *Joy of Life* (1905–06), with its ecstatic wedding of color to fluid, eroticized line. Moreover, the eruptive force of Picasso's passion could even be translated into language; for in words as well, he made love to Marie-Thérèse, describing her rapturously and chromatically in the image-ridden, unpunctuated

flow of his poetry of 1935, where her "cheveux blonds," her "bras couleur lilas," her "bleu de corsage"[32] recall such painted images as the supernal blend of blond hair, lilac flesh, and blue bodice in *The Dream*. And if we sense, too, that Picasso's eagerness to reexperience the fullest range of kindergarten colors corresponds to a childlike joy and rebirth synonymous with the universal symbolism of the rainbow (another recurrent image in his poetry),[33] we may even find such a metaphor literally depicted in a 1932 landscape of the château of Boisgeloup in the rain (p. 354). Here the gray, wet skies of Normandy are suddenly dispelled by a sweeping rainbow (dominated by red and yellow arcs) that embraces the rural retreat from sky to earth. The artist's euphoria has resurrected a shop-worn symbol.

But this rainbow palette could also be demonized, as in a startlingly ugly image of another enthroned woman painted on January 22, 1932, only two days before *The Dream* and traditionally titled *Repose* (p. 355). Although most of the women of 1932 evoke an ideal Marie-Thérèse as a tender, compliant creature of ample, voluptuous curves, this one appears a frightening intruder, close to the ogress who menaced the works of the late 1920s with shrieking maw, pointed tongue, and predatory limbs, a *femme fatale* who might be viewed as both a mythic

The Red Armchair (Marie-Thérèse). December 16, 1931. Oil and enamel on panel, 51½ × 39″ (130.8 × 99 cm). Zervos VII, 334. The Art Institute of Chicago. Gift of Mr. and Mrs. Daniel Saidenberg

Head of Marie-Thérèse. 1931. Plaster, 27 × 23⅝ × 4″ (69 × 60 × 10 cm). Spies 130, I. Private collection

Surrealist monster and a psychological portrait of the witch Olga, the legal enemy of his adulterous bliss.[34] But as John Richardson put it, referring to some of the mixed identities of 1928, "Picasso would not be Picasso if . . . he did not sometimes scramble his carefully differentiated images and perversely see the beloved mistress and hated wife in terms of each other."[35] Master of every kind of witchcraft, Picasso seems here to imagine Olga's evil

spirit, like Gauguin's frightening specter, invading the very body and soul of Marie-Thérèse. Now the full spectrum of complementary colors, from lilac flesh to yellow breast, has turned strident and threatening, the chromatic counterpart of a coarse sexual display that offers a shrill contrast to the gentle, caressing disclosures of *The Dream.* Another wanton daughter of *Les Demoiselles d'Avignon,* the sitter strikes a pose of sexual lure. With arms withdrawn

Paul Gauguin. *The Spirit of the Dead Watching*. 1892. Oil on burlap mounted on canvas, 28¾ × 36½" (72.5 × 92.5 cm). Albright-Knox Art Gallery, Buffalo, New York. A. Conger Goodyear Collection, 1965

Self-Portrait with Reclining Nude. 1902–03. Ink and watercolor on paper, 6⅞ × 9⅛" (17.6 × 23.2 cm). Zervos XXI, 283. D.B. IV, 5. Museu Picasso, Barcelona

behind a cushioned head, breasts wildly askew, and legs both joined and provocatively parted, she becomes a grotesque reincarnation of Goya's brazen *Naked Maja*; and her body parts, which fuse with the armchair's own arms and legs, are defined by ungainly, twisted contours and bony, muscular textures at opposite poles to the mellifluous curves and pneumatic flesh of the ideal Marie-Thérèse. Above all, the head, with its dangerous bristle of hair and its staring but pupilless eyes aligned above and below a vaginal, lipsticked mouth with exposed teeth, conjures up a grinning sexual sorceress in her lair. So powerful is her presence that even the familiar diamond-shaped wallpaper patterns seem drained of color and geometric stability, now fluttering toward the glowing sitter like moths to a flame. Apparently, Olga's evil spirit had not yet been exorcised, even in Marie-Thérèse's inner sanctum.

A different kind of metamorphic magic is found only five days later in a painting of January 27, 1932, *Woman in a Red Armchair* (p. 353). Shifting, as he often did, from the insistently flat to the emphatically modeled, from chromatic abundance to monochrome austerity, Picasso now resumes the painted and drawn sculptural language of the many beachside fantasies of the late 1920s, when Marie-Thérèse and her friends, frolicking with beach balls or approaching, key in hand, a bathing cabana, would be transformed into weathered monuments that loom like prehistoric fossils over the horizon. Here the familiar red armchair, its color seemingly dulled by time, becomes a crude, archaic throne, as stony as the anatomical fragments that rest upon it in a balance both solid and precarious. The head, tilted backward with crescent-eye closed, as well as the rounded anatomies recall the posture of chair-bound sleep in *The Dream*, permitting us to whiff

the scent of a now skeletal Marie-Thérèse. As for the rest of her body, it has been reassembled in a *tour de force* of Surrealist paleontology familiar to the paintings of Tanguy and the sculptures of Moore. Her bone of a neck is bent to support the reclining head; her back has become a solid stone, like that of a chair; two smaller spheres double as breasts; two arms reach to their chair-arm counterparts for regal stability; and, finally, the largest sphere distills buttocks and pelvis on the chair seat into a single, centralized support for these acrobatic fossils. Fantastic reinventions of the human body were always at the core of Picasso's genius; and, here, as in many of the materialized as well as imaginary drawn and painted sculptures she inspired in the years 1931–33 (p. 350, 351), Marie-Thérèse has been re-created as a cluster of rotund fragments, suggesting both archaeological relics of totemic power that have endured from a remote civilization and rudimentary, almost fetal, organisms that quiver with a new life.

Such regressions reached still more complex levels when Picasso introduced a variety of mirrors into Marie-Thérèse's pictorial sanctuary. In *The Mirror* (p. 356), a painting of March 12, 1932, she has fallen into so profound a sleep that her lilac flesh has sunk in total abandon to the bottom of the canvas. Leo Steinberg has pointed out the continuity of the theme of sleepwatchers in Picasso's long career;[36] here it flourishes again, perhaps made even more intense in such works by implying rather than depicting the sleepwatcher. "Combien je l'aime maintenant qu'elle dort" (How much I love her now that she's sleeping)[37] is how Picasso would later describe, in a poem of 1935, the voyeuristic rapture so evident in this and other paintings of his often somnolent mistress. But what

Woman with a Flower. April 10, 1932. Oil on canvas, 63¾ × 51¼″ (162 × 130 cm). Zervos VII, 381. Private collection

Seated Woman and Head of a Bearded Man. 1932. Ink and pencil on paper, 10⅞ × 10″ (27.5 × 25.5 cm). Museum Ludwig, Collection Ludwig, Cologne, Germany

vitality. In this sexual context, the erect, vertical silhouette of the mirror's outer swivel frame with its protruding knob (a recurrent symbol in Picasso, as Lydia Gasman has shown)[39] provides the single, potent male element in a horizontal terrain of female hills and valleys. Cycles of night and day are also suggested. The diamond wallpaper pattern, now a taut geometric foil to Marie-Thérèse's undulant flesh, twinkles with a bluish nocturnal phosphorescence, whereas the mirror image, by contrast, embraces the glaring, life-giving energy of solar heat. It is a fusion of night and day that often appears in Picasso's recreations of Marie-Thérèse as a goddess of love and fertility who exists in cosmic harmony with sun and moon.

For even a minor artist, the inclusion of a mirror adds, both literally and figuratively, new dimensions of space and symbol; but for Picasso, the potential was staggering. As usual, he could conjure up, like a spiritualist, the ghosts of mirrors past, genealogical tables culled from old and new art that, when applied to the mythical aura of Marie-Thérèse, might range from Velázquez's *Venus,* whose mirror adds a frontal to her dorsal view, to the society portraits of Ingres, whose glassy reflections lend yet further mysteries of psychological remoteness to his

was a commonplace of their domestic life here prompts a magical journey through the looking glass. Picasso, in fact, has divided her body into two parts, adored from two angles of vision—one, a still palpable Marie-Thérèse, viewed frontally from head to waist; and two, an impalpable reflection of what would be the rear view of her lower body from buttocks to relaxed leg. Such fragmentation of a passive female nude permits her body to be scrutinized as wondrous erotic topography, a vision paralleled in the photographs of reclining nudes, their useless heads cropped by the frame, that Picasso's friend Brassaï would publish the following year in the first issue of *Minotaure.*[38]

However, Picasso's sexual enthrallment moves still further into an image of woman as a procreative goddess in perfect tune with nature. The Marie-Thérèse of the foreground, curled in on herself with two protective arms, has regressed to so early a stage of human development that, like an infant or an embryo, she instinctively sucks her thumb. Indeed, her head, with its crescent-moon eye closed in total self-absorption, is fetal and seedlike, and the vulval shape of her yellow hair further enriches this uterine imagery. It is the reflection of the hair, in fact, that carries us into the field of the mirror, animating the yellow contours of the frame with the throb of life. Within this swelling enclosure that warps the mirror's geometry, the domain of the womb becomes an imaginary human landscape. Above the buttocks, a burning crescent of red heats the source of generative power, from whose groin a leaf in complementary green coils upward with newborn

Marie-Thérèse at 6, Cité d'Alfort at Alforville, with Dolly, her mother's dog. 1932. Photograph by Picasso. Collection Maya Picasso

Sculptured Head (Marie-Thérèse). 1932. Charcoal on canvas, 36¼ × 28¾″ (92 × 73 cm). Not in Zervos. Collection Beyeler, Switzerland

The Dream (Marie-Thérèse). January 24, 1932. Oil on canvas, 51¼ × 38⅛″ (130 × 97 cm). Zervos VII, 364. Collection Sally Ganz

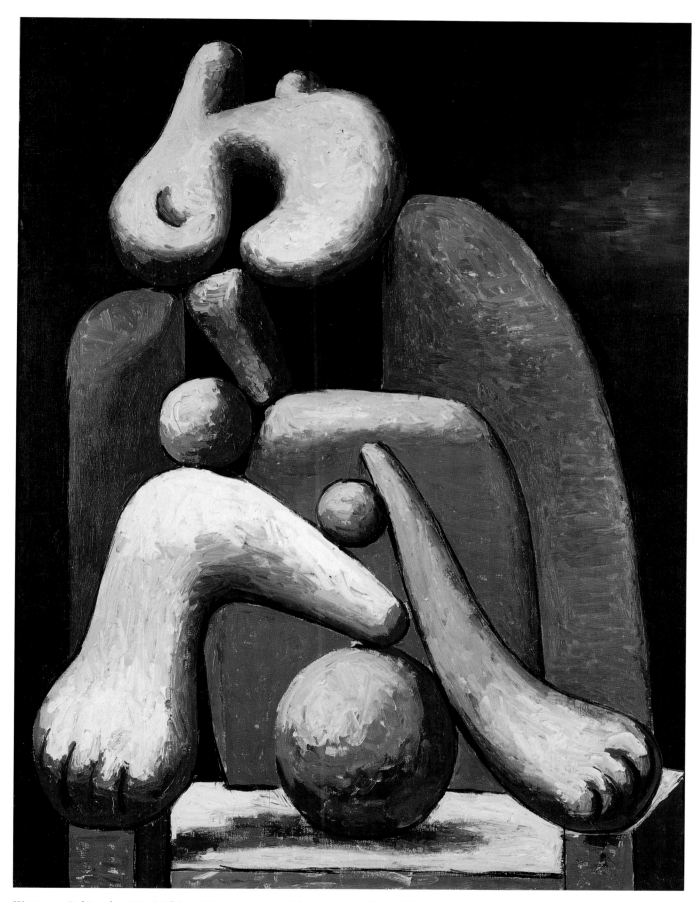

Woman in a Red Armchair (Marie-Thérèse). January 27, 1932. Oil on canvas, 51¼ × 38¼″ (130 × 97 cm). Zervos VII, 330. Musée Picasso, Paris

Village in the Rain. 1932. Oil on canvas, 18⅛ × 18⅛″ (46 × 46 cm). Collection Marina Picasso, courtesy Galerie Jan Krugier, Geneva

imperturbable sitters. And in 1932, the year of his birth centenary and a major retrospective, Manet might well enter this pantheon, especially with a painting of 1876, *Before the Mirror* (p. 358), which then belonged to Justin K. Thannhauser, who in that very year was organizing a Picasso retrospective for Zurich.[40] Like Picasso's mirror, Manet's is, in fact, a cheval glass, the word for which, in both French and Spanish, *psyché* and *psiquis*, gives it another mysterious layer, surely not lost on Picasso, who could see a mirror not only as an image of the soul or of death, but who, in his poetry, could refer to "the mirror's black light" and the way in which the mirror's "open mouth is ready to devour the sun."[41]

It is before such a magical mirror that Marie-Thérèse stands in her most famous transformation, painted on March 14, two days after *The Mirror*. The *Girl Before a Mirror* (p. 357), in fact, embraces such a multitude of symbols that to think of it as "Marie-Thérèse before a Mirror" would tether it to a prosaic situation grossly at odds with its metamorphic poetry,[42] which endlessly enriches the traditional motif of feminine vanity before a looking glass that ranges from Renaissance Venuses to, in our own century, works by artists as far afield as Otto Dix[43] and Norman Rockwell.[44] To be sure, in Picasso's re-creation of this archetype, we may still recognize Marie-Thérèse's personal code in the sitter's hair and profile, not to mention her rounded, lilac flesh; but she so far transcends the earthbound limitations of a portrait that, as in the case of de Kooning's famous series, we might now wish to refer to her as "Woman," evoking in a Jungian way the coexistence of many cultural archetypes. It is a telling coinci-

dence that in the same year, 1932, Jung himself, prompted by the Zurich retrospective, wrote an essay on Picasso which, though intended to demonstrate that the fractured, contradictory language of the art reflected the abnormal conflicts of schizophrenia, nevertheless made many relevant observations about the newest works of 1931–32, which included the *Girl Before a Mirror*.[45] Jung comments, for instance, on their brutal collision of color and on their insistent wedding of opposites: light and darkness, above and below, white and black, male and female, and even the light and dark anima. Moreover, in his fascination with archetypes, he speaks of Picasso's identity with Harlequin (today a commonplace of Picasso studies) and of his search for abstract female personae — the Eternal Feminine, whether Eve, Helen of Troy, Mary, or the gnostic demon Sophia. Despite their negative bias, Jung's insights may still be useful in directing our attention to Picasso's protean genius for fusing the widest spectrum of primal, and often contradictory, symbols in a pictorial language which, like James Joyce's in *Finnegans Wake* (1922–39), carries the ordinary phenomena of metaphorical puns and rhymes ("girth and mirth," "surf and turf," "imagineering") to unprecedented depths of elemental meaning.

Marie-Thérèse's head is just such a marvel of compression, merging, for instance, one of the most pervasive cultural myths about women inherited from the later nineteenth century, the polarity between the virgin and the whore, archetypes that haunted Picasso from his earliest years, when he could alternate between Madonna-like mothers and female creatures of sexual depravity, whether *Salome* or *Les Demoiselles d'Avignon*. So it is that the profile view of the head extends to an enclosing contour of white radiance that bleaches the stripe pattern to an ethereal pallor and suggests the chastity of both halo and veil. The half-hidden frontal view, however, becomes a cosmetic mask of sexual lure: the half-mouth lipsticked, the cheek rouged, the skin brazenly gilded. Such a duality, of course, echoes in countless other directions, including the evocative imagery of the sun and moon's cycles around the earth, a metaphor verbally distilled with a wizardry worthy of Picasso in Martin Amis's novel *The Information*, where a character, Gina, is described as "Mother Earth. Bipolar, sublunar, circumsolar."[46] In this context of astronomical rhythms, it is not surprising that the theme of the girl before a mirror has even been described as "a girl before her mirror image counting the days when her period is due to find out whether or not she could be pregnant, thus becoming connected with the moon and the sun and concerned with giving life and facing death."[47] And one should remember, too, that the ecliptical wedding of the sun and moon has a deep resonance in the iconography of that most Spanish of Christian images, the Virgin of the Immaculate Con-

Repose. January 22, 1932. Oil on canvas, 63¾ × 51¼″ (162 × 130 cm). Zervos VII, 361. Private collection

The Mirror (Marie-Thérèse). March 12, 1932. Oil on canvas, 51½ × 38⅛″ (130.7 × 97 cm). Zervos VII, 378. Private collection, Monaco

ception, who joins in her body the same two heavenly radiances.[48] But even in terms of the myths of the 1920s and 1930s, this intense physiognomic contrast gives visual form to the ever more popularized Freudian concept of clashing but coexisting aspects of the human mind, a tug between the conscious and the subconscious, the overt and the repressed. Indeed, such a concept had become so pervasive that, even apart from the Surrealists' programmatic efforts to release what Freud had called the id, a major playwright, Eugene O'Neill, could create a drama, *Strange Interlude* (1928), in which the female protagonist plays a double persona, speaking in frequent asides that disclose her hidden emotional life.

Such invisible worlds, imagined by Freud and Jung,

Girl Before a Mirror (Marie-Thérèse). March 1932. Oil on canvas, 64 × 51¼″ (162.3 × 130.2 cm). Zervos VII, 322. The Museum of Modern Art, New York. Gift of Mrs. Simon Guggenheim plumbed far into a dark, instinctual level that for Picasso, as for the culture into which he was born in the late nineteenth century, seemed far more potent in the female of the species, the procreative goddess who is foretold in this image of a young girl embracing and peering into a destiny that would wed her to the cycles of nature. It is a concept that extends and deepens a major theme of Symbolism, most familiar in Edvard Munch's variations on the three stages of a woman's life, moving from innocence, to sexual consummation, to withering old age. (Coincidentally, in a canvas also of 1932, Munch repeated the theme once more.[49]) Picasso, in fact, had already painted such an allegorical drama in *La Vie* of 1903; but now, with his fully developed genius for metamorphic imagery, he could probe much further into these human ultimates. There is room here for only a suggestion of the endless readings that can be intuited, though rarely fixed, in Picasso's meditation on a young girl's coming of age, a physical, psychological, and sexual evolution that he had known firsthand with Marie-Thérèse, who was then twenty-two (as Picasso himself approached his fiftieth birthday and a major retrospective), but who had been under the master's passionate surveillance since perhaps her later teens. Nevertheless, most readings tend to cluster around the motif of contrasting and cyclical

changes, reinforced by the high-keyed oppositions of complementary colors, such as the orange and blue oval frame that gives the mirror a magical vibrancy.

If the contemplative girl, in the ripeness of puberty, still appears constrained and virginal in the angular corseting of her swelling body (possibly a recall of the literal corseting in Manet's painting), the uterine image in the mirror releases such repressions, even warping the uncomfortably acute collar-pyramid upon which she must support her tensely watchful head. Moreover, the promise of sexual union and procreation revealed in Picasso's familiar genital puns (such as the visual rhyming of upright arm and breasts with erect phallus and testicles)[50] is fulfilled in the mirror, where one breast, part fruit and part ovum, seems fertilized by a black spot, generating a coiling green shoot already seen sprouting from the female groin in *The Mirror* of March 12. And if a life cycle is beginning, it is also ending, for the mirror image is haunted by the specter of death, a universal symbol, but one of particularly Spanish inflection, as evidenced in a painting by Picasso's friend and compatriot José Gutiérrez Solana, *The Mirror of Death* (c. 1928–29; below).[51] In fact, Picasso's mirror image almost literally illustrates the English phrase "from womb to tomb": before our eyes, the tough enclosure of burgeoning life,

Edouard Manet. *Before the Mirror.* 1876. Oil on canvas, 36¼ × 28⅛″ (92.1 × 71.4 cm). Solomon R. Guggenheim Museum, New York. Thannhauser Collection, Gift of Justin K. Thannhauser, 1978

José Gutiérrez Solana. *The Mirror of Death.* c. 1928–29. Oil on canvas, 32¼ × 26½″ (81.9 × 67.3 cm). Private collection

ROBERT ROSENBLUM

Woman with Book (Marie-Thérèse). 1932. Oil on canvas, 51³/₈ × 38¹/₂″ (130.5 × 97.8 cm). Zervos VIII, 70. The Norton Simon Foundation, Pasadena, Calif. Estate of Robert Ellis Simon, 1969

Jean-Auguste-Dominique Ingres. *Madame Inès Moitessier.* 1856. Oil on canvas, 47¹/₄ × 36¹/₄″ (120 × 92 cm). The National Gallery, London

with fetal head and developing internal organs, becomes a mummy's shrouded coffin, with an Egyptoid spirit head painted upon it, perhaps yet another memory of Gauguin's spirit of death. And, as always, Picasso is observing and guarding his female possession. As Jung had recognized in the same year, Picasso's alter ego might well be identified with Harlequin. Here, in fact, as so often before in his work, the diamond harlequin pattern, now of the wallpaper, can become a coded symbol of the artist's own presence, a heraldic field that proclaims his territory and that, when reaching, at the left, the body of his now mythical beloved, burns with the national colors of Spain, red and yellow.

His cryptic presence may be seen as well in another of the great mirror paintings of 1932, the *Woman with Book* (above),[52] a more recognizable domestic portrait of Marie-Thérèse that re-creates her in the role of one of Ingres' great late portraits, that of Madame Inès Moitessier (1856; above, right). Looked at from one point of view, such translations of Old Master art into the language of contemporary portraiture have ample precedent, whether one considers, say, the way Reynolds painted his own portrait in the guise of a Rembrandt self-portrait or the way Manet made Victorine Meurent masquerade unclothed as Titian's *Venus.* But in the case of Picasso, such quotational

portraiture has a more magical, almost voodoolike flavor, as if the ghost of the Old Master painting had been miraculously reincarnated through the presence of a living person in Picasso's life. Marie-Thérèse's predecessor, Olga, had already had the power to resuscitate several of Ingres' portraits, especially that of Madame Devaucey; and now, Ingres' *grande dame* of the Second Empire is miraculously metamorphosed into a no less mysterious female persona, captured reading in a darkened room that conveys an aura of nighttime privacy. The sibylline posture, which Ingres himself paraphrased from a Roman personification of Arcadia, gives Marie-Thérèse a sphinx-like remoteness at odds with the intense assault of colors and the provocative exposure of nipples; and this psychological distance is given an extra dimension of mystery through the profile reflected in the mirror, again a quotation from Ingres' portrait. It can, of course, be read almost literally as the reflection of Marie-Thérèse's own head, seen in its familiar classicizing guise; but it is also Picasso's coded classicizing profile for himself. The phantom in the looking glass now fuses artist and sitter, lover and beloved, in a single silhouette that is, at once, a real reflection, like Madame Moitessier's, and a poetic fantasy of voyeurism and possession that secretly tells how Picasso, as always, is on the scene.

Jean-Auguste-Dominique Ingres. *Odalisque with a Slave*. 1839–40. Oil on canvas mounted on panel, 28⅜ × 39½″ (72.1 × 100.3 cm). Courtesy the Fogg Art Museum, Harvard University Art Museums, Cambridge, Mass. Bequest of Grenville L. Winthrop

nature's fecundity, beauty, and sexuality as conveyed through a fantastic spectrum of hybrid creatures, from Wagnerian flower maidens and generative earth mothers to tentacular *femmes fatales*, was an international commonplace in the work of those Symbolist artists who helped to nurture Picasso's budding genius at the turn of the century.[54] And on quite another level, Picasso's imagery intersects the grossest popular humor, in which the anatomy of sexual arousal is likened to various fruits, as evidenced in a French postcard of 1917 that illustrates through still life what might be on the mind of a sex-starved soldier (p. 362).[55]

It is the kind of metaphor, whether exalted or vulgar, that helps us to understand the now common identification of a major still life of March 2, 1931,[56] as a disguised portrait of Marie-Thérèse, whose symbolic colors and ripe, burgeoning body pervade this domestic set piece of pitcher, *compotier*, and fruit on a three-legged *gueridon* (p. 362). As is often cited, Picasso himself, when questioned about the painting by Pierre Daix in 1970, outlined with pointed finger those contours that evoked Marie-Thérèse's body,[57] creating a subliminal double image that becomes far more overt in the botanical humanoids that soon followed. And in this still life, too, Picasso, lord and master, may be present in the form of the sun-drenched yellow pitcher (on a red cloth), an erect vertical shape that, proud as the crowing roosters Picasso painted, drew, and sculpted in the 1930s, presides over a hothouse of fruit bursting with erotic vitality.[58] As John Richardson has noted, a pitcher is often a code for the artist himself, "a bit like a Toby jar."[59] In this guise it seems very much part of the sexual entanglements above and below the tabletop, a role also played by the yellow-and-red pitchers that dominate two earlier still lifes of 1931.[60]

In yet another guise, the ghost of Ingres hovers as well over many of the images of Marie-Thérèse in the voluptuous release of sleep. On April 4, 1932, just three weeks after the *Girl Before a Mirror*, Picasso re-created in a *Sleeping Nude* (opposite) the serpents' nests of rounded, yielding flesh that Ingres had invented for his harem beauties (above). Now, Marie-Thérèse, cradled in an earth-colored couch, weds the nocturnal goddess of love to the diurnal fertility of sun-baked soil in a pictorial *aubade* that blanches her still-dormant lilac flesh with the heat of the morning sun through the window. Its rays penetrate the room, creating an astonishing wallpaper pattern that wriggles and glows around the upper half of her body like a spermatic assault on an egg. And in a transformation worthy of Ovid, whose *Metamorphoses* Picasso had illustrated in 1930, her body turns into a tree of life. Her fetal head, still under the spell of a crescent-moon eye closed within its dark womb, seems to generate the vital energy that turns her blond hair into a seedpod and her breasts into ripening red and green fruit, a double entendre so convincing that the bottom still life of two green leaves and two pears becomes one with her eroticized anatomy.

As usual, Picasso can muster the broadest visual genealogies, evoking, for one, the fantastic double images (heads composed of fruit, flowers, vegetables) by the sixteenth-century painter Arcimboldo, who had become an ancestral favorite of the Surrealists (p. 362).[53] For another, the concept of woman as a personification of

Although Marie-Thérèse's biological regressions most often move back into botanical and embryonic domains, she can also be transformed into a submarine creature, appropriate to her passion for swimming, as well as for cavorting with beach balls, both recurrent themes in Picasso's repertory of the late 1920s and early 1930s. In *Bather with Beach Ball* of August 30, 1932 (p. 363), as in other paintings of that great vintage year, the corporeal presence of Marie-Thérèse now dominates the world, swollen into a ballooning giantess, an unexpected preview of the pneumatic cartoon characters that float on high in Macy's annual Thanksgiving Day parade. (Apropos, Museum of Modern Art legend has it that, to add a bit of outdoor pageantry to the 1980 Picasso retrospective, an unrealized scheme would have set aloft a three-dimensional version of this bathing beauty.) But unlike most images prompted by Marie-Thérèse in 1932, this one, at first comically clumsy in its airborne athletics, quickly becomes grotesquely ugly, as if the demon Olga may have once more possessed her rival's placid spirit.

At first, we recognize many of the attributes of the teen-ager who, summering at Dinard, was actually photographed in a bathing suit, beach ball in hand (p. 67). There is the smooth flow of her seedpod hair, the spheroid

Sleeping Nude (Marie-Thérèse). April 4, 1932. Oil on canvas, 51¼ × 63¾″ (130 × 161.7 cm). Zervos VII, 332. Musée Picasso, Paris. (Colorplate, p. 71)

anatomy, and even the color code of yellow and violet on her skintight bathing suit. But another kind of being, more predatory than seductive, appears to inhabit her spirit and body, transforming her into a humanoid kin of a rubbery, gray squid. Jet-propelled across the blue sky, her bulbous head, with its two round, staring, lidless eyes and its vertical air vent, both mouth and vagina, mindlessly hunts its prey, the hair streaking behind like waterborne tentacles. The prey, of course, is presumably nothing but a beach ball, but it will never be caught. Rendered in two dimensions, as opposed to the creature's emphatically modeled three, it also becomes the most remote astral body, which its pursuer stupidly grasps at with tumescent, fingerless hands, as demanding and as ignorant as a child reaching for the moon. A voracious creature, perhaps the specter of Olga, has momentarily invaded this seaside romp on what the diminutive tricolor, which shuttles us dizzily from near to far, round to flat, tiny to huge, proclaims as French territory. And as usual, Picasso is secretly present.

As revealed by Lydia Gasman in her illuminating readings of some of the artist's key symbols, the beach cabana (or, in Spanish, *caseta*) was a recurrent prop in Picasso's work,[61] a secret shelter fraught with sexual memories that had become a synonym of a mysterious doorway (here half open and half shut) into the darker recesses of the artist's mind. And it can be added that Picasso may also be symbolically present (and, as usual, erotically possessive) in the seven yellow triangles on the bathing suit, which look like delirious fragments flung from the diamond har-

lequin patterns familiar to the wallpaper of 1932, now almost branding Marie-Thérèse's body on her breasts, navel, groin, and buttocks.

In surveying the emotional and pictorial graph of Marie-Thérèse's covert and overt presence in Picasso's life and art, there is no doubt that 1932 marks the peak of fever-pitch intensity and achievement, a year of rapturous masterpieces that reach a new and unfamiliar summit in both his painting and sculpture. But characteristically for the protean Picasso, he could also play out his love affairs on lesser stages, especially in the copious print production of the early 1930s, where his magical couplings with Marie-Thérèse would be disguised in a multitude of roles. At times they appear together in an imaginary artist's studio, where a classically bearded painter or sculptor transforms her ideal features into exquisitely drawn contours or a worshiped bust on a pedestal (p. 363); or, remaining in an antique milieu, they might break loose from the mental and optical concentration demanded by art and join their bodies in erotic tussles capable of turning Picasso's sexual alter ego into minotaur, centaur, faun, or even an Athenian rapist from the 1934 illustration to *Lysistrata*.

Nevertheless, Marie-Thérèse also remained for a few more years on center stage, figuring in many canvases of 1933 and 1934 that often provided later variations on the grand themes of 1932. Such is the case in *Nude Asleep in a Landscape* of August 4, 1934 (p. 365),[62] yet another homage to Ingres' *odalisques*, now recalled even in the exotic red-and-yellow fabric of the small pillow upon which her

Giuseppe Arcimboldo. *Summer.* 1563. Oil on wood, 26⅜ × 20″ (67 × 50.8 cm). Kunsthistorisches Museum, Vienna

Still Life on a Pedestal Table. March 2, 1931. Oil on canvas, 76¾ × 51¼″ (194 × 130 cm). Zervos VII, 317. Musée Picasso, Paris. (Colorplate, p. 69)

Postcard. *Les Fruits préférés du Soldat*

hand rests. At first, everything fits into the mold shaped in 1932 for the sleeping Marie-Thérèse. Here again is the lilac flesh, the yellow seedpod hair, the crescent-moon eye; and here, too, is the constellation of black dots that mark out the erogenous zones of nipples, navel, vulva, and anus. And once more, the sleeper is equated with nature's irrepressible bounty, so that philodendron leaves (so conspicuous in 1932), as well as flowers, appear to sprout from her loins. But within these now familiar formulas, there is a restlessness that leaves one imperfection after another, as if the ecstatic ideal of serenity and pleasure attained in 1932 could no longer be sustained. The contours of her body seem alternately slack and taut, a rhythmic conflict distilled in her hand; the greenery, whether above or below the angular white sheet, has a windswept, ragged quality; and the paint surfaces, mostly brushy, irregular, and impulsive, undermine the earlier images of what Brooks Adams described as "the absolute embodiment of non-threatening womanhood and sensual bliss."[63]

Such falls from grace can often be discerned in the portrait heads that follow the supernal perfection of 1932. For example, a small square of canvas, painted in 1932 but then reworked in 1934 (p. 364), begins to gnarl and knot Marie-Thérèse's placid features into a profound restlessness, as do many of the sculptural prints and drawings of 1933 (p. 364). Indeed, Mary Mathews Gedo, in her psycho-

Bather with Beach Ball (Marie-Thérèse). August 30, 1932. Oil on canvas, 57⅝ × 45⅛″ (146.2 × 114.6 cm). Zervos VIII, 147. The Museum of Modern Art, New York. Partial gift of an anonymous donor and promised gift of Ronald S. Lauder. (Colorplate, p. 65)

Muse Showing a Thoughtful Marie-Thérèse Her Sculpted Portrait (1st state). March 17, 1933. Etching and drypoint, 10½ × 7⅝″ (26.7 × 19.4 cm). Geiser/Baer II, 299. Private collection

analytic readings of Picasso, has even speculated, on the evidence of the art, that there must have been some private disaster in the couple's life in 1932–33, perhaps a pregnancy terminated by abortion or miscarriage.[64] We may never be able to confirm or deny such an intuition; but at least we do know that tensions with Olga reached an explosive point by 1935, a period which Picasso himself described as the worst in his life. Divorce was considered and then dropped because of legal complications, while, at the same time, his liaison with Marie-Thérèse was literally to bear the metaphorical fruit of his painted dreams of her fertility. Their child, María de la Concepción (named after Picasso's sister Concepción, who died of diphtheria in 1895 at the age of eight), was born on September 5, 1935.[65] The family would call her Maya.

As if to grasp the realities of the immense new fact of his second child, a girl, Picasso made many small and candid drawings of their domestic life, private vignettes often rendered with the Old Master warmth and *chiaroscuro* of a Rembrandt, whose portrait, in fact, began to figure in many of Picasso's prints of 1933–34. In one of November 15, 1935 (p. 366), in which Marie-Thérèse turns her round breast to her bare-bottomed infant daughter, the archetypal theme of maternity, a major motif of the early work that was explored once again after Paulo's birth in 1921, returns a third time to the master's repertory in a perfect

fusion of heroic Renaissance grandeur and modern Parisian domesticity; and in other, simpler drawings of the same months, Picasso, the new father, stares at Maya, recording, for instance, on December 24 the specifics of the baby's returned gaze and frizzy hair, but also adding a strange hint of her mother's double physiognomy, suggested by the intense contrast of light and shadow on the two sides of the head (p. 366). And in a pencil portrait of Marie-Thérèse, made three days later (p. 366), Picasso maintains this literalism of observed fact, resuming here the familiar situation of quietly watching her as she wafts off into a daydream, but now bringing back to a more prosaic reality the poetic flights of 1932, when her catnaps could carry us off on voyages to uncharted depths of the psyche. Similarly, in another portrait drawing of the following year, dated July 28, 1936 (p. 367), the intense, confrontational mode that reaches oracular mystery in 1932 is tethered to an earthbound individual, whose uneasy expression, again emphasized by opposition of light and darkness, seems to pertain more to domestic anxieties than to the riddle of the sphinx.

Of course, Picasso, at this or any other time, could never stop turning the people and things around him into the elaborate fictions of his art. So it is, for example, that his new situation could inspire such classicizing drawings as those penned in April 1936 (p. 368). Many of the props

Head of Marie-Thérèse. 1932–34. Oil on canvas, 18¹⁄₈ × 18¹⁄₈″ (46 × 46 cm). Not in Zervos. Private collection

Head of Marie-Thérèse (20th state). February 18, 1933. Scraper and drypoint, 12⁵⁄₈ × 9″ (32 × 22.9 cm). Geiser/Baer II, 288. Musée Picasso, Paris

here—shutters, wallpaper, palm trees, Mediterranean balcony views—reflect the family's new quarters in Juan-les-Pins, where, under his father's family name, Ruiz, Picasso, Marie-Thérèse, and Maya lived virtually in secret for more than a month. But this fresh setting could also become a theatrical backdrop for new roles that would re-create the trio in an antique drama, repeating with variations the classicizing family narratives inspired more than a decade earlier by the birth of Paulo. Here, the father, wreathed and bearded like an antique bust, can further distance his identity by holding a mask; or elsewhere, he can become a tender surrogate mother, while a mysteriously impassive Marie-Thérèse looks on. And from the same period of family seclusion, other fantasies emerged, revealing Picasso's usual multiplicity of invention. In one little drawing of April 3 (p. 370), he offers on the same page a perfect example of his double-track imagination, capturing below a *chiaroscuro* vignette of Marie-Thérèse rapt in indoor concentration, whereas above, he transforms her into a monumental sculpture that, on the very same day, he would also render as a small painting (p. 371). Resurrecting the monstrous beach-side giantesses of the late 1920s, he desiccates Marie-Thérèse's body through

Nude Asleep in a Landscape (Marie-Thérèse). August 4, 1934. Oil on canvas, 63¾ × 51¼″ (162 × 130 cm). Not in Zervos. Musée Picasso, Paris

Marie-Thérèse Nursing Maya. November 15, 1935. Pen and brown ink on paper, 11½ × 17″ (29 × 43 cm). Not in Zervos. Private collection

Maya at Three and a Half Months Old. December 24, 1935. Pencil on paper, 13⅜ × 10″ (34 × 25.5 cm). Not in Zervos. Private collection

Portrait of Marie-Thérèse. December 27, 1935. Pencil on paper, 10⅞ × 13½″ (27.5 × 34.3 cm). Not in Zervos. Private collection

Portrait of Marie-Thérèse. July 28, 1936. Pen, black ink, and gray wash on paper, 20⅛ × 13½″ (51 × 34.3 cm). Not in Zervos. Thaw Collection. The Pierpont Morgan Library, New York

the language of open, linear sculpture. From what appear to be coils of wicker, a basketwork skeleton is constructed through which we see the bluest Mediterranean trinity of coast, sea, and sky. The rotundities of her breast and torso, like the mysteries of her twinned physiognomies, have now become fleshless armatures, bleached in the sun, a shell of memory no longer inhabited by a living person.

Even in more casual and recognizable images of Marie-Thérèse from these reclusive weeks in Juan-les-Pins, we sense a dissolution of her earlier persona. In a sun-drenched window view of April 13 (p. 369), burning with intense yellows and oranges, her crossed hands, once soft and pliant, have become as spiky and brittle as artichokes; and her blue eyes, one frontal, one in profile, register pri-

Man with a Mask and Woman with a Child (Marie-Thérèse and Maya). April 23, 1936. Pen, India ink, and wash on paper, 25⅝ × 21¾″ (65 × 50 cm). Zervos VIII, 278. Musée Picasso, Paris

Family Scene (Marie-Thérèse and Maya). April 27, 1936. India ink on paper, 24½ × 18⅞″ (62 × 48 cm). Zervos VIII, 281. Private collection

Marie-Thérèse Walter nursing Maya Picasso. Juan-les-Pins, March or April 1936. Photograph by Picasso. Collection Maya Picasso

Picasso and his daughter, Maya. Le Tremblay-sur-Mauldre, March 1937. Photograph by Marie-Thérèse Walter. Collection Maya Picasso

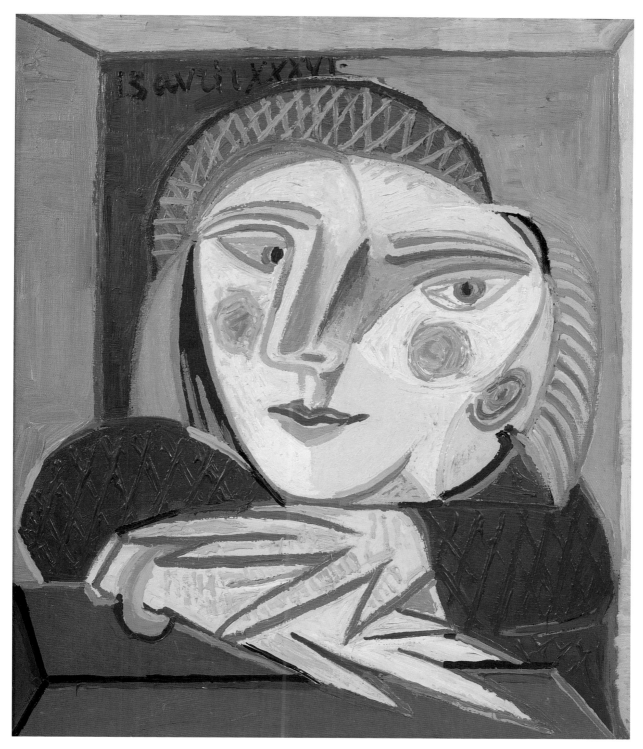

Woman at a Window (Marie-Thérèse). April 13, 1936. Oil on canvas, 21⅝ × 17¾″ (55 × 45 cm). Not in Zervos. Private collection

vate stress rather than eternal feminine magic. Most startling of this group is the hideous head of May 1 (p. 73), which has become so familiar an image through the work of Jasper Johns, who began to quote it in 1986,[66] that its disarming impact may now have been dulled. But here a barely identifiable Marie-Thérèse, the inevitable inspiration during this short and cloistered sojourn on the

Riviera, projects something near hysteria. Her colors still cling to her in the faint lilac flesh and the yellow stripes of the pedestal, but panic and disorder reign. The image first suggests a sculptured portrait bust on a base, of a kind familiar to the repertory of the early 1930s, but the violet support is now a bony neck[67] (similar to the skeleton anatomies of Christ in the 1932 variations on Grünewald's

Study for Portrait of a Young Woman; Marie-Thérèse Reading. April 3, 1936. Pen and India ink on paper, 10¼ × 6⅞″ (26 × 17.5 cm). Not in Zervos. Musée Picasso, Paris

Studies for Portrait of a Young Woman. April 4, 1936. India ink on paper, 10¼ × 6⅞″ (26 × 17.5 cm). Not in Zervos. Musée Picasso, Paris

Crucifixion), resting in turn on a pedestal that is also to be read as a constricting collar compressing her shoulders and ragged breasts. As for the head, topped by a straw hat whose coarse weave is related to the beach fantasy of April 3, it appears to be toppling, its nostrils and mouth frozen in warped curves of anxiety. When read as a frontal view, its hideous eyes, sliced at the pupils (perhaps a memory of Dalí's and Buñuel's *Le Chien Andalou* of 1928–29), stare at us in fixed terror or, when read as a side view, gaze helplessly to the left and right. A nightmare of paralysis and disintegration, she is, almost literally, a fallen idol.

With 20/20 biographical hindsight, it is, of course, tempting to read this painting as a decapitating finale to Marie-Thérèse's reign; for, in fact, she had gradually been replaced by Dora Maar, whom Picasso had met the winter before through the Paul Eluard circle and with whom he was to begin a passionate new liaison. But this would be a drastic, one-to-one simplification of the complex parallel, divergent, and intersecting dialogues between Picasso's life and art. In fact, he continued to create more familiar and tranquil images of Marie-Thérèse until the end of the

decade; but once more mirroring domestic realities, he would now often make virtual pendants of these iconic images in which Marie-Thérèse, on her armchair throne, was challenged by Dora Maar, as if one playing-card queen were conspiring against her rival. So it is in the temporarily majestic portrait of January 6, 1937 (p. 373), in which Marie-Thérèse resumes the meditative pose of Ingres' *Madame Moitessier* that had been more magically reinvented in 1932. And here, too, Picasso may be cryptically present, not only in the Spanish red-and-yellow of her straw hat, but more familiarly coded in the red-and-yellow harlequin patterns of the chairback. But this poise is again threatened by the angular and cramping distortions of the box space in which she is caged, a space in which the low ceiling and crazily tilted floor plane undo the semblance of commanding centrality and timeless calm. The point becomes clearer when we see this in tandem with a portrait of Dora Maar of the same year,[68] which also reflects the Ingresque head-to-hand posture but suddenly presides with a new authority, iconically centered in a more rigid box space (p. 391). Like a chameleon,

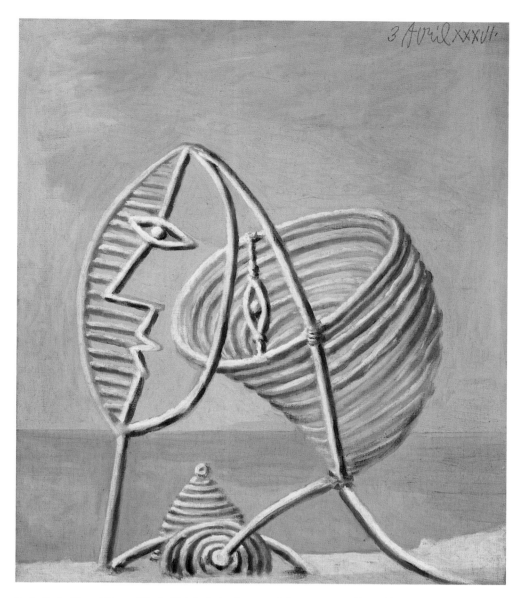

Portrait of a Young Woman (Marie-Thérèse). April 3, 1936. Oil on canvas, 21⅞ × 18⅛″ (55.5 × 46 cm). Not in Zervos. Musée Picasso, Paris

she has adapted to the yellow-and-violet complementaries of Marie-Thérèse, but gives them a new cosmetic blush of Parisian chic and vitality. And the spiky hands that Marie-Thérèse began to display in 1935–36 now end in bright red fingernail polish, an attribute of Dora Maar, conspicuous even in black-and-white photographs of her.

If this dark-haired, cosmopolitan, and well-educated woman seems to be given equal time with her blond rival (whom he had begun to see only once or twice a week), there is no question in the faces of the two portraits of 1937 which of them is the newcomer, a visual confirmation of Picasso's remark to John Richardson that "it must be painful for a girl to see in a painting that she is on the way out."[69] And in a portrait of Marie-Thérèse of March 11 (p. 336), by which time she and Maya had been removed from his Parisian life to the rural seclusion of

Ambroise Vollard's home at Le Tremblay-sur-Mauldre, not far from the château of Versailles, she seems to be camouflaged to the point of disappearance by the country setting of rough-surfaced wooden planes that drain her of flesh, color, and energy. Her head stiffly gripped by window handle and wall, she sits immobilized in the imprisoning rectilinear frame of an unpainted wooden chair that, in turn, locks into perpendicular place with the balcony grille and shutters. The once vivid colors of the rainbow are now muffled,[70] and her hands—a restless tangle of phallic fingers—are clasped over a tight plaid skirt in an image of lonely repression. Marie-Thérèse, one feels, has been walled up forever in the country. Almost a year later, in a drawing of January 8, 1938, she is still caged, her fingers still locked together, in the same wooden chair (p. 372).

Woman with Joined Hands (Marie-Thérèse). January 8, 1938. Pencil, charcoal, and oil wash on canvas, 31⅞ × 23⅝″ (81 × 60 cm). Not in Zervos. Collection Mr. and Mrs. Marshall Cogan

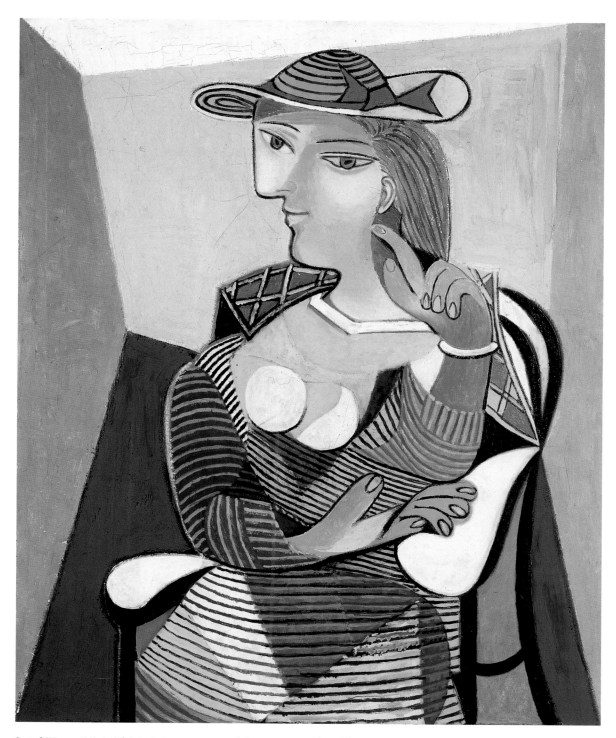

Seated Woman (Marie-Thérèse). January 6, 1937. Oil on canvas, 39⅜ × 31⅞″ (100 × 81 cm). Zervos VIII, 324. Musée Picasso, Paris

But elsewhere, she could be released from this fictional straitjacket, especially when maternal duty called. In a painting of January 22, 1938, the wooden chair remains, but the sitter now relaxes in order to embrace Maya with such total absorption that the bodies of mother and daughter become almost one in a union whose ineffable sweetness of color and sentiment skirts with greeting-card kitsch (p. 375). Yet Picasso adds a bizarre edge of genetic mystery to this popular formula, transforming Maya into a clone of her mother, whether in the odd inheritance of green nostrils and lipsticked blue lips, the identical coiffure of yellow-green hair, or the interchangeable scramble of mother's and daughter's hands. And as was the case with Paulo in the early 1920s, Maya would also inspire her own full-length portraits, state occasions for which she would be as fancily posed and dressed as an *infanta* by Velázquez.

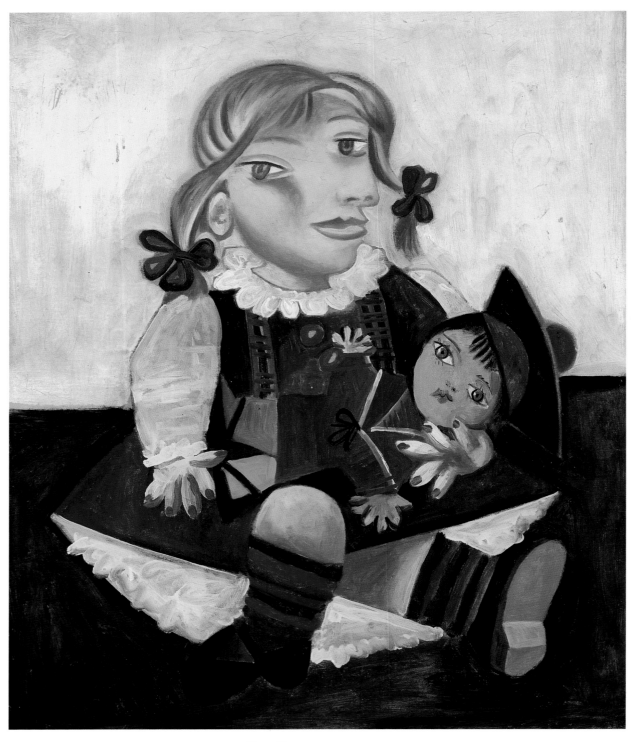

Maya with a Doll. January 16, 1938. Oil on canvas, 28¾ × 23⅝″ (73 × 60 cm). Zervos IX, 99. Musée Picasso, Paris

In one of January 16, 1938, she looms large, almost illustrating—to feminize Wordsworth's phrase—that the child is mother of the woman (above). Here, with the gravity of a Madonna, she herself assumes the maternal role, cradling in her lap a female doll in a sailor suit, a then familiar costume for children of either sex. And Marie-Thérèse's color code goes through strange muta-

tions, too, turning Maya's unblinking eyes a hypnotic purple that complements her now beribboned yellow-green hair. But even more metaphoric in terms of the Picasso family tree is a portrait of Maya in a sailor suit, painted exactly a week later (p. 377). The hat she sports bears Picasso's name (which doubles as a crude signature) in bold letters, evoking a juvenile self-portrait by the

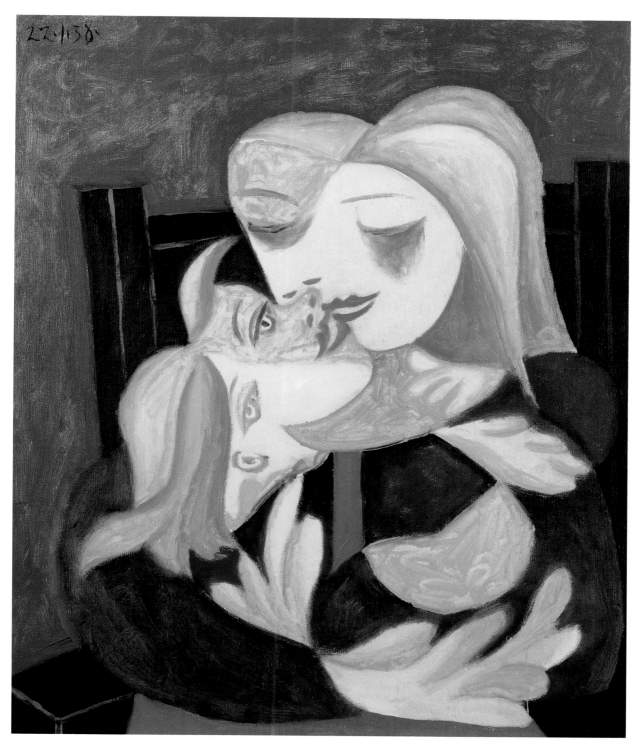

Mother and Child (Marie-Thérèse and Maya). January 22, 1938. Oil on canvas, 25⅝ × 21¼″ (65 × 54 cm). Not in Zervos.
Private collection

artist. Indeed, when the American soldier Pfc. Jerome Seckler discussed this painting with Picasso at the 1944 Salon d'Automne, suggesting that it was a self-portrait, the artist, never one to deny any imaginative reading of his work, concurred, adding for support that he always wore a sailor's striped jersey as an undershirt.[71] But even when Picasso paints a portrait of somebody else, he may also include himself, especially if the sitter is a family member. For example, in 1924, when Paulo was three years old, his father painted him in a harlequin costume, projecting one of his own alter egos onto his son. As for this ungainly child, who clumsily grasps a butterfly net but seems incapable of using it, identity may also be double, as if Picasso the father were merging with the

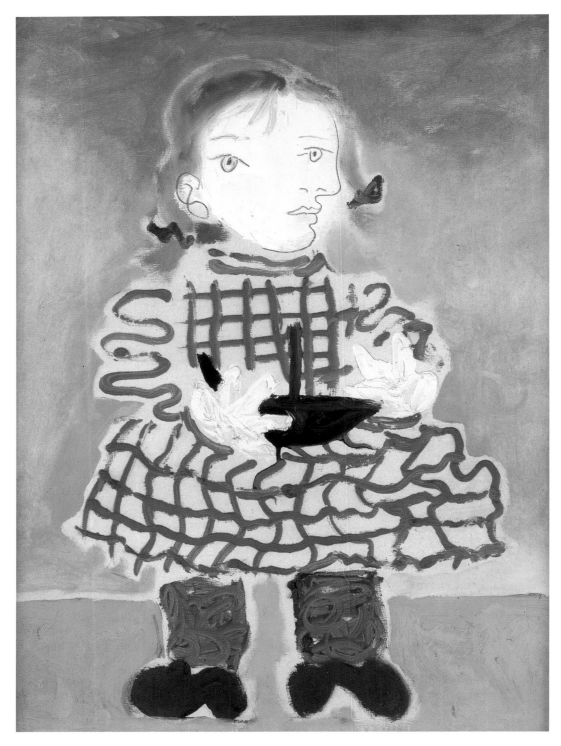

Maya in a Pinafore. c. 1938. Oil on plywood, 28¾ × 21¼″ (73 × 54 cm). Not in Zervos. Private collection

costumed image of his daughter, whose blond hair recalls her mother's. In fact, the very sex of the child is bluntly and surprisingly suggested by the gnarled oval on the tree trunk that appears between her awkwardly widespread legs, which, like those of Maya in other childhood portraits, terminate in hooflike shoes. And as usual, apart from the possessive and mystical fusion of parent and child, Picasso may be absorbing as well remembrances of other artists' portraits of children. The analogy with the flat, primitive charm of Henri Rousseau's icons of children, so well known to Picasso, has often been mentioned;[72] but it may also be that Picasso is recalling a youthful pictorial dialogue with Matisse. In 1906 Picasso made a modest little gouache portrait of Michael and

Maya in a Sailor Suit. January 23, 1938. Oil on canvas, 47⅞ × 34″ (121.6 × 86.3 cm). Zervos IX, 104. The Museum of Modern Art, New York. Gift of Jacqueline Picasso

Sarah Stein's son, Allan, but was totally outshone the next year by his perpetual rival, Matisse, who painted a large and vigorous outdoor portrait of the boy holding a butterfly net.[73] Could this new version of a butterfly hunter be Picasso's belated riposte?

In another child's portrait of 1938 (opposite), now clearly of Maya (who holds a toy ship that looks as if it might have been painted by the three-year-old that she then was), we again sense the ghosts of Rousseau and Matisse in the mixture of a frontality so crude that the shod and stockinged feet turn away from each other at 180 degrees and of a virtuosity so dazzling that the swiftly abbreviated grid patterns of the red plaid dress are flexible enough to stiffen or to rustle. But this willfully infantile

Portrait of Emilie Marguerite Walter (Mémé). October 21, 1939. Oil and pencil on canvas, 16⅛ × 13″ (41 × 33 cm). Zervos IX, 367. Private collection

style of kindergarten colors and coarse paint dabs (so appropriate to the sitter's age) suddenly matures into an unexpected linear grace in the head, rendered as a yet unformed version of the doubled physiognomies her father had created for her mother. Under the yellow hair, tinged with the green vitality of nature, the wide, blank whiteness of the child's nascent face, viewed frontally, merges unexpectedly with the perfect, classical profile that Picasso had already created as an ideal symbol for both himself and the child's mother. And five years later, in a charcoal drawing of August 29, 1943, Maya, now almost eight, fits even more closely into the classicizing profile silhouette invented for her parents (p. 383).

In Picasso's often irreverent hands, such fluid identities, genetically appropriate when dealing with parents and their offspring, could at times produce comical pairings,

Emilie Marguerite Walter (mother of Marie-Thérèse Walter and grandmother of Maya Picasso). Paris, 1939. Photograph by Photomaton. Collection Maya Picasso

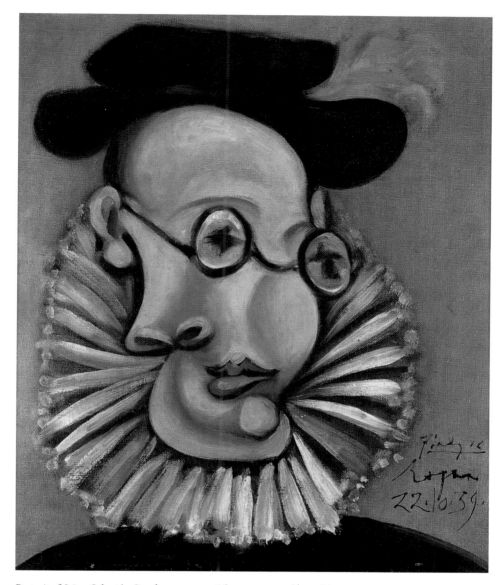

Portrait of Jaime Sabartés. October 22, 1939. Oil on canvas, 18½ × 15″ (45.7 × 38 cm). Zervos IX, 366. Museu Picasso, Barcelona

as in two portraits painted on two consecutive days, October 21 and 22, 1939. In the first one (opposite), he records the beloved matriarch of his new part-time family, Marie-Thérèse's Swedish mother, Emilie Marguerite Walter. After January 13, 1939, when Picasso's own mother, María Picasso López, died in Barcelona, Maya's maternal grandmother must have helped to fill an even larger emotional gap with her warming presence, registered in this portrait. A comforting image of gray-haired sweetness and propriety in black dress and high white collar, she is nevertheless transformed by bizarre facial contortions that permit a pair of thick-lensed eyeglasses to slip over to one side of a figure-eight nose and that can plant a discreetly lipsticked mouth at a rakish, smiling angle in an amorphous swell of pink flesh. No wonder Mémé (as French grandmothers are called) laughed when she saw her picture.[74] But a photograph of the lady also proves how sharp Picasso's observations were, right down to the slightly uneven twist of the sitter's thin-lipped mouth (opposite).

On the following day, Picasso fit a completely different sitter into this twisted mold, his friend and first biographer Jaime Sabartés (above). Grandma's collar now becomes a Spanish gentleman's ruff, and her spectacles continue to meander over the bridge of his nose to an adjacent cheek that, like hers, mixes flesh and putty. Within forty-eight hours, Picasso turned Swedish grandmother and Spanish friend into whimsically grotesque siblings who might well fall under the comic rubric of photographic look-alikes, "Separated at birth?"

But there were portrait pairings of 1939 that bore far more psychological weight, namely, those of Maya's

Bust of a Woman Leaning on One Elbow. January 1, 1939. Oil on canvas, 25⅝ × 21¼″ (65 × 54 cm). Not in Zervos. Galerie Louise Leiris, Paris

mother and her successor Dora Maar. Already in 1937, Picasso would occasionally paint the two women as rival queens, creating a variation of the dynastic wars that, a decade earlier, had finally dethroned Olga and inaugurated the reign of Marie-Thérèse. Now, in 1939, Picasso juxtaposed the old and the new monarch even more programmatically in twinned canvases that showed the

women in identical postures (above and opposite), usually inflected by the claustrophobic melancholy that mirrored the grimness of Europe in that terrible year. As if to objectify as well as to minimize the differences between his new and former lovers, he would place them in the same physical and psychological mold, comparing what would appear ever more superficial distinctions between

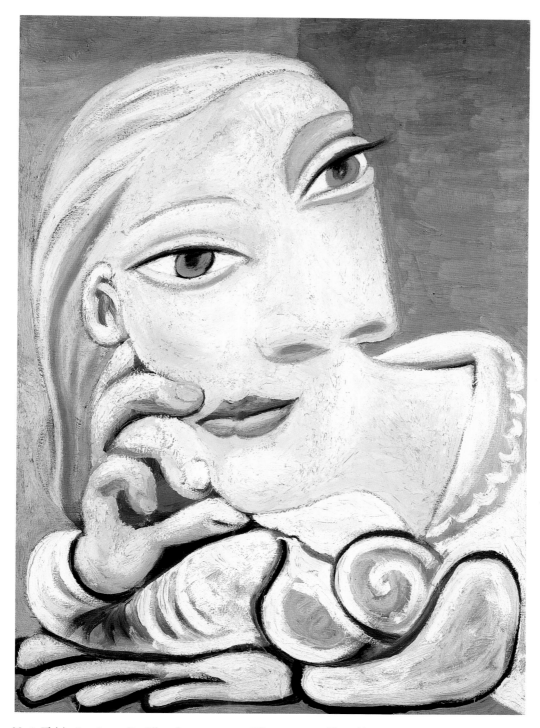

Marie-Thérèse Leaning on One Elbow. January 7, 1939. Oil on canvas, 25⅝ × 18⅛″ (65 × 46 cm). Not in Zervos. Private collection

blond and dark beauty, softness and angularity, languor and alertness. And in life, too, he would repeat the bigamous domestic situations of the years with Olga and Marie-Thérèse. After the outbreak of war in September 1939, he moved temporarily to Royan, where Marie-Thérèse and Maya were installed at a villa and where Dora Maar and he would share a hotel room. Both inside and outside his studio, Picasso could contemplate his pantheon of goddesses and demons, venerating them, comparing them, magically fusing them, and, finally, letting them return to earth.

Notes

In a letter of November 24, 1995, Maya Widmaier Picasso was kind enough to provide me with some factual details that may help to correct familiar errors in the biographical accounts of these years. I have tried to incorporate them here.

1. Judi Freeman, *Picasso and the Weeping Women: The Years of Marie-Thérèse Walter & Dora Maar* (Los Angeles: Los Angeles County Museum of Art, 1994).

2. Alfred H. Barr, Jr., *Picasso: Fifty Years of His Art* (New York: The Museum of Modern Art, 1946), pp. 201, 266.

3. Ibid., p. 175.

4. *Picasso: Peintures, 1900–1955* (Paris: Musée des Arts Décoratifs, 1955), p. 20.

5. Barr, *Picasso*, p. 158.

6. André Level, *Picasso* (Paris: G. Crès, 1928).

7. For the fullest account of these cryptic monograms, see Adam Gopnik, "P Loves MT: A Note on the First Appearance of Marie-Thérèse Walter in the Picasso Theater," *Marsyas* (Institute of Fine Arts, New York University) 21 (1981–82), pp. 57–60.

8. The manuscript, dated November 20, 1935, is illustrated in Marie-Laure Bernadac and Christine Piot, eds., *Picasso: Collected Writings* (New York: Abbeville, 1989), p. 45. ("Fleur plus douce que le miel 𝓜 tu es mon feu de joie.")

9. First pointed out, I believe, by Maurice Jardot in the 1955 Paris catalogue (see n. 4, above), no. 26, and then often repeated.

10. For an early account of "Job" and cryptic names in Picasso's Cubist work, see William Rubin, *Picasso in the Collection of the Museum of Modern Art* (New York: The Museum of Modern Art, 1972), p. 100.

11. For a vivid, illustrated account of this liaison, see John Richardson, "Picasso's Secret Love," *House and Garden* 159, no. 10 (October 1987), pp. 174–82, 252–54.

12. As disclosed in Pierre Daix, "On a Hidden Portrait of Marie-Thérèse," *Art in America* 71, no. 8 (September 1983), pp. 124–29.

13. Picasso's account of his first encounter with Marie-Thérèse is told in Françoise Gilot and Carleton Lake, *Life with Picasso* (New York: McGraw-Hill, 1964), p. 235. Marie-Thérèse herself added more details in two later interviews: Barry Ferrell, "His Women: The wonder is that he found time to paint," *Life*, special Picasso double issue, 65, no. 26 (December 27, 1968), p. 74; and Pierre Cabanne, "Picasso et les joies de la paternité," *L'Oeil*, no. 226 (May 1974), pp. 2–11.

14. Herbert T. Schwarz, *Picasso and Marie-Thérèse Walter, 1925–1927* (Montmagny, Quebec: Editions Isabeau, 1988). It should be said, however, that Maya Widmaier Picasso insists that January 8, 1927, was the date of their first encounter. Moreover, Marie-Thérèse, in a handwritten inscription on a Picasso manuscript of January 3, 1936, avowed that she loved him for nine years ("et dire que je t'aime depuis 9 ans") and that on January 11, 1936, Picasso referred to the anniversary of this love ("aujord'hui anniversaire de cet amour"; see Bernadac and Piot, *Picasso*, pp. 393, 89). This certainly suggests that January 1927 marked a significant emotional event. Nevertheless, the date may not have been that of their first encounter, but of a major turning point, sexual or otherwise, in their relationship.

15. These details are recounted in what remains the fullest and most detailed presentation of Marie-Thérèse's role in Picasso's life and art: John Richardson, "Picasso and Marie-Thérèse Walter," in *Through the Eye of Picasso, 1928–1934; The Dinard Sketchbook and Related Paintings and Sculpture* (New York: William Beadleston, 1985), n.p. Most of this material was then incorporated in an expanded version with many new observations: John Richardson, "Picasso and l'Amour Fou," *New York Review of Books* 32, no. 20 (December 19, 1985), pp. 59–68.

16. The sketchbook is presented, with an essay by Rosalind E. Krauss, in Arnold Glimcher and Marc Glimcher, eds., *Je suis le cahier: The Sketchbooks of Picasso* (New York: Pace Gallery, 1986), pp. 113–39. Believing, like most scholars at the time, that Marie-Thérèse had not entered Picasso's life until January 1927, Krauss makes a case for the artist having invented her features in his art of 1926 and earlier before meeting their real-life counterpart. Although this principle is often true for Picasso, it may have to be altered somewhat in this case to accommodate the new biographical evidence.

17. This is pointed out by Schwarz, *Picasso and Marie-Thérèse Walter*, p. 90. The pencil drawing in question is at the lower right of a sheet containing four drawings of musical instruments on a table (below) and is illustrated twice in Zervos (V, 406 and VII, 415), where the inscribed date, "novembre 1925," is clearly visible above it. However, this particular drawing was apparently cut out later from the whole sheet (presumably the other three suffered the same commercial fate), thereby losing the inscribed date above it. In this altered state, it appeared for sale at Sotheby's, New York (May 8, 1991, lot 175), where, on the basis of the Zervos illustration, the date is still given as November 1925. A new signature (probably fake) appears at the lower right, since the original signature (at the lower left) was separated from this drawing when it was cut out of the whole sheet.

18. See ibid., p. 80.

19. The familiar account would have her placed in a *colonie de vacances*, but Maya Widmaier Picasso informs me that it was, in fact, a *pension de famille*.

20. See Rubin, *Picasso in the Collection of The Museum of Modern Art*, p. 72.

21. As pointed out by John Richardson ("Picasso and Marie-Thérèse Walter," n. p.), the conversion of the stables into a sculpture studio took place in fall 1930, not fall 1931.

22. On this plaster relief, see Elizabeth Cowling and John Golding, *Picasso: Sculptor/Painter* (London: Tate Gallery, 1994), no. 80, where an analogy with Roman coins is suggested.

23. In 1970 I incorrectly presumed that Picasso's relationship with Marie-Thérèse began in 1931. See Robert Rosenblum, "Picasso and the Anatomy of Eroticism," in Theodore Bowie and Cornelia V. Christenson, eds., *Studies in Erotic Art* (New York: Basic Books, 1970), p. 347, n. 23. In 1972 William Rubin, also on the evidence of the work, narrowed the date down to summer 1931. See his *Picasso in the Collection of The Museum of Modern Art*, p. 226, n. 1.

24. For the impact of Gauguin's painting on Picasso, see John Richardson, *A Life of Picasso, Volume 1: 1881–1906* (New York: Random House, 1991), p. 264; and William Rubin et al., *Les Demoiselles d'Avignon*, Studies in Modern Art 3 (New York: The Museum of Modern Art, 1994), p. 95.

25. See Linda Nochlin, "Picasso's Color Schemes and Gambits," *Art in America* 68, no. 10 (December 1980), pp. 105–23, 177–83, especially part II, pp. 120–23, 177–80.

26. The presence of the Saint Bernard was pointed out in Richardson, "Picasso and Marie-Thérèse Walter," n. p.

27. On the dog Kasbec's presence in the Dora Maar portraits, see my comments on the *Bust of a Woman Wearing a Striped Hat* (June 3, 1939) in *Picasso from the Musée Picasso, Paris* (Minneapolis: Walker Art Center, 1980), p. 75.

28. The work was shown in Picasso's retrospective at the Galerie Georges Petit, Paris.

29. On the symbolism of the ace of clubs, see Jean Sutherland Boggs, *Picasso & Things* (Cleveland, Ohio: Cleveland Museum of Art, 1992), no. 54.

30. Rivalry with Matisse at this time (1930-32) was briefly suggested in Pierre Daix, *Picasso: Life and Art* (New York: HarperCollins, 1993), p. 221. See also Michael C. FitzGerald, *Making Modernism: Picasso and the Creation of the Market for Twentieth-Century Art* (New York: Farrar, Straus and Giroux, 1995), p. 202.

31. For a color reproduction of this painting (Smith College Museum of Art, Northampton,

Sheet of four drawings of musical instruments on a table. November 1925. Pencil, 7⅞ x 15¾″ (20 x 40 cm). Zervos VII, 415. Original sheet no longer in the form shown in Zervos

Mass.), see Jack Cowart and Dominique Fourcade, *Henri Matisse: The Early Years in Nice, 1916–1930* (Washington, D.C.: National Gallery of Art, 1986), p. 230.

32. For these phrases from his poetry, see Bernadac and Piot, *Picasso*, p. XXI.

33. Ibid., p. XVI.

34. I have discussed elsewhere Picasso's use of the myth in both broad terms ("The Fatal Women of Picasso and De Kooning," *ARTnews*, 84, no. 8 [October 1985], pp. 98–103) and in relation to the monstrous women of the late 1920s ("Picasso and the Anatomy of Eroticism," pp. 337–50).

35. In Richardson, "Picasso and Marie-Thérèse Walter," n. p.

36. Leo Steinberg, "Picasso's Sleepwatchers," in *Other Criteria: Confrontations with Twentieth-Century Art* (New York: Oxford University Press, 1972), pp. 93–114.

37. Bernadac and Piot, *Picasso*, p. 30 (poem of October 21, 1935).

38. The relevant Brassaï photographs are illustrated in my "Picasso and the Anatomy of Eroticism," fig. 233.

39. As discussed in her richly provocative and informative doctoral thesis: Lydia Gasman, "Mystery, Magic, and Love in Picasso, 1925–1938: Picasso and the Surrealist Poets," 6 vols., Ph.D. diss., Columbia University, New York, 1981, part II, B, chap. 10.

40. The relevance of Manet's painting was first pointed out in Carla Gottlieb, "Picasso's 'Girl Before a Mirror,'" *Journal of Aesthetics and Art Criticism* 24, no. 4 (summer 1966), pp. 509–18. I elaborated on it in Robert Rosenblum, "Picasso's 'Girl Before a Mirror': Some Recent Reflections," *Source: Notes in the History of Art* (New York) 1, no. 3 (spring 1982), pp. 1–4.

41. Bernadac and Piot, *Picasso*, p. XXII.

42. The fullest account of this masterpiece remains that by William Rubin in *Picasso in the Collection of The Museum of Modern Art*, pp. 138–41.

43. Dix's *Girl Before a Mirror* of 1921 (destroyed during the war) also depicts an oval cheval glass. See Fritz Löffler, *Otto Dix 1891–1969: Oeuvres der Gemälde* (Recklinghausen: Verlag Aurel Bongers, 1981), no. 1921/8.

44. Rockwell's painting *Girl at the Mirror* (1954) is in the Norman Rockwell Museum, Stockbridge, Massachusetts.

45. Jung's essay, "Picasso," originally published in the *Neue Zürcher Zeitung* (Zurich) 153, no. 2 (November 13, 1932), is conveniently reprinted in translation in Marilyn McCully, ed., *A Picasso Anthology: Documents, Criticism, Reminiscences* (Princeton, N.J.: Princeton University Press, 1982), pp. 182–86. For a full account of the circumstances surrounding Jung's essay, see Reinhold Hohl, "C. J. Jung on Picasso (and Joyce)," *Source: Notes in the History of Art* (New York) 3, no. 1 (fall 1983), pp. 10–18.

46. Martin Amis, *The Information* (New York: Harmony Books, 1995), p. 169.

47. Hohl, "C. J. Jung on Picasso (and Joyce)," pp. 15–16.

48. I have suggested elsewhere the possible relevance of the Spanish Virgin of the Immaculate Conception for the central figure of *Les Demoiselles d'Avignon*, a blasphemous quo-tation from El Greco's *Assumption of the Virgin* (Art Institute of Chicago) in which the crescent-shaped melon slice doubles as the crescent moon on which the virgin-whore floats ("The Spanishness of Picasso's Still Lifes," in Jonathan Brown, ed., *Picasso and the Spanish Tradition* [forthcoming]).

49. Munch-Museet, Oslo (OKK M375).

50. For more on these sexual puns, see my "Picasso and the Anatomy of Eroticism"; and László Glózer, *Picasso und der Surrealismus* (Cologne: M. DuMont Schauberg, 1974), pp. 56–69.

51. I have elaborated on the connection with Solana's painting in "Picasso's 'Girl Before a Mirror': Some Recent Reflections," pp. 1–4.

52. For a full presentation of this painting, see Robert Rosenblum, "Picasso's 'Woman with a Book,'" *Arts Magazine* 51, no. 5 (January 1977), pp. 100–105.

53. Arcimboldo's father-figure stature for the Surrealists was codified by his inclusion, with two illustrations, as the earliest ancestor of Surrealism in the pioneering catalogue: Alfred H. Barr, Jr., ed., *Fantastic Art, Dada, Surrealism* (New York: The Museum of Modern Art, 1936).

54. For a characteristic example, see *La Nature* (1897), a painting by the Belgian Symbolist Léon Frédéric, illustrated most recently in *Lost Paradise: Symbolist Europe* (Montreal: The Montreal Museum of Fine Arts, 1995), fig. 364.

55. This postcard comes from Paul Hammond, *French Undressing: Naughty Postcards from 1900 to 1920* (London: Bloomsbury Books, 1976), p. 134.

56. This date, often misread as March 11, 1931, is justified in Pierre Daix, *La Vie de peintre de Pablo Picasso* (Paris: Editions du Seuil, 1977), p. 231.

57. Ibid.

58. For further discussion of this still life, see my own essay, "Large Still Life on a Pedestal Table," in *Picasso from the Musée Picasso*, pp. 65–67; and Boggs, *Picasso & Things*, no. 93.

59. Richardson, "Picasso and l'Amour Fou," p. 66.

60. See Boggs, *Picasso & Things*, nos. 91, 92.

61. In Gasman, "Mystery, Magic, and Love." The material on the cabana is more conveniently summarized in her "Picasso's *Caseta*: His Memories and His Poems," in Mordechai Omer, ed., *Picasso and Literature* (Tel Aviv University, The Genia Schreiber University Art Gallery, 1989), pp. 114–27.

62. See also my essay, "Nude in a Garden," in *Picasso from the Musée Picasso*, pp. 69–71.

63. Brooks Adams, "Cry Me a River," *Los Angeles Times* (calendar), February 13, 1994, pp. 3–4.

64. Mary Mathews Gedo, *Picasso: Art as Autobiography* (Chicago: University of Chicago Press, 1980), p. 149. To pursue such gynecological speculations further, the still life of February 13, 1932, suggests menstrual cycles (in the lunar sequence of the three yellow and lilac apples in the *compotier*) and menstrual blood (in the unusual staining and streaking of red paint in the harlequin-pattern wallpaper behind). It is illustrated in color in Ulrich Weisner, ed., *Picassos Surrealismus: Werke 1925–1937* (Bielefeld: Kunsthalle Bielefeld, 1991), p. 74; also briefly discussed in Dorothy Kosinski, "Körperdinge—Picasso und Bataille," in Weisner, p. 237. As part of the speculative medical history, Maya Widmaier Picasso informs me that in 1932, her mother, always a passionate swimmer, contracted a spirochetal disease by swimming in the infected waters of the Marne.

65. Maya Widmaier Picasso has confirmed this birth date, which is given as September 5, 1935, in many biographies and chronologies.

66. See Nan Rosenthal, *The Drawings of Jasper Johns* (Washington, D.C.: National Gallery of Art, 1990), p. 33.

67. Nochlin ("Picasso's Color Schemes," p. 186, n. 106) also reads in the neck the image of a hatstand, equally appropriate to the fancy millinery.

68. These complementary portraits of Marie-Thérèse Walter and Dora Maar are compared as well in Freeman, *Picasso and the Weeping Women*, pp. 175–77.

69. See Richardson, "Picasso and l'Amour Fou," p. 68.

70. Nochlin ("Picasso's Color Schemes," p. 179) reads a metaphorical parallel here between the faded passion and the faded colors and comments also on the "unsympathetic context of simultaneous breakdown and constraint."

71. See Barr, *Picasso*, p. 268.

72. Ibid., p. 265; and Carolyn Lachner and William Rubin, "Henri Rousseau and Modernism," in *Henri Rousseau* (New York: The Museum of Modern Art, 1985), p. 62.

73. On the Picasso and Matisse portraits of Allan Stein, see Jack Flam, *Matisse: The Man and His Art, 1869–1918* (Ithaca and London: Cornell University Press, 1986), p. 217.

74. As recounted in "Picasso par Maya, fille de Pablo," *Air France Madame*, no. 1 (1986?), pp. 74–81.

The Artist's Daughter, Maya. August 29, 1943. Charcoal on paper, 14½ × 12¼″ (37 × 31 cm). Zervos XIII, 94. Private collection

Woman in an Armchair (Dora). 1941–42. Oil on canvas, 51⅜ × 38⅜″ (130.5 × 97.5 cm). Zervos XI, 374. Öffentliche Kunstsammlung Basel, Kunstmuseum

"For Charming Dora": Portraits of Dora Maar

BRIGITTE LÉAL

While the name Dora Maar,[1] for most true enthusiasts of Picasso's work, conjures up one of the greatest moments of his creative efforts, and while her role not only as a primary inspiration of the war years—linked, moreover, to the history of *Guernica*[2]—but also as a confirmed artist has scarcely been contested, it must be acknowledged that the impact of her personality on Picasso's art has never been truly assessed, any more than the decisive significance and scope of the stylistic upheaval she engendered. The reasons for this respectful distance on the part of specialized critics follow partly from the silence and dignity Dora Maar obstinately maintained in the face of the dark myth with which she was, quite despite herself, surrounded.

For every Roland Penrose, a friendly witness to her romance with Picasso, who hailed her intelligence,[3] and every Michel Leiris, who, though caustic by nature, described her in his *Journal* as "friendly and attractive,"[4] how many others have uttered hasty and, dare we say, "male chauvinist"[5] judgments, which, repeated tirelessly throughout the biographies, have incessantly demonized one of the rare creative women in Picasso's orbit and established the myth of a "powerful and solitary" Dora Maar.

Their *terribilità* no doubt explains why the innumerable, very different portraits that Picasso did of her remain among the finest achievements of his art, at a time when he was engaged in a sort of third path, verging on

Surrealist representation while rejecting strict representation and, naturally, abstraction. Today, more than ever, the fascination that the image of this admirable, but suffering and alienated, face exerts on us incontestably ensues from its coinciding with our modern consciousness of the body in its threefold dimension of precariousness, ambiguity, and monstrosity. There is no doubt that by signing these portraits, Picasso tolled the final bell for the reign of ideal beauty and opened the way for the aesthetic tyranny of a sort of terrible and tragic beauty, the fruit of our contemporary history. In spite of its typically Surrealist aura, the story of Picasso and Dora Maar has the magnitude of a Shakespearean drama, borrowing its masks from Greek myth, but lacking neither passion, madness, history, nor even the presence of God.

At first glance, nothing really distinguishes the evolution of the cycle of Dora Maar portraits from that of other female models who preceded her. At the outset, we always find intimate and tender sketches, quickly followed by a series of great classical portraits, often marked by melancholy. Ultimately, the beloved face is crystallized into a representation that is specific to it, in which it submits to the dominant plastic research (thus Fernande Olivier incarnates Cubism and Olga Khokhlova classicism) without losing any of its truth. Caricatures (the contorted dancers of the 1920s) and monsters (Olga as an Erinye) always betray the end of a relationship.

Paintings and drawings project and exorcise Picasso's

Composition. August 1, 1936. Ink on paper, 13⅝ × 20⅛″ (34.5 × 51 cm). Zervos VIII, 295. Private collection

private conflicts: in the Rescue series of 1932, Marie-Thérèse Walter is the victim of a symbolic death. Later, in June of 1938, a series of drawings returns to a 1927 theme of the cabana attacked by a monster brandishing a key like a weapon, and distinctly describes two or three incontestably female figures,[6] represented in the form of spiders, who are fighting over entrance to the cabana and possession of a crab, both symbolizing the person of Picasso.[7] In a 1938 portrait (p. 392) we recognize Dora Maar, for once almost cheerful, in any case triumphant, holding the key to the kingdom tightly in her fingers.

Theatrically orchestrated by Dora, the scene of Picasso's and Dora's meeting at the Deux Magots, in fall of 1935, so typically surrealist that one might think it apocryphal, is a peak in the category of "mad love," assured by the imprescriptible accessories of Bretonian eroticism: glove, knife, chance, blood.[8] In these games of cat-and-mouse and sadomasochistic rituals, Picasso intended to remain master. Faithful to his method of releasing intimate drama through drawing, he did two sketches on August 1 and September 1, 1936 (above and p. 87, bottom), constituting two facets of a sort of "primal scene" of their relationship, the immutable rules of which he had established

based on his absolute domination and his lover's total submission. In the first, we recognize the young photographer, her face and body significantly covered, timidly penetrating the lair of a well-known figure in the private Picassian mythology: his alter ego, the bearded and laurel-wreathed god, armed with his majestic scepter, emblem of his absolute authority. The following scene is unequivocal, since we again find the Minotaur smitten with young flesh, reenacting with Dora Maar the scenario of erotic initiation repeated so many times with Marie-Thérèse in the *Vollard Suite*.

This inscription in a tailor-made mythic dimension and its recurring *topos* perhaps explains why, beyond the anecdotal, Picasso the Minotaur chose to depict Dora, at the start of their romance, as Harpy (opposite), another mythical creature with the head of a woman and the body of a bird equipped with sharp claws, an incarnation of the male phantasm of the evil and fearsome woman.[9] At the same time he drew sketches of her, done "by heart," as he noted affectionately in the margins of the paper.[10] Like the first drawings depicting Olga in Barcelona in 1917, with long hair and sometimes holding a teddy bear in her arms[11]—the only affectionate portraits

Dora Maar in the Form of a Bird. September 28, 1936. Pencil, 10⅝ × 8¼″ (27 × 21 cm). Zervos VIII, 297. Private collection

that he ever did of her—these are intimate and spontaneous sketches of the modern young woman of whom he dreamed, her hair cropped like a boy's and ruffled by the wind; she is a vibrant image of youth and freedom, a sort of female Rimbaud. To please him she agreed to let her hair grow and to braid it, thereby emphasizing the pure oval of her face, made slightly heavy by a strong chin, and he drew new portraits.[12] In spite of all the deformations that he would later cause her features to undergo, this face of an Oriental idol, with its marked iconic character, impenetrable, hard, and unsmiling, and whose haughty beauty is enhanced by makeup and sophisticated finery, would remain the standard pattern of her iconography to the end.[13]

Indeed, if Marie-Thérèse incarnated a wild beauty, a sporty and healthy "beautiful plant," Dora Maar is the perfect prototype of the surrealist Egeria, capricious and eccentric, a direct descendant of the Baudelairean idol who is "accomplishing a kind of duty, when she devotes herself to appearing magical and supernatural."[14] The most provocative emblem of her somewhat flashy elegance is the little over-ornate hat that Picasso places on her head (he would soon give the object a ridiculous [p. 393], then grotesque, and even threatening, aspect, particularly in a whole series of brightly colored paintings of

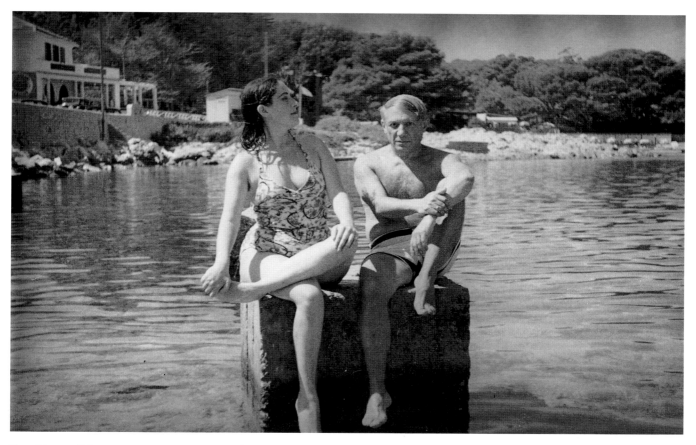

Dora Maar and Picasso. Mougins, summer 1937. Photograph by Roland Penrose. Lee Miller Archives

Head of a Woman. 1936. Oil on wood panel, 18⅞ × 13⅝″ (48 × 34.5 cm). Zervos VIII, 304. Private collection

Head of a Woman. 1936. Oil on canvas, 25⅞ × 21¼″ (65 × 54 cm). Zervos VIII, 305. Private collection

Head of a Woman. 1936. Oil on canvas, 21⅝ × 18⅛″ (55 × 46 cm). Zervos VIII, 306. Private collection

Head of a Woman. 1936. Oil on canvas, 25⅞ × 21¼″ (65 × 54 cm). Zervos VIII, 307. Private collection

Portrait of Dora Maar. 1936. Oil on canvas, 25⅝ × 21¼″ (65 × 54 cm). Zervos VIII, 302. Private collection

1938).[15] In its preciousness and fetishistic vocation, the feminine hat was, like the glove, an erotic accessory highly prized by the Surrealists. Thus Paul Eluard took advantage of the *Art Sauvage* exhibition organized by Charles Ratton in 1937—where one could see all sorts of African headgear with shells that would greatly inspire Man Ray—to bestow moving praise on the female hat:

"Among the objects tangled in the web of life, the female hat is one of those that require the most insight, the most audacity. A head must dare to wear a crown."[16] A crown of daffodils, an urchin's beret, or a cool straw hat for Marie-Thérèse, painted like a Manet;[17] nets, veils, and the great wings of a voracious insect for Dora:[18] even their respective ornaments point to the glaring differences in

Weeping Woman (Dora). 1937. Oil on canvas, 23⅝ × 19¼″ (60 × 49 cm). Zervos IX, 73. Tate Gallery, London

Dora Maar Seated. 1937. Oil on canvas, 36¼ × 25⅝″ (92 × 65 cm). Zervos VIII, 331. Musée Picasso, Paris

Dora Maar. Mougins, summer 1937. Photograph by Lee Miller. Lee Miller Archives

Woman Holding a Key. 1938. Oil on canvas, 39⅜ × 31⅞″ (100 × 81 cm). Zervos IX, 144. Private collection

temperament between the two women. Nothing reveals the total divergence of their psychologies better than the parallel portraits that Picasso, not without perversity, constantly drew of both of them, purposely confusing their clothes.

The most eloquent example of this is the 1937 "diptych" in the Musée Picasso of Dora and Marie-Thérèse (pp. 373 and 391), especially since each of these paintings shows the sitter in a similar position, a bust facing front, in the classic pose of melancholy but without morbid ostentation, seated in an armchair in a cramped, narrow space. For Marie-Thérèse, supple lines, curving forms, and pastel and light colors suggest a casual sensuality, a cheerful plenitude. For Dora, there are broken lines, acute, even jagged, angles, like the scarlet claws of her nails; the colors are loud and uneven. The black wings of her blouse recall a bird of prey, caged in a sort of barred cell.

While in portraits of Marie-Thérèse stripes appear in a range of pastel colors that always have a summery and childlike connotation, in the portraits of Dora stripes proliferate until they cover the figure and background entirely, becoming an eloquent statement of the intensely emotional character of her image. What is one to think of the meaning of this network of concentric lines that, not content to bud prettily on her clothes, begins progres-

sively to invade every part of her body in order to end up covering her totally with a fine tattoo that transforms her into some barbarous idol?[19] In a final metamorphosis, with strong sexual connotations, these lines evoke a spider with enormous elytrons pulling its tentacular threads from the four corners of the page (p. 396).[20] Picasso would explain himself more or less to Françoise Gilot about this likening of Dora to an insect by confiding that he considered her "a Kafkaesque personality."[21] Indeed, the derogatory and even diabolic function of stripes in the Western imagination encourages us to interpret their obsessive proliferation here as a metaphor of madness and confinement.[22] In the portrait of 1937 (p. 391) the profusion of stripes in the background already evoked prison bars. In one of the later portraits of Dora (p. 403), the most pathetic, no doubt, in its very "Balthusian" distancing effect, her unattractive striped dress clearly functions as an archetype reflecting a prisoner's garb.[23]

There is a pathological, prisonlike, exotic, but also erotic dimension to the Picassian stripe when it is woven into golden braids punctuating Dora's waist in a tight-fitting coat, at once suggestive and protective. In *The Yellow Sweater* (p. 398), instead of the usual ravishing hands, fine and lacquered, two paws emerge, their thick, gray skin banishing Dora once again to the animal kingdom.[24]

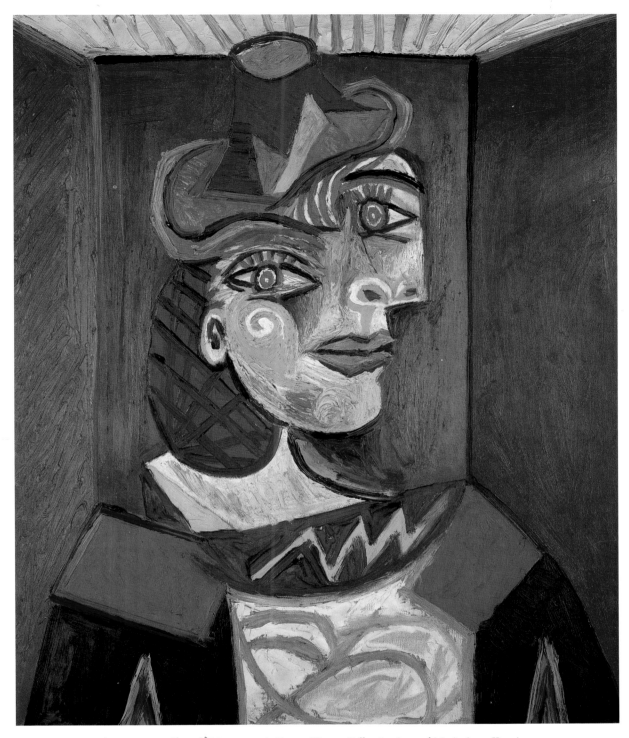

Dora Maar. 1938. Oil on canvas, 25⅝ × 21¼″ (65 × 54 cm). Zervos IX, 119. Collection Jan and Marie-Anne Krugier

Alfred H. Barr, Jr., saw the influence of Arcimboldo,[25] reintroduced by the Surrealists, in all of Picasso's faces of men and women created in the summer of 1938, with their skin scarred, corded, caned, woven like the straw of their hats, indeed, completely transformed into balls of wool or cord following the example of the spectacular *Seated Woman with a Hat* from the Menil collection (p. 394).

Its obscene form, of a radical syntheticism (the body of the woman and the armchair blended, the mouth/anus, and the phallic nose), is directly derived from the hairy monster in *Dream and Lie of Franco* (1936) and constitutes the summit of Picasso's investigations into the polymorphous and allotropic body, in which wild lines and hallucinatory colors, totally freed from organic representation,

Seated Woman with a Hat (Dora). September 10, 1938. Oil and sand on wood panel, 21⅝ × 18⅛″ (55 × 46 cm). Zervos IX, 228. The Menil Collection, Houston. Gift of Dominique de Menil

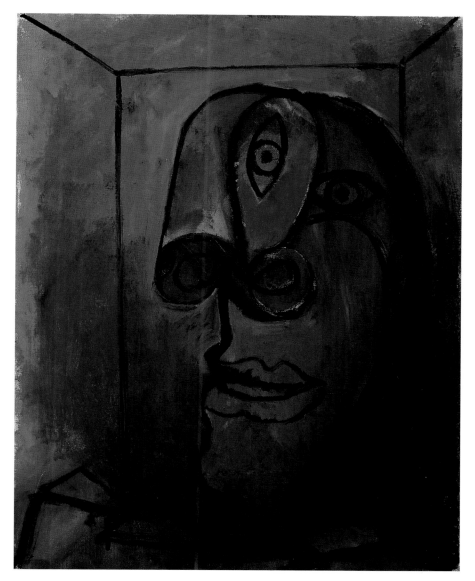

Head of a Woman (Dora). 1938. Oil on canvas, 25⅝ × 19¾″ (65 × 50 cm). Zervos IX, 216. Private collection

participate in a single hysterical image. Picasso claimed that his vision of Dora as the hysterical woman was wholly objective. "For me she's the weeping woman. For years I've painted her in tortured forms, not through sadism, and not with pleasure, either; just obeying a vision that forced itself on me. It was the deep reality, not the superficial one."[26]

As early as November 1936, less than four months after the start of their relationship, Picasso depicted Dora as melancholic, her hand pressed to her forehead (p. 389). Her face, which until now had remained intact, for the first time underwent the famous frontal/profile split which, though scarcely perceptible here, nevertheless suggests a "black mood," a temperament prone to withdrawal, to introspection; the hollowness of the cheek is most likely a sign of the mind's flight, a schizophrenic slide.

Indeed, the images that follow, also done in November of 1936, clearly portray her as an insane woman (p. 388): her grimacing and swollen face, dilated eyes, and convulsive postures recall quite unambiguously the "passionate poses" of hysterical women abundantly photographed at the end of the nineteenth century. These photographs were widely distributed in the 1920s by the Surrealists (especially by Breton and Aragon in an issue of *La Révolution surréaliste* of 1928), who embraced any source likely to nourish their reflections on the necessary disordering of the senses and the mind.[27] These images could also be interpreted as apotropaic representations by a painter confronted with a personality who confused and fascinated him at the same time. In 1938 Picasso noted, in the margin of a portrait of Dora (p. 406), her eyes twinkling like stars, catlike and magical: "Afghan

Dora Maar Seated in a Wicker Chair. April 29, 1938. Pen and ink, gouache, oil pastel, and crayon on paper, 30½ × 22⅜″ (77.5 × 56.9 cm). Zervos IX, 132. The Jacques and Natasha Gelman Collection

cat/chameleon/bear!" Equally projected is a premonitory vision of the rapid psychological degradation of a woman whom Picasso "had made . . . unhappy in a very concrete way"—to repeat the remarks Gilot attributed to Eluard—witness in 1945 the nervous breakdown from which Dora was rescued by Dr. Jacques Lacan.[28]

This stylization of Dora Maar's face, first as weeping woman, then as dog/woman glued to her chair of torture,[29] and finally as cadaver, as crucified carcass, more and more disfigured and monstrous, is certainly a vision of the world, the sign of universal catastrophe.

We shall not return here to the well-known genesis of the Weeping Woman series of 1937, which, as Alfred Barr had remarked, appeared as a postscript to *Guernica* (it would seem that the profile of the woman at the window holding the lantern is that of Dora Maar), as well as the etchings of *Dream and Lie of Franco*, which illustrate a text based on the obsessive repetition of the word "cry": "Cries of children cries of women cries of birds cries of flowers, etc."[30] Rather than paint the war, Picasso chose to paint the cry, taking up the most universal image of suffering in order to do so: that of Mary Magdalen pouring forth tears for eternity to express her sorrow for human folly. One sensational painting is the so-called "*Tête Penrose*" (p. 390), with the colors of the Catalan flag

and the eyes truly out of the head (drawn as if outside the face, they take on an otherworldly turn in the manner of Redon); but in spite of the strident colors and the deformations pushed to paroxysm, Dora Maar's features and even her beauty remain identifiable,[31] while at the same time comparable figures painted by Picasso's compatriot Miró (especially the extraordinary *Head of a Woman* of 1938) and the figures in his "savage paintings" that reflect the same despair in the face of Spain's political situation are stylized in organic elementary forms, degraded to the point of animality and tossed about in a chaotic space.

Picasso preferred to isolate his monsters in a cube (for example, *Bust of a Woman* of January 1, 1939), which forces them into immobility and deprives them of every illustrative characteristic, especially when they are viewed in closeup. In 1939, when the fusion of Dora's face and the snout of his dog Kasbec is definitively achieved,[32] one would not think of laughing at this hybrid monster, though it is clearly the result of a phallic combination, so evident does its symbolic meaning seem. From then on Picasso rejected the earlier rainbow-colored palette for colors of mourning where—as Christian Zervos has pointed out[33]—there is no lack of the grayish-green

Seated Woman (Dora). 1938. Ink, gouache, and colored chalk on paper, 30⅛ × 21⅝″ (76.5 × 55 cm). Zervos IX, 133. Collection Beyeler, Switzerland

Portrait of Dora in a Garden. December 10, 1938. Oil on canvas, 51½ × 38¼″ (131 × 97 cm). Zervos IX, 232. Collection Mr. and Mrs. Daniel Saidenberg

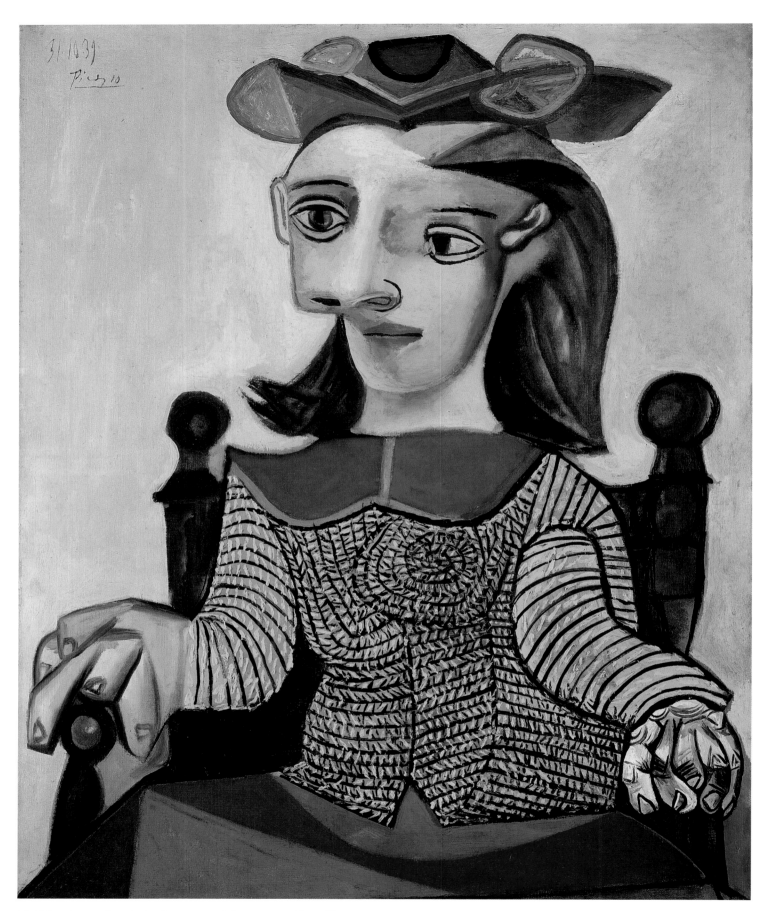

The Yellow Sweater (Dora). October 31, 1939. Oil on canvas, 31⁷⁄₈ × 25⁷⁄₈″ (81 × 65 cm). Not in Zervos. Berggruen Collection

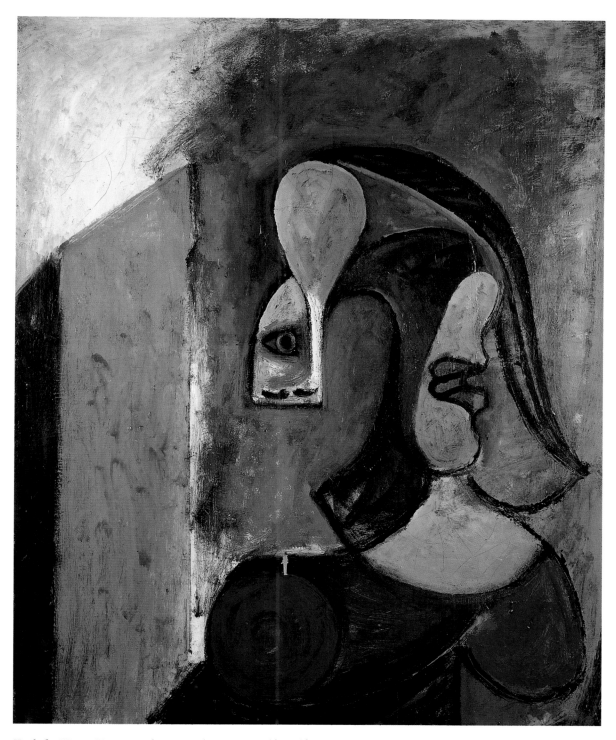

Head of a Woman (Dora). April 1, 1939. Oil on canvas, 36¼ × 28¾″ (92 × 73 cm). Zervos IX, 282. Collection Mrs. Lindy Bergman

of the German uniform that reinforces the particularly macabre nature of the *Head of a Woman* of June 11, 1940 (p. 400), in which the features of Dora, Kasbec, and a skull gritting its teeth in rage become amalgamated.

The monumental dimensions of the canvas, the gigantic proportions of the figure, and the excessiveness of the displacements and enlargements of the organs incon-

testably accentuate the dramatic scope of *Woman Dressing Her Hair*, painted at Royan in June 1940 (p. 401), which confirms the function of Dora's face as allegorical *topos*. This is not a private portrait; there is no attempt at psychology, just the image of a carcass with very prominent ribs, of the tortured or seemingly crucified remains evoking all the violence of the war.[34]

Sketches of Dora Maar and Death's-Heads. 1940. Pencil
on paper, 8⅝ × 7½″ (22 × 19 cm). Not in Zervos.
Private collection

Head of a Woman (Dora). June 11, 1940. Oil on paper, 25½ × 17¾″ (64.8 × 45 cm). Zervos X, 526. Musée
Picasso, Paris

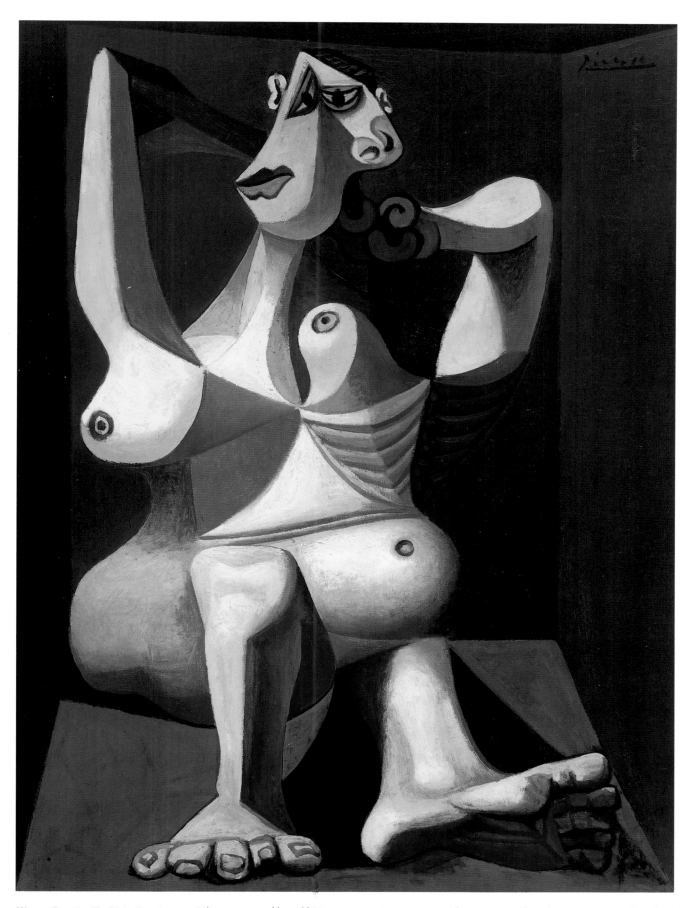

Woman Dressing Her Hair (Dora). 1940. Oil on canvas, 51¼ × 38¼″ (130 × 97 cm). Zervos X, 302. The Museum of Modern Art, New York. Gift of Louise Reinhardt Smith

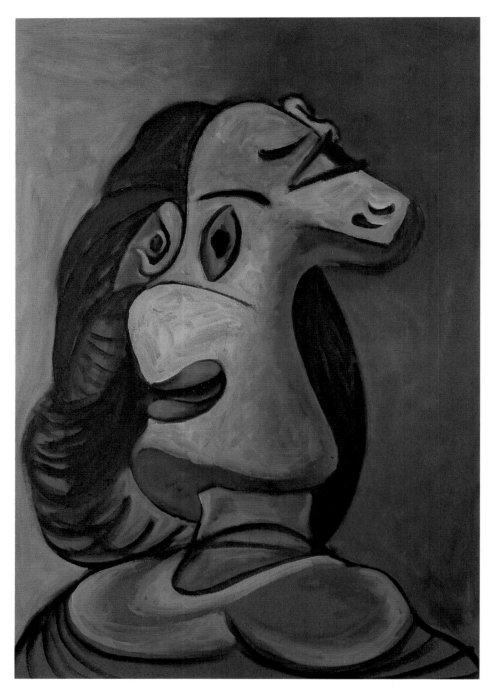

Head of a Woman (Dora). 1941. Oil on canvas, 21⅝ × 15″ (55 × 38 cm). Zervos XI, 143. Národní Galerie, Prague

Dora Maar. c. 1941. Photograph by Rogi André. Cabinet des Estampes et de la Photographie, Bibliothèque Nationale de France, Paris

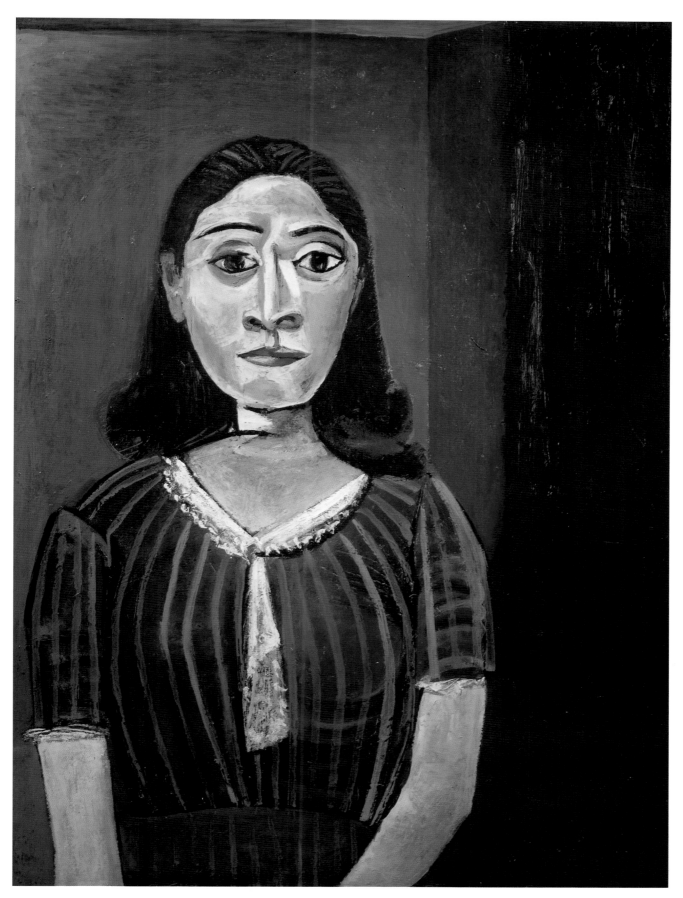

Portrait of Dora Maar. October 9, 1942. Oil on panel, 36¼ × 28¾″ (92 × 73 cm). Zervos XII, 154. Collection Stephen Hahn, New York

Picasso's studio at 7, rue des Grands-Augustins, Paris, c. 1939. Improvised arrangement of works of the same "generation," which includes a series of portraits of the previous two years placed in front of the large pasted paper-and-gouache *Women at Their Toilette*, of 1938 (Zervos IX, 103). Included in the group are the *Portrait of Nusch Eluard* (p. 83) and *Dora Maar Seated* (p. 391). Photograph by Dora Maar. Musée Picasso, Paris, Picasso Archives

"Similarities! . . . We all love the prehistoric paintings, but no one resembles them!" Picasso would say to André Malraux, unveiling for him, at the end of the war, his latest portraits, "intransigent works [that] were creating a world of painting that had never before existed."[35] Yet one can still recognize the significance of Dora's features in the series Woman in an Armchair, repeated in an obsessional way during the war years. The rigidity of a sphinx, the strict frontality, the body treated in an "Arcimboldesque" variant of Curvilinear Cubism, in geometric volumes brought into relief by the interlace of black rings and a very dense mesh of lines, often brightly colored—all of these describe *Woman in a Wicker Chair* (p. 407). The essentially illustrative and decorative quality of these portraits seems to deviate from the Surrealist canon of "convulsive" beauty that perfectly suited Dora's psychology. In actual fact, in their absolute distance in relation to life, they embody the height of modern beauty as Breton envisioned it, based on the principle of vital disorder, which the figure of Dora Maar, in her extreme mutability, her real, spiritual restlessness, will forever incarnate.

Woman in Green (Dora). 1944. Oil on canvas, 51¼ × 38¼″ (130 × 97 cm). Zervos XIII, 49. Private collection

NOTES

The first three words of this essay's title, "For Charming Dora," are a translation of a dedication written in Catalan by Picasso in a copy of Georges Buffon's *Histoire naturelle*. He gave this book to Dora Maar. Playing on the name "Buffon," Picasso's words were "Per Dora Maar tan rebuffon." This essay was translated from the French by Jeanine Herman.

1. According to the notarial deed of November 15, 1944, which made her owner of a house in Ménerbes, in the Vaucluse region, her real name was "Markovitch Henriette Dora," born on November 22, 1907, in Paris. This document refers to her as an "artist-painter," whereas in 1936, when Picasso met her, she was working as a professional photographer at 29, rue d'Astorg in the eighth arrondissement of Paris (Henri Bolle, "Autour de Picasso à Ménerbes en 1946," in *Mémoires de l'Académie du Vaucluse*, 8th ser., vol. 1, 1992).

2. Dora is generally identified as the model for the woman with the lantern, but, above all, she was the only photographer allowed to record the seven successive stages of *Guernica* between May and June 1937. All of these photographs were published in a special issue of *Cahiers d'art* in 1937.

3. Penrose, vacationing with Lee Miller in Mougins in 1937 and with Dora and Picasso, recalled "the variety of ways in which the presence and intelligence of Dora Maar nourished Picasso's inspiration" (*Picasso: His Life and Work* [Berkeley and Los Angeles: University of California Press, 1981], p. 340).

4. Michel Leiris, *Journal, 1922–1989* (Paris: Gallimard, 1992), p. 298, dated January 7, 1936, when Dora Maar was still seeing Georges Bataille. According to Michel Surya, who was Bataille's biographer, Dora was one of Bataille's numerous mistresses and collaborators, particularly in the context of "Contre-Attaque," the "band of revolutionaries" he formed between October 1935 and May 1936.

5. Professional rivalry doubtless explains Brassaï's initial opinion of her ("prone to tempests and outbursts"), which, sadly, has become canonical (Brassaï, *Conversations avec Picasso* [Paris: Gallimard, 1964], p. 63); but Marcel Duhamel's assessment of her as "pigheaded," quoted by Pierre Daix (*Raconte pas ta vie* [Paris: Le Mercure de France, 1973], p. 355), is even more brutal.

6. Zervos IX, 164 and 172.

7. Lydia Gasman bluntly titles these drawings *Dora Maar and Marie-Thérèse at the Cabana* and takes the crab for a scorpion, which was Picasso's astrological sign. Lydia Gasman, "Mystery, Magic, and Love in Picasso, 1925–1938: Picasso and the Surrealist Poets," Ph.D. diss., Columbia University, New York, 1981, pls. 172 and 173, vol. III, p. 1709, and chap. V, pt. I, "The Cabana Series."

8. "She was wearing black gloves with little pink flowers appliquéed on them. She took off the gloves and picked up a long, pointed knife, which she began to drive into the table between her outstretched fingers to see how close she

could come to each finger without actually cutting herself. From time to time she missed by a tiny fraction of an inch and before she stopped playing with the knife, her hand was covered with blood" (Françoise Gilot and Carleton Lake, *Life with Picasso* [New York: McGraw-Hill, 1964], pp. 85–86). Breton was naturally a master at describing unexpected encounters with "mad love." See especially his novel *Nadja* (1928), in which gloves play a significant role.

9. He would continue to depict Dora in this manner, since we find her as a bird with small horns on her head and her eyes spoked with rays until 1941 (Zervos XI, 103 and 104), when he depicted himself as a winged Minotaur, making them two of a kind (Zervos XI, 105). Picasso always claimed his monstrous dimension by showing himself as a Minotaur in erotic situations.

10. Zervos VIII, 289.

11. Zervos III, 39.

12. Zervos VIII, 298–300.

13. The evolution of Dora Maar portraits does not follow a straight course, beginning with positive representations and ending with monstrous ones, but alternates regularly between realistic portraits and tormented apparitions. In the years 1941–42, we still find many "normal" representations of Dora (notably Zervos XI, 273, 106, and 145, similar to the sculpture installed in the St.-Germain-des-Prés square). There is a series of drawings (Zervos XI, 96, 97, 101, 102, and particularly 98) in which the face is framed so tightly that it almost loses its human aspect.

14. Charles Baudelaire, "In Praise of Cosmetics," in *The Painter of Modern Life and Other Essays* (London: Phaidon Press, 1964), p. 33. In this chapter Baudelaire premonitorily praises the beauty of the savage, who alone has understood the "lofty spiritual significance of the toilet" (p. 32).

15. Zervos IX, 119–25.

16. Text titled "La Mode au Congo," quoted by Jean-Charles Gateau, in *Paul Eluard et la peinture surréaliste* (Geneva: Librairie Droz, 1982), p. 212; originally published in *Marianne*, May 5, 1937, and reprinted in *Oeuvres complètes* (Paris: Gallimard, 1968), vol. 2, pp. 850–51.

17. *Woman in a Straw Hat* of June 25, 1938, seems directly derived from a portrait of Mery Laurent by Manet titled *Autumn* (1881; Rouart-Wildenstein, 1975, no. 193).

18. André Breton's *Nadja* is described as having a fascination for extravagant hats and also "enjoyed imagining herself as a butterfly whose

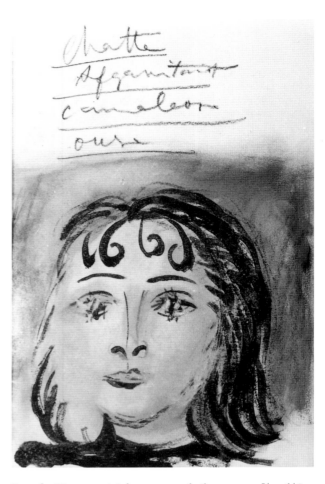

Face of a Woman. 1938. Ink, crayon, and oil on paper, 9⅞ × 6¼″ (25 × 16 cm). Not in Zervos. Private collection

body consisted of a Mazda (Nadja) bulb toward which rose a charmed snake" (*Nadja* [New York: Grove Press, 1960], p. 129).

19. Zervos IX, 118. Need we recall that Picasso's discovery of primitive art prompted him, beginning in 1907, to streak faces with bands of strong color (for example, *Mother and Child*, summer 1907; Zervos II¹, 38)? In addition to the marked emotional power of this painting, the resurgence of an anti-illusionist use of color, which is specific to the portraits of Dora Maar, signaled a new surge of primitivism in Picasso.

20. Zervos IX, 131, 146, and 147. If the sexual symbolism of the spider is too banal to consider at length, we shall examine more closely this intrusion of figures by a line, a practice equally indebted to non-European art (one thinks in particular of the masks from New Guinea that Breton appreciated for their elements "finely assembled by lines of light colors"; *Rêve I, Alentours*, in *Oeuvres complètes* [Paris: Editions Gallimard, 1988], vol. 1, p. 387). We may also note Giacometti's later use of these "lines of force" in the face, which Jean-Paul Sartre justifiably understood "as the expression of the intimate relations of a being with himself" ("Les Peintures de Giacometti," in *Situations IV* [Paris, Gallimard, 1964], p. 355).

21. Gilot, *Life with Picasso*, p. 92. Picasso also confided to Gilot that he had decorated the walls of Dora's apartment with insects!

22. The reference book in French on the history of stripes is Michel Pastoureau, *L'Etoffe du diable* (Paris: Editions du Seuil, 1991). A revealing poem written by Picasso in a notebook on March 11, 1937, evokes "behind its bars desire so confined in its prison" ("derrière ses barreaux le désir si à l'étroit dans sa prison"; Marie-Laure Bernadac and Christine Piot, eds., *Picasso: Collected Writings* [New York: Abbeville Press, 1989], p. 161).

23. Dora herself told James Lord the unpleasant story of this portrait—initially entrusted to Cocteau and ultimately painted over entirely by Picasso—which coincided with the death of her mother. She had a small window in the right-hand corner painted over, which, to her taste, too blatantly accentuated the prisonlike aspect of the space (James Lord, *Picasso and Dora* [New York: Farrar Straus Giroux, 1993], pp. 121–22).

24. These paws clearly recall those of the unidentifiable monster reproduced by Dora in one of her most famous photographs, the *Portrait of Ubu*, of 1936.

25. Alfred H. Barr, Jr., in *Picasso: Fifty Years of His Art* (New York: The Museum of Modern Art, 1946), p. 219, alludes to Arcimboldo in commenting on *Man with an Ice Cream Cone* of August 20, 1938, a sort of male equivalent to the portraits of Dora, who, in the contemporary painting *Night Fishing at Antibes*, is also shown licking an ice cream cone.

26. Gilot, *Life with Picasso*, p. 122.

27. See the plates of "passionate poses in 1878" illustrating the article devoted to the fifty-year anniversary of hysteria by Breton and Aragon in *La Révolution surréaliste*, no. 11 (March 15, 1928).

28. Gilot, *Life with Picasso*, p. 89.

29. In 1945 Picasso confided to André Malraux: "Dora, for me, was always a weeping woman. . . . And it's important, because women are suffering machines. . . . When I paint a woman in an armchair, the armchair implies old age or death, right? So, too bad for her" (André Malraux, *Picasso's Mask* [New York: Holt, Rinehart and Winston, 1976], p. 138).

30. Penrose, *Picasso: His Life and Work*, p. 298.

31. The metaphoric character of the representation did not prevent Picasso from also considering it a veritable portrait of Dora, whom he described, not without irony, in one of his poems of February 18, 1937, as "devilishly enticing in her disguise of tears and a marvelous hat" ("diablement séduisante dans son déguisement de larmes et chapeautée à merveille"; Bernadac and Piot, eds., *Picasso: Collected Writings*, p. 156).

32. Picasso here emphatically makes use of the sexual symbolism of the elongated nose as snout, which is a psychoanalytical commonplace, but the morbid symbolism of the dog—quintessential animal of the melancholic type—was certainly not unknown to him.

33. Christian Zervos, introduction to volume X of his catalogue of Picasso's work.

34. This unbearable image was certainly an important model for some of Francis Bacon's paintings (*Painting*, 1946), in which one again finds the idea of the crucified, slaughtered carcass, a fascination with tortured flesh, and the confusion between man and animal.

35. Malraux, *Picasso's Mask*, pp. 125 and 111.

Woman in a Wicker Chair. 1944. Oil on canvas, 39⅜ × 31⅞″ (100 × 81 cm). Zervos XIII, 328. Private collection

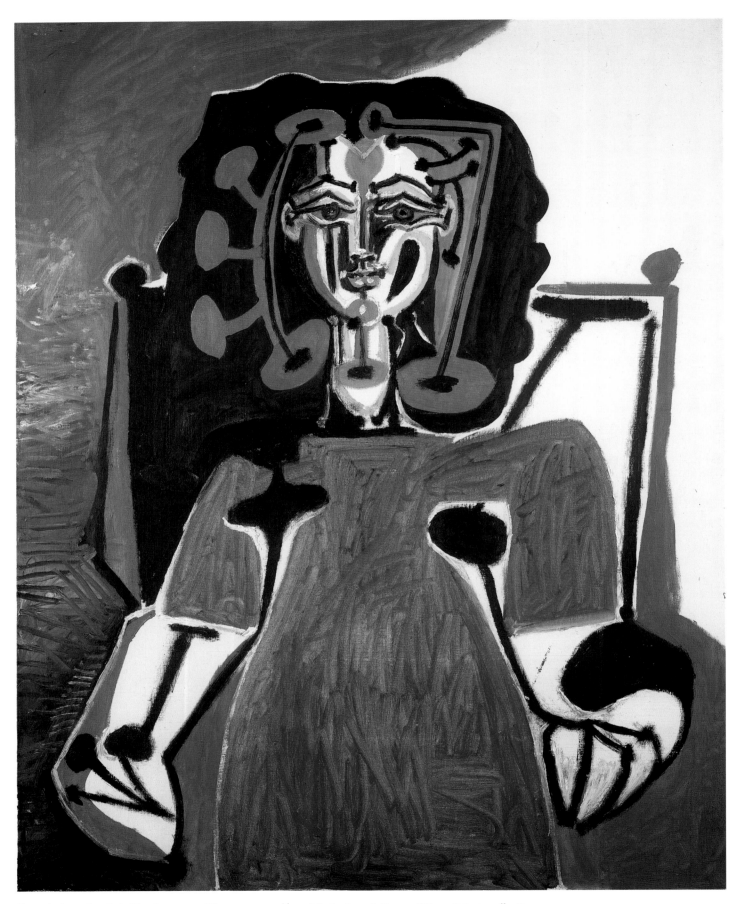

Françoise in an Armchair. March 23, 1949. Oil on canvas, 45½ × 35″ (116 × 89 cm). Zervos XV, 141. Private collection

A Triangle of Ambitions: Art, Politics, and Family during the Postwar Years with Françoise Gilot

MICHAEL C. FITZGERALD

With the end of World War II, Picasso was overwhelmed by an outpouring of admiration that swept away the cold, dark silence of the war years and raised him to a level of public acclaim never before experienced by a living vanguard artist. No longer known primarily for artistic innovations that left many observers puzzled or enraged, Picasso became the first modern artist to step from the relative isolation of the avant-garde into the mainstream of society and assume a role of moral conscience in contemporary life. Intensely observed by worldwide audiences, he sought to fulfill the vast expectations placed upon him by a multitude of groups ranging from such close friends in the Communist Party as Paul Eluard and Louis Aragon to the representatives of artistic, benevolent, and political organizations that constantly importuned him. While seeking to live up to his public stature, Picasso, already in his sixties, also fought to renew his art and cultivate his private life. At the center of these three competing, often contradictory, ambitions, Picasso could no longer often impose the distance, clarity, and control that had made his earlier career so remarkably productive; increasingly, his successes were shadowed by failures and missteps. As his partner during most of the first decade after the war, Françoise Gilot, a young painter whom he had met in May 1943, contributed to an artistic dialogue that funneled through these conflicts and produced a body of work that is both intimately related—and at the same time often opposed—to the "public" Picasso.

Fame was not thrust upon him by chance; Picasso had sought it from the beginning of his career, and he frankly reveled in its achievement. Having established an international reputation and amassed great wealth by the late 1920s, Picasso had seen his artistic stature confirmed by a series of major retrospectives during the 1930s. He had participated vigorously in most of these projects, and he unequivocally affirmed to his friend Brassaï the importance of widespread acclaim. Rejecting the notion that an artist should work "for oneself, for 'the love of art' and scorn success," Picasso claimed not simply the right to earn a living but proclaimed that public recognition was essential for the fulfillment of art: "An artist has a need for success. And not simply to be able to live, but above all to realize his work." In his opinion, art was not complete without garnering respect and influencing others.[1] The cornerstone of this approval, an "apotheosis" according to Brassaï, had been *Picasso: Forty Years of His Art*, the exhibition that had opened in New York in November of 1939, two months after Germany began World War II.[2]

This exhibition had set the stage for the postwar Picasso. Not only had it anointed him as the preeminent twentieth-century artist; it had expanded the definition of his achievement to include the artist's political commitment to the Spanish Republic, as well as his recent aesthetic innovations: surrounded by forty studies, the *Guernica* mural stood as Picasso's greatest contribution in

Bacchanal. 1944. Watercolor and gouache on paper, 12 × 16″ (30.5 × 40.5 cm). Zervos XIV, 35. Private collection

Nicolas Poussin. *Bacchanal: The Triumph of Pan.* 1638–39. Oil on canvas, 54¾ × 61¾″ (139 × 157 cm). The Louvre, Paris

the immediately preceding years. Despite the cessation of most artistic events in Europe during the war, Picasso emerged at the liberation of Paris with his reputation not only intact but greatly enhanced. He had remained in Paris during the Occupation, refused the special treatment offered him by the Nazis, and probably aided members of the Resistance. His long-standing reputation for artistic rebellion was transformed in public accounts to embrace political defiance as well.[3] Summarizing a visit four days after VE Day, Brassaï described the situation: "Picasso's studio was invaded. . . . His courageous attitude had made him a flag bearer, and the entire world wanted to salute him as the symbol of regained liberty. Poets, painters, art critics, museum directors, writers dressed in allied military uniforms; officers or simple soldiers, climbed en masse up the rugged stairs. . . . He [his name] had become as popular in Red China, in Soviet Russia as he had been in the United States since his great exhibition in New York." Somewhat ruefully, Picasso quipped, "Yes,

The Charnel House. 1944–45; dated 1945. Oil and charcoal on canvas, 78⅝ × 98½″ (199.8 × 250.1 cm). Zervos XIV, 76. The Museum of Modern Art, New York. Mrs. Sam A. Lewisohn Bequest (by exchange) and Mrs. Marya Bernard Fund in memory of her husband Dr. Bernard Bernard and anonymous funds

it's an invasion! Paris was liberated, but me, I was, and I am, continually under siege."[4]

In the decade following the war, Picasso's public reputation would be profoundly affected by paintings devoted to political themes: *The Charnel House* (1944–45), *Monument to the Spanish Dead* (1947), *Massacre in Korea* (1951), *War* and *Peace* (1952), and the drawing of Stalin's portrait (1953). Except for the first, these pictures reflect Picasso's allegiance to the French Communist Party, which he had announced in the fall of 1944, and they perpetuate the image of him as a figure who had gone beyond the art world to take a position in the pantheon of "world-historical" figures.[5] Yet, as his remark about being under siege suggests, Picasso soon found his fame constraining, and his global acclamation cast him into a ring of political adversaries more treacherous than the bullfights he so admired. His earnest and often explicit efforts to support the program of the Communist Party would be challenged by Party officials as well as art critics and political

enemies. Reflecting both the widespread paranoia of the Cold War years and his own qualitative judgments about the work involved, Alfred H. Barr, Jr., did not include either of Picasso's two postwar political easel paintings in the exhibition he organized at The Museum of Modern Art to commemorate the artist's seventy-fifth birthday in 1957.[6]

Although the public, political side of Picasso's art made the best news, it was not his primary achievement during the postwar decade. No matter how much the problem fascinates scholars, it now seems clear that Picasso's efforts to engage the Party's program were generally unsuccessful, in part because he rejected fundamental tenets of Communist ideology, especially as he found them put into practice. Rather than the handful of programmatic pictures, it is Picasso's still lifes, portraits, and figure paintings that constitute his major work of these years. Yet because Picasso did not put the majority up for sale at the time, so that they later passed to heirs

Two Women in an Interior. April 12, 1944. Oil on canvas, 28¾ × 36¼″ (73 × 92 cm). Zervos XIII, 251. Private collection

Two Women in an Interior. April 15, 1944. Oil on canvas, 28¾ × 36¼″ (73 × 92 cm). Zervos XIII, 252. Private collection

Portrait of Françoise. July 28, 1944. Charcoal on paper, 25¾ × 19¾″ (65 × 50 cm). Zervos XIV, 36. Private collection

Portrait of Françoise. April 15, 1944. Oil on paper, 25¾ × 19¾″ (65 × 50 cm). Zervos XIII, 270. Private collection

who mostly wished to retain them, many of these paintings—particularly the portraits—are relatively little known among art historians and even less by general audiences. Moreover, the portraits of Françoise and their children, Claude and Paloma, not only constitute a remarkable group of private images; they also frequently infuse the more public pictures with a welcome element of playfulness and renew a dialogue with past art that would increasingly propel Picasso's late career.

The nature of Picasso's postwar work is best established not by such pictures as *The Charnel House* but by the *Bacchanal* (pp. 411, 410), which he painted during the liberation of Paris. As an evocation of suffering during the war, *The Charnel House* has no parallel in Picasso's postwar art or that of his contemporaries, yet it is fundamentally a retrospective work. Its subject of a family brutally murdered in their home, and its grisaille Cubist-Expressionist style make it a pendant to *Guernica*. Like that great mural, *The Charnel House* is a generalized cry of outrage against brutality. During the course of developing his composition, Picasso substituted a common still life for the crowing cock that would have symbolized France's ultimate triumph. The *Bacchanal* is no more explicit. Painted during the street fighting of August 1944, this gouache is a variation on a painting by Poussin in the Louvre (p. 410).

Characteristically, Picasso leaped over the immediate circumstances ("gunshots everywhere . . . tanks slamming into the building") to evoke the celebration that would follow victory.[7] Even then, Picasso's dialogue was as much with past art as with current events. By choosing Poussin as his starting point, Picasso was embracing classical French culture (as many artists had done after World War I) and declaring both its continuing significance—and his role in the vanguard of its vital embodiment. Painted little more than a month before Picasso announced that he had joined the Communist Party, *Bacchanal* conveys the exuberant strength of this modern master without being freighted with political messages.

Besides selecting a Cubist idiom over Poussin's classicizing one, Picasso primarily departed from his source by transforming the two women dancing near the statue of Pan. Extending the proportions of his composition so that the woman embracing the statue stands at the center of his design, Picasso uncovered both women's bodies and metamorphosed them into pliable creatures whose swelling breasts and diminutive heads signal sensual abandon. Although Picasso painted this small gouache in Marie-Thérèse's apartment, and his figures evoke some images of her from nearly twenty years earlier, these carousing revelers are not simply persistent ghosts. Their

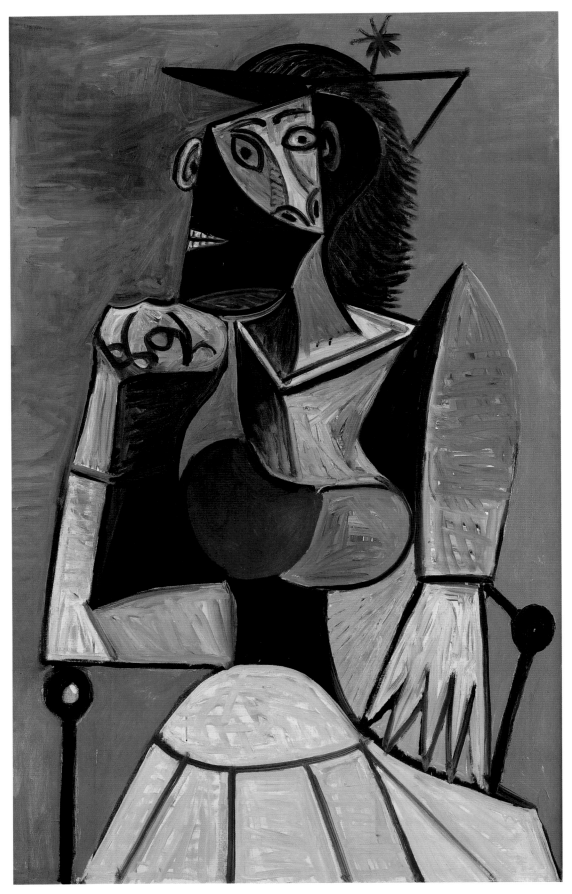

Seated Woman (Françoise). March 5, 1945. Oil on canvas, 51¾ × 31⅞″ (131.5 × 81 cm). Zervos XIV, 77. Musée Picasso, Paris primary source was living and immediate, Françoise Gilot.[8]

On July 28, 1944, he had drawn her face, distinguished by its wide, oval shape, large eyes, and straight nose surrounded by flowing waves of hair; her encompassing gaze (often transposed to an unblinking owl) would appear frequently in his work of the later 1940s and early 1950s (p. 413, left). Having met by chance over dinner in May 1943, Picasso and Françoise saw little of each other until the end of the year, when she began making regular visits to his studio to see his current work and show hers to him. After encountering Françoise on one of these occasions in early December, Brassaï recorded his impression of her compelling presence: "Rue des Grands-Augustins—I met Françoise Gilot. . . . I have known her for three years. . . . Very young—seventeen or eighteen years old—passionate about painting, eager for advice, impatient to prove her talent, . . . I was struck by the vitality of this girl, by her tenacity to triumph over obstacles. Her entire personality radiated an impression of freshness and restless vitality."[9] Throughout their years together, Picasso tapped this energy and channeled it to his art.

In April 1944 he made perhaps his first attempts to convey both Françoise's inquiring visage and her fecund body. On the fifteenth, he sketched two bust-length portraits that bear Françoise's features, without resolving to strict likenesses (p. 413, right). That day he also made the second of two paintings (the first is dated April 12) that not only define his conception of her body but map her increasing grasp on his imagination (p. 412). Both paintings depict two women in an interior. One woman, wearing a long-sleeved dark dress, sits in a chair near a corner of the room. Next to her, a naked figure stands before an open window, whose light shines into the space and reflects off the mirror next to the seated woman. The implied comparison between these two figures could not present a greater contrast: one seated, the other standing; one fully covered, the other nude; one in shadow, the other illuminated. In the first painting, the seated woman receives far greater definition than does the standing figure. Positioned as Picasso had frequently portrayed her during the previous seven years, the seated woman is identifiable, despite its stylization, as a portrait of Dora Maar. In the second version, however, her features are reduced beyond recognition. Picasso has shifted the focus of the composition to her counterpart, who now stands as a radiant presence rather than as an amorphous apparition. Her body is voluptuously developed, and her head bares the open features and lush hair of the portraits of Françoise he painted the same day. She has materialized in his art, and she dominates the composition by her statuesque presence and the backdrop of light streaming through the tall window. Even the bright ray reflecting off the armoire leaves Dora in shadow.

Head of a Woman. January 30, 1945. Oil on canvas, 18⅛ × 14⅞″ (46 × 38 cm). Zervos XIV, 63. Private collection

Although Picasso's friendship with Dora would linger for another year or two and Françoise would not officially join his life until April 1946, images of his new interest would punctuate his art from this time forward. Her physique appears regularly in his sketches (May 26 and June 27, 1944) before joining the revelers in the *Bacchanal* that August.[10] Françoise's youthful vitality and mature dedication to art revivified Picasso's spirits as he stepped beyond the oppressive years of the Occupation and sought to create an art that would address the challenges of the postwar world. Her frolicking image at the center of Picasso's revision of Poussin's masterpiece connects past and present through a shared commitment to art as their primary means of expression. In a contemporary self-portrait, Picasso even depicted himself as an adolescent.[11]

Although Picasso did not portray Françoise as an artist until later, her professionalism played an essential role in their relationship from the beginning. Soon after they met, Picasso visited an exhibition of her work (the first, a two-person show with a friend named Geneviève), and she regularly brought her work to his studio so that she could benefit from his advice, as well as advance the growing romance. In late 1944 Françoise began to draw portraits of Picasso that parallel Picasso's ones of her. Executed from memory in her Neuilly studio and without Picasso's knowledge (she did not show them to him until much later), the series stretches into the next year and includes two basic groups: studies of his naked torso and

Woman-Flower (unfinished state). 1946. Oil on canvas, 57½ × 35″ (146 × 89 cm). Not in Zervos. Repainted in 1946. Unique photographic print, courtesy Sidney Janis Gallery, New York

of his head. Most are devoted to the latter; they shift from naturalistic sketches to highly stylized renderings that reduce his features to a pair of deep eyes, a blocky jaw, and a helmetlike cranium. A painting of 1944 is the most abstract (p. 443, center).

Picasso's portraits of Françoise also were not drawn from life; yet the dialogue between artist and subject influenced their form. Françoise was not interested in truly naturalistic images, and, unlike in the cases of Picasso's other wives and mistresses, there are almost none that reproduce her features strictly. Moreover, until the spring of 1946, the couple sought to keep their relationship secret, particularly from Dora, so Françoise's likeness in Picasso's work could have betrayed them. In two paintings, however, Picasso confirmed the disguised subject when he gave them to Françoise; she kept them in her studio until she moved to the rue des Grands-Augustins. Painted on January 30, 1945, this pair of heads records the waved hairstyle she wore in those years, but neither of them bears a likeness of her face (p. 415) nor

the characterization Picasso had developed the previous year. Only her mouth remains in place. No longer dominant, her eyes are shifted to the left side of her face, and her nose is drawn in profile, so that the image may be read as either a frontal or a side view.

Within the context of portraiture, this radical reconfiguration of Françoise's face takes a step beyond Picasso's previous renderings of her; yet it does so by adopting techniques that he had employed for many years. Similarly, one of his first large portraits of Françoise, generally called *Seated Woman* (p. 414), does not differ greatly from his contemporary pictures of other figures. Françoise's staring eyes and ample bosom are evident, but the dynamic of this powerful painting lies elsewhere. Picasso created an image that plays off the figure's static, seated pose to create an effect of great force. By choosing a canvas with proportions that emphasize its verticality and then constructing the image from a low viewpoint that accentuates the figure's height, he contradicted the essential stability of the pose. Instead of a sedentary figure (her chin is planted on her right arm, which in turn is braced on the armchair, while her left arm rests on her hip), Picasso orchestrated a series of Cubist dislocations that turns the body into an assemblage of twisted masses. The modeled, frontal view of Françoise's face is framed between a profile of her cranium (on the right) and a flat, masklike plane that meets her fist (only the schematic rendering of a mouth and an ear, which doubles as a displaced eye, identifies this form as the remainder of her profile). The convolutions are matched by the angular, disjointed thrusts of her arms. These pictures are primarily focused on formal and painterly issues of concern to both artists; they engage the question of portraiture only indirectly.

The point is obvious when *Seated Woman* is compared to Picasso's quintessential portrait of Françoise, *Woman-Flower*, which he painted a little more than a year later (opposite). Standing rather than seated, the figure in *Woman-Flower* rises up an even more vertical canvas, and during this passage the body seems to shed nearly all of its mass as it blossoms into an iconic image of Françoise's face. Although apparently effortless in the final painting, this coupling of a striking stylistic departure with a multivalent portrayal of Françoise is the result of a laborious process that harnessed nearly the full range of Picasso's artistic concerns at the beginning of the postwar epoch.

As is so often the case with his finest portraits, *Woman-Flower* melds Picasso's conception of the individual he is portraying with the personal and aesthetic issues that then drove his art. In this case, domestic arrangements were a catalyst.[12] Finding Picasso's affection toward her increasingly controlling, Françoise had avoided him for much of 1945, although she returned for a memorable visit on her birthday (November 26); on December 2,

Woman-Flower (Françoise). 1946. Oil on canvas, 57½ × 35″ (146 × 89 cm). Zervos XIV, 167. Private collection, courtesy Thomas Ammann Fine Art, Zurich

Picasso drew an idealized portrait of her in a lithograph.[13] Still, Françoise did not accept his pressing invitations to move in with him until the following April, when she settled in the Grands-Augustins studio after Picasso had traveled to her hideaway in the south and finally convinced her to sever her ties with her family in order to join him. Predictably, this conquest stimulated Picasso to produce a cluster of portraits. But the form taken by these pictures frames the union between two other forces: Picasso's dialogue with another artist and his remembrance of his own past work.

The other artist was, of course, Matisse. Heightened by Françoise's respect for him and Matisse's appreciation of her, Picasso began a new phase of their long-running

Head of a Woman (Françoise). 1946. Oil wash, black stone, and charcoal on plywood, 25⅝ × 21¼″ (65 × 54 cm). Not in Zervos. Private collection, courtesy Galerie Jan Krugier, Geneva

friendly competition. As Françoise recounted, she and Picasso paid a visit to Matisse while in the south during the early spring of 1946.[14] Their relationship was still secret, and Picasso introduced her simply as a young artist of interest. With apparent nonchalance, Matisse responded by describing how he would paint her portrait. Picasso reacted as if Matisse had become his rival in love as well as in art; he seemed goaded to possess Françoise more fully through his art and demonstrate his superiority to Matisse in the same act.

If Matisse's attraction to Françoise helped stimulate Picasso to begin *Woman-Flower*, his initial efforts did not engage Matisse's art. *Woman-Flower* started as a composition remarkably different from its final form; in fact, it resembled *Seated Woman* in several ways. Picasso painted a fairly naturalistic image of Françoise sitting

on a wide African chair with her hands resting on its arms. (The original configuration is discernible under later accumulations of pigment.) Having sketched this arrangement, however, Picasso reversed course and chose to depict Françoise standing. This radical reorientation marks Picasso's shift from executing an almost generic composition of a seated woman—a format he had used for decades—to an intricately modulated portrait of Françoise, a portrait not only of the individual but also of her place in his art. Picasso told her, "No, it's just not your style. A realistic portrait wouldn't represent you at all." And he continued, "I don't see you seated. You're not at all the passive type. I only see you standing."[15] In order to convey Françoise's independence, Picasso did far more than simply shift her posture or obscure her features. At first he drew her standing firmly on two feet; yet he soon

Portrait of Françoise. May 20, 1946. Lead pencil, charcoal, and colored pencil on paper, 26 × 20″
(66 × 50.6 cm). Not in Zervos. Musée Picasso, Paris

reduced her legs to a single stem, whose quavering outline, as it modulates up to a tiny waist and on to a wider
torso, suggests both delicacy and assertion.

Thanks to Sidney and Harriet Janis, who visited Picasso
during the spring of 1946, we have a photograph of the
painting in an unfinished, intermediate state (p. 416); it
enables us to follow Picasso's extensive revision of the
figure.[16] The legs and lower torso are already thinned,
although Picasso would overpaint the straight shaft that
then supported her body. (Unfortunately, in the photograph the floor is cropped off so that the bottom of the
painting is not visible.) The very substantial differences in
the upper body demonstrate Picasso's desire not only to
depict Françoise standing but to impart an impression of
lift and bounce to the entire figure. As the photograph
records, Picasso significantly altered the balance of

Françoise's body, beginning with the placement of her
arms. He detached her right arm from her shoulder and
connected it below her bosom; for balance, he narrowed
her left arm and retained only a segment of the previous
outline that had swelled from her breast. Picasso said that
he wanted to lighten the figure; the left arm had been
"too heavy" and the right misdirected: "A falling form is
never beautiful. Besides, it isn't in harmony with the
rhythm of your nature. I need to find something that stays
up in the air." As Françoise remarked, "I noticed often at
that period that his pictorial decisions were made half
for plastic reasons, half for symbolic ones."[17] Continuing
his motif, Picasso reshaped her breasts and pointed the
nipples in opposite directions, as if they were independent
orbs bobbing in space. The most startling transformation,
however, is the rendering of Françoise's head. Picasso

Portrait of Françoise Gilot by Endre Rozsda. Paris, January 1943. Private collection

Portrait of Françoise. 1946. Pencil and collage on paper, 15⅜ × 11¾″ (39 × 30 cm). Not in Zervos. Private collection

expunged her shoulders and thinned her neck to the point that her head seems in danger of toppling; its equilibrium depends on the twisting fronds that have replaced her full head of hair.

As Picasso resolved his conception of Françoise, he reintroduced Matisse into the conversation. His rival had been quite precise about how he would portray her. He would paint her hair olive green and her face light blue, and he would be sure to emphasize both the circumflex-like arch of her eyebrows and the way they seem to meet her nose at the forehead. During the visit, Picasso had deflected Matisse's intense concentration on Françoise by suggesting that his friend would choose these colors only to match the Oriental carpet he would no doubt include in the painting, thereby implying that Matisse's art was essentially decorative. In his own portrait, Picasso created an image that is firmly opposed to the luxurious settings found in many of Matisse's paintings. (Its only decorative element is the strip of red flooring, which Matisse apparently suggested, barely visible at the bottom of the composition.[18]) Picasso took possession of Matisse's Françoise by placing her in a radically reduced composition and making explicit the analogies Matisse may have implied by his choice of colors. The green hair becomes the broad leaves of a plant, her slim body and oval head like the stalk and bloom of a sunflower. Yet the flower's radiance

has been transferred to the background; her blue tonality injects a lunar coolness that counterpoints the burgeoning metaphor of the "woman-flower." In fleeing one form of Matisse's art, however, Picasso may have embraced another. Speaking of Matisse's method of drawing, Picasso had told Brassaï, "Matisse makes a drawing, then he recopies it. . . . He recopies it five times, ten times, always purifying its features. He is persuaded that the last, the most stripped down, is the best, the purest, the definitive."[19] (It is probably not fortuitous that Picasso hung Matisse's highly simplified portrait of his daughter Marguerite, which Françoise greatly admired, in his studio during this time.[20])

The path to *Woman-Flower*'s extremely reductive image lies not only through Matisse's past art but also his most recent innovation. Matisse's adoption of scissors and painted paper as his primary medium—he called it "drawing with scissors"—provided a revolutionary outlet for this aspect of his art. Françoise recorded that Matisse was sitting in bed cutting forms from sheets of prepared paper when she and Picasso visited; not surprisingly, Picasso jumped on the idea. Although descended from collage and *papiers collés*, which Picasso and Braque had invented before World War I, Matisse's technique differed significantly from theirs. Picasso's cutouts are generally flat silhouettes and are rarely shaped to mimic more than a fraction of the contours of the objects they represent; sometimes, only their placement in the composition defines their identity. Matisse, on the other hand, not only maintained the shape of his subjects, but trimmed, or "carved," their contours to imply volume as well.[21] Picasso used Matisse's variation on the technique of *papiers collés* to define the honed shape of Françoise's face. Painting a sheet of paper blue, he cut out a series of variations and then pinned one after the other to the canvas. Having found an acceptable model, he then copied it into the painting, leaving no evidence of his procedure.

A contemporary exchange reminds us that Françoise was not the passive subject of a dialogue between Picasso and Matisse. Playfully exploring the possibilities of Matisse's new technique, she and Picasso made cutouts the focus of a series of drawings: he cut and pasted blue ovoids onto a sheet before drawing her features; she then cut a hole in another sheet, pasted the cutout behind, and drew her self-portrait on top (p. 443, right). In another image of Françoise, Picasso found a different way to schematize her: a tracery of overlapping lines resolve her face and hair while absorbing them in a fluid web (p. 418).

If *Woman-Flower* is a remarkable testament to Picasso's ability to meet the challenge he perceived in Matisse's words, its success rests equally on the store of his own images that he had amassed in previous decades. Picasso's metamorphosis of Françoise's "green hair" into leaves and his elaboration of this motif into a symbolic personification of his lover as a flowering reed go back nearly fifteen years to images he had created of Marie-Thérèse. His first characterization of Françoise in the *Bacchanal* and preceding studies recalled the fluid anatomies of his images of Marie-Thérèse cavorting on the beach in the late 1920s. In *Woman-Flower*, he shifted his attention from the grand series of the early 1930s, in which his reduction of Marie-Thérèse's pliant flesh to rounded pods is frequently paired with foliage that seems to sprout from her body (p. 361). Picasso's linkage of these two young and beautiful women is not surprising; yet *Woman-Flower* is not merely a recapitulation of past conceits. In the portraits of Marie-Thérèse, Picasso generally insinuated a fruitlike metaphor from his mistress's dreamy, mental abandon and luxuriant, supine posture. In *Woman-Flower*, he created an image that is at once a seamless union of the two realms and an icon of riveting human intelligence. No longer merely juxtaposed to the figure or vaguely intertwined with it, leaves now sprout directly from Françoise's head, thereby minting an integrated

The Rape of Europa (unfinished state). 1946. Oil on canvas, 76⅞ × 51¼″ (195 × 130 cm). Not in Zervos. Painted over in 1946. Unique photographic print, courtesy Sidney Janis Gallery, New York

Woman with Knife and Bull's Head. June 6–19, 1946. Oil on wood, 51¼ × 38¼″ (130 × 97 cm). Not in Zervos. Private collection

Faun and Centaur. August 24, 1946. Ink on paper, 19¾ × 25¾" (50 × 65 cm). Zervos XIV, 220. Private collection

Fauns and Nude Woman. August 26, 1946. Ink on paper, 19¾ × 25¾" (50 × 65 cm). Zervos XIV, 225. Private collection

symbolic form, whose believability is abetted by the taut armature that embraces both nearly abstract signs and naturalistic passages. Françoise's erect stance and piercing, hieratic stare convey a beaconlike rationality rather than a descent to a more primeval state, however desirable may be the liberation the latter implies. So when Picasso told Françoise, "You're like a growing plant. . . . I've never felt impelled to portray anyone else this way,"²² he was flattering her by overlooking his past and not entirely telling a lie: his portrayals of Marie-Thérèse generally suggest a luxuriant fruit more than a striving blossom.

Woman-Flower not only became Picasso's "signature" portrait of Françoise; it also initiated a reengagement with allegory that would inflect many of his following images of her and permeate his more public works as well. A little more than a month after finishing the portrait, Picasso included it in an exhibition of his work held at the Louis Carré gallery in Paris during June and July of 1946. The cover of the catalogue bore a likeness of Françoise, and the exhibition showcased his portraits of her; the prominence and frequency of her image among the pictures on view made the couple's relationship official, much as had his placement of a portrait of Olga on the cover of the catalogue of his first exhibition with Paul Rosenberg in 1919. In the weeks following the completion of *Woman-Flower*, his productivity continued unabated; yet his obsession with his new partner transformed Françoise into increasingly hostile personages.

Opposite *Woman-Flower* in Carré's main gallery hung a painting Picasso had finished on June 6, eight days before the exhibition opened—*The Rape of Europa* (p. 421; a month and a day separate the dates of completion of the two pictures). Although unusual in these years, Picasso's choice of a mythological subject continues the

engagement with classicism he had revisited two years earlier, in 1944, and advances the dialogue with preceding art that would grow to dominate his last decades. Yet as its placement in the Carré display suggests, this image is not simply a modern variation on an ancient theme: it appropriates a traditional subject to develop Picasso's conception of Françoise. He admitted as much in a conversation with Matisse during December 1947. Discussing the topic of portraiture, Picasso queried Matisse about why he had chosen a kneeling posture for Françoise in a cutout portrait he had made of her: "Do you associate her in your mind with a posture of devotion? Or with praying, perhaps? I can tell you she is just the opposite, quite a rebellious character, without consideration or respect—a nihilist! I can imagine her only standing erect or proudly riding a horse." Matisse then retorted, "Nevertheless, there is a reclining nude in the Museum of

Dance on the Beach. 1946. Graphite and watercolor on paper, 19⅞ × 25½" (50.5 × 65 cm). Not in Zervos. Private collection, France

Joy of Life. 1946. Oil on board, 47¼ × 98½″ (120 × 250 cm). Zervos XIV, 289. Musée Picasso, Château Grimaldi, Antibes

Antibes who seems to be taken from—." Picasso interrupted, "No, no, that painting originated from an old habit of painting reclining nudes. The one I did in the spring of 1946 with Europa riding Zeus in the shape of a bull is much more to the point."[23]

Indeed, the title of this painting is misleading, because "Europa" is not being raped. Sitting on top of the bull, she is the dominant one, who subdues the beast by holding both his tail and a horn. Now a monumental figure, whose imposing proportions contradict the much slighter *Woman-Flower*, Europa nonetheless exhibits the buxom torso and schematic, rectilinear physiognomy that Picasso derived from Françoise's features.[24] In formulating this characterization, Picasso probably once again returned to those deeply conflicted years of the late 1920s and early 1930s, in this instance to the elemental settings and aggressive angularity of his "bone" figures, such as *Seated Bather* (1930; p. 64), a picture he said derived from Olga. The dialogue became even more intense in the painting *Woman with Knife and Bull's Head* (p. 421), which he began the day after completing *Europa*. Repeating Europa's pose, Picasso reduced the bull to little more than a head (in the woman's left hand) and added a butcher knife (in her right). Instead of the *Seated Bather*'s jagged mandibles, Picasso armed this woman with a modern version of the sword Judith used to cut off Holofernes's head: Surrealist metamorphosis is wedded to historical precedent, much as Picasso had done in *Woman with Stiletto (Death of Marat)* (p. 330). The references to those years multiply further when one realizes that the figure in *Woman with Knife* does not grasp the head of a bull, but rather that of a minotaur (distin-guished by its snoutless, human face).[25] If Picasso considered *The Rape of Europa* an emblem of Françoise's "rebellious character," then the bull she rides presumably personifies himself, as does the trophy minotaur.

These abundant evocations of Picasso's bitter conflicts with Olga and his blissful idylls with Marie-Thérèse conflate to help shape his conception of Françoise in the first years of their relationship. The image of Dora does not seem to reappear after the *Interiors* of 1944, even though she was both Françoise's immediate predecessor and the primary precedent in his life for an affair with an artist. Perhaps, Picasso was too eager to renew his art through Françoise to allow Dora to remain and cloud the present with memories of the war years. Unlike Olga, who, as his legal wife, could not be entirely dismissed after he lost interest in her, Dora was apparently more easily put aside. Only in the early 1950s, toward the end of his relationship with Françoise, do references to Dora return. Nor are there allusions to the contemporary Olga or Marie-Thérèse.

Picasso built his conception of Françoise in part on a remembered contrast between an Olga-like will and a Marie-Thérèse–like fecundity. Similar to his subtle variations on his transformations of Marie-Thérèse, however, Picasso far from duplicated the harpy image Olga had inspired. It was Françoise's independence, not her dependence, that troubled him and drove him to stage battles in his art, as well as in his life with her. Moreover, Picasso's decision to portray Françoise in classical guises stems from both her interests and a shift of locale. Françoise had received a traditional French education, which she frequently drew upon to explore arcane myths with

Picasso. His return to the Côte d'Azur (after being denied access to the area during the war) helped precipitate a classical revival in his art that drew him increasingly into a dialogue with earlier masters. It also stimulated him to take up ceramics. He rapidly transformed this ancient medium and, in the process, used it during the late 1940s and early 1950s to make many portraits of Françoise and their children.[26]

Through the remainder of 1946, Picasso elaborated the imagined and real confrontations between himself and Françoise, but, increasingly, their personal relationship became absorbed into larger themes. In August he made a series of drawings that show a pitched battle between a faun and a centaur (p. 422, top left) and end with the faun standing in mourning over his foe.[27] Yet Picasso immediately proposed an alternative: the series resumes with the centaur's resurrection, now as a beautiful woman, whose dance is joined by the joyous faun (p. 422, top right). The woman bears Françoise's features, and Françoise's birth sign of Sagittarius links her with the centaur as well.[28] Apparently, Picasso composed a fantasy to fulfill his desire for Françoise to submit to his authority and then topped it off with a scene of the idyllic life that would follow. Meanwhile, she made a sketch of Picasso pushing a piece of fruit into her mouth, which she called *Adam Forcing Eve to Eat an Apple*.[29]

Characteristically, Picasso did not keep these games private. He used the final, celebratory drawing as the basis for a watercolor, *Dance on the Beach* (p. 422, bottom), and he appropriated its female dancer for the central figure in the *Joy of Life* (p. 423). Both of these works were painted in the Grimaldi castle. *The Joy of Life* was given to

Picasso and Françoise Gilot in the garden at La Galloise, Vallauris, summer 1948. Photograph by Robert Capa. Musée Picasso, Paris, Picasso Archives

the museum at Antibes. Matisse was quite right to perceive Françoise's reclining figure in another of these paintings (presumably the *Nymph*);[30] yet the distinction made by Picasso is accurate: they are no longer primarily concerned with portraiture. The pictures echo the theme of the *Bacchanal* and stem from a long tradition of pastoral subjects. They address public audiences concerned with other issues and not privy to Picasso's personal life.

Although he would continue to portray Françoise in many guises—as a kind of fortress, as a puzzle of brilliant hues in *Bust of Françoise* (opposite), and as an almost waiflike sculptural apparition in *Head of a Woman* (p. 426)—the obsession with portraiture that had driven his art since late April of 1946 was subsiding. During that summer, Picasso's art took a turn away from easel pictures, a shift that would guide his painting into the early 1950s. In part this reorientation occurred because the curator of the museum at Antibes offered him rooms in the Grimaldi castle as a studio and encouraged him to donate the work he made there for display in the museum. In many ways, however, this circumstance was merely the catalyst that prompted Picasso to fulfill a growing desire to create art that primarily engaged, by means of mural painting, a larger audience. Matisse's increasing involvement in large decorative projects, which would culminate in the Vence chapel (completed in 1951), no doubt stimulated his competitive spirit and found a response in Picasso's version of the *Joy of Life*, Matisse's old subject. Indeed, Picasso's *Joy of Life* became the centerpiece of his installation at the Antibes museum. Besides creating works for this museum, Picasso would soon donate an important group of his recent paintings to the Musée d'Art Moderne in Paris (in 1947), following the museum's acquisition of major works by Matisse and Braque in 1945 and 1946. Despite a continuing reluctance to purchase works, the French museums, which had neglected Picasso and his peers until the end of World War II, accorded them increasing respect. Such respect not only fed Picasso's self-esteem and sense of competition with his contemporaries but also drew him into a more intensive dialogue with past masters. Jean Cassou's offer to display the paintings Picasso had donated next to specified works in the Louvre (Picasso selected Zurbarán, Delacroix, and Courbet), particularly galvanized the artist's interest.[31] Moreover, acclaim by France's cultural establishment was paired with equal prominence, if not equal commendation, within the Communist Party, both in France and abroad.

In advance of a Party Congress in March 1945, Picasso had drawn several portraits of Maurice Thorez, the general secretary of the French Communist Party (p. 428). Although Picasso's choice to depict Thorez at this moment confirms his adherence to the Party, Picasso's delicate, almost effete, rendering of the minister seems far from engaged in any political program. In February

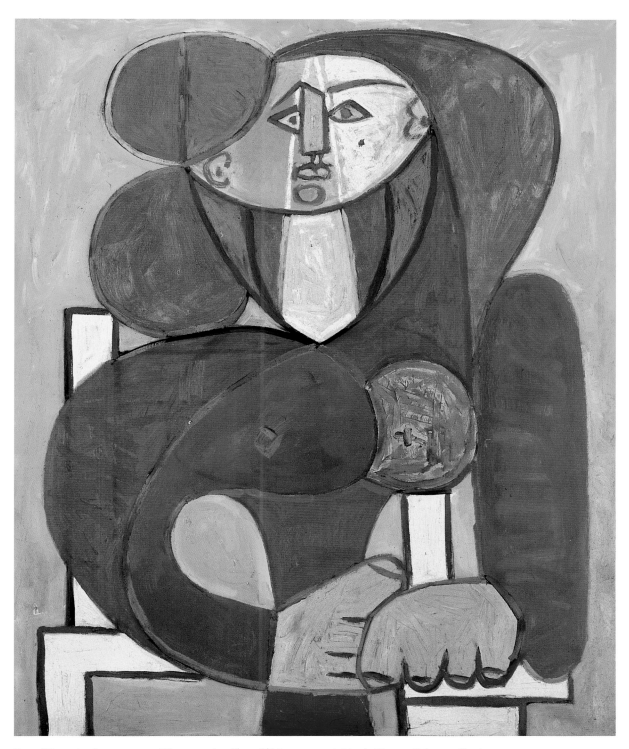

Bust of Françoise. June 17, 1946. Oil on wood, 39⅜ × 31½″ (100 × 80 cm). Not in Zervos. Private collection

and March of 1946, Picasso had participated in the exhibition *Art and Resistance* by including the recently completed *Charnel House* and possibly the *Monument to the Spanish Dead*.[32] The latter painting, which Picasso inscribed January 31, 1947, conveys little of the horror and anguish so powerfully captured in *The Charnel House*. Its almost burlesque assembly of standard motifs—a bust,

banner, bugle, and skull, among others—totters between slipping into a traditional mold and parodying the convention. Despite his presumably authentic desire to commemorate the Spaniards who died defending France against the Nazis, Picasso apparently could, in this case, neither create a new form of monument (as he had in *Guernica*) nor accept an old one. This diffidence would

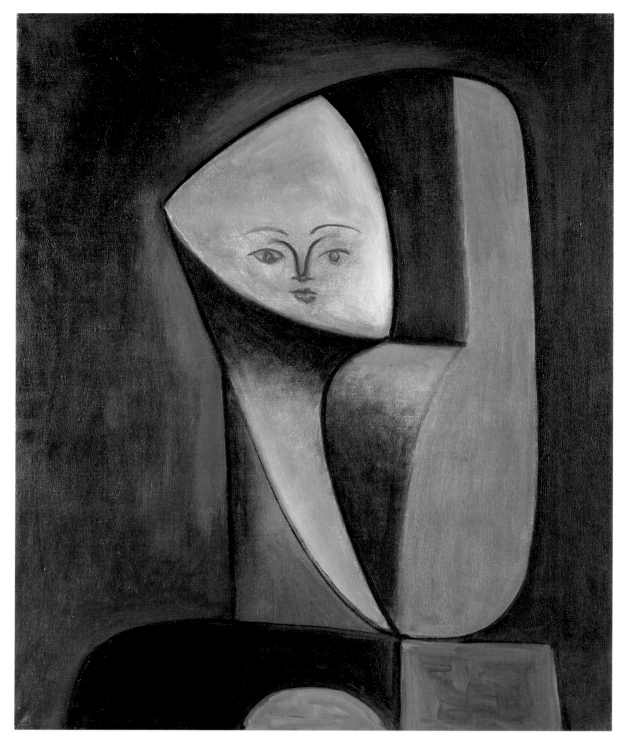

Head of a Woman (Françoise). December 30, 1946. Oil on canvas, 36¼ × 28¾″ (92 × 73 cm). Zervos XIV, 284. Private collection

characterize most of his political works of the following few years, even though he devoted many hours to attending Party conferences (Warsaw in 1948, Sheffield in 1950) and received the Lenin Peace Prize in 1950 for his efforts.

More than any other picture, *Massacre in Korea* (p. 428) epitomizes Picasso's awkward involvement in world politics during the decade after World War II. Both Pierre

Daix, who participated in many of Picasso's political activities, and Françoise, who did not, have described the artist's pained and confused response to the lukewarm reception of this painting, a picture in which he attempted to create an image that would galvanize opposition to the United States military involvement in the Korean War.[33] (I doubt that future historians will judge it any more

Studies for Head of a Woman (Françoise). January 1, 1947. Lead pencil on paper, 12⅞ × 19¾″ (32.5 × 50 cm). Zervos XV, 24. Private collection

effective as a political statement or as a work of art.) In accommodating himself halfway to the Party's demands for realistic images that could inspire diverse audiences, Picasso blunted the expressive power of his art. But even if he had not compromised aesthetically, it is unlikely the picture would have been convincing; notwithstanding the savagery of the conflict, Korea was probably too alien to focus his creativity. Picasso's sources of inspiration were direct, immediate, and generally closer to home.

Despite some efforts to cooperate with the Party's political program, Picasso ridiculed its aesthetic directives. He instantly flouted its repudiation of abstraction (in many of his finest works of the period, such as *The Kitchen*, 1948),[34] but, most significantly, engaged himself almost totally with themes outside its program, subjects which a Stalinist would probably call "decadent": intimate examinations of his family, and reflections on his place in the history of art. Picasso had joined the Party primarily in solidarity with his friends and as an expression of support for the Resistance organization that seemed to symbolize both opposition to Fascism and hope for social renewal at the end of the war, not because he shared its specific ideology. In February 1950 he contradicted the Party's emphasis on Courbet as a critic of bourgeois soci-

ety by painting a variation on *Women on the Banks of the Seine* that submerges social content in inventive stylistic initiatives, and a variation on a portrait of a painter by El Greco, through which Picasso links himself to an elite artistic tradition.[35] But perhaps the most blatant demonstration of Picasso's fundamental differences with the Party is his continuing participation in the capitalistic art market at a time when he was wealthy enough to withdraw from it.

Partly due to Picasso's cooperation with the Party, the market for his art remained sluggish until the mid-1950s, and this period of relative commercial inactivity had a significant impact on the public's access to his work.[36] Despite several retrospectives in museums or public halls during the late 1940s and early 1950s,[37] Picasso's recent paintings were not widely exhibited or readily available for sale because the steady stream of exhibitions in galleries that had served to showcase his new work since 1919 (except for a wartime halt) dwindled during the early postwar years. In Paris, Louis Carré held two major Picasso exhibitions in the mid-1940s, and in New York Samuel Kootz held two small ones, but Picasso did not develop lasting ties to either of these dealers, nor did he revive his prewar relationship with Paul Rosenberg.[38]

Portrait of Maurice Thorez. May 23, 1945. Lead pencil on paper. Zervos XIV, 112. Private collection

Even after Picasso concluded an agreement with Daniel-Henry Kahnweiler for the Galerie Louise Leiris to become his exclusive agent in 1947, the gallery did not hold an exhibition of his paintings until May of 1953. This limited exposure in commercial galleries reflects the fact that Picasso sold a relatively small number of paintings during the decade following the war. Instead, he accumulated a cache of pictures that is only now coming to light.

These many canvases that depict Picasso's family—Françoise and their children, Claude and Paloma—constitute a sanctuary from the conflicts that roiled Picasso's public life during the late 1940s and early 1950s. After the enthrallment of the spring and summer of 1946, Picasso's portraits of Françoise are more detached. Many subordinate his perceptions of her character to the role she continued to play as an intermediary between himself and Matisse. During their frequent stays in the south, Picasso and Françoise regularly visited Matisse in his villa at Vence or Nice-Cimiez, and as Françoise's long-standing admiration for Matisse developed into a warm friendship, including exchanges of letters and drawings, she employed the esteem in which both masters held her to ease the sometimes prickly relations between them. In one series, which he painted in March of 1949, Picasso returned to the challenge of Matisse's cut papers that he had explored in *Woman-Flower*. Instead of scissoring paper to stand for

Massacre in Korea. January 18, 1951. Oil on plywood, 43⅜ × 82⅝″ (110 × 210 cm). Zervos XV, 173. Musée Picasso, Paris

Woman in an Armchair (Françoise). 1949. Oil on canvas, 45⅝ × 35⅛″ (116 × 89 cm). Zervos XV, 128. Private collection

Françoise's head, he took a lithograph he had recently modeled on her face and copied it onto the canvas, while preserving its black-and-white palette, Cubist architecture, and the sharp edges of its sheet to stand in contrast to the fluid surrounding figure (above). Besides a possible reference to Matisse in this collage effect, Picasso rendered Françoise's body as a puzzlelike pattern of curvilinear sections, whose bright hues of red, yellow, blue, and pink as well as their unmodeled flatness evoke both Matisse's cutouts and the structure of his last paintings. In a contemporaneous portrait of her (p. 408), Picasso recast her head in the calligraphic style of his recent illustrations of Gongora's *Vingt Poèmes*.[39]

With the birth of Claude on May 15, 1947 (followed by

the birth of Paloma on April 19, 1949), Picasso's portraits are increasingly devoted to his children with Françoise. Unlike the earlier pictures of his first son, Paulo (born in 1921), which generally present the youngster in a formal pose and fancy dress, and the more uninhibited portraits of Maya (born in 1935), the images of Claude and Paloma reflect Picasso's joyful immersion in their world, and a liberation from adult expectations. Even in his portrait of Claude wearing a costume brought back from a Party conference in Poland, the composition has a spontaneous feel, due to Claude's position next to an open door (as if he has just toddled into a room) and the costume's dominance of all except Claude's head and multicolored ball (right). As if seated on the floor, we meet Claude's gaze and join his ramble through the house. This viewpoint, the child's rather than the adult's, was one of Picasso's primary strategies to lend his subjects a stature not normally accorded children and simultaneously to draw us into the youngster's mind; he used it regularly in his portraits of Claude as well as of Paloma. In *Claude Drawing* (p. 434), the son looks directly at us and seems to assume his father's role as portraitist, even though Picasso, of course, controlled the image. Picasso frequently used Claude's love of drawing (below) to link father and son in these portraits; in tandem, his portraits of Paloma regularly associate her with Françoise.

Having brought us into sympathy with the child's universe, Picasso then immerses us in their world by inverting an old canard against modern art. He took the conventional dismissal of non-naturalistic styles as

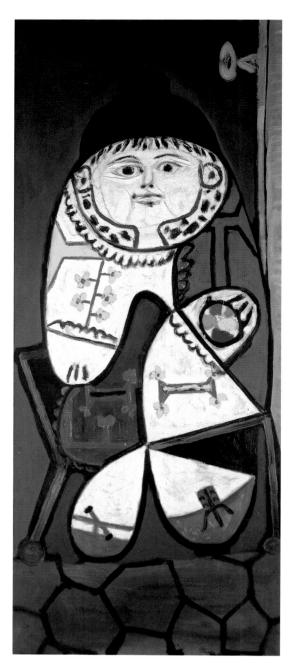

Claude in a Polish Costume. 1948. Oil on canvas, 46⅞ × 19¾″ (119 × 50 cm). Zervos XV, 101. Private collection

Picasso with Paloma, and Claude looking at his portrait of Picasso, at La Galloise, Vallauris, possibly Christmas 1953. Photograph by Edward Quinn

"something a child could do" and employed it to project the perceptions of a youngster not yet adjusted to his or her own body, or certain of how to navigate the outside world. In *Paloma with an Orange* (p. 432), her disarticulated arms and scrambled features are not simply Cubist riffs (as they primarily are in the 1944 portrait of Françoise, *Seated Woman*); here they convey the bumbling, uncoordinated gestures of a two-year-old. In paintings such as *Claude and Paloma at Play* (opposite), Picasso not only distinguished each child's demeanor (Claude watchful versus Paloma oblivious) but also makes us a part of an environment shaped by their sensibilities: everything from floor

Claude and Paloma at Play. 1950. Oil and enamel on plywood. 46½ × 57⅛″ (118 × 145 cm). Zervos XV, 163. Private collection

tiles to drapes wobbles and swirls with their rambunctious games. Photographs record Picasso's own participation in the communal drawings (p. 442); however, Picasso rarely chose to portray himself with the children.[40]

In contrast to these images of Claude and Paloma, Picasso's portraits of Françoise with the children are generally more sober. A few are dazzling simplifications. In *Françoise Gilot with Paloma and Claude* (p. 437), each figure is reduced to a flat, white silhouette that floats on a block of red, blue, or yellow. Yet each person is identifiable and distinguished by a characteristic activity (Françoise reclining on a couch, Paloma tending a train, and Claude driving a car). This bold, formal solution suggests not only Matisse's cutout technique but also his early images of his own family.[41] If the asymmetry of Françoise's eyes

leaves the impression that she may be less at ease than are her children, she is rarely portrayed as playing with the kids. Most of the images showing the three together present Françoise engaged in reading or drawing, while the children amuse themselves with toys. Lying on a couch or seated at a table, she is physically close to them, yet intellectually detached and elevated above their arena of the floor.

By 1950 Picasso and Françoise were drifting apart. He continued to devote much of his spare time to Party politics. (He had been attending a peace conference in Paris the day Paloma was born.) After Paloma's birth, Françoise became increasingly preoccupied with two activities in which Picasso took a small role: raising their children and developing her own art. She refused Picasso's urging for

Paloma with an Orange. 1951. Enamel on plywood, 42½ × 35⅛ (108 × 89 cm). Zervos XV, 175. Private collection

Paloma with a Doll. December 23, 1952–January 3, 1953. India ink on paper, 26 × 19⅞″ (66 × 50.5 cm). Not in Zervos. Private collection

a third child (her decision may have prompted him to make two sculptures of a pregnant woman in 1949–50).[42] Instead, she returned to painting after a hiatus of several years. Picasso's portraits of her reflect this change, a growing separation that would lead her to end the relationship in September 1953.

During these last years, Picasso's portraits present a characterization of Françoise radically different from the one that had introduced her in his art. Instead of being associated with Marie-Thérèse's voluptuous form or Olga's rigid mentality, Françoise—still only twenty-eight years old—now took on features that Picasso had previously used to depict her predecessor, Dora. In a drawing of August 23, 1950, the Weeping Woman reappears as a

Claude Drawing. 1951. Oil on canvas, 18⅛ × 15″ (46 × 38 cm). Not in Zervos. Private collection

portrait of Françoise (p. 438, top). Adopting a characteristic pose (in profile with hair streaming down her back), Picasso conflated a schema he had often used to portray Dora with a portrait of Françoise; inside the contours of the profile, he inscribed a frontal likeness of the younger woman, so that the image is subject to a dual reading.

Françoise's large eyes, long nose, and full mouth are heavily outlined and shaded; even though she is dry-eyed, the rendering evokes the incision-like tracts of the Weeping Woman's tears (not all of which show signs of crying). By the following March, she seems to have become more wan, at least as depicted in Picasso's portraits (p. 439). As

Paloma in Blue. 1952. Oil on plywood, 31⅞ × 25⅝″ (81 × 65 cm). Zervos XV, 202. Private collection

Françoise continued to refuse to bear another child and increasingly matched Picasso's devotion to his affairs with her own concentration on her art and the children, he aged her substantially. But these images do not merely return to the portraits of Dora. Instead of writhing in anguish, Françoise stands impassive, independent. Even

in *Head of Françoise* (p. 438), in which Picasso carved her features with heavy, black lines and swelled her tear ducts to bursting, nothing flows; her lips remain firmly closed, and the network of lines resolves into a benign pattern.

In other portraits, Picasso paired Paloma with her mother, mirroring the match of himself with Claude.

Paloma at Three Years Old. 1952. Oil on canvas, 16⅛ × 13″ (41 × 33 cm). Zervos XV, 209. Private collection

He made a whimsical sculpture of Françoise carrying Paloma on her shoulders that seems almost to merge the two into a single figure (p. 444). And he painted a portrait of Paloma (above) that is a pendant to *Head of Françoise*. Yet here the mood is nearly serene because the mesh of lines is less dense, the segments less overlapped, and the colors brighter. At the end of 1952, Picasso returned to this motif in a drawing that is devoid of color but is a masterpiece of graphic display (p. 433). With a variety of touches rarely seen since van Gogh's reed drawings, Picasso covered most of the sheet with a fluctuating array of dots, dashes, and strokes that densely model Paloma's eyes, nose, mouth, chin, and cheeks before diffusing to suggest a shadowy background and to outline lightly the doll she grasps with her tiny hands. Earlier in December, he had portrayed her in much the same pose, but in a

style of monumental volumes rather than flat patterns (p. 435).

As in 1946, when Picasso's portraits of Françoise spilled over into his paintings for the Antibes museum, in 1952–53 his portraits of Claude and Paloma infused his public murals, *War* and *Peace* (p. 445). Claude was the model for the classical soldier who stands guard against an assortment of fantastic creatures intended to symbolize the threat of germ weaponry in *War*. In *Peace*, both children and their mother populate the Matissean idyll of arcadian pleasure Picasso imagined as an alternative to the dangers of modern technology. Claude is particularly apparent, as a child who drives the winged horse and as a child who balances in midair.[43]

In 1953 both Picasso's private and public worlds exploded. To comply with Louis Aragon's request for a

Françoise Gilot with Paloma and Claude. 1951. Enamel on plywood, 44⅞ × 57½″ (114 × 146 cm). Zervos XV, 191. Private collection

Picasso and Françoise Gilot with their children, Claude and Paloma, in the garden at La Galloise, Vallauris, 1953. Photograph by Edward Quinn. Musée Picasso, Paris, Picasso Archives

Portrait of a Woman (Françoise). August 23, 1950. Pencil on paper, 25⅞ × 19⅞″ (65.5 × 50.5 cm). Not in Zervos. Collection Marina Picasso, courtesy Galerie Jan Krugier, Geneva

Head of Françoise. 1952. Oil on canvas, 18⅛ × 15″ (46 × 38 cm). Zervos XV, 206. Private collection

portrait of Stalin, who had died on March 5, Picasso drew a simplified image based on a photograph of Stalin as a young man (p. 445). When Aragon published the sketch in *Les Lettres françaises,* a scandal erupted among French Communists. Apparently, many believed the portrait was disrespectful because it did not depict the Soviet leader in glory or illustrate the details of his aged features; the French Communist Party officially condemned it. Relations between the artist and the Party were never fully restored, and three years later Picasso welcomed the display of his art by Hungarians revolting against Soviet rule.[44] At the end of the Stalin controversy, Françoise left for Paris with the children. Her decision was the culmination of two years during which they had drifted apart and Picasso had conducted several affairs, most prominently with Geneviève Laporte. Although the family was reunited in Vallauris during the summer, Françoise's departure in March marked the end of their relationship and the renewal of her professional activities, first as a painter and later as a writer as well.[45] During a visit the following May, Picasso painted several portraits of the children alone or with their mother (in each, Claude's engagement in drawing is the primary activity), but these are postscripts.

The portraits he painted in December 1953 reflect Picasso's meditation on his isolation, and his expectation that there would be no reconciliation: a black figure, a stand-in for the artist, paints while Paloma plays behind him (p. 441, left), or he appears as a shadow cast over a voluptuous nude, evoking Françoise, who reclines in his bedroom (p. 441, right). Yet, the most haunting image is a drawing, which, according to Picasso's inscription, links the last day of 1953 with the first day of 1954 (p. 442, top). On December 31, when the children had returned to Vallauris for the holidays but Françoise remained elsewhere, Picasso began to sketch a tender scene of Claude and Paloma handing a bouquet of flowers to their mother, who sits with a pet boxer on her lap. Presumably, as the drawing developed into the next day, he added the profile of himself that looms in the background and the pair of arms that reach around his children's shoulders and support a vase for the flowers. This may also have been the moment when he reworked Claude's head so heavily that the paper tore, and he heightened Françoise's features. Picasso's inclusion of himself in a family portrait is extremely rare, yet his presence affirms his separation from them. His profile is out of proportion to the others, too large to join the group, and his large black eye is not directed toward the children, despite his embrace.[46] Since the mid-1920s, Picasso had used a profile silhouette to represent himself, frequently in the context of domestic scenes. In 1944 he had celebrated the beginning of his affair with Françoise and the end of the war by filling out this shell to portray himself as a youth. Now, the profile

Woman Drawing (Françoise). March 13, 1951. Oil on plywood, 45⅝ × 35″ (116 × 89 cm). Zervos XV, 178. Private collection

Seated Nude (Françoise). 1953. Oil on canvas, 51¼ × 37¾″ (130.2 × 95.9 cm). Zervos XV, 292. The St. Louis Art Museum. Gift of Joseph Pulitzer, Jr.

In Front of the Garden. December 28, 1953. Oil on wood panel, 51¼ × 38¼ (130 × 97 cm). Zervos XVI, 97. Private collection

The Shadow. December 29, 1953. Oil and charcoal on canvas, 51 × 38″ (129.5 × 96.5 cm). Zervos XVI, 100. Musée Picasso, Paris

bears the features of a far older, bald man—Picasso at the age of seventy-four.

By the end of 1953, Picasso's hopes for humanity that had welled up with the end of the war had largely collapsed; they were preserved only in utopian compositions, such as *Peace*. The ambassadorial role Picasso had accepted, if grudgingly, with the liberation of Paris had been turned into a farce by partisan politics. His personal life was shattered, and the market for his art still appeared hobbled by his political affiliation. In the remaining nineteen years of his life, Picasso would never return to the

social activity he had engaged in during the previous nine, despite the overwhelming acclaim for his art that would soon expand at a seemingly exponential rate. Instead of attempting to reestablish his public role by engaging political issues or rebuilding his private life with a new family, Picasso would withdraw to his studio with a new companion and increasingly turn his attention to the past of his own art and that of art history. As Picasso said following Matisse's death in November 1954, his old rival had left him a "legacy" he had to pursue.[47]

Family of the Artist. December 31, 1953–January 1, 1954.
Ink on paper, 12¾ × 19⅞″ (32.5 × 50.5 cm). Not in
Zervos. Private collection

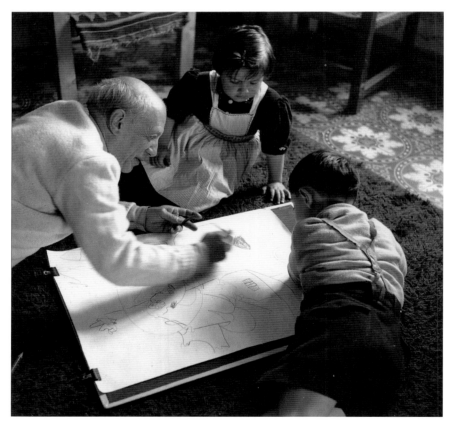

Picasso drawing with Claude and Paloma, at La Galloise, Vallauris, possibly Christmas 1953.
Photograph by Edward Quinn

NOTES

I would especially like to thank Claude Ruiz-Picasso and Françoise Gilot for their generous cooperation in preparing this essay. During several meetings in the fall of 1994, Claude contributed significantly to the process of developing the basic themes of my research, he gave me access to the archives of his mother's art, and he enhanced my understanding of the work of both of his parents. In two interviews, conducted in December 1994 and in June 1995, Françoise was most helpful, by offering extremely precise recollections and candid discussions of the period.

1. Brassaï, *Conversations avec Picasso* (Paris: Editions Gallimard, 1964), pp. 161–62.

2. Ibid., p. 52.

3. The most recent accounts of this period are Werner Spies, *Picasso: Die Zeit nach Guernica 1937–1973* (Berlin: Nationalgalerie Staatliche Museen, 1992), and Frances Morris, ed., *Paris Post War: Art and Existentialism 1945–1955* (London: The Tate Gallery, 1993).

4. Brassaï, *Conversations*, p. 182.

5. Picasso's increasing involvement in politics was highlighted by his participation in the 1944 Salon d'Automne. Dubbed the "Liberation Salon," it marked the first time Picasso had participated in a French salon. The organizers devoted a special section to seventy-four of his paintings and five of his sculptures; protests, sometimes violent, resulted. Picasso had announced his allegiance to the French Communist Party in anticipation of the exhibition's opening on October 6.

6. *Picasso: 75th Anniversary Exhibition*, May 22–September 8, 1957. While preparing an earlier version of this exhibition in 1954, Barr discussed with René d'Harnoncourt, the Museum's director, whether they should include "the problematic pictures such as the *Korea*, *War* and *Peace*," and whether "Picasso, who is capricious and might well be guided by his Party friends, may insist on the inclusion of such pictures as the *Korea* and he may also insist that we invite him to this country or he will cancel the exhibition." The McCarran Act would have banned Picasso from entering the United States because of his membership in the Communist Party. Barr also reminded d'Harnoncourt how difficult Picasso had been when the Museum organized the retrospective in 1939: "I remember Paul Rosenberg's warning to me that 'Picasso is a devil.' I didn't believe him until one day after we had been working together in the most cordial way, Picasso suddenly turned on me with an extraordinary ferocity and made a completely unreasonable ultimatum about the inclusion of four mediocre works which I had set aside for consideration and then had decided to discard. He insisted that I take them or he would cancel the show. He is not a reasonable man and the immense diet of flattery he has fed on, his age and his sense of power have certainly increased since 1939" (letter dated June 15, 1954, The Museum of Modern Art Archives, Alfred H. Barr, Jr., Papers, Box 11, subgroup V, series A). For the incident in 1939, see Michael C. FitzGerald, *Making Modernism: Picasso and the Creation of the Market for Twentieth-Century Art* (New York: Farrar, Straus and Giroux, 1995), pp. 254–55.

7. Brassaï, *Conversations*, p. 260.

8. Françoise Gilot's two books, *Life with Picasso*, with Carleton Lake (New York: McGraw-Hill, 1964) and *Matisse and Picasso: A Friendship in Art* (London: Bloomsbury, 1990), are essential sources. Citations of *Life with Picasso* that follow refer to the New American Library edition (New York, 1965).

9. Brassaï, *Conversations*, p. 124.

10. These drawings are Zervos XIII, 271–72, and 320, among others.

11. This brush-and-ink drawing, dated August 13–15, 1944, is in the collection of The Museum of Modern Art, New York. In conversation with the author, Françoise Gilot identified this and other drawings as self-portraits by Picasso. Their profile format and the outline of the profile correspond to his self-portraits from the mid-1920s. Jean Sutherland Boggs has asserted that Picasso "painted himself as one of the quieter figures—a youth solemnly bearing a basket of fruit" in his version of Poussin's *Bacchanal* ("The Last Thirty Years," in Roland Penrose and John Golding, eds., *Picasso in Retrospect* [New York: Praeger, 1973], p. 198).

12. See Françoise Gilot's account of this painting's development in *Life with Picasso*, pp. 89–115.

13. Ernst-Gerhard Güse and Bernd Rau, *Pablo Picasso, die Lithographien* (Stuttgart: G. Hatje, 1988), no. 61.

14. See Gilot's accounts in both *Life with Picasso*, pp. 93–94, and *Matisse and Picasso*, pp. 23–25.

15. Gilot, *Life with Picasso*, p. 111.

16. See Harriet and Sidney Janis, *Picasso: The Recent Years 1939–46* (Garden City: Doubleday, 1946). My thanks to Jeffrey Figley of the Sidney Janis Gallery for his help in obtaining a photograph of the painting in its unfinished state.

17. Gilot, *Life with Picasso*, p. 112.

18. Gilot, *Matisse and Picasso*, p. 23.

19. Brassaï, *Conversations*, p. 71.

20. Many years earlier, Matisse had given *Portrait of Marguerite* (1907) to Picasso. It is now in the collection of the Musée Picasso, Paris (T.49). Between December 5, 1945, and January 17, 1946, Picasso made a lithograph, *Bull*, in a series of eleven progressive states that shows a similar reductive process (Fernand Mourlot, *Picasso Lithographs* [Boston: Boston Book and Art Publisher, 1970], pp. 27–30, no. 17).

21. See John Elderfield, *The Cut-Outs of Henri Matisse* (New York: Braziller, 1978), p. 10.

22. Gilot, *Life with Picasso*, p. 113.

23. Gilot, *Matisse and Picasso*, pp. 76–77.

24. In conversation with the author, Gilot

Françoise Gilot. *Portrait of Picasso as a Mask*. 1944. Pencil on paper, 26 × 20″ (66 × 50.8 cm). Collection Françoise Gilot

Françoise Gilot. *Sorcerer's Mask (Portrait of Pablo Picasso)*. 1944. Oil on masonite, 21¾ × 18″ (55.3 × 45.7 cm). Collection Françoise Gilot

Françoise Gilot. *Self-Portrait with Two of Diamonds*. 1946. Pencil and *papier collé*, 26 × 20⅛″ (66 × 51 cm). Collection Françoise Gilot

Woman Carrying a Child. 1953. Painted wood and section of palm leaf, 68⅛ × 21¼ × 13¾″ (173 × 54 × 35 cm). Spies 478. Private collection

stated that Picasso overpainted *The Rape of Europa* during the fall of 1946. In a letter to Alfred H. Barr, Jr., dated December 21, 1946, Louis Carré wrote that the painting "no longer exists" (The Museum of Modern Art Archives, Alfred H. Barr, Jr., Papers, Box 15, subgroup VI, series A). According to an article in *Time* (July 8, 1946), it had been priced at the equivalent of $13,000 during Carré's exhibition. My thanks to Jeffrey Figley of the Sidney Janis Gallery for his help in obtaining a photograph of the painting.

25. The painting was given the title *Woman with Knife and Bull's Head* at the time of the inventory of Picasso's estate.

26. See Claude Ruiz-Picasso's account of his father's work at the Madoura pottery works, "The Valley of Gold: Picasso as Potter," in Elizabeth Cowling and John Golding, *Picasso: Sculptor/Painter* (London: The Tate Gallery, 1994), pp. 223–27.

27. Zervos XIV, 202–27.

28. She was born on November 26. Sagittarius is often symbolized as a centaur.

29. No. G574 in Gilot's archives.

30. Zervos XIV, 17.

31. Gilot, *Life with Picasso*, pp. 190–92. My thanks to Susan Grace Galassi for having discussed with me Picasso's variations on other artists' work. Her book on this subject is scheduled to be published by Abrams in 1996.

32. *Monument to the Spanish Dead* (1945–47) is in the collection of the Museo Nacional Centro de Arte Reina Sofía in Madrid.

33. For Daix's account of these years, see *Picasso: Life and Art* (New York: HarperCollins, 1993), pp. 277–311.

34. Zervos XV, 106.

35. *Women on the Banks of the Seine, after Courbet* (Zervos XV, 164); *Portrait of a Painter, after El Greco* (Zervos XV, 165).

36. Despite his considerable wealth, Picasso consistently demanded prices for his work that surpassed those received by his peers, especially Matisse and Braque. Apparently, Picasso took this commercial success as a matter of prestige, a demonstration of the world's recognition of his artistic achievement. During the period of his association with the French Communist Party, however, some American collectors, who constituted the largest pool of his buyers, seemed hesitant to acquire his paintings. In turn, many of the leading dealers, including Paul Rosenberg (who had represented Picasso from 1918 to 1940), refused to pay the high prices Picasso required. Rosenberg, at least, doubted that he could sell the pictures profitably in the near future. For Françoise Gilot's discussion of Picasso's relations with Rosenberg, Louis Carré, Samuel Kootz, and Daniel-Henry Kahnweiler, see *Life with Picasso*, pp. 168–71. In conversation with the author, she stated that the agreement between Picasso and Kahnweiler in 1947 (which reestablished a commercial relationship that had effectively ended in 1914) was based on the purchase of prints— not paintings—because Kahnweiler believed that Picasso was demanding too much for his oils.

37. During these years, Picasso's paintings were shown at several noncommercial exhibitions, particularly at the Maison de la Pensée Française in Paris in 1949, and the retrospectives held in Lyon, Rome, Milan, and São Paulo in 1953, but the paintings were returned to his possession after these shows closed.

38. After the exhibition in June 1946, Carré held a few shows of Picasso's work but they were based on stock he had not sold or pictures he acquired on the secondary market—not paintings directly from Picasso's studio. Kootz held two shows with work he acquired from Picasso: January 27–February 15, 1947 (ten paintings), and January 26–February 14, 1948 (fourteen paintings of 1941–47). For Picasso's relationship with Rosenberg and involvement in the art market from 1900 to 1940, see FitzGerald, *Making Modernism*. During the war, Picasso sold a small number of works to Carré and probably traded a few through Martin Fabiani, a dealer who was later condemned for collaborating with the Nazis. On July 28, 1943, Picasso drew a series of portraits of Fabiani in the artist's studio on the rue des Grands-Augustins. Fabiani described the session in *Quand j'étais marchand de tableaux* (Paris: Julliard, 1976), p. 127.

39. Paris: Les Grands Peintres Modernes et le Livre, 1948.

40. For a discussion of Picasso's portrayals of children throughout his career, see Werner Spies, *Picasso's World of Children* (Munich: Prestel-Verlag, 1994).

41. Particularly *The Painter's Family*, 1911 (The State Hermitage Museum, St. Petersburg).

42. See Cowling and Golding, *Picasso: Sculptor/Painter*, pp. 275–76. Gilot stated her belief that the sculptures were inspired by her recent pregnancies and reflect Picasso's wish that she would bear him a third child (*Life with Picasso*, p. 295).

43. For a discussion of these murals, see Kirsten Hoving Keen, "Picasso's Communist Interlude: The Murals of 'War' and 'Peace,'" *The Burlington Magazine* 122 (July 1980), pp. 464–70.

44. In a letter dated December 16, 1956, Roland Penrose wrote to Alfred H. Barr, Jr., concerning Picasso's response on learning that Hungarians protesting against Soviet rule had held aloft a reproduction of the *Massacre in Korea*: "He seems relieved that he is no longer, unlike many French intellectuals, identified with the party line on this particular issue." Penrose also told Barr that Picasso had signed an open letter to *L'Humanité* protesting the French Communist Party's support for the Soviet's suppression of the revolt. On January 16, 1957, Barr replied: "Of course I am pleased that he signed the open letter to *L'Humanité*, but I can't help feeling a certain sense of disgust that it should have taken him so long to declare what has been so painfully obvious to the rest of the world, namely that the communist press everywhere is a great deal more corrupt than the non-communist press." All correspondence in The Museum of Modern Art Archives, Alfred H. Barr, Jr., Papers, Box 2, Subgroup II, series C.

45. For Gilot's work as a artist, see *Françoise*

Gilot: An Artist's Journey, introduction and interview by Barbara Haskell, foreword by Danièle Giraudy (New York: The Atlantic Monthly Press, 1987).

46. In September 1953, Picasso made a number of ink drawings showing silhouettes of himself, Françoise, Claude, and Paloma. For example, see Gilot, *Life with Picasso*, illustration following p. 176. As if to emphasize the breakup of his family, Picasso appears not to have depicted the entire group until after Françoise had left.

47. Cited in Roland Penrose, *Picasso: His Life and Work* (New York: Harper and Row, 1973), p. 406. Responding to Penrose's remark that his recent variations on Delacroix's *Women of Algiers* reminded him of Matisse's *odalisques*, Picasso said, "You are right, when Matisse died he left his odalisques to me as a legacy."

Portrait of Stalin in *Les Lettres françaises*, March 12–19, 1953

War. 1952. Oil on wood fiber, 40⅛ × 185″ (102 × 470 cm). Zervos XV, 196. Temple of Peace, Vallauris

Peace. 1952. Oil on wood fiber, 40⅛ × 185″ (102 × 470 cm). Zervos XV, 197. Temple of Peace, Vallauris

Jacqueline Sitting. October 8, 1954. Oil on canvas, 57½ × 44⅞" (146 × 114 cm). Zervos XVI, 328. Private collection

The Jacqueline Portraits in the Pattern of Picasso's Art

WILLIAM RUBIN

If The Museum of Modern Art's exhaustive 1980 retrospective of Picasso's work succeeded, it was in part by unexpectedly disclosing an artist less given to sudden changes in style than to incremental advances. Only by bringing together a sufficient number of paintings with a comparable representation of drawings and sculptures was it possible to provide a context for the familiar "monuments" that would make visible their filiation within Picasso's imagery. An artist whose career had seemed mercurial, characterized by a patchwork of contrasting styles, was revealed as a focused—indeed, sometimes relentless—explorer of even the most remote implications of his pictorial inventions.

It also became clearer than before that changes in Picasso's painting, while often interrelated with events in his private life, had a quite evident logic of their own, subject to a dialectic (see p. 37) deriving as much from temperament and instinct as from intellect. In some phases of Picasso's career, the crucial 1906 Gosol period for example, the 1980 retrospective was able to explore close-up, as it were, the processes of what we may characterize as the artist's pictorial thought. This kind of study was renewed in the 1984 examination of *The Young Picasso* at the Bern Museum, the 1988 *Les Demoiselles d'Avignon* exhibition at the Musée Picasso in Paris, and The Museum of Modern Art's 1989 scrutiny of the Picasso and Braque dialogue. As a result of these and other in-depth reviews of small areas in the artist's oeuvre, particularly those organized by the Museu Picasso in Barcelona, critics and public began increasingly to perceive a kind of continuity in the artist's career where none seemed to have existed before—a consistency as regards his fundamental approach to making art. This integrality was not the conventional one provided by a signature style, but constituted instead a unity of mind, eye, temperament, and purpose on the part of a single individual who had tasked himself with probing the nature and testing the limits of pictorial representation—an inquiry that often took precedence over the fullest possible realization of individual paintings and sculptures.

Picasso's explorations of new (but also renewed) ways of imaging effectively questioned, short-circuited, and ultimately overrode prevailing assumptions about style. His development presupposed that style—what Mark Rothko and other of my Abstract Expressionist friends used to call "my image"—was in a sense a trap into which artists could fall far too willingly, closing themselves off from the richest possible pictorial materialization of their thoughts and identities. Picasso transgressed style in part by questioning its implicit historicity and by inundating his various manners with alternatives, which his work threw off like mutations in the process of natural selection. All artists generate some of these alternatives, but the commitment to a concept of style often

Portrait of Sylvette David. April 21, 1954. Lead pencil on paper, 12⅝ × 9⅜″ (32 × 24 cm). Zervos XVI, 284. Private collection

constrains them from following them up. Picasso, as observed in my introductory essay, made no bones about his distaste for the constraints of style. This stance took no small courage; the only other twentieth-century artists who consciously induced multiple manners in their work —Max Ernst and André Masson, for example—found that posture detrimental to their careers.

That I return here to a consideration of style follows from the fact that Picasso's portrayals of his second wife, Jacqueline Roque, not only constitute the largest single group of his portraits, but dominate the work of the artist's seventies and eighties. These would be precisely the years in question if art historians were to measure Picasso for an *Altersstil*, or old-age style. To the extent that it is possible to use this term in relation to twentieth-century art, the late *papiers découpés* of Matisse must surely constitute its most logical model, one whose distinctiveness reveals not only a distillation but a sublimation of the artist's earlier work.

The articulation of Picasso's career shows a very different kind of pattern. That his late work does *not* in fact reveal an *Altersstil*, even in the sense exemplified by Matisse's, Bonnard's, and Mondrian's later works (and especially not in the sense of those of Michelangelo, Titian, or Rembrandt) should hardly come as a surprise, for Picasso was without a signature style to begin with.[1] But consideration of the Jacqueline portraits nevertheless raises the question of how the dynamics of Picasso's late

work compare with and relate to those of his prior career, and whether the last decades of his art cannot be said to have betrayed consistent differences or particular inflections that were incumbent upon his advanced age.

We see an enormous stylistic variety and range of mediums in Picasso's work over the almost twenty years of the Jacqueline portraits. A number of superb works were realized throughout this period, although, in the final ten years of the artist's life, proportionately fewer of these were paintings and more were drawings and prints. Picasso and Jacqueline had first met in 1952,[2] and the artist began making portraits of her in the spring of 1954. Thirteen of the seventeen oils of Jacqueline chosen for this exhibition were painted during the first decade of their relationship. Only four come from the final ten years, although these are among the best. Indeed, the last of these portraits, the poignant and sumptuously painted Jacqueline of 1971 (p. 481), is one of the most moving of Picasso's paintings, a consummation of his imagery of his wife.

The accepted model for Picasso's career consists of a succession of "periods": Blue, Rose, Iberian, "African," Cubist, Neoclassical, etc. Skeptics of his art have tended to interpret this changing sequence as reflecting a shallowness and lack of conviction on Picasso's part, a superabundance of talent as over and against genius and, above all, a lack of unity in his work. Braque, for example, at a time of great dissatisfaction with Picasso for seemingly having deserted Cubism for Neoclassicism, wrote Kahnweiler denigrating his erstwhile colleague as a "virtuoso full of talent," and arguing that "the only real constant in this artist [Picasso] is his temperament."[3] Braque was perhaps being less critical here than he intended, for Cézanne himself had emphasized "temperament" as the primary requisite of a great painter.[4] And if we place such qualities as ambition, daring, intellect, wit, energy, and persistence under the general rubric of temperament, we are well on the way to understanding the cohesiveness of Picasso's oeuvre.

To be sure, the aim of Braque's angry letter was, quite contrarily, to establish Picasso as the paradigm of the "antigenius," the antithesis, in effect, of Cézanne, and to cast him as a painter whose astonishing talent blinded one to the (implied) shallowness of his message. But Braque, like many later critics of Picasso, oversimplified and misconstrued the dynamics of his art. Given the Spaniard's enormous gifts, virtuosity was something that he not surprisingly considered a great danger precisely if and when an artist remained for a long period in a single, unchanging style. Such a commitment doomed the painter, Picasso felt, to a self-imposed academicism.[5] Hence, within the unique dialectic of Picasso's development, his recurrent changes in style represented less an exercise of

Jacqueline with Flowers. June 3, 1954. Oil on canvas, 39⅜ × 31⅞″ (100 × 81 cm). Zervos XVI, 325. Private collection

talent than a reaction *against* the dangers of virtuosity.

Style was clearly associated in Picasso's mind with received values and ideas, and he placed virtuosity in the same category inasmuch as it also can be defined only by reference to prior models.[6] Picasso considered virtuosity a Satan he had to get behind him. While arguably the most brilliant draftsman since Leonardo (if a man of a less mature though more focused ego than the Italian master),

he sometimes clearly succumbed to it. Most geniuses in the plastic arts are not menaced by such an excess of talent, which is all virtuosity really is. Cézanne, for one, had little talent. But he had the mind, eye, and—in his art, at least—the ethical stamina to turn that absence to advantage.[7] Talent is cheap; it can be found in any art school. Picasso understood early on that the payoff was on genius —not on the hand that executes, but on the mind and

Head of a Woman (Jacqueline). October 18, 1954. Ink on paper, 14 × 10⅝″ (35.5 × 27 cm). Zervos XVI, 335. Private collection

imagination that tells it what to do.

In a lecture almost half a century ago, Meyer Schapiro argued that those who saw Picasso's art as without focus and unity had missed the over-arching coherence of it.[8] This could not be grasped, Schapiro said, by searching in it for the usual patterns of order (as exemplified by A-B-A, A-B-A-C-A-D, etc., or A-A′-A″-A‴ and the like). Picasso's career, Schapiro suggested, might be better likened to the letters A-B-C-D-E-F-G, etc., that is, the sequence of the entire alphabet—its oneness made up of unique, hence different, parts within an extended but ultimately closed system. The unity was not in the structure or style of Picasso's successive works so much as in the way the author had been able to imprint himself on all its aspects. Indeed, if temperament means the particular tuning of the mind and spirit, it is precisely temperament that provides the viewer of even Picasso's failed pictures with a minimal visual reward often absent from the bad pictures of other good painters: the excitement of the transmutation into purely plastic energy of an extraordinary and convincing temperament.

We have by now become sufficiently familiar with Picasso's heretofore unknown or little known work to see that even the "model" Schapiro had proposed implies the legitimacy of the received periodicity of supposedly successive styles and fails to take into account the *cumulative*

aspect of the artist's stylistic inventions which, once acquired, remained permanently accessible to him in the form of an *a priori* vocabulary. One has only to list the attributes that account for the names of each of Picasso's so-called periods to become aware of the problems of the traditional periodicity, not the least of which is the assumption that these "periods" denote, like the letters of the alphabet, comparable *kinds* of entities. Yet what prompts us to use the term "Blue" for Picasso's pictures of 1903 or "African" for those of 1907 is different both in nature and in kind from what has led to the characterization of the work of 1907–14 as Cubist, or some of the work of 1915–23 as Neoclassical.

Several of Picasso's "periods" did not even mark any real change in style. The Rose period, for example, differed from the preceding Blue period primarily in that the dominant tonality, an inherited Symbolist mood-creating device, shifted from Blue to Rose. Although Picasso's attitude toward his subjects became more affirmative and less sentimental, his drawing more decisive, and his brushwork freer and more emphatic, the Rose period portraits are ultimately *in the same style* as most of those of the Blue period. Indeed, there are greater differences in the morphologies of style within the Blue period works of 1903 alone, between portraits such as that of Sabartés (p. 239) or Carlota Valdivia (*Celestina*, p. 243) and the stylized, highly attenuated, more generic Grecoesque images, such as the *Old Guitarist*,[9] than there are between the characteristic portraits of the two "periods." Picasso's

Head of a Woman (Jacqueline). December 9, 1954. Ink on paper, 16⅞ × 13⅝″ (43 × 34.5 cm). Zervos XVI, 337. Private collection

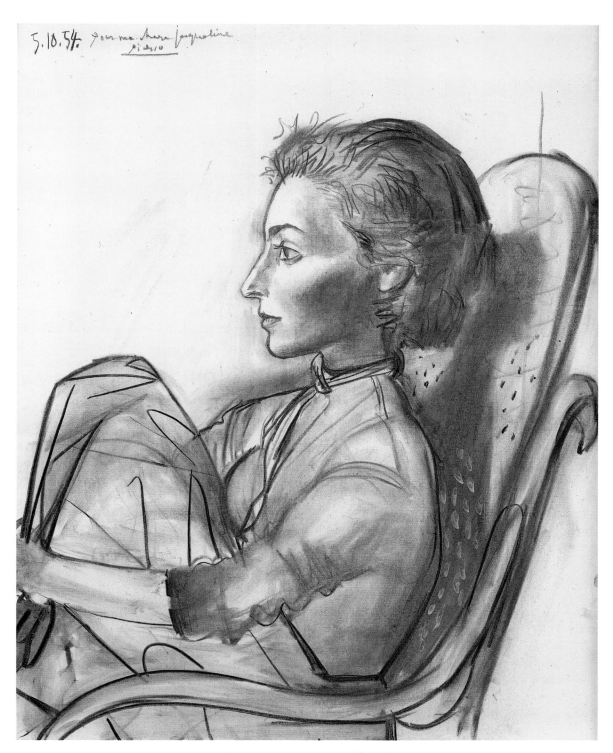

Jacqueline with Folded Legs. October 5, 1954. Oil and charcoal on canvas, 36¼ × 28¾″ (92 × 73 cm). Zervos XVI, 326. Private collection

development resists theoretical (indeed, logical) characterization as much as Mondrian's invites it. Its "messiness" was mirrored in his human relationships and in the seeming disorder[10] and heterogeneity of his studios, which reflected Picasso's art as much as Mondrian's studios mirrored his.

To recognize the significant stylistic dualism existing in the work of the year 1903 alone is to understand that, even before the astonishing caesura represented by *Les Demoiselles d'Avignon*, Picasso's development was far from the monolinear one assumed by use of the familiar periodicity and exemplified in a career like Mondrian's. Any vestiges of such a linear chronological thread disappear definitively in Picasso's work during the "Iberian" period

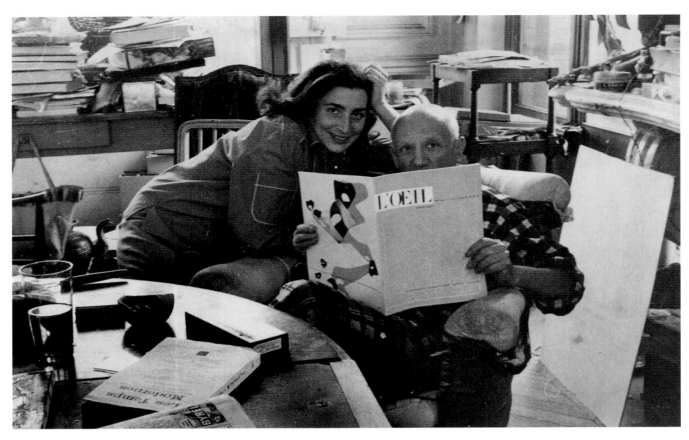

Picasso and Jacqueline Roque reading *L'Oeil*, in the dining room of La Californie, above Cannes, 1957. Photograph by Roland Penrose. Lee Miller Archives

of 1906, when he began working in a manner more conceptual than perceptual. It is between Gosol and the *Demoiselles* that his art passes from the stylized to the transformative, and its rate of change begins to accelerate exponentially; in the year that separates the Gosol works from the *Demoiselles*, one can distinguish at least half a dozen substyles jostling and tumbling over each other. By the time of the great canvas, it has become a question of Picasso's using multiple styles not simply in the same month, week, or day, but in the same picture.

One of the tasks of Picasso criticism in the last two decades has been to atomize the traditional "periodistic" visualization of his work with a view to anatomizing it in a truer form. Cubism, for example, had already been subdivided during Alfred H. Barr, Jr.'s generation into Analytic and Synthetic phases.[11] But the next generation found this two-part schema inadequate. First *Les Demoiselles d'Avignon*, long taken to have been Cubism's foundation, had to be almost entirely severed from its definition in order for the term to make any sense as a style. Then the "primitivist" Cubism of 1908, as in the portraits of Madame Putman (p. 272), Fernande (p. 271), and especially the two formerly overlooked monuments —the various stages of *Three Women* (St. Petersburg) and *Bread and Fruitdish on a Table* (Basel)[12]—had to be modi-

fied by the prefix "early" to identify it as a mode that preceded "Analytic" Cubism; the latter would be used now only for pictures dating from the summer of 1909 at Horta through the immediately succeeding yéars.

Yet the increased knowledge of the differences between the sculpturally modeled Horta pictures of 1909, the abstract and more painterly scaffoldings of those from Cadaqués a year later, and the luminous, highly painterly canvases from Céret of 1911 led to the term "early Analytic Cubism" in order to mark off those 1909 pictures from the works of 1910, to which the "early" was no longer applicable, and those of Céret and Paris from 1911 and early 1912, for which the prefix "high" was frequently added.

The illusoriness of Cubism's periodicity, even as modified by the introduction of these salami-slicing, substylistic terms, became painfully clear in the *Picasso and Braque* exhibition. There, one witnessed the unfolding in Picasso's work of a continuous if complex fabric of ideas (further enriched by his dialogue with Braque), whose sometimes meandering formulations entirely resisted the teleology heretofore imprinted on Cubism by the critics, art historians, and museologists of the 1920s, 1930s, and 1940s. For the most part, these writers had extrapolated

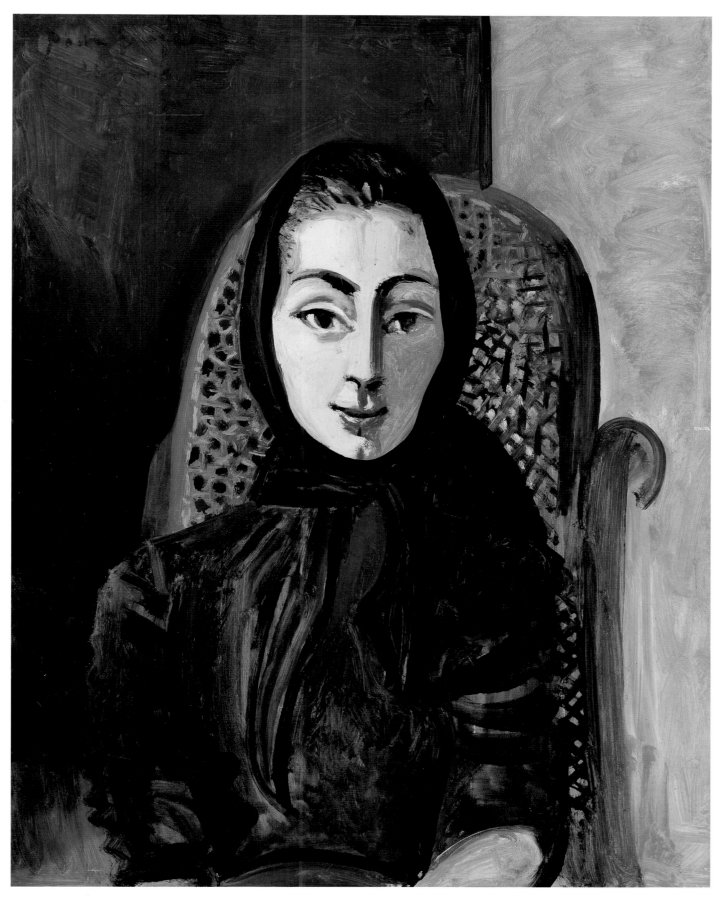

Jacqueline in a Black Scarf. October 11, 1954. Oil on canvas, 36¼ × 28¾″ (92 × 73 cm). Zervos XVI, 331. Private collection

Women of Algiers, after Delacroix. December 13, 1954. Oil on canvas, 22 × 28¾″ (60 × 73 cm). Zervos XVI, 342. Private collection

their ideas from conclusions Mondrian (and, to a lesser extent, Malevich, Delaunay, and Kupka) drew from Picasso's and Braque's work.

We know that periodicity, even at its most sophisticated, involves deeply problematic generalizations imposed on history to give it an order that makes it manageable for discourse. We are all aware that we do not go to sleep one night in the Romanesque period and get up the next morning in the Gothic. But the absolute mincemeat made of even the most developed periodicity for Cubism by the evidence of the Picasso and Braque show suggested that, while we probably must continue to use "period" terminology for reasons of convenience, we must constantly remind ourselves of the ultimate erroneousness of this sort of schema as regards the shape of Picasso's career in general and his Cubism in particular. That means confronting a surprising fact: during the five years separating primitivist early Cubism of 1908 from the Synthetic Cubism of 1912–13 (and its concomitants,

collage and construction), there are greater differences in style and conception in Picasso's art, quantitatively speaking, than those which distinguish the styles of the Romanesque and Gothic periods at their most different.

Cubism, as referring to Picasso's art of 1908 to 1914, can hardly be interpreted, then, as representing a single coherent style. There is not a season, hardly a month, during these years in which Picasso's pictures do not reflect profound quantitative changes in anything we might seriously define with the latter word. The only common denominator that remains from the dynamic of those years is the continuously transformative character of the work itself. But this cannot be said to constitute the unifying principle of Cubism inasmuch as, to a greater or lesser degree, it characterizes the concatenation of his career as a whole.

Thus, the changes in Picasso's work, throughout his career, have no evolutionary or teleological destiny. They

Study for Women of Algiers, after Delacroix. December 21, 1954. Ink on paper, 13⅝ × 17⅛″ (34.5 × 43.5 cm). Zervos XVI, 344. Musée Picasso, Paris

Study for Women of Algiers, after Delacroix. January 23, 1955. Pen and ink on paper,
16⅝ × 21⅝″ (42.1 × 55 cm). Zervos XVI, 350. Musée Picasso, Paris

Women of Algiers, after Delacroix. February 14, 1955. Oil on canvas, 45 × 57½″ (114.2 × 146 cm). Zervos XVI, 360. Collection Sally Ganz

are guided rather by the inclusionist tendencies of an artist fascinated, above all, by the nature of representation itself. Picasso accepts that he is, to some extent, bound by his moment in history. He feels it incumbent upon him, however, not only to develop new forms that express his own spirit and thus those of his epoch, but to re-explore past art to discover whatever aspects of its language might once again be rendered viable—in effect, to exploit the presentness of the past.

As Picasso expands the range of his artistic language, no discovery is ever lost; new ideas may linger unused for years before being explored, presumably because new contexts will not yet have warranted their exploitation. But they are never forgotten. As the vocabulary of modalities, morphologies, and styles of Picasso's art begins to accelerate in 1906–07, the artist sometimes puts out ideas and absorbs influences with which he will only really come to grips four to fifteen years later.[13] But by 1914, the four prevailing tendencies of his career—Cubist, classicist, expressionist, and surreal—are already evident, though evidences of the latter two are relatively fragmen-

tary; they would be the object of particular exploration in the period between the two world wars.

Picasso continued to add new discoveries to his expanding gamut of styles during the years immediately following World War II, spent largely with Françoise Gilot, and through the first decade of his life with Jacqueline. But the frequency of new ideas during those years diminished. Except for a few moments of crisis—"black-holes," relatively speaking, in his career[14]—Picasso had maintained an altogether remarkable creative intensity between 1906 and 1939. Only the standard he himself had set permits us to say that there are fewer inventions during the 1940s, 1950s, and 1960s than before, for the *best* work of those years was still remarkable by the standards of any other artist.

In 1954, the year of his definitive break with Françoise, Picasso executed the only large series of pictures that reflect a real inauthenticity of feeling—the portraits for which Sylvette David modeled.[15] Many of these suffer from a pouting, modish notion of chic that belongs more to the model (and the predilections of her generation)

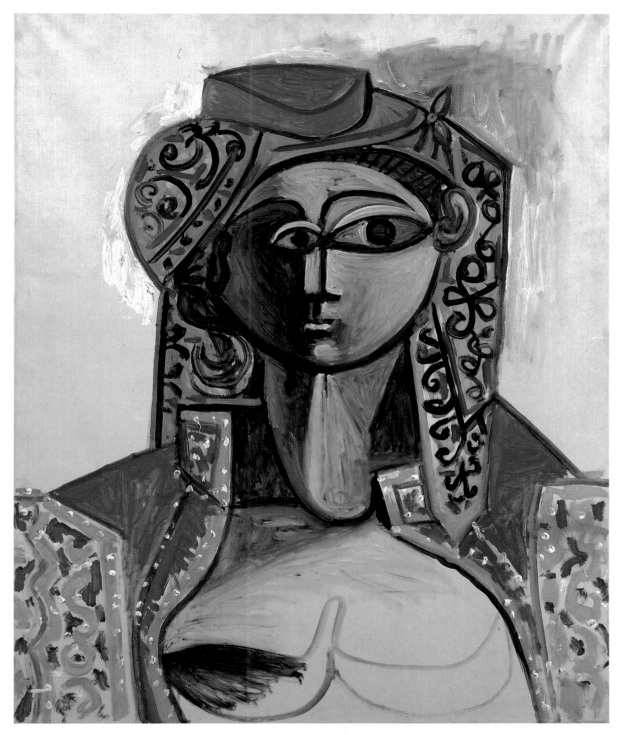

Jacqueline in a Turkish Jacket. November 1955. Oil on canvas, 31⅞ × 25⅝″ (81 × 65 cm). Not in Zervos. Private collection

than to the taste of Picasso himself. This series sounded a momentary knell in the artist's work that seems successfully to have reminded Picasso that he, at least, could only make great art from subjects that truly involved him. One has but to compare the Sylvette portraits with those of Jacqueline made later in that same year to see why, unlike Matisse, Picasso had eschewed models virtually all his mature life, preferring to paint individuals whose lives had

both impinged on, and had real significance for, his own.

Picasso's continuing psychic stamina was reflected in his ability to repress the profound hurt and distraction caused by Françoise's definitive parting from him, an acceptance of the inevitable that opened the way for what would become a final great love of his life. Françoise may have made the same mistake as some others before her: that of assuming Picasso's love for her would give her

Bust of a Woman (Jacqueline). January 21, 1955. Drypoint, 13½ × 9¹⁵⁄₁₆″ (34.3 × 25.3 cm). Geiser/Baer IV, 914. Private collection

of the Musée Picasso in Paris, she seemed to have sensed her earthly mission accomplished.

Jacqueline with Flowers (p. 449), Picasso's first painting of his future second wife, well captures certain of her features, such as her patrician nose and small chin. But it is a view of her that is inhabited—not surprisingly, given the characteristic "carry-over" in the artist's imagery—by the elongated neck and concomitant concerns for elegance that had marked the immediately prior Sylvette series (p. 448). This "mannerist" elongation (it was no more an attribute of Sylvette's neck than of Jacqueline's) would disappear from the artist's images of the latter in the course of the following year (1955), as Picasso's relationship with her deepened.

The most important stylistic influence inhabiting *Jacqueline with Flowers* is that of Matisse, with whom Picasso had renewed his personal dialogue a few years earlier. Not that one would mistake the drawing style here, with its mordant sculptural edge or the picture's dense, hard color, for that of Matisse. But the painting does pay homage to the French master in its open-ended planarity and in the decorative patterning of Jacqueline's dress and the flowers below and behind her. Jacqueline's almost frontal eye, inscribed on the profile of her head, though by now somewhat formulaic, also functions inevitably as a reference to the *Demoiselles* and, by implication, to the contemporaneous ritual that

primacy in his life. But Picasso had always made clear that the primary and only permanent bond in his life was with his art—and that love of women (or children) would, if necessary, be sacrificed to its purposes.

Jacqueline never forced Picasso to choose; his relationship with her was not the agonizing, novelistic kind of love that the artist had experienced in certain of his earlier liaisons. Picasso did not have to win Jacqueline from another man, nor struggle to keep her. Her understated, gentle, and loving personality combined with her unconditional commitment to him provided an emotionally stable life and a dependable *foyer* over a longer period of time than he had ever before enjoyed. The dissatisfactions, rages, and moments of depression continued, of course. But they were less frequent than in prior years, and Jacqueline knew how to brush aside and defuse Picasso's provocations and incitements to the kind of emotional *agon* that had characterized, in particular, his liaisons with Dora Maar and Françoise Gilot. Especially during the final decade, Jacqueline's presence was constant, day and night, dutifully keeping Picasso company in his studio or sitting at work in her adjacent alcove. Jacqueline's selfless patience and protectiveness inevitably took their toll. After Picasso died, she was unable to reconstruct a life for herself and, following the opening

Jacqueline as Lola de Valence, after Manet. October 4, 1955. India ink on paper, 12⅝ × 9½″ (32 × 24 cm). Zervos XVI, 479. Private collection

3.5.55.

4.5.55.

Portrait of Jacqueline. May 3, 1955. Charcoal and India ink on paper, 26 × 19⅞″ (66 × 50.5 cm). Zervos XVI, 389. Private collection

Portrait of Jacqueline. May 4, 1955. Charcoal and India ink on paper, 25⅝ × 19⅝″ (65 × 50 cm). Zervos XVI, 390. Private collection

Jacqueline as an Equestrian, after Velázquez. March 10, 1959. India ink and colored pencil on paper, 14½ × 10⅝″ (37 × 27 cm). Zervos XVIII, 367. Private collection

cemented Picasso's friendship with Matisse: their exchange of paintings.[16]

The frontal eye in *Jacqueline with Flowers* was used primarily to communicate the pride of an almost imperious gaze, a kind of feminine counterpart to Picasso's own *mirada fuerte*.[17] When I met Jacqueline with the painter fifteen years later, her pronounced, erect carriage and focused, intense gaze were constant aspects of her body language. But John Richardson's impressions of her were somewhat different, suggesting that certain of her expressions were unconsciously absorbed over time from Picasso's images of her, which reinforced the artist's fantasies about the prophetic nature of his art.[18]

October 1954 witnessed a number of Picasso's best early portraits of Jacqueline. *Jacqueline with Folded Legs* (p. 451), an endearing charcoal-on-canvas profile portrait, shows the sitter poised in her rocking chair. It was probably intended originally as the early stage of a painting that would have formed a pair with the oil of three days later (p. 446). As was almost certainly also the case with such superb charcoal portraits on canvas as those of Marie-Thérèse (p. 372) and Nusch Eluard (p. 84), the artist must have realized that his preparation was so perfect in its own right that he determined not to paint over it. A soft-focus realism similar to that of the large charcoal drawing was deployed in characterizing Jacqueline in an

Jacqueline Roque (detail) at La Californie, 1956. Photograph by André Villers

Jacqueline in a Head Scarf. December 28, 1955. Linocut, 21⅝ × 20⅛″ (54.9 × 51.1 cm). Geiser/Baer IV, 1033. Collection Marina Picasso, courtesy Galerie Jan Krugier, Geneva

Portrait of a Woman (Jacqueline). December 29, 1955. Lithograph, 25³⁄₁₆ × 14¹⁵⁄₁₆″ (64 × 38 cm). Bloch 780. Museu Picasso, Barcelona

Portrait of Jacqueline. December 30–31, 1955. Pen and India ink over linocut proof of print illustrated above, 26 × 20″ (66 × 58 cm). Zervos XVI, 525. Museum Ludwig, Collection Ludwig, Cologne

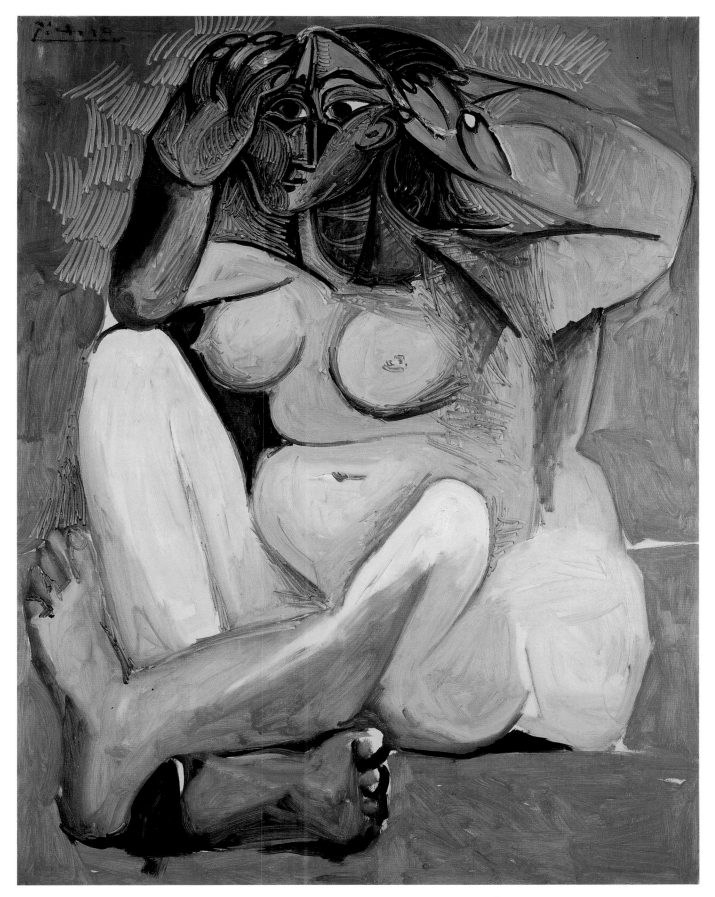

Seated Nude (Jacqueline). January 3, 1956. Oil on canvas, 46 × 35″ (117 × 89 cm). Zervos XVII, 2. Private collection

Jacqueline Roque at La Californie (detail), 1956. Photograph by André Villers

Head of a Woman (Jacqueline). January 25, 1957. Colored crayon on paper, 25⅞ × 20⅛″ (65.7 × 51.1 cm). Not in Zervos. Private collection

oil of the following week: the tender *Jacqueline in a Black Scarf* (p. 453), in which the sitter is again shown in her rocking chair but now with the directness of a frontal view. Despite the pervasive painterliness of this picture, Picasso has modeled Jacqueline's head in a more sculptural manner than elsewhere in the image. This decision, in combination with her serene, internalized gaze and the manner in which the black scarf encircles her face, recalls the 1906 Gosol portraits of Fernande.[19]

I spoke in my introductory essay about Picasso's habit of associating the women in his life with figures from earlier paintings by the masters he admired. Among the artists with whom Jacqueline was paired were Delacroix, Velázquez, and Manet (see, for example, her equestrian portrait, a gloss on Velázquez's royal portraits such as *Baltasar Carlos on Horseback*, and her personification as Manet's *Lola de Valence*, pp. 458, 459). Picasso had paraphrased (and parodied) the paintings of early Spanish and French masters since his youth. These did not represent an attempt to outstrip the earlier artists or improve upon their work, as is sometimes suggested. Certainly Picasso, like most other great artists, felt himself in competition with the best painters of the past as well as those of the present. But his paraphrases always reflected a deep and affectionate affinity with the painters evoked; and

Picasso's psychology in them, though not competitive, was anodynely cannibalistic. By taking apart and reconstituting another artist's picture, Picasso could better digest that painter's particular "magic." Whatever Picasso extrapolated from a painter's work, the result was always intended as an autonomous object, no different in kind from Picasso's other paintings.

Paraphrases such as those that compare Jacqueline to Manet's Lola de Valence are to be found here and there, with varying frequency, throughout Picasso's career, largely in drawings. But large groups or "series" of paintings and drawings based on a single work begin only in the 1950s (those extrapolated in 1932 from the *Crucifixion* panel of Grünewald's Isenheim Altarpiece were all drawings). These late groups were less paraphrases than extended variations on a theme, and they sometimes carried Picasso so far from his original source that, without their contexts, we might not always recognize them for what they are.[20]

The stage had been set for Picasso's late series of Old Master variations by the extraordinary success of his 1950 paraphrase of Courbet's *Women on the Banks of the Seine*.[21] This relatively little known large painting in the Basel Kunstmuseum is one of Picasso's great masterpieces, a picture that one might even prefer to Courbet's superb

Portrait of Jacqueline. February 13, 1957. Collage and charcoal on paper, 26 × 20⅛″ (66 × 51 cm). Not in Zervos. Private collection

Head of a Woman. February 14, 1957. Gouache, colored pencil, and ink on paper, 26 × 19¾″ (66 × 50 cm). Zervos XVII, 330. Private collection

antecedent. Picasso had often admired and studied Delacroix's *Women of Algiers* on his visits to the Louvre, and the sketches of figures from it drawn in the Royan notebook of 1940[22] indicate that a project for some kind of encounter with this particular Delacroix painting had percolated in Picasso's mind for at least fifteen years before he undertook his extraordinary variations on it.

As to why Picasso's interest in *Woman of Algiers* was renewed in 1954, a few reasons suggest themselves. Picasso was obviously struck by the subsequently much-noticed resemblance between Jacqueline and the woman crouching on the right in the Louvre version of *Women of Algiers*; this unusual "omen" might have been consciously or unconsciously an aspect of Picasso's initial attraction to her. (The resemblance exists mainly in the 1834 Louvre version of Delacroix's masterpiece, p. 484, left, not in the 1849 one in the Montpellier Museum, p. 484, right, though Picasso would exploit elements of the latter version as well in the course of his variations on them.) Marie-Laure Bernadac has characterized Jacqueline as "the ultimate odalisque" in terms of "her physique, in her strange like-ness to one of the women in the [Delacroix] painting, in her temperament, her calm, her sensuous nature."[23]

The immediate trigger, however, for Picasso's varia-tions on Delacroix's *Women of Algiers* was most probably the death of Matisse in November 1954. "Why shouldn't

one inherit something from one's friends?"[24] Picasso later remarked apropos of Matisse's *odalisques*, which the artist liked to imagine Matisse "had left to me as a legacy."[25] Orientalism was, of course, nothing new for Picasso, who had been virtually traumatized by Ingres' *Turkish Bath*, when it re-emerged into public view in 1905.[26] Indeed, one of the earliest anticipations of *Les Demoiselles d'Avignon* in Picasso's work had been the Ingres-inspired *Harem*,[27] which he painted at Gosol in summer 1906; this work celebrated the happiness of Picasso's first months of being truly alone with Fernande Olivier, whose face and figure would provide the starting point for all the *odal-isques* in that picture.

Now Picasso was embarking with Jacqueline on what he no doubt hoped would be a parallel period of happiness. Jacqueline manifestly inhabited Delacroix's Orientalist vision in the Louvre; Picasso would assert his rights again to the dream of the Levant that he associated, as a result of the work Matisse did there, with that artist's long sojourn on the Côte d'Azur (so opposite in spirit from Picasso's Paris-oriented, *engagé* life). It was surely not by accident that, just a month after the completion of his *Women of Algiers* variations, while he was still at work on "postludes" showing Jacqueline dressed in Turkish garb (p. 457), Picasso purchased for their idyll a spacious villa, La Californie, in Cannes. Its bastardized

Portrait of a Woman. May 13, 1959. Lead pencil on paper, 16½ × 13″ (42 × 33 cm). Zervos XVIII, 480. Private collection

to despair, foreshadowing the Jacqueline that one often discovered in Mougins following the painter's death. No other portrait of Jacqueline in any medium so totally captures these tragic aspects of her nature; next to this, her visualization four years later as the *Mater Dolorosa* (below) appears almost a caricature (and perhaps was partly so intended). The artist's daily portrayals of her document a regained composure; we might imagine that the Cubistic and architecturally structured lithographic portrait made of her the following day (p. 460) was Picasso's attempt "magically" to prop her up, while the India ink drawing made over a lightly printed proof of the linocut itself (p. 460), executed a day later, records Jacqueline's uneasy return to the world of the living.

Surely one of the most extraordinarily inventive portraits Picasso ever painted is the *Seated Nude* of 1959 (opposite). Its particular resonance derives from a harmonious melding and resolution of contraries—expressionist "distortion" and Cubist-derived structure. Rarely was Picasso able to make so imperiously manifest the sheer power and sureness of the aesthetic decision-making process. In few other portraits has he derived so much tension from the analogies and contrasts between the structure of the figure and that of the chair in which she

architecture featured, as Penrose and Richardson have observed,[28] virtually Neo-Moorish window motifs that smacked of the ambiance in which Picasso had pictured Jacqueline in his Delacroix paraphrases.

Picasso had begun his series of *Women of Algiers* on December 13, 1954, with a small oil sketch (p. 454) loosely based on the earlier Louvre version with which he was intimately familiar, but probably also with his eye cocked on a reproduction of the Montpellier version; clear in his memory was probably also Cézanne's *Afternoon in Naples*,[29] which had partially inspired his 1901 parody of Manet's *Olympia*. In this first Delacroix variation, there is no direct reference to Jacqueline, whose presence only becomes visible in the India ink sketch of December 21 (p, 455, top). And while there are occasional hints of her in subsequent compositions (such as the oil sketch of January 16, 1955), she does not really appear again until her reincarnation as the *odalisque* with the hookah on the left of the final variation (p. 456). Of course, the real drama of Picasso's *Women of Algiers* has to do not with Jacqueline but with that extended exploration of pictorial means analyzed so closely in Leo Steinberg's classic text[30] —a remarkably profound and detailed plotting of Picasso's intricate artistic thought.

The end of 1955 would witness Picasso's most penetrating image of Jacqueline, a linoleum print (p. 460, top right) that plumbs her fragile equilibrium and her vulnerability

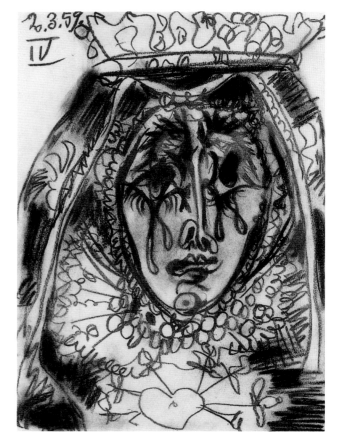

Mater Dolorosa. March 2, 1959. Lithographic crayon on paper, 14⅝ × 10⅝″ (37 × 27 cm). Zervos XVIII, 338. Private collection

Seated Nude (Jacqueline). 1959. Oil on canvas, 57½ × 45″ (146 × 114.2 cm). Zervos XVIII, 308. Private collection

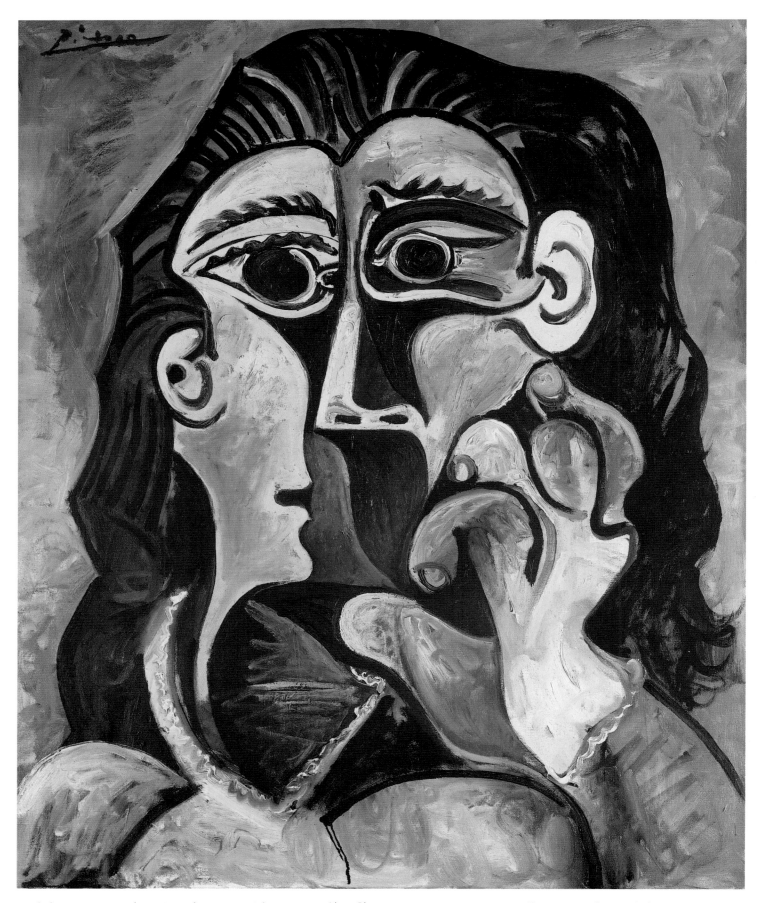

Head of a Woman (Jacqueline). December 18, 1961. Oil on canvas, 39⅜ × 31⅞″ (100 × 81 cm). Zervos XXIII, 1. Collection M. and W. Staehelin

Head of a Woman (Jacqueline). December 20, 1961. Lead pencil on paper, 12⅝ × 9½″ (32 × 24 cm). Zervos XX, 163. Private collection

Head of a Woman (Jacqueline). December 21, 1961. Linocut, 25³⁄₁₆ × 20⅞″ (64 × 53 cm). Geiser/Baer V, 1278. Museu Picasso, Barcelona

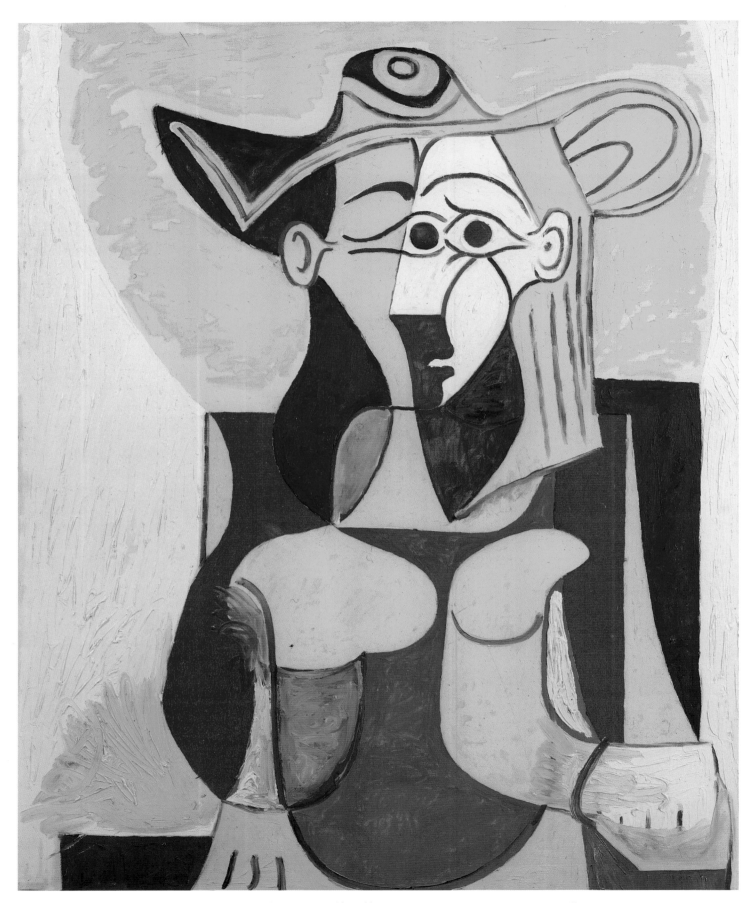

Woman in an Armchair (Jacqueline). January 2, 1962. Oil on canvas, 63¾ × 51¼″ (162 × 130 cm). Zervos XX, 179. Private collection

Woman in a Yellow Hat (Jacqueline). December 19, 1961–January 20, 1962. Oil on canvas, 36 × 28¾″ (91.5 × 73 cm). Zervos XX, 162. Private collection

sits, or between the silhouette of figure and chair together as opposed to the shaping of the residual background areas of wall and floor. The power of the self-inhibiting rectangle formed by Jacqueline's two arms, right breast, and exaggerated clasped hands is remarkable. The parallelism between the chair's right arm and Jacqueline's left upper arm obliges us to compare the architecture of her tightly locked but animated form with that of the inani-

mate object on which she sits, and to find the latter comparatively lacking in tensile strength. Even the continuous diagonal formed by her right lower leg and foot, and the vertical of the left one, play a more emphatic structural role in the composition than the solidly rectilinear legs of the chair.

Few portraits by Picasso boast a more extraordinary asymmetry of the human face than this *Seated Nude*. The manner in which Jacqueline's right cheek is pulled out laterally in a way that allows its plane to "double" as that of her forearm, and her right ear to approach her elbow so as to enhance the analogy between the two shapes, is pictorial invention at its highest. The "down and dirty" flesh tones of Jacqueline's body are one with the *expressivo* of her underarm hair, whose prickly patterns creep up to the top of her head; its rhythms are echoed in the brushwork, the sureness and determination of which make many "gestural" pictures of the 1950s look finicky by comparison.

Jacqueline's entire pose is one which emphasizes the containment and closure—if not the denial—of the self, psychological states made all the more poignant by the beggarliness of the homely props, such as the bottle of water and the high-heeled shoes. The latter are very consciously fixed at right angles to show simultaneously the objects' front and side views, with one parallel to the picture plane, the other moving through space but tilted upward. Thus the two together form a microcosm that re-enacts the fundamental plastic tension at work in the figure as a whole.

Perhaps because of their astonishing number, Picasso's individual pictures usually appear more a part of an ongoing exploration of ideas than do the successive pictures of other artists. The four portraits of Jacqueline begun between December 18 and 21, 1961 (two oils, one drawing, and a linocut), provide an excellent illustration of the degree to which Picasso's pictures are linked with one another even in the absence of conscious serial intent. The concatenation of these four images does not follow the type of logic we find in such series as the eleven states of *Bull*[31] (where, for example, the eleven representations pass from total painterliness to total linearity), or even in the looser series such as *Women of Algiers*. Yet the interrelationships are unmistakable, even though the order of the works sometimes contains surprises. Inasmuch as Picasso dated most of his work by the calendar day, at least from his middle years onward, we are facilitated in pursuing the task Picasso bequeathed us in undertaking this practice: to help "learn more about man in general through the study of the creative man." "I often think about such a science," Picasso continued, "and I want to leave to posterity a documentation that will be as complete as possible."[32]

If Picasso's dating did not indicate otherwise, one would probably assume that the pencil drawing of Jacqueline with her head leaning on her hand, dated December 20, 1961 (p. 467, top), preceded—indeed, served as a sketch for—the monumental oil of December 18 (p. 466). Certainly that daring canvas, which attains its

Two Busts of a Woman (Jacqueline). May 13, 1962. Lead pencil on paper, 10⅝ × 16½" (27 × 42 cm). Zervos XX, 221. Private collection

Seated Woman (Jacqueline). May 13–June 16, 1962. Oil on canvas, 57½ × 44⅞″ (146 × 114 cm). Zervos XX, 227. Collection M. and Mme Claude Laurens, Paris

Small Bust of a Woman (Jacqueline). February 15–March 7, 1962. Lithograph, 13¾ × 10⅝″ (35 × 27 cm). Geiser/Baer V, 1300. Museu Picasso, Barcelona

Head of a Woman (Jacqueline). May 20, 1962. Conté crayon on paper, 16½ × 10⅝″ (42 × 27 cm). Zervos XX, 228. Private collection

Jacqueline at Notre-Dame-de-Vie, Mougins, 1961. Photograph by Jacqueline Picasso. Private collection

looming monumentality as a result of its combination of absolute scale and close cropping by the frame, is the more challenging image of the two and seemingly the more developed. Picasso's emphatic contouring of Jacqueline's hair, the saliency of her features, and the sureness with which the shaded areas are determined all mark this canvas as one of the artist's real successes, while the beauties of the pencil drawing (which, to be sure, take account of a certain sadness in Jacqueline's mien) are only perceived through an uneven and, in some passages, unsure web of markings. The distancing of Jacqueline within the illusioned space of this drawing and the framing of her image are also comparatively more conventional. Given what we know of the dates of the two images, we have to imagine Picasso, in effect, stepping back from the boldness of his canvas.

Upon closer inspection of the pictorial context for these three days in December, we discover that the painting and the drawing were, in fact, separated by the laying-in, on December 19, of another painting, the lyrical *Woman in a Yellow Hat* (p. 469), which would undergo its final revision—probably the whole of the hat and chignon, and perhaps some of the yellows and reds in the face—only in January of the following year. This bust view of Jacqueline, which shows her leaning on her right

Bust of a Woman (Jacqueline). May 20, 1962. Colored pencil on paper, 16½ × 10⅝" (42 × 27 cm). Zervos XX, 229. Private collection.

Head of a Woman on a Green Background (Jacqueline). May 5–August 2, 1962. Oil on canvas, 28¾ × 21⅝" (73 × 55 cm). Zervos XX, 231. Private collection

hand rather than her left, is set in a comparatively conventional manner within the space and framing edge of the canvas. And in tandem with the perspective of the hat brim, these decisions push the figure into a deeper (if still somewhat shallow) space compared to the oil of the day before.

If the drawing of December 20 is clearly based upon the large canvas of December 18, its recession into space was nevertheless obviously inflected by the oil begun on the nineteenth. The differences between them suggest that, after executing the large canvas, Picasso wanted further to develop certain aspects of Jacqueline which fall generally under the rubric of the polarized or divided personality. For Picasso, this meant achieving through a conflation of images the simultaneous presentation of an outgoing or "public" self and a more subjective, psychologically withdrawn "private" self. From the mid-1920s onward, Picasso had used for this purpose variations on his celebrated "double-face," which usually discloses the darker, private self in the form of a shaded or more darkly colored profile enclosed within the silhouette of a full-front face. This trope, the possibilities of which Picasso appears first to have noticed in winter 1908–09, while abstracting in a Cubist manner the light and dark shading in the face of his standing *Bather*,[33] became his

most frequently employed visual symbol (although it never reappears in exactly the same form). By shrinking Jacqueline's giant thumb (as it appears in the large oil), and by pulling the fourth and fifth fingers of her hand sufficiently to the right, Picasso makes room in the pencil drawing for a clearer division of the head into two distinct and expressively contrasting aspects. His interest in asymmetry also leads him to a greater contrast in the figuration of Jacqueline's eyes. Though somewhat different in size in the large oil, both had been figured there with the same patterns; in the drawing, however, Jacqueline's eyes have been represented divergently, her left, more shrunken and more deeply recessed into its socket than her right. The result heightens those suggestions of malaise already present in the large painting and renders manifest the potentially darker self within the personality.

One day after the drawing, Picasso returned to the same image in a linoleum print (p. 467, bottom). Here the technique itself ensured a flatter and more inherently abstract image, in which linearity and planarity would dominate, and where any suggestion of modeling would necessarily be raw and simple. In some respects this print is the most striking of the four images in the group we are considering. The Cubist elements that had remained largely a matter of infrastructure in the large canvas of

Sketches for Bust of a Woman. May 21, 1962. Pencil on paper, each image: 16½ × 10⅝″ (42 × 27 cm). Zervos XX, 234–42.
Private collections

December 18 become more evident here, but are set off, at the same time, against a more intensely expressionist component carried largely by the contrast between Jacqueline's eyes. For the first time in this succession of works, Picasso forcefully articulates the eyebrows and lashes. Unlike the intensely expressive and intricate drawing lavished on the eyes, the hand supporting Jacqueline's head is now relatively "de-characterized" to the point that its abstract form can virtually be read as part of the plane of the face. Although Picasso fills the picture field with the head itself almost as much here as in the large oil, the linocut does not communicate as much of the looming grandeur of the personage found in the canvas, where it is achieved not only by the scale relationship of its silhouette to the field as a whole, but by its larger-than-life-size image.

During the period of the works we have just been discussing, Picasso was absorbed in making his flat metal cutout sculptures, of which the giant head in Chicago is probably the best known. A number of these cutouts can be considered portraits of Jacqueline,[34] although in the Chicago work the artist has conflated his wife's head with the snout of Kabul, the couple's Afghan hound (opposite and right). These sculptures lie outside the purview of the exhibition (for reasons of space), hence this book. But we must observe that, as was usually the

Bust of a Woman (Jacqueline). May 28, 1962. Oil on canvas, 42⅜ × 19½″ (107.5 × 49.5 cm). Zervos XX, 243. Private collection

Jacqueline Seated with Kabul. May 31–June 7, 1962. Oil on canvas, 57½ × 44⅞″ (146 × 114 cm). Zervos XX, 244. Private collection

case with Picasso, his sculptural investigations cross-fertilized his painting (and both emerge, ultimately, from his practice of drawing). Here the series that closes with the painted counterpart of the Chicago sculpture (p. 473, right) is clearly less accomplished than the portrait of Jacqueline as a *Seated Woman* completed on June 16, 1962 —equally related in general to the cutout sculptures. Realized in subtle tones of black, white, and warmed-up grays—a palette with which Picasso could not go wrong —this image endows Jacqueline with regal stability (p. 471).

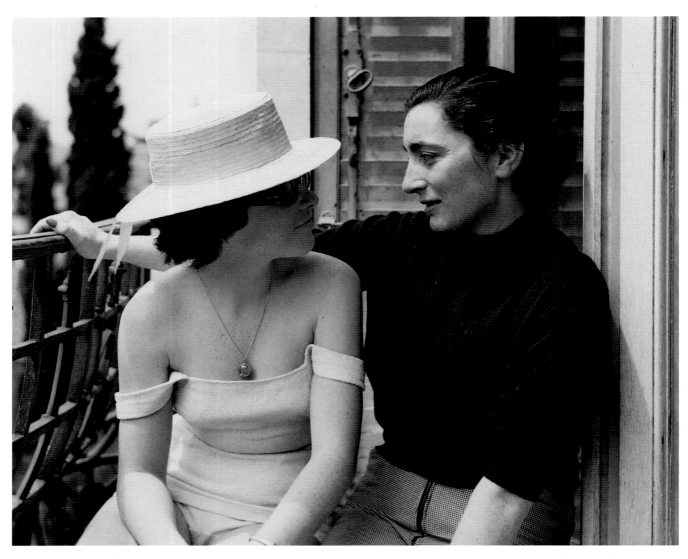

Jacqueline Picasso and her daughter, Catherine Hutin-Blay (detail), at La Californie. Photograph by Jacqueline Picasso. Private collection

The years 1963 and 1964 found Picasso focusing more than ever on images of Jacqueline, most of them exploring a kind of painterliness that contrasted markedly with the illusioned *découpage* of the 1962 *Seated Woman. Large Profile* (opposite) of January 7, 1963, has an airiness, a kind of transparency, that depends in part upon its brushed-out and relaxed facture. Jacqueline's head acquires a formal dignity through the heraldic absoluteness of her profile, while the immensity of the image is reinforced by the fact that her head is sized much larger than life. If she seems made out of some otherworldly, lighter-than-air substance in this 1963 portrait, the *Nude in an Armchair* (p. 478), finished in June of the following year, has brought her back down to earth. This comfortable and intimate portrait has a fleshiness that is less a quality described or illusioned by the painter than a property of the pigment itself.

From the mid- to the late 1960s, Picasso pressed his language of pictorial signs into a very economical shorthand that lent itself more readily to a generic type of imagery than to the particularizations congruent with the type of portraiture we have been discussing. By 1969, however, we find him returning to less staccato images of Jacqueline that are easily recognizable. The palette and brushwork of these images convey a tenderness and delicacy—indeed, a certain empathy with their subject—that were but intermittently delineated before.

Only a lifetime of drawing with a brush could have produced the homely grace of Jacqueline's contouring in *Woman on a Pillow* of July 10, 1969 (p. 479). Here, everything that belongs to the laureate hand of the younger Picasso has been set aside. The awkwardness of the image is willed—and full of feeling. This is not a question of the loss of dexterity in old age. Picasso had remained capable of remarkably controlled and highly refined drawing virtually until his final days, as his graphic work

Large Profile (Jacqueline). January 7, 1963. Oil on canvas, 51¼ × 38¼″ (130 × 97 cm). Zervos XXIII, 117. Kunstsammlung Nordrhein-Westfalen, Düsseldorf

Nude in an Armchair (Jacqueline). May 2-8–June 7, 1964. Oil on canvas, 45⅝ × 31¾″ (116 × 80.5 cm). Zervos XXIV, 138. Private collection

demonstrates; indeed, some etchings made in his ninety-first year have a blinding virtuoso brilliance that have made them popular among collectors. Such technical finesse had been necessary to explicate the complex and detailed narrative situations with which those prints and drawings often dealt. It would have been entirely alien to the simple iconic directness of his figure paintings, as

in *Woman on a Pillow*. If there is any virtuosic element in this canvas, it is not in the drawing but in the subtlety of gradations in the gray-blue shading and the relaxed, nuanced manner in which that tone is warmed by ochers and cooled by whites. This is a virtuosity of the eye rather than the hand, and comes as close as modernism probably ever gets to the spirit of late Titian.

WILLIAM RUBIN

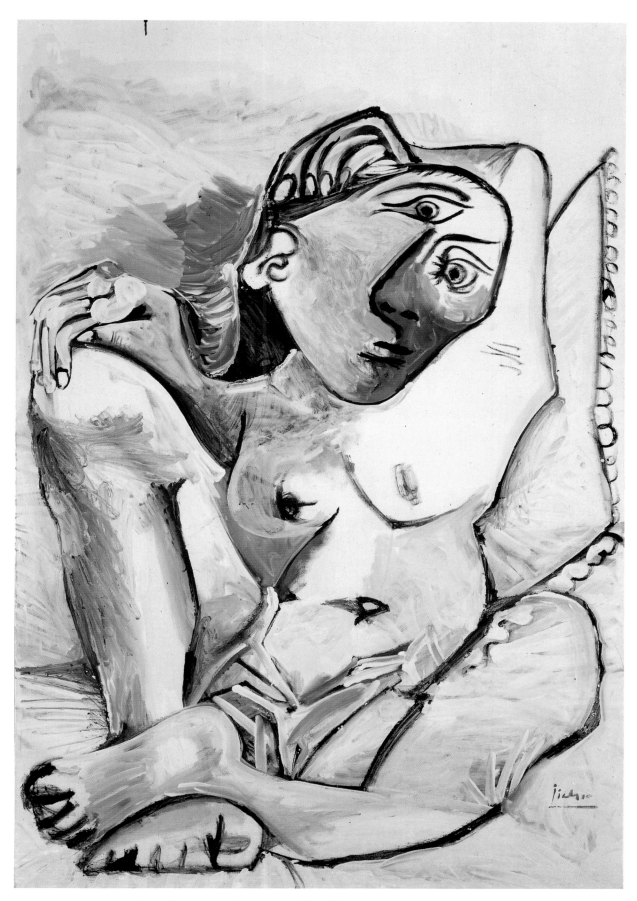

Woman on a Pillow (Jacqueline). July 10, 1969. Oil on canvas, 76¾ × 51¼″ (195 × 130 cm). Zervos XXXI, 315. Musée Picasso, Paris

Pablo and Jacqueline Picasso at Notre-Dame-de-Vie, Mougins, 1961. Photograph by Jacqueline Picasso. Private collection

Picasso was in his mid-seventies when he began living with Jacqueline. During their years at La Californie, he managed to maintain a large number of contacts with old and new friends, including, as before, painters as well as poets. As the artists of his own generation and those of the next disappeared, Picasso's contacts with the ongoing tradition of modern painting became fewer, and the several practicing painters he continued to see in his eighties were no longer drawn from their generation's handful of creative vanguardists, the caliber of artist with whom Picasso had maintained a dialogue for half a century. This isolation—enforced primarily by age but also, to some extent, by celebrity—did not serve Picasso as well as it did such painters as Bonnard and Matisse. As an artist whose temperament responded strongly to challenge, and whose emotional sources were drawn from the drama of urban sociability, loss of milieu and absence of contact with the cutting edge of modernism stripped Picasso's work of some of its cultural urgency.

Another painter might have worked less; ever the fighter, Picasso responded by working more. If Matisse's late work reflects a coming to terms with mortality, Picasso's shows him obstinately fighting against the dying of the light. With more stability and calm in his daily life during his last ten years, Picasso turned for drama to the narrative of his own past—as that could now be filtered and relived through the sentiments and sensibility of old

age; this produced a remarkable flowering in Picasso's prints and drawings, mediums which lent themselves far better to such "narratives" than did the inherently "iconic" vocabulary of modern painting. Picasso's isolation drew the painter increasingly into a dialogue with artists of the past, not only variations on particular works by the Old Masters, but in the appropriation of subject types such as the Musketeers, which reflected his particular affinities with the Baroque masters.

Even when painting such generic types, however, Picasso always seems to have wanted some real, some particular person in mind. We are not surprised that, before embarking on the series of Musketeers, he asked Piero Crommelynck to "model" a hat and cape the artist had on hand and that many of the Musketeers bore some resemblance to Piero. It is not, therefore, surprising that many of the most deeply felt pictures of his final years should have been inspired by Jacqueline, by then the only significant presence in his life. Few of his more generic late pictures contain the subtleties of emotion expressed in the superb portrait of Jacqueline of September 14, 1971 (opposite); few balance so clearly the passion of the pure painter with the love and compassion of the man. The style of this picture does not constitute an *Altersstil*. But the canvas reflects the abandon made possible by a long lifetime of painting culture, which Picasso could take for granted.

Seated Woman (Jacqueline). September 14, 1971. Oil on canvas, 57½ × 44⅞″ (146 × 114 cm). Zervos XXXIII, 181. Private collection

NOTES

1. Though Picasso is known throughout the world more for his Blue period than for anything else, even the art of those years constitutes less a style than simply a Symbolist decision to paint in a single, pervasive hue; as Verlaine had instructed: "pas de couleur, rien que la nuance." Within that hue limitation, Picasso actually worked in at least two quite different styles. See p. 450.

2. Françoise Gilot wrote that during the fall of 1952, when she had already begun to think of separating from Picasso, Madame Ramié [who with her husband ran the Madoura pottery in Vallauris], "imported a young cousin of hers named Jacqueline Roque to be a salesgirl at the pottery. . . . She spoke a little Spanish and since very little pottery was sold in winter, her chief occupation appeared to be holding conversations in Spanish with Pablo. . . . A week after I left Vallauris on September 30, Pablo came to Paris and stayed two weeks. Within a week of the time he got back to the Midi, Jacqueline Roque had taken over. 'One can't leave that poor man alone like that, at his age. I must look after him.' That was the substance of the quotations that were passed along to me at the time" (Françoise Gilot and Carlton Lake, *Life with Picasso* [New York: McGraw-Hill, 1964], p. 358).

John Richardson was more precise, specifying that "Jacqueline Hutin [Roque had been her maiden name] entered Picasso's life in the summer of 1952, shortly after she went to work in the Galerie Madoura. This gallery—in the rue d'Antibes at Cannes—was the retail outlet for the artist's Vallauris potters, the Ramiés. Over the next two years Picasso saw more and more of this attractive young divorcée, but did not introduce her into his work until summer 1954." Richardson adds in a note that "Jacqueline was no relation of Madame Ramié, as most biographers have assumed, but a casual acquaintance of her daughter-in-law, Hugvette" (John Richardson, "L'Epoque Jacqueline," in *Late Picasso: Paintings, Sculpture, Drawings, Prints 1953–1972* [London: Tate Gallery, 1988], pp. 17, 48, n. 1); original French edition, *Le Dernier Picasso* (Paris: Musée National d'Art Moderne, Centre Georges Pompidou, 1988).

3. Letter of October 8, 1919, from Braque in Sorgues to Kahnweiler in Bern, following Braque's return from the front (cited in Isabelle Monod-Fontaine et al., *Daniel-Henry Kahnweiler: Marchand, éditeur, écrivain* [Paris: Musée National d'Art Moderne, Centre Georges Pompidou, 1984], p. 126); in English translation in William Rubin, *Picasso and Braque: Pioneering Cubism* (New York: The Museum of Modern Art, 1989), pp. 51–52, and n. 159.

4. Typical of Cézanne's remarks concerning temperament is the one contained in a letter of February 22, 1903: "I have nothing to hide in art," Cezanne wrote Charles Camoin. "Primary force alone, *id est* temperament, can bring a person to the end he must attain" (cited in John Rewald, *Cézanne: A Biography* [New York: Harry N. Abrams, 1986], p. 228).

5. The substance of the views attributed here to Picasso is drawn from my notes of two conversations with him in July 1970. These notes, recorded in the evenings of the conversations in question, after I had returned to my summer home, did not attempt to reconstruct verbatim any part of these conversations (which would have been impossible without a recording device, never acceptable to Picasso). In attempting to set down the gist of Picasso's observations, I paraphrased them in English, though any individual word I happened to remember was recorded in the original French.

6. Conversation with the artist, July 1970.

7. I say "in his art, at least" because Cézanne showed much less of his temperament, willpower, and ethical stamina in many of his life activities than in his work. That he was aware of his incapacity to order equally well his life as his art is revealed by a letter he wrote to Chocquet in 1886, the year of his marriage: "Chance has not favored me with an equal self-assurance [i.e., the intellectual equilibrium that characterizes you]; it is the only regret I have about things on this earth" (cited in Rewald, *Cézanne: A Biography*, p. 127). His self-awareness of the weaker side of his personality is further described by Rewald: "Little by little, this lack of 'intellectual equilibrium,' his dread of life and doubtless also of death, as well as the influence of his mother and sister, made of Cézanne, who had been inveterately anti-clerical, a churchgoing Catholic. 'It is fear!' he explained to Paul Alexis in 1891. 'I feel that I have only a few days left on earth—and then what? I believe I shall survive and do not want to risk roasting in *eternum.*'" Although Cézanne went to Mass, he considered it a sign of weakness and mockingly referred to it as taking his "'slice of the Middle Ages.' He hated priests and was afraid of getting into their 'clutches,' and this aversion even extended to religion, which he called 'moral hygiene'" (Rewald, p. 127).

8. This observation and the substance of the following sentences are taken from notes recorded by the late Professor Albert Elsen, Jr., from lectures by Professor Meyer Schapiro at Columbia University during the school year 1950–51. Elsen had made these notes available to this author, who missed this lecture at the time.

9. Zervos I, 202.

10. Describing the boulevard de Clichy studio, to which Picasso moved in September 1909, Fernande wrote: "He worked in a large, airy studio, which no one could enter without permission, where nothing could be touched and where, as usual, the chaos—which never remotely resembled those carefully worked-on states of disorder designed to appeal to visitors and show the host in a flattering light—had to be treated with respect. . . . The studio was never cleaned unless Picasso gave orders for it to be. No sweeping was done because he couldn't stand dust, except as it lay in its undisturbed state. Dust in the air and sticking to his wet canvases made him wild with rage" (Fernande Olivier, *Picasso and His Friends* [New York: Appleton-Century, 1965], pp. 135, 136).

Brassaï described his first meeting with Picasso, which occurred in 1932 at the rue La Boétie apartment that Picasso used as a studio: "I began then to survey my strange surroundings. I had expected an artist's studio, and this was an apartment converted into a kind of warehouse. Certainly no characteristically middle-class dwelling was ever so uncharacteristically furnished. There were four or five rooms—each with a marble fireplace surmounted by a mirror—entirely emptied of any customary furniture and littered with stacks of paintings, cartons, wrapped packages, pails of all sizes, many of them containing the molds for his statues, piles of books, reams of paper, odds and ends of everything, placed wherever there was an inch of space, along the walls and even spread across the floors, all covered with a thick layer of dust. . . . The floors were dull and lusterless, long since deprived of any polish, coated here and there with splotches of paint, and strewn with a carpet of cigarette butts. Picasso had stood his easel in the largest and best-lit room—and this was the only room that contained any furniture. . . . Madame Picasso never came up to this apartment" (Brassaï, *Picasso and Company*, translated by Francis Price [Garden City, N.Y.: Doubleday, 1966], p. 5); originally published as *Conversations avec Picasso* (Paris: Editions Gallimard, 1964).

Sabartés had ample opportunities to observe Picasso's "studio and/or living" habits, having moved into rue La Boétie in November 1935, at the artist's request, to live with him: "Observing him at close range and pondering his strange ways, I sometimes think that perhaps he does not dare exert pressure upon events for fear that the air displaced by a voluntary gesture may shatter the equilibrium of his life and change his fate. Who knows?" (Jaime Sabartés, *Picasso. An Intimate Portrait*, translated by Angel Flores [New York: Prentice-Hall, 1948], p. 106). "When he finally got out of bed, he would take the letters and papers and pile them on the buffet, or a chair, or a table, or even in the dining room or bathroom. This new pile is added to another pile begun some other time, with the same care and the same aim. Everything has been placed here or there in order not to mix this with that, with the intention of going over it later more carefully; but he always receives new mail and never finds an opportunity to reread any of it. Thus it is that the piles overflow on tables and chairs, and nothing can be touched or put in order until the day and the hour of the final sorting. . . . The mantelpiece in the dining room is laden with things. . . . Obviously, it would never have occurred to him to build up this cluttering labyrinth of bagatelles did he not have a mania for collecting everything, without rhyme or reason. His pockets testify to this: filled with papers, nails, keys, pieces of cardboard, pebbles, pieces of bone, a pocketknife, a small knife, notebooks for his literary lucubrations, matchboxes, cigarettes, cigarette lighters without fluid . . . letters and bills, very crumpled or totally shredded—irretrievably ruined—because of his fear of losing them!—seashells, a stone which suggested something to him on seeing it on the ground, pieces of string, ribbons, buttons, an eraser, a pencil stump, his fountain pen, etc. Of course his coat is very heavy and his pockets bulge and finally split. When he returns from his summer trips, he brings along vast quantities of stones, shells, pieces of glass and porcelain smoothed by the sea, fishbones, jawbones of animals, at times whole skulls—in short, anything that attracted his attention on the beach. . . . He keeps to this day ties which he wore as a child, his first drawings and paintings, packs of Spanish cigarettes, matchboxes of olden days, some full and some empty, and of the most diverse origin, cigars of different brands, chunks of bread, . . . mandolins and other musical instruments, Negro sculptures, castanets—in short, everything he has ever laid hands upon for however brief a moment" (Sabartés, *An Intimate Portrait,* pp. 107–11).

"After three years, in spite of the attentions of Jacqueline Roque," wrote Roland Penrose of La Californie, "the situation has not changed much. Incongruous objects, crowded together, become more deeply hedged in by a forest of newcomers. Packing-cases are opened to see what is inside, then left packed. Flowers stand desiccated in their vases. Food, clothing, toys, books, lamps, presents of all descriptions, and objets d'art pile up on top of each other like the crusts of the earth. Yet strangely enough, in spite of all this, there is no squalor. As the visitor grows used to the disorder, details of fascinating interest catch the eye. A Sicilian marionette in golden armour hangs from a lamp standard, a cage of noisy tropical birds can be seen among books and papers, a small self-portrait of the Douanier Rousseau and a night landscape by Max Ernst emerge from piles of ceramics. . . . The quality essential to every object in this heterogeneous collection is its value to Picasso in his work. Everywhere there are signs of his activity, everything has gone through his hands and been scrutinized by him before taking its place in this agglomeration. Canvases, ceramics, tiles, plates, bronze and plaster sculptures, bulging portfolios crammed with drawings and engravings mingle with things that have been brought there intentionally or by chance. All have their significance and their place in the alchemist's den in which he lives" (Roland Penrose, *Picasso: His Life and Work* [London: Victor Gollancz, 1958], p. 357).

To the above, this author would add only that Picasso seemed to know the precise location of every book, bibelot, object, and work of art in any of his studios or ancillary rooms.

11. The division of Cubism into Analytic and Synthetic phases was first proposed in *Documents: Archéologie, Beaux-Arts, Ethnographie, Variétés* 2, no. 3 (1930), pp. 180, 181, issued as an *Hommage à Picasso.* No author was indicated for this "Notice Documentaire," but it was probably Carl Einstein (as the same definition occurs, as we shall see, in a publication by Einstein the following year). *Documents,* on whose editorial board Einstein sat, categorized Picasso's Cubism as follows: "1910–1914 Période qui peut être dite celle du CUBISME ANALYTIQUE. C'est la phase héroïque du cubisme; 1914–18 Vers 1914, commence ce qu'on appelle fréquemment le CUBISME SYNTHETIQUE. A la description des objets par détails séparés dont la

somme restituait les objets primitifs, se substitue une manière moins énumératrice d'en rendre compte." This definition of the two phases of Cubism recurs in the third edition of Carl Einstein's *Die Kunst des 20. Jahrhunderts* (Berlin: Propyläen-Verlag, 1931). It had been absent from the first and second editions, published in 1926 and 1928, respectively. In the chronological outline of Picasso's career up to 1928 (p. 87), one reads: "1910–14 die Zeit des analytischen Kubismus; 1914–18 der synthetische Kubismus." Einstein's chronology is only approximate. Had Kahnweiler been responsible for this division, as is sometimes suggested, he would surely have begun Synthetic Cubism in 1913, or even in the autumn of 1912, as he was close enough to the actual events not to have made the same mistake that was made in *Documents.*

12. Even though *Three Women* (and many of its studies) and *Bread and Fruitdish on a Table* were published in 1942 by Zervos (II¹, 101–08, and 134, respectively), they dropped out of the canonical history of Cubism as a result of the absence of these paintings from Barr's monographs on Picasso (1939 and 1946). Only in 1964 did Pierre Daix identify the importance of *Three Women* in Picasso's oeuvre and reproduce it, for the first time in color (Pierre Daix, *Picasso* [Paris: Somogy, 1964]); its greatness was not measured until the publication of Leo Steinberg's magisterial text, "Resisting Cézanne: Picasso's Three Women," *Art in America* 66 (November 1978), pp. 114–33. The importance of *Bread and Fruitdish on a Table* was not recognized until the 1970s.

13. The stylistic multiplicity Picasso aborded in *Les Demoiselles d'Avignon* was, for example, resurrected only from 1912 onward in works featuring *trompe l'oeil* collage. This multiplicity of styles is not unrelated to Picasso's very first *papier collé,* the 1908 *Bathers* (Zervos II¹, 66), which would go without suite until autumn 1912. The collage/construction implications of some of the tribal art that Picasso had collected between 1907 and 1911 were only fully assimilated into his own work beginning in 1912. By the same token the "proto-Surrealism" of Picasso's 1913 painting and drawing would only really flourish again subsequent to Picasso's links with Surrealist poets and artists in 1925.

14. The most important of these was the period 1934–36—a bleak one, indeed, during which Picasso was confronted by events such as the breakup of his marriage with Olga and its ensuing complications: the birth of his daughter Maya, not without difficult consequences; full separation from Olga; the beginning of his involvement with Dora Maar; and the deteriorating political situation in Spain. Picasso's work in 1935 was numerically minuscule as compared to that of the preceding or following years.

15. During the tortuous process of Françoise Gilot's ending of her liaison with Picasso in 1953/54, he made the acquaintance of the conventionally very pretty Sylvette David, the fiancée of a young English chair designer, who personally attended all the sessions in which his fiancée modeled for the painter. According to

Françoise, it was during the spring of 1953 that Picasso became intrigued by the silhouettes of Sylvette and her young English fiancé, who designed and assembled very unusual chairs. Having purchased a number of these chairs for La Galloise, Picasso "decided that Sylvette, with her blond pony tail and long bangs, had very pictorial features and he began to make portraits of her. . . . The first few portraits he did with enthusiasm, and then he began to drag his heels like a schoolboy doing homework on his vacation. The pleasure was shrinking. One day he reproached me: 'You don't seem at all unhappy about it. You should refuse to admit another face into my painting. If you knew how Marie-Thérèse suffered when I began making portraits of Dora Maar and how unhappy Dora was when I went back to painting Marie-Thérèse. But you—you're a monster of indifference'" (Gilot and Lake, *Life with Picasso,* p. 352).

16. In early 1907, as he was working up the *Demoiselles,* Picasso exchanged a powerful still life (Daix 66) with Matisse. In return, he chose Matisse's "primitivist" portrait of his daughter Marguerite, just recently completed, in which the "conceptualized" profile nose in the frontal face paralleled Picasso's own visualization of the moment.

17. *Mirada fuerte* is, besides *machismo,* another prominent Andalusian characteristic. Picasso, who was born in Málaga, remained deeply Andalusian at heart. Richardson has stressed the importance of Picasso's preoccupation with the *mirada fuerte,* especially in his old age. "Being Andalusian, [Picasso] . . . was at the mercy of that other Andalusian obsession, the *mirada fuerte* (literally, 'strong gazing')." Citing a definition from David D. Gilmore's *Aggression and Community: Paradoxes of Andalusian Culture* (New Haven: Yale University Press, 1987), Richardson finds it relevant to Picasso: "'In Andalusia the eye is akin to a sexual organ . . . looking too intently at a woman is akin to ocular rape'" (John Richardson with the collaboration of Marilyn McCully, *A Life of Picasso, Volume 1: 1881–1906* [New York: Random House, 1991], p. 10).

18. Richardson, writing about Picasso's portraits of Jacqueline, observed: "Jacqueline had a far from easy time. Picasso manipulated people —often by way of his work—as ruthlessly as he manipulated form. . . . Once the image had been established, Picasso did not hesitate to manipulate it in ingenious and occasionally diabolical ways, manipulating Jacqueline's feelings in the process. Subtle adjustments to the portraits enabled Picasso to worship or humiliate or test her . . . and even on occasion predict one of her frequent bouts of illness. This prediction might take the form of a drawing like one done on Saint Valentine's Day, 1957, in which Jacqueline's anguished portrait is superimposed over a network of zigzag lines in fever-chart pink. When Jacqueline, who was nothing if not suggestible, fell ill the following day, the artist could take pride in his prophetic powers" (John Richardson, "The Catch in the Late Picasso," *The New York Review of Books* 31, no. 12 [July 19, 1984], p. 24); reprinted as "Picasso's Last Years," in *Pablo Picasso: Meeting in Montreal* (Montreal

Museum of Fine Arts, 1985), pp. 102–03.

19. See Daix XV, 47.

20. For example, certain oils such as Zervos XVII, 370, 371, and 374, from the Meninas series would be difficult to identify without knowledge of their context in the oeuvre.

21. Zervos XV, 164.

22. Picasso's sketches of figures from Delacroix's *Women of Algiers* in the Royan sketchbook of 1940 (Musée Picasso, Paris, M.P. 1879), are reproduced in Marie-Laure Bernadac, "Picasso 1953–1972: Painting as Model," in *Late Picasso*, p. 56, figs. 18, 20.

23. Ibid., p. 55.

24. Daniel-Henry Kahnweiler, "Entretiens avec Picasso au sujet des Femmes d'Alger," *Aujourd'hui*, no. 4, 1955.

25. "[Picasso] said with a laugh, 'when Matisse died he left his odalisques to me as a legacy, and this is my idea of the orient though I have never been there'" (Penrose, *Picasso: His Life and Work*, pp. 351–52).

26. Picasso saw the *Turkish Bath* at the retrospective exhibition organized in homage to Ingres and held during the Salon d'Automne at the Grand Palais, Paris, October–November 1905.

27. Zervos I, 321.

28. "The grandiose Villa La Californie . . . had an Orientalist air. He had put so much thought into the 'Women of Algiers,' Picasso told Daix, that he ended up with a house that, as it were, matched them" (Richardson, "L'Epoque Jacqueline," p. 19).

29. Lionello Venturi, *Cézanne: son art—son oeuvre* (Paris: Paul Rosenberg, 1936), no. 224.

30. Leo Steinberg, "The Algerian Women and Picasso at Large" (1972), in Steinberg, *Other Criteria: Confrontations with Twentieth-Century Art* (London: Oxford University Press, 1976), pp. 124–234. An article containing some indications from this chapter had been published a year earlier under the title "Picasso and Drawing as if to Possess," in *Artforum* 10, no. 2 (October 1971), pp. 44–53.

31. *Bull.* Paris, December 5, 1945–January 17, 1946. Eleven progressive states of the same lithograph published in Fernand Mourlot, *Picasso Lithographs,* translated by Jean Didry (Boston: Book and Art Publisher, 1970), pp. 27–30; 17, states I–XI. The eleven states were reproduced in William Rubin, ed., *Pablo Picasso: A Retrospective* (New York: The Museum of Modern Art, 1980), pp. 390–91.

32. On Monday, December 6, 1943, Picasso explained to Brassaï: "Why do you think I date everything I do? Because it is not sufficient to know an artist's works—it is also necessary to know when he did them, why, how, under what circumstances. . . . Some day there will undoubtedly be a science—it may be called the science of man—which will seek to learn more about man in general through the study of the creative man. I often think about such a science, and I want to leave to posterity a documentation that will be as complete as possible. That's why I put a date on everything I do" (Brassaï, *Picasso and Company*, 1966, p. 100).

33. Zervos II¹, 111. Robert Rosenblum's observations regarding the origin of the "double-face" in the 1908–09 *Bather* were cited by this author in *Picasso in the Collection of The Museum of Modern Art* (New York: The Museum of Modern Art, 1972), p. 227, nn. 5 and 6.

34. Spies, 620 and 626.

Eugène Delacroix. *The Women of Algiers.* 1834. Oil on canvas, 69¹¹⁄₁₆ × 89³⁄₈″ (177 × 227 cm). The Louvre, Paris

Eugène Delacroix. *The Women of Algiers.* 1849. Oil on canvas, 33¹⁄₁₆ × 43¹¹⁄₁₆″ (84 × 111 cm). Musée Fabre, Montpellier

Lenders to the Exhibition

The Baltimore Museum of Art
Museu Picasso, Barcelona
Öffentliche Kunstsammlung Basel, Kunstmuseum
The Art Institute of Chicago
Museum Ludwig, Cologne
Columbus Museum of Art
The Detroit Institute of Arts
Kunstsammlung Nordrhein-Westfalen, Düsseldorf
The Menil Collection, Houston
Tate Gallery, London
Pushkin State Museum of Fine Arts, Moscow
The Metropolitan Museum of Art, New York
The Museum of Modern Art, New York
The Pierpont Morgan Library, Thaw Collection, New York
Musée National d'Art Moderne, Centre National d'Art et de Culture Georges Pompidou, Paris
Musée Picasso, Paris
Národní Galerie, Prague
The St. Louis Art Museum
The State Hermitage Museum, St. Petersburg
The Hakone Open-Air Museum, Tokyo
Art Gallery of Ontario, Toronto
Museum of Modern Art, Toyama
National Gallery of Art, Washington, D.C.
Worcester Art Museum

Alsdorf Collection, Chicago
Heinz Berggruen
Mrs. Lindy Bergman
Beyeler Collection, Basel
Gilbert de Botton, St. Moritz
Mrs. Henry Brandon
Mr. and Mrs. Marshall Cogan
Mrs. Sally Ganz
Mrs. Jacques Gelman
Stephen Hahn, New York
Jan and Marie-Anne Krugier
M. and Mme Claude Laurens, Paris
Susan and Lewis Manilow
Marina Picasso
Mrs. Daniel Saidenberg
Estate of Florene M. Schoenborn
M. and W. Staehelin
Mrs. John Hay Whitney
Anonymous lenders

Thomas Ammann Fine Art AG, Zurich
Galerie Cazeau-de La Béraudière, Paris
Fuji Television Gallery Co., Ltd.
Galerie Jan Krugier, Geneva
Galerie Louise Leiris, Paris

Acknowledgments

Mounting an exhibition of this scale and importance necessitates the assistance and collaboration of a great number of individuals and institutions. I have been fortunate in the generous help I have received from people outside The Museum of Modern Art, the extraordinary dedication of the Museum's staff members, and the support and encouragement of its former director, Richard E. Oldenburg; Glenn D. Lowry, Director; and the members of the Board of Trustees—especially Chairman Emeritus David Rockefeller, Chairman Ronald S. Lauder, and President Agnes Gund.

This project could hardly have been contemplated, not to say realized, without the cooperation of Picasso's heirs and their families. Maya Widmaier Picasso, Claude Ruiz-Picasso, Bernard Ruiz-Picasso, Marina Picasso, Christine Ruiz-Picasso, and Jacqueline Picasso's daughter Catherine Hutin-Blay have not only lent generously, but their high level of personal cooperation, their willingness to search out and deal with questions of documentation, and finally their encouragement have all made this project a more enjoyable one for me and for my staff.

Claude Ruiz-Picasso has also served as a special advisor, as have Pierre Daix and John Richardson; their contributions are visible throughout the publication and exhibition. Brigitte Baer, on whose work we have depended for all our print documentation, has also been extremely helpful with advice, and Maya Widmaier Picasso has helped us to avoid a number of historical errors in our book.

Our heartfelt gratitude goes to the lenders—institutions, private individuals, and galleries (listed on page 485)—whose sacrifice in parting with works in their collections has made possible the realization of this exhibition. Foremost among the lending institutions, the Musée Picasso, Paris, merits our deepest appreciation. Gérard Régnier, Director, has generously approved our numerous loan requests, and Hélène Seckel, Chief Curator, has provided invaluable advice, information, and scholarly contributions throughout the preparation of this show. To her I offer my very particular gratitude. From the same institution, Brigitte Léal, Curator, and Anne Baldassari, Curator of Archives and Photography, have helped with many inquiries; along with Hélène Seckel they should also be thanked for the essays they have contributed to this volume. I would also like to express my gratitude to Irène Bizot, General Administrator at the Réunion des Musées Nationaux, for her constant and wise help, which reprises her collegial participation in previous shows.

The Museu Picasso, Barcelona, is another institution whose numerous loans have much enriched our exhibition. We owe a special word of thanks to its director, Maria-Teresa Ocaña. The Musée National d'Art Moderne, Centre National d'Art et de Culture Georges Pompidou, Paris, continues its role as a most cooperative lender to the Museum; we would like particularly to thank its director, Germain Viatte, and its chief curator, Madame Isabelle Monod-Fontaine. Other museums around the world have opened their collections to us and provided much needed documentation. Russian museums, in particular, continue to be generous lenders. We want to thank Dr. Mikhail Piotrovski, Director, The State Hermitage Museum, St. Petersburg, and Dr. Albert Kostenevich, Chief Curator of Modern European Painting. At The Pushkin State Museum of Fine Arts, Moscow, we thank Irina Antonova, Director; Alla Butrova, Deputy Director; and Inna Orn, Head of Foreign Relations. At the Národní Galerie, Prague, we thank the former director, Dr. Jirí Sevcík, and Director Martin Zlatohlávek, as well as Dr. Olga Uhrova, Curator-in-Chief. Dr. Peter Ludwig and Dr. Alfred M. Fischer, Curator, the Ludwig Museum, Cologne, have graciously lent three important works. We owe special thanks to Nicholas Serota, Director, the Tate Gallery, London, and to Katharina Schmidt, Director, Öffentliche Kunstsammlung Basel, both of whom continue the extraordinary level of participation they have established in the past. Our thanks for loans and/or help with this book go to Dr. Armin Zweite, Director, Kunstsammlung Nordrhein-Westfalen, Düssseldorf; Dr. Christophe von Tavel, Kunstmuseum Bern; Dr. Felix Baumann, Director, Kunsthaus Zurich; Shinya Ueda, Director, The Hakone Open-Air Museum, Tokyo; Chicanao Yagi, Director, the Museum of Modern Art, Toyama.

The participating American museums have been equally supportive and generous to us, and we would like to extend our gratitude to Arnold L. Lehman, Director, The Baltimore Museum of Art, and Brenda Richardson, Deputy Director for Art and Curator, Modern Painting & Sculpture; James N. Wood, Director, Charles F. Stuckey, former Frances and Thomas Dittmer Curator of Twentieth-Century Painting and Sculpture, and Suzanne Folds McCullagh, Curator of Earlier Prints & Drawings, The Art Institute of Chicago; Irvin M. Lippman, Executive Director, the Columbus Museum of Art; Samuel Sachs II, Director, The Detroit Institute of Arts; Mrs. John de Menil and Paul Winkler, Director, The Menil Collection; Philippe de Montebello, Director, The Metropolitan Museum of Art, and William S. Lieberman, Jacques and Natasha Gelman Chairman of 20th-Century Art, who was particularly helpful; James Burke, Director, and Sidney M. Goldstein, Associate Director, The St. Louis Art Museum; Maxwell L. Anderson, Director, the Art Gallery of Ontario, Toronto, and its former chief curator, Alan G. Wilkinson; Earl A. Powell III, Director, and Alan Shestack, Deputy Director, the National Gallery of Art, Washington, D.C.; and James A. Welu, Director, Worcester Art Museum.

Continuing with private lenders, I wish to acknowledge Ernst Beyeler, Heinz Berggruen, Gilbert de Botton, Mrs. Henry Brandon, Mr. and Mrs. Marshall Cogan, Eugene Thaw (whose loans were facilitated by Charles E. Pierce, Jr., Director, The Pierpont Morgan Library, and by Stephanie Wiles, Associate Curator of Drawings and Prints), Mrs. Sally Ganz, Mrs. Jacques Gelman, Stephen Hahn, M. and Mme Claude Laurens, Susan and Lewis Manilow, Mrs. Daniel Saidenberg, M. and W. Staehelin, and Mrs. John Hay Whitney. The late Mrs. Florene M. Schoenborn, whose lawyer, Stewart G. Rosenblum, is currently endeavoring to fulfill her wishes, and the late Mrs. Louise Reinhardt Smith will forever remain in our memory as very special lenders and benefactors to this institution. I want further to acknowledge with gratitude those private collectors who have chosen to remain totally anonymous.

Several gallery directors and dealers have facilitated our loan requests or acted as intermediaries: we are indebted to William Acquavella in New York, Doris Ammann in Zurich, William Beadleston in New York, Marc Blondeau in Paris, Galerie Cazeau-de La Béraudière in Paris, Richard Gray in Chicago, Mariko Goto at the Fuji Television Gallery in Tokyo, Quentin Laurens at the Galerie Louise Leiris in Paris, and Lionel Prejger in Paris. Jan Krugier and his assistant Evelyne Ferlay have played an important role in helping out with numerous inquiries as well as loans. We would also like to thank Jean-Marie Rouquette, Chief Curator of Arles Museums; Doug Hall, Director, the Queensland Museum, Brisbane; and James Cuno, Director of the Harvard Art Museums, for assistance in many crucial areas.

Other individuals helped us trace the works we were considering, generously made their time available to us, enriched us with their special expertise, and on occasion negotiated certain loans for us. In this category, we would like to thank Jeffrey Deitch, President of Jeffrey Deitch Inc., Art Advisory Services; Arne Glimcher, Chairman of Pace-Wildenstein, and his assistant Eileen Costello; Alexandra Schwartz, Director of Pace Master Prints; John Leighton, Curator of 19th-Century Paintings, The National Gallery, London; Thomas M. Messer, Director Emeritus, Solomon R. Guggenheim Museum; Christopher Burge, Chairman of Christie's; Wendy Luers; David Nash, formerly executive vice president of Sotheby's New York; Harumi Kohara, formerly at Sotheby's Japan; Angela Rosengart; and Werner Spies.

Almost all The Museum of Modern Art's departments have participated in one way or another in the preparation of this publication and exhibition. I am especially grateful to Kirk Varnedoe, Chief Curator of Painting and Sculpture, who has been a staunch supporter of this project as well as a major contributor to this book. As in the past, James S. Snyder, formerly deputy director for planning and program support, has diligently helped with Russian loans and various other matters. Beverly M. Wolff, Secretary and General Counsel, provided expertise in legal matters which has been invaluable. In the same area, Stephen W. Clark, Assistant General Counsel, has offered invaluable help. I am also indebted to the development group for its unstinting efforts in obtaining funding for the exhibition and publication, particularly Michael Margitich, Deputy Director for Development; Monika Dillon, Director, Major Gifts; Brett Cobb, Director of Development and Membership; and John L. Wielk, Manager, Exhibition and Project Funding.

Peter Galassi, Chief Curator, Department of Photography, has given important help on questions of Picasso's experimental photographs. Riva Castleman, formerly chief curator in the Department of Prints and Illustrated Books, and her staff, including Andrea Feldman, Assistant Curator, and Starr Figura, Curatorial Assistant, have all helped with inquiries and print loans. I have been fortunate to benefit from the expertise of Richard L. Palmer, Coordinator of Exhibitions; he has been outstanding in his meticulousness, especially in matters related to U.S. indemnity. I am also indebted to his staff: Eleni Cocordas, Associate Coordinator; Rosette Bakish, Executive Secretary; and Maria DeMarco, Assistant to the Coordinator. Special thanks are due the departments of Registration and Conservation, especially Diane Farynyk, Registrar; Meryl Cohen, Associate Registrar, who handled foreign loans; Elena Amatangelo, Assistant Registrar, U.S. loans; Jana Joyce, Registrar Assistant, New York loans; Pete Omlor, Manager, Art Handling and Preparation; and James Coddington, Senior Conservator; Anny Aviram, Conservator; Karl Buchberg, Conservator; and Michael Duffy, Associate Conservator. Their work has ensured the transport, handling, and safest display possible for all the objects. In addition, James Coddington's transmitted infrared Vidicon Images and infrared examinations have yielded some interesting insight into one of the paintings in the exhibition. Helping with the technical examination was intern Suzanne Siano.

I am ever more indebted to the particular installation skills of Jerome Neuner, Director of Exhibition Design and Production. Special thanks are also due Karen Meyerhoff, Assistant Director in that department, and to the indefatigable Pedro Perez, Conservation Framer, his team in the workshops, and Steven Jo, Production Manager and Frameshop Coordinator. Jessica Schwartz, Director of Public Information, and her staff, including Elisa Behnk, Assistant Director, Alexandra Partow, Press Representative, and Tavia Fortt, Writer/Editor, have all been most efficient in their efforts to bring an enlightened audience to this exhibition. Patterson Sims, who recently joined the Museum as Deputy Director for Education and Research Support, generously agreed to prepare the introductory brochure for the exhibition. Jo Pike, Director of Visitor Services, and her staff merit a special acknowledgment for their well-planned services for the public. I would also like to express my thanks to Joan Tenney Howard, Director of Special Events, and to her staff for organizing the exhibition's opening festivities. Ethel Shein, Director of Special Programming and Protocol, has, as always, acted as troubleshooter and my personal hand-holder through it all.

The publication of this book of multiple essays has been an enormous task. In one connection or another, I have already acknowledged several of the authors above, with the exception of Michael C. FitzGerald, Marilyn McCully, and Robert Rosenblum, whom I wish to thank here. The editing and the production of the book have been admirably handled by the Department of Publications. I owe a particular debt of gratitude to Osa Brown, Director; Harriet Schoenholz Bee, Managing Editor; Barbara Ross, Associate Editor; Nancy T. Kranz, Manager, Promotion and Special Services; and especially Amanda Freymann, Production Manager, with whom it has been a very great pleasure to work and who is largely responsible for the exceptional beauty of this book. I would also like to thank Cynthia Ehrhardt, Senior Production Assistant, and Dorothée Horps, Business Manager, for their important contributions. Joanne Greenspun, who served as project editor for this complicated book, undertook the principal share of the editorial work, which she accomplished graciously, deftly, and with superb professionalism. It was a pleasure to work once again with Steven Schoenfelder, who designed this book with all the elegance and speed he has made his trademark. Thanks are also due Mikki Carpenter, Director of Photographic Services and Permissions, as well as Kate Keller, Chief Fine Arts Photographer, Tom Griesel, Senior Photo Lab Technician, and Rosa Laster Smith, Photo Lab Technician. In Graphics, Emily Waters, Assistant Director; John Calvelli, Senior Graphic Designer; Jean Garrett, Graphic Designer; and John Donahue, Production Manager, have ably handled the wall texts and labels as well as the graphic needs of the entire exhibition. In Sales and Marketing I wish to thank Louise Chinn, Director, and Kara Orr, Paper Products Manager.

In the Department of Painting and Sculpture the early stages of this project were handled by Lynn Zelevansky, formerly curatorial assistant. We were most fortunate in having Fereshteh Daftari, Curatorial Assistant, to take on the role of principal exhibition assistant and fulfill this demanding role with intelligence and expertise. As the head of the curatorial support team, she has worked extraordinarily hard to coordinate this project, and we are deeply appreciative. Carolyn Lanchner, Curator, was personally helpful to me in preparing my texts, as was writer and art historian Pepe Karmel, who generously took over the responsibility for overseeing the audio tour for the exhibition. None of the people working intimately on this exhibition could have survived psychologically were it not for the lively participation of my assistant Anne Lampe in every aspect of this exhibition; her energy and constant good humor always raised our spirits when things went wrong or when work on the book seemed to lag. She has been an unbeatable collaborator.

Kathleen Robbins, Research Assistant, pursued the statistical research at the Musée Picasso in Paris, and in New York she engaged in numerous tasks, including the collection of photographic materials and the preparation of the majority of the captions for the book. Several interns helped us along the way on both book and exhibition: Pascaline Marre undertook a thorough statistical research; Yves Théoret, among other things, helped in the preparation of the study and indemnity albums; Christine Stotz and R. Dale Tucker were invaluable in ordering photographs and preparing captions for some of the essays in the book; and Lisa Zeitz helped Judith Cousins, Curator for Research in the department.

Judith Cousins has, once again, served as guarantor for the scholarly seriousness of this endeavor. As in the case of many other exhibitions and books, I cannot imagine how we could ever do without her. She, in turn, has naturally had to call upon many other people, whose special help in researching various problems or in the procuring of documentary photographs must be recognized. In addition to those whose names appear elsewhere above, they are: Philippe Arbaizar, Frédérique Barret, Marie-Laure Bernadac, Catherine Biedermann, Salvador Bonet, Yve-Alain Bois, Gilberte Brassaï, Edward Burns, Pierre-Yves Butzbach, Carole Callow, Henri Cartier-Bresson, Carrie T. Chalmers, Micheline Charton, Mary Chan, Stephen Cohen, Victoria Combalia Dexeus, Ellen Cordes, Neil Cox, Lydia Cresswell-Jones, Piero Crommelynck, Léonor Cuahonte, Caroline de Lambertye, Marie-Noelle Delorme, Christian Derouet, Ines Dickmann, Virginia Dodier, Honoria Murphy Donnelly, Deirdre Donohue, Catalina Draper, Janis Ekdahl, Sol Enjuanes Puyol, Pierrot Eugène, Adrienne Fischier, Daniel Fermon, Jane Fluegel, Yves de Fontbrune, Phyllis Freeman, Sylvie Fresnault, Phillippe Garner, Lydia Gasman, Françoise Gilot, Colette Giraudon, Jacques and Jacqueline Gojard, Béatrice Hatala, Marc Hauvette, Maureen D. Heher, Nancy Herrault, Eumie Imm Stroukoff, Colta Ives, Maurice Jardot, Mme Kaganowich, Beatrice Kernan, Billy Klüver and Julie Martin, Gibert Krill, Jay Kruger, Suzanne Kudielka, Claude Laugier, Kathy Lee, Ariane Lopez-Huici, Dora Maar, Janice Madhu, Marta Marton, Yves Mathieu, Lisa Messinger, Kimi Mikami, Yvan de Monbrizon, Jean-Paul Morel, Ulrich Mosch, Diane Moss, Jane Necol, Enrique Negre Gomez, Mary Ann Newman, Richard Ogar, Karen Otis, Joanne Paradise, Melissa Piper, Philippe Peltier, John Pennino, Valérie Phillippe, Edith and Sidney Posel, Nicole Prevot, Christoph Pudelko, Edward Quinn, Mathias Rastofer, Nancy Reynolds, Michèle Richet, Hélène Rogier, Lydia Roman, Deborah Rothschild, Endre Rozsda, Sheila Schwartz, Herbert T. Schwarz, R. Josue Seckel, Suzanne Slesin, Daniel Starr, Jonas Storsve, Joseph Struble, Jeanne Sudour, Michael Sweeney, Christine Swenson, Genevieve Taillade, Antoine Terrasse, Lucien Treillard, Anne Umland, Amanda Vaill, Pierre Vidal, George Vilinbahkov, Andre Villers, Brigitte Vincens, Ornella Volta, Ingo F. Walther, Donna Welton, Gerrard White, Patricia Willis, Elizabeth Wisniewsky, Helen Wright, and Chloe R. Ziegler.

William Rubin

Photograph Credits

Photographs of works of art reproduced in this volume have been provided in most cases by the owners or custodians of the works, identified in the captions. Individual works of art appearing herein may be protected by copyright in the United States of America or elsewhere, and may thus not be reproduced in any form without the permission of the copyright owners. The following and/or other photograph credits appear at the request of the artist's heirs and representatives, and/or the owners of individual works.

Rose Adler, Universités de Paris, Bibliothèque Littéraire Jacques Doucet (copyright by Béatrice Hatala, 1994): 282 bottom right. Courtesy Albright-Knox Art Gallery, Buffalo: 348 left. Courtesy Thomas Ammann Fine Art, Zurich: 128 bottom left; 288; 417. Rogi André, © Sagem: 402 right. I. Andréani, Musée d'Art et d'Histoire, Saint-Denis: 78 left. Studio Antonin, © Musée Picasso, Paris/© R.M.N., Agence Photographique: 212 left. Archivo Fotográfico Museo Nacional Centro de Arte Reina Sofia: 341 right. © Arxiu Fotogràfic de Museus, Ajuntament de Barcelona, courtesy Museu Picasso, Barcelona: 58 bottom left, bottom right; 112 right; 113; 115 top; 116 top, bottom center; 119 bottom right; 120 top right; 130; 148 top center; 226 top; 231; 232 bottom left, bottom right; 233; 235 top; 238; 240 left; 249; 305; 348 right; 379; 460 bottom left; 467 bottom; 472 top left; 475 left. James Austin, University of East Anglia, Norwich, England: 264 right. Courtesy The Baltimore Museum of Art: 51; 138 top left; 258 left; 264 left; 319 right. Studio Photo Bampuis, Juan Les Pins, courtesy Musée Picasso, Antibes: 423. © 1995 The Barnes Foundation: 140 bottom. Eric Baudouin: 28 top; 54 top; 143 bottom; 303 right; 304 top; 321; 322 top; 323; 355; 426; 431; 437 top; 446. Courtesy William Beadleston Inc., New York: 408. Dean Beasom, National Gallery of Art, Washington: 117. Courtesy Musée des Beaux Arts, Orléans: 192 left. Courtesy Galerie Beyeler, Basel: 44; 351; 396. © BHVP/Leyris: 185 top right. Thérèse Bonney: 282 top right. Courtesy the Family of Henry Brandon: 188 top left. Brassaï, © Estate Brassaï: 86 right; 158 top left, top right. The Brooklyn Museum of Art: 99 center. Martin Bühler, Öffentliche Kunstsammlung Basel: 135 bottom right; 327; 384. Foundation E. G. Bührle Collection, Zurich: 136 bottom. Courtesy Collection Edward Burns: 266 bottom. © Robert Capa/Magnum: 424. © Henri Cartier-Bresson: 175. Carlo Catenazzi, AGO, Art Gallery of Ontario, Toronto: 260. Courtesy Galerie Cazeau-de La Béraudière, Paris: 190 bottom. © 1994 The Art Institute of Chicago, All rights reserved: 211 center right; 285. © 1995 The Art Institute of Chicago, All rights reserved: 245; 259. © 1996 The Art Institute of Chicago, All rights reserved: 58 top; 317; 340 left; 346. Franco Cianetti, courtesy Ingo F. Walther (copyright from Du/Atlantis, October 1966): 284 bottom right. Columbus Museum of Art: 35 left; 289. Courtesy Christie's, New York: 229; 356. © The Cleveland Museum of Art: 129 right; 145 right; 316 top left. Christian Crampont, Paris: 28 top; 48 top left, top right, bottom left, bottom right; 56 bottom; 66 top left, top right; 318 right; 319 left; 406. Prudence Cuming Associates Limited: 435. ©1995 D. James Dee: 372. ©The Detroit Institute of Arts, 1995: 273. Ali Elai. Courtesy Stephen Hahn: 403. Jacques Faujour, Saint-Maur-des-Fossés: 24; 25 top, bottom; 26 top left, top right; 27 top left, top right, bottom. Feulard, © Musée Picasso,

Paris/© R.M.N., Agence Photographique: 213 top left. Courtesy Fuji Television Gallery, Tokyo: 173. Agustin Clavijo Garcia, Màlaga: 226 bottom right. © Françoise Gilot: 443 left, center, and right. Patrick Goetelen, courtesy Galerie Jan Krugier, Geneva: 22; 52 top left, bottom left; 272 top; 303 center; 347; 354; 393; 418; 438 top; 460 top right. Courtesy Richard Gray Gallery, Chicago: 465. Paul Guillaume, copyprint from André Billy, *Guillaume Apollinaire* (Paris: Pierre Seghers, 1967): 198 bottom left. The Hakone Open-Air Museum, Tokyo: 165; 170 right. © President and Fellows, Harvard College, Harvard University Art Museums: 128 bottom right; 360. Béatrice Hatala: 128 top; 185 bottom right; 186; 197 left. David Heald, © The Solomon R. Guggenheim Foundation, New York: 211 bottom left; 358 left. © Her Majesty Queen Elizabeth II: 91 top left; 93 bottom; 94 left, right; 95; 96 top left, top right, bottom left, bottom right; 97. Michael Herling, courtesy Sprengel Museum, Hannover: 274. Paul Hester, The Menil Collection, Houston: 76 top right; 394. The State Hermitage Museum, St. Petersburg: 219 bottom right; 271; 272 bottom. Courtesy Collection Ricardo Huelin: 235 bottom. Imageart, Antibes: 16; 30 bottom; 31 top right; 43; 109 bottom left; 142; 163; 184 top, bottom left; 234; 257 left; 395; 400 top; 449; 451; 453; 457; 459 top left; 468; 478; 481. Courtesy Sidney Janis Gallery, New York: 416; 421 left. Herbert Josse, Paris: 268. Kate Keller, The Museum of Modern Art, New York: 284 bottom left. Kate Keller, © 1994 The Museum of Modern Art, New York: 261. Kate Keller, © 1995 The Museum of Modern Art: 64; 65; 133; 363 left; back cover. Courtesy Kimbell Art Museum, Fort Worth: 211 bottom right. Bernd Kirtz: 375. Bob Kolbrener: 281. Courtesy Kunsthistorisches Museum, Vienna: 362 top left. Kunstsammlung Nordrhein-Westfalen, Düsseldorf: 477. Peter Lauri, Bern: 56 top. Lauros-Giraudon: 143 top left. Courtesy Galerie Louise Leiris, Paris: 169; 170 top left, bottom left; 172 right; 228 bottom; 380. Studio Levitsky, © Musée Picasso, Paris/© R.M.N., Agence Photographique: 213 bottom left. David A. Loggie, The Pierpont Morgan Library, New York: 310 bottom left; 367. Dora Maar: 12. © 1996 Dora Maar/© R.M.N., Agence Photographique: 404. Courtesy Susan and Lewis Manilow: 263. Man Ray, © 1996 ADAGP/Man Ray Trust, Paris: 82 bottom; 83 bottom; 318 top left. Man Ray, © 1996 ADAGP/Man Ray Trust, Paris/© R.M.N., Agence Photographique: 310 top right. Ervin Marton: frontispiece. James Mathews, The Museum of Modern Art, New York: 411. © The Metropolitan Museum of Art, New York, All rights reserved: 120 top left; 287 right; 299 right. © 1983 The Metropolitan Museum of Art, New York: 267. © 1984 The Metropolitan Museum of Art, New York: 236 bottom left. © 1994 The Metropolitan Museum of Art, New York: 57; 131. © 1995 The Metropolitan Museum of Art, New York: 29; 265; 277. G. Meunier, © R.M.N., Agence Photographique: 189 bottom left. Lee Miller, © Lee Miller Archives: 392 left. The Minneapolis Institute of Arts: 150 top left. MNAC Photographic Service (Calveras/Sagristà), Museu d'Art de Catalunya, Barcelona: 252 right; 262. Gerald Murphy: 52. © Musées de la Ville de Paris: 32. The Museum of Modern Art, New York: 75; 76 center left, center right, bottom left, bottom right; 93 top; 103; 114 top; 115 bottom left; 134; 138 bottom; 145 left; 146; 147 top left; 152 top, bottom; 154 top left, top right, center left, bottom left, bottom right; 155; 161 top; 168 top; 279; 280 top. Národní Galerie, Prague:

Index of Illustrations

This index is divided into three parts. The first consists of works by Picasso, listed alphabetically by title. The second section gives works by other artists, listed alphabetically by artist. The third gives photographs of Picasso's portrait subjects and associates, listed alphabetically by the name of the subject, and views of Picasso's studios. Page numbers are given in bold-face type for works that appear in color.

VAN GOGH
A DOCUMENTARY BIOGRAPHY

A.M. AND RENILDE HAMMACHER

VAN GOGH

A DOCUMENTARY BIOGRAPHY

232 ILLUSTRATIONS
48 IN COLOUR

THAMES AND HUDSON

CONTENTS

FOREWORD

The composition of this book has necessitated a fresh re-reading of well-known documents, as well as research in less familiar fields: among others, the artistic affinities of the period when Van Gogh was not yet a painter. The material is so rich that our initial selection, already much reduced, has had to be subjected for practical reasons to a further process of cutting. This delicate operation was done, in collaboration with the authors, by Thames and Hudson, the book's originating publishers, who also undertook the task of collecting picture material – a matter of increasing difficulty since the owners of works of art have become more and more anonymous.

We have to thank the director of the Rijksmuseum Vincent van Gogh, Amsterdam, Johan van der Woek, and his staff members Han van Krimpen and Miss Fieke Pabst, for opening the archives to us and facilitating an investigation of numerous photographic negatives, and the three children of the late Engineer Dr V.W. van Gogh, now trustees of the Van Gogh Foundation, who gave permission for investigation of the Foundation's archives and reproduction of works. Another main source of works by Van Gogh, the Rijksmuseum Kröller-Müller at Otterlo, has also been highly co-operative. Our thanks are due also to the many other museums and private collections whose contributions have enriched the illustration sections of this book.

We feel a debt of special gratitude to Dr P.J.J. van Thiel, director of the Department of Paintings at the Rijksmuseum, Amsterdam, who unhesitatingly furnished us with unpublished information on the famous Trippenhuis, so dear to Van Gogh and a main source of his knowledge of seventeenth-century Dutch painting. Dr van Thiel has made a special study of the subject, and has been preparing a publication on the function of the Trippenhuis as museum before the Rijksmuseum was constructed. Mr J.M. van der Hock-Ostende of the Gemeentearchief in Amsterdam, Madame Claudine Lemaire of the Bibliothèque Royale in Brussels, and Mr Carlos van Hasselt, Curator of the Frits Lugt Collection (Custodia) in Paris, all gave their assistance in the search for a number of rare, or even untraceable, illustrations.

A.M. HAMMACHER
RENILDE HAMMACHER–VAN DEN BRANDE

All the quoted documents, except where there is an indication to the contrary, are letters from Vincent van Gogh (1853–90) to his brother Theo (1857–91). The original language is Dutch except in those documents marked F. (French) or E. (English).

INTRODUCTION

Just before Vincent van Gogh died, young Albert Aurier – man of letters, poet and philosopher – wrote an article in which he set out to explore the essence of the artist's work, still at that time known only within a small circle. After Vincent's death Aurier wanted to write a biography using the correspondence with Theo which he had borrowed. He had difficulty in finding a publisher, and the book remained unwritten. Nowadays, more than ninety years later, it would be hard to find a publisher who did not aspire to publish a book about Van Gogh, despite the flood of publications which have been attracting readers all over the world for several generations. The number of specialized art-historical and psychological studies of the Van Gogh phenomenon is very much smaller, although some most welcome and detailed research has been carried out, mainly in recent years, and mostly dealing with specific, limited areas. The purpose of the present book, however, is to study the artist's entire personality. It concentrates, more than previous work has done, on the area where art merges into life and vice versa.

Although the reader will find here a large number of fragments from the letters, and from family and other sources, this book should not be seen as an anthology. It is meant rather as an invitation to return to the sources themselves, and as a reading of those sources. Fragmentation is always painful – even if, as in this instance, its purpose is to find the key to an important whole.

Perhaps the most extraordinary thing about Van Gogh's life is the fact that he did not discover his artistic vocation until his twenty-eighth year. Little is known of his childhood and adolescence; but the experiences of the eight years between the ages of nineteen and twenty-seven are vividly reported by Vincent himself, and his interests and obsessions carry clues to the origins of his later work, and above all to the nature of the tensions and inhibitions that gave his adult life its curious and fascinating combination of frustration, achievement and self-destructiveness.

I am convinced that the early part of Van Gogh's adult life – his life as a non-artist – is of fundamental importance in relation to his work, and deserves as close study as the later, creative phase of his career. All this is a problem area, but it is one Vincent himself was always aware of, and one which never ceased to haunt him.

Those eight years of preparation brought a series of failures and much tentative searching. They provided the tilth, the reservoir for a life which was lived with intensity and devoted to a pictorial incarnation of one man's world. The vehemence with which Vincent always rejected anything that, in his family's eyes, represented a socially acceptable means of earning a living, was for many years a blind force; activated by suffering, it eventually developed into a force that was clear-sighted. In this study, full attention is devoted to that process. The letters not only reflect the origins of an artistic output, but constitute an enthralling source in which we can discover the structure of a personality, still unaware of a hesitant and dormant creative power which was not yet ready to become a will to create.

For most of the time, Vincent was prey to an inner tension that he himself did not know how to interpret. His reading, for example, was never for relaxation; it was always purposeful, even compulsive, although there is evidence of a strong affinity to certain writers rather than of any premeditated system of selection. His reactions to external impressions were strong and idiosyncratic. Object and subject constantly merged. Conscious and unconscious reactions to stimuli can be traced in his actions, his habits – such as that of studying his reflection in a mirror, the child's first form of self-examination – and eccentricities of behaviour. Problems with clothes started early; he never ate or drank sensibly; he showed great delicacy, as well as sensitivity, in conversation and in making small gestures and gifts; his reactions were violent when the power of passion began to make itself felt, long before he was able to come to terms with that of love. The contradictions of those eight crucial years are the marks of a period of artistic gestation. Trying to find one's way in all this has meant discovering a number of basic motifs so deeply rooted that they played a part in his work until the very end.

Psychoanalytical opinion has held that the still-birth of his namesake one year before his own birth had some influence on Vincent's earliest emotions. No information has been produced to make me consider this in any way likely. The earliest letters known to us were written in 1872. Information about his youth is inadequate. Even the reminiscences published by his sister, Elisabeth H. du Quesne-van Gogh, twenty years after his death (1910), fail to rise above the customary awe and lack of comprehension for a temperament that seemed merely 'strange' to those around him.

'Strange' was the only word relatives, acquaintances, schoolfellows and teachers could find to describe a child who for obscure reasons held aloof from his environment. We possess no clues to suggest a motive for this isolation. One thing that seems clear is that it does not conform to any of the familiar stereotypes of the 'gifted child'; it was not accompanied by an early and seemingly effortless mastery of technique in one discipline or another, as was observed in such individuals as Mozart, Pascal, Flaubert or Picasso. His early drawings are unremarkable. Nor, in consequence, did Vincent have the fragile support of the gifted child's characteristic self-confidence or self-conceit. He manifested only the negative aspects of a potential but deeply hidden creativity.

Vincent showed no signs of maladjustment in his school work. Why his education was broken off in March 1868 remains a mystery. It was the first of a series of enterprises in his life that were abruptly left unfinished, in this case presumably through no fault of his own. The most likely explanation is that there was simply not enough money for the parson's family, with its ever-present financial anxieties, to continue this somewhat expensive undertaking, which included the cost of full board and lodging. It was more than a year *9, 10* (July 1869) before his uncle Vincent, a prominent member of Goupil & Cie, an international firm of art dealers, was able to take on the sixteen-year-old youth as a trainee at the organization's branch at The Hague. Nothing is known about how Vincent spent his time between leaving Tilburg and joining his uncle at The Hague.

It was to be another three years before Vincent provided a record, and a reticent one at that, of how he had fared in his first job at Goupil's. And it was only then, at the age of nineteen, that a penetrating spiritual awareness of painting and literature became apparent: childishly, conventionally formulated at first, and then becoming ever stronger, like a slowly rising tide. He did not have to reach far back into the past. The seventeenth century was close to him, the eighteenth century less so; but he had a thorough knowledge of the art of his own time, in so far as the 1860s and 1870s contained elements to which he felt attracted. This knowledge was in fact so thorough that once his creative instinct, with inflexible psychic force, had overcome all resistance, its content was largely determined by this absorption with the art of the nineteenth century. Literature, painting and drawing – all seen in relationship to the Bible – were the disciplines that we shall be able to follow through a gradually changing appreciation based on inward struggle.

During the years before becoming a painter, Vincent developed a notable predilection for twilight and night, which became even more apparent during the last phases of his life as a painter, at Arles and Saint-Rémy. The first and last light of day promoted a state of mind in which his emotions, thoughts and bodily senses were absorbed in what he saw, intensifying his experience and giving him the ecstatic sense of being absorbed in the macrocosm. Often he rose at four a.m. or walked to meet the dusk late in the evening. Many a time he sat without shelter by a pond, or in a churchyard or a field, waiting for the dawn and listening to the first bird song.

Superficially, such a tendency might be considered a mere romantic inclination, had it not also been a specific symptom of an ecstatic disposition (see, inter alia, Marghanita Laski on *Ecstasy*, London 1961, 1980). Ecstatic experience takes a wide range of possible forms, from the erotic to the abstract, from a visionary transformation of everyday life to states of sensitivity that can culminate in visual and auditory paranormal experiences. In Van Gogh's case, the two states of mind – losing himself in the twilight and awakening – whereby his spiritual existence was released from both the past and the present, came to have a fundamental and long-lasting effect on his existence and subsequently on his creativity. Through such profound experiences of Nature, in its most elemental and universal manifestation, his inwardly lonely life was transformed and united with a greater whole.

Fascinated by the Montagne Sainte-Victoire, Cézanne for many years felt the need to go there before five o'clock in the morning to witness the awakening of light and nature in complete solitude. There is no record of what sensations he actually experienced there. We know more about a similar compulsion on the part of Charles Baudelaire (1820–67) and Arthur Rimbaud (1854–91), the latter a contemporary of Van Gogh, to experience the eternal repetition of the awakening and death of light and the world. Georges Poulet has written a profound analysis of this psychic condition (*La Poésie éclatée*, Paris 1980). The work of both poets manifests profound reactions to the awakening of the world or the transition to night. However, the inspiring power of these ecstatic moments allows for differences in the way they are assimilated and in their effect. This applies to Vincent, whose world was unlike that of Baudelaire with his devotion to night and artificial light. Vincent, like Rimbaud, was as sensitive to the victory of the rising sun as to that of the night.

It was above all during those eight years before Vincent became a painter that he wrote the descriptions of exhausting nocturnal or evening walks which recur like a refrain in the text of his letters. These experiences, seen with hindsight, were probably the best of his tormented life. Later, particularly after his year of painting at The Hague, in 1881–82, Vincent's predisposition for ecstatic experiences acquired an active aspect, both in Holland and the South of France, where colour sometimes escalated to paroxysm.

His sense of affinity to night and twilight continued to make itself felt even in Provence, where – stimulated by Impressionism and by his body's craving for warmth – his love of the sun appeared, superficially at least, to cast out all northern gloom and even gave him a false reputation of being a 'sunlight' artist. Star-filled night skies at Arles inspired several drawings and paintings *156* which are among his finest works. At Auvers in 1890, in his last few months of life, the blue of the sky acquires a value which eliminates from scenes such as the view of the little church and the background of Dr Gachet's portrait any definition of day, evening or night. It is true that most of the harvest scenes with the high note of yellow, with which he himself characterized Arles, constitute a maximum and exhaustive realization of his endeavours to express the effect of the sun; but this was never free from 'the shadow of death' seen in the figures of reapers, or 'the shadow of evil' in the cypresses.

205, 216

141

207

In the years before he was an artist, his whole attitude towards the dark, towards dusk, towards mourning for what is lost, towards the romantic and psychoanalytical linking of Eros and Thanatos, love and death, became concentrated, with obsessional persistence, in the figure of the 'woman in black'. This figure then appeared in his early Hague drawings and paintings, and later in those produced in Brabant – in autumnal landscapes or as an individual worn down by cares and sorrows (the woman Christine with whom he lived at The Hague); but it had germinated and developed in his mind from 1873 onwards, before there was any question of his starting to paint.

70, 71, 76

56

Its origin lay in a complex interaction of factors. Among these were the 'heavy blow' of his first unsuccessful infatuation, in London, with Eugenia Loyer, and the rise of his great admiration for Jules Michelet, whose *L'Amour* was one of his favourite books. Michelet – more than Carlyle or Longfellow, whom he also read at this time – meant to him the crystallization of his awakening feelings for women, not only as mothers of children, but also as stimulators of psychic energy and imagination. In his letters, we shall find the details of his fluctuating feelings for Michelet and the latter's evocations and imaginings of the 'woman in black'. Other writers were also having an effect on him in those same years, 1873–76. There was John Bunyan's seventeenth-century allegory *The Pilgrim's Progress*, with its fascinating character, the attractive vampire-like female who features as the Temptress on the Pilgrimage; H.W. Longfellow, the American with many readers in Europe, who wrote the history of the legend of the Plymouth colony (*The Courtship of Miles Standish*, 1858) and *Evangeline*, a rhyming tale of Anglo-French tensions, sealing the fate of Acadia; George Eliot (*Janet's Repentance*); and Charlotte Brontë (*Shirley*). There was in Vincent's imagination a strange mixture of puritanism and adventurousness. Passionate females in difficult circumstances fascinated him. At the same time, the cold fire of fanatical piety was developing in him as a substitute for his extinguished passion for Eugenia.

From the time of his employment at Goupil, Vincent had on the walls of his small rooms in Paris, London, Dordrecht and Amsterdam, two pictures of women whom he admired, or who at all events occupied his mind to a remarkable degree. They were the portrait in the Louvre of the *Woman in Mourning* which had inspired Michelet, and a drawing from the tomb effigy of Anne of Brittany, whose name reminded him of rocks and the sea (the link with landscape), and who responded to his admiration for a strong, combative, loving image of womanhood.

18

19

The religious feeling which held him prisoner, through obsessive passion rather than through the warmth of genuine love, has nevertheless been rather caricatured by his biographers. The suggestion that he lived for no other purpose for three years in the late 1870s is contradicted by his passion for literature and art, which, far from weakening after his days in London, Paris and Amsterdam, was asserting itself with increasing vigour. Yet he was aware that he was 'imprisoned in something'. I call that having a psychological block. He remained his own prisoner until he had come to accept the consequences of not wanting to become a biblical scholar, as would have been required of him had he sought entry to the ministry. The questions requiring an answer were 'What is it that I might be?' and 'What purpose might I serve?' He could answer them only by eliminating the block. Instead, he tried to adapt in behaviour and clothing, thereby holding back whatever might be struggling for release.

It was in his clothing that Vincent sought to show the outside world to what category of people he felt it was his calling to belong: the poor. He had arguments to provide a motive for neglecting his clothes when, after leaving Goupil, he no longer possessed the means to dress like the class to which his family belonged. But his family, and Theo in particular, had observed that even during his final year at Goupil in 1875, after his spell of depression in London and the onset of his fanatical piety, some measure of neglect was already noticeable. Theo understood this to be one of the reasons why Goupil wanted to get rid of him – although Vincent denied this, advancing the deeper reason of his aversion to the practices of the world of art dealers. In London in 1873 he had conformed to some extent to the conventions of his environment by acquiring the top hat he then continued to wear at Dordrecht in the Netherlands, three years later – where it did deviate from local custom. (It was also, by this time, noticeably decrepit.)

It was in the Borinage, where he preached among the miners in 1879–80, that he tried hardest to achieve his aim, not to be distinguishable – inwardly, but above all outwardly – from those among whom he had to perform his mission. He did all he could to avoid standing out among them by loaning his good clothes if help was needed at the time of accidents, as well as by neglecting himself physically, and by reducing his food requirements to the barest necessities. He managed to achieve the very opposite of what he had hoped for, and drew attention to himself, not only because people had seen him arrive looking *Hollands proper* – well-dressed and clean as it behoved a Dutchman – but also because of his social role and manners, which clearly reflected his different origins. Local tradition suggests that it was the very artificiality of his attempted adaptation which aroused notice. It was not expected of him. His goodness and commitment were remembered with deep respect, but as a deviation, as something special. There were memories of his old military coat, his shabby cap, and how he slept in a small hut without furniture even though not driven to it through lack of money.

His longing for primeval purity, his Adamistic, ecstatic character, remained apparent in his clothing even when he became an artist, and so continued to be a challenge to his family. They, in fact, did their best on several occasions to smarten Vincent up a little, as may be seen in some rather touching letters from his parents. In his defence, he pointed to his occupation rather than bringing forward any social or political arguments. Painting was a messy job, and he had to work unobtrusively in slum streets, in the rain and mud. He went on to air his objections to the bourgeois life indulged in by some painters who were prospering in a material sense.

In Antwerp, however, on his way to Paris after leaving the Netherlands for good, his attitude was modified to some extent. He found it necessary to do something about his clothes. His Paris self-portraits of 1885–88 show him *115–117* conforming to an astonishing degree to the environment where Theo had to carry on his business as an art dealer. It is obvious that the hat, collar and tie, and respectable suit which we see in his self-portraits would not have been specially assumed for the purpose of self-examination in a mirror. (Although the fur hat and paint-smeared smock were still obviously essential for his work out of doors in all weathers at Asnières.)

He was working with Paul Signac and Emile Bernard, and even had a number of acquaintances of aristocratic descent. Toulouse-Lautrec's unrival-led profile portrait in pastels must reflect Van Gogh's image as it appeared in Paris, without any extravagances in dress and with the appearance of a gentleman. It is remarkable that it was Lautrec who saw him like this, whereas he was always out to stress the elements in a person's appearance whereby he might turn them, with barely suppressed irony or malice, into caricatures stressing decay, vice and the exhaustion of passion. To him Vincent looked impassioned but controlled, vehement and quick to react, but neither unrestrained nor confused.

114

Vincent was not wholly uninterested in politics, but such interest as he had did not affect either his bearing or his behaviour. On one occasion, in an unusual mood, he was tempted to apply the divisions of the 1848 barricades to himself and his brother, assigning Theo to the side of Guizot and himself to Michelet's. He once spoke of his own 'socialism', and referred to an ideal 'revolution'. But he never showed any signs of a commitment other than one based on sentiment and on his own psychological make-up. Not once in his letters did he mention the name of Marx or that of Bakunin, who had a considerable reputation among artists in France. In Belgium in the late 1870s, Vincent hardly mentions the negligence on the part of the mine-owners, or the social unrest among the population which was to lead to revolt in 1885; he speaks of strikes in one letter (130) which was written in 1879, the year in which Bakunin (more popular in France and in anarchist Wallonia than Marx) broke with Marx at the International. But his preoccupations at the time when he was living among the industrial poor were markedly religious rather than political. He wrote in praise of Courbet, but failed to respond to his political action, with its well-known and unhappy end. Vincent's compassion was fundamentally directed towards individuals.

More, perhaps, than he would admit to himself, Vincent remained deeply inspired by the figure of Christ, even after he had come to place the Bible and the Church alongside and not above other matters. He was congenitally better at giving than at receiving, although he set out to correct this in himself after he had experienced the adverse consequences of giving alone.

There is no evidence that his life's sufferings ever caused him to rebel, either in the Borinage, or in London or Brabant. He wanted to do good, to give personal help. In this context, his repetition, in Provence, of an inscription quoted in an old newspaper as having been found on an ancient tombstone between Arles and Carpentras, acquires a profound significance. It expressed something he knew only too well. 'Thebe, daughter of Thelhui, priestess of Osiris, who never complained of anyone.' 'Never complained' implies a great deal. It means an acknowledgment and understanding, if not total acceptance, of the basic truth that suffering is constant and there is no complaining.

Vincent's sole, but absolute, act of revolt was directed against himself – his suicide. All manner of speculations have been made, referring to rational as well as irrational impulses. However, from an early age there were slight, and subsequently more serious, signs of his predisposition, of his reactions to happenings frequently initiated by himself. There is coherence in these signs. Gradually, the realization grew of an end dimly perceived earlier on. He became more and more aware of his existence in the service of a specific task, imposed from within. His ecstatic disposition laid him open to the absorbing, totally possessive power of an idea which overcomes all opposition. Pulling the trigger was the final deed brought about by what, ten years earlier on, he had termed his 'active melancholy'.

The mystery of his sickness, and the series of crises, can no longer be solved by medical science. It has remained nameless, since it cannot be identified by that final deed alone. The final deed was an actual, but not an inevitable, consequence of the syndrome. It went beyond this and was closely linked with creative power and creative instinct. The presumed syndrome and subsequent suicide have caused a great deal of misunderstanding in writings about Van Gogh. An art historian is clearly in no way competent to define the syndrome itself, but he cannot ignore the possibility of a link existing between Vincent's sickness or predisposition and his artistic output. Conversely, psychiatric studies have rarely had a sufficiently aesthetic slant to do justice to the problem. The symbolic explanation of Vincent van Gogh along psychoanalytical lines (Graetz) suffers from the same defect, i.e. that the aesthetic and art-historical aspect cannot be ignored with impunity. Not only because of his link with Roger Fry, Charles Mauron inspires confidence in this respect, displaying a discipline that is aesthetically well orientated.

In a book like this it would be an omission to dispose of Vincent's sickness with a few generalities. The reader will find the details in the Arles and Saint-Rémy/Auvers sections. It is appropriate to recall here that the now obsolete and schematic routine data noted by the doctors at the institutions at Arles and Saint-Rémy do not constitute the only information available for contemporary psychiatrists to work on. The dates of pre-crisis exaltation as well as the crisis situations in his life – including, it should be remembered, his pre-painting years – can be worked out with some accuracy. There were periods of being out of humour; there was insomnia. We know very little about his dreams, but a great deal about his eating and drinking habits; smoking (he several times quoted Dickens on smoking as an antidote to suicidal thoughts); fears; hallucinations, both auditory and visual; his sense, not of persecution, but certainly of isolation; statements about his sexuality in certain circumstances; evidence of possibly faulty treatment of venereal disease. When leaving Paris, Vincent feared total paralysis.

The information given to the psychiatrist at Arles about epileptics in his family was provided by Vincent himself. As far as we know, it was not refuted by Theo. At Saint-Rémy, Dr Rey gave epilepsy as his own diagnosis, with some reservations. Family records on the Van Gogh side provide no record of epilepsy; and the Van Goghs – the uncles at least – were mostly clear-sighted, realistic people earning good money. On the Carbentus side of his mother's family the evidence is different: artistic and musical talent occurred, but also nervousness, depressions and neuroses. It seems it is too late now to devote more attention to this neglected area of Vincent's ancestry; but there is some information concerning the generation to which Vincent himself belonged. After working as a teacher for some years, his favourite sister Willemien was admitted to a psychiatric institution; she died in one, after many years (undated letter from Mrs van Gogh, Van Gogh Archive). Without any knowledge of her symptoms, and relying solely on his own powers of observation, Vincent himself had, in a photograph, seen signs of madness in the eyes of his sober and quiet sister.

The epilepsy hypothesis appears to have been rejected by most modern psychiatrists because of the absence of convulsive conditions; yet the idea of epilepsy occasionally turns up again. Fernand Destaing (*La Souffrance et le génie*, Paris 1980) refers to the modern change in the concept of epilepsy, in that convulsions are not invariably present; despite many errors in Destaing's summary of Van Gogh's life, the possibility of epilepsy is once again a live issue.

The aspect of interest to us – however inconclusive the diagnosis must remain – is the question of how his predisposition helped to determine the form and quality of his art. Ignoring his sickness is a misjudgment of its character; trying to show that the sickness was the cause of some of the aesthetic phenomena in Vincent's art is turning the matter back to front. The known facts are too numerous for one not to agree with Van Gogh himself, who said that the output which, after years of preparation, he finally produced at speed in the space of ten years meant exhausting his physical and psychic strength and destroying his health. His psychological disposition – including his unconscious – possessed a reservoir of energy comparable to the fertile soil which has to be ploughed, sown, manured, and rained on, before its latent forces can be realized. Such forces included the sickness which could not fail to make itself felt after Vincent had whipped up all his nerves into a paroxysm in order to produce his work. Tensed beyond the limits, he could not be saved by any relaxation of tension. Relaxation became disorientation.

Without such transgression of the limits, many a work by Van Gogh would never have acquired the quality which causes it to affect people who remain totally unconscious of what is enacted within it. Van Gogh was aware of this. He remembered – or rather continued to feel – the impression made on him in *17* 1873 by the wild-eyed portrait of the mad Hugo van der Goes in a painting by Wauters. And in 1888 that same image of Van der Goes returned to him as he was drawing up his own balance-sheet. He always had occasional lucid moments, of such existential power that at the age of thirty (1883) he was able to state, 'I must complete a certain amount of work in just a few years' (309), knowing it would depend on the first ten years and reckoning on having between six and ten. In the event, he had seven. In the same year, 1883, he knew that the wound caused by rejected and forbidden love 'cannot heal', that it goes too deep and '*after years and years* will be as it was on the first day' (312). The decisions were taken then, and it is there, in his sense of obligation towards his work and the wound caused by love, that the two sources of his art lie linked; sources which determined all that was to follow.

A.M. HAMMACHER

I

THE ART TRADE AND RELIGION

'Homesick for the land of pictures'

Vincent wrote the earliest of his extant letters in August 1872, when he was nineteen and Theo a fifteen-year-old schoolboy. He wrote from The Hague, where he had been working for the art dealers Goupil & Cie since the age of sixteen (1869).

Thanks for your letter. I was glad to hear you arrived home safely. I missed you the first few days; it was strange not to find you when I came home in the evening. We have had pleasant days together, and between times have taken many a nice walk and done some sightseeing.

What terrible weather! You must have suffered from the heat on your walks to Oisterwijk. Yesterday there were races to celebrate the Exhibition; but the illumination and the fireworks were put off because of the bad weather, so it is just as well that you did not stay to see them. Compliments from the Haanebeek and Roos families. (1, Aug. 1872.)

9
10
Goupil & Cie, founded in Paris by Adolphe Goupil in 1827, now incorporated the Hague business founded by Vincent's uncle, another Vincent Willem van Gogh, who was still active as a partner in the parent company. Centres of the art trade such as this should not be underestimated as sources of knowledge and connoisseurship. Both Vincent and Theo made their first contact with art through 'Uncle Cent'' s collection, and met their first artists through working for Goupil. Business at The Hague bore a mixed character at this time and consisted of the production and sale of engravings, etchings, lithographs, and photographs of works of art as well as the sale of paintings.

Art dealers made considerable profits at that time out of reproductions; and they were gradually beginning to deal in contemporary art. Goupil in The Hague was already selling works by artists who belonged to contemporary groups, the French Barbizon School (Théodore Rousseau, Charles-François Daubigny, Narcisse-Virgile Diaz, Jules Dupré, Constant Troyon) and the Dutch Hague School (Anton Mauve, Jozef Israëls, Thijs and Jacob Maris, H.W. Mesdag, Johannes Bosboom, H.J. Weissenbruch).

62, 63
59, 64, 90
25, 61

Vincent has left little record of the kind of work he did for the firm at The Hague. When he left he took with him a reference signed by H.C. Tersteeg, who managed the branch on behalf of Vincent's uncle. The letters of this period, immature though they are, show signs of regular visits to the major art galleries and pronounced, if conventionally expressed, preferences.

The young Vincent was intensely attached to his parental home and his family, so that his transfer to London in 1873, although intended as promotion, immediately aroused his fears of homesickness. Theo, meanwhile, started working for Goupil in Brussels.

... Be sure to tell me more about the pictures you see. A fortnight ago I was in Amsterdam to see an exhibition of the pictures that are going from here to Vienna. It was very interesting, and I am curious to know what impression the Dutch artists will make in Vienna. I am also curious to see the English painters; we see so little of them because almost everything remains in England. ... (5, 17 Mar. 1873.)

It is easy to overlook the postscript:

Theo, I strongly advise you to smoke a pipe; it is a good remedy for the blues, which I happen to have had now and then lately. ... (5, 17 Mar. 1873.)

Vincent was to remain inseparable from his pipe all his life; and not long before the end he was to refer to its value as an antidote to thoughts of suicide:

Every day I take the remedy which the incomparable Dickens prescribes against suicide. It consists of a glass of wine, a piece of bread and cheese, and a pipe of tobacco. (Vincent to Wil van Gogh, WII, 10 Apr. 1889, F.)

G.H. Boughton. *'On the hill by the sea lies buried Rose Standish'*. From H.W. Longfellow, *The Courtship of Miles Standish*.

20–22

In London, Vincent's first impressions of English art were not altogether favourable. He was still unfamiliar with the artists who were to be his enduring love, the draughtsmen who produced the illustrations for weeklies and other publications. Soon however, he began to take considerable interest in the competent, if mediocre, painter George Henry Boughton, whom he long continued to mention in his letters. It was characteristic of Vincent that even at an early age he was not only impressed by famous names and great masters, but also had an eye for lesser artists provided they gave evidence of genuine sentiments and something that went beyond modish competence. Boughton attracted him because of his serious understanding of landscape and because he occasionally chose pilgrims and particularly Puritans as his subjects. Boughton also inspired Vincent to reread Longfellow's *Evangeline* and *The Courtship of Miles Standish*. From an early age Vincent had been aware of the interaction between literature and painting.

... At first English art did not appeal to me; one must get used to it. But there are here, among other, Millais, who has painted *The Huguenot*, *Ophelia*, etc., of which I think you know the engravings; his things are beautiful. Then there is Boughton, whose *Puritans Going to Church* is in our Galerie Photographique; I have seen wonderful things by him. Among the old painters, Constable was a landscape painter who lived about thirty years ago [*sic*]; he is splendid – his work reminds me of Diaz and Daubigny. Then there are Reynolds and Gainsborough, whose forte was very beautiful ladies' portraits, and Turner, whose engravings you must have seen. ...

Sometime you must write me if there are any photographs of Wauters's work besides *Hugo Van der Goes* and *Mary of Burgundy*; and if you know about any photographs of pictures by Lagye and De Braekeleer. I don't mean the elder Braekeleer, but, I think, a son of his who had three beautiful pictures called *Antwerp*, *The School* and *The Atlas* at the last exhibition in Brussels. (10, 20 July 1873.)

97

It is remarkable that he was collecting photographs of paintings and specifically mentioned Emile Wauters' painting of *Hugo van der Goes in the Red Monastery*, where the artist is shown, wild-eyed and staring, as a small choir endeavours to calm his mind with music. This image of Hugo van der Goes was to remain with Vincent until his dying day. He clearly identified with him; such thinking was fundamental to his way of reading, seeing and hearing.

17

Vincent walked a great deal and became familiar with London and the surrounding countryside.

... I walk as much as I can, but I am very busy. It is very beautiful here (though it is in the city). The lilacs and hawthorn and laburnums are in bloom in every garden, and the chestnut trees are beautiful. If one really loves nature, one can find beauty everywhere. But still I sometimes long for Holland and especially for home. ... (16, 13 Apr. 1874.)

Such walks were to become an indispensable element in his experience of nature, as well as in the activation of his inner life. They were true wanderings and pilgrimages, and reflect an intense inner life, which long remained in a receptive, passive state.

He visited the museums, but seems to have despised the traditional London sights and failed to visit the Tower, Crystal Palace and Madame Tussaud's. He was fascinated by the people, their way of life, and the scenes he encountered in the streets. In spite of permanent homesickness, his nationalism weakened.

... I live a rich life here, 'having nothing, yet possessing all'. At times I am inclined to believe that I am gradually turning into a cosmopolite; that is, neither a Dutchman, nor an Englishman, nor yet a Frenchman, but simply a *man*. And as a homeland, the whole world, *i.e.* a small spot in the world where we are sent to stay. We have not got there yet, though I am straining after it, and perhaps may grasp it. And as my ideal, what Mauve called, 'That is *it*.' (Vincent to Carolien van Stockum-Hannebeek, 13a, 1874.)

The Mauve whom Vincent here and afterwards approvingly quotes was the distinguished Hague painter Anton Mauve, who was married to Vincent's maternal aunt Jet. His most significant allegiance, however, was to the philosophical historian Jules Michelet; and a letter from London quotes the following fragment from the chapter 'Les Aspirations de l'automne' in Michelet's *L'Amour*:

'From here I see a lady, I see her walk pensively in a not very large garden, bereft of its flowers early in the season, but sheltered, as you see them behind our cliffs in France or the dunes of Holland. The exotic shrubs have already been put back into the conservatory. The fallen leaves reveal a number of statues. An artistic luxury which contrasts a little with the lady's very simple, modest, dignified dress, of which the black (or grey) silk is almost imperceptibly brightened by a lilac ribbon.

'But haven't I seen her already in the museums of Amsterdam or The Hague? She reminds me of a lady by Philippe de Champaigne [*n.b.* in the Louvre – V. v. G.], who took my heart, so candid, so honest, sufficiently intelligent, yet simple, without the cunning to extricate herself from the ruses of the world. This woman has remained in my mind for thirty years, persistently coming back to me, making me say: 'But what was she called? What happened to her? Did she know some happiness? And how did she cope with life?' (Vincent to Carolien and Willem van Stockum, 11, Oct. 1873.)

Vincent was a solitary, and an intensely religious, youth. His imagination was captured by the image of womanhood he found above all in Michelet. In London in 1873, he was humiliated by the rejection of his love for Eugenia, the daughter of his widowed landlady Ursula Loyer. Eugenia proved to be secretly engaged to be married. Vincent apparently failed to respect the fact, nor had he any sympathy with Eugenia's boyfriend whom he wished to supplant. His forceful nature, and what he later considered to have been half imagination and half genuine love, brought about a sense of injury and a state of introversion which distracted his mind from the harsh reality of having to earn a living. Much later, he gave an acute analysis of his state of mind at this time.

... What kind of love did I feel, when I was twenty? It is difficult to define – my physical passions were very weak then, perhaps because of a few years of great poverty and hard work. But my intellectual passions were very strong, meaning that without asking anything in return, without wanting any pity, I wanted only to give, not to receive. Foolish, wrong, exaggerated, proud, rash – for in love one must not only give, but also take; and, reversing it, one must not only take but also give. Whoever deviates either to the right or to the left fails, there is no help for it. So I fell, but it was a wonder that I got up again. ... (157, 12 Nov. 1881.)

In 1873, Vincent was unable to put these feelings into words in his letters; we know of the episode with Eugenia only because Theo later told his wife Johanna, who tells the story in her introduction to the *Complete Letters* (erroneously calling the daughter by the mother's name). Theo mentioned it also in letters to his parents (unfortunately not all preserved in the Van Gogh Archive).

In the summer of 1874 Vincent visited his parents at Helvoirt (they had moved there from nearby Zundert in 1871) in order to escort his sister Anna to

England, where she was to seek employment. His parents were disappointed to find him 'silent and depressed, and also more and more religious'.

I am glad you have read Michelet and that you understand him so well. Such a book [*L'Amour*] teaches us that there is much more in love than people generally suppose.

To me that book has been both a revelation and a Gospel at the same time: 'There is no such thing as an old woman.' (That does not mean that there are no old women, but that a woman is not old as long as she loves and is loved.) And then such a chapter as 'The Aspirations of Autumn' – how beautiful it is.

That a woman is quite a different being from a man, and a being that we do not yet know – at least, only quite superficially, as you said – yes, I am sure of it. And that man and wife can be one, that is to say, one whole and not two halves, yes, I believe that too.

Anna is in good spirits; we take beautiful walks together. It is so beautiful here, if only one has an open and simple eye, without many beams in it. But if one has that, it is beautiful everywhere.

That picture by Thijs Maris which Mr Tersteeg has bought must be beautiful. I have already heard about it, and I myself have bought and sold one quite similar.

Since I have been back in England, my love for drawing has stopped, but perhaps I will take it up again some day or other. I am reading a great deal just now. . . . (20, 31 July 1874.)

Only in his musings about man and wife is there evidence of his passion for womanhood and its mysterious force, a passion governed by the impelling power of Michelet's writing. Ever in search of self-understanding, Vincent seems to have been intuitively attracted to Michelet's intensely emotional personality and way of thinking, so aptly described by Georges Poulet:

Michelet is a creature who starts off by refusing ever to unburden himself, to open his heart to others, to the outside world; and who furthermore cannot concentrate his thoughts on any single object without a deliberate expenditure of energy. There is nothing spontaneous in his conduct. Self-isolation and restriction are in this instance the consequences of a considered decision. Michelet starts his life by forcing his nature. Or rather, in his explicit acts of will he is obeying one of the essential characteristics of that nature. He does violence to himself because there is violence in his temperament. (Georges Poulet, *Etudes sur le temps humain*, Paris 1968.)

Vincent now left the Loyers and their infants' school and went to lodge without board at Ivy Cottage, 395 Kennington Road. He attached no importance to his drawings; and since creativity in the true sense of the word hardly comes into them at all, it would be wrong to attach importance to them.

. . . With the money I gave you, you must buy Alphonse Karr's *Voyage autour de mon jardin*. Be sure to do that – I want you to read it.

Anna and I walk every evening. Autumn is coming fast and that makes nature more serious and more intimate still. We are going to move to a house quite covered with ivy; I will soon write more from there. Compliments to anybody who may inquire after me. (21, 10 Aug. 1874.)

Ivy and moss appealed to him wherever he found them, and ivy became a symbol, one of the underlying themes in his work. In Christian symbolism it represents death, immortality and affection. In 1876, visiting his sister Anna at another Ivy Cottage, at Welwyn, he found a *Mater Dolorosa* in her room, framed in ivy (letter 69). At Isleworth, one autumn evening that same year, he was moved by the sight of 'the church with the ivy, and the churchyard with the weeping willows on the banks of the Thames' (letter 76). At Dordrecht he quoted Dickens (from memory):

172

. . . The window of my room looks out on a garden with pine trees and poplars, and the backs of old houses covered with ivy. 'A strange old plant is the ivy green,' says Dickens. The view from my window can be solemn and more or less gloomy, but you ought to see it in the morning sun – how different it is then. When I look at it, I am often reminded of a letter from you in which you speak of such a house covered with ivy – do you remember? . . . (84, 21 Jan. 1877.)

Later still, struggling with his Latin and Greek in Amsterdam in 1878, he was to reflect that 'patience will help me through. I hope to remember the ivy, "which stealeth on though he wears no wings"; as the ivy creeps along the walls, so the pen must crawl over the paper' (letter 95). At Arles, years later, he wrote, in a curious attempt to comfort his sister Willemien, who was nursing a sick relative:

. . . The ivy loves the old branchless willow – every spring the ivy loves the trunk of the old oak tree – and in the same way cancer, that mysterious plant, so often fastens on people whose lives were nothing but love and devotion. However terrible the mystery of these sufferings may be, yet there is in reality something sweet and pathetically touching about it, which has the same effect as seeing the abundant growth of green moss on the old thatched roof. . . . (Vincent to Wil, W11, 10 Apr. 1889, F.)

One of the last letters written during Vincent's first spell at Goupil's in London includes a remarkable description of one of Thijs Maris' most popular works, *Souvenir of Amsterdam*, painted in Paris with the aid of a stereoscopic photograph. Vincent has clearly studied the painting; he describes it with uncommon precision, and makes a telling assessment of its quality.

Thanks for your letter. I copied in your little book 'Meeresstille' [Calm Sea] by Heine, didn't I? Some time ago I saw a picture by Thijs Maris that reminded me of it. It represents an old Dutch town with rows of brownish-red houses with stepped gables and high stoops; grey roofs; and white or yellow doors, window frames and cornices. There are canals with ships and a large white drawbridge under which a barge with a man at the tiller passes the little house of the bridgekeeper, who is seen through the window, sitting alone in his little office. Farther on is a stone bridge across the canal, over which some people and a cart with white horses are passing.

And there is life everywhere: a porter with his wheelbarrow; a man leaning against the railing of the bridge and looking into the water; women in black with white bonnets.

In the foreground is a brick-paved quay with a black rail; in the distance a church spire rises above the houses. A greyish white sky is above.

It is a small picture, and the artist was looking down on the scene. The subject is almost the same as that of the big J. Maris, *Amsterdam*, which you probably know; but this is talent and the other, genius. . . . (24, 6 Apr. 1875.)

His final letter briefly but unmistakably reflects a sombre mood. His art dealer uncle C.M. van Gogh had visited London, together with Tersteeg.

. . . Aye, boy, 'What shall we say?' C.M. and Mr Tersteeg have been here and left again last Saturday. In my opinion they went too often to the Crystal Palace and other places where they had nothing particular to do. I think they might just as well have come to see the place where I live. I hope and believe that I am not what many people think I am just now. We shall see, some time must pass; probably they will say the same of you a few years hence, at least if you remain what you are: my brother in both senses of the word. . . .

[PS.] 'If one is to act in this world, one must be dead to oneself. The nation that makes itself the missionary of a religious idea no longer has any fatherland but that idea.

'A man does not exist here below simply in order to be happy, or even in order to be honest. He is here to achieve great things for society, to attain nobility, and to rise above the common round in which almost every individual drags out his existence.' (RENAN.) (26, 8 May 1875.)

Vincent had developed a new awareness of his own personality, and at the same time a sense of estrangement. Being different meant – and this was to prove fundamental over a long period of inner growth – the detachment of his social ego from his family tradition. This tradition decided, with authority based on the desire for status rather than money, what kind of career the children of the Reverend Theodorus van Gogh and his wife Anna van Gogh-Carbentus should have.

6, 7

The members of his family were seriously worried by Vincent's sombre mood. He was clearly suffering from dissatisfaction with life and the world, although the nature of his dissatisfaction was as incomprehensible to himself as it was to them. They put their heads together, in 1874, and Uncle Vincent, who had more understanding of his nephew's psychological problems than the others, had him transferred to Paris for a while (October–December). When the experiment failed, Vincent was sent back to London. Nevertheless, Paris was to bring matters to a head.

Vincent now clearly began to subordinate his social ego to the undefined being which contained his true self and its psychic structure. He was unable to write about this. For those who can read there are ample indications in views on painting and literature which are far from commonplace, as well as an obsessive and constrained (or unfree) religious life which had an increasingly disruptive effect on his relations with his family and their traditional bourgeois values.

Ernest Meissonier. *The Reader* (see also *pl. 11*).

In May 1875 Vincent was transferred permanently to Paris. He knew he would be under special observation after the doubts felt about him in London.

Uncle Vincent has been here again. I have been with him pretty often and have talked things over. I asked him if there was any chance of getting you here in Paris. At first he wouldn't hear of it and said it was much better for you to stay in The Hague. I persisted, however, and you may be sure he will keep it in mind. When he comes to The Hague he probably will talk to you about it. Be as calm as you can and let him say whatever he likes: it will do you no harm, and probably you will want his help later on. You must not speak about me if you can avoid it.

He is enormously clever. When I was here last winter, one of the things he said to me was, 'Supernatural things I may not know, but I know everything about natural things.' I do not know if those were the exact words, but that was the meaning.

I can also tell you that one of his favourite pictures is *Lost Illusions* by Gleyre.

Sainte-Beuve said, 'In most men there exists a poet who died young, whom the man survived.' And Musset said, 'Know that often a dormant poet is hidden within us, always young and alive.' I think Uncle Vincent belongs to the first group. So you know whom you are dealing with. You can ask him straight out if he can have you transferred here or to London.

Thank you for the letter I got this morning and for the poem by Rückert. Have you a copy of his poems? I should like to know him better. As soon as there is a chance I shall send you a *18* French Bible and the *Imitation of Christ*. The latter was probably the favourite book of the lady painted by Ph. de Champaigne. At the Louvre there is a portrait of her daughter, a nun, also by Ph. de Ch.; she has the *Imitation* on the chair beside her. . . .

[PS.] Do you have the photographs after Meissonier in the gallery? Look at them often; he has painted *men*. Probably you know his *Smoker at the Window* and *Young Man at Breakfast*. (31, 15 July 1875.)

His reading now centred on the Bible (in French) and Thomas à Kempis' *Imitation of Christ*; which had a significant influence on his convictions and even on his style of writing. He soon became an ardent visitor to the Louvre and the Luxembourg museum. Two contemporary painters that Vincent mentioned at this time were to be of lasting importance to him: Ernest Meissonier and the painter-poet from Northern France, Jules Breton.

... Yesterday I saw the Corot exhibition. In it was the picture, *The Garden of Olives*; I am glad he painted that. To the right, a group of olive trees, dark against the glimmering blue sky; in the background, hills covered with shrubs and a few large ivy-grown trees over which the evening star shines.

At the Salon there are three very fine Corots; the best of them, painted shortly before his death, *Female Woodcutters*, will probably be reproduced as a woodcut in *L'Illustration* or *Le Monde Illustré*.

Of course I have also been to the Louvre and the Luxembourg. The Ruysdaels at the Louvre are splendid, especially *The Copse*, *The Stockade*, and *The Shaft of Sunlight*. I wish you could see the little Rembrandts there; *The Men of Emmaus* and its counterpart, *The Philosophers*.

Some time ago I saw Jules Breton with his wife and two daughters. His figure reminded me of J. Maris, but he has dark hair. As soon as there is an opportunity I will send you a book of his, *Les Champs et la mer*, which contains all his poems. He has a beautiful picture at the Salon, *St John's Eve*. Peasant girls dancing on a summer evening around a St John's fire; in the background, the village with a church and the moon over it. ...

[PS.] I have taken a little room in Montmartre which I am sure you would like. It is small, but it overlooks a little garden full of ivy and wild vines.

I will tell you what engravings I have on the wall. ... (27, 31 May 1875.)

His letters make no mention of his own work at the Goupil gallery, but include a remarkably detailed description – reminiscent of that of Thijs Maris' *Souvenir of Amsterdam* – of the striking Adriaan van Ostade group portrait in the Louvre, which is unusual for this painter in its choice of subject.

... Last Sunday I was at the Louvre (on Sundays I generally go there or to the Luxembourg). I wish you could see Van Ostade, his own family – himself, his wife and, I think, eight children. They are all in black – the wife and daughters with white caps and kerchiefs – in a stately old-Dutch room with a fireplace, large oak panels and ceiling, and whitewashed walls with pictures in black frames. In the corner of the room is a large bed with blue curtains and quilt.

The Rembrandt, *The Men of Emmaus*, which I wrote you about, has been engraved; Messrs. Goupil & Co. will publish the engraving next autumn. ... (35, 2 Sept. 1875.)

... Theo, I want to make a suggestion that may perhaps surprise you. Do not read Michelet any longer or *any* other book (except the Bible), until we have seen each other at Christmas, and do as I told you: go out in the evening often, dropping in on Van Stockum, Borchers and the like. I don't think you will regret it; you will feel much freer once you start this regimen.

Beware of the words I underlined in your letter [*still sadness*]. ... (36a, 8 Sept. 1875.)

The tone of Vincent's letters to his younger brother was becoming peremptory, and, with the zeal of a youthful Savonarola, he even went so far as to check later whether Theo had destroyed his copy of Michelet. Michelet had become an admired but dangerous writer. The text Vincent had quoted in London about the 'woman in black' continued to stir his imagination, although he urged its destruction. In July 1875 the picture was still on the wall of his room in Montmartre (letter 30).

With their frequently highflown, sermonizing tone and their profusion of Biblical texts (necessarily omitted here), conjoined with Thomas à Kempis' intense style of argument, his letters at this time do not make easy reading. He was unable as yet to formulate his ideas, and therefore borrowed much from other writers, although his sentiments were genuine and personal. This permeation of Vincent's feelings and thoughts with the spirit of the medieval lay religious movement of the *Devotio moderna*, from which Thomas à Kempis stemmed, was to be of importance all his life. Appealing directly to the individual, it preached a pure and humble way of life and the need to fight

Thomas à Kempis (1379/80–1471). From a medieval ms. of the *Imitation of Christ*.

temptation. Both in Paris and on his return to England, Vincent had a picture of Thomas à Kempis on his wall (letter 33). It was a lithograph, untraceable today, of a painting by a now forgotten Spanish artist called Luis Ruyperez or Ruipérez (1833–67), a pupil of Meissonier, who at one time had a considerable reputation as a portrait and genre painter.

During the same period in Paris Vincent also quoted (from memory) the following lines from Christina Rossetti's poem 'Uphill':

> *Does the road wind uphill all the way?*
> *Yes to the very end.*
> *Will the day's journey take the whole long day?*
> *From morn to night, my friend.* (41, 6 Oct. 1875.)

(In writings about Van Gogh, reference is always made to his 'misquoting', although in this instance it consisted merely of 'go' instead of 'wind', 'the journey' instead of 'the day's journey' and 'till' instead of 'to'. This seems quite excusable in someone who seems to have been able to jot down from memory anything he had found deeply moving.)

He did not reflect to any great extent on his visual impressions of paintings, since their impact was mainly emotional. This provides a clue to what was passing through his mind at this time. Since leaving London Vincent had arrived in a zone of pain and suffering, and his thinking was dominated by a desire to know the meaning of the sorrow and what it had to convey to him, rather than by a wish to complain. He failed to assimilate the outer world, but let himself be permeated with whatever his unconscious self made him select. He digested it, but his religious life was not creative; hence its forced aspect, which he carried to the utmost extreme before discovering that it was doing violence to his nature.

In December 1875 he decided to go home to Holland for Christmas. His employer, the new proprietor of Goupil in Paris, Boussod, did not approve, but Vincent seemed oblivious of his displeasure. He had become a man overwhelmingly absorbed in his own problems, seeking dawn and dusk rather than the light of day. Back in Paris after Christmas, he wrote laconically to Theo:

I have not written to you since we saw each other; in the meantime something has happened that did not come altogether unexpectedly. When I saw M. Boussod again, I asked him if he approved of my being employed in the house for another year, and said that I hoped he had no serious complaints against me. But the latter was indeed the case, and in the end he forced me, as it were, to say that I would leave on the first of April, thanking the gentlemen for all that I might have learned in their house.

When the apple is ripe, a soft breeze makes it fall from the tree; such was the case here; in a sense I have done things that have been very wrong, and therefore I have but little to say. . . . (30, 10 Jan. 1876.)

Meanwhile his real, that is to say his inner, life – that of seeing, reading and evaluating – continued. All this seems to have counted for far more with him than the loss of prospects in the art trade.

. . . I have just read a very fine book by [George] Eliot, *Scenes from Clerical Life*; three tales, especially the last one, 'Janet's Repentance', struck me very much. It is the story of a clergyman who lived chiefly among the inhabitants of the squalid streets of a town; his study looked out on gardens with cabbage stalks, etc., and on the red roofs and smoking chimneys of poor tenements. For his dinner he usually had nothing but underdone mutton and watery potatoes. He died at the age of thirty-four. During his long illness he was nursed by a woman who had been a drunkard, but by his teaching, and leaning as it were on him, had conquered her weakness and found rest for her soul. . . . (55, 19 Feb. 1876.)

It would be hard to avoid the impression that there was a psychic link between Vincent's experiences and intentions later on in The Hague, relating to the alcoholic prostitute Christine, and the story he had read in Paris in 1876. He read with so much intensity that it seems as if, whenever his reading had activated his still unconscious desires and driving force, it could years later, totally detached from the actual moment, occasionally make itself felt not as a memory, but as something new and contemporary or resurgent.

To his parents, with their constant financial anxieties and obsessive concern for social appearances, Vincent's dismissal naturally came as a severe blow. They could hardly be expected to come anywhere near comprehending a problem which Vincent himself was still engaged in elucidating. His father wrote to Theo:

He leaves Paris at eight o'clock this evening. What will be passing through his mind – and through ours! You will understand something of all this. It is a bitter blow. And yet I have always continued to write and encourage him, and I also pointed out to him the possibility of starting up on his own if he was still keen on his occupation. Uncle Cent started up with a miniature business, and he went so far in the world, and Uncle Cor ditto. *If only he could gain some life and energy!* and fight his way through with fresh vigour – whatever he does and wishes to do, it will have to come from himself. (Father to Theo, 31 Mar. 1876.)

Vincent's father had had no sign that the 'life and energy' that his son had failed to devote to business were abundantly present in his inner life. His parents complained that the letter they received from him on 31 March was

. . . only about paintings . . . without a word about his birthday or anything else . . . How he loves art, and how deeply he will feel having to take leave of it all. I need not tell you how sad we are, and it must be a great disappointment to you as well . . . (Mother to Theo, Apr. 1876.)

Arriving at Etten on 1 April 1876, one day after his twenty-third birthday, Vincent came face to face with the hard reality of needing to find another job. Naturally drawn to the religious tradition in the family, more so than to the world of commerce, and devoted as he was to the Bible and the works of Thomas à Kempis and John Bunyan (*A Pilgrim's Progress*), he felt a strong desire to preach the Gospel to the poor. His sense of reality, however, was still far from strong.

He decided to try to teach and preach, although unqualified for either, and took up a post, in return for board and lodging only, as assistant master at the small private school run by a minister, the Rev. William Port Stokes, at Ramsgate in south-eastern England.

And now Vincent has left us. We have had such pleasant days with him. His impending departure gave us all a difficult day; we took communion together at De Hoeven, and Father found it hard to have to preach a sermon at five o'clock after Vincent had left at four. (Mother to Theo, 16 Apr. 1876.)

Vincent felt impelled to tell his parents about his crossing to Ramsgate and his never-ending difficulty in saying farewell, always experiencing his departures in symbolic depth. It is possible to observe a fundamental fusion of inner and external worlds, which existed long before the revelation of his will to create, and which ever afterwards gave his vision of reality a quality of its own.

You have probably received my telegram, but you will be glad to hear some more particulars. On the train I wrote down a few things, and I am sending them to you, so that you will know all about my journey.

Friday.

In thought we will stay together today. Which do you think is better . . . the joy of meeting or the sorrow of parting? We have often parted before; this time there was more sorrow in it than there used to be, but also more courage because of the firmer hope, the stronger desire, for God's blessing. And didn't nature seem to share our feelings, everything looked so grey and dull a few hours ago.

Now I am looking across the vast expanse of meadows, and everything is very quiet; the sun is disappearing again behind the grey clouds, but sheds a golden light over the fields.

These first hours after our parting – which you are spending in church, and I at the station and on the train – how we are longing for each other and how we think of the others, of Theo and Anna and the other little sisters and the brother. Just now we passed Zevenbergen; I thought of the day you took me there, and I stood on the steps at Mr Provily's, looking after your carriage on the wet road; and then of that evening when my father came to visit me for the first time. And of that first homecoming at Christmas!

Saturday and Sunday.

On the steamer I thought often of Anna – everything reminded me of our journey together.

The weather was clear, and the river was especially beautiful, and also the view, seen from the sea, of the dunes, dazzling white in the sun. The last I saw of Holland was a little grey church spire. I stayed on deck until sunset, but then it became too cold and rough.

At dawn the next morning on the train from Harwich to London it was beautiful to see the black fields and green meadows with sheep and lambs and an occasional thornbush and a few large oak trees with dark twigs and grey moss-covered trunks; the shimmering blue sky with a few stars still, and a bank of grey clouds at the horizon. Before sunrise I had already heard the lark. When we were near the last station before London, the sun rose. The bank of grey clouds had disappeared and there was the sun, as simple and grand as ever I saw it, a real Easter sun. The grass sparkled with dew and night frost. But I still prefer that grey hour when we parted.

Saturday afternoon I stayed on deck till the sun had set. The water was fairly dark blue with rather high white-crested waves as far as one could see. The coast had already disappeared from sight. The sky was one vast light blue, without a single little cloud. And the sunset cast a streak of glittering light on the water. It was indeed a grand and majestic sight, but still the simpler, quieter things touch one so much more deeply. . . .

At one o'clock I arrived at Mr Stokes's; he was not home but will be back tonight. During his absence his place was taken by his son (twenty-three years old, I think), a teacher in London. I saw Mrs Stokes at dinner. There are twenty-four boys from ten to fourteen years old. (It is a pleasant sight to see them at their dinner.) So the school is not large. The window looks out on the sea. . . . Yesterday everything was grey. In the evening we went with the boys to church. On the wall of the church was written: 'Lo, I am with you always, even unto the end of the world.'

The boys go to bed at eight o'clock, and they rise at six.

There is another assistant teacher, seventeen years old. He, four boys and myself sleep in another house near by, where I have a little room that is waiting for some prints on the wall. (Vincent to parents, 60, 17 Apr. 1876.)

In the nine months he now spent in England, at Ramsgate and Isleworth, Vincent occupied lowly and ill-rewarded posts at private schools, living in a constant state of self-scrutiny. In this he was aided by his explorations of nature, in the external world of earth and sky. A sense of darkness and confinement often yielded to moments of religious ecstasy. Periods of desolation were transformed into tense, devout moods in which he could scale the heights of ecstatic experience. Those nine months passed in an inner twilight.

It is not enough to select just one of the wonderful descriptions of his remarkable walks. Apparent repetitions in fact never do repeat, but reflect a renewed penetration to the source, an absorbing, an ecstatic experience, clearly nourished by powerful driving forces from his unconscious self. Walking, for him as for Wordsworth and Coleridge, was a passion: the finest condition for engendering the required state of loneliness in which he could scrutinize his inner life and at the same time lose himself in the external world of nature familiar to him since his childhood in Brabant. He loved the nights, rose early, and did not mind spending the night out of doors. In Arles he was to say that 'night is even more richly coloured than day'.

Vincent's sense of affinity with anything gnarled or thorny, or anything which clings like ivy or moss, is already apparent in a few lines from a letter written soon after he arrived at Ramsgate.

... Now I am going to tell you about a walk we took yesterday. It was to an inlet of the sea, and the road there led through fields of young corn and along hedges of hawthorn, etc. Once there, we saw to our left a steep two-storey-high ridge of sand and stone. On top of it were old gnarled hawthorn bushes – their black and grey moss-covered stems and branches were all bent to one side by the wind; there were also a few elder bushes.

The ground we walked on was all covered with big grey stones, chalk and shells. To the right lay the sea as calm as a pond, reflecting the light of the transparent grey sky where the sun was setting. The tide was out and the water very low. ... (63, 28 Apr. 1876.)

One of Vincent's last Ramsgate letters conveys much of his state of mind, and his perennial fascination with the 'poetry of parting'. The precise phraseology, more mature now than during his first stay in London, and the ecstatic, stilled tone with which he experienced and reported the appearance of first light, birdsong, the sight of the sea at night, and his evening wanderings, either in the country or in the streets of London, are signs that his walks were the great moments, the profound experiences of those nine months.

... Did I tell you about the storm I watched recently? The sea was yellowish, especially near the shore; on the horizon a strip of light, and above it immense dark grey clouds from which the rain poured down in slanting streaks. The wind blew the dust from the little white path on the rocks into the sea and bent the blooming hawthorn bushes and wallflowers that grow on the rocks. To the right were fields of young green corn, and in the distance the town looked like the towns that Albrecht Dürer used to etch. A town with its turrets, mills, slate roofs and houses built in Gothic style, and below, the harbour between two jetties which project far into the sea.

I also saw the sea last Sunday night. Everything was dark and grey, but in the horizon the day began to dawn. It was still very early, but a lark was already singing. So were the nightingales in the gardens near the sea. In the distance shone the light from the lighthouse, the guard ship, etc.

From the window of my room that same night I looked on the roofs of the houses that can be seen from there and on the tops of the elm trees, dark against the night sky. Over those roofs one single star, but a beautiful, large, friendly one. And I thought of you all and of my own past years and of our home, and in me arose the words and the emotion: 'Keep me from being a son that maketh ashamed; give my Thy blessing, not because I deserve it, but for my mother's sake. Thou art love, cover all things. Without Thy continued blessings we succeed in nothing.'

Enclosed is a little drawing of the view from the school window through which the boys wave good-bye to their parents when they are going back to the station after a visit. None of us will ever forget the view from the window. *You ought to have seen* it this week when it rained, especially in the twilight when the lamps were lit and their light was reflected in the wet street.

On such days Mr Stokes is sometimes in a bad temper, and when the boys make more noise than he likes, they occasionally have to go without their supper. I wish you could see them looking from the window then, it is rather melancholy: they have so little else except their meals to look forward to and to help them pass their days. ... (67, 31 May 1876.)

Drawing from letter 67.

Stokes closed his school at Ramsgate in the summer of 1876 and moved it to Isleworth, a few miles up the Thames from London. On 12 June Vincent followed, taking the opportunity to visit his sister Anna at Welwyn in Hertfordshire, north of the city.

Last Monday I started from Ramsgate to London. It is a long walk; when I left it was very hot, and it stayed so until the evening, when I arrived in Canterbury. I went still a little farther that same evening, till I arrived at a few large beech and elm trees near a little pond; there I rested for a while. At half past three in the morning the birds began to sing at sight of dawn and I set off again. It was fine to walk then.

In the afternoon I arrived at Chatham. There one can see in the distance between partly flooded low-lying meadows, with elm trees here and there, the Thames full of ships. I believe the weather is always grey. I met a cart which took me a few miles farther, but then the driver went into an inn and I thought that he would stay a long time, so I continued on my way.

But to continue. One night I stayed at Mr Reid's and the next day at Mr Gladwell's, where they were very, very kind. Mr Gladwell kissed me good night that evening and it did me good; may it be given to me in the future to prove my friendship for his son now and then.

I wanted to go on to Welwyn that very evening, but they kept me back literally by force because of the pouring rain. However, when it began to let up about four o'clock in the morning, I set off for Welwyn. First a long walk from one end of the city to the other. In the afternoon at five o'clock I was with our sister and was very glad to see her. She is looking well, and you would like her little room as much as I do, with the *Good Friday*, *Christ in the Garden of Olives*, *Mater Dolorosa* framed in ivy. . . . (69, 17 June 1876.)

Professionally, Vincent's prospects remained dim. He wrote to Theo from Isleworth:

The time may come when I shall look back with a certain melancholy on the 'fleshpots of Egypt' connected with other situations – that is, the bigger salaries and the higher worldly esteem – this I foresee.

Mr Stokes says that he definitely cannot give me any salary because he can get teachers enough for just board and lodging, and that is true. But will it be possible for me to continue this way? I am afraid not; it will be decided soon enough.

But, boy, however this may be, one thing I can repeat: these few months have bound me so strongly to the sphere that extends from schoolmaster to clergyman, as much by the pleasures connected with those professions as by the thorns which have pricked me, that I cannot draw back any more. So I have to go on! . . .

Last week I was at Hampton Court to see the beautiful gardens and long avenues of chestnut and lime trees, where many crows and rooks have their nests, and also to see the palace and the pictures. Among other things there are many portraits by Holbein which are very beautiful; two splendid Rembrandts (the portrait of his wife, and of a rabbi); beautiful Italian portraits by Bellini, Titian; a picture by Leonardo da Vinci; cartoons by Mantegna; a beautiful picture by S. Ruysdael; a still life of fruit by Cuyp, etc. I wish you had been there with me; it was a pleasure to see pictures again.

And involuntarily I thought of the persons who had lived there at Hampton Court, of Charles I and his wife (it was she who said, 'I thank Thee, my God, for having made me queen, but an unhappy queen') at whose grave Bossuet spoke from the fullness of his heart. Do you have Bossuet's *Oraisons funèbres*? In it you will find that speech (there is a very cheap edition, I think for 50 centimes); and I thought also of Lord and Lady Russell, who must have been there very often too (Guizot described their lives in *L'Amour dans le mariage* – you must read that when you can lay your hands on it).

Enclosed, a feather from one of the rooks there. . . . (70, 5 July 1876.)

Early in July, Vincent moved to another private school in Isleworth, kept by a Methodist minister, the Rev. T. Slade Jones, who not only paid him a salary (unlike Stokes) but was to remain a friend.

It is Saturday again and I am writing once more. How I long to see you all again. Oh! my longing is sometimes so strong. Drop me a line soon, to tell me how things are.

Last Wednesday we took a long walk to a village an hour from here. The road led through meadows and fields, along hedges of hawthorn, full of blackberries and traveller's joy, and an occasional large elm tree. It was so beautiful when the sun set behind the grey clouds and the shadows were long. By chance we came upon Mr Stokes's school; several of the boys I knew are still there. The clouds stayed red long after the sun had set and the dusk had settled over the fields; and in the distance we saw the lamps lit in the village.

While I was writing to you, I was called to Mr Jones, who asked if I would walk to London to collect some money for him. And when I came home in the evening, hurrah! there was a letter from Father with news of you. How I should like to be with you both, my boy. And thank God there is some improvement, though you are still weak. And you will be longing to see Mother, and now that I hear that you are going home with her, I think of Conscience's words:

'I was ill. My mind was fatigued, my soul disillusioned, my body suffering. I, whom God has endowed at least with mental energy, and with a vast instinct for affection, I was sinking into the depths of the bitterest discouragement, and I felt with horror the deadly poison that was entering my withered heart. I spent three months on the Heath – you know that fair land where the soul returns to itself and enjoys a delectable repose, where all is calm and peace; where the soul, in the presence of God's immaculate creation, shakes off the yoke of convention, forgets society and frees itself from its fetters with the vigour of youth reborn; where every thought forms a prayer, where all that is out of harmony with the freshness and freedom of nature departs from the heart. Oh! there the tired soul finds tranquillity, there the exhausted man regains his youthful strength. So passed my days of sickness. . . . And the evenings? To sit beneath the wide canopy of the fireplace, feet in the ashes, gazing up at a star which sends down its ray through the opening of the chimney, as if to send me an appeal; or deep in a vague reverie, watching the flames as they are born, rise, pant, flicker, succeed each other, as if out of desire to lick the pot with their fiery tongues, and reflecting that this is human life: we are born, we work, we love, we grow, and we vanish!' [Henri Conscience, *Le Conscrit*, preface.]

Mr Jones has promised me that I shall not have to teach so much in future, but may work more in his parish, visiting the people, talking with them, etc. May God give it His blessing.

Now I am going to tell you about my walk to London. I left here at twelve o'clock in the morning and reached my destination between five and six. When I came into the part of town where most of the picture galleries are, around the Strand, I met many acquaintances: it was dinnertime, so many were in the street, leaving the office or going back there. First I met a young clergyman with whom I became acquainted when he preached here once. After that, Mr Wallis's employee and then one of the Messrs. Wallis, whose house I visited occasionally; now he has two children. Then I met Mr Reid and Mr Richardson, who are already old friends. Last year about this time Mr Richardson was in Paris and we walked together to Père Lachaise.

After that I went to Van Wisselingh, where I saw sketches for two church windows. In the middle of one window was a portrait of a middle-aged lady – oh, such a noble face – with the words 'Thy will be done' over it; and in the other window, a portrait of her daughter with the words, 'Faith is the substance of things hoped for, the evidence of things not seen.' There, and in Messrs. Goupil & Co.'s gallery, I saw beautiful pictures and drawings. It is such an intense delight to be so often reminded of Holland by art. . . . Then to the place where I had to collect the money for Mr Jones. The suburbs of London have a peculiar charm; between the little houses and gardens there are open spots covered with grass and generally with a church or school or workhouse in the middle among the trees and shrubs. It can be so beautiful there when the sun is setting red in the thin evening mist.

Yesterday evening it was like that, and afterward I wished you could have seen those London streets when the twilight began to fall and the lamps were lit and everybody went home. Everything showed that it was Saturday night, and in all that bustle there was peace, one felt the need of and the excitement at the approaching Sunday. Oh, those Sundays, and all that is done and accomplished on those Sundays, it is such a comfort for those poor districts and crowded streets.

In the City it was dark, but it was a beautiful walk along the row of churches one has to pass. Near the Strand I caught a bus which took me quite a long way; it was already pretty late. I passed Mr Jones's little church and saw another one in the distance, with a light still burning at that hour; I entered and found it to be a very beautiful little Catholic church where a few women were praying. Then I came to that dark park which I have already written you about; from it I saw far away the lights of Isleworth and the church with the ivy, and the churchyard with the weeping willows on the banks of the Thames.

Tomorrow for the second time I shall get some small salary for my new work, and with it buy a pair of new boots and a new hat. And then, God willing, I shall gird myself up again.

Everywhere in the London streets they sell scented violets, which bloom here twice a year. I bought some for Mrs Jones to make her forget the pipe I smoke now and then, especially late in the evening in the playground, but the tobacco here is rather a gloomy weed. . . . (76, 7/8 Oct. 1876.)

The sermon Vincent preached at Richmond, towards the end of his final nine months in England, was a great moment for him. It is a mixture of personal experience and borrowed formulations – quoted, as usual, from memory. It shows how powerful and workable a synthesis he had developed between literature and the Bible, as well as between literature and his sentiments about painting and nature. An irresistible fusion of painting, narrative and landscape had taken place in his imagination, and he included all three elements in his conception of a 'picture'.

The entire sermon is permeated with the spirit of Puritanism, and in particular with that of Methodism, which, at this time more than later, was in tune with Vincent's own character. Since 1875 he had been a passionate reader of Bunyan, of whom it is said that in England there are more editions of his work than of any other writer except Shakespeare. After a dramatic experience of conversion, Bunyan had taken to preaching among the ordinary, poor people whom the established Church neglected. For this and his non-conformist views he spent years in prison. His personal style of devotion, and his simple, measured style of writing, in which allegory alternated with realism, were highly congenial to Vincent.

In composing his sermon, Vincent used symbolic images made up of elements such as the pilgrim's journey to the Heavenly City through the Valley of the Shadow of Death, his meeting with the woman in black (which for Vincent had become an almost obsessive image since his encounter with Michelet's description of the portrait by Champaigne); the constant question, *18* 'Is there far still to go?' (frequently quoted from Christina Rossetti's 'Uphill'), and, lastly, Boughton's lost painting which Vincent called *The Pilgrim's Progress*. Here he followed his own imagination, and provided the only genuine section of the sermon. The confusion of elements makes it typical of his later work.

. . . Our life is a pilgrim's progress. I once saw a very beautiful picture: it was a landscape at evening. In the distance on the right-hand side a row of hills appeared blue in the evening mist. Above those hills the splendour of the sunset, the grey clouds with their linings of silver and gold and purple. The landscape is a plain or heath covered with grass and its yellow leaves, for it was in autumn. Through the landscape a road leads to a high mountain far, far away, on the top of that mountain is a city whereon the setting sun casts a glory. On the road walks a pilgrim, staff in hand. He has been walking for a good long while already and he is very tired. And now he meets a woman, a figure in black, that makes one think of St Paul's word: As being sorrowful yet always rejoicing. That Angel of God has been placed there to encourage the pilgrims and to answer their questions and the pilgrim asks her: 'Does the road go uphill then all the way?'

And the answer is: 'Yes to the very end.'
And he asks again: 'And will the journey take all day long?'
And the answer is: 'From morn till night my friend.'
And the pilgrim goes on sorrowful yet always rejoicing – sorrowful because it is so far off and the road so long. Hopeful as he looks up to the eternal city far away, resplendent in the evening glow. . . . (CLVG, I, 90.)

. . . Theo, your brother has preached for the first time, last Sunday, in God's dwelling, of which is written 'In this place, I will give peace.' Enclosed a copy of what I said. My it be the first of many.

It was a clear autumn day and a beautiful walk from here to Richmond along the Thames, in which the great chestnut trees with their load of yellow leaves and the clear blue sky were mirrored. Through the tops of the trees one could see that part of Richmond which lies on the hill: the houses with their red roofs, uncurtained windows and green gardens; and the grey spire high above them; and below, the long grey bridge with the tall poplars on either side, over which the people passed like little black figures.

When I was standing in the pulpit, I felt like somebody who, emerging from a dark cave underground, comes back to the friendly daylight. It is a delightful thought that in the future wherever I go, I shall preach the Gospel; to do that *well*, one must have the Gospel in one's heart. May the Lord give it to me. . . .

Yesterday evening I was again at Richmond, and walked through a large grassy field surrounded by trees and houses, over which the church spire rises. The dew was lying on the grass and the twilight was falling: on one side the sky was still aglow from the setting sun, on the other, the moon was rising. Under the trees an old lady with beautiful grey hair was walking, dressed in black. In the middle of the grass plot the boys had lit a bonfire which one could see flickering from afar. I thought of the lines: 'Once at the evening of my life, tired from care and strife, I'll bring Thee praise more loud and fair, for each day given to me here.' (79, 7 Oct. 1876.)

Vincent went home for Christmas in December 1876, and never returned to England. His prospects there appeared non-existent, and it was decided that he would try something new.

. . . A few days ago Mr Braat from Dordrecht came to visit Uncle Vincent, and they talked about me; Uncle asked Mr Braat if he had a place for me in his business, should I want one. Mr Braat thought so, and said that I should just come and talk it over. So I went there early yesterday morning; I thought I could not let it go by without seeing what it was. We arranged that I should come for a week after New Year's to try it out, and after that we will see. There are many things that make it desirable; being back in Holland near Father and Mother, and also near you and all the others. Then the salary would certainly be better than at Mr Jones's, and it is one's duty to think of that because later in life a man needs more.

As to the religious work, I still do not give it up. Father has so many interests and he is so versatile, I hope that in whatever circumstances I may be, something similar will develop in me. The change will be that, instead of teaching the boys, I shall work in a bookshop. . . .

So it is quite possible that I shall go there.

Yesterday evening I was at Uncle Vincent's to tell him that I had gone to Dordrecht at once. It was a stormy night; you can imagine how beautiful the road to Prinsenhage was with the dark clouds and their silver linings.

I just entered for a minute the Catholic church where evening service was being held. It was a beautiful sight, all those peasants and peasant women in their black dresses and white caps, and the church looked so cheerful in the evening light. . . . (83, 31 Dec. 1876.)

Vincent spent just over three months (14 January–2 May 1877) working for the Blussé & Van Braam bookshop. Thirty-seven years later, when Vincent was famous, a Rotterdam journalist made some enquiries at Dordrecht, and talked to one of Braat's sons (whose brother Frans had been a colleague of Theo's at Goupil).

In theory Vincent had the show goods, and now and then the delivery goods, under his care – but whenever anyone looked at what he was doing, it was found that instead of working, he was translating the Bible into French, German and English, in four columns, with the Dutch text in addition.

He was puttering at this mostly. At other times when you happened to look, you caught him making little sketches, such silly pen-and-ink drawings, a little tree with a lot of branches and side branches and twigs – nobody ever saw anything else in it. (Although it turned out that afterward, when this work had come so much into vogue, Mr Braat had taken a good look through Vincent's little desk from top to bottom! – But not the slightest vestige of his handiwork was to be found, neither outside nor in.) . . .

'Well, shortly afterward Vincent went to Amsterdam and was taken in by his uncle, the rear admiral, in whose house he started studying Latin and Greek in an attic. Since then I have lost sight of him – I cannot say I was particularly interested. No, he was not an attractive boy, with those small, narrowed, peering eyes of his, and, in fact, he was always a bit unsociable.

'And then I remember well that he always preferred to wear a top hat, a bit of respectability he had brought back from England; but such a hat – you were afraid you might tear its brim off if you took hold of it. I have often puzzled over his exact age, but I cannot work out, for instance, whether he was old enough to be called up for the militia.'

But he was certainly obliging, and physically very strong, though he did not look it. During one of those frequent floods Mr Braat had admired his physical strength and good nature. At the time he lived in Tolbrugstraatje – in a room with whitewashed walls, my informant believed, on which he had made all kinds of sketches and crude drawings. But his landlord, who did not like this at all, had repainted them later on. However this may have been – that particular night everything was flooded. Without hesitating for a moment, Van Gogh rushed out of the house and waded through the water to his employer's house in order to warn him. For Blussé & Van Braam's storehouse was next door to his boarding-house. All the next morning he was lifting those heavy wet sacks of paper and carrying them upstairs. After all these years Mr Braat still spoke with admiration of so much physical strength.

Also, Van Gogh was always as compliant as possible. For all that, he now and then could irritate the old gentleman into peevishness: 'Good heavens! that boy's standing there translating the Bible again.' But he could not be trusted to serve the public and such, except perhaps to sell a quire of letter paper or a halfpenny print once in a while. For he had not the slightest knowledge of the book trade, and he did not make any attempt to learn.

On the contrary, he was excessively interested in religion. 'On Sunday he always went to church, preferably an orthodox one. – And during the week, well, we started work here at eight o'clock in the morning; at one o'clock he went home to lunch until three; and then he came back in the evening for a few hours. For the rest, he had no intercourse with anybody; he led an absolutely solitary life. He took many walks all over the island, but always alone. In the shop he hardly spoke a word. In short, he was something of a recluse.' . . . (M.J. Brusse, 'Onder de mensen', *Nieuwe Rotterdamse Courant*, 26 May, 2 June 1914, CLVG, I, 108–09.)

At Dordrecht he continued with even greater intensity the twilit life of his days in Isleworth, went to church, including the Eglise Wallonne, and did some drawing. The thirteen letters dating from this period also refer to frequent visits to museums and art galleries. Once again he continued to go for a great many walks, insisted that Theo and his father accompanied him to the museum, and extolled Ary Scheffer, chiefly because of the subject matter of paintings such as *Christ in Gethsemane, Portrait of The Artist's Mother, Christ the Comforter*. His predilection for ivy was a continuation of his English love of Dickens' 'strange old plant'.

38
39

. . . The two prints, *Christus Consolator* and *Remunerator*, which you gave me are hanging in my little room – I saw the pictures at the museum, as well as Scheffer's *Christ in Gethsemane*, which is unforgettable. Then there is a sketch of *Les Douleurs de la Terre* and several drawings, a sketch of his studio, and, as you know, the portrait of his mother. There are still other fine pictures, for instance, Achenbach and Schelfhout and Koekkoek and also a fine Allebé – an old man near the stove. Shall we look at them together someday? . . .

The window of my room looks out on a garden with pine trees and poplars, and the backs of old houses covered with ivy. 'A strange old plant is the ivy green,' says Dickens. The view from my window can be solemn and more or less gloomy, but you ought to see it in the morning sun – how different it is then. When I look at it, I am often reminded of a letter from you in which you speak of such a house covered with ivy – do you remember? . . .

30   If you can afford it – if I can, I will do the same – you must subscribe to the Catholic *Illustration* of this year; there are prints in it from London by Doré – the wharves on the Thames, Westminster, Whitechapel, the underground railway, etc. . . . (84, 21 Jan. 1877.)

. . . Oh, that I may be shown the way to devote my life more fully to the service of God and the Gospel. I keep praying for it and, in all humility, I think I shall be heard. Humanly speaking, one would say it cannot happen; but when I think seriously about it and penetrate the surface of what is impossible to man, then my soul is in communion with God, for it is possible to Him Who speaketh, and it is, Who commandeth, and it stands firmly.

Oh! Theo, Theo boy, if I might only succeed in this! If that heavy depression because everything I have undertaken has failed, and that torrent of reproaches which I have heard and felt, might be taken from me; and if there might be given to me both the necessary opportunity and the strength to develop fully and to persevere in that course for which my father and I would thank the Lord so fervently. . . . (92, 15 Apr. 1877.)

This letter shows how his family's reproaches had wounded him. However, his proposal to study for admission to university at Amsterdam, after giving up his job at the bookshop, was approved by all the family except his Uncle Vincent, who lacked confidence in it. His final letter from Dordrecht mentions three separate church attendances. After a morning service at the French church he quoted the text of the sermon, taken from I Corinthians 13.12, which had deeply impressed him: 'For now we see through a glass, darkly; but then face to face: now I know in part, but then shall I know even as also I am known.'

In letter 641a, written shortly before his death in 1890, he quoted it, following his mother's departure from Nuenen, to allude to the ultimate farewell. This text, quoted in its Dutch form ('in a mirror, by a dark reason'), obsessed him for years.

. . . In the afternoon I was in the Great Church to hear the Reverend Mr Keller van Hoorn; his text was, 'Our Father.' In the evening I heard the Reverend Mr Greeff, whom I also heard the first Sunday night I was here in Dordrecht. May the Lord bless thee and keep thee. The Lord make His face to shine upon thee, and give thee peace. The Lord make thee pray high prayers and think high thoughts. The Lord be thy keeper and the shade upon thy right hand. May He be with thee always until the end of the world.

After church I walked along the path behind the station where we walked together; my thoughts were full of you, and I wished we might be together. I walked on to the churchyard at the end of a black cinder track through the meadows – they looked so beautiful in the twilight. The churchyard reminds me of that drawing by Apol in *Eigen Haard*; a moat surrounds it, and there is a house circled by pine trees – last night a light was shining kindly through the windows – it is an old house, and looks like a parsonage. . . .

Much good may be in store for us in the future; let us learn to repeat with Father, 'I never despair'; and with Uncle Jan, 'The devil is never so black but you can look him in the face.' . . .

Between times I have worked through the whole story of Christ from a catechism book of Uncle Stricker's and copied the texts; they reminded me of so many pictures by Rembrandt and others. I hope and believe I will not repent my choosing to try to become a Christian and a Christian worker. Yes, everything in my past experience may contribute to it: through the acquaintance with cities such as London and Paris and life in schools like those at Ramsgate and Isleworth, one is strongly drawn and attached to many things and books from the Bible – for instance, the Acts of the Apostles. Knowledge of and love for the work and life of men like Jules Breton, Millet, Jacque, Rembrandt, Bosboom and so many others may become a source of new thoughts. What a resemblance there is between the work and life of Father and that of those men; I value Father's higher still. . . . (94, 30 April 1877.)

The twenty-six letters Vincent wrote as a theological student in Amsterdam between May 1877 and July 1878 reflect the same two driving forces within him: religion and art. His devotion to art and to literature was increasing rather than diminishing, and it was further stimulated by the paintings then exhibited by the State in the Trippenhuis (Cuypers' Rijksmuseum was not yet *12–14* built). This interest was in fact gaining ground on his obligation to learn Latin, Greek and other subjects so as to be admitted to the University. He still remained firmly tied to the family circle, and had a room in an official residence in the Amsterdam naval dockyard, where his Uncle Jan was officer *42* commanding. He called regularly on his aunt Catrina Gerardina Carbentus and her husband J.P. Stricker, a prominent clergyman. One of the Strickers' *43* daughters was married to a clergyman by the name of Vos, and Vincent enjoyed visiting the young couple as well. After she was widowed a few years later, this cousin, Cornelia Adriana (Kee), born 21 March 1846, was to *49* become the object of Vincent's great and unrequited love.

Outside the family circle his tutor Dr M.B. Mendes da Costa was the only person with whom he was able to talk freely without fear of offending the authoritarian sensibilities of clerics like his Uncle Stricker – for whom Vincent, however, had considerable affection. Mendes da Costa wrote a frank memoir many years later.

. . . Our first meeting, of so much importance to the relationship between master and pupil, was very pleasant indeed. The seemingly reticent young man – our ages differed but little, for I was twenty-six then, and he was undoubtedly over twenty – immediately felt at home, and notwithstanding his lank reddish hair and his many freckles, his appearance was far from unattractive to me. In passing, let me say that it is not very clear to me why his sister [Lies] speaks of his 'more or less rough exterior'; it is possible that, after the time when I knew him, because of his untidiness and his growing a beard, his outward appearance lost something of its charming quaintness; but most decidedly it can never have been rough, neither his nervous hands, nor his countenance, which might have been considered homely, but which expressed so much and hid so much more.

I succeeded in winning his confidence and friendship very soon, which was so essential in this case; and as his studies were prompted by the best of intentions, we made comparatively good progress in the beginning – I was soon able to let him translate an easy Latin author. Needless to say, he, who was so fanatically devout in those days, at once started using this little bit of Latin knowledge to read Thomas à Kempis in the original.

So far everything went well, including mathematics, which he had begun studying with another master in the meantime; but after a short time the Greek verbs became too much for him. However I might set about it, whatever trick I might invent to enliven the lessons, it was no use. 'Mendes,' he would say – we did not 'mister' each other any more – 'Mendes, do you seriously believe that such horrors are indispensable to a man who wants to do what I want to do: give peace to poor creatures and reconcile them to their existence here on earth?'

And I, who as his master naturally could not agree, but who felt in my heart of hearts that he – mind, I say *he*, Vincent van Gogh! – was quite right, I put up the most formidable defence I was capable of; but it was no use.

'John Bunyan's *Pilgrim's Progress* is of much more use to me, and Thomas à Kempis and a translation of the Bible; and I don't want anything more.' I really do not know how many times he told me this, nor how many times I went to the Reverend Mr Stricker to discuss the matter, after which it was decided again and again that Vincent ought to have another try.

But before long the trouble would start afresh, and then he would come to me in the morning with an announcement I knew so well, 'Mendes, last night I used the cudgel again,' or, 'Mendes, last night I got myself locked out again.' It should be observed that this was some sort of self-chastisement resorted to whenever he thought he had neglected a duty. .... (M.B. Mendes da Costa, *Het Algemeen Handelsblad* (Amsterdam), 2 Dec. 1910, CLVG, I, 169–70.)

Vincent's parents showed touching solicitude for the neglected appearance of their twenty-four-year-old son.

We have smartened him up a little by putting him in the hands of the best tailor in Breda. Would you care to perform an act of mercy and have his *chevelure* metamorphosed by a clever barber? Here in Etten there is no one suitable, but I think a Hague *friseur* would be able to make something of it. (Mother to Theo, 7 May 1877.)

His first letter from Amsterdam to Theo in The Hague proves once more that art, painting, and the pictures he wanted to hang on his own wall, were taking precedence over his studies.

... I am sending you something for your collection by the same mail, namely a lithograph after J. Maris which might be called *A Poor Man in the Kingdom of God* and a lithograph after Mollinger – I never saw it before, did you?

A Jewish bookseller who gets me the Latin and Greek books I want had a large number of prints, and I could choose from them very cheaply, thirteen for 70 cents. I took some for my little room to give it the right atmosphere, for that is necessary to get new thoughts and ideas. I will tell you what they are, then you will know how my room looks and what is hanging there: one after Jamin (it also hangs in your room); one after M. Maris, the little boy going to school; five after Bosboom, Van der Maaten's *Funeral Procession through the Cornfields*; Israëls, poor man on a snowy winter road; and Ostade, studio. Then there is still an Allebé, a little old woman carrying her hot water and live coals on a winter morning along a snow-covered street. I sent the last one to Cor for his birthday. The Jew had a lot more fine things, but I could not afford any more, and though I like to put some up in my room, I am not going to make a collection.

Yesterday Uncle Cor sent me a lot of old paper, like the sheet on which I am writing now; isn't it delightful for writing my exercises on?

I have a lot of work to do and it is not very easy, but patience will help me through. I hope to remember the ivy 'which stealeth on though he wears no wings'; as the ivy creeps along the walls, so the pen must crawl over the paper.

Every day I take a long walk. Lately I came through a very nice part of town; I went along the Buitenkant to the Dutch Railway station, where I saw men working with sand carts near the IJ, and I passed through many narrow streets with gardens full of ivy. Somehow it reminded me of Ramsgate. Near the station I turned to the left, where all the windmills are, along a canal with elm trees; everything there reminds one of Rembrandt's etchings.

How is Mrs Tersteeg, and have you been to see Mauve? Keep courage, there may be good days in store for us, if God will grant us life and bless what we undertake. Will you ever hear me preach in some little church? May God grant it – I believe that He will. ...

[PS.] Yesterday I saw a portrait of Michelet; I looked at it carefully and thought of 'his life of ink and paper'. At night I am tired and I cannot get up as early as I wish, but I will get over that, and hope to force myself to it. (95, 19 May 1877.)

Thomas Couture. *Jules Michelet* (detail).

Michelet was now fully restored to Vincent's affections. His letters give a lively impression of insuperable distaste for his studies and a conflicting desire to complete them so as to confound those who would otherwise condemn him.

The idea, a central one in the minds of many nineteenth-century artists and writers, of a 'wasted life' – *une vie, une existence, manquée* – here makes its first appearance in Vincent's letters, long before the related idea of sacrificing all human happiness in the cause of art. Vincent was ultimately to make that sacrifice, but would never cease to be tormented by the sense of the life he had missed.

... A phrase in your letter struck me: 'I wish I were far away from everything; I am the cause of all, and bring only sorrow to everybody; I alone have brought all this misery on myself and others.' These words struck me because that same feeling, exactly the same, neither more nor less, is also on my conscience.

When I think of the past; when I think of the future of almost invincible difficulties, of much and difficult work which I do not like – which I, or rather my evil self, would like to shirk; when I think of the many watching me who will know where the fault is if I do not succeed, who will not make trivial reproaches, but as they are well tried and trained in everything that is right and virtuous and pure gold, the expression on their faces will seem to say, We have helped you and have been a light unto you, we have done for you what we could – have you honestly tried? What is our reward and the fruit of our labour now? See! when I think of all this and of so many other things like it too numerous to mention, of all the difficulties and cares that do not lessen as we advance in life – of sorrow, of disappointment, of the fear of failure, of disgrace – then I also know the longing, I wish I were far away from everything!

And yet I go on, but prudently and hoping to have the strength to resist those things, so that I shall know how to answer the reproaches that threaten me, and believing that, notwithstanding everything that seems against me, I yet shall reach the aim I am striving for, and if God wills it, find favour in the eyes of some I love and of those who will come after me. ... (98, 30 May 1877.)

His anxieties were counterbalanced, as they had been in England, by his profound sensitivity to all he observed and enjoyed in the way of light, sky and especially people, in and around Amsterdam.

You remember that night at Dordrecht when we walked together through the town, around the Great Church and through so many streets, and along the canals – in which the old houses and the lights from the windows were reflected? You spoke then about the description of a day in London by Théophile Gautier, the coachman for a wedding party in front of the door of a church on a stormy foggy day: I saw it all before me. If that struck you, you will also appreciate the pages I enclose. I read them on a very stormy day last week: it was in the evening, and the sunset threw a ruddy glow on the grey evening clouds, against which the masts of the ships and the row of old houses and trees stood out; and everything was reflected in the water, and the sky threw a strange light on the black earth, on the green grass with daisies and buttercups, and on the bushes of white and purple lilacs, and on the elderberry bushes of the garden in the yard.

In London I had read that book of Lamartine's, and I was very much struck by it; the last pages especially made a deep impression on me again. Tell me what you think of it. These places mentioned in it – Hampton Court with its avenues of linden trees full of rookeries; Whitehall overgrown with ivy at the back; and the square bordering St James's Park where one can see Westminster Abbey – they are all before me, and the weather and the gloomy atmosphere: it keeps me from sleeping. ...

[PS.] Today when I passed the flower market on the Singel, I saw something very pretty. A peasant was standing selling a whole bunch of pots with all kinds of flowers and plants; ivy was behind it, and his little girl was sitting between it all, such a child as Maris would have painted, so simple in her black bonnet, and with a pair of bright, smiling eyes. She was knitting; the man praised his wares – and if I could have spared the money I should have liked only too well to buy some – and he said, pointing unintentionally at his little daughter also, 'Doesn't it look pretty?'

(5 June)

Yesterday evening I was at Stricker's ... We walked along the Buitenkant and the embankment near the East railway. I cannot describe to you how beautiful it was there in the twilight. Rembrandt, Michel and others have sometimes painted it: the ground dark, the sky still lit by the glow of the setting sun, the row of houses and steeples against it, lights in the windows everywhere, and the whole mirrored in the water. And the people and the carriages like little black figures, such as one sees sometimes in a Rembrandt. We were so struck by the beauty of it that we began to talk about many things.

I sat up writing late last night and was up again early this morning, it was such beautiful weather. At night there is also a beautiful view of the yard; everything is dead quiet then, and the lamps are burning and the starlit sky is over it all.

'When all sounds cease, God's voice is heard under the stars.'

Write me soon and tell me if that part about Cromwell isn't taken from the very heart of London.

Youth of Cromwell [Lamartine, *Cromwell*]
'The family soon lost its wealth. He retired to a small estate he possessed amidst the marshes of Huntingdon. The barren, rough and morose character of this shore district, the monotonous horizon, the muddy river, the clouded skies, the meagre trees, the infrequent cottages, the rude habits of the inhabitants, were such as to make the young man's nature concentrated and gloomy. The soul of a land seems to enter into that of man. Often a lively, ardent and profound faith seems to emanate from a poor and dismal country; like country, like man. The soul is a mirror before it becomes a home. . . .' (100, 5 June 1877.)

Vincent now began to teach a Sunday-school class, and enjoyed it, because he felt he could achieve something positive and of use to the children. His father thought otherwise, and felt he should not allow matters of secondary importance to distract him from his studies. Vincent persevered, and his letters home became infrequent.

He really takes no pleasure in life, always walking around with head bent, although we have done all we could to bring him to some honourable goal in life. It is as if he deliberately chooses whatever leads to trouble. (Parents to Theo, 1877.)

At home they clearly felt that another disaster was imminent. This impression was not false; but his parents remained totally unaware of what lay behind his actions in 'deliberately choosing' the hard way: the pressure from his unconscious self which held him back from a path which was ultimately the wrong one, even though he was still unaware of the power of his own artistic genius.

In the summer of 1877 he wrote, as he had done before, of Dickens' frugal remedy for suicidal thoughts:

. . . I got up early and saw the workmen arrive in the yard while the sun was shining brightly. You would be intrigued by the sight – that long line of black figures, big and small, first in the narrow street where the sun just peeps in, and later in the yard. Then I breakfasted on a piece of dry bread and a glass of beer – that is what Dickens advises for those who are on the point of committing suicide, as being a good way to keep them, at least for some time, from their purpose. And even if one is not in such a mood, it is right to do it occasionally, while thinking, for instance, of Rembrandt's picture, *The Men of Emmaus*. . . . (106, 18 Aug. 1877.)

His tendency to view matters ecstatically was now well developed. After a frightening sensation he had experienced when looking into a dark cellar, he managed to express with great clarity how ordinary things can be transfigured.

. . . This morning I saw a big dark wine cellar and warehouse, with the doors standing open; for a moment I had an awful vision in my mind's eye – you know what I mean – men with lights were running back and forth in the dark vault. It is true you can see this daily, but there are moments when the common everyday things make an extraordinary impression and have a deep significance and a different aspect. De Groux knew so well how to put it in his pictures 96 and especially in his lithographs. . . . (108, 4 Sept. 1877.)

Vincent's ecstatic disposition was also manifest in the obsessional persistence with which he continued to dwell on the *Imitation of Christ*. He even began to observe a resemblance to Thomas à Kempis (as portrayed by Ruiperez) in his tutor Mendes.

. . . This morning I had a talk with Mendes about M. Maris, and showed him that lithograph of those three children, and also *A Baptism*, and he understood them very well. Mendes reminds me now and then of the *Imitation of Jesus Christ*, by Ruyperez. . . . (106, 18 Aug. 1877.)

. . . How would a man like Father, who so often goes long distances, even in the night with a lantern, to visit a sick or dying man, to speak with him about One whose word is a light even in the night of suffering and agony – how would he feel about Rembrandt's etchings, for instance, *The Flight into Egypt in the Night* or the *Burial of Jesus*? The collection in the Trippenhuis is splendid, I saw many I had never seen before; they also told me there about drawings by Rembrandt at the Fodor Museum. . . .

But I am up to my ears in my work, for it is becoming clear to me what I really must know what *they* know and what inspires *those* whom I should like to follow. 'Search the scriptures' is not written in vain, but is a good guide; I should like to become the kind of scribe who brings forth old and new things from his treasure.

I spent Monday evening with Vos and Kee; they love each other truly, and one can easily perceive that where love dwells, God commands His blessing. It is a nice home, though it is a great pity that he could not remain a preacher. When one sees them sitting side by side in the evening, in the kindly lamplight of the little living room, quite close to the bedroom of their boy, who wakes up every now and then and asks his mother for something, it is an idyll. On the other hand, they have known days of anxiety and sleepless nights and fears and troubles. . . .

Twilight is falling – 'blessed twilight', Dickens called it, and indeed he was right. Blessed twilight, especially when two or three are together in harmony of mind and, like scribes, bring forth old and new things from their treasure. Blessed twilight, when two or three are gathered in His name and He is in the midst of them, and blessed is he who knows these things and follows them, too.

Rembrandt knew that, for from the rich treasure of his heart he produced, among other things, that drawing in sepia, charcoal, ink, etc., which is in the British Museum, representing the house in Bethany. In that room twilight has fallen; the figure of our Lord, noble and 40 impressive, stands out serious and dark against the window, which the evening twilight is filtering through. At Jesus's feet sits Mary who has chosen the good part, which shall not be taken away from her; Martha is in the room busy with something or other – if I remember correctly, she is stoking the fire, or something like that. I hope I forget neither that drawing nor what it seems to say to me: 'I am the light of the world: he that followeth me shall not walk in darkness, but shall have the light of life.' . . .

Such are the things twilight tells to those who have ears to hear and a heart to understand and believe in God – blessed twilight! And it is also twilight in that picture by Ruyperez, the *Imitation of Jesus Christ*, as well as in another etching by Rembrandt, *David Praying to God*.

But it is not always blessed twilight, as you can see from my handwriting; I am sitting upstairs by the lamp, for there are visitors downstairs and I cannot sit there with my books. . . . (110, 18 Sept. 1877.)

Akin to this twilight obsession were his romantic dreams and imagined love of Anne of Brittany, whose image (from a Goupil drawing course) had hung 19 on his wall of his room since his early days in London, together with Michelet's 'woman in black'. The last independent Duchess of Brittany in the late fifteenth and early sixteenth centuries, Anne was twice Queen of France, married first to Charles VIII and then to Louis XII. This brave woman defended the lost Breton cause, and died at the age of thirty-seven.

... I have walked a great deal this week; there is no harm in knowing the city well.

Today while I was working I had in front of me a page from the *Cours de Dessin Bargue* (the drawing examples) part 1, No. 39, 'Anne of Brittany'. It was hanging in my room in London with No. 53; 'A Young Citizen' was hanging in between. What I liked and admired in the beginning, I like and admire still. The expression on Anne of Brittany's face is noble, and reminds one of the sea and the rocky coasts. I should like to know her history someday. She is a real king's daughter. De Lemud would have drawn her figure well. ... (115, 4 Dec. 1877.)

Vincent owned Flemish, Dutch, Latin and French editions of the *Imitation of Christ* and read them critically, noting that they had sometimes been unduly 'adapted' by clerical editors. He presented his tutor Mendes with a Latin edition and discussed with him the principle of 'hating one's own life' for the sake of the universal.

... This week I had a conversation with Mendes about 'the man who hates not his own life, cannot be my disciple'. Mendes asserted that that expression was too strong, but I held that it was the simple truth; and doesn't Thomas à Kempis say the same thing when he speaks about knowing and hating oneself? When we look at others who have done more than we and are better than we, we very soon begin to hate our own life because it is not as good as others'. Look at a man like Thomas à Kempis, who wrote his little book with a simplicity and sincerity unequalled by any other writer, either before or since; or, in another sphere, look at Millet's work or Jules Dupré's *The Large Oaks* – that is *it*. ... (116, 9 Dec. 1877.)

60
62

Vincent must also have found this line of reasoning in Michelet, who continued to influence his ideas on women.

... Uncle Cor asked me today if I didn't like *Phryne* by Gérôme. I told him that I would rather see a homely woman by Israëls or Millet, or an old woman by Edouard Frère: for what's the use of a beautiful body such as Phryne's? Animals have it too, perhaps even more than men; but the soul, as it lives in the people painted by Israëls or Millet or Frère, that is what animals never have. Is not life given us to become richer in spirit, even though the outward appearance may suffer? I feel very little sympathy for the figure by Gérôme. I can find no sign of spirituality in it, and a pair of hands which show they have worked are more beautiful than those of this figure. The difference is greater still between such a beautiful girl and a man like Parker or Thomas à Kempis or those Meissonier painted; one can no more love and have sympathy for two such disparate things than one can serve two masters.

Uncle Cor then asked me if I should feel no attraction for a beautiful woman or girl. I answered that I would feel more attraction for, and would rather come into contact with, one who was ugly or old or poor or in some way unhappy, but who, through experience and sorrow, had gained a mind and a soul. ... (117, 9 Jan. 1878.)

90

36

159, 160

Vincent first wrote about Fildes' *The Empty Chair* when he was still in London. We have also observed how oversensitive were his reactions to saying farewell. The famous empty chairs belonging to himself and Gauguin which he painted in Arles have given rise to both matter-of-fact and symbolic interpretations. In view of his account of bursting into tears at the sight of his father's empty chair after a visit, and his continuing emotional reactions to partings, the appearance of the image of the empty chair, particularly when his nerves were in an overwrought state as they were at Arles, seems wholly in keeping with a character abnormally sensitive to symbols.

... As you know, Father has been here, and I am so glad he came. Together we went to see Mendes, Uncle Stricker and Uncle Cor and the two Meyes families, and the most pleasant recollection of Father's visit is of a morning we spent together in my little room, correcting some work and talking over several things. You can imagine how the days flew by. After I had seen Father off at the station and had watched the train go out of sight, even the smoke of it, I came home to my room and saw Father's chair standing near the little table on which the books and copybooks of the day before were still lying; and though I know that we shall see each other again pretty soon, I cried like a child. ... (118, 10 Feb. 1878.)

The profoundly significant moment had now arrived when Vincent could unhesitatingly accept art as a main source of inspiration alongside the Bible. He had doubts about taking 'the wrong road', but not about the value of opposition or difficulties as long as there was an ultimate goal to which one could devote oneself totally. In June 1878 he took the decision to abandon his academic studies, and to train in Belgium as a lay evangelist. His mother wrote to Theo, now in Paris:

... Pa has written to him so firmly that he should continue with his lessons for another three months so as to allow himself time to think matters over clearly and calmly. Pa has also written to Belgium, and there comes the reply, just as I have got this far. ... 'Decent, clever people should be able to manage there, even without examinations.' I am always so concerned that wherever Vincent goes and whatever he does, he will always give up everywhere, because of his strangeness and odd ideas and notions about life. ... (Mother to Theo, 7 June 1878.)

Vincent arrived home at Etten on 8 July, and in the following week went with his father to see 'Master' Bokma, the principal of the school of evangelism at Laeken, near Brussels. His former headmaster, Mr Jones, came from England specially to be present, a remarkable proof of the impression Vincent must have made during his short time at Isleworth.

I suppose Father has written to you that we went to Brussels last week, along with the Rev. Mr Jones from Isleworth, who stayed here over Sunday. The impression of that journey was satisfactory, in that I think I shall find my work there sometime – the course certainly is shorter and less expensive than in Holland. ... And they do not even require that you quite finish the course, before you can apply for a place as evangelist. What is wanted is the talent to give popular and attractive lectures to people, more short and interesting than long and learned. So they require less knowledge of ancient languages and less theological study (though everything one knows is an asset), but they value more highly fitness for practical work and the faith that comes from the heart.

Still, there are many obstacles to overcome. First, one does not acquire at once, but only by long practice, a talent for speaking to people with seriousness and feeling, fluency and ease; what one says must have meaning and purpose and some persuasiveness to rouse one's listeners so that they will try to root their convictions in truth. In short, one must be a popular orator to succeed there. *Ces messieurs* in Brussels wanted me to come for three months to become better acquainted, but that would again cause too much expense, and this must be avoided as much as possible. Therefore I am staying in Etten for the present, doing some preparatory work; from here I can occasionally visit both the Reverend Mr Pietersen in Mechlin and the Reverend Mr de Jong in Brussels, and in that way become mutually better acquainted. How long this will take depends entirely on what they say over there. Father and I have just written them again.

Now I will try to write as well as I can some compositions which will prove useful to me later: I am writing one now on Rembrandt's picture, *The House of the Carpenter*, in the Louvre. ... (123, 22 July 1878.)

... I wonder if the exhibition of pictures there [in Brussels] will still be open then – I should like very much to see it. I am eager to hear from you. I hope to write you more as soon as I am in Brussels; also about the exhibition – at least if it isn't already closed. ... (125, 15 Aug. 1878.)

Once at Laeken, he immediately started sketching, but realized that it would probably distract him from his work. A single underlined paragraph shows how strong the power and significance of art had become to him, and how little regard he had for his assessment by the Training School for Evangelists. He was to stay at Laeken only for the probationary period.

Drawing from letter 126.

I enclose that hasty little sketch, *Au Charbonnage*. I should like to begin making rough sketches of some of the many things that I meet on my way, but as it would probably keep me from my real work, it is better not to start. As soon as I came home, I began a sermon about the barren fig tree, Luke 13: 6–9. The little drawing *Au Charbonnage* is not particularly remarkable, but I made it because one sees here so many people who work in the coal mines, and they are a rather distinctive type. This little house stands not far from the road; it is a small inn which adjoins the big coal shed, and the workmen come to eat their bread and drink their glass of beer there during the lunch hour. . . .

How rich art is; if one can only remember what one has seen, one is never without food for thought or truly lonely, never alone. . . . (126, dated 15 Nov. 1878.)

He left Brussels for a six months' probationary period as a lay evangelist at Wasmes, near Mons, in the Borinage mining district in the south of Belgium. There he soon became, in the phrase he later used, 'homesick for the land of pictures'.

. . . As for me, I am sure you realize that here in the Borinage there are no pictures; generally speaking, they do not even know what a picture is. So of course I have not seen anything in the way of art since I left Brussels. Notwithstanding, the country is very picturesque and very unique here: everything *speaks*, as it were, and is full of character. Lately, during the dark days before Christmas, the ground was covered with snow; then everything reminded one of the medieval pictures by Peasant Brueghel, for instance, and of those by the many who have known how to express so remarkably well that peculiar effect of red and green, black and white. At every moment I am reminded here of the work of Thijs Maris or of Albrecht Dürer. There are sunken roads, overgrown with thornbushes, and old, gnarled trees with their fantastic roots, which perfectly resemble that road on the etching by Dürer, *Death and the Knight*. So, a few days ago, it was an intriguing sight to see the miners going home in the white snow in the evening at twilight. Those people are quite black. When they come out of the dark mines into daylight, they look exactly like chimney sweeps. Their houses are very small, and might better be called huts; they are scattered along the sunken roads, and in the wood, and on the slopes of the hills. Here and there one can see moss-covered roofs, and in the evening the light shines kindly through the small-paned windows. . . . (127, 26 Dec. 1878.)

It is not the purpose of this book to recount in detail Vincent's sufferings during his period as an evangelist in the Borinage; but it is necessary to point out his extraordinary capacity for using suffering, both to gain access to the most profound knowledge and to activate his creative powers. The letters recount Vincent's experiences amidst the ordinary working people, whom he had first observed in artists' drawings for *The Graphic* and other magazines when he was in England, and among whom he had dreamed of working. Influenced partly by what he had read and partly by the English Methodists, he saw opportunities ahead of him which would satisfy his Adamistic longing for primeval simplicity and justice, his Thomas à Kempis-like humility and distaste for the rich, as well as his sense of fellowship with the poor.

With a certain logic, this English image of Christianity led at last to a direct confrontation with reality when he reached the Borinage. Alongside this, a creative power had been developing in his psychical make-up which then became an urge to create. Initially he ignored the urge, but he could no longer do so when his evangelical work had to come to an end. Not only the qualities later censured by the ecclesiastical assessors in Brussels, but also the effect, no doubt unconscious, of the powerful growth of his creativity, must have contributed to his failure to rise above a fanatical and immoderate display of compassion which surprised and sometimes touched people but did not convince them. In the same way, his style of preaching, violent in emotion but intolerably laden with borrowed formulations, failed to impress.

30–37

In the Borinage, deliberately avoiding contact with Theo or his parents, Vincent now came face to face with real poverty for the first time. The 'dry bread', the diet of which he constantly spoke in England, Paris and Amsterdam, had been his by choice; it had never been necessary. He had always stayed in or near the homes of relatives or friends who were solvent. Announced with so much emphasis, such self-mortification struck a forced and not wholly genuine note. It was genuinely willed, and yet there was an undercurrent of self-pity, of mixed motives. In the Borinage things were different. In this respect too, the experience marked a turning-point and proved a test of endurance.

Because he now seldom wrote to anyone, even Theo, Vincent was totally on his own. He forwent the therapy of letter-writing which except for this period and one or two others, helped him all his life to bear both the strain of his sense of vacuity and the pressure of a rich and emotional world of images, as well as the condition of his body, through putting them into words. His relations with the miners were good, and he gave an almost dispassionate, realistic account of going down the Marcasse mine, one of the most dangerous.   *47*

... Most of the miners are thin and pale from fever; they look tired and emaciated, weather-beaten and aged before their time. On the whole the women are faded and worn. Around the mine are poor miners' huts, a few dead trees black from smoke, thorn hedges, dunghills, ash dumps, heaps of useless coal, etc. Maris could make a wonderful picture of it.

I will try to make a little sketch of it presently to give you an idea of how it looks.

I had a good guide, a man who has already worked there for thirty-three years; kind and patient, he explained everything well and tried to make it clear to me.

So together we went down 700 metres and explored the most hidden corners of that underworld. The *maintenages* or *gredins* [cells where the miners work] which are situated farthest from the exit are called *caches*.

This mine has five levels, but the three upper ones have been exhausted and abandoned; they are no longer worked because there is no more coal. A picture of the *maintenages* would be something new and unheard of – or rather, never before seen. Imagine a row of cells in a rather narrow, low passage, shored up with rough timber. In each of those cells a miner in a coarse linen suit, filthy and black as a chimney sweep, is busy hewing coal by the pale light of a small lamp. The miner can stand erect in some cells; in others, he lies on the ground (⌷⌷⌷⌷ *tailles à droit*, ⌷⌷⌷ *tailles à plat*). The arrangement is more or less like the cells in a beehive, or like a dark, gloomy passage in an underground prison, or like a row of small weaving looms, or rather more like a row of baking ovens such as the peasants have, or like the partitions in a crypt. The tunnels themselves are like the big chimneys of the Brabant farms.

The water leaks through in some, and the light of the miner's lamp makes a curious effect, reflected as in a stalactite cave. Some of the miners work in the *maintenages*, others load the cut coal into small carts that run on rails, like a tramcar. This is mostly done by children, boys as well as girls. There is also a stable yard down there, 700 metres underground, with about seven old horses which pull a great many of those carts to the so-called *accrochage*, the place from which they are pulled up to the surface. Other miners repair the old galleries to prevent their collapse or make new galleries in the coal vein. As the mariners ashore are homesick for the sea, notwithstanding all the dangers and hardships which threaten them, so the miner would rather be under the ground than above it. The villages here look desolate and dead and forsaken; life goes on underground instead of above. One might live here for years and never know the real state of things unless one went down in the mines.

People here are very ignorant and untaught – most of them cannot read – but at the same time they are intelligent and quick at their difficult work; brave and frank, they are short but square-shouldered, with melancholy deep-set eyes. They are skilful at many things, and work terribly hard. They have a nervous temperament – I do not mean weak, but very sensitive. They have an innate, deep-rooted hatred and a strong mistrust of anyone who is domineering. With miners one must have a miner's character and temperament, and no pretentious pride or mastery, or one will never get along with them or gain their confidence.

Did I tell you at the time about the miner who was so badly hurt by a firedamp explosion? Thank God, he has recovered and is going out again, and is beginning to walk some distance just for exercise; his hands are still weak and it will be some time before he can use them for his work, but he is out of danger. Since that time there have been many cases of typhoid and malignant fever, of what they call *la sotte fièvre*, which gives them bad dreams like nightmares and makes them delirious. So again there are many sickly and bedridden people – emaciated, weak, and miserable. . . . (129, April 1879.)

Vincent's official time as an evangelist in the Borinage lasted only from January to July 1879. His appointment was not renewed, on the grounds of his inaptitude for preaching. He stayed in the area for another year, continuing his work in spite of lack of means and the distress of his family. There was even a rift between the two brothers; no letter from Vincent survives from the period between April, when he wrote his account of the coalmine, and October, when Theo paid him a visit and the first steps to reconciliation were taken.

. . . While I am remembering your visit gratefully, I of course think over our discussions too. I have heard them before, even a great many of them, and often. Plans for improvement and change and gathering energy; do not be annoyed, but I am a little afraid – because I sometimes followed them, and the result was poor. How many things have been discussed that later proved to be impracticable.

How fresh my memory of that time in Amsterdam is. You were there yourself, so you know how things were planned and discussed, argued and considered, talked over with wisdom, with the best intentions, and yet how miserable the result was, how ridiculous the whole undertaking, how utterly foolish. I still shudder when I think of it.

It was the worst time I have ever lived through. How desirable and attractive have become the difficult days, full of care, here in this poor country, in these uncivilized surroundings, compared to that. I fear a similar result if I follow wise advice given with the best intentions.

Such experiences are too dreadful – the harm, the sorrow, the affliction is too great – not to try on both sides to become wiser by this dearly bought experience. . . .

And now if you should conclude from what I say that I wanted to call you a quack because of your advice, you would have quite misunderstood me, as I do not think this of you at all. On the other hand, you would also be mistaken if you thought that I would do well to follow your advice literally to become an engraver of bill headings and visiting cards, or a bookkeeper or a carpenter's apprentice – or else to devote myself to being a baker – or many similar things (curiously different and hard to combine) that other people advise me.

But, you say, I do not expect you to take that advice literally; I was just afraid you were too fond of spending your days in idleness, and I thought you had to put an end to it.

May I observe that this is a rather strange sort of 'idleness'. It is somewhat difficult for me to defend myself, but I should be very sorry if, sooner or later, you could not see it differently. I am not sure it would be right to combat such an accusation by becoming a baker, for instance. It would indeed be a decisive answer (always supposing that it were possible to assume, quick as lightning, the form of a baker, a barber or a librarian); but at the same time it would be a foolish answer, more or less like the action of the man who, when reproached with cruelty for riding a donkey, immediately dismounted and continued his way with the donkey on his shoulders.

Now, all jesting aside, I really think it would be better if the relation between us became more friendly on both sides. If I had to believe that I were troublesome to you or to the people at home, or were in your way, of no good to anyone, and if I should be obliged to feel like an intruder or an outcast, so that I were better off dead, and if I should have to try to keep out of your way more and more – if I thought this were really the case, a feeling of anguish would overwhelm me, and I should have to struggle against despair. . . . (132, 15 Oct. 1879.)

Vincent's moment of truth came with a grim journey on foot, early in 1880, to Courrières, about 70 kilometres or 45 miles to the west, over the French *29, 58* border, the home of the painter-poet Jules Breton. The journey is related in a (later) letter, which represents Vincent's *De Profundis*, with all the details of its martyrdom. This experience saw the awakening of that power which had been blocked for years but was now in process of transformation, as if by miracle, into a will to create.

... I had undertaken a walking tour mostly in Pas-de-Calais, not the Channel [coast], but the department or province. I had undertaken the trip hoping to find some kind of work there if possible. I would have accepted anything. But after all, perhaps I went involuntarily, I can't exactly say why.

I had said to myself, You must see Courrières. I had only 10 fr. in my pocket, and having started by train, I was soon out of money; I was on the road for a week, I had a long, weary walk of it. Anyhow, I saw Courrières, and the outside of M. Jules Breton's studio. The outside of the studio was rather disappointing: it was quite newly built of brick, with a Methodist regularity, an inhospitable, chilly and irritating aspect. If I could only have seen the interior, I would certainly not have given a thought to the exterior, I am sure of that. But what shall I say of the interior? I was not able to catch a glimpse, for I lacked the courage to enter and introduce myself. ...

But I have at least seen the country around Courrières, the haystacks, the brown earth or almost coffee-coloured clay, with whitish spots here and there where the marl appears, which seems very unusual to those of us who are accustomed to black earth. And the French sky seemed to me very much clearer and more limpid than the smoky, foggy sky of the Borinage. Besides, there were farms and sheds which, the Lord be praised, still retained their moss-covered thatched roofs. I also saw flocks of crows made famous by the pictures of Daubigny and Millet. Not to mention, as I ought to have in the first place, the characteristic and picturesque figures of the different travellers, diggers, woodcutters, peasants driving horses, and here and there the silhouette of a woman in a white cap. Even in Courrières there was a *charbonnage* or mine. I saw the day shift coming up in the twilight: there were no women in men's clothes as in the Borinage, only miners with tired and miserable faces, blackened by the coal dust, clad in tattered miners' clothes, and one of them in an old soldier's cape.

Though the journey was almost too much for me, and I came back overcome by fatigue, with sore feet, and quite melancholy, I do not regret it, for I had seen interesting things, and one learns to take a different but correct view of the hardships of real misery. Occasionally I earned some crusts of bread along the road in exchange for some drawings which I had in my valise. But when the 10 fr. were all gone, I had to spend the last nights in the open air, once in an abandoned wagon, which was white with frost the next morning – rather a bad resting place; once in a pile of faggots; and one time that was a little better, in a haystack, where I succeeded in making a rather more comfortable berth – but then a drizzling rain did not exactly further my well-being.

Well, even in that deep misery I felt my energy revive, and I said to myself, In spite of everything I shall rise again: I will take up my pencil, which I have forsaken in my great discouragement, and I will go on with my drawing. From that moment everything has seemed transformed for me; and now I have started and my pencil has become somewhat docile, becoming more so every day. The too long and too great poverty had discouraged me so much that I could not do anything.

Another thing which I saw during that excursion was the villages of the weavers.

The miners and the weavers still constitute a race apart from other labourers and artisans, and I feel a great sympathy for them. I should be very happy if someday I could draw them, so that those unknown or little-known types would be brought before the eyes of the people. The man from the depth of the abyss, *de profundis* – that is the miner; the other, with his dreamy air, somewhat absent-minded, almost a somnambulist – that is the weaver. I have been living among them for two years, and have learned a little of their unique character, at least that of the miners especially. And increasingly I find something touching and almost sad in these poor, obscure labourers – of the lowest order, so to speak, and the most despised – who are generally represented as a race of criminals and thieves by a perhaps vivid but very false and unjust imagination. (136, 24 Sept. 1880, F.)

At this time, between October 1879 and July 1880, there was silence once more between Vincent and Theo. Only a gift of fifty francs from Theo compelled Vincent to write again, which he did with reluctance, and (for the first time) in French. Amid an apparent welter of disparate ideas, this letter contains an evaluation of his own past, and an analysis of his true self, which was to form the driving force for his future actions. It does not mention the decision to 'take up my pencil', which with hindsight he was to consider the most significant result of the journey to Courrières.

I am writing to you with some reluctance, not having done so in such a long time, for many reasons.

To a certain degree you have become a stranger to me, and I have become the same to you, more than you may think; perhaps it would be better for us not to continue in this way. Probably I would not have written you even now if I were not under the obligation and necessity of doing so, if you yourself had not given me cause. At Etten I learned that you had sent 50 francs for me; well, I have accepted them. Certainly with reluctance, certainly with a rather melancholy feeling, but I am up against a stone wall and in a sort of mess. How can I do otherwise? So I am writing to thank you.

Perhaps you know I am back in the Borinage. Father would rather I stay in the neighbourhood of Etten; I refused, and in this I think I acted for the best. Involuntarily, I have become more or less a kind of impossible and suspect personage in the family, at least somebody whom they do not trust, so how could I in any way be of any use to anybody? Therefore, above all, I think the best and most reasonable thing for me to do is to go away and keep at a convenient distance, so that I cease to exist for you all.

As moulting time – when they change their feathers – is for birds, so adversity or misfortune is the difficult time for us human beings. One can stay in it – in that time of moulting – one can also emerge renewed; but anyhow it must not be done in public and it is not at all amusing, therefore the only thing to do is to hide oneself. Well, so be it.

Now, though it is very difficult, almost impossible, to regain the confidence of a whole family, which is not quite free from prejudices and other qualities equally fashionable and honourable, I do not quite despair that by and by, slowly but surely, a cordial understanding may be renewed between some of us. And in the very first place, I should like to see that *entente cordiale*, not to put it stronger, re-established between Father and me; and I desire no less to see it re-established between us two. An *entente cordiale* is infinitely better than misunderstandings.

Now I must bore you with certain abstract things, but I hope you will listen to them patiently. I am a man of passions, capable of and subject to doing more or less foolish things, which I happen to repent, more or less, afterward. Now and then I speak and act too hastily, when it would have been better to wait patiently. I think other people sometimes make the same mistakes. Well, this being the case, what's to be done? Must I consider myself a dangerous man, incapable of anything? I don't think so. But the problem is to try every means to put those selfsame passions to good use. For instance, to name one of the passions, I have a more or less irresistible passion for books, and I continually want to instruct myself, to study if you like, just as much as I want to eat my bread. *You* certainly will be able to understand this. When I was in other surroundings, in the surroundings of pictures and works of art, you know how I had a violent passion for them, reaching the highest pitch of enthusiasm. And I am not sorry about it, for even now, *far from that land, I am often homesick for the land of pictures.*

You remember perhaps that I knew well (and perhaps I know still) who Rembrandt was, or Millet, or Jules Dupré or Delacroix or Millais or M. Maris. Well, now I do not have those surroundings any more – yet that thing called soul, they say it never dies, but lives on and continues to search forever and ever and ever. So instead of giving way to this homesickness, I said to myself: That land, or the fatherland, is everywhere. So instead of giving in to despair, I chose the part of active melancholy – in so far as I possessed the power of activity – in other words, I preferred the melancholy which hopes and aspires and seeks to that which despairs in stagnation and woe. So I studied somewhat seriously the books within my reach like the Bible, and the *Révolution française* by Michelet, and last winter, Shakespeare and a few by Victor Hugo and Dickens, and Beecher Stowe, and lately Aeschylus, and then several others, less classical, several great 'minor masters'. You know, those 'minor masters' include people like Fabritius or Bida.

Now he who is absorbed in all this is sometimes *choquant*, shocking, to others, and sometimes unwittingly sins against certain forms and customs and social conventions. It is a pity, however, when this is taken in bad part. For instance, you know that I have often neglected my appearance; I admit it, and I admit that it is shocking. But look here, poverty and want have their share in the cause, and also profound discouragement; and then, it is sometimes a good way to assure the solitude necessary for concentrating on whatever study preoccupies one. A very necessary study is that of medicine; there is scarcely anybody who does not try to know a little of it, who does not try to understand what it is about, and you see I do not yet know one word about it. All this absorbs and preoccupies one – all this gives one something to dream about, to reflect on and to think about.

Now for more than five years – I do not know exactly how long – I have been more or less without employment, wandering here and there. You say, Since a certain time you have gone down, you have deteriorated, you have not done anything. Is this quite true?

It is true that occasionally I have earned my crust of bread, occasionally a friend has given it to me in charity. I have lived as I could, as luck would have it, haphazardly. It is true that I have lost the confidence of many; it is true that my financial affairs are in a sad state; it is true that the future is only too gloomy; it is true that I might have done better; it is true that I've lost time in terms of earning my bread; it is true that even my studies are in a rather sad and hopeless condition, and that my needs are greater – infinitely greater – than my possessions. But is this what you call 'going down', is that what you call 'doing nothing'?

You will perhaps say, But why didn't you continue as they wanted you to – they wanted you to go through the university?

My only answer is, the expenses were too heavy, and besides, that future was not much better than the one on the road now before me.

But I must continue on the path I have taken now. If I don't do anything, if I don't study, if I don't go on seeking any longer, I am lost. Then woe is me. That is how I look at it: to continue, to continue, that is what is necessary.

But you will ask, What is your definite aim?

That aim becomes more definite, will stand out slowly and surely, as the rough draft becomes a sketch, and the sketch becomes a picture – little by little, by working seriously on it, by pondering over the idea, vague at first, over the thought that was fleeting and passing, till it gets fixed.

I must tell you that with evangelists it is the same as with artists. There is an old academic school, often detestable, tyrannical, the accumulation of horrors, men who wear a cuirass, a steel armour, of prejudices and conventions; when these people are in charge of affairs, they dispose of positions, and by a system of red tape they try to keep their protégés in their places and to exclude the other man. Their God is like the God of Shakespeare's drunken Falstaff, 'the inside of a church'; indeed, by a curious chance some of these evangelical (???) gentlemen find themselves with the same point of view on spiritual things as that drunken character (perhaps they would be somewhat surprised to discover this if they were capable of human emotions). But there is little fear of their blindness ever changing to clear-sightedness in such matters. . . .

For the moment it seems that things are going very badly with me, and it has already been so for a considerable time and may continue awhile in the future; but after everything has seemed to go wrong, perhaps a time will come when things will go right. I don't count on it, perhaps it will never happen; but if there is a change for the better, I should consider it so much gain, I should be contented, I should say, At last! you see *there was something after all!* . . .

But I always think that the best way to know God is to love many things. Love a friend, a wife, something – whatever you like – you will be on the way to knowing more about Him; that is what I say to myself. But one must love with a lofty and serious intimate sympathy, with strength, with intelligence; and one must always try to know deeper, better and more. That leads to God, that leads to unwavering faith.

To give you an example: someone loves Rembrandt, but seriously – that man will know there is a God, he will surely believe it. Someone studies the history of the French Revolution – he will not be unbelieving, he will see that in great things also there is a sovereign power manifesting itself. Maybe for a short time somebody takes a free course at the great university of Hardship, and pays attention to the things he sees with his eyes and hears with his ears, and thinks them over; he, too, will end in believing, and he will perhaps have learned more than he can tell. To try to understand the real significance of what the great artists, the serious masters, tell us in their masterpieces, *that* leads to God; one man wrote or told it in a book; another, in a picture. Then simply read the Gospel and the Bible: it makes you think, and think much, and think all the time. Well, think much and think all the time, it raises your thoughts above the ordinary level without your knowing it. We know how to read – well then, let us read!

It is true that there may be moments when one becomes somewhat absent-minded, somewhat visionary; some become too absent-minded, too visionary. This is perhaps the case with me, but it is my own fault; maybe there is some excuse after all – I was absorbed, preoccupied, troubled, for some reason – but one overcomes this. The dreamer sometimes falls into a well, but is said to get out of it afterward. And the absent-minded man also has his lucid intervals in compensation. He is sometimes a person who has his reasons for being as he is, but they are not always understood at first, or are unconsciously forgotten most of the time, from lack of interest. A man who has been tossed back and forth for a long time, as if on a stormy sea, at last reaches his destination; a man who has seemed good-for-nothing and incapable of any employment, any function, ends in finding one and becoming active and capable of action – he shows himself quite different from what he seemed at first.

I write somewhat at random whatever comes to my pen. I should be very glad if you could see in me something more than an idle fellow. Because there are two kinds of idleness, which are a great contrast to each other. There is the man who is idle from laziness and from lack of character, from the baseness of his nature. If you like, you may take me for such a one.

On the other hand, there is the idle man who is idle in spite of himself, who is inwardly consumed by a great longing for action but does nothing, because it is impossible for him to do anything, because he seems to be imprisoned in some cage, because he does not possess what he needs to become productive, because circumstances bring him inevitably to that point. Such a man does not always know what he could do, but he instinctively feels, I am good for something, my life has a purpose after all, I know that I could be quite a different man! How can I be useful, of what service can I be? There is something inside of me, what can it be? This is quite a different kind of idle man; if you like, you may take me for such a one! . . .

One cannot always tell what it is that keeps us shut in, confines us, seems to bury us; nevertheless, one feels certain barriers, certain gates, certain walls. Is all this imagination, fantasy? I don't think so. And one asks, 'My God! is it for long, is it for ever, is it for all eternity?'

Do you know what frees one from this captivity? It is every deep, serious affection. Being friends, being brothers, love, that is what opens the prison by some supreme power, by some magic force. Without this, one remains in prison. Where sympathy is renewed, life is restored.

And the prison is also called prejudice, misunderstanding, fatal ignorance of one thing or another, distrust, false shame.

But to speak of other things, if I have come down in the world, you, on the contrary, have risen. If I have lost the sympathy of some, you, on the contrary, have gained it. That makes me very happy – I say it in all sincerity – and always will. If you hadn't much seriousness or depth, I would fear that it would not last; but as I think you are very serious and of great depth, I believe that it will. But I should be very glad if it were possible for you to see me as something more than an idle man of the worst type. . . . (133, July 1880, F.)

Vincent was now inwardly mature, but the process of maturation had been a long one. It was only now that he was ready to formulate for himself the basic principles of drawing whether from nature or from artistic exemplars. Formulations of the state of his soul, examinations of his image in the mirror (Who am I? What do I look like?) – these had been present all along; so had his understanding of other people's paintings and drawings; what he had never formulated was what he himself might have to express, in drawing and painting, out of the totality of his emotional experience of life.

The second important point was the restoration of the original unity of the arts. This was no vague concept but a concrete one, tried by experience and substantiated by examples. Literature, painting and the Bible were seen as streams that ultimately sprang from a single source. This was to make his modernism, right up to the Auvers period, almost at the end of the century, something different from that of all the other modern artists – Naturalists, Realists, Impressionists or Symbolists – of his time. These long letters should be read in the knowledge of the value of what he has left us, and every line will tell not only of *la grande université de la misère*, the great university of Hardship; not only of the cry of despair, 'How long, my God!', but also of a perfectly lucid realization of the pathetic social state in which he was living. Equally lucid and strong was his faith that sooner or later, almost certainly later, things would take a turn for the better.

Vincent now began to draw in earnest. His remark that he was now looking at things in an entirely new way implicitly dismisses, as of no significance, his previous impulses to draw at The Hague, in England, and at Amsterdam.

. . . If you still have the book with the etchings after Michel, please lend me that sometime, too, but there is no hurry. For the moment I have enough to keep me busy, but I should like to see those landscapes again, for now I look at things with other eyes than I did before I began to draw.

I hope that you will not be too dissatisfied with the drawings after Millet when you see them; those little wood engravings are admirable.

As I already have twenty prints after Millet, you can understand that if you could send me some more, I would make them readily, for I try to study that master seriously. I know that the large etching of *The Diggers* is rare, but be on the lookout for it, and tell me what it will cost. Someday or other I shall earn a few pennies with some drawings of miners; I should like to have that print and *The Copse* as soon as I am able to buy it, even if it is rather expensive. The other day I bought for 2.50 francs two volumes of the *Musée Universel*, in which I found a large number of interesting woodcuts, including three of Millet's.

I cannot tell you the pleasure Mr Tersteeg gave me by letting me have the *Exercices au fusain* and the *Cours de dessin Bargue* for a while. I worked almost a whole fortnight on the former, from early morning until night, and daily I seem to feel that it invigorates my pencil. . . . (135, Sept. 1880, F.)

. . . Between times I am reading a book on anatomy and another on perspective which Mr Tersteeg also sent me. The style is very dry, and at times those books are terribly irritating, but still I think I do well to study them.

So you see that I am in a rage of work, though for the moment it does not produce very brilliant results. But I hope these thorns will bear their white blossoms in due time, and that this apparently sterile struggle is no other than the labour of childbirth. First the pain, then the joy. . . . (136, 24 Sept. 1880, F.)

Eventually, he could stand the isolation and hardship of the Borinage no longer. With autumn coming on, he moved to Brussels.

. . . Boy, if I had stayed in Cuesmes a month longer, I should have fallen ill with misery. You must not imagine that I live richly here, for my chief food is dry bread and some potatoes or chestnuts which people sell here on the street corners, but by having a somewhat better room and by occasionally taking a somewhat better meal in a restaurant whenever I can afford it, I shall get on very well. But for almost two years I have had a hard time in Borinage – it was no pleasure trip, I assure you. The expenses here will be somewhat more than 60 fr., which cannot be helped. Drawing materials, studies to copy – for instance, for anatomy – all cost money, and yet they are strictly necessary: only in this way shall I obtain a fair return, otherwise I could never succeed. . . . (138, 1 Nov. 1880.)

Vincent made the acquaintance of a young Dutch artist, Anton Ridder van Rappard, who was to become a friend and correspondent, and began to have thoughts of living and working with a fellow-artist.

81, 85

. . . I have also been to see Mr Van Rappard, who now lives at Rue Traversière 6a, and had a talk with him. He is a fine-looking man; of his work I saw only a few small pen-and-ink landscapes. But judging from the way he lives, he must be wealthy, and I do not know whether he is the person with whom I might live and work, because of financial reasons. But I certainly shall go and visit him again. He impressed me as one who takes things seriously. . . . (138, 1 Nov. 1880.)

Vincent was staying at a small hotel, now demolished, at 72 Boulevard du Midi, for 50 francs a month including a daily supply of bread and coffee, which he found expensive. His father was sending him 60 francs a month. Van Rappard, as well as others, had advised him to work at the Academy, where he enrolled, but hesitated to follow up his enrolment. At all events it has never been proved that he actually attended the school. Van Rappard allowed him to work in his studio for a while. Academies, like universities, were to Vincent respectable but disastrous institutions. In an academy one might benefit, when short of money, by seeking contact with other students and being allowed to work from the nude in heated premises without having to pay. He also benefited from lessons in perspective from an unidentified, mediocre painter with sound technical skills, and managed to borrow a good illustration of a skeleton from him. He now started a procedure that was to continue throughout the rest of his life, and began to supply, first to his parents and later only to Theo, three or four times a month the painful details of his expenditure and the reasons why he could not make ends meet. We know all the details of his worn-out trousers, coats, underwear and shoes; but money to buy his working materials and to pay his models was of paramount importance from then onwards.

The idea of living with Theo in Paris had already passed through the brothers' minds (letter 136, 24 Sept. 1880: 'It would certainly be my great and ardent wish to go to Paris or to Barbizon or elsewhere. But how could I, when I do not earn a cent?') Cost alone was a consideration in reaching a decision whether Vincent would now go and live at Heyst, Calmphout, Schaerbeek, Katwijk, Scheveningen, or with his parents at Etten. On 12 April 1881 he was able to report that he was leaving for Etten the same day.

1 Vincent van Gogh as a boy
Vincent was born on 31 March 1853, at Zundert in Brabant, one year after the stillbirth of a first Vincent Willem. His disconcerting gaze – with 'those small, narrowed, piercing eyes of his', in the words of a later acquaintance (p. 31) – is recorded in only two photographs. This, the earlier, bears an inscription to say that it was taken in Brussels (where his uncle Hein lived from 1863 onwards). If it is true that the photograph represents Vincent as a boy of thirteen (1866), it might have been taken between the end of his time at boarding-school at Zevenbergen and the beginning of his secondary education at Tilburg. There, although near the top of his class, he stayed for only two years; he left school in March 1868, for reasons still unexplained.

2,3 Vincent's grandparents
Vincent van Gogh (1789–1874), pastor at Breda from 1822
onwards, married in 1811 Elisabeth Huberta Vrijdag
(1790–1875), who came of a Swiss family (Freytag). Of
their six sons, no less than three married girls from the
Carbentus family.

4,5 The church and town hall of Zundert
These were the first public buildings Vincent saw; the town
hall at Auvers, at the end of his life, was curiously similar (*203*).

Opposite:

8 The house where Vincent and Theo were born, in 1853
and 1857 respectively

6 Theodorus van Gogh

7 Anna Cornelia van Gogh-Carbentus

The painter's father (1822–85) was the only one of the twelve children of Vincent and Elisabeth Huberta van Gogh to follow his father's theological vocation. He became pastor of Zundert on 1 April 1849 and married Anna Cornelia Carbentus (1819–1907). They moved to Helvoirt in 1871, and in 1875 to Nuenen, where Theodorus van Gogh died. Vincent's mother (daughter of Willem Carbentus, one of the best bookbinders of his time, who worked for the Dutch Court) combined certain artistic abilities with a strong character and perseverance.

9 Interior of Goupil & Cie (ancienne maison
Vincent van Gogh), Plaats 14, The Hague

10 Vincent van Gogh (1820–88)

11 Rembrandt van Rijn. *Burgomaster Ja*
Six 1647

The setting of an art gallery like Goupil &
Cie, where the young Vincent van Gogh
began to learn the art trade, was of a
Victorian opulence. The founder of the
Hague branch was Vincent's uncle
Vincent, his father's brother and married
to a sister of young Vincent's mother. This
uncle's cultivated appreciation of literature
and art, his understanding of the tensions
which his nephew underwent, meant a
great deal to Vincent on several occasions
during his troubled early career. Vincent,
always ready to link his impressions of
people with those of pictures, wrote of the
etching *Burgomaster Six* by Rembrandt: 'I
sometimes think they [Uncle Vincent and
another uncle, Cor] must have resembled
him when they were younger' (37). Of
Uncle Vincent, he wrote 'the poet died
young in him, the man survived' (81).

12 The Trippenhuis, Amsterdam
13 Henri de Braekeleer.
Staalmeesterszaal, in the Trippenhuis, 1883
14 August Jernberg. *The 'Night Watch' in the Trippenhuis*, 1885

Vincent, the apprentice art dealer, passionately desired to extend his knowledge of painting. The Trippenhuis in Amsterdam was a former private mansion arranged as a State museum. He often went there, and in his letters analysed his experiences. He even had an exact memory of the hanging.

Faces

15 Vincent van Gogh, c.1872

16 Theo van Gogh, c.1888–90

The second of the two photographs of
Vincent is lost, after having been
reproduced in the first edition
(Amsterdam 1914) of the *Letters*. By
comparison with the earliest photograph
(*1*), there is already a cloud over the
features, a resentfulness, a confirmation of
his later confessions that his years at The
Hague were far from happy. Theo's face,
with its piercing gaze, is known to us from
a much later photograph.

Vincent felt the need to create, on the walls of the places where he lived, a visual confrontation with admired pictures and faces. Three examples tell of his psychological obsessions. Two, the mad Hugo van der Goes and the 'woman in black', of whom he read in Michelet, continued to haunt him, even years later. In London, as early as 1873–74, there hung in his room a plate showing a detail of the tomb effigy of Anne of Brittany; but he wrote of it only in 1877, ('she is a real king's daughter').

17 Emile Wauters. *Hugo van der Goes at the Red Monastery* (detail), 1872

18 French School. (formerly attrib. Philippe de Champaigne). *Woman in Mourning*, 17th c.

19 Bargue. *Cours de Dessin*, I.39

Puritans and exiles

20 G.H. Boughton. *Early Puritans of New England Going to Worship*, 1867
21 G.H. Boughton. *The Landing of the Pilgrim Fathers*, 1869
22 G.H. Boughton. *Deserted*, 1859

From the time of his first stay in London (1873), Vincent admired George Henry Boughton (1834–1905), born in England, educated in America and Holland. Boughton's love for New England, the Pilgrim Fathers, and the Puritans generally, his feeling for a special kind of landscape, and his motifs from Brabant, coincided with Vincent's own ideas. Boughton showed a marked interest in the bleak Dutch landscape.

23 J.E. Millais. *Chill October*, 1870
24 J.E. Millais. *The Lost Piece of Silver*
(*The Lost Mite*)

John Everett Millais (1829–96) aroused
Vincent's warm appreciation with a
landscape, *Chill October*. As with
Boughton's *Deserted*, this was doubtless
because it shows a feeling for landscape
similar to that which Van Gogh himself
was later to express. He was excited to
receive, from Anton Mauve, a
confirmation of his own high opinion of
Chill October. Millais' *The Lost Mite*
attracted Vincent's attention by showing 'a
young woman who early in the morning,
at dawn, is looking for the mite she has
lost' (102, 15 July 1877).

25 Mathijs (Thijs) Maris. *Souvenir of
Amsterdam*, 1871
Thijs Maris' painting, from memory, of a
corner of Amsterdam received a lyrical
description from Vincent in letter 24. Thijs
Maris was a typical, introverted, isolated
Dutch painter, living outside his own
country and full of nostalgia and dreams.
Vincent defended him against those who
ridiculed him: he saw him as 'the
personification of everything high and
noble' (268). 'I spoke once or twice to
Thijs Maris. I dared not speak to
Boughton because his presence overawed
me' (332).

26 Rembrandt van Rijn. *The Men of Emmaus*
The *Men of Emmaus* of Rembrandt in the Louvre was to Vincent an image of human and supernatural elements emanating from a simple realistic motif; it even became a measure for his own impressions. 'Don't you think that when [Uncle Jan and Uncle Cor] sit together, as often happens of an evening, in that lovely, restful room which you also know, it is a sight which warms the heart, especially if one looks at them with love as I do? And yet the *Men of Emmaus* of Rembrandt is even more beautiful, and it might have been the same . . . . What they lack, their homes and families also lack' (108).

27 Jacob van Ruisdael. *The Copse*
The Copse was also in the Louvre. He longed for an engraving of it for his wall, and when he received one (by Daubigny), he expressed his enthusiasm with his relative Anton Mauve's catch-phrase, 'That is *it*!' (*Dat is het*).

28 Adriaen van Ostade, *Family Portrait*, 1654
A surprise for Vincent in Paris in 1875 was the family group by Van Ostade; Vincent thought it was the painter's own family, but this now seems doubtful. This delicately painted, lively and skilfully composed group received a detailed description in letter 35, proving the intensity with which Vincent looked at paintings.

29 Jules Breton. *Blessing of the Harvest in Artois*, 1857
Jules Breton (1827–1906) had a great influence on Vincent, both as a poet and as a painter. He saw this *Blessing of the Harvest* in the Luxembourg in 1875.

Serious sentiment

31 Anonymous. *The Mineshaft (Rescue Team Going Down after a Firedamp Explosion)*

30 Gustave Doré. *Exercise Yard at Newgate Gaol*, 1872

32 Auguste Lançon. *Men Shovelling Snow*, 1881

33 Hubert van Herkomer. *Sunday at Chelsea Hospital*, 1871

34 Edwin Buckman. *People Waiting for Ration Tickets in Paris*, 1870

37 M.W. Ridley. *Heads of the People: the Miner*, 1876

35 Luke Fildes. *Homeless and Hungry*, 1877

36 Luke Fildes. *The Empty Chair, Gad's Hill, June 9th, 1870*

The great gain of Vincent's first stay in England was not his experience of painting but his discovery of the high graphic quality of the English illustrated magazines. The images on these two pages, all collected by Vincent himself, give some idea of his feeling for the way in which ordinary people lived and worked. He started collecting in earnest only after his return to Holland and his decision to become an artist. 'At night when I cannot sleep, which often happens, I look at the wood engravings with renewed pleasure' (229).

His collection included Gustave Doré's famous *Exercise Yard at Newgate Gaol*, here squared up by Vincent for the copy he made in the last year of his life; a number of coalmining and urban subjects; Fildes' view of Dickens' study the morning after his death, which was to have repercussions in Vincent's own art; and Herkomer's *Sunday at Chelsea Hospital*, home of British military pensioners. '[The English artists] choose subjects which are as true as Gavarni's or Daumier's, but have something noble and a more serious sentiment.'

38 Ary Scheffer. *Christ on the Mount of Olives*, 1839

39 Ary Scheffer. *Christus Consolator (Christ the Comforter)*, 1837

Christ the Comforter

Leaving England for good at the end of 1878, Vincent was a prey to religious obsessions reflected in his admiration of Ary Scheffer's *Christs*, with their overblown pathos. It was a moment of great weakness. A rare example of his imagination and its moods is given by Vincent in a sensitive description of a Rembrandt drawing he had seen in London, all inspired by his poetic feelings of 'blessed twilight' (109).

40 Attrib. Rembrandt. *Christ with Mary and Martha (The House at Bethany)*, c.1650

42 Vice-Admiral Johannes
van Gogh (1817–85)
43 The Rev. Johannes
P. Stricker

41 Marinewerf (dockyard commandant's house),
Amsterdam, in 1890

Amsterdam

His environment in Amsterdam in 1878, in the house of his
uncle the Vice-Admiral, could not have been more
comfortable; he must have seemed even more of an odd-
man-out than usual in such a setting. The same was true of
the house of the Rev. J.P. Stricker and his wife, a sister of
Vincent's mother. The cemetery entrance is a reminder of
some magnificent paintings and drawings of similar
avenues, done later in Brabant.

44 Oosterbegraafplaats, Oosterpark, Amsterdam

The Borinage

46 Coal-heaver, Jul.–Aug. 1879

Greater contrast is unthinkable than that between the comfort of Amsterdam and the bleakness and squalor of the Borinage, on the Belgian–French border, where Vincent settled late in 1878 as a lay preacher. In his work among the small evangelical community of Wasmes and Cuesmes, Vincent used a small book of seventy metrical psalms. He underlined a number of texts; as here, from Psalm 77: 'in the day of my trouble I sought the Lord . . . I remembered God, and was troubled'. In this, the phase of Vincent's life which led up to his decision to become an artist, he felt an increasing urge to draw. This *Coal-heaver* is one of the few examples to have survived destruction.

47 Vincent's psalter

II

THE DUTCH PERIOD

*'In a few years I must finish
a certain body of work'*

1881 Etten
1881–1883 The Hague
1883 Drenthe
1883–1885 Nuenen

Since 22 October 1875 Vincent's father had been minister at Etten, again in Brabant, not far from Eindhoven and the Belgian border. Vincent had already taken refuge there three times, on the failure of successive attempts to find his way in life. He now returned with the intention of making Etten, for reasons of cheapness, the base of a new and lifelong career as a painter. No one – except Theo, who was away working for Goupil in Paris – had any confidence in his chances of success.

50–53 The months Vincent now spent at Etten bore witness above all to the onset of an intense concentration on nature, the human figure and the landscape. Almost everything he drew at Etten is a primitive Vincent, the work of a man who was not to be satisfied with external appearances only.

… Nature certainly is 'intangible', yet one must seize her, and with a strong hand. And then after one has struggled and wrestled with nature, sometimes she becomes a little more docile and yielding. I do not mean to say that I have reached that point already – no one thinks so less than I – but somehow I get on better. The struggle with nature sometimes reminds one of what Shakespeare calls 'the taming of the shrew' (that means conquering the opposition by perseverance, *bon gré et mal gré*). In many things, but especially in drawing, I think that 'holding tight is better than letting go'.

More and more I feel that drawing the figure is a good thing which indirectly has a good influence on drawing landscape. If one draws a willow as if it were a living being – and after all, it really is – then the surroundings follow in due course if one has concentrated all one's attention only on that same tree, not giving up until one has put some life into it. … (152, 12–15 Oct. 1881.)

The idea of triumph through persistence – significantly seen in terms of victory over a woman – accompanies the other obsession of Vincent's stay at Etten. To add to the existing family tensions, Vincent now fell in love with his 49 thirty-five-year-old cousin Kee. Since her husband's death in October 1878 she had been living with her parents, the Strickers, in Amsterdam. In 1881 she came with her four-year-old son to stay with her aunt and uncle at Etten.

There is something in my heart that I must tell you; perhaps you know about it already and it is no news to you. I want to tell you that this summer a deep love has grown in my heart for Kee; but when I told her this, she answered me that to her, past and future remained one, so she could never return my feelings.

Then there was a terrible indecision within me about what to do. Should I accept her 'no, never, never'; or, considering the question not finished or decided, should I keep some hope and not give up?

I chose the latter. And up to now I do not repent the decision, though I am still confronted by the 'no, never, never'. Of course, since that time I have met with many *petites misères de la vie humaine* which, written in a book, would perhaps serve to amuse some people, but can hardly be termed pleasant sensations if one has to experience them oneself. …

Kee herself thinks she will never change her mind, and the older people try to convince me that she cannot; yet they are afraid of that change. The older people will change in this affair, not when Kee changes her mind, but only when I have become somebody who earns at least 1000 guilders a year. Again forgive me the harsh outlines in which I draw things. You will perhaps hear it said of me that I try to force the situation, and similar expressions, but anybody will understand that forcing is absurd in love. …

Rappard has been here; he brought water colours with him which were very good. Mauve will come here soon, I hope, otherwise I shall go to him. I am drawing a good deal, and believe I am improving; I work more with the brush than before. It is so cold now that I draw exclusively from the figure indoors, a seamstress, a basket weaver, etc. … (153, 3 Nov. 1881.)

This major development should be seen in relation to his new-found will to activate the creative powers of which he had at last become aware. By virtue of what Vincent called 'the mourning in her', Kee also represented Michelet's 'woman in black'. It was a uniquely important event.

... My love has made me resolute, and I feel energy – new, healthy energy in me. Just the way everybody else who really loves feels. So what I want to say, brother, is no more nor less than that I firmly believe that any man is unconscious of some peculiar great hidden force, deeply hidden in him, until sooner or later he is awakened by meeting someone of whom he says, 'She, and no other.' ...

Boy, I must see her face again and speak to her once more; if I do not do it soon, something will happen at the silver wedding which would perhaps do me great harm. Don't ask me to go into it. If you were in love too, you would understand; because you are not in love, I should not be able to make it clear to you.

Theo, I want money for the trip to Amsterdam; if I have but just enough, I will go. Father and Mother have promised not to oppose this if only I leave them out of the matter, as it were.

Brother, if you send it to me, I will make lots of drawings for you of the Heike, and whatever you want. And they would not get worse if the 'no, never, never' began to thaw. For *aimer encore* is also the best recipe for *dessiner encore*.

Could you help me with the money, boy? If it is only 20 fr., Father will perhaps give me another 10 (leaving him out of it, 'pretending not to know') and then I'm off like a flash. You understand, old fellow! (157, 12 Nov. 1881.)

It proved quite impossible to bridge the gulf existing between, on the one hand, his own love and the sense of liberation which he described so haltingly to Theo, and, on the other, the inability of his mother and father to show even the very smallest measure of understanding.

... And now that I have got so far, Father would say, Because you write letters to Kee and therefore make trouble between us (*for this is the chief reason*, for whatever they may say of my being too unconventional, or the like, it is just talk), because difficulties arise, I am showing you the door.

Isn't it too bad, and wouldn't it be ridiculous to stop work that has been started, and is beginning to succeed, for that reason? ... No, no, no, there is something wrong, it cannot be right that they want to put me out of the house just at this moment. There is no excuse, and it would thwart me in my work. So I cannot allow it. ... (159, 18 Nov. 1881.)

Vincent's pleas to Theo for money to go and see Kee in Amsterdam were pathetic. And yet, at the same time, he wrote another of his wise and beautifully phrased assessments of his own and Theo's ideas about their generation and the future, managing, as ever, to rise above personal concerns and take a broad view.

... We are full-grown men now, and stand like soldiers in the rank and file of our generation. We do not belong to the same generation as Father and Mother and Uncle Stricker. We must be more faithful to the modern than to the old – to look back towards the old is fatal. ... (160, 19 Nov. 1881.)

His visit to Kee's house in Amsterdam brought matters to a head.

... I went there thinking, Perhaps the 'no, never, never' is thawing, the weather is so mild.

And on a certain evening I strolled along the Keizersgracht looking for the house, and I found it. I rang the bell and heard that the family was still at dinner. But then I was asked to come in. But they were all there except Kee. And they all had a plate before them, but there was not one too many, and this little detail struck me. They wanted me to believe that Kee was out, and had taken away her plate, but I knew that she was there, and I thought this rather like a play or a farce. After some time I asked (after the usual greeting and small talk), 'But where is Kee?'

67

Then Uncle repeated my question, saying to his wife, 'Mother, where is Kee?'

And Mother answered, 'Kee is out.'

For the moment I did not inquire further, and talked a little about the exhibition at Arti, etc. But after dinner the others disappeared and Uncle S. and his wife and the undersigned remained alone and settled down to discuss the 'case in question'. Uncle S. opened the discussion as a minister and a father, and said that he was just about to send a letter to the undersigned, and that he would read the letter aloud.

But I asked again, 'Where is Kee?' (For I knew that she was in town.)

Then Uncle S. said, 'Kee left the house as soon as she heard that you were here.' . . .

And – do you want me to tell you the rest, boy? It is somewhat risky to be a realist, but Theo, Theo, you yourself are also a realist – oh, bear with my realism. I told you that to some my secrets are not secrets. I do not take it back, think what you will of me, and whether or not you approve of what I did is of less consequence.

I continue. From Amsterdam I went to Haarlem and spent a few hours pleasantly with our little sister Willemien, and I walked with her. In the evening I went to The Hague, and at about seven o'clock I arrived at Mauve's.

And I said, Listen, Mauve, you intended to come to Etten and were to initiate me, more or less, into the mysteries of the palette; but I thought it would not be a matter of a few days, so I have come to you, and if you agree, I shall stay four to six weeks, or more or less if you say so, and then we must see what we can do. It is very bold of me to ask so much of you, but you see, 'the sword is in my loins'.

Then Mauve said, Did you bring anything with you? Yes, here are a few studies. And then he praised them a great deal too much, at the same time criticizing, but too little. Well, the next day we put up a still life and he began by telling me, This is the way to keep your palette. And since then I've made a few painted studies, and then later, two water colours.

So that is the result of the work, but working with the hands and brains is not everything in life. . . .

Then I thought, I should like to be with a woman – I cannot live without love, without a woman. I would not value life at all, if there were not something infinite, something deep, something real.

But then I said to myself, You said 'she, and no other', and now you would go to another woman; it is unreasonable, it is contrary to all logic. . . .

But under the circumstances I fought a great battle within myself, and in the battle some things remained victorious, things which I knew of physic and hygienics and had learned by bitter experience. One cannot live too long without a woman with impunity. And I do not think that what some people call God, and others, supreme being, and other, nature, is unreasonable and without pity; and in short, I came to the conclusion, I must see whether I can find a woman.

And, dear me, I hadn't far to look. I found a woman, not young, not beautiful, nothing remarkable, if you like, but perhaps you are somewhat curious. She was rather tall and strongly built; she did not have a lady's hands like Kee, but the hands of one who works much; but she was not coarse or common, and had something very womanly about her. She reminded me of some curious figure by Chardin or Frère, or perhaps Jan Steen. Well, what the French call *une ouvrière*. She had had many cares, one could see that, and life had been hard for her; oh, she was not distinguished, nothing extraordinary, nothing unusual. 'Every woman at every age can, if she loves and is a good woman, give a man, not the infinity of a moment, but a moment of infinity.' . . .

That woman has not cheated me – oh, he who regards all such women as cheats, how wrong he is, and how little understanding he shows. That woman was very good to me, very good, very kind – in what way I shall not tell my brother Theo, because I suspect my brother Theo of having had some such experience. So much the better for him. Did we spend much money together? No, for I did not have much, and I said to her, Listen, you and I don't need to make ourselves drunk to feel something for each other; just put what I can spare in your pocket. And I wish I could have spared more, for she was worth it.

And we talked about everything, about her life, about her cares, about her misery, about her health, and with her I had a more interesting conversation than, for instance, with my very learned, professorial cousin. (164, *c*.21 Dec. 1881.)

Nearly five months later, Vincent gave his brother more details, but moved the meeting with 'the woman' from December to January, *after* the writing of letter 164. The later letter (193) certainly refers to Christine Clasina (Sien) Hoornik; the earlier one presumably also does so.

... That cold terrible reception in Amsterdam was too much for me, my eyes were opened at last.

Enough. Then Mauve diverted and encouraged me; I threw myself into my work with all my strength. Then toward the end of January, after I had been thrown over by Mauve and had been ill for a few days, I met Christine.

Theo, you say that if I had really loved Kee, I shouldn't have done this. But do you understand better now that I couldn't go any further after what happened in Amsterdam – should I have despaired then? Why should an honest man despair – I am no criminal – I don't deserve to be treated in such an inhuman way. Well, what can they do this time? It's true they got the best of me, they thwarted me there in Amsterdam. But I'm not asking their advice any more now, and being of age, I ask you, Am I free to marry – yes or no? Am I free to put on a workman's clothes and live like a workman – yes or no? Whom am I responsible to, who will try to force me?

To hell with anyone who wants to hinder me. ... (193, 14 May 1882.)

... You must know, Theo, that Mauve has sent me a paintbox with paint, brushes, palette, palette knife, oil, turpentine – in short, everything necessary. So it is now settled that I shall begin to paint, and I am glad things have gone so far.

Well, I have been drawing a good deal recently, especially studies of the figure. ... I am now longing to hear what Mauve will have to say. The other day I made some drawings of children, too, and liked it very much.

These are days of great beauty in tone and colour; after I have made some progress in painting, I will succeed in expressing a little of it. But we must stick to the point, and now that I have begun drawing the figure, I will continue it until I am more advanced; and when I work in the open air, it is to make studies of trees, viewing the trees like real figures. ...

But, Theo, I am so very happy with my paintbox, and I think my getting it now, after having drawn almost exclusively for at least a year, better than if I had started with it immediately. I think you will agree with me in this. ...

For, Theo, with painting my real career begins. Don't you think I am right to consider it so? ... (165, December 1881.)

He was to find himself back in The Hague sooner than he had expected.

Thanks for your letter and the enclosed. I was at Etten again when I received it; as I told you, I had arranged this with Mauve. But now you see I am back again in The Hague. On Christmas Day I had a violent scene with Father, and it went so far that Father told me I had better leave the house. Well, he said it so decidedly that I actually left the same day.

The real reason was that I did not go to church, and also said that if going to church was compulsory and if I was *forced* to go, I certainly should never go again out of courtesy, as I had done rather regularly all the time I was at Etten. But oh, in truth there was much more at the back of it all, including the whole story of what happened this summer between Kee and me.

I do not remember ever having been in such a rage in my life. I frankly said that I thought their whole system of religion horrible, and just because I had gone too deeply into those questions during a miserable period in my life, I did not want to think of them any more, and must keep clear of them as of something fatal.

Was I *too* angry, *too* violent? Maybe – but even so, it is settled now, once and for all. ... (166, 29 Dec. 1881.)

Vincent's entire output at The Hague, between Christmas 1881 and September 1883, was produced in an atmosphere of mostly ambiguous emotions, thoughts and actions, the origins of which are to be found at Etten. He never thought of The Hague as a place where he might settle permanently.

52–53

69

Drawing from letter 166.

54, 57   Vincent's relationship with Christine – whom he at first referred to as Sien, but after a while merely as 'the woman', suggesting a change in his feelings towards her – developed into settled cohabitation. The affair represented a challenge to his family, and to society, which, without ever fully believing in it himself, he wanted to carry through by marrying her. He had to defend his intentions to everyone. In view of his Adamistic condemnation of the bourgeois world, and of hypocrisy in the Church, he did not find it hard to do so.

... It happens often enough that I am at quite a loss as to what to do. Now this morning I felt so miserable that I went to bed; I had a headache and was feverish from worry because I dread this week so much, and do not know how to get through it. And then I got up, but went back to bed again; now I feel a little better, but I wanted you to know that I did not exaggerate in yesterday's letter. If only I continue working hard, it will not be long before I earn something with my work; but meanwhile I am greatly harassed by scarcity of funds. ... Sometimes my clothes need repairing, and Mauve has already given me a few hints about that too, which I shall certainly carry out; but it cannot all be done at once. You know my clothes are chiefly old things of yours which have been altered for me, or a few have been bought ready-made and are of poor material. So they look shabby, and especially all my dabbling in paint makes keeping them decent even more difficult; it is the same with boots. My underwear is also beginning to fall apart. You know that I have been without means for a long time already, and then many things get dilapidated.

And sometimes one involuntarily becomes terribly depressed, if only for a moment, often just when one is feeling cheerful, as I really am even now. That's what happened this morning; these are evil hours when one feels quite helpless and faint with overexertion. ...

Now that I can work at Pulchri [art club] with a model two evenings a week, perhaps four days with the model would be enough if necessary; and now I have found that old woman, it needn't be so expensive as it was at first when I had a new one every day. For I have already had several models, but they are either too expensive or they think it's too far to come here, or they make objections afterward and do not come back. But I think I have hit on the right one in this old woman. (172, 22 Jan. 1882.)

... Well, my youth is gone – not my love of life or my energy, but I mean the time when one feels so lighthearted and carefree. I really say, So much the better, now there are much better things, after all. ... (173, 26 Jan. 1882.)

He was in close touch with only a small circle of acquaintances consisting mainly of Mauve and Tersteeg (with both of whom he quarrelled) and the painters Weissenbruch, van der Weele and Georg Hendrik Breitner. The highly-strung, irritable Mauve gave him good advice, and professionally Vincent always had the greatest respect for him. This is understandable when one studies Mauve's work, unfortunately out of fashion at the present time.

. . . At present Weissenbruch is the only one allowed to see Mauve, and I thought I would go and have a talk with him. So today I went to his studio, the attic which you know too. As soon as he saw me, he began to laugh and said, 'I am sure you have come to talk about Mauve'; he knew at once why I came, and I did not have to explain.

Then he told me that the reason for his visiting me was really that Mauve, who was doubtful about me, had sent Weissenbruch to get his opinion about my work.

And Weissenbruch then told Mauve, He draws confoundedly well, I could work from his studies myself.

And he added, 'They call me "the merciless sword", and I am; I would not have said that to Mauve if I had found no good in your studies.'

Now as long as Mauve is ill or too busy with his large picture, I may go to Weissenbruch if I want to find out anything, and Weissenbruch told me that I need not worry about the change in Mauve's attitude toward me.

Then I asked Weissenbruch what he thought of my pen drawings. 'These are the best,' he said.

I told him that Tersteeg had scolded me about them. 'Pay no attention to it,' he said. 'When Mauve said you were a born painter, Tersteeg said No, and Mauve then took your part against Tersteeg – I was there. If it happens again, I will take your part too, now that I have seen your work.'

I do not care so much about that 'taking my part,' but I must say that sometimes I cannot bear Tersteeg's saying to me over and over again, 'You must begin to think about earning your own living.' I think it is such a dreadful expression, and then it is all I can do to keep calm. I work as hard as I can and do not spare myself, so I deserve my bread, and they ought not to reproach me with not having been able to sell anything up to now.

I tell you these details because I do not understand why you have neither written nor sent me anything this month.

Is it possible that you have heard something from Tersteeg that has influenced you?

I can assure you once more that I work hard to make progress on things which would be easy to sell, that is, water colours, but I cannot succeed immediately. If I succeed in making them by and by, it would still be rapid progress, considering the short time I have been working. But I cannot succeed right away. . . . (175, 13 Feb. 1882.)

[PS.] *Theo, it is almost miraculous!!!*

First comes your registered letter, second, C. M. asks me to make 12 small pen drawings for him, views of The Hague, apropos of some that were ready. (The *Paddemoes*, the *Geest* and the *Vleersteeg* were finished.) At 2.50 guilders apiece, price fixed by me, with the promise that if they suit him, he will take 12 more at his own price, which will be higher than mine. In the third place, I just met Mauve, happily delivered of his large picture, and he promised to come and see me soon. So '*ça va, ça marche, ça ira encore!*'

And another thing touched me – very, very deeply. I had told the model not to come today – I didn't say why, but nevertheless the poor woman came, and I protested. 'Yes, but I have not come to pose – I just came to see if you had something for dinner.' She had brought me a dish of beans and potatoes. These are things that make life worth living after all. . . .

The following words in Sensier's *Life of Millet* appealed to me, and touched me very much, sayings of Millet's: 'Art is a battle – in art you have to risk your own skin.' 'Work like a whole gang of Blacks: I would rather say nothing than express myself feebly.' . . . (180, 11 March 1882.)

The correspondence also contains the one remark that proves that Theo had encouraged him to become an artist. By now, Vincent was unsuccessfully urging Theo to follow suit. There is a remarkable coherence in all that he was experiencing and reading, and in what he admired in others; and in his work all this was sometimes embodied in a single figure (185, *Sorrow*).

. . . In my opinion the enclosed is the best figure I have drawn yet, therefore I thought I should send it to you. It is not the study from the model, and yet it is directly after the model. You should know that I had two underlayers beneath my paper. I had been working hard to get the

Sorrow, Apr. 1882.
Inscribed 'How can it be that there is in the world one woman alone – deserted? MICHELET'.

right contour; when I took the drawing from the board, it had been imprinted quite correctly on the two underlayers, and I finished them immediately according to the first study. So this one is even fresher than the first. I am keeping the other two for myself, I wouldn't like to part with them. ... (186, *c*.10 Apr. 1882.)

Mauve's behaviour towards Vincent became less encouraging, and Vincent was distressed. He suspected that people's opinion of him was being adversely affected by the fact that he was living with Sien.

Today I met Mauve and had a very painful conversation with him, which made it clear to me that Mauve and I are separated forever. Mauve has gone so far that he cannot retract, at least he certainly wouldn't want to. I had asked him to come and see my work and then talk things over. Mauve refused point-blank: 'I will certainly not come to see you, that's all over.'

At last he said, 'You have a vicious character.' At this I turned around – it was in the dunes – and walked home alone.

Mauve takes offence at my having said, 'I am an artist' – which I won't take back, because, of course, these words connote, 'Always seeking without absolutely finding.' It is just the opposite of saying, 'I know, I have found it.'

As far as I know, that word means, 'I am seeking, I am striving, I am in it with all my heart.'

I have ears, Theo. If somebody says, 'You have a vicious character,' what should I do next?

I turned around and went back alone, but with a heavy heart because Mauve had dared to say this to me. I shall not ask him to explain it, nor shall I excuse myself. And still – and still – and still – ! I wish Mauve were sorry for it.

They suspect me of something – it is in the air – I am keeping something back. Vincent is hiding something that cannot stand the light.

Well, gentlemen, I will tell you, you who prize good manners and culture, and rightly so if only it be the true kind: Which is the more delicate, refined, manly – to desert a woman or to stand by a forsaken woman?

Last winter I met a pregnant woman, deserted by the man whose child she carried. A pregnant woman who had to walk the streets in winter, had to earn her bread, you understand how.

I took this woman for a model, and have worked with her all winter. I could not pay her the full wages of a model, but that did not prevent my paying her rent, and, thank God, so far I have been able to protect her and her child from hunger and cold by sharing my own bread with her. ... The woman is now attached to me like a tame dove. For my part, I can only marry once, and how can I do better than marry her? It is the only way to help her; otherwise misery would force her back into her old ways, which end in a precipice. She has no money, but she helps me earn money in my profession. ... (192, late Apr. 1882.)

Mauve's own temperament made him a difficult mentor for any young artist. In 1885 he moved to Laren, which was the home of the portrait painter Jan Veth (whom Vincent, incidentally, had met at Dordrecht). Veth was a placid and easy-going person, very unlike Vincent; but he wrote to his future biographer, Jan Huizinga:

Mr Mauve lives here. He once corrected my work. Although he gave me much encouragement, I must say that he more or less demolished everything I had done. ... I don't know anyone else who is so guided by momentary impressions as Mauve. If he suddenly discovers something in one's work that is not too bad, he positively falls over himself to be pleasant. On the other hand, if he has anything at all against one, or if he is in a bad mood, then he is absolutely impossible to live with. He has a great heart and a weak head; he is very childlike, very passionate, and the only reason why he ranks so high as a human being is that he is such a great artist. (Jan Huizinga, *Leven en werk van Jan Veth*, Haarlem 1927, p.819.)

During the summer of 1882 Vincent was lonely and much given to reflection. Sien was in a maternity hospital in Leyden, while he himself had been treated for venereal disease at a Hague hospital and was due to return there. His greatest problems, those relating to work and money, were often summarized with notable clarity, while his analyses of the creative process show an ever-increasing awareness of what took place prior to the actual work of painting.

... In life it is the same as in drawing – one must sometimes act quickly and decisively, attack a thing with energy, trace the outlines as quickly as lightning.

This is no time for hesitation or doubt; the hand must not tremble, nor must the eye wander, but remain fixed on what is before one. And one must be so absorbed in it that in a short time something has been brought onto the paper or the canvas which was not there before, in such a way that later one hardly knows how it was hammered off. The period of discussing and thinking must precede the decisive action. There is little room for reflection or argument in the *action* itself.

To act quickly is the function of a man, and one has to go through much before one is able to do it. The pilot sometimes succeeds in using a storm to make headway, instead of being wrecked by it.

What I wanted to say to you again is this: I have no great plans for the future; if momentarily I feel rising within me the desire for a life without care, for *prosperity*, each time I go fondly back to the trouble and the cares, to a *life full of hardship*, and think, It is better this way; I learn more from it, it does not degrade me, this is not the road on which one perishes. (197, 12/13 May 1882.)

... You know I wrote you a lot about Kee last year, so I think you know what went on in my mind. Don't think that I exaggerated my feelings then; I had a strong, passionate love for her, quite different from that for Sien. When I unexpectedly learned in Amsterdam that she had a kind of aversion to me, that she considered my behaviour as coercing her and refused even to see me, and that 'she left her own house as soon as I entered it' – then, but not before, that love for her received a death blow. And I only perceived this when I awoke to reality here at The Hague this winter.

I then felt an inexpressible melancholy inside, which I cannot possibly describe. I know that then I often, often thought of a manly saying of father Millet's: 'It has always seemed to me that suicide was the deed of a dishonest man.'

The emptiness, the unutterable misery within me made me think, Yes, I can understand people drowning themselves. But I was far from approving this. I found strength in the above-mentioned saying, and thought it much better to take heart and find a remedy in work. ... It is hard, very hard, aye, quite impossible to consider last year's love an illusion, as Father and Mother do, but I say, *'Though it never will be, it might have been.'* ...

The feeling between Sien and me is *real*; it is no dream, it is reality. I think it is a great blessing that my thoughts and energy have found a fixed goal and a definite direction. ...

Do not imagine that I think myself perfect, or that I think that many people's taking me for a disagreeable character is no fault of mine. I am often terribly melancholy, irritable, hungering and thirsting, as it were, for sympathy; and when I do not get it, I try to act indifferently, speak sharply, and often even pour oil on the fire. I do not like to be in company, and often find it painful and difficult to mingle with people, to speak with them. But do you know what the cause is – if not at all, of a great deal of this? Simply nervousness; I am terribly sensitive, physically as well as morally, the nervousness having developed during those miserable years which drained my health. Ask any doctor, and he will understand at once that nights spent in the cold street or in the open, the anxiety to get bread, a continual strain because I was out of work, the estrangement from friends and family, caused at least three-fourths of my peculiarities of temper, and that those disagreeable moods or times of depression must be ascribed to this. But you, or anyone who will take the trouble to think it over, will not condemn me, I hope, because of it, nor find me unbearable. I try to fight it off, but that does not change my temperament; and even though this may be my bad side, confound it, I have a good side too, and can't they credit me with that also? ... (212, 6 July 1882.)

Vincent's father now seems to have made an attempt, or at least a proposal, to have his son committed to a mental home at Gheel (in Belgium). Vincent never managed to forget this. It was mentioned in the course of a stormy interview with Tersteeg in which Vincent's former employer, in his own tactless, not to say insulting manner, fairly accurately expressed the family's point of view.

This time I have to tell you something about a visit from Mr Tersteeg. This morning, he came here and saw Sien and the children. I could have wished that he had shown a kind face to a young little mother just out of childbed. But that was asking too much.

Dear Theo, he spoke to me in a way which you can perhaps imagine.

'What was the meaning of that woman and that child?'

'How could I think of living with a woman, and children into the bargain?'

'Wasn't it just as ridiculous as driving my own four-in-hand all over town?'

To which I answered that this was certainly quite a different case.

'Had I gone mad? It was certainly the result of an unsound mind and temperament.'

I told him that I had just received the most reassuring information from persons more competent that he, namely the physicians at the hospital, as much about the condition of my body as about the power of my mind to stand exertion. . . .

As for my constitution – Tersteeg is not my physician and he does not understand my constitution in the least – when I want information on the subject, I shall go to my own doctor and ask for it, but I absolutely refuse to discuss it with him any more. But it is certain that there are few things more harmful either to the woman or to myself than visits like that one we just went through. Avoiding these is absolutely one of the first medical orders I shall have to carry out. *Never* has a doctor told me that there was something abnormal about me in the way and in the sense Tersteeg dared to tell me this morning. That I was not able to think or that my mind was deranged. No doctor has told me this, neither in the past nor in the present; certainly I have a nervous constitution, but there is definitely no real harm in that. So those were serious insults on Tersteeg's part, just as they were on Pa's, but even worse, when he wanted to send me to Gheel. I cannot take such things lying down. I am looking forward to discussing my indisposition further with you, what caused it, etc. . . . (216, 18 July 1882.)

Van Gogh remained faithful to the subjects he had loved so much in the days before he started painting. Once again his walls were covered with Boughtons, Millets, Ruysdaels, Herkomers and De Groux. The nineteenth century, with its many constituent layers, remained part of him – although he had progressed far beyond it, and nothing of that tradition is in fact to be seen in his original work. He saw himself clearly to be a man of his time.

. . . Personally, I find in many modern pictures a peculiar charm which the old masters do not have.

24, 33 For me one of the highest and noblest expressions of art is always that of the English, for instance, Millais and Herkomer and Frank Holl. What I mean about the difference between the old masters and the modern ones is this – perhaps the modern ones are deeper thinkers.

23 There is a great difference in sentiment between *Chill October* by Millais and *Bleaching Ground at Overveen* by Ruysdael; and also between *Irish Emigrants* by Holl and *The Bible Reading* by Rembrandt. Rembrandt and Ruysdael are sublime, for us as well as for their contemporaries; but there is something in the modern painters that appeals to us more personally and intimately.

It is the same with the wood engravings by Swain and those of the old German masters.

So, I think it was a mistake a few years ago when the modern painters went through a period of imitating the old masters.

Therefore I think old Millet is right in saying, 'I think it absurd that men should wish to seem other than they are.' It seems like a commonplace saying, yet it is fathomless, as deep as the ocean, and personally I think one would do well to take it to heart. . . . (218, 21 July 1882.)

. . . I saw a dead willow trunk there [Scheveningen], just the thing for Barye, for instance. It was hanging over a pool that was covered with reeds, quite alone and melancholy, and its bark was moss-covered and scaly, somewhat like the skin of a serpent – greenish, yellowish, but mostly a dull black, with bare white spots and knotted branches. I am going to attack it tomorrow morning.

I also did a bleaching-ground at Scheveningen right on the spot, washed in at one sitting, almost without preparation, on a piece of very coarse torchon [unbleached linen]. Enclosed a few small sketches of it. . . .

. . . You see I am quite taken up by landscape, but it is because Sien is not yet fit to pose; nevertheless, the figure remains the principal thing for me.

When you come, I shall take care to be near the house as long as you are in town so you will know where to find me; and then while you attend to business and pay your calls, I will go on drawing as usual. I can meet you by appointment wherever you wish, but for several reasons it is better for us both, I think, if I do not go with you to see Tersteeg or Mauve, etc. And then, I am so used to my working clothes, in which I can lie or sit on the sand or the grass, whichever is necessary (for in the dunes I never use a chair, only an old fish basket sometimes); so my dress is a little too Robinson Crusoe-like for paying calls with you. . . . (220, 26 July 1882.)

Vincent's discussions of the creative process set him apart from the Hague painters, in spite of similarities of subject-matter. He was looking at their studios, however, and visited the Post and Mesdag collections, where he saw numerous works by French artists such as Daubigny, Courbet, Breton, Rousseau and Millet. His descriptions of landscape have a precision, an awareness of structure, light and colour, which still make them a joy to read.

You must not take it amiss if I write you again – it is only to tell you that painting is such a joy to me.

Last Saturday night I attacked a thing I had been dreaming of for a long time. It is a view of the flat green meadows, with haycocks. It is crossed by a cinder path running along a ditch. And on the horizon in the middle of the picture the sun is setting, fiery red. I cannot possibly draw the effect in such a hurry, but this is the composition.

But it was purely a question of colour and tone, the variety of the sky's colour scheme – first a violet haze, with the red sun half covered by a dark purple cloud which had a brilliant fine red border; near the sun reflections of vermilion, but above it a streak of yellow, turning into green and then into blue, the so-called *cerulean blue*; and then here and there violet and grey clouds, catching reflections from the sun.

The ground was a kind of carpetlike texture of green, grey and brown, but variegated and full of vibration – in this colourful soil the water in the ditch sparkles.

It is something that Emile Breton, for instance, might paint.

Then I have painted a huge mass of dune ground – thickly painted and sticky.

And as for these two, the small marine and the potato field, *I am sure no one could tell that they are my first painted studies.*

To tell you the truth, it surprises me a little. I had expected the first things to be a failure, though I supposed they would improve later on; but thought I say so myself, they are not bad at all, and I repeat, it surprises me a little. . . .

As you perhaps know, there is an exhibition of the Black and White Society. There is a drawing by Mauve – a woman at a weaving loom, probably in Drenthe – which I think superb.

No doubt you saw some of them at Tersteeg's. There are splendid things by Israëls – including a portrait of Weissenbruch, with a pipe in his mouth and his palette in his hand. By Weissenbruch himself, beautiful things – landscapes and also a marine.

There is a very large drawing by J. Maris, a splendid town view. A beautiful W. Maris, among other things, a sow with a litter of pigs, and cows. Neuhuys, Duchâtel, Mesdag. By the last, besides a fine large marine, two Swiss landscapes which I think rather stupid and dull. But the large marine is splendid. . . .

But this much I want to tell you – while painting, I feel a power of colour in me that I did not possess before, things of broadness and strength.

Now I am not going to send you things *at once* – let it ripen a little first – but know that I am full of ambition and believe that for the present I am making progress. . . .

Neither do I believe that it will hinder me if my health should give way a little from time to time. As far as I can see, the painters who occasionally cannot work for a week or two are not the worst ones. It may be because they are the ones 'who risk their own skins', as old Millet says. That doesn't matter, and in my opinion one must not spare oneself when there is something important to do. If a short period of exhaustion follows, it will soon pass, and so much is gained that one harvests one's studies just the way a farmer harvests his crops. Now for myself, I have not yet thought of taking a rest. . . . (225, 15 Aug. 1882.)

His letters are full of interesting information about his intelligent but also compulsive manner of working, and about the various stages in the development of his conceptions. Applying the paint to the canvas straight from the tube was one of his technical innovations; it was more than just a spontaneous impulse to achieve an immediate result.

. . . The wood is becoming quite autumnal – there are effects of colour which I very rarely find painted in Dutch pictures.

In the woods, yesterday toward evening, I was busy painting a rather sloping ground covered with dry, mouldered beech leaves. This ground was light and dark reddish-brown, made more so by the shadows of trees casting more or less dark streaks over it, sometimes half blotted out. The problem was – and I found it very difficult – to get the depth of colour, the enormous force and solidity of that ground – and while painting it I perceived for the very first time how much light there still was in that dusk – to keep that light and at the same time the glow and depth of that rich colour.

For you cannot imagine any carpet as splendid as that deep brownish-red in the glow of an autumn evening sun, tempered by the trees.

From that ground young beech trees spring up which catch light on one side and are brilliant green there; the shadowy sides of those stems are a warm, deep black-green.

Behind those saplings, behind that brownish-red soil, is a sky very delicate, bluish-grey, warm, hardly blue, all aglow – and against it all is a hazy border of green and a network of little stems and yellowish leaves. A few figures of wood gatherers are wandering around like dark masses of mysterious shadows. The white cap of a woman bending to reach a dry branch stands out suddenly against the deep red-brown of the ground. A skirt catches the light – a shadow is cast – a dark silhouette of a man appears above the underbrush. A white bonnet, a cap, a shoulder, the bust of a woman moulds itself against the sky. Those figures are large and full of poetry – in the twilight of that deep shadowy tone they appear as enormous terracottas being modelled in a studio. . . .

It struck me how sturdily those little stems were rooted in the ground. I began painting them with a brush, but because the surface was already so heavily covered, a brush stroke was lost in it – then I squeezed the roots and trunks in from the tube, and modelled it a little with the brush. Yes – now they stand there rising from the ground, strongly rooted in it.

In a certain way I am glad I have not *learned* painting, because then I might have *learned* to pass by such effects as this. Now I say, No, this is just what I want – if it is impossible, it is impossible; I will try it, though I do not know how it ought to be done. *I do not know myself how I paint it.* I sit down with a white board before the spot that strikes me, I look at what is before my eyes, I say to myself, That white board must become something; I come back dissatisfied – I put it away, and when I have rested a little, I go and look at it with a kind of fear. Then I am still dissatisfied, because I still have that splendid scene too clearly in my mind to be satisfied with what I made of it. But I find in my work an echo of what struck me, after all. . . .

You see I am absorbed in painting with all my strength; I am absorbed in colour – until now I have restrained myself, and I am not sorry for it. If I had not drawn so much, I should not be able to catch the feeling of and get hold of a figure that looks like an unfinished terracotta. But now I feel myself on the open sea – the painting must be continued with all the strength I can give it. . . . (228, Sept. 1882.)

Vincent always retained the old academic distinction between *studies* and completed *paintings*, and often returned to the theme, even as late as Arles. To him it was essential to distinguish between the work produced as a direct reflection of what had inspired him, either because it caught his eye or for analytical reasons, and that in which inwardly inspired elements played an active part in transforming the given subject.

I consider making studies like sowing, and making pictures like reaping.

I believe one gets sounder ideas when the thoughts arise from direct contact with things than when one looks at them with the set purpose of finding certain facts in them.

It is the same with the question of the colour scheme. There are colours which harmonize together wonderfully, but I try my best to make it as I see it, before I set to work to make it as I feel it. And yet feeling is a great thing, and without it one would not be able to do anything. . . .

It is already late. I have not slept well these last few nights. It is all that beautiful autumn scenery that I have on my mind, and the desire to profit by it. But I wish I *could* sleep at the right time, and I try my best, for it makes me nervous; but there is no help for it. . . . (233, 19 Sept. 1882.)

The descriptions of the search for his themes are far from sentimental; nor are they deliberately symbolic. They correspond quite naturally to the emotions he felt in a period of increasingly intense loneliness. Themes such as trodden grass by the roadside, frozen cabbages, rusty rails in yellow sand, hungry crows, a low grey sky, were such as could be observed, and transformed into music, only by a man whose inner life was embodied in just such images.

. . . Your description of that night effect again struck me as very beautiful. It looks very different here today, but beautiful in its own way, for instance, the grounds near the Rhine railway station: in the foreground, the cinder path with the poplars, which are beginning to lose their leaves; then the ditch full of duckweed, with a high bank covered with faded grass and rushes; then the grey or brown-grey soil of spaded potato fields, or plots planted with greenish purple-red cabbage, here and there the very fresh green of newly sprouted autumn weeds, above which rise bean stalks with faded stems and the reddish or green or black bean pods; behind this stretch of ground, the red-rusted or black rails in yellow sand; here and there stacks of old timber – heaps of coal – discarded railway carriages; higher up to the right, a few roofs and the freight depot – to the left, a far-reaching view of the damp green meadows, shut off far away at the horizon by a greyish streak, in which one can still distinguish trees, red roofs and black factory chimneys. Above it, a somewhat yellowish yet grey sky, very chilly and wintry, hanging low; there are occasional bursts of rain, and many hungry crows are flying around. Still, a great deal of light falls on everything; it shows even more when a few little figures in blue or white smocks move over the ground, so that shoulders and heads catch the light. . . .

But it's on days like this that one would like to go and see some friend or would like a friend to come to the house; and it's on days like this that one has an empty feeling when one can go nowhere and nobody comes. But it's then that I feel how much the work means to me, how it gives tone to life, apart from approval or disapproval; and on days which would otherwise make one melancholy, one is glad to have a will. . . . (238, Oct. 1882.)

The profound emotion with which he interpreted certain natural phenomena is more evident in his letters than in the works he produced at this time.

. . . At times I feel a great desire to be in London again. I should so much love to know more about printing and wood engravings.

I feel a power in me which I must develop, a fire that I may not quench, but must keep ablaze, though I do not know to what end it will lead me, and shouldn't be surprised if it were a gloomy one. In times like these, what should one wish for? What is relatively the happiest fate? . . .

Sometimes I have such a longing to do landscape, just as I crave a long walk to refresh myself; and in all nature, for instance in trees, I see expression and soul, so to speak. A row of pollard willows sometimes resembles a procession of almshouse men. Young corn has something inexpressibly pure and tender about it, which awakens the same emotion as the expression of a sleeping baby, for instance.

The trodden grass at the roadside looks tired and dusty like the people of the slums. A few days ago, when it had been snowing, I saw a group of Savoy cabbages standing frozen and benumbed, and it reminded me of a group of women in their thin petticoats and old shawls which I had seen standing in a little hot-water-and-coal shop early in the morning. . . .

When one is in a sombre mood, how good it is to walk on the barren beach and look at the greyish-green sea with the long white streaks of the waves. But if one feels the need of something grand, something infinite, something that makes one feel aware of God, one need not go far to find it. I think I see something deeper, more infinite, more eternal than the ocean in the expression of the eyes of a little baby when it wakes in the morning, and coos or laughs because it sees the sun shining on its cradle. If there is a 'ray from on high', perhaps one can find it there. (242, ?5 Nov. 1882.)

Vincent was already longing for some form of collaboration, the beginnings of a desire to work as a group, which he could not achieve in The Hague.

. . . The truth is that whenever different people love the same thing and work at it together, their union makes strength; combined, they can do more than if their separate energies were each striving in a different direction. By working together one becomes stronger and a whole is formed, though the personality of each need not be blotted out by working together. And therefore I wish that Rappard were entirely better; we do not really work together, but we have the same thoughts about many things. He is recovering, though, and we are already fussing over our wood engravings again. . . . (262, 25/29 Jan. 1883.)

In 1883 he drew up a balance sheet of his thirty years, and was conscious of his desolate face in the mirror, and of the oppressive weight of the judgment of those who regarded him as a failure. Later, his emergent idea that 'life is only a kind of sowing time, and the harvest is not here' was to develop into a fundamental belief.

. . . Sometimes I cannot believe that I am only thirty years old, I feel so much older.

I feel older *only* when I think that most people who know me consider me a failure, and that it might really be so if some things do not change for the better; and when I think *it might be so*, I feel it so intensely that it quite depresses me and makes me as downhearted as if it were really so. In a calmer and more normal mood I am sometimes glad that thirty years have passed, and not without teaching me something for the future, and I feel strength and energy for the next thirty years, if I live that long.

And in my imagination I see years of serious work ahead of me, and happier than the first thirty.

How it will be in reality doesn't depend *only* on myself, the world and circumstances must also contribute to it.

What concerns me and what I am responsible for is making the most of the circumstances and trying my best to make progress.

For the working man, the age of thirty is just the beginning of a period of some stability, and as such, one feels young and full of energy.

But at the same time a chapter of life is closed; it makes one melancholy, thinking some things will never come back. And it is no silly sentimentalism to feel a certain regret. Well, many things really begin at the age of thirty, and certainly all is not over then. But one doesn't expect to get from life what one has already learned it cannot give; rather one begins to see more and more clearly that life is only a kind of sowing time, and the harvest is not here.

Perhaps that's the reason why one is sometimes indifferent to the world's opinion, and if that opinion depresses us all too strongly, we may shake it off.

Perhaps I had better tear up this letter again. . . . (265, 8 Feb. 1883.)

His melancholy could be gentle as well as bitter; he gave an unprejudiced and sympathetic response to Theo, who like himself had taken pity on a sick woman and was unsure whether to marry her. His mood of intense loneliness persisted; it was at this time that he began to be affected by the shortcomings of 'the woman', and by the lack of response to his work.

... Yes, I often think of what you wrote recently. I think there must be a great difference between the woman you met and the one I have already lived with for a full year, but what they have in common is their misfortune and their sex.

Don't you also think that if one meets someone in such a way – I mean, so weak and defenceless – something makes one surrender completely, so that one cannot imagine ever being able to desert such a person? Generally speaking, such an encounter is an apparition. Have you read Erckmann-Chatrian's *Madame Thérèse*? It has a description of a woman who is recovering – very touching and beautiful; it is a simple book, but at the same time, deep.

If you don't know *Madame Thérèse*, do read it. I think she will like it too, and be touched by it.

At times I regret that the woman with whom I live understands neither books nor art. But (though she definitely can't) doesn't my still being so attached to her prove that there is something sincere between us? Perhaps she will learn later on, and it may strengthen the bond between us; but now, with the children, you will understand that she has her hands full already. And especially because of the children she comes into contact with reality, and involuntarily she learns. Books and reality and art are alike to me. Somebody out of touch with real life would bore me, but somebody right in the midst of it knows and feels naturally.

If I did not look for art in reality, I should probably find her stupid; as it is I only wish it were otherwise, but after all I am contented with things as they are. .... (266, 11 Feb. 1883.)

Vincent's depressions were deepening. The relationship with 'the woman' only exacerbated his longing for contact at a deeper level, and the situation between them deteriorated rapidly. He was soon to leave her and her children. This was the moment when he made his lucid assessment – discussed in the Introduction, p.14 – of his chances of survival. Depressions which one cannot, in Vincent's words, 'exactly account for' may sometimes obscure the view of the future, or else clarify an inexplicable sudden insight into a development and its duration. Vincent experienced both phenomena. He both foresaw the duration of his creative life, and wished himself already dead.

[PS.] In fact, I have no real friend but you, and when I am in low spirits, I always think of you. I only wish you were here, that we might again talk together about moving to the country.

Except for what I told you about, there is nothing particular the matter with me, and things are going well – but perhaps I am a little feverish or something – I feel miserable. I had to pay money right and left – landlord, paint, baker, grocer, shoemaker, heaven knows what – and only a little is left. But the worst is that after many such weeks, one feels one's resistance ebbing, and is overcome by a pervading feeling of weariness.

If you can't send anything at once, brother, at all events try to write me by return of mail if possible. And as to the future, if there is some danger, tell it straight out, '*homme avisé en vaut deux* [forewarned is forearmed]', it is better to know exactly what one has to fight against.

I have tried to work a little today, but suddenly I was overcome by a depression which I cannot exactly account for. At such moments one wishes one were made of iron, and regrets that one is only flesh and blood. ...

And now I thought, I am sorry that I didn't fall ill and die in the Borinage that time, instead of taking up painting, for I am only a burden to you. And yet I cannot help it, for one must go through many phases to become a good painter, and what one makes in the meantime is not exactly bad if one tries one's utmost; but there ought to be people who see it in the light of its tendency and objective, and who do not ask the impossible.

Things are looking dark now. If it were only for me, but there is the thought of the woman and the children, poor creatures whom one would keep safe, and feels responsible for.

The woman has been doing well recently.

I cannot talk about it with them, but for myself it became too much today. Work is the only remedy; if that does not help, one breaks down.

And you see the trouble is that the possibility of working depends on selling the work, for there are expenses – the more one works, the greater the expenses are (though the latter is not true in every respect). When one does not sell and has no other income, it is impossible to make the progress which would otherwise follow of its own accord.

The fact is, brother, that the general state of affairs oppressed me more than I could bear, and I am telling you my thoughts. I only wish you would come soon. And do write soon, for I need it. Of course there is nobody but you that I can speak to about it, for it does not concern other people, and they have nothing to do with it. (302, 22 July 1883.)

[PS.] Without any definite motive, I can't help adding a thought which often occurs to me. Not only did I begin drawing relatively late in life, but it may also be that I shall not live for so very many years.

If I think of that in a coldly calculating manner, as if I were making an estimate of something, it is in the nature of things that I cannot possibly know anything definite about it.

But in comparison with various persons whose lives one might happen to know, or in comparison with some people with whom one is supposed to have many things in common, one can draw some conclusions which are not completely without foundation. Therefore, as to the time ahead in which I shall still be able to work, I think I may safely presume: that my body will keep a certain number of years *quand bien même* – a certain number, between six and ten, for instance. I can assume this the more safely as at present there is no immediate *quand bien même*.

This is the period which I can firmly count on; for the rest, it would be speculating too much at random to dare say something definite about myself, because whether or not there will be anything after that time depends especially on those, let's say, first ten years.

If one wears oneself out too much in those years, one doesn't live past forty; if one is strong enough to resist certain shocks which generally attack one then, to solve some more or less complicated physical difficulties, then between forty to fifty one is again in a new, relatively normal fairway.

But for the present, such calculations are irrelevant; as I said, one can only take plans for a period of between five and ten years into account. I do *not* intend to spare myself, nor to avoid emotions or difficulties – I don't care much whether I live a longer or a shorter time; besides, I am not competent to take care of my physique the way a physician, for instance, can.

So I go on like an ignoramus who knows only one thing: '*In a few years I must finish a certain body of work.*' I need not rush myself too much – there is no good in that, but I must work on in complete calmness and serenity, as regularly and fixedly as possible, as concisely and pointedly as possible. The world concerns me only in so far as I feel a certain indebtedness and duty toward it because I have walked this earth for thirty years, and, out of gratitude, want to leave some souvenir in the shape of drawings or pictures – not made to please a certain taste in art, but to express a sincere human feeling. So this work is my aim – and when one concentrates on that one idea, everything one does is simplified in that it is not chaotic, but all done with one object in mind. . . . (309, 4/8 Aug. 1883.)

He re-examined not only the fate of Christine and her children, but also the situation regarding Kee with which it was so inextricably linked.

. . . I would rather give up everything than put too heavy a burden on your shoulders. Then I shall definitely go to London at once to work at *anything*, even carrying parcels, and I will leave art till better times, at least the painting and having a studio. When I look back on the past, I always run up against the same never-quite-cleared-up fatal facts which coincided in the months from August 1881 till February 1882. . . . (312, 17 Aug. 1883.)

. . . There is no anguish greater than the soul's struggle between duty and love, both in their highest meaning. When I tell you I choose my duty, you will understand everything.

A simple word about it during our walk made me feel that absolutely nothing is changed within me in that respect, that it is and remains a wound which I carry with me; it lies deep and cannot be healed. After years it will be the same as it was the first day. . . .

And my own future is a cup that will not pass from me unless I drink it.

So '*Fiat voluntas.*' . . . (313, 18 Aug. 1883.)

Intermingled with all this, the conflict about clothes was one of the recurrent signs of Vincent's self-protective obsession with personal autonomy. Eccentricities of dress had been given as the explanation for his dismissal from Goupil in 1876; seven years later, the memory still rankled.

... As to my clothes, dear brother, I put on what was given me, without wanting more, without asking for more. I have worn clothes I got from Father and from you, which sometimes do not fit me the way they ought to because of the difference in our sizes. If you will drop the matter of defects in my attire, I shall remain content with what I have, and even be grateful for little, though of course later I hope to remind you of it and say, 'Theo, do you remember the time when I walked about in a long clergyman's coat of Father's?' etc. It seems to me that it is infinitely better to take things as they are *now*, and laugh over them together later, when we have made our way, rather than quarrel about them now.

For the moment I have the suit you brought for me to wear when I go out, and more things that are still quite presentable. But you must excuse my not putting them on in the studio or when I work out-of-doors – it would be spoiling them recklessly, for one always gets some stains on one's clothes while painting, especially if one tries to catch an effect even in rain and storm. ...

[PS.] I do not hesitate about the work.

You have read [Alphonse Daudet's] *Fromont Jeune et Riszler aîné*, haven't you? Of course I do not find you in Fromont Jeune, but in Riszler aîné – in his being absorbed in his work, his resoluteness *there*, for the rest a simple fellow and rather careless and shortsighted, wanting little for himself, so that he himself did not change when he became rich – I find some likeness to myself.

All my ideas about my work are so well ordered, so definite, that I think you would do well to accept what I say: Let me go my own way, just as I am. My drawings will become good, even if we continue as we have till now; but as their turning out well depends a little on the money for my obligations and expenses – and not just on my efforts – be as liberal as you can about the money, and if you see a chance of finding any help from others, don't neglect it. But in fact, I have said everything I have to say in these few lines. ...

You must not let my conduct when I left Goupil's deceive you as to my real character. If business had meant to me then what art does now, I would have acted more resolutely. But then I was in doubt whether it was my career or not, and I was more passive. When they said to me, 'Hadn't you better go,' I replied, 'You think I had better go, so I shall go' – no more. At the time more things were left unspoken than said aloud.

If they had acted differently then, if they had said, 'We do not understand your behaviour on this or that occasion, explain it,' things would have turned out differently. ...

But they did not ask me anything, but just said, 'You are an honest and active employee, but you set a bad example to the others.' And I did not say anything in reply because I did not want to have any influence on my staying or not.

But I could have said a lot of things in reply if I had cared to, and such things as I believe would have made it possible for me to stay.

I tell you this because I do not understand why you do not know that the reason then was quite another than my manner of dressing. ... (315, 20/21 Aug. 1883.)

Leaving The Hague disposed of his main problem, which was how to resolve the 'Kee-Christine' situation in a manner acceptable both to himself and to the outside world. Here he was considering not only the two women, but above all the question whether, because of his work as a painter, he would have to abandon forever any idea of having what he called a *real* life with a wife and children.

... You write about your walk that Sunday in Ville d'Avray; at the same moment on the same day, I too was walking alone, and I too want to tell you something about that walk, when our thoughts probably met again. As I wrote you, I had spoken to the woman – we felt that in the future it would be impossible for us to stay together, nay, that we should make each other unhappy, yet we both felt how strongly we are attached to each other – and then I went far out into the country to have a talk with nature. Well, I walked to Voorburg and from there to Leidendam. You know the scenery there, splendid trees, majestic and serene, right next to horrible green toy summerhouses and all the absurdities the heavy fancy of retired Dutchmen can invent in the form of flower plots, arbours and porches. Most of the houses very ugly; some, however, old and stately. Now at that very moment, high over the meadows, boundless as the desert, one mass of clouds after the other came sailing on, and the wind first struck the row of country houses with their clumps of trees on the other side of the canal, bordered by the black cinder path. Those trees were superb; there was drama in each *figure* I was going to say, but I mean in each tree. But the scene as a whole was even more beautiful than those scourged trees viewed apart, because at that moment even those absurd little summerhouses assumed a curious character, dripping with rain and dishevelled.

It seemed to me an image of how even a man of absurd deportment and conventions, or another one full of eccentricities and caprice, may become a dramatic figure of a peculiar type, if only real sorrow strikes him – a calamity befalls him. And the thought crossed my mind, how at moments when today's deteriorating society is society seen against the light of a renewal, it stands out as a large, gloomy silhouette.

Yes, for me, the drama of storm in nature, the drama of sorrow in life, is the most impressive. . . . (319, *c.* 4 Sept. 1883.)

In sorrow, Vincent took leave of Sien and her children and left for Hoogeveen, in the north-eastern province of Drenthe, on 11 September 1883. He speaks of sorrow so often that he seems to accept it as the inescapable condition of his life; there is in him a cult of sorrow.

The twenty-two letters he wrote in the next three months contain a wealth of material. Intermingled with a recapitulation of his past life, some magnificent pages bear witness to the dramatic, symphonic way in which he experienced nature. The difference between his state of mind now and in the Borinage is striking. Vincent had found a distant horizon, and was now capable of seeing the darkness and suffering of his own life in a wider, universal context.

In Drenthe, he straightaway discovered another strange little graveyard. He had already visited many: Père Lachaise in Paris, the Jewish cemetery and Oosterse Begraafplaats in Amsterdam, where he went to pick snowdrops, the village churchyards of Brabant, and those in England which he frequently recalled along with the ivy he associated with them.

Your letter just arrived, so I know that the mail will reach me regularly.

70 Some days ago I wrote you a line to tell you a few things about the country around here. Everything is beautiful here, wherever one goes. The heath is much vaster than in Brabant, at least near Zundert or Etten – a little monotonous in the afternoon, and especially when the sun shines, but I would not miss that very effect, which I tried vainly to paint several times. Nor is the sea always picturesque; but those moments and effects, too, must be studied if one does not want to be deceived in their real character. Then the heath is sometimes far from attractive at that hot midday hour – it is aggravating, monotonous, and wearying like the desert, as inhospitable and hostile, so to speak. Painting it in that blazing light and rendering the planes vanishing into infinity makes one dizzy.

However, one must not suppose it has to be taken sentimentally; on the contrary, that is what it hardly ever is. In the evening when a poor little figure is moving through the twilight – when the vast sun-scorched earth stands out darkly against the delicate lilac hues of the evening sky, and the very last little dark-blue line at the horizon separates the earth from the sky – that same aggravating, monotonous spot can be as sublime as a Jules Dupré. . . .

Yesterday I found one of the most curious cemeteries I ever saw. Imagine a patch of heath surrounded by a hedge of thickly grown little pine trees, so that one would think it just an ordinary little pine wood. There is an entrance, however, a short avenue, and then one sees a number of graves overgrown with grass and heather. Many of them marked with white posts bearing the names. . . . (325, *c.* 17 Sept. 1883.)

His basic problem was to find some means of earning a living so that he could relieve the burden on Theo; his brother was thinking of emigrating to America because of career problems. Vincent approached their art dealer uncle in Amsterdam, C.M. van Gogh, without success. Like a drowning man, he now let all his troubles pass rapidly before his mind's eye.

... I was very sceptical about the plan of studying, whether the promise to carry it through was sincere and well considered. I then thought that they had made the plan rashly and that I had approved of it rashly. And in my opinion it always remains an excellent thing that a stop was put to it then, which I brought about on purpose and arranged so that the shame of giving it up fell on me, and on nobody else. You understand that I, who have learned other languages, might have managed to master that miserable little bit of Latin – which I declared, however, to be too much for me. This was a fake, because I then preferred not to explain to my protectors that the whole university, the theological faculty at least, is, in my eyes, an inexpressible mess, a breeding place of Pharisaism. ...

I tell you, brother, I am not good from a clergyman's point of view. I know full well that, frankly speaking, prostitutes are bad, but I feel something human in them which prevents me from feeling the slightest scruple about associating with them; I see nothing very wrong in them. I haven't the slightest regret about any past or present association with them. If our society were pure and well regulated, yes, then they would be seducers; but now, in my opinion, one may often consider them more as sisters of charity.

And *now*, as in other periods when civilization is in a decline, the corruption of society has turned all the relations of good and evil upside down, and one falls back logically upon the old saying, 'The first shall be last, and the last shall be first.'

Like you, I have visited Père Lachaise. I have seen there graves of marble, for which I have an indescribable respect. I feel the same respect before the humble tombstone of Béranger's mistress, which I looked for on purpose (if I remember correctly, it is in a corner behind his own), and there I particularly remembered Corot's mistress too. Silent muses these women were, and in the emotion of those gentle masters, in the intimacy, the pathos of their poetry, I always feel a woman's influence everywhere. ... (326, 22 Sept. 1883.)

His current misery was so total as to have its comic side.

As I feel the need to speak out frankly, I cannot hide from you that I am overcome by a feeling of great anxiety, depression, a *je ne sais quoi* of discouragement and despair more than I can tell. And if I cannot find comfort, it will be too overwhelming.

I take it so much to heart that I do not get on better with people in general; it worries me a great deal, because so much of my success in carrying out my work depends on it.

Besides, the fate of the woman and the fate of my poor little boy and the other child cut my heart to shreds. I would like to help them still, and I cannot. I am at a point where I need some credit, some confidence and warmth, and, look here, I find no confidence. You are an exception, but it makes me feel even more how hopeless everything is just because you have to bear the brunt of it all.

And if I look at my equipment, everything is too miserable, too insufficient, too dilapidated. We have gloomy rainy days here, and when I come to the corner of the garret where I have settled down, it is curiously melancholy there; through one single glass pane the light falls on an empty colour box, on a bundle of worn-out brushes, in short, it is so curiously melancholy that fortunately it also has a comical aspect, enough not to make one weep over it, but to take it gaily. For all that, it is very disproportionate to my plans, very disproportionate to the seriousness of my work – so here is an end of the gaiety. ... (328, *c.* 26 Sept. 1883.)

In the meantime he would not and could not go on like that, without food or shelter, the eternal wanderer, a vagabond. From the viewpoint of his personal shipwreck, he took a close look at the world of art dealers, going over all the things that might have been different at Goupil's. He tried to persuade Theo to stop working for the firm and become a painter too, although this would clearly have meant the end of his financial support and therefore a disaster for the Van Gogh family as well as for the woman Theo was helping in Paris.

... But as to that despairing struggle without getting light anywhere, I know how awful it is too – with all one's energy one cannot do anything, and thinks oneself crazy, or Heaven knows what. In London how often I stood drawing on the Thames Embankment, on my way home from Southampton Street in the evening, and it came to nothing. If there had been somebody then to tell me what perspective was, how much misery I should have been spared, how much further I should be now! Well, let bygones be bygones. It has not been so. I spoke once or twice to Thijs Maris. I dared not speak to Boughton because his presence overawed me; but I did not find it there either, that help with the very *first* things, the A B C.

Let me repeat now that I believe in you as an artist, and that you may become so still, yes, that in a very short time you would think over in all calmness whether you are an artist or not, whether you would succeed in producing something or not, if you learned to spell the above-mentioned A B C and if at the same time you wandered through the cornfields and the moors, to renew what you yourself express as 'I used to feel myself part of nature; now I do not feel that way any longer.'

Let me tell you, brother, that I myself have experienced so deeply, so very deeply what you say there. That I have been through a period of nervous, arid overstraining – there were days when I could not see anything in the most beautiful landscape just because I did not feel myself part of it. It is the street and the office and the care and the nerves that make it so.

Do not be angry with me when I say that at this moment your soul is sick – it is true, you know; it is not right for you not to feel yourself part of nature, and I think the most important thing is to restore that. I must look into my own past to find why I lived in that stony, arid mood for years, and why it became worse instead of better, though I tried to remedy it.

Not only did I feel hardened instead of sensitive toward nature, but, much worse still, I felt exactly the same toward people.

They said I was out of my mind, but I knew myself that it was not true, for the very reason that I felt my own disease deep within me, and tried to remedy it. I exhausted myself in hopeless, unsuccessful efforts, it is true, but because of that fixed idea of reaching a normal point of view again, I never mistook my own desperate doings, worryings and drudgings for my real innermost self. At least I always felt, 'Just let me do something, be somewhere, and it *must* redress itself. I will rise above it, let me keep hold of patience to redress things.'

This was the ground which gave way under my feet; think how miserable anyone would be if such a ground gave way. I had been with Goupil for six years. I was rooted there, and I thought that if I left them, I could look back on six years of clean work, and that if I presented myself elsewhere, I might refer to my past with full assurance. . . . All right, but by and by a person out of work, *l'homme de quelque part*, becomes a suspicious character. . . . (332, 12 Oct. 1883.)

. . . It seems to me that the whole art business is rotten – to tell you the truth, I doubt if the present enormous prices, even for masterpieces, will last. A *je ne sais quoi* has passed over it which has chilled everything – and enthusiasm has been put to flight. Is this of great influence on the artists? Not at all, for generally the greatest of them personally profited but little from those enormous prices, except in their last period, when they were already famous, and they – Millet and others, particularly Corot – would not have painted less, or less beautifully, without that enormous rise. And whatever may be said of the art business, for the present it will remain so that he who can make a thing worth seeing will always find certain persons interested in it, who will make it possible for him to earn a living.

I would rather have 150 francs a month as a painter than 1500 francs a month in another position, even as an art dealer. . . . (335, *c.* 22 Oct. 1883.)

Some time ago you wrote me about a certain difference in our respective physiognomies. All right. And your conclusion was that I was more of a thinker. What can I say to that? I do feel in myself a faculty for thinking, but that faculty is not what I feel specially organized in me. I think myself to be something other than specially a thinker. When I think of you, I see very characteristic action, that is well and good, but also most decidedly not isolated but on the contrary accompanied by so much sentiment, and real *thought* too, that for me the conclusion is that there is more resemblance than difference between you and me. I do not say there is no difference – but having learned to know you better of late, the difference seems smaller to me than I used to think sometimes in former years.

When I consider our temperament and type of physiognomy, I find similarity, and a very pronounced resemblance between, for instance, the Puritans and ourselves besides. I mean the people in Cromwell's time or thereabouts, the little group of men and women who sailed from the Old World to America in the *Mayflower*, and settled there, firmly resolved to live simple lives. . . .

If I mention the Pilgrim Fathers, it is because of the physiognomy, to show you that certain reddish-haired people with square foreheads are neither only thinkers nor only men of action, but usually combine both elements. In one of Boughton's pictures I know a little figure of one of those Puritans, for which I should think *you* had posed if I didn't know better. It is exactly, exactly the same physiognomy – a small silhouette on a rock against a background of sea and fog; I can show you myself also, that is to say, that *variation* of the same physiognomy, but my profile is less characteristic. . . .

20, 21

I myself have sometimes thought about that being a thinker, but more and more it becomes clear to me that it was not my vocation, and because of the unfortunate prejudice that a man who feels the need to think things over is *not* practical, and belongs only among the dreamers, because this prejudice is greatly respected in Society, I often met with rebuffs because I didn't keep things to myself enough.

But since then that very history of the Puritans, and the history of Cromwell, as for instance Carlyle gives it, made me see that thinking and acting do not exclude each other, and that the sharp dividing lines which are drawn nowadays between thinking and acting – as if the one excluded the other – do not really exist. As to doubting whether one is an artist or not – that question is too much of an abstraction. . . . (338, 29 Oct. 1883.)

Again he wrote about his problems with women, describing the situation in increasingly powerful terms. At the same time however – and this typifies the greatness of Vincent's vision – he was totally responsive to the tremendous drama of nature that was being enacted on the autumnal heathland.

. . . Imagine a trip across the heath at three o'clock in the morning, in an open cart (I went with the landlord, who had to go to the market in Assen), along a road, or *diek* as they call it here, which had been banked up with mud instead of sand. It was even more curious than going by barge. At the first glimpse of dawn, when everywhere the cocks began to crow near the cottages scattered all over the heath and the few cottages we passed – surrounded by thin poplars whose yellow leaves one could hear drop to earth – an old stumpy tower in a churchyard, with earthen wall and beech hedge – the level landscapes of heath or cornfields – it all, all, all became exactly like the most beautiful Corots. A quietness, a mystery, a peace, as only he has painted it.

But when we arrived at Zweeloo at six o'clock in the morning, it was still quite dark; I saw the real Corots even earlier in the morning.

The entrance to the village was splendid: Enormous mossy roofs of houses, stables, sheepfolds, barns.

The broad-fronted houses here stand between oak trees of a splendid bronze. In the moss are tones of gold green; in the ground, tones of reddish, or bluish or yellowish dark lilac grey; in the green of the cornfields, tones of inexpressible purity; on the wet trunks, tones of black, contrasting with the golden rain of whirling, clustering autumn leaves – hanging in loose tufts, as if they had been blown there, and with the sky glimmering through them – from the poplars, the birches, the lime and apple trees.

The sky smooth and clear, luminous, not white but a lilac which can hardly be deciphered, white shimmering with red, blue and yellow in which everything is reflected, and which one feels everywhere above one, which is vaporous and merges into the thin mist below – harmonizing everything in a gamut of delicate grey. I didn't find a single painter in Zweeloo, however, and people said *none* ever came *in winter*.

I, on the contrary, hope to be there *just* this winter.

As there were no painters, I decided not to wait for my landlord's return, but to walk back, and to make some drawings on the way. So I began a sketch of that little apple orchard, of which Liebermann made his large picture. And then I walked back along the road we had driven over early in the morning.

For the moment the whole country around Zweeloo is entirely covered – as far as the eye can see – with young corn, the very, very tenderest green I know.

With a sky over it of a delicate lilac-white, which gives an effect – I don't think it can be painted, but which is for me the keynote that one must know in order to understand the keynotes of other effects.

A black patch of earth – flat – infinite – a clear sky of delicate lilac-white. The young corn sprouts from that earth, it is almost mouldy-looking with that corn. That's what the good fertile parts of Drenthe are basically; the whole in a hazy atmosphere. Think of Brion's *The Last Day of Creation*; yesterday it seemed to me that I understood the meaning of that picture.

The poor soil of Drenthe is just the same – but the black earth is even blacker still – like soot – not lilac-black like the furrows, and drearily covered with ever-rotting heather and peat. I see that everywhere, the incidentals on the infinite background: on the moors, the peat sheds; in the fertile parts, the very primitive gigantic structures of farms and sheepfolds, with low, very low little walls and enormous mossy roofs. Oak trees all around them.

When one has walked through that country for hours and hours; one feels that there is really nothing but infinite earth – that green mould of corn or heather, that infinite sky. Horses and men seem no larger than fleas. One is not aware of anything, be it ever so large in itself; one only knows that there is earth and sky. However, in one's quality of a little speck noticing other little specks – leaving the infinite apart – one finds every little speck to be a Millet.

I passed a little old church exactly, exactly *The Church at Gréville* in Millet's little picture in the Luxembourg; instead of the little peasant with his spade in that picture, there was here a shepherd with a flock of sheep walking along the hedge. There was not a glimpse of the true sea in the background, but only of the sea of young corn, the sea of furrows instead of the sea of waves.

The effect produced was the same. Then I saw ploughmen, very busy – a sandcart, a shepherd, road menders, dungcarts. In a little roadside inn I drew an old woman at the spinning-wheel, a dark little silhouette out of a fairy tale – a dark little silhouette against a light window, through which one saw the clear sky, and a small path through the delicate green, and a few geese pecking at grass.

And then when twilight fell – imagine the quiet, the peace of it all! Imagine then a little avenue of poplars with autumn leaves, imagine a wide muddy road, all black mud, with an infinite heath to the right and an endless heath to the left, a few black triangular silhouettes of sod-built huts, through the little windows of which shines the red light of the little fire, with a few pools of dirty yellowish water that reflect the sky, and in which trunks lie rotting; imagine that swamp in the evening twilight, with a white sky over it, everywhere the contrast of black and white. And in that swamp a rough figure – the shepherd – a heap of oval masses, half wool, half mud, jostling each other, pushing each other – the flock. You see them coming – you find yourself in the midst of them – you turn around and follow them. Slowly and reluctantly they trudge along the muddy road. However, the farm looms in the distance – a few mossy roofs and piles of straw and peat between the poplars.

The sheepfold is again like the silhouette of a triangle – dark. The door is wide open like the entrance to a dark cave. Through the chinks of the boards behind it gleams the light of the sky. The whole caravan of masses of wool and mud disappear into that cave – the shepherd and a woman with a lantern shut the doors behind them.

That coming home of the flock in the twilight was the finale of the symphony I heard yesterday.

That day passed like a dream, all day I was so absorbed in that poignant music that I literally forgot even food and drink – I had a piece of brown bread and a cup of coffee in the little inn where I drew the spinning-wheel. The day was over, and from dawn till twilight, or rather from one night till the other, I had lost myself in that symphony. . . . (340, Oct.–Nov. 1883.)

Life in Drenthe proved intolerable, despite its wealth of inspiration, and Vincent was forced to take refuge in his parents' home. They had moved from Etten to nearby Nuenen in September 1883.

. . . So for several reasons I made up my mind to go home for a while. A thing which, however, I was very loath to do.

My journey began with a good six-hour walk across the heath – to Hoogeveen. On a stormy afternoon in rain and snow.

That walk cheered me greatly, or rather my feelings were so in sympathy with nature that it calmed me more than anything. I thought that perhaps going back home might give me a clearer insight into questions of how to act. . . . (344, *c.* 5 Dec. 1883.)

Vincent's relations with his parents remained difficult, now that he had come to stay with them indefinitely.

I was lying awake half the night, Theo, after I wrote you last night.

I am sick at heart about the fact that, coming back after two years' absence, the welcome home was kind and cordial in every respect, but basically there has been no change whatever, not the slightest, in what I must call the most extreme blindness and ignorance as to the insight into our mutual position. And I again feel almost unbearably disturbed and perplexed.

The fact is that things were going extremely well until the moment when Father – not just in the heat of passion, but also because he was 'tired of it' – banished me from the house. It ought to have been understood then that this was supremely important to my success or failure – that things were made ten times more difficult for me by this – almost insupportable. . . .

Nothing, nothing of all that.

In Father's mind there was not then, there is not now, the faintest shadow of a doubt that what he did was the right thing.

Father does not know remorse like you and me and any man who is human.

Father believes in his own righteousness, whereas you and I and other human creatures are imbued with the feeling that we *consist* of errors and efforts of the lost souls. I commiserate with people like Father – *in my heart of hearts I cannot be angry with him* – because I think they are more unhappy than I. Why do I think them unhappy? – because the good within them is wrongly applied, so that it acts like evil – because the *light* within them is black and spreads darkness, obscurity around them. . . .

[Written in the margin] They think *they did no harm at the time,* this is *too* bad. (345, 6/7 Dec. 1883.)

The tone of his letters to Theo became almost hostile as he pursued, obsessively, the argument he had started in Drenthe, about the art trade and Theo's position in it. Seemingly coherent lines of reasoning are followed by untenable conclusions; his greatest desire is to recapture something of the aspirations that the brothers had shared in youth.

. . . I thought of you, brother, during that long walk across the heath in the evening, in the storm. I thought of a passage, I don't know from what book: 'Two eyes watched, lightened by true tears.' I thought, *I am disillusioned.* I thought, I have believed in many things which I now know are really sorry fallacies – I thought, Those eyes of mine, here on this gloomy evening, wide awake in this deserted region – if they have been full of tears at times, why shouldn't these have been wrung from me by a sorrow that disenchants – yes – and disturbs illusions – but at the same time – makes one wide *awake.*

I thought, *Is it possible* that Theo is satisfied with many things that worry me?

Is it possible that it is only my own melancholy when I cannot enjoy some things as I used to do? . . . (344, *c.* 5 Dec. 1883.)

I do not beg for your mediation, I do not beg for anything personal on your part; but I ask you point-blank how we stand – are you a 'Van Gogh' too? I have always looked upon you as 'Theo'.

In character I am rather different from the various members of the family, and essentially. I am *not* a 'Van Gogh'. If you became a 'personality' – if you were going to play a part in the world – like Father or C.M., or even V. – all right, I should not try to interfere, I should take you at your own valuation, I should be silent about it; but our ways would diverge so much that I should not think it advisable to continue our financial relations. I hope you will understand what I want to express. If not, you'll have to give it time. . . . (345a, 7/8 Dec. 1883.)

Friction between Vincent and his parents culminated in the image of himself as a dog.

I feel what Father and Mother think of me *instinctively* (I do not say *intelligently*).

They feel the same dread of taking me into the house as they would about taking a big rough dog. He would run into the room with wet paws – and he is so rough. He will be in everybody's way. *And he barks so loud.* In short, he is a foul beast.

All right – but the beast has a human history, and though only a dog, he has a human soul, and even a very sensitive one, that makes him feel what people think of him, which an ordinary dog cannot do.

And I, admitting that I am a kind of dog, leave them alone. . . . (346, Dec. 1883.)

. . . Without being personal, just for the sake of an impartial character study, as if I did not speak about you and me but about strangers, for the sake of analysis, I point out to you once more how it was last summer. I see two brothers walking about in The Hague (*see them as strangers*, do not think of yourself and me).

One says, 'I must maintain a certain standing, I must stay in business, I don't think I shall become a painter.'

The other says, 'I am getting to be like a dog, I feel that the future will probably make me more ugly and rough, and I foresee that "a certain *poverty*" will be my fate, but, but *I shall be a painter.*'

So the one – a certain standing as an art dealer.

The other – poverty and painter.

And I see those same brothers in former years, when you had just entered the world of pictures, when you just began to read, etc., etc. – I see them near the mill at Rijswijk or, for instance, on a walk to Chaam in winter across the snowy heath early in the morning! *Feeling, thinking* and *believing* so exactly alike that I ask myself, Are those the same??? The question is, How will things turn out – will they separate forever, or will they forever follow the same path? . . . (347, Dec. 1883.)

Seeing Sien again on a brief visit to The Hague brought to the surface Vincent's resentment of Theo's part in his decision to leave; he wrote of losing his respect for Theo. The strain on the brothers' relationship was growing; and Vincent even went so far as to say that he could no longer accept Theo's support. His outbursts of anger were short-lived, however, and he was quick to retract. They mainly fastened on Theo's lack of success in promoting his work; for at this time Vincent was still expecting something to come of sales and exhibitions.

. . . Well, our friendship, brother, has received a bad shock from this, and if you were to say we certainly did not make a mistake, and if it should appear to me that you are still in the same frame of mind – then I should not be able to respect you as much as in the past. Because at the time I respected you for the very fact that, at a moment when others cut me because of my being with her, you were the one to help me keep her alive. I do not say there was no need for a change or a modification, but – I think we, or rather I, have gone too far.

As I now have a studio here, more than one financial difficulty is less ruinous perhaps.

I will end by saying: Please think it over – but if your state of mind remains the same as last summer after what I have said, I cannot feel the same respect for you as in the past. For the rest, I have resolved never to speak another word with you about a possible change in your circumstances and your career, for it is as if I see two natures in you, struggling within your breast – a phenomenon I perceive in myself too, but it may be that some problems are solved because of my being four years older, problems which in your case are more or less in a state of ferment. . . . (350, 25–28 Dec. 1883.)

. . . Just listen – after having read your letter about the drawings, I at once sent you a new water colour of a weaver, and five pen drawings. For my part I will also tell you frankly that I think it true what you say, that my work must become much better still, but at the same time, that your energy to sell them for me may become somewhat stronger too.

You have *never sold a single one for me* – neither for much nor for little – and in fact *you have not even tried.*

You see, I am not *angry* about it, but – we must call things by their names. In the long run, I would certainly not put up with that.

You, on your part, can also continue to speak out frankly.

As to being salable or unsalable, that is an old file, on which I do not intend to blunt my teeth. Well, you see my answer is that I send you some new ones, and I will go on doing so very willingly – I ask no better.

But I insist on your speaking out quite frankly – that is what I like best – whether you intend to interest yourself in them henceforth, or whether your dignity does not allow it. Leaving the past for what it was, I must face the future, and apart from what you think of it, I decidedly intend to try and sell them. . . . (358, *c.* 1 Mar. 1884.)

One of these days I am going to send you another pen-and-ink drawing of a weaver – larger than the other five; the loom seen from the front – it will make this little series of drawings more complete; I believe they will look best if you have them mounted on grey Ingres.

It would rather disappoint me if you sent these little weavers back to me. And if none of the people you know would care to take them, I should think that you might take them for yourself, as the beginning of a collection of pen-and-ink drawings of Brabant artisans.

Which I should love to make, and which, as I shall be in Brabant pretty often now, I should be very eager to do.

On condition of making a series of them, which must be kept together, I will price them low, so that though I might make many drawings of the same kind, they might be kept together. But I, for my part, will agree to what you think best.

And you see it is not my aim to break off relations with you; I only wanted to point out that it seemed necessary to me that, when I send the pen drawings, you at least show them to somebody. . . . (359, *c.* 9 Mar. 1884.)

Vincent's friendship with the unhappy Margo (or Margot) Begemann, who was living at Nuenen with her parents, friends and neighbours of the parson's family, complicated his position at home and in the village community when Margo tried to poison herself. His account is remarkably calm and rational, showing unmistakable insight into suicide attempts and the symptoms of poisoning. Margo undoubtedly loved him, and the question of marriage arose. Family opposition flared up again, although there is no evidence that Vincent was particularly keen. Once, as a break in the silent endurance of a permanent sorrow, the image of Kee fleetingly reappeared.

. . . Something terrible has happened, Theo, which hardly anybody here knows, or suspects, or may ever know, so for heaven's sake keep it to yourself. To tell you everything, I should have to fill a volume – I can't do it. Margot Begemann took poison in a moment of despair; after she had had a discussion with her family and they slandered her and me, she became so upset that she did it (in a moment of decided *mania*, I think). Theo, I had already consulted the doctor about certain symptoms of hers three days before; I had secretly warned her brother that I was afraid she would get brain fever, and that I was sorry to state that, in my eyes, the Begemann family acted extremely imprudently in speaking to her the way they did. This had no effect, at least no other than that they told me to wait two years, which I decidedly refused to do, saying that *if* there was a question of marriage, it had to be very soon or not at all.

Well, Theo, you have read *Mme Bovary* – do you remember the first Mme Bovary who died in a nervous attack? Here it was something like that, but complicated by her having taken poison.

She had often said when we were quietly walking together, 'I wish I could die now' – I had never paid any attention to it.

One morning, however, she slipped to the ground. At first I only thought it was weakness. But it got worse and worse. Spasms, she lost her power of speech, and mumbled all kinds of things that were only half intelligible, and sank to the ground with many jerks and convulsions, and so on. In any case it was different from a nervous collapse, though there was a great similarity, and suddenly I grew suspicious, and said – Did you happen to swallow something? She screamed 'Yes'. Well, then I took matters in hand and no mistake – she insisted on my swearing that I should never tell anybody – I said, That's all right, I'll swear anything you like, but only on condition that you throw that stuff up immediately – so put your finger down your throat until you puke, or else I'll call the others. Well, now you understand the rest. . . .

But for heaven's sake, what is the meaning of that standing, and of that religion, which the respectable people maintain? – oh, they are perfectly *absurd*, making society a kind of lunatic asylum, a perfectly topsy-turvy world – oh, that mysticism. You will understand how everything, everything passed through my mind these last few days, and how absorbed I was in this sad story.

Now that she has tried this and failed, I think it has given her such a fright that she will not readily try it a second time; the failure of a suicide is the best remedy against a future suicide. . . . (375, Sept. 1884.)

[PS.] . . . It is a pity that I didn't meet her *before*, for instance, ten years ago. Now she gives me the impression of a Cremona violin which has been spoiled by bad, bungling repairers.

And the condition she was in when I met her proved to be rather too damaged.

But originally it was a rare specimen of great value, and *even now* she has, in spite of drawbacks, great value.

The only thing I ever saw again of Kee was a picture taken a year later; was she changed for the worse? On the contrary, *more interesting*.

That disturbing the tranquillity of a woman, as theological people call it (sometimes theologians *sans le savoir*), is sometimes *the breaking of stagnation or melancholy*, which steals over many people, and is *worse* than *death itself*. Some people think it terrible to hurl them back into life, into love, and one must consider very carefully how far one may go. But if one does it with motives other than egoism, well, then the women themselves will sometimes get *angry*, and may even hate instead of love, *que soit*.

But they will *not easily despise* the man who did it, while they do despise the men who have extinguished the manliness in themselves. Well, those are the deep things of life. . . . (377, Sept. 1884.)

After his earlier signs of interest in paint and the original techniques he had thought out at The Hague, Vincent became totally engrossed in rules of colour and drawing – 'the line' – at this time. Through lack of knowledge of the Impressionists, he looked mainly to Delacroix, not realizing that the latter was also a welcome source for the French avant-garde, Signac and Lautrec in particular.

. . . Please write me some more details about the Manet exhibition: tell me which of his pictures are there. I have always found Manet's work very original. Do you know that article of Zola's on Manet? I am sorry to have seen so very few of his pictures. I should especially like to see his figures of nude women. I do not think it exaggerated that some people, for instance Zola, *rave* about him, although I, for my part, do not think he can be reckoned among the very first of this century. But his is a talent which *certainly* has its *raison d'être*, and that is a great thing in itself. The article which Zola wrote about him is published in the volume *Mes Haines*. For my part, I cannot agree with Zola's *conclusions*, as if Manet were a man who opens a new future to modern ideas of art; I consider *Millet*, not Manet, to be that essentially modern painter who opened a new horizon to many. (355. *c.* 24 Jan. 1884.)

. . . The *laws* of colours are unutterably beautiful, just because they are *not accidental*. In the same way that people nowadays no longer believe in fantastic *miracles*, no longer believe in a God who capriciously and despotically flies from one thing to another, but begin to feel more respect and admiration for and faith in nature – in the same way, and for the same reasons, I think that in art, the old-fashioned idea of innate genius, inspiration, etc., must be, I do not say put aside, but thoroughly reconsidered, verified – and greatly modified. However, I do not deny the existence of genius, or even its being innate. But I certainly do deny the inference that theory and instruction should, as a matter of course, always be useless.

The same thing which I applied in the woman spinning and the old man spooling yarn, I hope, or rather I shall try, to do much *better* later on.

But in these two studies from life *I have been a little more myself* than I succeeded in being in most of the other studies – except perhaps in some of my drawings. . . . (371, July 1884.)

Enclosed you will find some interesting pages about *colour*, namely the great principles which Delacroix believed in.

Add to this *'les anciens ne prenaient pas par la ligne, mais par les milieux'*, that means, starting with the circular or elliptical bases of the masses, instead of with the contour.

I found the exact words for the latter in Gigoux's book, but the fact itself had already preoccupied me a long time. I believe the fuller of sentiment a thing one makes is, and the more true to nature, the more it is criticized and the more animosity it rouses, but after all, in the end it will rise above criticism. . . .

[Enclosure:] . . . 'The ancients admitted only three primary colours: yellow, red and blue, and the modern painters do not admit any others. In fact, these three colours are the only indissoluble and irreducible ones. . . .' (401, Summer 1885.)

. . . *There is a school – I believe – of impressionists. But I know very little about it.* But I do know who the original and most important masters are, around whom – as around an axis – the landscape and peasant painters will revolve. Delacroix, Corot, Millet and the rest. That is my own opinion, not properly formulated.

I mean there are (rather than persons) rules or principles or fundamental truths for *drawing* as well as for *colour*, which *one proves to fall back on* when one finds out an actual truth.

In drawing, for instance – that question of drawing the figure starting with the circle – that is, to say, using the elliptical planes as a foundation. A thing which the ancient Greeks already knew, and which will remain valid till the end of the world. . . . (402, Summer 1885.)

He could not resist seeking every opportunity to place Theo in a position opposed to him instead of alongside him. A prospective Delacroix exhibition in Paris provided a reason for mentioning *Liberty on the Barricade*, which he thought referred to the revolution of 1848. (In fact, this famous canvas was inspired by the revolt of 1830.)

. . . You tell me that within a short time there will be an exhibition of Delacroix's work. All right. You will certainly see there a picture, *La Barricade*, which I know only from biographies of Delacroix. I believe it was painted in 1848. You also know a lithograph by De Lemud, I believe; if it is not by him, then by Daumier, also representing the barricade of 1848. I wish you could just imagine that you and I had lived in that year 1848, or some such period, for on the occasion of Napoleon's coup d'état, there was again something of the kind. I will not make any offensive remarks – that has never been my object – I try to make it clear to you in how far the difference that has sprung up between us is connected with the general drift of society, and, as such, is something quite different from premeditated reproaches. So take that period of 1848. . . .

I begin with Guizot and Louis-Philippe, were they bad or tyrannical? Not exactly; in my opinion they were people like Father and Grandfather, for instance, like old Goupil. In short, people with a very venerable appearance, deep – serious – but if one looks at them a little more closely and sharply, they have something gloomy, dull, stale, so much so that it makes one sick. Is this saying too much??? . . . But my opinion is, if you and I had lived *then*, you would have been on the Guizot side, and I on the Michelet side. And both remaining consistent, with a certain melancholy, we might have confronted each other as direct enemies, for instance on such a barricade, you before it as a soldier of the government, I behind it, as a revolutionary or rebel. . . . (379, Sept. 1884.)

The only nearby town he visited occasionally was Eindhoven. He even made a few acquaintances there and gave some lessons to amateurs, including Willem van de Wakker and Anton Kerssemakers. His keen theoretical interest in rules of colour and music also led him to take some pianoforte lessons. He designed

Drawing from letter 402.

six panels representing peasant life for the dining room of a rich goldsmith called Hermans. He provided the sketches, the goldsmith copied them, and Vincent made the copies into paintings. The rich gentleman failed to pay for his services.

To writers, Mallarmé among others, a blank sheet of paper frequently represents a paralysing challenge. Vincent described an analogous experience with a new canvas. He even likened it to life itself, and perhaps to women. It was characteristic of him that he proceeded to make a fierce attack on the unwritten, the unsullied.

... You do not know how paralysing that staring of a blank canvas is; it says to the painter, *You can't do anything*. The canvas stares at you like an idiot, and it hypnotizes some painters, so that they themselves become idiots. Many painters are afraid of the blank canvas, but the blank canvas is afraid of the really passionate painter who is daring – and who has once and for all broken that spell of 'you cannot'.

Life itself is also for ever turning toward a man an infinitely vacant, discouraging, hopeless, blank side on which nothing is written, no more than on a blank canvas. But however vacant and vain and *dead* life may present itself, the man of faith, of energy, of warmth, and who knows something, does not let himself be led astray by it. He steps in and acts and builds up, in short he *breaks – ruins* they call it. ... (378, Oct. 1884.)

He wished, more cogently than ever before or later, that conventional morality might be renewed, but said nothing of changing the social structure.

... To me personally, an important difference between *before* and *after* the revolution – is the change in social position of women and the collaboration that is desired between men and women, with equal rights, equal freedom.

But I can find neither the words nor the time, nor the inclination, to go into this more deeply. Enough, the conventional morals are in my opinion quite *wrong*, and I hope they will be *changed* and *renewed* in time. ... (388, *c.* 7 Dec. 1884.)

In his remote corner of Brabant he remained very much alive to what was going on in the art world, keeping in touch mainly through Theo and by reading. In 1884, for instance, he read about the Paris Salon in *L'Illustration*, which also included reproductions of work by Puvis de Chavannes. A critic's comment that the medieval or Neo-Gothic style of artists like Leys was being superseded by realism in the style of De Groux reinforced his own convictions.

94, 97
96

... And at this very moment I could tell you some new names of people who are hammering again on the same old anvil which De Groux hammered on. If it had pleased De Groux at that time to dress his Brabant characters in medieval costumes, he would have run parallel with Leys in genius, and also in fortune.

However, he didn't, and *now*, years later, there is a considerable reaction against that medievalism, though Leys always remains Leys, and Thijs Maris, Thijs Maris, and Victor Hugo's *Notre Dame, Notre Dame*.

But the realism *not wanted* then is *in demand* now, and there is more need of it than ever.

The realism that has character and a serious sentiment.

I can tell you that for my part I shall try to keep a straight course, and shall paint the simplest, the most common things. ... (390, 15–17 Dec. 1884.)

The year 1885 began in deep depression, and letter 392 is characteristic of the coherence between the elements within and beyond Vincent's mental and sentimental receptiveness. His realism was essentially symbolic, although he did not use the actual symbolic signs which caused problems in the emerging Symbolist writing and art. His concern, since Courrières, with the dying breed of weavers fitted in with this mood. He must have been prepared to understand their social decline by Charlotte Brontë's novel *Shirley*, an astonishing pre-Zola social document which he had read in 1881 (148).

... I've hardly ever begun a year with a gloomier aspect, in a gloomier mood, nor do I expect any future of success, but a future of strife.

It is dreary outside, the fields a mass of lumps of black earth and some snow, with mostly days of mist and mire in between, the red sun in the evening and in the morning, crows, withered grass, and faded, rotting green, black shrubs, and the branches of the poplars and willows rigid, like wire, against the dismal sky. This is what I see in passing, and it is quite in harmony with the interiors, very gloomy, these dark winter days.

It is also in harmony with the physiognomy of the peasants and weavers. I don't hear the latter complain, but they have a hard time of it. A weaver who works steadily weaves, say, a piece of 60 yards a week. While he weaves, a woman must spool for him, that is supply the shuttles with yarn, so there are two who work and have to live on it.

On that piece of cloth he makes a net profit, for instance, of 4.50 guilders a week, and nowadays when he takes it to the manufacturer, he is often told that he cannot take another piece home for one or two weeks. So not only are wages low, but work is pretty scarce too.

Consequently, there is often something agitated and restless about these people.

It is a different spirit from that of the miners, among whom I lived during a year of strikes and many accidents. That was even worse, yet it is often pathetic here too; the people are quiet, and literally *nowhere* have I heard anything resembling rebellious speeches.

But they look as little cheerful as the old cab horses or the sheep transported by steamer to England. ... (392, Jan. 1885.)

Vincent's premonitions (letter 392) proved to be right; his father died suddenly on 26 March 1885. Although his reactions were sober, the rhythm of his work was momentarily disturbed. He was full of what was to be the most mature and powerful achievement of his Brabant period: *The Potato Eaters*. It was not directly inspired by works by Zola such as *Germinal*, but reading Zola did encourage him to work on a scheme which was the result of the powerful impression made on him by peasants eating their frugal meal in their lamp-lit hovel. Vincent had already found himself a place to work at the home of the Roman Catholic sexton, one Schafrath, so that he would not longer be tied to the family circle at the parsonage which was increasingly ill-disposed towards him. His sisters, particularly Anna, had become a great source of annoyance. The death of his father provided him with an excuse to move in with Schafrath. He had two rooms there, a small dark one which he used as a studio, and an attic room to sleep in. He neglected himself, going short of food and sleep. The urge to paint, and thereby progress towards a solution to his problems, always proved stronger than his instinct for self-preservation.

I have wondered a little at not having heard from you yet. You will say that you have been too busy to think of it, and of course I understand this.

It is late in the evening, but I want to tell you once more how sincerely I hope that in the future our correspondence will become somewhat more animated than it has been of late.

Enclosed you will find two scratches of a few studies I made, while at the same time I am again working on those peasants around the dish of potatoes. I have just come home from this cottage and have been working at it by lamp-light, though I began it by daylight this time.

This is what the composition looks like.

I painted it on a rather large canvas, and as the sketch is now, I think there is some life in it.

Yet I am sure C.M., for instance, would find fault with the drawing, etc. Do you know what a positive argument against that is? That the beautiful effects of light in nature demand a very quick hand in drawing.

Now I know quite well that the great masters, especially in the period of their ripest experience, knew both how to be elaborate in the finishing and at the same time to keep a thing

Drawing from letter 399.

full of life. But certainly that will be beyond my power for the present. At the point I am now, however, I see a chance of giving a true impression of what I see.

Not always literally exact, or rather never exact, for one sees nature through one's own temperament.

The advice I want to give, you know, is the following: Don't let the time slip by; help me to work as much as possible, and from now on keep all the studies together.

I do not like to sign any of them yet, for I do not want them to circulate as pictures, which one would have to buy up again when one had some reputation. But it will be a good thing if you show them, for you will see that someday we shall find somebody who wants to do the same thing I propose to you now, namely make a collection of studies. . . .

You are looking for new ideas for the art trade; the idea of being *kind* to art lovers is not new, but it is one that *never gets old*.

Like that of guaranteeing a purchase. And I ask you, isn't it better for an art lover to possess from one painter, for instance, twenty quite different sketches at the same price which he in all fairness would have to pay for *one* finished picture which, as a salable article, had its value on the market? If I were in your place, as you know so many young painters who haven't a reputation yet, I would try to bring *painted studies* on the market, not as pictures, but mounted in some way on gilt Bristol, for instance, or black, or deep red. . . . (399, 11 Apr. 1885.)

. . . I will not send the *Potato Eaters* unless *I know for sure* there is *something* in it.

But I am getting on with it, and I think there are completely different things in it than you can ever have seen in my work. At least, so distinctly.

I mean the life especially. I paint this *from memory on the picture itself.* But you know yourself how many times I have painted these heads!

And then I drop in every night to correct some details on the spot.

But in the picture I give free scope to my own head in the sense of *thought* or imagination, which is not so much the case in *studies*, where no creative process is allowed, but where one finds food for one's imagination in reality, in order to make it exact.

But you know I wrote to M. Portier, 'Up till now I have made only *studies*, but the *pictures* will come.' And I will stick to that.

I intend to send soon a few more studies from nature too.

It is the *second* time that a saying of Delacroix's has meant so much to me. The first time it was his theory about colours, but later I read a conversation he had with other painters about the making, namely the *creation* of a picture.

He claimed that the best pictures are made from memory. *Par cœur!* he said, And about that conversation I read that, when all those worthy people were going home in the evening, Delacroix, with its usual vivacity and passion, loudly called after them in the middle of the boulevard, *Par cœur! par cœur!* probably to the great astonishment of the respectable passers-by. . . . (403, end April 1885.)

I just received *Germinal*, and started to read it at once. I have read about fifty pages, which I think splendid; I once travelled through those same parts on foot.

Enclosed is a sketch of a head, which I just brought home.

There was the same one among the last studies I sent you, namely the largest of all. But painted smoothly.

Now I have not smoothed down the brush stroke and in fact the colour is quite different too.

I haven't yet made a head so much 'painted with earth', and more will follow now.

If all goes well – if I earn a little more – so that I can travel more – then I hope to go and paint the miners' heads someday.

But I shall work on till I am absolute master of my hand, so that I can work even more quickly than now, and, for instance, bring home about thirty studies within a month. I do not know if we shall earn money, but if it is only enough to let me work terribly hard, I shall be satisfied; the main thing is to do what one wants to do. . . . (409, 15 May 1885.)

A lengthy passage from *Germinal* provides the best example of Van Gogh's method of quoting from the books he read. The quoted passage describes how the former student Souvarine saw his girlfriend, the anarchist Anouchka, executed by hanging in Moscow, a sublimely tragic moment when he amidst

Drawing from letter 409.

the crowds and she on the scaffold caught each other's eyes. If Van Gogh had the book in front of him, he deliberately limited the quotation to that unfathomable moment of life and death. He left out completely the reasons given for those looks and for the actual event, as well as its effect on the character Souvarine. The latter was not a Marxist but held views close to Bakunin's, and as an anarchist saw total destruction as the only means of creating a new and better world. A fervent reader of almost everything Zola wrote, in the course of his reading he blended his own thoughts with an active visual imagination. From the point of view of literary criticism this naturally produced a transformed image.

... '"Did I tell you how she died?"
'"Who do you mean?"
'"My woman over there in Russia."
'Etienne made a vague gesture, wondering at the trembling of the voice, and at this sudden need of confidence in this habitually reticent fellow, in his stoical detachment from others and from himself. He only knew that the woman was his mistress, and that she was hanged in Moscow.
'Souvarine resumed: "The last day in the square, I was there. ... It was raining – the clumsy fellows lost their heads, upset by the pelting rain, they had taken twenty minutes to hang four others. She stood waiting. She did not see me, she was looking for me in the crowd. I got on top of a stone pillar and she saw me, our eyes never left each other. Twice I wanted to cry out, to hurl myself over the heads to join her. But what would have been the good of it? One man less, one soldier less; and I guessed that she was saying no with her big fixed eyes, when they met mine."' ... (410, 1 June 1885.)

Totally absorbed in the complex problems of planning a figure composition such as the *Potato Eaters*, which Theo now showed to the Paris artist Charles Serret, Vincent still provided occasional flashes of evidence of his thoughts on the problems of painting out of doors as opposed to in a studio. Like his preoccupation with Delacroix, these were matters which had been digested by the Impressionists earlier on. But before his late initiation to Impressionism in Paris, Vincent – like Manet and Renoir, and to a lesser extent Monet and his followers – continued with figure painting, which was to enable him to resist total conversion to Impressionist theories.

He was increasingly anxious to exhibit his works in sequences. This approach was more modern than it seems, since Van Gogh thereby revealed the great importance of *continuity*. He was no longer concentrating on individual completed works, or on isolated major works, but on the general flow. His life's work was to be completed within a time he knew to be limited; and so he instinctively aimed for directness and above all speed. There were to be no real pauses, no gaps, no deviations; but, as in his letters, no real order either. As always, any arranging, setting in order, would have been rational interference.

... It won't be so very long before things we can show will become more important. You will notice yourself, and it is a fact which pleases me enormously, that more and more they begin to arrange exhibitions of one person, or of a very few who belong together.
This is something in the art world which I am sure contains more promise for the future than any other undertaking. It is a good thing they begin to understand that a Bouguereau does not show off well next to a Jacque, a figure by Beyle or Lhermitte does not do beside a Schelfhout or Koekkoek. Disperse the drawings of Raffaelli and judge for yourself whether it would be possible to get a good idea of that original artist. ...
... But *even* in this century, how relatively few among the innumerable painters want the figure – yes, above all – for the figure's sake, that is to say for the sake of line and modelling,

110

but cannot imagine it otherwise than in action, and want to do what the old masters avoided – even the old Dutch masters who clung to many conventional actions – and I repeat – want *to paint the action for the action's sake.*

So that the picture or the drawing has to be a drawing of the figure for the sake of the figure and the inexpressibly harmonious form of the human body, but at the same time a digging of carrots in the snow. Do I express myself clearly? I hope so, and just tell this to Serret. . . .

Tell him that I adore the figures by Michelangelo though the legs are undoubtedly too long, the hips and the backsides too large. Tell him that, for me, Millet and Lhermitte are the real artists for the very reason that they do not paint things as they are, traced in a dry analytical way, but as *they* – Millet, Lhermitte, Michelangelo – feel them. Tell him that my great longing is to learn to make those very incorrectnesses, those deviations, remodellings, changes in reality, so that they may become, yes, lies if you like – but truer than the literal truth. . . .

You recently wrote that Serret had spoken to you 'with conviction' about certain faults in the structure of the figures of *The Potato Eaters.*

But you will have seen from my answer that my own criticism also disapproves of them on that score, but I pointed out that this was an impression after my having seen the cottage in the dim lamplight for many evenings, after having painted forty heads, so it is clear that I started from a different point of view. . . .

Rather than say there must be character in a digger, I define it by saying, That peasant *must* be a peasant, that digger *must* dig, and then there will be something essentially modern in them. But I feel myself that from these very words conclusions may be drawn that I do not intend, even if I should add a whole oration. . . . (418, July–Aug. 1885.)

Van Gogh became impatient if his continuity, his élan, was checked. He would become nervous, charged with tension like a brooding storm, eruptive and anxious to force the birth-throes of his creation. Michelet said of himself, 'Grasp what is becoming a reality the moment it becomes a reality'; 'Let us seize them this very hour'; 'Time passes quickly, they will change.'

. . . What struck me most on seeing the old Dutch pictures again is that most of them *were painted quickly*, that these great masters, such as Frans Hals, a Rembrandt, a Ruysdael and so many others – dashed off a thing from the first stroke and did not retouch it so very much.

And please note this too – if it was right, *they left it as it was.* I have especially admired the hands by Rembrandt and Hals, certain hands in *The Syndics*, even in *The Jewish Bride*, and in Frans Hals, hands that lived, but were not finished in the sense they demand nowadays.

And heads too – eyes, nose, mouth done with a single stroke of the brush without any retouching whatever. Unger, Bracquemond have etched it well – just as it was painted – and one can see in their etchings the way of painting. . . .

Those are the things which I believe in, but every day I hate more and more those pictures which are light all over. It is a bad thing for me when they say that I have 'no technique'; it is possible that this will blow over, as I make no acquaintances among the painters; it is true that, on the contrary, *those who talk most about technique* are in my eyes weakest in it!

I wrote you so already. But when I show something of my work in Holland, I know beforehand what will be said, and by what kind of critics. Meanwhile I am going quietly to the *old Dutch masters*, and to the pictures by Israëls, and to those who have a direct affinity with Israëls, which the modern painters do not have. They are almost diametrically opposed to Israëls. . . .

What they call brightness is in many cases an ugly studio tone of a cheerless city studio. The dawn in the morning or the twilight in the evening does not seem to exist, there only seems to be midday, from 11 to 3, a very decent hour indeed, but – often insipid as a milksop. . . . (427, Oct. 1885.)

. . . 'The true painters are the ones who do not make local colour' – that was what Blanc and Delacroix discussed once.

Mightn't I presume to infer from it that a painter had better start from the colours on his palette than from the colours in nature? I mean, when one wants to paint, for instance, a head, and sharply observes the reality one has before one, then one may think: That head is a harmony of red-brown, violet, yellow, all of them broken – I will put a violet and a yellow and a red-brown on my palette and these will break each other. . . .

A portrait by Courbet is much truer – manly, free, painted in all kinds of beautiful deep tones of red-brown, of gold, of colder violet in the shadow with black as *repoussoir*, with a little bit of tinted white linen, as a rest for the eye – finer than a portrait by whomever you like, who has imitated the colour of the face with horribly punctilious *precision*.

A man's head or a woman's head, well observed and at leisure, is divinely beautiful, isn't it? Well, one loses that *general harmony* of tones in nature by painfully exact imitation; one keeps it by recreating in a parallel colour scale which may be not exactly, or even far from exactly, like the model. . . . (429, end Oct. 1885.)

Briefly leaving his quiet backwater, he paid a visit to Amsterdam to see the museum. His analysis of the colours in a work by Hals is so outstanding, lively and clear that only a painter who could also write well and was engrossed in the study of the rules of colour, could so record them from memory. As usual, he also had to mention Delacroix because this artist and his ideas formed part of the debate that was going on inside him.

. . . I do not know whether you remember the one to the left of the *Night Watch*, as pendant of *The Syndics*, there is a picture (unknown to me till now) by Frans Hals and P. Codde, about twenty officers full length. Did you ever notice that??? that alone – that one picture – is worth the trip to Amsterdam – especially for a colourist. There is a figure in it, the figure of the flag-bearer, in the extreme left corner, right against the frame – that figure is in grey, from top to toe, I shall call it pearl-grey – of a peculiar neutral tone, probably the result of orange and blue mixed in such a way that they neutralize each other – by varying that keynote, making it somewhat lighter here, somewhat darker there, the whole figure is as if it were painted with one same grey. But the leather boots are of a different material than the leggings, which differ from the folds of the trousers, which differ from the waistcoat – expressing a different material, differing in relation to colour – but all one family of grey. But just wait a moment! 88

Now into that grey he brings blue and orange – and some white; the waistcoat has satin bows of a divine soft blue, sash and flag orange – a white collar.

Orange, blanc, bleu, as the national colours were then – orange and blue, side by side, that most splendid colour scale, against a background of a grey, cleverly mixed by uniting just those two, let me call them poles of electricity (speaking of colours though) so that they annihilate each other against that grey and white. Further, we find in that picture – other orange scales against another blue, further, the most beautiful blacks against the most beautiful whites; the heads – about twenty of them, sparkling with life and spirit, and a technique! a colour! the figures of all those people superb and full size.

But that orange blanc blue fellow in the left corner . . . I seldom saw a more divinely beautiful figure. It is unique.

Delacroix would have raved about it – absolutely raved. I was literally rooted to the spot. Well you know *The Singer*, that laughing fellow – a bust in a greenish-black with carmine, carmine in the flesh colour too. . . .

Bürger has written about Rembrandt's *Jewish Bride*, just as he wrote about van der Meer of Delft, as he wrote about *The Sower* by Millet, as he wrote about Frans Hals, with devotion, and surpassing himself. *The Syndics* is perfect, is the most beautiful Rembrandt; but *The Jewish Bride* – not ranked so high, what an intimate, what an infinitely sympathetic picture it is, painted 'with a hand of fire'. You see, in *The Syndics* Rembrandt is true to nature, though *even there*, and always, he soars aloft, to the very highest height, the infinite; but Rembrandt could do more than that – if he did not have to be *literally* true, as in a portrait, when he was free to *idealize*, to be poet, that means Creator. That's what he is in *The Jewish Bride*. How Delacroix would have understood that picture. What a noble sentiment, infinitely deep. . . . 89

In Amsterdam I also saw pictures of today, Witkamp and others. Witkamp is one of the best, reminds one of Jules Breton; others whom I have in mind but I shall not name, who always talk about what *they* call technique, I found *weak in that very technique*.

You know all those cold grey tones which they think distinguished, but which are flat and uninteresting, childishly mixed. Nowadays they bring on the market ordinary colours purposely mixed with pure white, for the convenience of painters who paint in what they call a distinguished light colour scale. (426, 10/11 Oct, 1885.)

After years of longing to make a sale, and countless begging letters, to pay for essential expenditure, Vincent now had an opportunity to sell something to his Eindhoven acquaintance Kerssemakers.

You know those three pollard oaks at the bottom of the garden at home; I have laboured over them for the fourth time. I had been at them for three days with a canvas the size of, let's say, the *Cottage* and the *Country Churchyard* which you have.

The difficulty was in the tufts of havana-brown leaves: modelling them and giving them their form, colour and tone. In the evening I took it to that acquaintance of mine in Eindhoven, who has a rather stylish drawing-room, where we put it on the wall (grey paper, furniture black and gold). Well, never before have I been so convinced that I shall make things that do well, that I shall succeed in calculating my colours, so that I have it in my power to make the right effect. This was havana, soft green and white (grey), even *pure* white, direct from the tube (you see that I, for my part, though I speak about black, have no prejudice against the other extreme, even the utmost extreme).

Now, though that man has money, though he took a fancy to it, I felt such a glow of courage when I saw that it was good, that, as it hung there, it created an atmosphere by the soft melancholy harmony of that combination of colours, *that I could not sell it.*

But as he had a fancy for it, I gave it to him, and he accepted it just as I had intended, without many words, namely little more than, 'The thing is damned good.'

I don't think so yet myself. First I must see a little more of Chardin, Rembrandt, old Dutch and French painters, and think it over well – because I want to make it more elaborate with less paint than I used, for instance, in this thing. ... (431, 8–12 Nov. 1885.)

81, 85 The correspondence with Van Rappard had become acrimonious. His relationship with the artist had taken the form of an exchange of views with a colleague, and thus complemented what he wrote to Theo, but never more than that. Van Rappard's academic criticism of *The Potato Eaters* – proportions, anatomy, state of completion, suggestion of space – was based on the lithograph Vincent had made of it. It led to a impassioned series of letters in self-defence from Vincent, and, ultimately, to a final break.

... You will agree with me that such work is not meant seriously. Fortunately you can do better than that, but why then did you see and treat everything so superficially? Why didn't you study the movements? *Now* they are only posing. How far from true that coquettish little hand of the woman in the background is – and what connection is there between the coffeepot, the table and that hand that is lying on top of the handle? What on earth is that kettle doing? – it isn't standing, it isn't being lifted up – so what then? And why isn't that man to the right allowed to have a knee, a belly and lungs? Or are they located in his back? And why must his arm be a yard too short? And why must he do without one half of his nose? And why must that woman on the left have some sort of little tobacco-pipe stem with a little cube at the end for a nose?

And after that, while working in such a manner, you dare invoke the names of Millet and Breton? Come on! In my opinion art is too sublime a thing to be treated so nonchalantly. (Van Rappard to Vincent, R51a, 24 May 1885.)

I just received your letter – to my surprise. You are herewith getting it back. (Vincent to Van Rappard, R51, 24 May 1885.)

... Millet was mentioned. All right, my friend, I'll answer you.

You wrote, 'And such a one dares invoke Millet and Breton.'

My answer to that is that I most seriously advise you *not* to fight with me. As for me – I go my own way – you see? I don't want to pick a quarrel with anyone, so *not with you* either, even now. I should let you say whatever you liked; if you were to have more observations of the same kind, it would leave me stone cold, and that would be all. But for the moment I want to say this much, you have said more than once that I do not care for the form of the figure, it is beneath me to pay attention to it, and – my dear fellow – it is beneath you to say such an unwarranted thing. You have known me for years – just tell me, have you ever seen me work otherwise than after the model, never sparing expense, however heavy at times, though I am surely poor enough.

Not in your last letter, but repeatedly and ad nauseam in your previous letters you wrote about '*technique*', which was the reason for the letter to which you did not reply. What I answered to that, and what I will answer again is, There is the conventional meaning, which is being given more and more to the word technique, *and* the real meaning – *science*. Very well, Meissonier himself says, '*La science nul ne l'a*' [nobody has science]. . . . (Vincent to Van Rappard, R52, before 6 July 1885.)

. . . As for my work, that scene of the potato eaters – you saw the lithograph of it – is a subject that I tried to paint, being inspired by the peculiar light effect in that grimy cottage. It is kept in such a low scale of colours that the *light* colours, smeared on white paper, for instance, would look like ink stains; but on the canvas they stand out like lights because of the great forces opposed to them, for instance by putting on absolutely unmixed Prussian blue. My own criticism is that by paying attention to this, I lost sight of the form of the torsos. Heads and hands, however, were done very carefully; and as they were of the greatest importance and all the rest was nearly entirely dark (therefore *quite different* in effect from the lithograph), my painting the picture *as I did* is to be excused to a greater extent than you think. And besides, the real picture differs in design from *either* the rough sketch for it, which I still have and which I made in that cottage by the light of a little lamp, *or* from the lithograph.

I want to tell you further that I have drawn quite a number of heads since you were here, and quite a lot of peasants besides: diggers, weeders, harvesters. The thing that occupied my *83, 84* attention, either directly or indirectly, and was the great problem in all this, was colour. I mean the *breaking* of the colours – mixing red with green, blue with orange, yellow with violet, always the combination of the complementary colours, their influence on each other – of which nature is as full as of light and brown. Another problem – which engrosses me every day anew – is precisely the one I think you asserted I neglected: rendering the form and its modelling, its great lines and masses – one considers the contours in the *last* instead of the *first* place in doing this.

Herewith two sketches of smaller compositions – I painted both of them. Lately I have been working mostly on things of a smaller size. . . .

And as for other questions – I cannot always keep quiet under it; now and then it seems to me as though people were touching my body, so much do I feel taken up by the question, and so much is my conviction a part of myself.

It is true that there are faulty things in that lithograph as well as in my other work – certainly there are. But my other work proves so clearly that I render what I see that people cannot be justified, or speaking in good faith, when they judge my work otherwise than as a whole and in a broader way, taking into account my purpose and endeavour – namely to paint *le paysan chez soi*, peasants in their surroundings. . . . (Vincent to Van Rappard, R57, Sept. 1885.)

However little he agreed with his father, it was the death of Theodorus Van Gogh which made Vincent grasp the opportunity to cut himself loose first from the family home, then from Nuenen, and finally from the Netherlands. He had now found a pattern of life whereby each idea he had of moving came to fruition as soon as a phase in his work had been completed.

Theo was briefly informed of his brother's decision to go to Antwerp, a town suggested previously as one of the places where he might possibly sell some paintings and see some more works of art. The move was to be temporary, he thought, just for a few months, and then he would go back *if need be*. It does not sound very convincing.

. . . I must say I am longing for Antwerp now. Probably the first thing I shall do there will be to go and see the pictures by Leys in his *dining hall*, if it is open to the public. You know that *97*

Walk on the Ramparts, and those which Bracquemond etched, *The Table* and *The Servant Maid*.

I imagine it will be beautiful there this winter, especially the docks with snow.

Of course I shall take a few pictures with me, and they will be those that I would otherwise have sent to you one of these days. A big mill on the heath in the evening, and a view of the village behind a row of poplars with yellow leaves, a still life, and a number of drawings of figures. ... (434, 15–20 Nov. 1885.)

... I repeat, as to my rather sudden departure from here, if I hadn't had trouble with the models, I should have spent the winter here. But working steadily with models here is not so much hampered by the priest's opposition, which in itself would have been neutralized by my ignoring it completely, but the worst is that though I have the courage to stand my ground, people hesitate, and are more frightened than I thought they would be.

And I am not going to undertake it unless I am quite sure that they have the courage. Now it might help if I go away for a couple of months, and if it doesn't help, then not one of those to whom I gave something for it every week last winter will earn a penny with it this winter. ... (435, 18–22 Nov. 1885.)

His mother wrote an undated and unpublished letter (Van Gogh Museum Archives, Amsterdam): 'Friday morning – The Hague', in which she explained to Jo van Gogh-Bonger that, when moving from Nuenen to Breda on 30 March 1886, 'under unfavourable circumstances for assessing Vincent's work, perhaps we did not sufficiently appreciate the things we found'. Considering the few belongings Vincent took with him to Antwerp, and his large output, the work he left behind at Nuenen can hardly have been negligible, even allowing for what he had sent to Theo. There was a 'man who helped us clear up and move', and his mother thought it might well be possible that 'something was distributed from that quarter, but I do not know any facts'. She would get someone to ask the man. For the trade this became a welcome source when suggesting the possible provenance of works supposedly by Van Gogh. Van Gogh had left about seventy painted studies at The Hague (letter 329).

48 The Potato Eaters, 1885
The definitive version of *The Potato Eaters* is the synthesis of all the ideas of Vincent's Dutch period: all he had learned from Millet and Breton, and from reading Zola (*Germinal* and *La Terre*), his religious and moral conviction of the value of working people and their lives, his feeling of being bound to the earth, his union with the group that sits at night around the table. The tension of his creativity in the months from January to March 1885, before the definitive composition came to fruition, was enormous. Numerous heads of peasants were drawn. After growing up among the masters of the Hague School, and absorbing the masterpieces of the Dutch seventeenth century, Vincent now appeared in his maturity as a Dutch painter, an authentic genius, distancing himself with a sure hand from everyday aesthetic rules and fashions, with a mastery of proportion, colour and space. 'By continually witnessing peasant life, at all hours of the day, I have become so absorbed in it that I hardly think of anything else' (400).

Etten and Kee

'Well, the same thing that Weissenbruch has said about a landscape, a peat bog, Mauve said about a figure, i.e. an old peasant who sits brooding by the hearth, as if he saw things from the past rising in the glow of the fire or in the smoke' (177). In general the letters of the Etten period (1881) inform us better of his deep-rooted, violent and obdurate love for his cousin Kee than about his work. He discussed technical problems, briefly and unemotionally. The works themselves, however, show the development of a great power to express his own melancholy, gloomy temper.

49 Kee Vos-Stricker, 1879

51 Shacks, 1881

50 *Corner of a Garden with an Arbour*, June 1881

52 *Old Peasant by the Fire*, Nov. 1881
53 *Worn Out*, 1881

The Hague and Sien

In The Hague in the following year, 1882, he lived with Christine Hoornik (Sien), an alcoholic prostitute, whom with some of his old missionary zeal he attempted to rehabilitate. A series of seated or crouching figures, mostly female – and mostly of Sien – maintain the mood of the seated peasants of 1881.

54 *The Great Lady,* 1882

55 *Girl (Sien's Daughter with Shawl: Left Profile),* Jan. 1883

56 *Weeping Woman (Woman with her Head in her Hands, Seated on a Basket),* 1883

57 *Sien with a Cigar, Sitting on the Ground by a Stove,* Apr. 1882

103

Seen in The Hague

Vincent's background did not lie exclusively in Dutch, but also in English and French, art. He had adored the work of Breton since 1875. In The Hague he saw the collection of the Hague School painter H. W. Mesdag, in which Breton, Millet and Jacob Maris were represented by the three paintings seen here. Mesdag did not collect conventional fashionable subjects, but sought just the qualities which also appealed to Van Gogh. Millet was a mentor of his all his life; he constantly cited maxims, such as 'I would never do away with suffering, for it often is what makes artists express themselves most energetically'; 'Because I go to work in clogs, I shall manage'; and one which Van Gogh was to reaffirm at the cost of this own life: 'In art you have to risk your own skin' (406).

60 Jean-Francois Millet. *Fisherman's Wife, c.*1849

61 Jacob Maris. *Evening on the Dunes (Fisherman's Wife, Seated)*

Anton Mauve, who married one of Mrs Van Gogh's numerous sisters, Jet Carbentus, had the merit of teaching Van Gogh, in The Hague period, a considerable amount about the techniques of painting and drawing. Moreover, his critical spirit and total commitment to his own work enhanced his authority in Vincent's eyes. They fell out; Vincent is too readily blamed for this by his biographers, the volatile Mauve being at least as difficult as he was. Vincent never ceased to revere Mauve as an artist. Jacob Maris (1837–99) was the eldest of three brothers, all painters. Long considered to be the greatest Dutch artist of the century, he caught Vincent's imagination through his use of subdued warm colour (in his early work) and his scenes of the life of the poor.

Left:
58 Jules Breton. *The Harvest*
59 Anton Mauve. *Digging Potatoes*

62 Jules Dupré. *Evening*
63 Charles-François Daubigny. *Sunset at Villerville*, 1866
64 Anton Mauve. *Sale of Wood*, c.1881

Left:
Three more works with which Vincent saw in the Mesdag collection. Jules Dupré was a pure landscape painter, a mixture of French and English influences (Barbizon and Constable). This dark Dupré is an example of that painter's evolution towards a broader vision, suppressing details. A lifelong admirer of Daubigny, Vincent painted *Daubigny's Garden* at Auvers shortly before he died (*211*). Not only the English illustrators but the Hague artists Mauve and Breitner showed figures in groups, a theme which attracted Vincent principally during his Hague period.

Urban reality

Left:
65 *Roofs seen from the Artist's Attic Window,*
July 1882
66 *Road at Loosduinen,* 1882

Five drawings of 1882 show how fast, after leaving Etten in December 1881, Vincent gained his astonishing mastery of drawing. He left the famous masters of the Hague School behind him and developed a different and ultimately more modern style of expressive realism, combining an almost photographic exactness with an expressive use of perspective and a great feeling for space (65,66). His choice of subjects is modern (67,68): the fascination of urban and suburban life, deeply felt in all its ugliness. Vincent responded to his environment not as an aesthete, reacting against the surrounding squalor, but as an artist, responding imaginatively to an unspoken menace: a man with a presentiment of the rootless and disorientated urban culture that was to come.

67 *Gas-holders (The Gas Tanks of The Hague).* Mar. 1882
68 *Factory in The Hague (Sterkman's Factory),* Mar. 1882
69 *Entrance to the Pawnshop, The Hague,* Mar. 1882

Rural melancholy

70 Bridge at Nieuw Amsterdam (Drenthe), Nov. 1883
The silence, the melancholy of this poor, forgotten corner
of Drenthe are expressed by the delicate, pale colour of the
late autumn light. The symmetry of the composition is
unusual for Vincent.

71 Vicarage Garden with Figures, Oct.–Nov. 1885
Shortly before he left Nuenen for good in 1885, Vincent
was 'completely absorbed in the laws of colour', as
expounded by Delacroix. His composition here is stiff, but
the symphonic use of dark colours is deeply moving.

72 Work in the Fields, Oct. 1883
See *22*, a landscape by Boughton with tree trunks, a pool
and mud (as described by Vincent in letter 331); his long-
standing admiration for Boughton signified a serious
affinity.

73 Avenue of Willows with Shepherd and Peasant Woman, 1884
Vincent was strongly attracted by thorn bushes, gnarled
tree trunks, fantastic roots, pollard willows (127). Trunks
are drawn here more by circles than contours (in
accordance with Delacroix's theories).

Nuenen

Vincent's last stay with his parents was also the longest since childhood: at Nuenen, from December 1883 to November 1885. These were two years of intensive work, in the studio he rented from the local Catholic sacristan. Theodorus van Gogh was pastor of the little Reformed Church and lived in the vicarage. Here, as with all the other places where Vincent lived as an artist, photographs remind us how intense, and how exact, was the painter's experience of the tangible world.

76 *Lane of Poplars at Nuenen,* autumn 1885
In 1885, from early spring onwards, Vincent underwent a series of emotional shocks which stimulated his creative powers. His father died on 26 March. He left his parents' house, to live and work alone; trouble with the parish priest over rumours of misbehaviour with one of his models intensified his unrest. He created a

74 *The Vicarage at Nuenen,* autumn 1885
75 The vicarage at Nuenen

number of the masterpieces of his Dutch
phase. The *Lane of Poplars* is a revelation of
autumn colours, so rich that some art
historians have supposed that he retouched
it in Paris. There are other colourful
autumn lanes, all with the figure of the
'woman in black'. He had realized the
possiblities that Brabant offered; he was
ripe to leave.

77 *Coming out of Church in Nuenen*, Jan. 1884
78 Nuenen church

79 *Weaver, Facing Front*, July 1884
From the time he first read Charlotte
Brontë's *Shirley* (at Etten, 1881), and
through the Borinage and The Hague,
weavers had a mysterious fascination for
Van Gogh. This is one of his best paintings
of this subject, a monumental construction
with a towering figure working
energetically behind his loom.

80 *Woman Spinning*, 1885
The profile and structure of the seated
woman, and the paint, are elements of the
period which produced *The Potato Eaters*.
The Zola-like atmosphere and the brutish
expressions of the human figures are far
from any sentimental feeling.

81 Anton van Rappard. *The Brickworks*, 1885
82 Constantin Meunier. *The Brickmakers*
Vincent admired Constantin Meunier
more than he did Van Rappard, a friend
and contemporary whom he had known
since Brussels (1880). Vincent's
knowledge of Meunier was so great that
he could remember having seen a picture
by Meunier in the same spirit as one that
Van Rappard was engaged upon in 1885
(421).

83 *Peasant Woman Stooping, Aug. 1885*
84 *The Reaper with Cap, Moving to the Right, Aug. 1885*

Artists are children of their time; and two artists of different stature, like Van Gogh and Van Rappard, may share a common subject matter. The difference, when it comes to the survival of the artists' works, lies in their spirit. Van Rappard has left much good work; but he believed in the rules of the academies, and Van Gogh believed only in himself and in Delacroix. In the Dutch period, both his colour and his drawing attain an intensity of vision, in the depiction of human labour, that remains unequalled in art before or since. Mauve, in related themes, was delicate, serious, subtle, and his work is still of great value; so is that of his associate Breitner. But Vincent, capable of total spiritual commitment, fearless in transgressing the unwritten limitations that hemmed the artist in, became after his death the yardstick by which his contemporaries were measured.

85 Anton van Rappard. *Girl Holding a Brick Mould*, 1885
86 Anton Mauve. *The Potato-digger*
87 Georg Hendrik Breitner. *Couple Walking*

A hand of fire

88 Frans Hals and Pieter Codde. *The Company of Captain Reynier Reael . . .*, 1633–36
Vincent had a profound love of tradition; but he was never a mere follower. In October 1885, shortly before he left his native land for good, he stood for the last time in the new Rijksmuseum in Amsterdam. He was especially interested by one relatively little-known picture by Hals (finished by Codde), and in particular by the flagbearer at the left (letter 426, perhaps the best critical analysis he ever wrote).

89 Rembrandt van Rijn. *The Jewish Bride, c.*1666
Of Rembrandt's famous *Jewish Bride*, which he did not rank as high as The *Syndics*, he wrote: 'what an infinitely sympathetic picture it is, painted "with a hand of fire". In *The Jewish Bride* Rembrandt is a 'poet; that means "creator"'.

90 Jozef Israëls. *Alone in the World*, 1878
He must have absorbed pictures until he reached the point of exhaustion. About the work by Jozef Israëls, whom he had admired since his early days, he said, 'an old woman huddles together like a bundle of rags near the bedstead in which the corpse of her husband lies . . . let them jabber about technique as much as they like, in pharisaical, hollow, hypocritical terms'. Vincent thought it a masterpiece.

III

ANTWERP AND PARIS

'Colour seeking life'

1885–1886 Antwerp
1886–1888 Paris

In November 1885 Vincent left his native land, sadly, but with a feeling of relief. He was never to return. His letters from Antwerp, over the ensuing three months, are not on the same level of creative excitement as those from Drenthe or Brabant. Nevertheless, they are – and with Van Gogh it could hardly be otherwise – documents of great interest: by turns acute, stimulating, and almost haughty in his contempt for the Antwerp Academy.

97 ... I shall begin by telling you that I saw Leys's dining hall, you know, *The Walk on the Ramparts*, *The Skaters*, *The Reception* and *The Table*, and on a panel between the windows *St Luke*. To my astonishment the composition was somewhat different from the ultimate compositions, at least I imagine so – although I have not yet been able to compare photos of the *pictures* with them.

Then, it was painted in fresco – *i.e.* on the plaster of the wall. Now fresco really must and can last for centuries, but these have already faded considerably, and the one over the mantelpiece especially (part of *The Reception*) already shows some cracks. The highly ingenious son of Baron Leys has also improved the hall by having a door enlarged so that in *The Skaters*, the legs of the fellows standing on the bridge looking over the railings have been cut away, which makes a deplorable effect. Besides, the light is terribly bad there: now, that hall was originally painted – I imagine – to be used by lamplight. Therefore, because I honestly could not see anything, I gave the servant a tip and asked her to light the chandelier for me, and then I could see better.

After so much that had rather disappointed me – in the first place that the colour in the fresco, and, alas, I am afraid *bad* fresco, is not what we are used to from Leys – after so much that disappointed me – after all it is superb.

The maidservant, the woman near the baker's shop, the lovers and other figures in *The Walk on the Ramparts* – the bird's-eye view of the city, the silhouette of the towers and roofs against the sky, the bustle of skaters on the frozen moat – are superbly executed. ... (436, Nov. 1885.)

104 Amidst numerous impressions of the busy life of the port, and descriptions of several areas of the town, Van Gogh's discovery of Japanese prints – in Antwerp of all places – was to be significant for his entire future development. It seems simpler than in fact it is. He pinned a few pictures to the wall of his rented room, and some influence began to make itself felt in the way he looked at people in the town. There was also a link with a book, *Chérie*, by Edmond de Goncourt (1884). Jules de Goncourt had died, and in the introduction to *Chérie* Edmond spoke of their close collaboration. Vincent regretted that he and Theo were unable to work along similar lines. In one of Vincent's favourite books, *Germinie Lacerteux*, the Goncourts had proved that it was possible to maintain aesthetic standards and artistic values despite deep concern for their terrible subject, the misery of the poorer classes. At an early date the Goncourts had also introduced the subject of Japan and Japanese art into their writings and activity as collectors, even though they were not the first to do so.

Van Gogh bought some Japanese prints in Antwerp and fell in love with this particular art form, which, unbeknown to him, had already had a fruitful effect on Braquemond, Manet, the other Impressionists and Whistler.

... This morning I took a most satisfactory walk in the pouring rain, the object of this excursion being to get my things at the customhouse; the various dockyards and warehouses on the quays are splendid.

I have walked along the docks and the quays several times already, in all directions. Especially when one comes from the sand and the heath and the quiet of a peasant village, and has been in none but quiet surroundings for a long time, the contrast is curious. It is an unfathomable confusion. One of Goncourt's sayings was: 'Japonaiserie for ever.' Well, those docks are a famous Japonaiserie, fantastic, peculiar, unheard of – at least one can take this view of it.

I should like to walk there with you, just to know whether we see alike. One could make everything there, city views – figures of the most varied character – the ships as the principal things, with water and sky a delicate grey – but above all – Japonaiserie. I mean, the figures are always in action, one sees them in the queerest surroundings, everything fantastic, and at all moments interesting contrasts present themselves.

A white horse in the mud, in a corner where heaps of merchandise are lying covered with oilcloth – against the old smoky black walls of the warehouse. Quite simple, but an effect of Black and White.

Through the window of a very elegant English bar, one will look out on the dirtiest mud, and on a ship from which, for instance, attractive merchandise like hides and buffalo horns is being unloaded by hideous dock hands or exotic sailors; a very dainty, very fair young English girl is standing at the window looking at it, or at something else. . . . There will be Flemish sailors, with almost exaggeratedly healthy faces, with broad shoulders, strong and plump, and thoroughly Antwerp folk, eating mussels, or drinking beer, and all this will happen with a lot of noise and bustle – by way of contrast – a tiny figure in black with her little hands pressed against her body comes stealing noiselessly along the grey walls. Framed by raven-black hair – a small oval face, brown? orange-yellow? I don't know. For a moment she lifts her eyelids, and looks with a slanting glance out of a pair of jet-black eyes. It is a Chinese girl, mysterious, quiet like a mouse – small, bedbug-like in character. What a contrast to that group of Flemish mussel eaters.

Another contrast – one passes through a very narrow street, between tremendously high houses, warehouses, and sheds.

But down below in the street pubs for all nationalities with masculine and feminine individuals to match, shops selling eatables, seamen's clothes, glaringly colourful and crowded.

That street is long; every moment one sees something striking. Now and again there is a noise, intenser than anywhere else, when a quarrel is going on; for instance, there you are walking, looking about, and suddenly there is a loud cheering and all kinds of shouting. In broad daylight a sailor is being thrown out of a brothel by the girls, and pursued by a furious fellow and a string of prostitutes, of whom he seems rather afraid – at least I saw him scramble over a heap of sacks and disappear through a warehouse window. . . .

And so my studio is all fixed up. If I could get good models for almost nothing, I should not be afraid of anything.

I do not think it so very bad either that I have not got so much money as to be able to force things by paying for them. Perhaps the idea of making portraits and having them paid for by posing is the safer way, because in a city it is not the same as it is with the peasants. Well, one thing is sure, Antwerp is very curious and fine for a painter.

My studio is not bad, especially as I have pinned a lot of little Japanese prints on the wall, *104* which amuse me very much. You know those little women's figures in gardens, or on the beach, horsemen, flowers, knotty thorn branches. . . . (437, 28 Nov. 1885.)

Of course he was familiar with Rubens' art, but it was only after moving to Antwerp that he made a thorough analysis of his work and discovered its value to himself. We can share his fascination with some of the artist's less popular paintings, not prime examples of his art but possessing a wealth of fine qualities.

. . . Rubens is certainly making a strong impression on me; I think his drawing tremendously good – I mean the drawing of heads and hands in themselves. I am quite carried away by his way of drawing the lines in a face with streaks of pure red, or of modelling the figures of the hands by the same kind of streaks. I go to the museum fairly often, and then I look at little else but a few heads and hands of his and of Jordaens'. I know he is not as intimate as Hals and Rembrandt, but in themselves those heads are so alive.

Probably I don't look at those which are generally admired most. I look for fragments like, for instance, those blonde heads in *St Theresa in Purgatory*. I am now looking for a blonde *98* model just because of Rubens. But you must not be angry if I tell you that I cannot make both ends meet this month. I have bought some more colours and two new kinds of drawing brushes which suit me splendidly and with which I can work more accurately. . . . (430, 8–15 Dec. 1885.)

He was a close student of contemporary art in Antwerp. Apart from Leys, he was also familiar with Henri de Braekeleer, Constantin Meunier, Félicien Rops and Henri de Groux, and updated his views on them. The younger artists of whom he took special note included Edgard Farasyn and Jan Verhas, who, a hundred years later, again appear to stand out amidst many mediocrities, and to have some quality – albeit of local value only.

. . . I have seen two collections of modern pictures, first, what was bought at the exhibition for the raffle, and then a collection of pictures that was for sale.

So I saw several fine things, two studies by Henri de Braekeleer; you know that he is absolutely different from the old De Braekeleer, I mean the one who is a famous colourist, and who analyses rigorously. He is somewhat like Manet, that is to say as original as Manet.

One study was of a woman in a studio, or some such interior, with Japanese objects; the woman wore a costume of yellow and black. The flesh colour, white with carmine. In the surroundings, all kinds of quaint little tones. The other one was a half-finished study of a landscape. Yellow, faded, flat fields as far as the eye can see, crossed by a black cinder path, with a ditch alongside; over it, a sky of lilac grey, with accents of carmined lilac. Far away the little red patch of vermilion of a roof, and two little black trees. Hardly anything, and yet for me a great deal, because of the peculiar sentiment in the juxtaposition of colours. I also saw an old study by De Groux, a woman beside a cradle, somewhat like an old Israëls.

Further, what shall I say about those modern pictures? I thought many of them *splendid*, and then I mean especially the work of the colourists, or of those who try to be so, who look everywhere for mother-of-pearl-like combinations in the light parts. But to me it is not always perfect by a long shot; it is too affected. I prefer to see a simple brush stroke and a less far-fetched, difficult colour. More simplicity, in short that intelligent simplicity which is not afraid of frank technique.

I like Rubens just for his ingenuous way of painting, his working with the simplest means.

I don't count Henri de Braekeleer among those who look for mother-of-pearl effects everywhere, because his is a curious, very interesting endeavour to be literally true, and he stands quite apart. I also saw various grey paintings, including a printing shop by Mertens, a picture by Verhaert representing his own studio, where he himself is sitting etching and his wife standing behind him. . . . (439, 8–15 Dec. 1885.)

91 He also made a remarkable discovery in the Andrieskerk or church of St Andrew (1523), in the poor fisherman's quarter: a superb stained glass window which he described from memory – there were no catalogues at the time. The thoroughness of his powers of observation and concentration on the colours in particular is remarkable. After his studies in Brabant, he felt colour was the most important thing for him as a painter. Stained glass windows had long fascinated him, in England for instance, while the related technique of Cloisonnism (see p. 195) occupied his mind at Arles for a while.

. . . By the way, let me begin by answering your question of some time ago, about the picture by Franck or Francken at Saint-André, which I saw today. I think it is a good picture – especially fine in sentiment – the sentiment is not very Flemish or Rubens-like. It reminds one more of Murillo. The colour is warm, in a reddish colour scheme like Jordaens sometimes is.

The shadows in the flesh are very strong, that is what Rubens has not, and Jordaens often has, and it gives something mysterious to the picture which one must appreciate in that school.

I could not get near enough to analyse the technique close up, which would have been well worth while. The head of Christ is less conventional than the Flemish painters usually conceive it.

But I imagine I can also do it in that way, and the picture did not tell me anything new. And as I am not satisfied with what I can do now, and try to make progress – enough – let's talk about other pictures. What struck me in that church was a sketch by Van Dyck or Rubens (?), *The Deposition from the Cross*, which hung high, but seemed very beautiful to me. Much sentiment in the pale corpse – this by the way.

There is a painted window which I think superb – very, very curious. A beach, a green sea with a castle on the rocks, a sparkling blue sky of the most beautiful tones of blue, greenish, whitish, deeper, higher of tone.

An enormous three-master, quaint and phantasmal, stands out against the sky, diffusion everywhere, light in the dark, dark in the light. In the blue a figure of the Holy Virgin, bright yellow, white, orange. Higher up the window reappears dark green, with black, with fiery red.

Well – do you remember it? It is very beautiful, and Leys would certainly have fallen in love with it, or James Tissot in his old style or Thijs Maris.

I saw some pictures bought for the Musée Moderne, by Verhas and Farasyn. . . . (443, Jan. 1886.)

During Vincent's months in Antwerp one problem urgently required a solution: where was he to go now that he specifically wanted to make studies from the nude and was anxious to find an environment where he could gain constructive help? He decided, late and reluctantly, on the Academy. *103*

. . . Always to be in a state of exile, forever having to make great efforts, always half measures! But never mind – the family stranger than strangers is one fact – and being through with Holland is a second fact. *It is quite a relief.*

That is my only feeling, and yet I have been so deeply attached to it all that at first the estrangement drove me crazy. . . .

About models this month I think I shall go and see Verlat, who is the director of the academy here – and I must see what the conditions are, and if one could work there from the nude. I shall take a portrait and some drawings with me then. . . . (443, early Jan. 1886.)

Karel Verlat (1824–90) was a talented, ambitious, superficial man, authoritarian as a teacher. He had worked in Paris for eighteen years and failed to progress beyond a glorification of tradition. Vincent could hardly object to Verlat's conviction that drawing was of prime importance; but he naturally came into conflict with the anti-Delacroix doctrine that contour must dominate. Van Gogh thought Verlat's colour hard, as did the critic Max Rooses (*Oude en nieuwe Kunst*, Ghent 1896). But Verlat did urge his students to go to the Near East, because of the southern light; it is conceivable that this may have roused something in Van Gogh.

The thought of entering the studio of Fernand Cormon, in Paris, was already in Vincent's mind; although *any* established painter was likely to object strongly to his manner of working.

. . . I am sorry to have to tell you more categorically that I am literally worn out and overworked. Just think, I went to live in my own studio (in Nuenen) on 1 May and I have not had a hot dinner more than perhaps six or seven times since. I do not want you to tell Mother that I am not well, for good reasons, for perhaps she would begin to worry, thinking that it was not kind to let things happen as they did, namely – that I did not stay at home to avoid these very consequences.

I will not mention it, so don't you, either.

But I have lived *then*, and I do *here*, without any money for a dinner, because the work costs me too much, and I have relied too much on my being strong enough to stand it.

What the doctor tells me is that I absolutely must *take better care of myself*, and until I feel stronger I must take more rest.

It is an *absolute* breakdown.

Now I have made it worse by smoking a great deal, which I did the more because then one does not feel an empty stomach so much. . . .

What we must do, and where the greatest trouble lies, is this. To pay the models oneself is too great a burden; as long as one hasn't enough money, one must use the opportunities offered by the studios like those of Verlat or Cormon. And one must live in the artists' world, and work at the clubs where one shares the cost of the models. . . .

For speaking of Cormon, I think he would tell me much the same thing as Verlat, namely that I must draw from the nude or plaster casts for a year, just because I have always been drawing from life. . . .

Drawing in itself, the technique of it, comes easily enough to me. I am beginning to do it like writing, with the same ease. . . . (449, 3 Feb. 1886.)

I decidedly want to tell you that it would make me feel much better if you would approve of my coming to Paris much earlier than June or July. The more I think about it, the more anxious I am to do so.

Just think, if all goes well, and if I had good food, etc., all that time, which certainly will leave something to be desired, even in that case it will take about six months before I shall have recovered entirely. . . .

If I rent a garret in Paris, and bring my paintbox and drawing materials with me, then I can finish what is most pressing at once – those studies from the ancients, which certainly will help me a great deal when I go to Cormon's. I can go and draw either at the Louvre or at the Ecole des Beaux-Arts. . . .

After all I am glad I went to the academy, for the very reason that I have abundant opportunity to observe the results of *prendre par le contour*.

For that is what they do systematically, and that is why they nag me. 'First make a contour, your contour isn't right; I won't correct it if you do your modelling before having seriously fixed your contour.'

You see that it always comes to the same thing. And now you ought to see how flat, how lifeless and how insipid the results of that system are; oh, I can tell you I am very glad just to be able to see it close up. Like David, or even worse, like Pieneman in full bloom. I wanted to say at least twenty-five times, 'Your contour is a cheat, etc.'; but I have not thought it worth while to quarrel. Yet I irritate them even though I don't say anything; and they, me. . . .

They go so far as to say, 'Colour and modelling aren't much, one can learn that very quickly, it's the contour that is essential and the most difficult.' . . .

Just yesterday I finished the drawing I made for the evening class's competition. It is the figure of Germanicus that you know. Well, I am sure I shall place last, because all the drawings of the others are exactly alike, and mine is absolutely different. But I saw how that drawing they will think best was made. I was sitting just behind it, and it is correct, it is whatever you like, but it is *dead*, and that's what all the drawings I saw are. . . . (452, Feb. 1886.)

93 Vincent's short and turbulent involvement with the Antwerp Academy ended with the unanimous decision of the professorial board to send him back to repeat the elementary course. The decision was registered on 31 March, by which time he had left; so it seems unlikely that, as some have supposed, this humiliating decision prompted his departure. In any case, the value of his own inventions was confirmed to him by the opposition he had experienced.

In the face of apparently evasive answers from Theo, Vincent pursued the idea of coming to Paris, constantly varying the details of his proposals: should they put off the idea of living together, renting a separate attic for Vincent? Or should they share an apartment? (To which he added suggestions on how to divide it up.) He would like them to work, and think, together, even share a regular woman; and so on. It seems pointless to analyse in rational terms a decision which came to emotional fruition in sickness, exhaustion and grinding poverty.

Without a positive response from Theo, Vincent did the only thing that could advance his plans: he took a train to Paris.

Do not be cross with me for having come all at once like this; I have thought about it so much, and I believe that in this way we shall save time. Shall be at the Louvre from midday on or sooner if you like.

Please let me know at what time you could come to the Salle Carrée. As for the expenses, I tell you again, this comes to the same thing. I have some money left, of course, and I want to speak to you before I spend any of it. We'll fix things up, you'll see.

So, come as soon as possible. (459, early Mar. 1886, F.)

The famous brief letter Vincent wrote at the Gare du Nord and sent round to Goupil by messenger marks the beginning of a period of almost two years for which the kind of documentation which is otherwise available in such profusion, both before and afterwards, is all but lacking. The period therefore provides instructive examples of the kind of problems that occur when only the actual works of art – the objects which, after all, are of paramount and essential importance – are available.

The phase when Vincent heard a lot about the Impressionists, but did not know them, was not past. He now became familiar with the movement through what he saw in Theo's gallery and during his visits to art galleries, through the enthusiasm for Japonaiserie, and through contacts with artists whose work formed the sequel to Impressionism: Georges Seurat, Paul Signac, Emile Bernard, Emile Anquetin, Louis Angrand.

His arrival did not make life any easier for Theo, as the latter's friend Andries Bonger reported in his letters home.

. . . Did I tell you that Van Gogh has moved to Montmartre? They now have a big, spacious apartment (by Parisian standards) and their own household. They are now keeping their own cook *in optima forma*. Theo is still looking frightfully ill; he literally has no face left at all. The poor fellow has many cares. Moreover, his brother is making life rather a burden to him, and reproaches him with all kinds of things of which he is quite innocent. . . . (Andries Bonger to Bonger family, 462a, 23 June 1886.)

. . . It now appears that Theo's brother is here for good, at least for three years, in order to work in the painter Cormon's studio. I think I told you in the summer what a queer life this brother has led. The man hasn't the slightest notion of social conditions. He is always quarrelling with everybody. Consequently Theo has a lot of trouble getting along with him. (Andries Bonger to Bonger family, 462a, 1886.)

Vincent stayed only three or four months with Cormon. His letter to the young English painter Horace Mann Livens, who was studying in Antwerp, mentions that he had been obliged to give up figure painting entirely. *109*

Since I am here in Paris I have very often thought of yourself and work. You will remember that I liked your colour, your ideas on art and literature and I add, most of all your personality. I have already before now thought that I ought to let you know what I was doing where I was. But what refrained me was that I find living in Paris is much dearer than in Antwerp and not knowing what your circumstances are I dare not say come over to Paris from Antwerp without warning you that it costs one dearer, and that if poor, one has to suffer many things – as you may imagine – . But on the other hand there is more chance of selling. There is also a good chance of exchanging pictures with other artists.

In one word, with much energy, with a sincere personal feeling of colour in nature I would say an artist can get on here notwithstanding the many obstructions. And I intend remaining here still longer.

There is much to be seen here – for instance Delacroix, to name only one master. In Antwerp I did not even know what the impressionists were, now I have seen them and though *not* being one of the club yet I have much admired certain impressionists' pictures – *Degas* nude figure – *Claude Monet* landscape.

And now for what regards what I myself have been doing, I have lacked money for paying models else I had entirely given myself to figure painting. But I have made a series of colour studies in painting, simply flowers, red poppies, blue corn flowers and myosotys, white and rose roses, yellow chrysanthemums – seeking oppositions of blue with orange, red and green, yellow and violet seeking *les tons rompus et neutres* to harmonize brutal extremes. Trying to render intense colour and not a grey harmony.

Now after these gymnastics I lately did two heads which I dare say are better in light and colour than those I did before.

So as we said at the time: in *colour* seeking *life* the true drawing is modelling with colour.

I did a dozen landscapes too, frankly *green* frankly *blue*.

And so I am struggling for life and progress in art. . . .

[PS.] With regard my chances of sale look here, they are certainly not much but still *I do have* a beginning.

At the present moment I have found four dealers who have exhibited studies of mine. And I have exchanged studies with many artists.

Now the prices are 50 francs. Certainly not much – but – as far as I can see one must sell cheap to rise and even at costing price. And mind my dear fellow, Paris is Paris. There is but one Paris and however hard living may be here, and if it became worse and harder even – the french air clears up the brain and does good – a world of good.

I have been in Cormons studio for three or four months but I did not find that so useful as I had expected it to be. It may be my fault however, anyhow I left there too as I left Antwerp and since I worked alone, and fancy that since I feel my own self more.

Trade is slow here. The great dealers sell Millet, Delacroix, Corot, Daubigny, Dupré, a few other masters at exorbitant prices. They do little or nothing for young artists. The second class dealers contrariwise sell those at very low prices. If I asked more I would do nothing, I fancy. However I have faith in colour. Even with regards the price the public will pay for it in the long run. But for the present things are awfully hard. Therefore let anyone who risks to go over here consider there is no laying on roses at all.

What is to be gained is *progress* and what the deuce that is, it is to be found here. I dare say as certain anyone who has a solid position elsewhere let him stay where he is. But for adventurers as myself, I think they lose nothing in risking more. Especially as in my case I am not an adventurer by choice but by fate, and feeling nowhere so much myself a stranger as in my family and country. – Kindly remember me to your landlady Mrs Roosmalen and say her that if she will exhibit something of my work I will send her a small picture of mine. (Vincent to H.M. Livens, 459a, Aug.–Oct. 1886, e.)

Emile Bernard wrote to the poet and critic Albert Aurier two months later, giving some information about Vincent's approach to life studies. It is certain that Bernard caused dissension at Cormon's studio and took part in a campaign against Cormon, who totally rejected the new colour theories.

After writing to his mother on 12 January 1886 that Vincent – then still in Antwerp – was going to concentrate on portraiture, Theo was not able until eleven months later to report that Vincent had really begun to paint portraits, 'which have turned out well, but he always does it for nothing! It is a pity he is not developing any inclination to earn some money, for if he wanted to he could probably manage; but one cannot change people'. In March 1887 Theo wrote to Cor, the brother who was working as a labourer on the construction of the Eiffel Tower:

V. is continuing to study and he is working with talent. It is a pity though that his character is so against him. In the long run it is really impossible to get on with him. When he came here last year he was certainly difficult, but I thought there was some improvement all the same. Now he is his old self again and you simply cannot argue with him. This does not make things pleasant for me at home, and I am hoping for a change. There will probably be one, but it is unfortunate for him, since it would have been better for both of us if we had co-operated. (Theo to Cor, 11 Mar. 1887.)

While still in this mood, Theo declared his love to Dries Bonger's sister Jo; and relations between him and Vincent seem thereafter to have very markedly improved.

... We have made our peace, because there was no point in going on as we were. I hope it will last. For the time being there will be no changes and I am glad of it. For me it would have been strange to be living on my own again, and he would not have gained anything either. *I* asked him to stay. It may seem strange to you after what I wrote to you recently – but it is not weakness on my part, and since I am feeling much stronger than I did last winter I am full of hope that I shall be able to bring about an improvement in our relations. ... (Theo to Wil, 25 April 1887.)

The improvement in their relations was so great that they were both surprised to find how strong a bond there was between them. More than two years later Vincent even admitted to his mother from Saint-Rémy (letter 619), 'It is a good thing that I did not stay in Paris, for we, he and I, would have become too interested in each other'.

It is unfortunate that the more sensational aspects of the first difficult year, and the wreck of Theo's social life because of Vincent's boorishness, have had more publicity – as if they referred to the whole period – than has the second year when there was peace between them and a deep, mysterious attachment.

In an undated letter Vincent sent to Wil in 1887 (W1) there is evidence to show that it must have been written after Theo's visit to Holland in July–August. According to Vincent, Theo's sickly appearance on his return was largely accounted for by 'presumably a less cordial welcome from acquaintances and friends'. By way of allegory he referred to the germinating capacity inherent in every human being as in a grain of corn. 'Life is germination. The love in us is what the germinating capacity is in corn'. Vincent was certainly referring to Theo's love for Jo, which had met with little response in Amsterdam. He was more candid about himself when admitting to Wil that in Paris he had been involved in, 'not very decorous love affairs from which he usually extricated himself "ignominiously"' and recalled the days when he ought to have been in love but instead 'was absorbed in religious and socialistic devotions'.

Overall the Paris part of Van Gogh's oeuvre makes a less unified impression than the work produced in Brabant, but it is a more direct reflection of the vibrant, vital environment of painters who were roughly his contemporaries. The direct stimuli provided by Millet, Israëls, Mauve, De Groux and the English illustrators disappeared, and the painter of peasants donned a gentleman's suit except when he was working.

Van Gogh's initiation to Impressionism took place in 1886 only, his first year in Paris. Here, we believe, Paul Signac, ten years younger than he, was a *121* support to Vincent and his work even before 1887, when they worked out of doors at Asnières together until the end of May. Signac was well informed, and had known Seurat and Guillaumin since 1884, and Pissarro since 1885. Seurat, it seems, was more difficult for Vincent to approach. Vincent rated him highly, but knew himself well enough to realize that his own nature was the very opposite of Seurat's rational systematics. In his own evolution he fought shy of reducing his inventions to formulas which might then develop into mannerisms. It would be hard to call Van Gogh spontaneous in his work – his passion, his fury was the release of long-pent-up emotional energy. Manet, Renoir and above all Monet meant a great deal to him, but even so it would have been unthinkable for him to wish, as Monet did, to paint a series of impressions of the light on a cathedral at set times or in successive seasons.

Van Gogh's reservations about Impressionism were the result not only of his own firm roots in earlier nineteenth-century traditions but of his mistrust of the momentary 'impression', with its implication of passivity in experiencing the passing of time, the flowing of water, the drifting of the clouds. Vincent's melancholy was an active one, and each disappointment, as well as each success, activated a psychic energy. In his way of observing things, each moment was always linked to all kinds of previous moments. He came to regard himself as an Impressionist, because the term was synonymous with modernity in art; but he always looked beyond observation to the importance of imagination. As he was to write to Bernard from Arles:

... Sometimes I regret that I cannot make up my mind to work more at home and extempore. The imagination is certainly a faculty which we must develop, one which alone can lead us to the creation of a more exalting and consoling nature than the single brief glance at reality – which in our sight is ever changing, passing life a flash of lightning – can let us perceive. ... (Vincent to Emile Bernard, B3, April 1888, F.)

The most characteristic works Van Gogh produced in Paris are the self-portraits which – in the metropolis with all its exciting distractions – were the outcome of his need to keep an eye on himself both literally and figuratively. The problem whether several small portraits were painted in Paris or elsewhere will not be dealt with here. The style of painting reveals not only all the technical phases he passed through in the course of those two years, but also all the phases of his physical condition. The 'mirror test' remained indispensable to him until well into his Saint-Rémy period. Since Antwerp, and perhaps before, he had been looking at himself, even when he was not painting, like a doctor who mercilessly diagnoses his own condition. Such scrutiny went beyond the self-questioning of an artist immediately absorbed by the colour problem facing him on his palette and on the canvas. A summing-up of the final results conveys some detachment: 'My own adventures are restricted chiefly to making swift progress toward growing into a little old man, you know, with wrinkles, and a tough beard and a number of false teeth, and so on. But what does it matter? I have a dirty and hard profession ...' (W1, summer-autumn 1887).

Alongside the self-portraits there are several portraits of acquaintances in which the brushwork reaches the same pitch of intensity (Tanguy, Reid, Segatori); perhaps the most Impressionistic works of the period are the suburban landscapes. So far, there was no debt to the Cloisonnists.

By juxtaposing touches of contrasting colour in the *Self-portrait with Easel*, in certain sections of the Segatori portrait, and in one of the Tanguy portraits, Vincent created effects which would be hard to parallel in works of this period by Monet, or Renoir, or Signac. Perhaps rather too barbaric for French taste, these works reach a level of achievement which Vincent himself rarely surpassed even at Arles. They demonstrate that even without a close collaboration with Gauguin, such as was to take place during the autumn of 1888 at Arles, Vincent could already produce flat effects and find inspiration in the actual material of the paint itself, thus reducing the model to a secondary importance. One has only to compare the lap of the figure in *La Berceuse* (Arles, 1889) with that in *Segatori* (Paris, 1887), who is in the same pose, to see that, both in the emotive and the compositional use of colour, the later work is inferior to the earlier. The *Berceuse* is seated in front of a real background, a papered wall. *Segatori* has no background but a violent yellow surface which is

Self-portrait, 1887.

sometimes, we believe wrongly, considered to be an imitation of crinkly Japanese paper (*crépon*). This is neither paper nor wall, but a fantasy in yellow.

In Paris he paid repeated visits to Samuel Bing's shop to buy such Japanese colour woodcuts as were within his and Theo's means. By way of experiment he produced some reinterpretations of these works in oils. This enabled him to study the compositions in further detail, and in relation to his own ideas of colour, while transforming the graphic and material lightness of the originals into a totally Western, that is to say heavier, effect. The Japanese influence was not to mature until Arles, where there is little trace of Japanese subject matter in his work, but where he associated Japan with a kind of clarity and light that he could no longer call 'Impressionist'. His own imagination, in this sense, had become Japanese, and he was fascinated by such hints as he found in writers like Pierre Loti of the nature of Japanese, and in particular Zen Buddhist, thought and religion. He came to associate Japanese art with speed and spontaneity of execution, and to produce reed-pen drawings that are markedly Japanese in technique rather than subject matter.

The feelings with which Vincent left Paris were dangerously affected, if not yet dominated, by his sense of not having really lived, of *l'existence manquée*.

133–135

136–138

149–51

Thank you for your letter and what it contained. It depresses me to think that even when it's a success, painting never pays back what it costs.

I was touched by what you wrote about home – 'They are fairly well but still it is sad to see them.' A dozen years ago you would have sworn that at any rate the family would always prosper and get on. It would be a great satisfaction to Mother if your marriage came off, and for the sake of your health and your work you ought not to remain single.

As for me – I feel I am losing the desire for marriage and children, and now and then it saddens me that I should be feeling like that at thirty-five, just when it should be the opposite. And sometimes I have a grudge against this rotten painting. It was Richepin who said somewhere: 'The love of art makes one lose real love.' I think that is terribly true, but on the other hand real love makes you disgusted with art.

And at times I already feel old and broken, and yet still enough of a lover not to be a real enthusiast for painting. One must have ambition in order to succeed, and ambition seems to be absurd. I don't know what will come of it; above all I should like to be less of a burden to you – and that is not impossible in the future – for I hope to make such progress that you will be able to show my stuff boldly without compromising yourself.

And then I will take myself off somewhere down south, to get away from the sight of so many painters that disgust me as men. . . . (462, July–Aug. 1887, F.)

Reports of eccentric behaviour on Vincent's part, mostly late and unverifiable, serve only to underline the scarcity of clear biographical information about this phase in his life. It is tantalizing to know so little about the circles in which Vincent moved without Theo. What, for instance, was the role of the mysterious Comtesse de la Boissière and her daughter, of Asnières?

In any case, the relationship between the two brothers, which had been extremely strained, was fully restored by the time Vincent decided to leave Paris early in 1888. He was exhausted, nearly an alcoholic, and once more ready for a complete change of scene. He fitted in one visit to Seurat's studio before he left.

. . . Vincent left for the South last Sunday. He is going first to Arles to orient himself and then probably to Marseilles. . . . Years of worry and adversity have not made him any stronger and he felt a definite need to be in a more temperate climate. . . . I believe it will certainly do his health good and will also benefit his work. When he came here two years ago I did not think we would become so attached to each other, but the flat feels decidedly empty now that I am on my own again. If I find someone to live with I shall do so, but it is not easy to replace a person like Vincent. His knowledge and clear perception of the world are incredible. I am therefore convinced that if he has a few more years to live, he will make a name for himself. Through him, I came into contact with many painters among whom he is greatly respected. He is one of the champions of new ideas – or rather, as there is nothing new under the sun, of the regeneration of old ideas which have been corrupted by routine and have lost their colour. Furthermore, he has such a great heart that he is always trying to do something for others. So much the worse for those who do not know him or want to understand him. . . . (Theo to Wil, 24/26 Feb. 1888.)

91 The *Maris Stella* window, Andrieskerk, Antwerp, 16th century

After the excitement of his farewell to the old masters in Amsterdam, he wrote from Antwerp, where he arrived late in 1885, with less emotion about paintings and with more animation about the life of the port. But in the Andrieskerk in Antwerp, in January 1886, Vincent was impressed by a sixteenth-century window (the earliest one in the church, although he probably did not know this). The virgin is shown as *Maris Stella*, the Star of the Sea, protectress of mariners in distress. The symbolism of shipwreck, a recurrent element in other letters, is hidden in Vincent's account of this window to Theo, which reflects rather his close study of colour and colour theory: 'There is a painted window which I think superb – very, very curious. A beach, a green sea with a castle on the rocks, a sparkling blue sky of the most beautiful tones of blue, greenish, whitish, deeper, higher of tone. An enormous three-master, quaint and phantasmal, stands out against the sky, diffusion everywhere, light in the dark, dark in the light. In the blue a figure of the Holy Virgin, bright yellow, white, orange. Higher up the window reappears dark green, with black, with fiery red.'

Antwerp

Right:
96 Charles de Groux. *Benedicite*, 1861
Along with the same Antwerp artist's *The Paupers' Bench*, this was a favourite with Van Gogh from a very early age. Working on his own *The Potato Eaters* (*48*), and later, Vincent's memory of De Groux did not fade.

97 Henri de Braekeleer. *Baron Leys' Dining-room*, 1869
Henri Leys was a famous painter in his time, who moved from history (subjects from the Middle Ages) to daily life,

On arriving in Antwerp, Vincent was not in a hurry to go to the academy. Only on 18 January 1886 did he register for an evening class in drawing from the Antique (plaster casts) and the painting class (444).

Left, above:
92 The house where Vincent lodged, in Beeldekenstraat (Rue des Images)
Left:
93 Academie Royale des Beaux-Arts, Antwerp
Top:
94 Henri Leys. *Het Steen, Antwerp*
Above:
95 *The Marketplace, Antwerp*, 18 December 1885.

working in a sober and far from anecdotal style. Vincent liked his work, as is proved by the fact that his first visit in Antwerp was to Leys' dining-room, with its well-known murals by Leys himself. He was disappointed: 'Frescoes can last for centuries, but these are already faded considerably' (436). He nevertheless, curiously, did not give Leys up: 'after all, it is superb'. Another realist painter who interested Vincent in particular was Leys' nephew, Henri de Braekeleer. Vincent praised his 'curious . . . endeavour to be literally true'.

Flemish models

98 Peter Paul Rubens. *St Theresa Saving Bernardo de Mendoza from Purgatory* (detail), c.1638
Vincent was occupied in Antwerp with research into technical problems and other artists' handling of them. He was highly critical of Rubens from a psychological point of view, but interested by his use of colour, particularly in the flesh tones of this picture, modelled 'with streaks of pure red .... I don't look at those which are admired most. I look for fragments, like, for instance, those blonde heads in *St Theresa*' (439).

99 *Head of a Woman*, December 1885
'I have made two fairly big heads ... then also a study of a woman. In the woman's portrait I have brought lighter tones into the flesh, white tinted with carmine, vermilion, yellow, and a light background of grey-yellow' (439).

100 *Portrait of a Woman*, early Dec. 1885
Vincent was always seeing magnificent heads in Antwerp, and enjoyed his visits to the docks, where he studied the townspeople as well as those who came from the ships. He wanted to earn some money by doing portraits, but the reverse happened: he spent so much on paying models that he had not enough left to buy food.

133

101 Eugène Delacroix. *Study for the Panel 'War' on the Ceiling of the Salon du Roi, Palais Bourbon*, 1833–38

102 *Women Dancing*, early Dec. 1885

'Antwerp is beautiful in colour, and is worth while just for the subjects. One evening I saw a sailors' dance at the docks; . . . they behaved quite decently . . . nobody was drunk. Handsome girls, a figure that struck me as a splendid Jordaens or Velásquez, or Goya – was one in black silk, most likely a barmaid or such, with an ugly and irregular face, but lively and piquant *à la* Frans Hals' (438). He drew them in motion, with the energy of his admired Delacroix.

From Delacroix to Japan

103 *Female Nude*, Jan. 1886
Vincent now began to work at the Academy and in evening life classes. 'After having drawn for years from fully clothed models, to see the nude again . . .' (447). He remembered Géricault, Gros, Delacroix, and set out to draw 'like the Greeks': from the centre, the nucleus, not the contour.

104 Oko Kunisada II. *Two Girls Bathing*, 1868
It was in Antwerp that Vincent became actively interested in Japanese colour prints, which he bought on a small scale and without realizing at first that they were to have an increasing influence on his whole development. In Antwerp, *Japonisme* was in the air; the artist Henry van de Velde and the writer Max Elskamp were bringing out their *L'Eventail japonais*. There, too, Vincent bought this print.

105 Skull with Burning Cigarette, Dec. 1885

106 Félicien Rops. *The Husbands' Train*; *The Death of the Sinner*

107 *Hanging Skeleton and Black Cat*, Dec. 1885–Jan. 1886

An artist hungry for technical and anatomical knowledge, as Van Gogh was, inevitably studies the skeleton: and here 'the drawing of the mass instead of outlines' (449) takes on a macabre twist. It was in Antwerp in 1885 that Vincent painted the curious and unexplained *Skull with Burning Cigarette*, a striking *memento mori* that is not without a connection with his own state: faint, overstrained, undernourished. Its black humour might also have a link with what he remembered and admired of the work of Félicien Rops, the Belgian illustrator; in 1873 he possessed a copy of Rops's *Uilenspiegel*, a kind of satirical-critical *Journal des arts*. Rops would have made a good illustrator of Baudelaire.

108 Rue Lepic, Montmartre, late 19th c.
Theo moved to a new apartment, at No.
54 rue Lepic, soon after Vincent's sudden
arrival in 1886.

109 Salon of the painter Fernand Cormon,
Paris
Leaving aside the vexed question of when
Vincent entered Cormon's studio, we
learn from Toulouse-Lautrec's friend
Gauzi that Vincent was 'an excellent
comrade but had to be left in peace'.
Cormon was not a success with his young
avant-garde pupils, but he did provide a
centre where Van Gogh could make
friends (Bernard, Lautrec, Russell,
Hartrick).

Paris at last

110 Jean-François Raffaelli. View of Montmartre
We recognize in this fine etching, owned by Theo, and the work of an artist highly appreciated by Van Gogh, the diagonal line of the slope of the hill common to many works of the time (Van Gogh, Angrand, Gauguin).

111 John P. Russell. *Vincent van Gogh,* Nov. 1886
Russell, a wealthy Australian, was to keep in touch with Vincent after he left Paris. He bought many Impressionist works, and received many drawings from Vincent.

112 Meyer de Haan. *Theo van Gogh, c.* 1889
Meyer de Haan, a Dutch painter, moved in with Theo after Vincent left Paris for Arles in 1888 (as did another Dutch artist, Joseph Isaäcson). As long as he could afford it, De Haan remained a financial support to his friend Gauguin; he was a man of a philosophical and religious turn of mind, who did his best work as an artist in Brittany with Gauguin.

113 Old Boots (*A Pair of Boots*), late 1886
This famous painting has elicited much symbolic interpretation on the lines that these are two brothers, worn down by life, but one standing firmer than the other; it has also been pointed out that the boots are not a pair. The image is so powerful as to cause most attempts to verbalize it to seem beside the point

Parisian mirror

114 Henri de Toulouse-Lautrec. *Vincent van Gogh*, 1886

115 Self-portrait with Easel, early 1888

116 Self-portrait with Grey Felt Hat, summer 1887

It was at the café Le Tambourin, in the Boulevard de Clichy, that Lautrec is said to have drawn this pastel of Vincent (*left-hand page*). All the man's energy and genius are expressed in the leonine tension of his pose. This is the most impressive image of Vincent in Paris as an outsider saw him, recognizably the man whom we see in the self-portraits.

117 Self-portrait, autumn 1887

These three self-portraits, taken together with the pastel by Lautrec, provide a close-up view of Vincent's forced existence in Paris, which brought him to the point of total exhaustion, 'almost an invalid and almost a drunkard' (544a). The last dates from early in 1888, just before he left; it is 'the face of death', painted in the mirror (W7).

141

Impressions at Theo's

118 Claude Monet. *Four Boats in Winter Quarters, Etretat,* 1885
Vincent greatly admired Monet, and among the works he remembered seeing at Theo's this seems particularly calculated to appeal to him, with its thick impasto and strong structural brush strokes.

119 Louis Anquetin. *Avenue de Clichy,* 1887
This view, with its leafless trees and warmly clad figures, was presumably painted in the autumn, and Vincent saw it 'not too many months before his departure from Paris' (B. Welsh-Ovcharov, *Vincent van Gogh: his Paris Period*, Utrecht 1976).

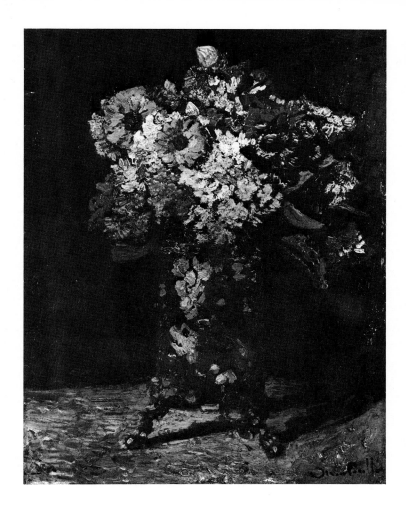

120 Adolphe Monticelli. *Vase of Flowers,*
1875–80
A work owned by Theo and praised by
Vincent. Vincent's relationship to the
works of Monticelli was a curious one.
Vincent analysed his passion for colour
with all his knowledge of Delacroix,
considering Monticelli also as a disciple.
He often discussed Monticelli's
personality, and identified himself with his
fate, which was to be underestimated as a
painter and slandered as a drunkard.

121 Paul Signac. *Still-life with*
Maupassant's Book 'Au Soleil', dated 1883
Vincent's firm friendship with Signac was
exceptional in that there was never a
quarrel between them. This still-life must
have had a strong influence on Vincent,
antedating that of the Montmartre views
by Signac which Rewald refers to, and
which were painted between 1884 and
1887. Signac was a source of information
for Vincent concerning Pontillist theory
and technique (Seurat himself being
difficult to approach).

Woman

122 Plaster Statuette, 1886–87
Less brutal than the few nudes we have that were done from life, the numerous ones done from casts are rarely the kind of academic work that the Antwerp professors could have acknowledged.

123 Nude Woman on a Bed, 1887
There is a drawing (F1404) for this, one of very few extant nudes by Van Gogh; there is a suggestion that after his death many were destroyed. Its character is exotic, even bestial.

124 The Italian Woman, with Carnations (La Segatori), winter 1887–88
This portrait of Agostina Segatori (proprietress of the Tambourin, with whom Vincent is said to have had an affair) is one of the peaks of Van Gogh's Paris achievement. We can easily forget the sitter, and the suggestions of folk art, Japan, and a few fellow painters (Monticelli, Guillaumin). Vincent creates here a modern, and greatly intensified, symphonic structure of contrasting coloured brush strokes, the synthesis of all he had absorbed since Nuenen concerning new possibilities for colour.

Asnières

125 Asnières, on the first loop of the Seine north of Paris, early 1887. Van Gogh (seen from behind) and Emile Bernard discuss the endless problems of art.

126 *Riverside Walk near Asnières*, early summer 1887
This Impressionistic style, almost immaterial in effect, with points of colour – *pointilles* – represents a very brief phase in Van Gogh's painting, although Impressionistic influences lasted longer in his drawing.

127 *Factory near the Pont de Clichy, Asnières*, summer 1887
The same year and season as *126*, but a great contrast: long, clear, rhythmical strokes, structuring and accentuating the forms; here and there a resemblance to Signac.

Right:
128 Bridge at Asnières, late 19th c.
It was the landscape itself that attracted the artists, rather than any mutual influence; they painted the same scenes consecutively, not concurrently. Photographs do not always make illuminating comparisons with paintings; but here the photograph, with the train on the bridge, shows how impressive were the compositional elements provided by these semi-artificial landscapes.

129 Emile Bernard. *Bridge at Asnières*, autumn 1887

130 Restaurant de la Sirène, Asnières, early summer 1887
Vincent never follows the Pointillist technique strictly,
setting up a static pattern of dots, but expresses a
movement that is between drawing and painting.

131 Bathing Place on the Seine, Asnières, summer 1887
An example of Vincent's use of the Manet-like, strong
structural brush stroke.

132 Factories at Asnières Seen from the Quai de Clichy,
summer 1887
Emile Bernard lived at Asnières with his parents; and the
two artists often met Signac there during the spring of
1887. All faced the same influences: the leadership of Seurat
(strict Pointillism) and the flat colours and strong outlines
derived from the Japanese (Anquetin). Asnières satisfied
Vincent's interest in landscape and in the semi-industrial
suburban scene (the *banlieue*).

Japan in Paris

133 Utagawa Kuniyoshi. *Portrait of a Woman Viewing Flowers, with an Inset of Local Industry, Bitchu Province*, 1852 The clean-cut, flat silhouette and the pose have a striking similarity to one of the two portraits of Madame Ginoux, painted in Arles (155), which was painted with 'Japanese' speed in less than an hour. The use of Japanese prints in the background is itself a Japanese practice.

Opposite page:
134 Utagawa Hiroshige. *Plum Trees in Flower,* 1857
135 Utagawa Hiroshige. *Shower on the Ohashi Bridge near Ataka,* 1857

This page:
136 *Flowering Plum Tree,* first half 1887
137 *The Bridge in the Rain,* summer 1887

Vincent possessed twelve prints from the series *Famous Places in Edo*; and the two oil paintings on the right are enlarged copies, made by squaring up the originals, and with added Japanese lettering (including, it is said, a clearly legible advertisement for a brothel).

138 Japonaiserie: Oiran, summer 1887
After a print, *The Actor,* by Kesai Yeisen (1790–1848), with variations Van Gogh took from various sources (including *Paris illustré*). His copies of Japanese prints are typical Western interpretations, with line subordinated to colour.

139 Père Tanguy, autumn 1887
A larger and more detailed version (F636) has in the
background only Japanese prints. This one, the earlier, has
also an autumn still-life by Van Gogh himself (F383); here,
the sitter has more tension and vitality, the expression is
more direct.

IV

ARLES

*'Something greater than I,
which is my life – the power to create'*

1888–1889 Arles

Vincent's output in Arles is largely a continuation of the best work he had done in his last few months in Paris. Colour now came to dominate more and more; in his drawings the line improved immensely, particularly when drawn with a reed pen (a Japanese tool); the Impressionist influence waned. He developed the idea of a small collective of artists who might solve common problems in art or life more easily than an individual working alone. With characteristic generosity and drive, he proposed to use his rented Maison Jaune in Arles as a modest centre of work and debate for himself and guests. The idea began to take shape with the longed-for arrival of Gauguin in October 1888, and ended in disaster at Christmas with Gauguin's hasty departure and Vincent's admission to the local hospital. Vincent failed to save his health, but succeeded in rescuing his work from defeat and ruin. The interest in religion that had disappeared in Paris, as well as an increasing interest in the possibility of life after death, were to complicate his spiritual life to a considerable degree.

... When I left you at the station to go south, very miserable, almost an invalid and almost a drunkard, I still felt vaguely that we had put our very heart into our discussions with so many interesting people and artists that winter, but I hadn't the courage to hope.

After continued efforts on your part and mine, now at last something is beginning to show on the horizon: Hope. ... (544a, 29 Sept. 1888, F.)

196

He had abandoned the abject image of himself as a dog, and now likened himself and his friends to worn-out cab horses.

But, old boy, you know, I feel as though I were in Japan – I say no more than that, and mind, I haven't seen anything in its usual splendour yet.

That's why – even although I'm vexed that just now expenses are heavy and the pictures worthless – that's why I don't despair of the future success of this idea of a long sojourn in the Midi.

Here I am seeing new things, I am learning, and if I take it easy, my body doesn't refuse to function.

For many reasons I should like to get some sort of little retreat, where the poor cab horses of Paris – that is, you and several of our friends, the poor impressionists – could go out to pasture when they get too beat up.

I was present at the inquiry into a crime committed at the door of a brothel here; two Italians killed two Zouaves. I seized the opportunity to go into one of the brothels in a small street called 'des ricolettes'.

That is the extent of my amorous adventures among the Arlésiennes. The mob *all but* (the Southerner, like Tartarin, being more energetic in good intentions than in action) – the mob, I repeat, all but lynched the murderers confined in the town hall, but in retaliation all the Italians – men and women, the Savoyard monkeys included – have been forced to leave town.

I should not have told you about this, except that it means I've seen the streets of this town full of excited crowds. And it was indeed a fine sight.

I made my last three studies with the perspective frame I told you about. I attach some importance to the use of the frame because it seems not unlikely to me that in the near future many artists will make use of it, just as the old German and Italian painters certainly did, and, as I am inclined to think, the Flemish too. The modern use of it may differ from the ancient practice, but in the same way isn't it true that in the process of painting in oils one gets very different effects today from those of the men who invented the process, Jan and Hubert van Eyck? And the moral of this is that it's my constant hope that I am not working for myself alone. I believe in the absolute necessity of a new art of colour, of design, and – of the artistic life. And if we work in that faith, it seems to me there is a chance that we do not hope in vain. ... (469, 17 Mar. 1888, F.)

Some of his work was accepted for the Salon des Indépendants in Paris. He insisted that his name be given as Vincent only, justifying this with the argument that it would be impossible for people to pronounce Van Gogh. However, this argument did not apply to the Netherlands and Belgium, where he had also regularly signed his works as Vincent. He had probably started doing so in Brabant to dissociate himself from his family. Vincent started a fashion among artists which has continued to this day.

. . . On the whole I'm very glad that [my works have] been put with the other impressionists.

But though it doesn't matter in the least this time, in the future my name ought to be put in the catalogue as I sign it on the canvas, namely Vincent and not Van Gogh, for the simple reason that they do not know how to pronounce the latter name here.

I return to you enclosed Tersteeg's and Russell's letters. It might perhaps be interesting to keep the artists' correspondence. . . .

[PS.] Paris doesn't pay: I'd be sorry to see the Seurats in a provincial museum or in a cellar, those pictures ought to stay in living hands – if only Tersteeg would. If three permanent exhibitions are started, there must be one great Seurat in Paris, one in London, and one in Marseilles. (471, 24 Mar. 1888, F.)

The news of Mauve's early death came as a blow to him. There was no rancour left about their erstwhile disagreements at The Hague. On the contrary, Vincent sent to his aunt Jet, Mauve's widow, the now popular *Flowering Tree, Souvenir of Mauve*, signed 'Vincent', although it was supposed first to have been signed 'Vincent Theo'. It is not known whether Theo had objected to the use of his name.

. . . I have been working on a size 20 canvas in the open air in an orchard, lilac ploughland, a reed fence, two pink peach trees against a sky of glorious blue and white. Probably the best landscape I have done. I had just brought it home when I received from our sister a Dutch notice in memory of Mauve, with his portrait (the portrait, very good), the text, poor and nothing in it, a pretty water colour. Something – I don't know what – took hold of me and brought a lump to my throat, and I wrote on my picture

SOUVENIR DE MAUVE
VINCENT THEO

and if you agree we two will send it, such as it is, to Mrs Mauve. I chose the best study I've painted here purposely; I don't know what they'll say about it at home, but that does not matter to us; it seemed to me that everything in memory of Mauve must be at once tender and very gay, and not a study in any graver key.

> '*O never think the dead are dead,*
> *So long as there are men alive,*
> *The dead will live, the dead will live.*'

That's how I feel it. Nothing sadder than that. . . . (472, 30/31 Mar. 1888, F.)

. . . The air here certainly does me good. I wish you could fill your lungs with it; one effect it has on me is comical enough – one small glass of brandy makes me tipsy here, so that as I don't have to fall back on stimulants to make my blood circulate, there is less strain on my constitution. The only thing is that my stomach has been terribly weak since I came here, but after all that's probably only a matter of time. I hope to make great progress this year, and indeed I need to. . . .

Mauve's death was a terrible blow to me. You will see that the pink peach trees were painted with a sort of passion.

I must also have a starry night with cypresses, or perhaps above all, a field of ripe corn; there are some wonderful nights here. I am in a continual fever of work. . . . (474, 9 Apr. 1888. F.)

Particularly in his letters from Arles, Van Gogh created, in words, an undefined environment for a strange continuity of thought which deviates totally from the rational discipline of continuity. It is not unlike a staccato played by a nervous violinist. There is also a simultaneity of memory and observation which constantly jostle each other. In the manuscripts of his letters acceleration and retardation are clearly visible, ignoring the rules of punctuation. The increases and decreases in the size of the writing follow a process of intense concentration and subsequent relaxation, as if he were trying to articulate a concept.

. . . I think there would be something to do here in portraits. Although the people are blankly ignorant of painting in general, they are much more artistic than in the North in their own persons and their manner of life. I have seen figures here quite as beautiful as those of Goya or Velásquez. They will put a touch of pink on a black frock, or devise a garment of white, yellow and pink, or else green and pink, or else *blue and yellow*, in which there is nothing to be altered from the artistic point of view. Seurat would find some very picturesque men's figures here in spite of their modern clothes.

Now, as for portraits, I am pretty sure they'd take the bait.

But first before I dare start along that line, I want my nerves steadier, and also to be settled in so that I could have people in my studio. And if I must tell you roughly what I figure it would take to get me quite well and acclimatized for good, it will mean a year, and to set me up completely, a cool thousand francs. If during the first year – the present year – I spend 100 francs on food and 100 francs on this house per month, you see there won't be a cent left in the budget for painting.

But at the end of that year I should have a decent establishment and my own health to show for it – of that I am sure. And in the meantime I should spend my time drawing every day, with two or three pictures a month besides.

In figuring what it would cost to set me up, I am also counting in a complete new set of linen and clothes and shoes.

And at the end of the year I should be a different man.

I should have a home of my own and the peace to get back my health. . . .

My poor Theo, our neurosis, etc., also comes from our way of life, which is a bit too artistic; but it is also a fatal inheritance, for in civilization the stock becomes enfeebled from one generation to the next. Take our sister Wil. She has never drunk or led a wild life, and yet we know a portrait of her in which she has the look of a madwoman. [*These last two sentences omitted in* CLVG.] If we want to face up to the true state of our own temperament we shall have to number ourselves among those who suffer from a neurosis whose origins lie far in the past. . . .

However, if we want to live and work, we must be very sensible and look after ourselves. Cold water, fresh air, simple good food, decent clothes, a decent bed, and no annoyances. And not to let oneself go with women, or with life that *is* life, as much as one would like to. . . . (481, 3/4 May 1888, F.)

. . . It is a filthy town this, with the old streets. As for the women of Arles that there's so much talk about – there is, isn't there? – do you want to know my real opinion of them? They are, no question about it, really charming, but no longer what they must have been. As things are now, they are more often like a Mignard than a Mantegna, for they are in their decadence. That doesn't prevent them from being beautiful – very beautiful, and I am talking now only of the type in the Roman style – rather boring and commonplace. But what exceptions there are!

There are women like a Fragonard and like a Renoir. And some that can't be labelled with anything that's been done yet in painting. The best thing to do would be to make portraits, all kinds of portraits of women and children. But I don't think that I am the man to do it. I'm not enough of a M. Bel Ami for that.

But I should be heartily glad if this Bel Ami of the Midi, which Monticelli was not – but was by way of being – whom I feel to be coming, though I know it isn't myself – I should be heartily glad, I say, if a kind of Guy de Maupassant in painting came along to paint the beautiful people and things here lightheartedly. As for me, I shall go on working and here and there among my work there will be things which will last, but who will be in figure painting what Claude Monet is in landscape? However, you must feel, as I do, that such a one will come. Rodin? He does not work in colour, he's not the one. But the painter of the future will be *a colourist such as has never yet existed*. Manet was working toward it, but as you know the impressionists have already got a stronger colour than Manet. But this painter who is to come – I can't imagine him living in little cafés, working away with a lot of false teeth, and going to the Zouaves' brothels, as I do. . . . (482, 3/4 May 1888, F.)

. . . We do not feel we are dying, but we do feel the truth that we are of small account, and that we are paying a hard price to be a link in the chain of artists, in health, in youth, in liberty, none of which we enjoy, any more than the cab horse that hauls a coachful of people out to enjoy the spring.

So what I wish for you; as for myself, is to succeed in getting back your health, because you must have that. That *Hope* by Puvis de Chavannes is so true. There is an art of the future, and *196* it is going to be so lovely and so young that even if we give up our youth for it, we must gain in serenity by it. Perhaps it is very silly to write all this, but I feel it so strongly; it seems to me that, like me, you have been suffering to see your youth pass away like a puff of smoke; but if it grows again, and comes to life in what you make, nothing has been lost, and the power to work is another youth. Take some pains then to get well, for we shall need your health. (489, *c.* 19 May 1888, F.)

[PS.] . . . So if it has come to this, that you have to travel around like this, with never any peace, it honestly kills any desire in me to get back my own ease of mind.

If you agree to these proposals, all right – but then ask these Goupils to take me on again, at my old wages, and take me with you on these journeys. People matter more than things, and the more trouble I take over pictures, the more pictures in themselves leave me cold. The reason why I try to make them is to be among the artists. You understand, it would make me wretched to be forcing you to make money. Rather, let's be together whatever happens. Where there's a will there's a way, and I think if you can get well now, you will be well for quite a number of years. But don't kill yourself now, either for me or for anybody else. You know the portrait of the elder Six, the man going away, his glove in his hand. Well, *live* until you go away like that; I can see you do so, married. You would carry it off well. Think it over, and consult [Dr] Gruby before you accept such a proposal. (492, *c.* 29 May 1888, F.)

I have thought of you [Gauguin] very often, and the reason why I did not write sooner is that I did not want to write empty phrases. The deal with Russell has not come off yet, but for all that Russell has bought some impressionists, e.g. Guillaumin and Bernard, so bide your time – he will come to it of his own accord, but after two refusals I could not possibly insist any longer, as the refusals also contained a promise for the future.

I wanted to let you know that I have just rented a four-room house here in Arles.

And that it would seem to me that if I could find another painter inclined to work in the South, and who, like myself, would be sufficiently absorbed in his work to be able to resign himself to living like a monk who goes to the brothel once a fortnight – who for the rest is tied up in his work, and not very willing to waste his time, it might be a good job. Being all alone, I am suffering a little under this isolation.

So I have often thought of telling you so frankly.

You know that my brother and I greatly appreciate your painting, and that we are most anxious to see you quietly settled down.

Now the fact is that my brother cannot send you money in Brittany and at the same time send me money in Provence. But are you willing to share with me here? If we combine, there may be enough for both of us, I am sure of it, in fact. Once having attacked the South, I don't see any reason to drop it.

I was ill when I came here, but now I am feeling better, and as a matter of fact, I am greatly attracted by the South, where working out-of-doors is possible nearly all the year round.

However, it seems to me that life is more expensive here, but on the other hand the chances of getting more pictures done are better. However this may be, if my brother were to send 250 francs a month for us both, we might share, should you care to come. Only in this case it would be necessary to have our meals at home as much as possible; we might engage some kind of charwoman for a few hours a day, so as to avoid all the expense of going to an inn.

And you would give my brother one picture a month; you could do what you like with the rest of your work. . . . (Vincent to Paul Gauguin, 494a, *c.* 5 June 1888, F.)

... If Gauguin were willing to join me, I think it would be a step forward for us. It would establish us squarely as the explorers of the South, and nobody could complain of that. I must manage to get the firmness of colouring that I got in the picture that kills the rest. ...

This last picture can bear the surroundings of red brick, with which my studio is paved. When I put it on the ground, with this background of red, *very red* brick, the colour of the picture does not become hollow or bleached. The country near Aix where Cézanne works is just the same as this, it is still the Crau. If coming home with my canvas, I say to myself, 'Look! I've got the very tones of old Cézanne!' I only mean that Cézanne like Zola is so absolutely part of the countryside, and knows it so intimately, that you must make the same calculations in your head to arrive at the same tones. Of course, if you saw them side by side, mine would hold their own, but there would be no resemblance. (497, 12–13 June 1888, F.)

141

161–62
147–48

He continued to work hard to make the Maison Jaune habitable at the lowest possible cost, painting sunflower decorations to welcome Gauguin. He was still pinning his hopes on the establishment of a centre for artists, although even he sometimes felt the idea was utopian. From time to time he went for longish excursions, for instance to the seaside at Saintes-Maries-de-la-Mer. A walk along the beach there inspired one of his wonderful brief description of ecstatic nocturnal experiences.

150–51

... One night I went for a walk by the sea along the empty shore. It was not gay, but neither was it sad – it was – beautiful. The deep blue sky was flecked with clouds of a blue deeper than the fundamental blue of intense cobalt, and others of a clearer blue, like the blue whiteness of the Milky Way. In the blue depth the stars were sparkling, greenish, yellow, white, pink, more brilliant, more sparklingly gemlike than at home – even in Paris: opals you might call them, emeralds, lapis lazuli, rubies, sapphires. The sea was very deep ultramarine – the shore a sort of violet and faint russet as I saw it, and on the dunes (they are about seventeen feet high) some bushes Prussian blue. ... (499, 22 June 1888, F.)

Despite repeated lapses into inactivity, his energies prevailed as a result of all he was seeing and inwardly experiencing of nature. These thoughts and sentiments may be summed up in one word, 'Japan'.

... I wish you could spend some time here, you would feel it after a while, one's sight changes: you see things with an eye more Japanese, you feel colour differently. The Japanese draw quickly, very quickly, like a lightning flash, because their nerves are finer, their feeling simpler.

I am convinced that I shall set my individuality free simply by staying on here.

I have only been here a few months, but tell me this – could I, in Paris have done the drawing of the boats *in an hour*? Even without the perspective frame, I do it now without measuring, just by letting my pen go. ...

Anquetin and Lautrec – I think – will not like what I am doing; there has been an article, it seems, in the *Revue Indépendante* on Anquetin, which called him the leader of a new trend, in which the Japanese influence is even more apparent. I have not read it, but anyway the leader of the Petit Boulevard is undoubtedly Seurat, and young Bernard has perhaps gone further in the Japanese style than Anquetin. Tell them that I have done a picture of boats, that and the *Pont de l'Anglais* could go to Anquetin. What Pissarro says is true, you most boldly exaggerate the effects of either harmony or discord which colours produce. It is the same as in drawing – accurate drawing, accurate colour, is perhaps not the essential thing to aim at, because the reflection of reality in a mirror, if it could be caught, colour and all, would not be a picture at all, no more than a photograph. ... (500, 23 June 1888, F.)

It is all too easy to overlook the way in which a person may be going through a crisis long before it leads to any specific act, and long before there is any reason for the outside world to intervene. The continual wane of Vincent's ambitions; his condition during harvest time when he devoted himself wholly to painting his theme and subsequently felt exhausted; the doubtful remedy he referred to; his sense of being old and broken before his time; all these add up to a kind of litany clearly indicating the destructive effect on a weak constitution of an excessive urge to create. The same process also included the lucid but sombre moments when Vincent summoned up supernatural images suggesting some form of life after death. These were dreams in which a longing for death lay barely concealed.

He kept returning to Monticelli, with whose irregularities he felt he had great affinity both as a man and as an artist.

... It certainly is a strange phenomenon that all artists, poets, musicians, painters, are unfortunate in material things – the happy ones as well – what you said lately about Guy de Maupassant is fresh proof of it. That brings up again the eternal question: Is the whole of life visible to us, or isn't it rather that this side of death we see only one hemisphere?

Painters – to take them alone – dead and buried speak to the next generation or to several succeeding generations through their work.

Is that all, or is there more to come? Perhaps death is not the hardest thing in a painter's life.

For my own part, I declare I know nothing whatever about it, but looking at the stars always makes me dream, as simply as I dream over the black dots representing towns and villages on a map. Why, I ask myself, shouldn't the shining dots of the sky be as accessible as the black dots on the map of France? Just as we take the train to get to Tarascon or Rouen, we take death to reach a star. One thing undoubtedly true in this reasoning is that we *cannot* get to a star while we are *alive*, any more than we can take the train when we are dead.

So to me it seems possible that cholera, gravel, tuberculosis and cancer are the celestial means of locomotion, just as steamboats, buses and railways are the terrestrial means. To die quietly of old age would be to go there on foot. ... (506, 1–3 Aug. 1888, F.)

... As for landscapes, I begin to find that some done more rapidly than ever are the best of what I do. For instance, the one I sent you the cartoon of, the harvest, and·the stacks too. It is true that I have to retouch the *whole* to rearrange the composition a bit, and to make the touch harmonious, but all the essential work was done in a single long sitting, and I change them as little as possible when I'm retouching.

But when I come home after a spell like that, I assure you my head is so tired that if that kind of work keeps recurring, as it has done since this harvest began, I become hopelessly absent-minded and incapable of heaps of ordinary things.

It is at times like these that the prospect of not being alone is not disagreeable.

And very often indeed I think of that excellent painter Monticelli – who they said was such a drinker, and off his head – when I come back myself from the mental labour of balancing the six essential colours, red – blue – yellow – orange – lilac – green. Sheer work and calculation, with one's mind strained to the utmost, like an actor on the stage in a difficult part, with a hundred things to think of at once in a single half hour.

After that, the only thing to bring ease and distraction, in my case and other people's too, is to stun oneself with a lot of drinking or heavy smoking. Not very virtuous, no doubt, but it's to return to the subject of Monticelli. I'd like to see a drunkard in front of a canvas or on the boards. It is too gross a lie, all the Roquette woman's malicious, Jesuitical slanders about Monticelli.

Monticelli, the logical colourist, able to pursue the most complicated calculations, subdivided according to the scales of tones that he was balancing, certainly overstrained his brain at this work, just as Delacroix did, and Richard Wagner. ... (507, *c.* 7 July 1888, F.)

In the meantime, aided by Pierre Loti's *Madame Chrysanthème*, Vincent was also endeavouring to enter factually into the spirit of a Japanese environment. This is why he could rightly claim that although one of his finest landscapes, *Harvest, La Crau*, superficially had nothing to do with Japan, it was the most *141* Japanese thing he had ever painted. This is because of its light and clarity, the absolute accuracy of each form and line, the colourfulness and detail which are present throughout the work yet never predominate. Viewed in this way, Cloisonnism never had the significance for him that it did for other artists. It was an end result created in Western style with a Japanese background, while Van Gogh – and this was only possible because of his ecstatic, Adamistic disposition – imagined that he was seeing and experiencing his subject from a genuine Japanese viewpoint.

... Have you read *Mme Chrysanthème*? It gave me the impression that the real Japanese have *nothing on their walls*, that description of the cloister or pagoda where there was *nothing* (the drawings and curiosities all being hidden in the drawers). That is how you must look at Japanese art, in a very bright room, quite bare, and open to the country. ... (509, 18 July 1888, F.)

You will already have received my letter of this morning, in which I enclosed the 50-fr. note for Bing, and there is still more I want to write you about this Bing business! The point is that we do not know enough about Japanese prints.

Fortunately we know more about the Japanese of France, the impressionists.

So Japanese art proper, already interred in collections, already impossible to find in Japan itself, is becoming of secondary interest.

But that doesn't mean that if I had a single day to see Paris again, I should not call at Bing's to see those very Hokusais and other drawings of the great period. Besides, Bing himself used to say to me, when I was admiring the ordinary prints, that after a while I should come to see that there are quite different things still. ... (511, 22 July 1888, F.)

In a few lines Vincent managed to reduce his own and Theo's condition to a sense of the *vie manquée* familiar from nineteenth-century French literature. It should be noted that this was not because he no longer had any faith in his art, but because he could never reconcile himself to the fact that what he called genuine living life had eluded him because of the compulsion, the imposition, of his creative work.

... These painter's fingers of mine are growing supple, even though the carcass is going to pieces. And the merchant's head for selling – and a long job to learn it is – is getting more experience too. In our situation, which you may well say is so precarious, we must not forget our advantages, and let's try to hang on to our patience to do the right thing and see clearly. Isn't it true, for instance, that in any case it is better if someday they say to you, 'Go to London,' than chuck you out, your services no longer being required?

I am getting older than you, and my ambition is to be less of a burden to you. And, if no actual obelisk of too pyramidal a catastrophe occurs, and there's no rain of frogs in the meantime, I hope to achieve it sometime. ...

My dear brother, if I were not broke and crazy with this blasted painting, what a dealer I'd make just for the impressionists. But there, I am broke. London is good, London is just what we need, but alas I feel I cannot do what I once could. But broken down and none too well myself, I do not see *any* misfortune in your going to London; if there is fog there, well, that seems to be increasing in Paris too.

What's wrong – basically – is that we are getting older, and must behave accordingly; that's *all there is to it*. Yet there is something *for* as well as *against*, and we must make the best of it. ... (513, 26/27 July 1888, F.)

... The more I am spent, ill, a broken pitcher, by so much more am I an artist – a creative artist – in this great renaissance of art of which we speak.

These things are surely so, but this eternally living art, and this renaissance, this green shoot springing from the roots of the old felled trunk, these are such abstract things that a kind of melancholy remains within us when we think that one could have created life at less cost than creating art. ... (514, 29 July 1888, F.)

The letters written between August and October, prior to Gauguin's ultimate arrival, contain indications that Van Gogh was on the verge of total collapse, though not in the sense of being confused. On the contrary, they are positive because of their wealth of profound thoughts on life and death; the overwhelming impressions of life and landscape; their lyricism about all that he still wished to do, details of what he was reading, painting and drawing, in between writing letters – complete Van Gogh, in fact. The letters need to be read in their entirety if one wishes to comprehend the power of the stream welling up from his unconscious self and sweeping him along without any chance of finding calmer waters.

Vincent was unable to escape the desire for totality, the constant reliving of previous experiences, always present as such in the actuality of what he was engaged in doing. Of course it goes without saying that there was in all this an element of regression – but dominated by the urge to transcend the moment: to possess the whole.

I think you were right to go to our uncle's funeral, since Mother seemed to be expecting you. The best way to cope with death is to accept the illustrious departed, whatever he was, as being the best man in the best of all possible worlds, where everything is for the best. Which not being contested, and consequently incontestable, doubtless all that remains to be done is to return laudably to our own pursuits. I am glad that our brother Cor has grown bigger and stronger than the rest of us. And he must be stupid if he does not get married, for he has nothing but that and his hands. With that and his hands, or his hands and that, and what he knows of machinery, I for one would like to be in his shoes, if I had any desire at all to be anyone else.

And meanwhile I am in my own hide, and my hide caught in the wheels of the Fine Arts, like wheat between the millstones. . . .

I have come to the end both of paints and canvas and I have already had to buy some here. And I must go back for even more. So please do send the letter so that I'll have it on Saturday morning.

Today I am probably going to start on the interior of the café where I eat, by gaslight, in the evening. It is what they call here a 'café de nuit' (they are fairly common here), staying open all night. Night prowlers can take refuge there when they have no money to pay for a lodging or are too tight to be taken in.

All those things – family, native land – are perhaps more attractive in the imagination of such people as us, who are doing pretty well without native land or family, than they are in reality. I always feel I am a traveller, going somewhere and to some destination. If I tell myself that the somewhere and the destination do not exist, that seems to me very reasonable and likely enough.

When the brothel bouncer kicks anyone out, he has a similar logic, argues well too, and is always right, I know. So at the end of my career I shall prove to be wrong. So be it. Then I shall find that not only the Arts but everything else were only dreams, that one was nothing at all oneself. If we are *as flimsy as that*, so much the better for us, for then there is nothing to be said against the unlimited possibility of future existence. Whence comes it that in the present instance of our uncle's death, the face of the deceased was calm, peaceful, and grave, whereas it is a fact that he was rarely that way while living, either in youth or age? I have often observed a similar effect as I looked on the dead as though to question them. And for me that is *one* proof, though not the most serious, of a life beyond the grave.

And in the same way a child in the cradle, if you watch it at leisure, has the infinite in its eyes. In short, I know *nothing* about it, but it is just this feeling of *not knowing* that makes the real life we are actually living now like a one-way journey on a train. You go fast, but cannot distinguish any object very clearly, and above all you do not see the engine.

It is rather curious that Uncle as well as Father believed in a future life. Not to mention Father, I have several times heard Uncle arguing about it.

Ah – but then, they were more assured than we are, and got angry if you dared to go into it more deeply.

I do not think much of the *future* life of artists *through their works*. Yes, artists perpetuate themselves by handing on the torch, Delacroix to the impressionists, etc. But is that all?

If the kind old mother of a family, with her rather limited ideas, and tortured by the

Christian system, is to be immortal as she believes, and seriously too – and I for one do not gainsay it – why should a consumptive or neurotic cab horse with vast ideas, like Delacroix and de Goncourt, be any less immortal?

Granted, it seems that the most empty-headed should feel the springing of this unaccountable hope most keenly.

Enough. What's the good of worrying about it? But living in the full tide of civilization, of Paris, of the Arts, why shouldn't one hold on to this old-womanish 'ego', if the women themselves would not find strength to create and do things without their instinctive belief in 'that is *it.*'

Then the doctors will tell us that not only Moses, Mahomet, Christ, Luther, Bunyan and others were mad, but Frans Hals, Rembrandt, Delacroix too, and also all the dear narrow-minded old women like our mother.

Ah – that's a serious matter – one might ask these doctors: Where then are the sane people?

Are they the brothel bouncers, who are always right? Probably. Then what to choose? Fortunately there is no choice. (518, 6 Aug. 1888, F.)

... What I learned in Paris is leaving me, and I am returning to the ideas I had in the country before I knew the impressionists. And I should not be surprised if the impressionists soon find fault with my way of working, for it has been fertilized by Delacroix's ideas rather than by theirs. Because instead of trying to reproduce exactly what I have before my eyes, I use colour more arbitrarily, in order to express myself forcibly. Well, let that be, as far as theory goes, but I'm going to give you an example of what I mean.

156 I should like to paint the portrait of an artist friend [Eugène Boch], a man who dreams great dreams, who works as the nightingale sings, because it is his nature. He'll be a blond man. I want to put my appreciation, the love I have for him, into the picture. So I paint him as he is, as faithfully as I can, to begin with.

But the picture is not yet finished. To finish it I am now going to be the arbitrary colourist. I exaggerate the fairness of the hair, I even get to orange tones, chromes and pale citron-yellow.

Behind the head, instead of painting the ordinary wall of the mean room, I paint infinity, a plain background of the richest, intensest blue that I can contrive, and by this simple combination of the bright head against the rich blue background, I get a mysterious effect, like a star in the depths of an azure sky. ... (520, 11 Aug. 1888, F.)

At the same time Vincent continued to take a technical and factual interest in the composition and quality of the paint he employed.

Would you like to ask Tasset's opinion on the following question? To me it seems as though the more finely a colour is brayed, the more it becomes saturated with oil. Now needless to say, we don't care overmuch for oil.

If we painted like M. Gérôme and the other delusive photographers, we should doubtless ask for very finely brayed colours. But we on the contrary do not object to the canvas having a rough look. If then, instead of braying the colour on the stone for God knows how many hours, it was brayed just long enough to make it manageable, without worrying too much about the fineness of the powder, you would get fresher colours which would perhaps darken less. If he wants to make a trial of it with the three chromes, the malachite, the vermilion, the orange lead, the cobalt, and the ultramarine, I am almost certain that at much less cost I should get colours which would be both fresher and more lasting. Then what would the price be? I'm sure this could be done. Probably also with the reds and the emerald, which are transparent. ... (527, 22 Aug. 1888, F.)

Painting at it is now promises to become more subtle – more like music and less like sculpture – and above all it promises *colour*. If only it keeps this promise. ...

As for stippling [*le pointillé*] and making haloes and other things, I think they are real discoveries, but we must already see to it that this technique does not become a universal dogma any more than any other. That is another reason why Seurat's *Grande Jatte*, the landscapes with broad stippling by Signac, and Anquetin's boat, will become in time even more personal and even more original.

About my clothes, certainly they were beginning to be the worse for wear, but only last week I bought a black velvet jacket of fairly good quality for 20 francs, and a new hat, so there is no hurry. . . . (528, 26 Aug. 1888, F.)

Nothing escaped his notice. The lyricism of his utterances, and the images he employed, 'a wedding of two complementary colours, . . . the mysterious vibrations of kindred tones', go beyond simple description; this is a reliving, while he was writing, of what had taken place. The abrupt switches of tone, as when he refers to his *Night Café* as 'the ugliest I have done', are part of his *164* ecstatic mood. In the context of what was being painted elsewhere at the time, these works represented historically a tremendous leap, even after *La Segatori* and the final self-portraits painted in Paris. This was the discovery of the *115, 124* *terribilità* of colour, which he knew lay concealed in Delacroix. His reflections *193* at this time were not concerned with any pre-existing religious or historical context; they were totally modern. From a literary point of view, that is to say in the context of the letters, Vincent now came closer to Huysmans than to Zola. The *fin-de-siècle* perversity of 'Louis XII green' and 'malachite' and the 'sulphurous smell of crime' is not exactly what the reader expects when Vincent expresses his frequently quoted desire to use his art 'to say something comforting, as music is comforting'; nor does it reflect that other side of him which started thinking about Giotto and Puvis while he was at Arles.

. . . Oh, my dear brother, sometimes I know so well what I want. I can very well do without God both in my life and in my painting, but I cannot, ill as I am, do without something which is greater than I, which is my life – the power to create.

And if, frustrated in the physical power, a man tries to create thoughts instead of children, he is still part of humanity.

And in a picture I want to say something comforting, as music is comforting. I want to paint men and women with that something of the eternal which the halo used to symbolize, and which we seek to convey by the actual radiance and vibration of our colouring.

Portraiture so understood does not become like an Ary Scheffer just because there is a blue sky in the background, as in *St Augustine*. For Ary Scheffer is so little of a colourist.

But it would be more in harmony with what Eug. Delacroix attempted and brought off in his *Tasso in Prison*, and many other pictures, representing a *real* man. Ah! portraiture, portraiture with the thoughts, the soul of the model in it, that is what I think must come. . . .

So I am always between two currents of thought, first the material difficulties, turning round and round to make a living; and second, the study of colour. I am always in hope of making a discovery there, to express the love of two lovers by a wedding of two complementary colours, their mingling and their opposition, the mysterious vibrations of kindred tones. To express the thought of a brow by the radiance of a light tone against a sombre background.

To express hope by some star, the eagerness of a soul by a sunset radiance. Certainly there is no delusive realism in that, but isn't it something that actually exists? . . . (531, 3 Sept. 1888, F.)

Thank you a thousand times for your kind letter and the 300 francs it contained; after some worrying weeks I have just had one of the very best. And just as the worries do not come singly, neither do the joys. For just because I am always bowed under this difficulty of paying my landlord, I made up my mind to take it gaily. I swore at the said landlord, who after all isn't a bad fellow, and told him that to revenge myself for paying him so much money for nothing, I would paint the whole of his rotten joint so as to repay myself. Then to the great joy *164* of the landlord, of the postman whom I had already painted, of the visiting night prowlers and *154* of myself, for three nights running I sat up to paint and went to bed during the day. I often think that the night is more alive and more richly coloured than the day.

Now, as for getting back the money I have paid to the landlord by means of my painting, I do not dwell on that, for the picture is one of the ugliest I have done. It is the equivalent, though different, of the *Potato Eaters*. *48*

I have tried to express the terrible passions of humanity by means of red and green.

The room is blood red and dark yellow with a green billiard table in the middle; there are four citron-yellow lamps with a glow of orange and green. Everywhere there is a clash and contrast of the most disparate reds and greens in the figures of little sleeping hooligans, in the empty, dreary room, in violet and blue. The blood-red and the yellow-green of the billiard table, for instance, contrast with the soft tender Louis XV green of the counter, on which there is a pink nosegay. The white coat of the landlord, awake in a corner of that furnace, turns citron-yellow, or pale luminous green. . . .

The *Night Café* carries on the style of the *Sower*, as do the head of the old peasant and of the poet also, if I manage to do this latter picture.

It is colour not locally true from the point of view of the delusive realist, but colour suggesting some emotion of an ardent temperament.

When Paul Mantz saw at the exhibition the violent and inspired sketch by Delacroix that we saw at the Champs-Elysées – the *Bark of Christ* – he turned away from it, exclaiming, 'I did not know that one could be so terrible with a little blue and green.'

Hokusai wrings the same cry from you, but he does it by his *line*, his *drawing*, just as you say in your letter – 'the waves are *claws* and the ship is caught in them, you feel it'.

Well, if you make the colour exact or the drawing exact, it won't give you sensations like that. . . . (533, 8 Sept. 1888, F.)

. . . In my picture of the *Night Café* I have tried to express the idea that the café is a place where one can ruin oneself, go mad or commit a crime. So I have tried to express, as it were, the powers of darkness in a low public house, by soft Louis XV green and malachite, contrasting with yellow-green and harsh blue-greens, and all this in an atmosphere like a devil's furnace, of pale sulphur.

And all with an appearance of Japanese gaiety, and the good nature of Tartarin.

But what would Monsieur Tersteeg say about this picture when he said before a Sisley – Sisley, the most discreet and gentle of the impressionists – 'I can't help thinking that the artist who painted that was a little tipsy'. If he saw my picture, he would say that it was delirium tremens in full swing.

I see absolutely nothing to object to in your suggestion of exhibiting once at the *Revue Indépendante*, provided, however, that I am no obstacle to the others who usually exhibit there. . . .

Just as I'm writing to you, the poor peasant who is like a caricature of Father happens to have come into the café. The resemblance is terrible, all the same. Especially the uncertainty and the weariness and the vagueness of the mouth. I still feel it is a pity that I have not been able to do it. . . . (534, Sept. 1888, F.)

. . . Ideas for my work are coming to me in swarms, so that though I'm alone, I have no time to think or to feel, I go on painting, like a steam engine. I think there will hardly ever be a standstill again. And my view is that you will never find a live studio ready-made, but that it is created from day to day by patient work and going on and on in one place. . . .

The idea of the *Sower* continues to haunt me all the time. Exaggerated studies like the *Sower* and like this *Night Café* usually seem to me atrociously ugly and bad, but when I am moved by something, as now by this little article on Dostoievsky, then these are the only ones which appear to have any deep meaning. . . . (535, 10 Sept. 1888, F.)

. . . The third picture this week is a portrait of myself, *almost colourless*, in grey tones against a background of pale malachite.

I purposely bought a mirror good enough to enable me to work from my image in default of a model, because if I can manage to paint the colouring of my own head, which is not to be done without some difficulty, I shall likewise be able to paint the heads of other good souls, men and women.

The problem of painting night scenes and effects on the spot and actually by night interests me enormously. This week I have done absolutely nothing but paint and sleep and have my meals. That means sittings of twelve hours, of six hours and so on, and then a sleep of twelve hours at a stretch. . . . (537, 16/17 Sept. 1888, F.)

In September and October 1888, prior to Gauguin's arrival on 23 October, Van Gogh experienced a medley of moods consisting of moments of rarest happiness, a lucidity which he felt as a blessing, a state of grace ('I can't help it, I feel my brain is lucid'), and a powerful need for religion, a word now used to denote a religion of nature. Vincent was impressed by Tolstoy's concept of an approaching inner, private revolution. Sentiments about music and a 'more musical' way of life had acquired that same metaphorical value; but it remains uncertain what this meant to him. He found it difficult to define the relationship between music and colour. What in the work of Delacroix and Monticelli he called 'suggestive colour' was, for him, a related quality.

I wrote to you already, early this morning, then I went away to go on with a picture of a garden in the sunshine. Then I brought it back and went out again with a blank canvas, and that also is finished. And now I want to write you again.

Because I have never had such a chance, nature here being so *extraordinarily* beautiful. Everywhere and all over the vault of heaven is a marvellous blue, and the sun sheds a radiance of pale sulphur, and it is soft and as lovely as the combination of heavenly blues and yellows in a Van der Meer of Delft. I cannot paint it as beautifully as that, but it absorbs me so much that I let myself go, never thinking of a single rule. . . .

School of Giotto. *Death of the Virgin*, 14th c.
This work, attributed to Giotto, was to be seen in the Montpellier museum when Van Gogh and Gauguin visited it.

I am so happy in the house and in my work that I even dare to think that this happiness will not always be limited to one, but that you will have a share in it and good luck to go with it.

Some time ago I read an article on Dante, Petrarch, Boccaccio, Giotto and Botticelli. Good Lord! it did make an impression on me, reading the letters of those men.

And Petrarch lived quite near here in Avignon, and I am seeing the same cypresses and oleanders.

I have tried to put something of that into one of the pictures painted in a very thick impasto, citron yellow and lime green. Giotto moved me most – *always in pain*, and always full of kindness and enthusiasm, as though he were already living in a different world from ours.

And besides, Giotto is extraordinary. I understand him better than the poets Dante, Petrarch and Boccaccio.

I always think that poetry is more *terrible* then painting, though painting is a dirtier and a much more worrying job. And then the painter never says anything, he holds his tongue, and I like that too.

My dear Theo, when you have seen the cypresses and the oleanders here, and the sun – and the day will come, you may be sure – then you will think even more often of the beautiful *Sweet Land* by Puvis de Chavannes, and many other pictures of his.

There is still a great deal of Greece all through the Tartarin and Daumier part of this queer country, where the good folk have the accent you know; there is a Venus of Arles just as there is a Venus of Lesbos, and one still feels the youth of it in spite of all. . . .

143, 148, 164 What is Seurat doing? I should not dare to show him the studies already sent, but the ones of the sunflowers, and the cabarets, and the gardens, I would like him to see those. I often think of his method, though I shall not follow it at all; but he is an original colourist, and Signac too, though to a different degree, the *pointilleurs* have discovered something new, and at all events I like them very much. But I myself – I tell you frankly – am returning more to what I was looking for before I came to Paris. I do not know if anyone before me has talked about suggestive colour, but Delacroix and Monticelli, without talking about it, did it.

But I have got back to where I was in Nuenen, when I made a vain attempt to learn music, so much did I already feel the relation between our colour and Wagner's music.

It is true that in impressionism I see the resurrection of Eugène Delacroix, but the interpretations of it are so divergent and in a way so irreconcilable that it will not be impressionism which will give us the final doctrine.

That is why I myself remain among the impressionists, because it professes nothing, and binds you to nothing, and as one of the comrades I need not declare my formula.

Good Lord, how you have to mess about in life. I only ask for time to study, and do you yourself really ask for anything but that? . . . (539, *c.* 18 Sept. 1888, F.)

I know quite well that I have already written you once today, but it has been such a lovely day again. My great regret is that you cannot see what I am seeing here.

Since seven o'clock this morning I have been sitting in front of something which after all is no great matter, a clipped round bush of cedar or cypress growing amid grass. You already know this clipped bush, because you have had a study of the garden. Enclosed also a sketch of my canvas, again a square size 30.

The bush is green, touched a little with bronze and various other tints.

The grass is bright, bright green, malachite touched with citron, and the sky is bright, bright blue.

The row of bushes in the background are all oleanders, raving mad; the blasted things are flowering so riotously they may well catch locomotor ataxia. They are loaded with fresh flowers, and quantities of faded flowers as well, and their green is continually renewing itself in fresh, strong shoots, apparently inexhaustibly.

A funereal cypress is standing over them, and some small figures are sauntering along a pink path.

This makes a pendant to another size 30 canvas of the same spot, only from a totally different angle, in which the whole garden is in quite different greens, under a sky of pale citron.

But isn't it true that this garden has a fantastic character which makes you quite able to imagine the poets of the Renaissance, Dante, Petrarch, Boccaccio, strolling among these bushes and over the flowery grass? It is true that I have left out some trees, but what I have kept in the composition is really there just as you see it. Only it has been overcrowded with some shrubs which are not in character. . . .

And to get at that character, the fundamental truth of it: that's three times now that I've painted the same spot.

It happens to be the garden just in front of my house. But this corner of the garden is a good example of what I was telling you, that to get at the real character of things here, you must look at them and paint them for a long time.

Perhaps you will see nothing from the sketch except that the line is now very simple. This picture is again painted very thickly, like its pendant with the yellow sky.

I hope to work again with Milliet tomorrow.

Today again from seven o'clock in the morning till six in the evening I worked without stirring except to take some food a step or two away. That is why the work is getting on fast.

But what will you say of it, and what shall I think of it myself, a little while from now?

I have a lover's insight or a lover's blindness for work just now.

Because these colours about me are all new to me, and give me an extraordinary exaltation.

I have no thought of fatigue, I shall do another picture this very night, and I shall bring it off.

If I tell you that it is very urgent for me to have:

>   6 large tubes of chrome yellow, 1 citron
>   6   ,,   ,,   malachite green
>   3   ,,   ,,   Prussian blue
>   10   ,,   ,,   zinc white
>   A big tube like the zinc white and flake white
>   Then that will be deducted from yesterday's order.
>   And 5 metres of canvas, too.

I can't help it, I feel my brain is lucid, and I want as far as possible to make sure of enough pictures to hold my own when the others are making a great show for the year '89. Seurat with two or three of his enormous canvases has enough for an exhibition of his own, Signac is a good worker and has enough as well, and Gauguin and Guillaumin too. So, whether we exhibit or not, I do want to have the series of studies *Decoration* for the same time. . . . (541, 23/24 Sept. 1888, F.)

. . . I have read another article on Wagner – 'Love in Music' – I think by the same author who wrote the book on Wagner. How one needs the same thing in painting.

It seems that in the book *My Religion*, Tolstoi implies that whatever happens in the way of violent revolution, there will also be a private and secret revolution in men, from which a new religion will be born, or rather something altogether new, which will have no name, but which will have the same effect of comforting, of making life possible, which the Christian religion used to have. It seems to me that the book ought to be very interesting.

In the end we shall have had enough of cynicism and scepticism and humbug, and we shall want to live more musically. How will that come about, and what will we really find? It would be interesting to be able to prophesy, but it is even better to be able to feel that kind of foreshadowing, instead of seeing absolutely nothing in the future beyond the disasters that are all the same bound to strike the modern world and civilization like terrible lightning, through a revolution or a war, or the bankruptcy of worm-eaten states. If we study Japanese art, we see a man who is undoubtedly wise, philosophic and intelligent, who spends his time doing what? In studying the distance between the earth and the moon? No. In studying Bismarck's policy? No. He studies a single blade of grass.

But this blade of grass leads him to draw every plant and then the seasons, the wide aspects of the countryside, then animals, then the human figure. So he passes his life, and life is too short to do the whole.

Come now, isn't it almost a true religion which these simple Japanese teach us, who live in nature as though they themselves were flowers?

And you cannot study Japanese art, it seems to me, without becoming much gayer and happier, and we must return to nature in spite of our education and our work in a world of convention. . . . (542, 25/26 Sept. 1888, F.)

... When I left you at the station to go south, very miserable, almost an invalid and almost a drunkard, I still felt vaguely that we had put our very heart into our discussions with so many interesting people and artists that winter, but I hadn't the courage to hope.

After continued efforts on your part and mine, now at last something is beginning to show on the horizon: Hope.

It does not matter if you stay with the Goupils or not, you have committed yourself to Gauguin body and soul.

So you will be one of the first, or the first, dealer-apostle. I can see my own painting coming to life, and likewise a work among the artists. For if you try to get money for us, I shall urge every man who comes within my reach to produce, and I will set them an example myself.

And if we stick to it, all this will help to make something more lasting than ourselves. ...
(544, *c.* 29 Sept. 1888, F.)

This morning I received your excellent letter, which I sent on to my brother; your concept of impressionism in general, of which your portrait is a symbol, is striking. I can't tell you how curious I am to see it – but this much I know in advance: this work is too important to allow me to make an exchange. But if you will keep it for us, my brother will take it at the first opportunity – which I asked him directly – if you agree, and let's hope that it will be soon.

For, once again, we are trying to hasten the possibility of your coming here. I must tell you that even while working I keep thinking incessantly of that plan to found a studio, which will have you and myself as permanent residents, but which the two of us would turn into a refuge and place of shelter for comrades at moments when they are encountering a setback in their struggle.

After you left Paris, my brother and I stayed together for a time, which will forever remain unforgettable to me! The discussions covered a wider field – with Guillaumin, with the Pissarros, father and son, with Seurat, whose acquaintance I had not made (I visited his studio only a few hours before my departure).

Often these discussions had to do with the problems that are so very near my brother's heart and mine, *i.e.* the measures to be taken to safeguard the material existence of painters and to safeguard the means of production (paints, canvases) and to safeguard, in their direct interest, their share in the price which, under the present circumstances, pictures only bring a long time after they leave the artists' possession.

When you are here, we are going to go over all these discussions.

However this may be, when I left Paris, seriously sick at heart and in body, and nearly an alcoholic because of my rising fury at my strength failing me – then I shut myself up within myself, without having the courage to hope!

Now, however, hope is breaking for me vaguely on the horizon; that hope in intermittent flashes, like a lighthouse, which has sometimes comforted me during my solitary life. ...
(Vincent to Gauguin, 544a, Sept.–Oct. 1888, F.)

The letter of 13 October saw the appearance of the first signs of a crisis: fatigue, even exhaustion; exceptionally tired eyes; immoderate need of sleep, on one occasion up to sixteen hours on end; difficulty in concentrating on writing; uneven size of handwriting which was sometimes large with an excessive number of separated letters; no inclination for drawing. To us this seems enough to suggest Vincent was on the verge of a breakdown. He himself foresaw such a possibility when he attempted to define his possible madness, ruling out persecution mania and allowing for a reduced production.

Thank you for your letter and the 50-franc note it contained. Thank you for writing more about the picture by these Dutch artists. I have had gas installed in the studio and in the kitchen, which has cost me 25 francs. If Gauguin and I were to work every night for a fortnight, shouldn't we get it back? Only as Gauguin may come any day, I do desperately need another 50 francs.

I am not ill, but without the slightest doubt I'd get ill if I did not eat plenty of food and if I did not stop painting for a few days. As a matter of fact, I am again pretty nearly reduced to the madness of Hugo van der Goes in Emile Wauters' picture. And if it were not that I have almost

196

a double nature, that of a monk and that of a painter, as it were, I should have been reduced, and that long ago, completely and utterly, to the aforesaid condition.

Yet even then I do not think that my madness could take the form of persecution mania, since when in a state of excitement my feelings lead me rather to the contemplation of eternity, and eternal life.

But in any case I must beware of my nerves, etc. . . . (556, 21/22 Oct. 1888, F.)

Gauguin's arrival on 23 October ostensibly brought peace. They began to prepare their own canvases and use cheaper paint; they shared cooking chores, and Gauguin did some extra shopping. Each sought his 'own' Arlésienne.

Thanks for your letter and the 50-fr. note. As you learned from my wire, Gauguin has arrived in good health. He even seems to me better than I am.

Of course he is very pleased with the sale you have effected, and I no less, since in this way certain expenses absolutely necessary for the installation need not wait, and will not weigh wholly on your shoulders. Gauguin will certainly write you today. He is very interesting as a man, and I have every confidence that we shall do loads of things with him. He will probably produce a great deal here, and I hope perhaps I shall too.

157

158

And then I dare hope that the burden will be a *little* less heavy for you, and I even hope, *much* less heavy. I myself realize the necessity of producing even to the extent of being mentally crushed and physically drained by it, just because after all I have no other means of ever getting back what we have spent.

I cannot help it that my pictures do not sell.

Nevertheless the time will come when people will see that they are worth more than the price of the paint and my own living, very meagre after all, that is put into them.

I have no other desire nor any other interest as to money or finance, than primarily to have no debts.

But my dear boy, my debt is so great that when I have paid it, which all the same I hope to succeed in doing, the pains of producing pictures will have taken my whole life from me, and it will seem to me then that I have not lived. The only thing is that perhaps the production of pictures will become a little more difficult for me, and as to numbers, there will not always be so many. . . . (557, 24 Oct. 1888, F.)

. . . Gauguin, in spite of himself and in spite of me, has more or less proved to me that it is time I was varying my work a little. I am beginning to compose from memory, and all my studies will still be useful for that sort of work, recalling to me things I have seen. What then does selling matter, unless we are absolutely pressed for money? . . . (563, 2–11 Dec. 1888, F.)

The visit Gauguin and Vincent made to Montpellier was something of a turning-point; their reactions to it led to fierce arguments. His letter of 23 December gives a suspiciously calm account of how Gauguin, upset by Arles and Vincent in particular, wanted to leave, while Vincent, understandably, found this hard to bear. Gauguin had come to symbolize some of his most passionate hopes, which were concerned partly with Theo's interest in tying Gauguin to his business, and partly with his own efforts to test the practicability of his scheme for a society of painters living and working together which would act as a cure for his own loneliness and give the Maison Jaune a purpose.

Yesterday Gauguin and I went to Montpellier to see the gallery there and especially the Brias room. There are a lot of portraits of Brias, by Delacroix, Ricard, Courbet, Cabanel, Couture, Verdier, Tassaert, and others. Then there are pictures by Delacroix, Courbet, Giotto, Paul Potter, Botticelli, Th. Rousseau, very fine. Brias was a benefactor of artists, I need say no more to you than that. In the portrait by Delacroix he is a gentleman with red beard and hair, uncommonly like you or me, and made me think of that poem by de Musset – 'Wherever I touched the earth – a miserable fellow in black sat down close to us, and looked at us like a brother'. It would have the same effect on you, I'm sure. Please go to that bookshop where they sell the lithographs after past and present artists, and see if you could get a not too expensive lithograph after Delacroix's *Tasso in the Madhouse*, since I think the figure there must have some affinity with this fine portrait of Brias. . . .

Gauguin and I talked a lot about Delacroix, Rembrandt, etc. Our arguments are terribly *electric*, sometimes we come out of them with our heads as exhausted as a used electric battery. We were in the midst of magic, for as Fromentin says so well: Rembrandt is above all a magician. . . .

Eugène Delacroix. *Alfred Bruyas*, 1853. Vincent always spelt his name Brias.

Tell Degas that Gauguin and I have been to see the portrait of Brias by Delacroix at Montpellier, for we have the courage to believe that *what is is*, and the portrait of Brias by Delacroix is as like you and me as another brother. . . . (564, *c.* 15–20 Dec. 1888, F.)

Thank you very much for your letter, for the 100-fr. note enclosed and also for the 50-fr. money order.

I think myself that Gauguin was a little out of sorts with the good town of Arles, the little yellow house where we work, and especially with me.

As a matter of fact, there are bound to be grave difficulties to overcome here too, for him as well as for me.

But these difficulties are more within ourselves than outside.

Altogether I think that either he will definitely go, or else definitely stay.

I told him to think it over and make his calculations all over again before doing anything.

Gauguin is very powerful, strongly creative, but just because of that he must have peace. Will he find it anywhere if he does not find it here?

I am waiting for him to make a decision with absolute serenity. . . . (565, 23 Dec. 1888, F.)

The very next day – Christmas Eve, often a bad time of year in Vincent's life – Gauguin called Theo to Arles after a series of dramatic developments. These have been over-emphasized in accounts of Vincent's life; a sensational approach does little to enhance our understanding of either the man or his work. The local paper carried the story the following week-end:

On Sunday last, at 11.30 p.m., one Vincent Vangogh, a painter, born in Holland, arrived at House of Tolerance [brothel] No. 1, asked for one Rachel, and handed her – his ear, saying 'Keep this and treasure it.' Then he disappeared. Informed of this action, which could only be that of a poor lunatic, the police went to the man's address the next morning and found him lying in bed and giving almost no sign of life. The unfortunate was admitted to hospital as an emergency case. . . . (*Le Forum républicain* (Arles), 30 Dec. 1888, F.)

On 1 January 1889 Emile Bernard wrote to the critic Albert Aurier, giving Gauguin's version of what had happened. Gauguin's attitude may be open to criticism, and his account of the events may be subject to correction; but this is after all the nearest to an immediate first-hand account that we have. The few artists who were close to Vincent were shaken by what had happened, and the event seems to have shocked them into a fuller realization of his true significance as an artist.

In the meantime Theo had become engaged to be married. He had come to believe that his overtures to Jo Bonger in the summer of 1888 had been definitely rejected, or at least discouraged. Since the failure of his suit in the summer, he had avoided his friend Andries Bonger in Paris. A few days before 21 December, Jo Bonger, who had been staying with her brother for a month, happened to meet Theo and asked to speak to him. She believed it to be her fault that Andries and Theo were avoiding each other. Relations improved at a stroke. After consultations with parents, their engagement was announced in Holland early in 1889.

The coincidence of this engagement and the crisis between Vincent and Gauguin has tempted some authors to attribute to it an active part in Vincent's derangement. In fact, however, although Vincent knew all about the estrangement between Theo and Jo (and had repeatedly urged his brother to marry), he knew nothing of the rapprochement. This news was given by Theo in a letter to his mother on 21 December, and in other to Lies, to Vincent, and other members of the family, which were not sent until 24 December. There is nothing to suggest that Theo wrote to Vincent before Christmas Eve.

Vincent's nervous condition had clearly deteriorated since the arrival of Gauguin, who had proved too strong a stimulus. Sunday 23 December was the date not of a first crisis, but of a final stage in a crisis which had been threatening and developing for months and became acute after their visit to Montpellier on 13 December. Following an earlier, interrupted crisis which lasted from the end of August and was particularly serious around 13 October, Gauguin was welcomed by a man who was undoubtedly exhausted by ecstatic states of mind, depressions and overwork. Gauguin too was subject to bouts of depression. His part in Vincent's derangement can be limited to the fact that he brought inflammable material with him.

I take the opportunity of my first absence from the hospital to write you a few words of very deep and sincere friendship. I often thought of you in the hospital, even at the height of fever and comparative weakness.

Look here – was my brother Theo's journey really necessary, old man?

Now at least do reassure him completely, and I entreat you, be confident yourself that after all no evil exists in this best of worlds in which everything is for the best.

Then I should like you to give my kind regards to good old Schuffenecker, to refrain, until after more mature reflection on both our parts, from speaking ill of our poor little yellow house, and to remember me to the painters whom I saw in Paris. I wish you prosperity in Paris, with a good handshake.

[PS.] Roulin has been truly kind to me, it was he who had the presence of mind to make me come out of that place before the others were convinced.

Please answer me. (Vincent to Gauguin, 566, 4 Jan. 1889, F.)

154

... You can see just what a disaster Gauguin's leaving is, because it has pushed us down again just when we had made a home and furnished it to take in our friends during bad times.

But we will keep the furniture, etc., in spite of it. And though everyone will be afraid of me now, in time that may disappear.

We are all mortal and subject to all the ailments that exist, and if the latter aren't of a particularly pleasant kind, what can one do about it? The best thing is to try to get rid of them.

I feel remorse too when I think of the trouble that, however involuntarily, I on my part caused Gauguin. But up to the last days I saw one thing only, that he was working with his mind divided between his desire to go to Paris to carry out his plans, and his life in Arles.

What will come of all this for him? . . .

Meanwhile the great thing is that your marriage should not be delayed. By getting married you will set Mother's mind at rest and make her happy, and it is after all almost a necessity in view of your position in society and in commerce. Will it be appreciated by the society to which you belong? Perhaps not, any more than the artists ever suspect that I have sometimes worked and suffered for the community. . . . So from me, your brother, you will not want banal congratulations and assurances that you are about to be transported straight into paradise. And with your wife you will not be lonely any more, which I could wish for our sister as well.

That, after your own marriage, is what I should set my heart on more than anything else. . . .

Whatever I think on other points, our father and mother were exemplary as a married couple.

And I shall never forget Mother at Father's death, when she said only one little word: it made me begin to love dear old Mother more than before. In fact, as a married couple our parents were exemplary, like Roulin and his wife, to cite another instance.

Well, take that same road. During my illness I saw again every room in the house at Zundert, every path, every plant in the garden, the views of the fields outside, the neighbours, the graveyard, the church, our kitchen garden at the back – down to a magpie's nest in a tall acacia in the graveyard.

It's because I still have earlier recollections of those first days than any of the rest of you. There is no one left who remembers all this but Mother and me. . . .

And after all I should like to go on exchanging my things with Gauguin even if sometimes it would mean a wrench to me too.

155   During your hasty visit did you see the portrait of Mme Ginoux in black and yellow? That portrait was painted in three-quarters of an hour. I must stop for the moment. . . . (573, 23 Jan. 1889, F.)

Paul Signac was the only artist to visit Vincent in hospital.

The last time I saw Vincent was in Arles in the spring of 1889. Then he was already in that town's asylum.

A few days before [sic] he had cut off the lobe of his ear under the circumstances you know of. But on the day of my visit he was quite sane, and the house physician gave me permission to go out with him. He had the famous bandage around his head and wore his fur cap. He led me to his apartments in Place Lamartine, where I saw his marvellous pictures, his

153, 164   masterpieces: *Les Aliscamps*, the *Night Café*, *La Berceuse*, the *Lock*, the *Saintes-Maries*, the *Starry Night*, etc. Imagine the splendour of those whitewashed walls, on which flowered those colourings in their full freshness.

Throughout the day he spoke to me of painting, literature, socialism. In the evening he was a little tired. There had been a terrific spell of mistral, and this may have enervated him. He wanted to drink about a quart of essence of turpentine from the bottle that was standing on the table in the room. It was high time to return to the asylum.

Next day I went to take leave of him; I went to Cassis; there he sent me a nice letter full of art and friendship, telling me how much pleasure my visit had afforded him, and illustrated with a fine drawing.

I never saw him again. . . . (Paul Signac, quoted from Gustav Cocquiot, *Vincent van Gogh*, Paris 1923; CLVG, III, 166–67.)

. . . I have seen Signac, and it has done me quite a lot of good. He was so good and straightforward and simple when the difficulty of forcing the door open presented itself – the police had closed up the house and destroyed the lock. They began by refusing to let us do it, but all the same we finally got in. I gave him as a keepsake a still life which had annoyed the good gendarmes of the town of Arles, because it represented two bloaters, and as you know they, the gendarmes, are called that. You remember that I did this same still life two or three times in Paris, and exchanged it once for a carpet in the old days. That is enough to show you how meddlesome and what idiots these people are.

I found Signac very quiet, though he is said to be so violent; he gave me the impression of someone who has balance and poise, that is all. Rarely or never have I had a conversation with an impressionist so free from discords or conflict on both sides. For instance he has been to see Jules Dupré, and he admires him. Doubtless you had a hand in his coming to stiffen my morale a bit, and thank you for it.

I took advantage of my outing to buy a book, *Ceux de la glèbe*, by Camille Lemonnier. I have devoured two chapters of it – it has such gravity, such depth! Wait till I send it to you. This is the first time in several months that I have had a book in my hands. That means a lot to me and does a good deal toward curing me.

Altogether there are several canvases to be sent to you, as Signac could see, he was not frightened by my painting as far as I saw. Signac thought, and it is perfectly true, that I looked healthy.

And with it I have the desire and the inclination for work. Still, of course, if I had to endure my work and my private life being interfered with every day by gendarmes and poisonous idlers of municipal electors petitioning the Mayor whom they have elected and who consequently depends on their votes, it would be no more than human of me to relapse all over again. I am inclined to think that Signac will tell you very much the same thing. In my opinion we must firmly oppose the loss of the furniture, etc. Then – my Lord – I must have liberty to carry on my handicraft.

M. Rey says that instead of eating enough and at regular times, I kept myself going on coffee and alcohol. I admit all that, but all the same it is true that to attain the high yellow note that I attained last summer, I really had to be pretty well keyed up. And that after all, an artist is a man with his work to do, and it is not for the first idler who comes along to crush him for good.

Am I to suffer imprisonment or the madhouse? Why not? Didn't Rochefort and Hugo, Quinet and others set an eternal example by submitting to exile, and the first even to a convict prison? But all I want to say is that this is a thing above the mere question of illness and health.

Naturally one is beside oneself in parallel cases. I do not say equivalent, being in a very inferior and secondary place to theirs, but I do say parallel.

And that is what the first and last cause of my aberration was. Do you know those words of a Dutch poet's – 'I am attached to the earth by more than earthly ties'?

That is what I have experienced in the midst of much suffering – above all – in my so-called mental illness. . . .

I am thinking of frankly accepting my role of madman, the way Degas acted the part of a notary. But there it is, I do not feel that altogether I have strength enough for such a part.

You talk to me of what you call 'the real South'. The reason why I shall never go there is above. I rightly leave that to men who have a more well-balanced mind, more integrity than I. I am only good for something intermediate, and second rate, and self-effaced.

However intense my feelings may be, or whatever power of expression I may acquire at an age when physical passions have lessened, I could never build an imposing structure on such a mouldy, shattered past. . . . (581, 24 Mar. 1889, F.)

After having rambled along the coast, I settled in Cassis. I am sending you my address so that you can let me know how you are getting on. I have written to your brother, but he has not answered me at all. (Paul Signac to Vincent, postcard, 583a, 4 Apr. 1889, F.)

Many thanks for your postcard and the information it contained. As to my brother's not having replied to your letter, I am inclined to think that it is hardly his fault. I myself have not heard from him for a fortnight. The fact is that he is in Holland, where he is getting married one of these days.

Well, look here, without denying the least bit in the world the advantages of marriage, once it has been contracted, and of being quietly settled down in one's own home, when I think of the obsequial pomp of the reception and the lamentable congratulations on the part of the two families (still in a state of civilization), not to mention the fortuitous appearances in those chemist's jars where the antediluvian civil and religious magistrates are kept – goodness gracious – mustn't one pity the poor wretch who is obliged, after having provided himself with the necessary documents, to repair to a locality, where, with a ferocity unequalled by the cruellest cannibals, he is married alive at a slow fire of receptions and the aforesaid funereal pomp.

I remain greatly obliged to you for your friendly and beneficial visit, which contributed considerably to raising my spirits. At present I am well, and I work at the sanatorium and its environs. I have just come back with two studies of orchards. . . . (Vincent to Paul Signac, 583b, April 1889, F.)

. . . And now I am returning to my portrait of *La Berceuse* for the fifth time. And when you see it, you will agree with me that it is nothing but a chromolithograph from the cheap shops, and again that it has not even the merit of being photographically correct in its proportions or in anything else.

But after all, I want to make a picture such as a sailor at sea who could not paint would imagine to himself when he thinks of his wife ashore.

They are very attentive to me at the hospital these days, and this as well as many other things upsets me and makes me rather confused.

Meanwhile I imagine that you would rather get married without all the ceremony and congratulations of a wedding, and I'm quite sure in advance that you will avoid them as much as possible. . . .

These last three months do seem so strange to me. Sometimes moods of indescribable mental anguish, sometimes moments when the veil of time and the fatality of circumstances seemed to be torn apart for an instant.

Certainly you are right after all, damn well right – even allowing for hope, the thing to do is to accept the probably disastrous reality. I am hoping once again to throw myself wholly into my work, in which I've fallen behind.

Oh, I must not forget to tell you a thing I have very often thought of. Quite accidentally I found in an article in an old newspaper some words written on an ancient tomb in the country between here and Carpentras.

Here is this very, very, very old epitaph, say dating from the time of Flaubert's *Salammbo*.
'Thebe, daughter of Thelhui, priestess of Osiris, who never complained of anyone.'

If you see Gauguin, you should tell him that. And I thought of a faded woman, you have the study of her at home, the woman who had such strange eyes whom I also met accidentally.

What does it mean, this 'she never complained of anyone'? Imagine a perfect eternity, why not, but don't let us forget that even in those old days reality had this – 'and she never complained of anyone'.

Do you remember that one Sunday good old Thomas came to see us and said, 'Ah but – are those the kind of women to make a man horny?'

It is not exactly a question of being horny, but from time to time in your life you feel thrilled through and through as if you were actually striking root in the soil. . . . (582, 29 Mar. 1889, F.)

. . . I settled my bill at the hospital today, and there is still almost enough for the rest of the month out of the money I still have on deposit. At the end of the month I should like to go to the hospital in Saint-Rémy, or another institution of this kind, of which M. Salles has told me. Forgive me if I don't go into details and argue the pros and cons of such a step. . . .
. . . What comforts me a little is that I am beginning to consider madness as a disease like any other and accept the thing as such, whereas during the crises themselves I thought that everything I imagined was real. Anyway, the fact is that I do not want to think or talk about it. You'll spare me any explanations, but I ask you and Messrs Salles and Rey to arrange things so that I can go there as a resident at the end of this month or the beginning of May.

Beginning again that painter's life I have been living, isolated in the studio so often, and without any other means of distraction than going to a café or a restaurant with all the neighbours criticizing, etc., *I can't face it*; going to live with another person, say another artist – difficult, very difficult – it's taking too much responsibility on oneself. I dare not even think of it.

So let's try three months to begin with, and afterward we shall see. . . . Certainly these last days were sad, with all the moving, taking away all my furniture, packing up the canvases that are going to you, but the thing I felt saddest about was that you had given me all these things with such brotherly love, and that for so many years you were always the one who supported me, and then to be obliged to come back and tell you this sorry tale – but it's difficult to express it as I felt it. The goodness you have shown me is not lost, because you had it and it remains for you; even if the material results should be nil, it remains for you all the more; but I can't say it as I felt it.

Meanwhile you do understand that if alcohol has undoubtedly been one of the great causes of my madness, then it came on very slowly and will go away slowly too, assuming it does go, of course. Or the same thing if it comes from smoking. ... (585, 21 Apr. 1889, F.)

Tomorrow being the first of May, I wish you a tolerable year, and above all health.

I should so like to be able to pass some physical strength on to you. At the moment I feel that I have more than enough. That doesn't mean that my head is still all that it ought to be.

How right Delacroix was, who lived on bread and wine only, and who succeeded in finding a manner of life in harmony with his profession. But the fatal question of money remains – Delacroix had property, Corot too. And Millet – Millet was a peasant and the son of a peasant. You will perhaps read with some interest the article which I have cut out of a Marseilles paper, because you will catch a glimpse of Monticelli in it, and I think the description of the picture representing a corner of the cemetery very interesting. But alas, that is still another lamentable story. How sad it is to think that a painter who succeeds, even only partially, involves in his turn half a dozen other artists who are worse failures than himself.

However, think of Pangloss, think of *Bouvard et Pécuchet*. I know it, then even that becomes clear, but perhaps these people do not know Pangloss or else forget all they know of him in the face of the fatal bite of actual despair and great grief.

And besides, under the name of optimism we are falling back once more into a religion which looks to me like the tail end of a kind of Buddhism. No harm in that; on the contrary, if you like.

I do not much like the article on Monet in the *Figaro*. How much superior that other article was in the *XIXme Siècle*! There you saw the pictures and this only contains commonplaces that depress me.

Today I am busy packing a case of pictures and studies. ...

This study, like some others, has got spoiled by moisture during my illness.

The flood water came to within a few feet of the house, and on top of that, the house itself had no fires in it during my absence, so when I came back, the walls were oozing water and saltpetre.

That touched me to the quick, not only the studio wrecked, but even the studies which would have been a souvenir of it ruined; it is so final, and my enthusiasm to found something very simple but lasting was so strong. It was a fight against the inevitable, or rather it was weakness of character on my part, for I am left with feelings of profound remorse, difficult to describe. I think that was the reason why I have cried out so much during the attacks, it was because I wanted to defend myself and could not do it. For it was not for myself, it was just for painters like the unfortunates the enclosed article speaks of that that studio would have been of some use. ...

If I were without your friendship, they would remorselessly drive me to suicide, and however cowardly I am, I should end by doing it. There, as you too will see, I hope, is the juncture where it is permissible for us to protest against society and defend ourselves. You can be fairly sure that the Marseilles artist who committed suicide did not in any way do it as the result of absinthe, for the simple reason that no one would have offered it to him and he couldn't have had anything to buy it with. Besides, he would drink it, not solely for pleasure, but because, being ill already, he needed it to keep himself going.

M. Salles has been to Saint-Rémy – they are not willing to let me paint outside the institution, nor to take me for less than 100 francs.

This information is pretty bad. If I could get out of it by enlisting in the Foreign Legion for five years, I think I'd prefer that. ...

If I cannot work unless under surveillance! and in an institution! – Good Lord, is it worth paying money for that! Certainly in that case I could work just as well in the barracks, even better. Anyway, I am thinking about it. You do the same. Let's remember that everything is always for the best in the best of worlds, which is not impossible. ... (588, 30 April 1889, F.)

Your kind letter did me good today, honestly – so now here's for Saint-Rémy. But I tell you once more, if on consideration and after consulting the doctor it should perhaps be either necessary or simply advisable and wise to enlist, let's give it the same consideration as everything else and have no prejudice against it. That's all! You must put aside any idea of sacrifice in it. The other day I again wrote our sister that all through my life, or at least most of it, I have sought something other than a martyr's career, for which I am not cut out.

If I find trouble or cause it, honestly, I am aghast at it. Certainly I should respect, I should heartily admire martyrs and the like, but you must know that in *Bouvard et Pécuchet*, for instance, there's something very different which accords better with these little lives of ours. ...

I see in the papers that there are some good things at the Salon.

Listen – do not become completely and exclusively impressionist; after all, if there is good in anything, don't let's lose sight of it. Certainly colour is progressing *primarily under the influence of* the impressionists, even when they go astray, but already Delacroix had reached more completeness than they.

And confound it all, Millet, who has hardly any colour, what work it is!

Madness is salutary in that one becomes less exclusive. ...

Ah, to paint figures as Claude Monet paints landscapes! That still, in spite of everything, remains to be done, unless one is to see only Monet in all the impressionists. For after all, in figure Delacroix, Millet, and several sculptors have done far better work than the impressionists and even J. Breton. In short, my boy, let's be fair, and, while withdrawing: I tell you whenever we think we are getting too old to class ourselves with the younger men, let us remember that in our time we have loved Millet, Breton, Israëls, Whistler, Delacroix and Leys.

And I'm quite sure that for my part I am pretty well convinced that I shall see no future beyond that, nor desire one.

Now society being what it is, we naturally cannot wish that it should conform to our personal needs. And so, though I am very, very glad to be going to Saint-Rémy, nevertheless it would be really fairer to men like myself to shove them into the Legion.

We can do nothing about it, it's more than likely that they would turn me down, at least here where what has happened to me is too well known, and above all exaggerated. I say this very, very seriously; physically I am better than I have been in years and years, and I could quite well be a soldier. Let's think this over again, even though I'm going to Saint-Rémy. ...

[PS.] ... So many distinctions in impressionism have *not* the importance that people have chosen to see in them. ...

They have lots of room here in the [Arles] hospital, there would be enough to make studios for a score or so of painters.

I really must make up my mind, it is only too true that lots of painters go mad, it is a life that makes you, to say the least, very absent-minded. If I throw myself fully into my work again, very good, but I shall always be cracked.

If I could enlist for five years, I should recover considerably and be more rational and more master of myself.

But one way or the other, it's all the same to me. ... (590, 3 May 1889, F.)

140 Self-portrait, Sept. 1888
Dedicated *à mon ami Paul Gauguin*. To his sister Willemien he wrote of doing a self-portrait 'in which I look like a Japanese' (w7); and to Theo he described it as 'almost *colourless*, in grey tones against a background of pale malachite' (537). To the dedicatee, Gauguin, he wrote of it as 'all ash-coloured. ... I also exaggerate my personality ... aimed at the character of a simple Bonze, worshipping the Eternal Buddha' (see also *147*). In one of his last Paris self-portraits (*117*) he was already conscious of a certain decay. This, the first painted at Arles, shows him in an even worse state, recalling Job 10.8: 'Thine hands have made me and fashioned me together round about; yet thou dost destroy me.'

141 *Harvest, La Crau, with Montmajour in the Background*, June 1888
Charles Mauron, in *Van Gogh au seuil de la Provence* (1959), wrote: 'Japan is no longer, for Vincent, simply "The land of gay colours", of colour prints, but that of Buddhist wisdom.' This is the link between the monk-like *Self-portrait* (previous page) and this lucid landscape, with its Dutch, Provençal and Japanese echoes.

Opposite page:
142 *Boats with Men unloading Sand*, Aug. 1888
'All of it seen from the quay above,' Vincent wrote to Bernard. 'No sky; it is only a sketch or rather a scribble, done during the full violence of the Mistral' (B15). A scribble, but a masterpiece of drawing with colour; it shows an unhesitating hand and eye. The tension of the outlines is stronger than that of a Japanese woodcut.

Above:
143 *The Poet's Garden: Sunshine in the Park*, Sept. 1888
September 1888 was a month in which ecstatic states alternated with deep depressions. His style varied from a light Parisian (positive) Impressionism to a bright, clear, lucid realism.
144 *The Stevedores*, end Aug. 1888

Sunflowers and sun

145 Sunflowers on the road from Arles to Tarascon, 1981
146 *The Road to Tarascon: Sky with Sun*, Aug. 1888

Since the destruction by fire, in 1945, of the wonderful
painting *Vincent on the Road to Tarascon* (F448), we are all
the more fortunate in the existence of this drawing. It is
astonishingly rich in different manners of drawing: ovals,
short straight lines, curves, a dance of dots and dashes of
different lengths, and stippling, together with a sun which
can only be described as an enormous vibration. The man
Vincent is invisible, but he is there.

147 Paul Gauguin. *Vincent Painting Sunflowers*, autumn
1888
148 *Fourteen Sunflowers*, summer 1888

Vincent started painting sunflowers in 1888 to decorate the
Maison Jaune to receive Gauguin. Gauguin, as a true
Symbolist, chose to paint an exhausted Vincent still
painting sunflowers out of season.

181

Profusion and rhythm

149 *A Garden*, July 1888
Van Gogh drew three different gardens at Arles; this is one of which he also made painted studies. The rich profusion of alternative means of suggesting detail – which is not, however, really detail at all, but a celebration of the luxuriant growth of grass and flowers – has been seen already in *The Road to Tarascon* (*146*).

150 *Sailing Boats Coming Ashore*, 2nd half June 1888
151 *Street at Saintes-Maries-de-la-Mer*, 2nd half June 1888
The same graphic richness reappears in the drawings, also done with a reed pen (a Japanese implement), which he made on his only visit to the Mediterranean, at Saintes-Maries. The drawing is almost an abstract rhythm; reality is subordinated to the musical imagination.

152 Patience Escalier, Aug. 1888

Vincent was linked by close friendship to four of the sitters for these paintings. The fifth, Patience Escalier, was a shepherd and gardener whom he saw in the Night Café (*164*); 'sunburned quality, tanned and airswept' (*520*). He remarked on the unlovely traces of uncertainty and weariness in Escalier's face, the 'vagueness of the mouth' associated with a 'terrible resemblance' to Vincent's own father. The resulting portrait has 'something of the eternal which the halo used to symbolize' (*531*).

153 *La Berceuse: Mme Augustine Roulin*, Jan 1889

154 *Joseph Roulin Seated at a Table*, Aug. 1888

155 *L'Arlésienne: Madame Ginoux*, Nov. 1888

156 *The Poet: Eugène Boch*, Sept. 1888

186

Gauguin

157 Paul Gauguin. *Vineyard at Arles with Breton Women*, 1888
158 *Memory of the Garden at Etten*, Nov. 1888

159 *Gauguin's Chair, Candle and Books (The Empty Chair)*, Dec. 1888
160 *Vincent's Chair with his Pipe and Tobacco Pouch*, Dec. 1888–Jan. 1889

These four paintings, which date from the period in which the two painters lived together at the Maison Jaune, reflect their shared life, and their impassioned and often stormy discussions of the current issues of art. The two *Empty Chairs*, deliberately contrasted, must be seen in the context of Vincent's own early reactions to empty chairs: the Fildes engraving (*36*); his tears at the sight of the empty chair his father had occupied during a visit to Amsterdam. Here symbolic and realistic feeling are in perfect balance, along with painterly expression through colour. Albert Aurier was right to stress Vincent's capacity to create modern symbols. The *Garden at Etten* was another combination of memory, sorrow, current poetic feelings, and imagination in the absence of the motif (Gauguin's advice to Vincent). For both artists, at times, a true, symbiotic collaboration was imminent. Vincent's tragic act of self-inflicted violence on 23 December brought the episode to a dramatic end.

'A devilish yellow'

161 The Maison Jaune, before its destruction in the Second World War. Vincent rented the wing on the right before it became a *Bar-Tabac*

162 *Vincent's House on the Place Lamartine, Arles (The Yellow House)*, Sept. 1888

163 *Vincent's Bedroom in the Maison Jaune*, Oct. 1888
164 *The Night Café*, Sept. 1888

Right:
In September and October 1888 Vincent still spoke of harmony and consolation, but cannot have been aware of the intensity of his colours: he felt that *Vincent's Bedroom* was suggestive 'of rest or of sleep in general'. *The Night Café*, on the other hand, is 'a place where one can ruin oneself, go mad or commit a crime' (533).

165 *Self-portrait with Bandaged Ear*, Jan. 1889
166 *Still-life on Table, with Book, Pipe, Candle, Letter and Onions*, Jan. 1889
167 *The Hospital Ward, Arles*, Apr.–Oct. 1889

All three works were painted in his studio at Arles after his stay in the local hospital and before he left for the hospital at Saint-Rémy; there he finished from memory the picture of the hospital ward. He was preoccupied with himself, his sickness, his state of mind and appearance (the mirror); everything around him, every object he painted, was an object of deep and more than purely artistic concern. The still-life is composed only of things with a special relation to his health; the book a health directory belonging to Dr Rey, the pipe a mainstay of his defences against depression. Arles continued to preoccupy him even at Saint-Rémy; he wanted to go back to see the people he loved. At the Maison Jaune he had tried to strike deep roots in this small Provençal town, which makes his enforced departure all the more tragic.

A hospital garden

168 Courtyard of the Arles hospital, 1981
169 *Courtyard of the Arles Hospital*, Apr.–
May 1889

In Paris Vincent had been too preoccupied
with theories of colour to attach great
significance to his drawings. His great
period of drawing seemed to be behind
him, with the peasants at Nuenen. In
Arles, we see the Impressionist context
disappear, the Japanese influence grow;
and there is a reconsideration of his Dutch
problems. His drawing in Arles is partly
classical: strong, sure, profoundly realistic.
After the late summer of 1888, something
happened inwardly. This drawing of the
hospital courtyard, a late Arles work,
shows a baroque movement, line more
freed from form, detail less important than
a constantly interrupted rhythm.

V

SAINT-RÉMY AND AUVERS

'Well, my own work, I am risking my life
for it and my reason has half foundered'

1889–1890 Saint-Rémy-de-Provence
1890 Auvers-sur-Oise

Life at Saint-Rémy meant struggling against the enclosed environment of the mental institution which Vincent believed himself to need. It was a struggle against his sickness, a struggle to save and preserve his creative powers through repeatedly interrupted, and sometimes forbidden, contacts with the overwhelming scenery beyond: 'I shall not conceal from you that being here is highly tedious, because of the monotony, and because the company of these unfortunates who do absolutely nothing is enervating' (614).

Time and again Vincent was insidiously debilitated by the destructive forces of his illness. Its roots lie in his childhood. This is a complex problem, since we are concerned with neurosis and, from his days at Arles onwards, with psychosis. According to Jean Delay's definition, neurosis is the psychological exaggeration of a character, a deviation which does not affect the personality or cause intellectual defects but leaves a way for suppressed energy and unbalanced emotions to escape from an impasse. Psychosis, however, is an organic process which does not benefit creativity. The personality is affected, intellectual deterioration takes place, and existing creative powers are checked (see the inaugural lecture by Professor Jean Delay, Paris, 'Névrose et création'; *Congrès des médecins aliénistes et neurologistes*, Liège, 19–26 July 1954, Masson, Paris).

It is disconcerting to find how precise an awareness Vincent had of what he experienced, heard and saw even when in a state of great emotional agitation. Even before those phenomena, which sprang from the unconscious and became conscious, were subjected to rational interpretation and suppression, Van Gogh dropped hints about them, sometimes breaking off and refusing to write more 'for fear of a relapse'. Vincent continued to work through his crises, except only at his worst periods, when his head felt empty, his energy had disappeared and the action involved in writing, reading and working became impossible. His great fear was that ultimately his creative powers might be affected. He himself mentioned that, despite the great effort involved, he had managed to complete several works and had even had ideas for new ones.

According to his letters, his stay at Saint-Rémy was marked by a constant preoccupation with attempts to account for his presence there. An 'accident like any other', he thought, but his reflections on the subject were sometimes cut short by irrational fear and horror. It was living on the borderline, and in the grip, of reason; living in the grip also of the community that was controlled by reason to the extent that was possible. And then suddenly again he was across the borderline, existing in a time and in a space in which the most violent emotions changed the image of time and space themselves. Vertiginous and mortal fears assailed him then.

Symptoms usually associated with schizophrenia occurred, but they were contradicted by others. He viewed things, as always, symbolically; he foresaw a catastrophic future for the world, but he was not subject to delusions in the medical sense. Similarly, with epilepsy: he knew it ran in his mother's family, but his symptoms were not conclusive proof of its presence.

Since Vincent managed time and again to transcend his syndrome, thereby eluding a whole succession of varying scientific diagnoses, the wisest opinion seems to me to be that of Jean Delay. He bases his views on writers, not on painters, but they apply to the relationship between neurosis and creativity in general. Delay said that the same phenomena that in some individuals can cause a neurosis to end in disaster can, in the case of certain gifted people, be transmuted into something of rare value. In these individuals – and this could apply literally to Van Gogh – all conflict is so intensely experienced (*vécu*) that it approaches the borderline of a crisis. In Arles, it seems to me, Vincent went over into a crisis of this kind, which at Saint-Rémy gained lasting, but intermittent, control over his life. Again and again he reverted to a state of neurosis, in which his powers of thought were unimpaired and his personality undistorted, and in which he was able to restore the disturbed equilibrium in his work.

... It is rather queer perhaps that the result of this terrible attack is that there is hardly any very definite desire or hope left in my mind, and I wonder if this is the way one thinks when, with the passions lessened, one descends the hill instead of climbing it. And anyhow, my sister, if you can believe, or almost believe, that everything is always for the best in the best of worlds, then perhaps you will also be able to believe that Paris is the best of the cities in it.

Have you noticed that the old cab horses there have large beautiful eyes, as heartbroken as Christians sometimes have? However it may be, we are neither savages nor peasants, and it is perhaps *even a duty* to like civilization (so called). ...

It may well be that I shall stay here long enough – I have never been so peaceful as here and in the hospital in Arles – to be able to paint a little at last. Quite near here there are some little mountains, grey and blue, and at their foot some very, very green cornfields and pines. ... (Vincent to Jo van Gogh-Bonger, 591, 9 May 1889, F.)

... I am again – speaking of my condition – so grateful for another thing. I gather from others that during their attacks they have also heard strange sounds and voices as I did, and that in their eyes too things seemed to be changing. And that lessens the horror that I retained at first of the attack I have had, and which, when it comes on you unawares, cannot but frighten you beyond measure. Once you know that it is part of the disease, you take it like anything else. If I had not seen other lunatics close up, I should not have been able to free myself from dwelling on it constantly. For the anguish and suffering are no joke once you are caught by an attack. Most epileptics bite their tongue and injure themselves. Rey told me that he had seen a case where someone had mutilated his own ear, as I did, and I think I heard a doctor here say, when he came to see me with the director, that he also had seen it before. I really think that once you know what it is, once you are conscious of your condition and of being subject to attacks, then you can do something yourself to prevent your being taken unawares by the suffering or the terror. Now that it has gone on decreasing for five months, I have good hope of getting over it, or at least of not having such violent attacks. There is someone here who has been shouting and talking like me *all the time* for a fortnight, he thinks he hears voices and words in the echoes of the corridors, probably because the nerves of the ear are diseased and too sensitive, and in my case it was my sight as well as my hearing, which according to what Rey told me one day is usual in the beginning of epilepsy. Then the shock was such that it sickened me even to move, and nothing would have pleased me better than never to have woken up again. At present this *horror of life* is less strong already and the melancholy less acute. But I have no *will*, hardly any desires or none at all, and hardly any wish for anything belonging to ordinary life, for instance almost no desire to see my friends, although I keep thinking about them. That is why I have not yet reached the point where I ought to think of leaving here; I should have this depression anywhere.

And it is only during these very last days that my aversion to life is in any way being radically modified. There is still some way to go from that to will and action. ... (592, 25 May 1889, F.)

Vincent regarded with some scepticism a new 'sect' which included artists such as Gauguin, Bernard and Anquetin. He was referring to Cloisonnism, first considered critically at the 1981 exhibition in Toronto and Amsterdam organized by Bogomila Welsh-Ovcharov, and in studies based on the exhibition.

119, 129, 157

... The thing is that among the number of things you make, there are always some that you have felt more or put more into and that you want to keep in spite of everything. When I see a picture that interests me, I can never help asking myself, 'In what house, room, corner of a room, in whose home would it do well, would it be in the right place?'

Thus the pictures of Hals, Rembrandt, Van der Meer [Vermeer], are only at home in an old Dutch house.

Now as to the impressionists – once again, if an interior is not complete without a work of art, neither is a picture complete if it is not in harmony with surroundings originating in and resulting from the period in which it was produced. And I do not know if the impressionists are better than their time or, on the contrary, are not yet so good. In a word, are there minds and interiors of homes more important than anything that has been expressed by painting? I am inclined to think so.

I have seen the announcement of a coming exhibition of impressionists called Gauguin, Bernard, Anquetin and other names. So I am inclined to think that a new sect has again been formed, no less infallible than those already existing.

Was that the exhibition you spoke of? What storms in teacups.

My health is all right, considering; I feel happier here with my work than I could be outside. By staying here a good long time, I shall have learned regular habits and in the long run the result will be more order in my life and less susceptibility. That will be so much to the good. . . . (594, *c.* 9 June 1889, F.)

. . . Thank you very much for the package of colours. Subtract them from the order sent since, but if you could manage it *not* for the quantity of white. Thank you also very heartily for the Shakespeare. It will help me not to forget the little English I know, but above all it is so fine. I have begun to read the series of which I knew least, which formerly, distracted by other things or not having the time, I could not read; the series of the kings: I have already read *Richard II*, *Henry IV* and half of *Henry V*. . . .

And so what Rembrandt has alone or almost alone among painters, that tenderness of gaze which we see, whether in the *Men of Emmaus* or in the *Jewish Bride* or in some such strange angelic figure as the picture you have had the good fortune to see, that heartbroken tenderness, that glimpse of a superhuman infinitude that seems so natural there – in many places you come upon it in Shakespeare too. And then above all he is full of portraits, grave or gay, like *Six* and like the *Traveller*, and like *Saskia*.

When I think of the impressionists and of all the problems of art nowadays, what lessons there are for us in that very thing. . . .

If they dare call themselves primitives, certainly they would do well to learn a little to be primitives as *men* before pronouncing the word primitive as a title, which would give them a right to anything whatever. But as for those who may be the cause of the impressionists' unhappiness, well, they are in a pretty serious predicament, even though they make light of it. . . .

How fine Zola's books will continue to be, just because there is life in them.

What has life in it too is that Mother is glad that you are married, and I think that this cannot be unpleasant to yourselves, you and Jo. But the separation from Cor will be harder on her than one can imagine. It is just in learning to suffer without complaint, in learning to look on pain without repugnance, that you risk vertigo, and yet it is possible, yet you may even catch a glimpse of a vague likelihood that on the other side of life we shall see good reason for the existence of pain, which seen from here sometimes so fills the whole horizon that it takes on the proportions of a hopeless deluge. We know very little about this, about its proportions, and it is better to look at a wheat field, even in the form of a picture. . . . (597, 30 June–4 July 1889, F.)

. . . Old man – don't let's forget that the little emotions are the great captains of our lives, and that we obey them without knowing it. . . . Don't forget henceforth that neither our spleen and melancholy, nor yet our feelings of good nature and common sense, are our sole guides, and above all not our final guardians; and if you find yourself faced with heavy responsibilities to be risked if not undertaken, honestly, let's not be *too* much concerned about each other. . . . (603, 6 July 1889, F.)

He retained his urge to work even when fresh attacks occurred.

I thank Jo very much for having written, and knowing that you want me to drop you a line, I must let you know that it is very difficult for me to write, my head is so disordered. So I am taking advantage of an interval. Dr Peyron is very kind to me and very patient. You can imagine that I am terribly distressed because the attacks have come back, when I was already beginning to hope that it would not return.

It would perhaps be a good thing if you wrote a few words to Dr Peyron to tell him that working on my pictures is almost a necessity for my recovery, for these days without anything to do, and without being able to go to the room they had allotted me to do my painting in, are almost unbearable.

(My friend Roulin has written me too.)

I have received a catalogue of the Gauguin, Bernard, Schuffenecker, etc., exhibition, which I find interesting. Gauguin has also written a kind letter, though a little vague and obscure, but after all I must say that I think they are right to have an exhibition among themselves.

For many days *my mind has been absolutely wandering*, as in Arles, quite as much if not worse, and presumably the attacks will come back again in the future; it is *abominable*.

For four days I have been unable to eat because of a swollen throat.

I hope it is not complaining too much if I tell you these details, but I do it to show you that I am not yet in a condition to go to Paris or to Pont-Aven, unless it were to Charenton. I no longer see any possibility of having courage or hope, but after all, it wasn't just yesterday that we found this job of ours wasn't a cheerful one. . . . (601, *c.* 17 Aug. 1889, F.)

He made no reference to thoughts of suicide, but his physician, Dr Peyron, mentioned them to Theo in a note enclosed with Vincent's letter of 3/4 September.

I add a few words to your brother's letter to inform you that he has quite recovered from a crisis, that he has completely regained his lucidity of mind, and that he has resumed painting as he used to do. His thoughts of suicide have disappeared, only disturbing dreams remain, but they tend to disappear too, and their intensity is less great. His appetite has returned, and he has resumed his usual mode of life. (Dr Peyron to Theo, 602a, 3/4 Sept. 1889, F.)

There is coherence between his despondency about the series of attacks and the irresistible re-emergence of his old longing for the North, in which the word 'North' has both personal and aesthetic connotations. He wanted to rid himself of the Impressionistic palette and see what he could achieve again with greys.

. . . Your telling me of Maus having been to see my canvases made me think a good deal about the Belgian painters just now and during my illness.

Then memories overwhelmed me like an avalanche, and I tried to reconstruct that whole school of modern Flemish artists, until I was as homesick as a lost dog.

Which does no good, because our way lies – forward, and retracing one's steps is forbidden and impossible. I mean, we can think about the past without letting ourselves be drowned in too sad a longing. . . .

Well, Henri Conscience is by no means a perfect writer, but here and there, and a little everywhere, what a painter! And what human kindness in what he said and intended. I have a preface of his in my head all the time (that of *Le Conscrit*), in one of his books where he says that he had been very ill and that during his illness, in spite of his efforts, he felt his affection for men grow faint, and that on long walks in the open fields his feeling of love returned. This fatality in suffering and despair – there, I wound up again for another spell – I thank him for it.

I am writing this letter little by little in the intervals when I am tired of painting. Work is going pretty well – I am struggling with a canvas begun some days before my indisposition, a *Reaper*; the study is all yellow, terribly thickly painted, but the subject was fine and simple. For I see in this reaper – a vague figure fighting like a devil in the midst of the heat to get to the end of his task – I see in him the image of death, in the sense that humanity might be the wheat he is reaping. So it is – if you like – the opposite of that sower I tried to do before. But there's nothing sad in this death, it goes its way in broad daylight with a sun flooding everything with a light of pure gold. . . .

My dear brother – it is always in between my work that I write to you – I am working like one actually possessed, more than ever I am in a dumb fury of work. And I think that this will help cure me. Perhaps something will happen to me like what Eug. Delacroix spoke of, 'I discovered painting when I no longer had any teeth or breath left', in the sense that my distressing illness makes me work with a dumb fury – very slowly – but from morning till night without slackening – and – the secret is probably this – work long and slowly. . . .

115–17 . . . And you will see this when you put the portrait with the light background that I have just finished next to the self-portraits in Paris, and that I look saner *now* than I did then, even much more so.

I am even inclined to think that the portrait will tell you how I am better than my letter, and that it will reassure you – it cost me some trouble to do. And then the *Reaper* is getting on, too, I think – it is very, very simple. . . .

There! The *Reaper* is finished, I think it will be one of those you keep at home – it is an image of death as the great book of nature speaks of it – but what I have sought is the 'almost smiling'. It is all yellow, except a line of violet hills, a pale fair yellow. I find it queer that I saw it like this from between the iron bars of a cell. . . . (604, 5–6 Sept. 1889, F.)

Although resisting the idea of being a martyr, he had some highly emotional thoughts about early Christians. His Adamism, his desire for a return to the origin of things, his liberation from the Church, re-awakened his weakened religious sentiments but now in a wider sense.

153 . . . And I must tell you – and you will see it in *La Berceuse*, however much of a failure and however feeble that attempt may be – if I had had the strength to continue, I should have made portraits of saints and holy women from life who would have seemed to belong to another age, and they would be middle-class women of the present day, and yet they would have had something in common with the very primitive Christians.

However, the emotions which that rouses are too strong, I shall stop at that, but later on, later on I do not say that I shall not return to the charge. . . . (605, 7 Sept. 1889, F.)

His critical faculties had remained intact. Dissatisfaction with his work referred particularly to *lines*, if these were impersonal or insensitive. He wanted them to be tauter and more considered. His ideas on Cloisonnism also came into this to some extent: here he is in agreement with Gauguin and Bernard.

. . . I am adding a study of flowers to the roll of canvases – nothing much, but after all I do not want to tear it up.

Altogether I think nothing in it *at all* good except the *Field of Wheat*, the *Mountain*, the *Orchard*, the *Olives* with the blue hills and the portrait and the *Entrance to the Quarry*, and the rest tells me *nothing*, because it lacks individual intention and feeling in the lines. Where these lines are tight and deliberate it begins to be a picture, even if it is exaggerated. That is a little what Gauguin and Bernard feel, they do not ask the correct shape of a tree at all, but they do insist that one can say if the shape is round or square – and honestly, they are right, exasperated as they are by certain people's photographic and fatuous perfection. They will not ask the correct tone of the mountains, but they will say: By God, the mountains were blue, were they? Then chuck on some blue and don't go telling me that it was a blue rather like this or that, it was blue, wasn't it? Good – make them blue and it's enough! . . . (607, 19 Sept. 1889, F.)

The idea of the North haunted him. Theo had found the address of a Dr Paul *205* Gachet, at Auvers-sur-Oise, north of Paris; Vincent might be able to live there under his supervision. Vincent hesitated between desire to leave as soon as possible after an attack and fear of leaving too soon.

... If I come North, even supposing that there were no room at this doctor's house, it is probably that after your recommendation and old Pissarro's he would find me board either with a family or quite simply at an inn. The main thing is to know the doctor, so that in case of an attack I do not fall into the hands of the police and get carried off to an asylum by force.

And I assure you that the North will interest me like a new country. ... (609, 5 Oct. 1889, F.)

The minor Dutch painter J.J. Isaäcson wrote an article which mentioned (in a footnote) some works by Vincent which he had seen in Theo's apartment. Vincent, disturbed perhaps by the vein of shallow mysticism which runs through Isaäcson's work, took no pleasure in this first taste of publicity.

... M. Peyron has told me again that there is a considerable improvement and that he has good hopes for me – and that he has no objection to my going to Arles just now.

And yet very often terrible fits of depression come over me, and besides the more my health comes back to normal, the more my brain can reason coldly, the more foolish it seems to me, and a thing against all reason, to be doing this painting which costs us so much and brings in nothing, not even the outlay. Then I feel very unhappy, and the trouble is that at my age it is damnably difficult to begin anything else.

In some Dutch newspaper which you put in with the Millets – I notice some Paris letters that I attribute to Isaäcson.

They are very subtle and one guesses the author to be a sorrowful creature, restless, with a rare tenderness – a tenderness which makes me instinctively think of H. Heine's *Reisebilder*.

No need to tell you that I think what he says of me in a note extremely exaggerated, and that's another reason why I should prefer him to say nothing about me. And in all these articles I find, side by side with very fine things, something, I don't quite know what, that seems to me unhealthy. ... (611, c. 25 Oct. 1889, F.)

Van Gogh made no secret of his criticism of contemporary adaptations of the symbols of Christ by Bernard and Gauguin. In his opinion they painted Christ in the Garden of Olives without understanding olive trees; he could convey his own mystical experiences by painting the trees alone. Supported by the example of Puvis de Chavannes, he wanted to prove that in this way he could paint sentiments that were both ancient and modern. He was at this time working long hours and slowly. His mania for speed was a thing of the past.

... The thing is that this month I have been working in the olive groves, because their *Christs in the Garden*, with nothing really observed, have got on my nerves. Of course with me there is no question of doing anything from the Bible – and I have written to Bernard and Gauguin too that I considered that our duty is thinking, not dreaming, so that when looking at their work I was astonished at their letting themselves go like that. For Bernard has sent me photos of his canvases. The trouble with them is that they are a sort of dream or nightmare – that they are erudite enough – you can see that it is someone who is gone on the primitives – but frankly the English Pre-Raphaelites did it much better, and then again Puvis and Delacroix, much more healthily than the Pre-Raphaelites. ... (615, c. 18 Nov. 1889, F.)

... Only we mustn't forget that an old crock is an old crock and so in no case do I have the right to any pretensions. I think that at home in Holland they always value painting more or less, so that an institution would hardly object to letting me do it. However, over and above painting, it would be important to have the opportunity for an occupation, and it would cost less. Hasn't the country, and working in it, always been to our taste? And aren't we rather indifferent, you as much as I, to the life of a big city? ...

So that means that I do not hesitate to make copies. I should so much like, if I had time to travel, to copy Giotto's work, that painter who would be as modern as Delacroix, if he were not primitive, yet so different from the other primitives. However, I have not seen much of his work, but there is one piece which is comforting. ... (623, Jan. 1890, F.)

Albert Aurier.

Vincent was deeply moved by two events which took place in January 1890: the birth of his namesake Vincent in Paris on 31 January, and the appearance in the *Mercure de France* of the first basic study of his work, by Albert Aurier (1865–92). Vincent was undoubtedly pleased, and wanted to send copies to three men, all of them art dealers. They were Alexander Reid, H.C. Tersteeg, and C.M. van Gogh. None of them was now a friend, but all had once had it in their power to help him.

Aurier was a student of law, who wrote, painted and drew; Rémy de Gourmont called him 'an innovator in art criticism'. It was therefore no jaded professional scribe who was the first to boost Vincent's work. Vincent had indeed transmitted a spark. Aurier was an ardent admirer of the Italian Primitives, and Vincent's interest in Giotto, which had developed in isolation, is thereby placed in a wider context.

... In the case of Vincent van Gogh, despite the sometimes disconcerting strangeness of his work, it is difficult ... to contest the naïve truthfulness of his art, the ingenuity of his concepts. Indeed, independently of that undefinable aroma of good faith and of things really seen which all his pictures exhale, his choice of subjects, the constant harmony of the most excessive colours, the honesty in the study of characters, the continuous search for the essential meaning of each object, a thousand significant details unquestionably proclaim his profound and almost childlike sincerity, his great love of nature and of truth – of his own truth. ... What particularizes his entire work is the excess, excess in strength, excess in nervousness, in violence of expression. In his categorical affirmation of the character of things, in his frequently headstrong simplification of forms, in his insolence in depicting the sun face to face, in the vehement ardour of his drawing and of his colour, and even in the slightest particularities of his technique, he reveals a powerful being, a male, a bold man, often brutal and sometimes ingenuously delicate. This can be seen in the almost orgiastic excesses of everything that he has painted; he is a fanatic, an enemy of bourgeois sobriety and of trifling details, a kind of drunken giant, better able to move mountains than to handle *bibelots*, an ebullient brain which irresistibly pours its lava into all the ravines of art, a terrible and highstrung genius, often sublime, sometimes grotesque, almost always on the edge of the pathological. Lastly and above all, he is a hyper-aesthete with obvious symptoms who perceives with abnormal and possibly even painful intensity the imperceptible and secret character of lines and forms, and even more of colours, of light, of the magic iridescence of shadows, of nuances which are invisible to healthy eyes. And that is why the realism of this neurotic, why his sincerity and his truth are so different. ...

This robust and true artist, with the brutal hands of a giant, with the nerves of a hysterical woman, with the soul of a mystic, so original and so alone in the midst of the pitiful art of our time, will he experience some day – anything is possible – the joy of rehabilitation, the repentant cajoleries of fashion? Possibly. But whatever happens, and even if it should become fashionable, as is very unlikely, to pay for his canvases the prices commanded by the dwarfish infamies of M. Meissonier, I do not think that much real sincerity will ever enter into the belated admiration of the public at large. Vincent van Gogh is both too simple and too subtle for the contemporary *esprit bourgeois*. He will never be fully understood except by his brothers, the true artists, and the happy ones among the little people, the very little people. ... (Albert Aurier, 'Les Isolés. Vincent van Gogh', *Mercure de France*, January 1890, quoted in translation from John Rewald, *Post-Impressionism*, revised edn, New York and London 1978, F.)

Many thanks for your article in the *Mercure de France*, which greatly surprised me. I like it very much as a work of art in itself, in my opinion your words produce colour, in short, I rediscover my canvases in your article, but better than they are, richer, more full of meaning. However, I feel uneasy in my mind when I reflect that what you say is due to others rather than to myself. For example, Monticelli in particular. Saying as you do: 'He is, as far as I know, the only painter who perceives the colouration of things with such intensity, with such a metallic, gem-like quality', be so kind as to go and see a certain bouquet by Monticelli at my brother's – a bouquet in white, forget-me-not blue and orange – then you will feel what I want to say. But the best, the most amazing Monticellis have long been in Scotland and England. In a museum in the North – the one in Lille, I believe – there is said to be a very marvel, rich in another way and certainly no less French than Watteau's *Départ pour Cythère*. At the moment M. Lauzet is engaged in reproducing some thirty works of Monticelli's.

Here you are; as far as I know, there is no colourist who is descended so straightly and directly from Delacroix, and yet I am of the opinion that Monticelli probably had Delacroix's colour theories only at secondhand; that is to say, that he got them more particularly from Diaz and Ziem. It seems to me that Monticelli's personal artistic temperament is exactly the same as that of the author of the *Decameron* – Boccaccio – a melancholic, somewhat resigned, unhappy man, who saw the wedding party of the world pass by, painting and analysing the lovers of his time – he, the one who had been left out of things. Oh! he no more imitated Boccaccio than Henri Leys imitated the primitives. You see, what I mean to say is that it seems there are things which have found their way to my name, which you could better say of Monticelli, to whom I owe so much. And further, I owe much to Paul Gauguin, with whom I worked in Arles for some months, and whom I already knew in Paris, for that matter.

Gauguin, that curious artist, that alien whose mien and the look in whose eyes vaguely remind one of Rembrandt's *Portrait of a Man* in the Galerie Lacaze – this friend of mine likes to make one feel that a good picture is equivalent to a good deed; not that he says so, but it is difficult to be on intimate terms with him without being aware of a certain moral responsibility. A few days before parting company, when my disease forced me to go into a lunatic asylum, I tried to paint 'his empty seat'.

It is a study of his armchair of sombre reddish-brown wood, the seat of greenish straw, and in the absent one's place a lighted torch and modern novels.

If an opportunity presents itself, be so kind as to have a look at this study, by way of a memento of him; it is done entirely in broken tones of green and red. Then you will perceive that your article would have been fairer, and consequently more powerful, I think, if, when discussing the question of the future of 'tropical painting' and of colours, you had done justice to Gauguin and Monticelli before speaking of me. *For the part which is allotted to me, or will be allotted to me, will remain, I assure you, very secondary.* . . .

And in conclusion, I declare that I do not understand why *you* should speak of Meissonier's 'Infamies'. It is possible that I have inherited from the excellent Mauve an absolutely unlimited admiration for Meissonier; Mauve's eulogies on Troyon and Meissonier used to be inexhaustible – a strange pair. . . .

In the next batch that I send my brother, I shall include a study of cypresses for you, if you will do me the favour of accepting it in remembrance of your article. I am still working on it at the moment, as I want to put in a little figure. The cypress is so characteristic of the scenery of Provence; you will feel it and say: 'Even the colour is black'. Until now I have not been able to do them as I feel them; the emotions that grip me in front of nature can cause me to lose consciousness, and then follows a fortnight during which I cannot work. Nevertheless, before leaving here I feel sure I shall return to the charge and attack the cypresses. The study I have set aside for you represents a group of them in the corner of a wheat field during a summer mistral. So it is a note of a certain nameless black in the restless gusty blue of the wide sky, and the vermilion of the poppies contrasting with this dark note.

You will see that this constitutes something like the combination of tones in those pretty Scotch tartans of green, blue, red, yellow, black, which at the time seemed so charming to you as well as to me, and which, alas, one hardly sees any more nowadays.

Meanwhile, dear Sir, accept my gratitude for your article. When I go to Paris in the spring, I certainly shall not fail to call on you to thank you in person. . . . (Vincent to Albert Aurier, 626a, 10/11 Feb. 1890, F.)

Proud of the honour bestowed upon him, he also wrote to the Ginoux family in Arles to tell them about the favourable publicity he was receiving. His sense of collectivity was genuine, and his sense of personality remained modest. He continued to regard himself as a link supported by his past and present.

Anna, a sister of his Belgian friend Boch, bought a canvas by Vincent at the *Vingtistes'* exhibition (*Les XX*) in Brussels for 400 francs, and a second Van Gogh from Tanguy a little later on. The tide was undoubtedly turning. The impressions of his work which a few visitors had gained at Theo's appartment in Paris, and at Tanguy's, must have been powerful indeed to achieve such avant-garde publicity suddenly. It came too late for Vincent, as would soon become apparent. He paid another visit to Arles on 22/23 February, and there followed a relatively long crisis which inhibited his writing and his work.

... What am I to say about these last two months? Things are not going well at all. I am sadder and more wretched than I can say, and I do not know at all where I have got to.

The order for paints is rather big, so let me wait for half of it if it is more convenient to you.

While I was ill I nevertheless did some little canvases from memory which you will see later, memories of the North, and now I have just finished a corner of a sunny meadow, which I think is fairly vigorous. You will see it soon. ...

Letters from home have come too, which I have not yet had the courage to read, I feel so melancholy. Please ask M. Aurier not to write any more articles on my painting, insist upon this, that to begin with he is mistaken about me, since I am too overwhelmed with grief to be able to face publicity. Making pictures distracts me, but if I hear them spoken of, it pains me more than he knows. ... (629, 30 Apr. 1890, F.)

... I have talked to M. Peyron about the situation and I told him that it was almost impossible for me to endure my lot here, and that not knowing at all with any clearness what line to take, I thought it preferable to return North.

If you think well of it and if you mention a date on which you would expect me in Paris, I will have myself accompanied part of the way, either to Tarascon, or to Lyons, by someone from here. Then you can wait for me or get someone to wait for me at the station in Paris. Do what seems best to you. I will leave my furniture temporarily where it is in Arles. It is with friends, and I am sure that they will send it when you want it, but the carriage and packing would be almost as much as it is worth. I think of it as a shipwreck – this journey. Well, we cannot do what we like, nor what we ought to do, either. As soon as I got out into the park, I got back all my lucidity for work; I have more ideas in my head than I could ever carry out, but without it clouding my mind. The brush strokes come like clockwork. So relying on that, I dare think that I shall find my balance in the North, once delivered from surroundings and circumstances which I do not understand or wish to understand. ... (630, 2 May 1890, F.)

... I have tried to be patient, up till now I have done no one any harm; is it fair to have me accompanied like a dangerous beast? No, thank you, I protest. If an attack comes, they know at every station what to do, and then I should let them do what they like.

But I dare believe that my mental balance will not fail me. I am so sorry to leave like this that my sorrow will be stronger than my madness, so I shall have, I think, the necessary poise. ... (631, May 1890, F.)

These are valuable data because of the lucidity of Vincent's reactions to his condition, his fitness to work and the tremendous influence of nature on his creative powers. He was aware that '*My sorrow will be stronger than my madness*' – an unforgettable statement in which he established the nature of a grief that transcended mental confusion. To us, and perhaps also to him, it had a cause but no longer a name: '*I think of it as a shipwreck, this journey.*' His final request from Saint-Rémy was to his landlord at Arles, to dispatch the looking-glass which for years had been an indispensable aid to his self-confrontations.

... The rest of the furniture, goodness yes, there is the mirror, for instance, which I should like to have. Will you kindly paste strips of paper across the glass to prevent its breaking? – but the two chests of drawers, the chairs, tables, you may keep for your trouble, and if there are extra expenses, please let me know.

I greatly regret I fell ill on the day I came to Arles to say good-bye to you all – after that I was ill for two months without being able to work. However, at present I am quite well again. ... (Vincent to Ginoux, 634a, 12/13 May 1890, F.)

Despite some qualms on the part of the Saint-Rémy doctor, and of Theo and Jo, Vincent left for Paris by night train on 16 May 1890 and arrived at 5 a.m.

the next day. He stayed for three days, with the idea of getting to know his sister-in-law and his young nephew, then three-and-a-half months old. There is nothing to suggest that any heated discussions about Theo's future in Paris took place at the time. However, Vincent did have some difficulty in getting used to Paris and normal family life. After three days he left by train for Auvers-sur-Oise, either by the last train on 19 May or next morning. On 2 June Theo and Jo were in a position to write calmly to Wil:

Vincent has been staying with us. He has never looked healthier, and his speech is quite normal again. He has had an operation, and all his teeth have gone because of the poor state of his stomach. However, he still feels that the fits may return and this is something he is afraid of. It seems that they come on suddenly, and that at Saint-Rémy nothing was done about them apart from making him rest. He writes that he is staying at an inn, c/o Ravoux, which suits him very well for the moment. . . . (Theo and Jo to Wil, 2 June 1890.)

I have been wanting to write you collectedly for several days already, but I've been absorbed in my work. This morning your letter arrived, for which I thank you, and for the 50-fr. note it contained. Yes, I think that for many reasons it would be good if we could be together again for a week of your holidays, if longer is impossible. I often think of you, Jo, and the little one, and I notice that the children here in the healthy open air look well. And yet even here it is difficult enough to bring them up, therefore it must be all the more terrible at times to keep them safe and sound in Paris on a fourth floor. But after all, we must take things as they come. M. Gachet says that a father and mother must naturally feed themselves up, he talks of taking 2 litres of beer a day, etc., in those circumstances. But you will certainly enjoy furthering your acquaintance with him, and he already counts on all of you coming, and talks about it every time I see him. He certainly seems to me as ill and distraught as you or me, and he is older and lost his wife several years ago, but he is very much the doctor, and his profession and faith still sustain him. We are great friends already, and as it happens, he already knew Brias of Montpellier and has the same idea of him that I have, that there you have someone significant in the history of modern art.

I am working at his portrait, the head with a white cap, very fair, very light; the hands also a light flesh tint, a blue frock coat and a cobalt blue background, leaning on a red table, on which are a yellow book and a foxglove plant with purple flowers. It has the same sentiment as the self-portrait I did when I left for this place.

M. Gachet is absolutely *fanatical* about this portrait, and wants me to do one for him, if I can, exactly like it. I should like to myself. He has now got so far as to understand the last portrait of the Arlésienne, of which you have one in pink; he always comes back to these two portraits when he comes to see the studies, and he understands them exactly, exactly, I tell you, as they are.

I hope to send you a portrait of him soon. Then I have painted two studies at his house, which I gave him last week, an aloe with marigolds and cypresses, then last Sunday some white roses, vines and a white figure in it.

I shall most probably also do the portrait of his daughter, who is nineteen years old, and with whom I imagine Jo would soon be friends.

Then I am looking forward to doing the portraits of all of you in the open air; yours, Jo's and the little one's. . . . And I am well. I go to bed at nine o'clock, but get up at five most of the time. I hope that it will not be unpleasant to meet again after a long absence. . . .

Now nothing, absolutely nothing, is keeping us here but Gachet – but he will remain a friend, I should think. I feel that I can do not too bad a picture every time I go to his house, and he will continue to ask me to dinner every Sunday or Monday.

But till now, though it is pleasant to do a picture there, it is rather a burden for me to dine and lunch there, for the good soul takes the trouble to have four- or five-course dinners, which is as dreadful for him as for me – for he certainly hasn't a strong digestion. The thing that has somewhat prevented me from protesting against it is that it recalls the old times to him, when there were those family dinners which we ourselves know so well. But the modern idea of eating one – or at most two – courses is certainly progress, as well as a remote return to real antiquity. Altogether father Gachet is very, yes, very like you and me. . . . (638, 3 June 1890, F.)

205

155

200

It seems unlikely that it will ever be possible to produce a reliable reconstruction of the sequence of the works, or of the letters exchanged between Auvers and Paris, in this period of Van Gogh's life. For those whose desire it is to set in order, arrange and rearrange, it seems hard to accept the abrupt, shocking and uneven aspects of his last works, verging as they do on disorientation and chaos. And yet the destruction, the attack on order, proves to be the reality of a process. The letters are comparatively short, for Vincent, and afford some insight into his moods, particularly in relation to Gachet (both in criticism and self-projection). The one to his mother, probably written on 11 or 12 June, after the visit from Theo and his family, has profound undertones. Although he had formerly resented his father more than his mother, both parents had been equally incapable of understanding art. Now, suddenly, he had no reservations about confiding to his mother the thoughts that were passing through his mind both as a man and as an artist. The passage he quoted from I Corinthians 13 had impressed him deeply as early as 1877 (see p. 32); and farewells had always had a more than normal effect on his emotions. 'Through a glass, darkly' meant for Vincent, above all, the confrontation with a mirror turned solely towards himself, as a means of heightening self-awareness.

What struck me in your letter was that you say that, having gone to Nuenen, you saw all those things again, 'being thankful that they were once yours', and now being able to leave them to others with a peaceful mind.

As through a glass, darkly – so it has remained; life and the why of saying good-bye and going away and the continuance of unrest, one does not understand more of it than that.

For me life might well continue being isolated. Those whom I have been most attached to – I never descried them otherwise than through a glass, darkly. And yet there is a reason for there occasionally being more harmony in my work now. Painting is something in itself. Last year I read in some book or other that writing a book or painting a picture was like having a child. This I will not accept as applicable to me – I have always thought that the latter was the more natural and the best – so I say, only *if* it were so, only *if* it were the same.

This is the very reason why at times I exert myself to the utmost, though it happens to be this very work that is least understood, and for me it is the only link between the past and the present.

Last Sunday Theo, his wife and their child were here, and we lunched at Dr Gachet's. . . . (Vincent to mother, 641a, 11/12 June 1890.)

What is it in St Paul's words that struck such a profound chord in Vincent that he never reasoned them out and yet never forgot them? In a brilliant essay ('Le miroir des enigmes', *Enquêtes 1937–1952*, Paris 1957, pp. 177–83), Jorge Luis Borges discusses the text and its various translations, and in particular the fascination it exercised on Léon Bloy. Van Gogh knew himself to be impelled by unconscious emotions and forces (*sans le savoir*), and craved ultimate knowledge of himself. Borges quotes a telling passage from Bloy: 'The terrifying immensity of the abysses of the sky is an illusion, an external reflection of *our own abyss, seen in a mirror*. . . . If we see the Milky Way, this means that it truly exists in our souls.' Surely this is what Van Gogh saw as he peered into his looking-glass.

'If the symbolic function functions, we are inside,' said Jacques Lacan, whose own mirror contemplations are well known in psychoanalytical literature (*Séminaire II*, Paris 1978, p. 48). He added: 'We are so much inside that we cannot get out.' To get out, to leave – this, presumably, was how Vincent interpreted St Paul – was the action required if he was to pass from his isolation to an inner universe.

Did Theo's and Jo's family problems then worry Vincent and cause a worsening of his condition? There had been great anxiety over the baby; but this had abated, and the child was taking ass's milk. Nor were financial worries as threatening as at other times; Theo still planned to set up in business on his own, and, although he later abandoned the plan (letter to Wil, 22 July), he was still hoping that a major turning-point lay ahead when he wrote to Vincent at the end of June:

We have gone through a period of the greatest anxiety; our dear little boy has been very ill, but fortunately the doctor, who was uneasy himself, told Jo, You are not going to lose the child because of this. . . .

Don't bother your head about me or about us, old fellow, but remember that what gives me the greatest pleasure is the knowledge that you are in good health and that you are busy with your work, which is admirable. You have too much ardour as it is, and we shall be ready for the battle for a long time to come yet, for we shall have to battle all through life without eating the oats of charity they give to old horses in the mansions of the great. We shall draw the plough until our strength forsakes us, and we shall still look with admiration at the sun or the moon, according to the hour. . . . (Theo to Vincent, T39, 30 June 1890, F.)

Between 5 and 15 July Vincent is thought to have stayed one further day with Theo in Paris; he was invited on Saturday 5 July and replied that day that he would come by 'the first train on Sunday' – presumably the next day. The well-known outcome of the visit was that all three became more tense, more tired and more agitated.

. . . It is certain, I think, that we are all of us thinking of the little one, and that Jo must say what she wishes. Theo, like myself, will, I believe, agree to her opinion. For myself, I can only say at the moment that I think we all need rest. I feel – a failure. So much for me – I feel that this is the lot which I accept and which will not change.

But one more reason, *putting aside all ambition*, we can live together for years without ruining each other. You see that with the canvases which are still at Saint-Rémy, there are at least eight with the four here, I am trying not to lose my skill. It is the absolute truth, however, that it is difficult to acquire a certain facility in production, and by ceasing to work, I shall lose it more quickly and more easily than the pains it has cost to acquire it. And the prospect grows darker, I see no happy future at all.

Write me by return mail if you haven't already written, and good handshakes for both in thought. I wish there were a possibility of seeing each other again soon with more collected minds. (Vincent to Theo and Jo, 648, July 1890, F.)

A letter from Jo was intended to make him realize that he had taken too serious a view of the situation.

Jo's letter was really like a gospel to me, a deliverance from the agony which had been caused by the hours I had shared with you which were a bit too difficult and trying for us all. It was no slight thing when we all felt our daily bread was in danger, no slight thing when for reasons other than that we felt that our means of subsistence were fragile.

Back here, I still felt very sad and continued to feel the storm which threatens you weighing on me too. What was to be done – you see, I generally try to be fairly cheerful, but my life is also threatened at the very root, and my steps are also wavering.

I feared – not altogether but yet a little – that being a burden to you, you felt me to be rather a thing to be dreaded, but Jo's letter proves to me clearly that you understand that for my part I am as much in toil and trouble as you are.

There – once back here I set to work again – though the brush almost slipped from my fingers, but knowing exactly what I wanted, I have painted three more big canvases since.

They are vast fields of wheat under troubled skies, and I did not need to go out of my way to try to express sadness and extreme loneliness. I hope you will see them soon – for I hope to bring them to you in Paris as soon as possible, since I almost think that these canvases will tell

206, 208

211 you what I cannot say in words, the health and restorative forces that I see in the country. Now the third canvas is Daubigny's garden, a picture I have been thinking about since I came here.

I hope with all my heart that the intended journey will give you a little distraction. . . . (Vincent to Theo and Jo, 649, ?9 July 1890, F.)

Reassurance could be of no avail to a state of mind which was waiting for the decision to pull the trigger – any more than the first signs of worldly success could have lifted him out of his deep depression at Saint-Rémy. Before anyone could have suspected, and after Theo's prospects appeared to have brightened, Vincent was about to write his last two letters. One of them (652) was found on him, undated and unsigned, by Theo after his death. Its two final paragraphs make this the more important of the two. Dr Jan Hulsker – surely with reason – thought it was written before the other. In its last sentence, Vincent summarized his own crisis, the fatal state of his body and mind from which his work sprang; what he then did to himself was not the consequence of Theo's precarious financial position.

Thanks for your kind letter and for the 50-fr. note it contained.

There are many things I should like to write you about, but I feel it is useless. I hope you have found those worthy gentlemen favourably disposed toward you.

Your reassuring me as to the peacefulness of your household was hardly worth the trouble, I think, having seen the weal and woe of it for myself. And I quite agree with you that rearing a boy on a fourth floor is a hell of a job for you as well as for Jo.

Since the thing that matters most is going well, why should I say more about things of less importance? My word, before we have a chance to talk business more collectedly, we shall probably have a long way to go.

The other painters, whatever they think, instinctively keep themselves at a distance from discussions about the actual trade.

Well, the truth is, we can only make our pictures speak. But yet, my dear brother, there is this that I have always told you, and I repeat it once more with all the earnestness that can be expressed by the effort of a mind diligently fixed on trying to do as well as possible – I tell you again that I shall always consider you to be something more than a simple dealer in Corots, that through my mediation you have your part in the actual production of some canvases, which will retain their calm even in the catastrophe.

For this is what we have got to, and this is all or at least the main thing that I can have to tell you at a moment of comparative crisis. At a moment when things are very strained between dealers in pictures of dead artists, and living artists.

Well, my own work, I am risking my life for it and my reason has half foundered because of it – that's all right – but you are not among the dealers in men as far as I know, and you can still choose your side, I think, acting with humanity, but que veux-tu? (652, 23/24 July 1890, not sent, F.)

Thanks for your letter of today and the 50-fr. note it contained.

Perhaps I'd rather write you about a lot of things, but to begin with, the desire to do so has completely left me, and then I feel it is useless.

I hope that you will have found those worthy gentlemen well disposed toward you.

As far as I'm concerned, I apply myself to my canvases with all my mind, I am trying to do as well as certain painters whom I have greatly loved and admired.

Now I'm back, what I think is that the painters themselves are fighting more and more with their backs to the wall.

Very well . . . but isn't the moment for trying to make them understand the usefulness of a union already gone? On the other hand a union, if it should take shape, would founder if the rest should have to founder. Then perhaps you would say that some dealers might combine on behalf of the impressionists, but that would be very short-lived. Altogether I think that personal initiative remains powerless, and having had experience of it, should we start again?

I noticed with pleasure that the Gauguin from Brittany which I saw was very beautiful, and I think that the others he has done there must be so too.

Drawing from letter 651.

Perhaps you will look at this sketch of Daubigny's garden. It is one of my most purposeful canvases. I add a sketch of some old thatched roofs and the sketches of two size 30 canvases representing vast fields of wheat after the rain. Hirschig asked me to beg you to be kind enough to order for him the list of paints enclosed at the same colour merchant's whose paints you send me.

Tasset can send them to him direct, cash on delivery, but then he would have to give him the 20 per cent reduction, which would be simplest. Or else you could put them in with the package of paints for me, adding the bill, or telling me how much the total is, and then he would send the money to you. You cannot get anything good in the way of paints here.

I have reduced my own order to the barest minimum. Hirschig is beginning to understand things a little, it seems to me; he has done a portrait of the old schoolmaster, he has got him well – and then he has some landscape studies which are like the Konings at your place, almost the same in colour. They will come to be quite like these perhaps, or like the things by Voerman which we saw together.

Good-bye now, and good luck in business, etc., remember me to Jo and handshakes in thought.

[PS.] Daubigny's garden, foreground of grass in green and pink. To the left a green and lilac *211* bush and the stem of a plant with whitish leaves. In the middle a border of roses, to the right a wicket, a wall, and above the wall a hazel tree with violet foliage. Then a lilac hedge, a row of rounded yellow lime trees, the house itself in the background, pink, with a roof of bluish tiles. A bench and three chairs, a figure in black with a yellow hat and in the foreground a black cat. Sky pale green. . . . (651, 23/24 July 1890, F.)

Vincent left the Ravoux hotel with his painting gear on 27 July 1890 and, once he was out of sight, shot himself with a revolver. The scanty information provided by local people who saw him on that day leaves us in some doubt about the exact spot where the attempt took place: on the way to Chaponval or Commenay, or behind a manure heap in the yard of a small farm in Rue Boucher. The location of the bullet – chest or stomach – was never established officially. As usual, the story of this suicide attempt has been explained in a multitude of ways, with the prior indications which, according to Van Gogh's letters, occurred repeatedly from 1873 onwards, carrying most weight.

The maturing of his will to escape from the mysterious process of dying a natural death was wholly in tune with his character. He had always broken tensions by forced departures or forced decisions. He could never wait and see, either in his work or in his life as an artist. As Maurice Blanchot wrote in his subtle analysis of the subject, 'there is in suicide a remarkable intention to abolish the future as a mystery of death; one wishes in some way to kill oneself so that the future may be without secrets' (*L'Espace littéraire*, Paris 1955, pp. 127–31).

The initial failure of his attempt changed his situation in a way that was significant. He had precipitated the very confrontation he had hoped to escape. This enabled him to listen to what those who kept watch by his bedside said, so that the lucid calm of expectancy could come over him. He smoked his pipe as he waited. He was at last allowed to see behind the glass, 'face to face', in the morning of 29 July 1890.

Did Auvers, after Arles and Saint-Rémy, mark a genuine conclusion? For Van Gogh himself, the problem of his return to the North because of sickness was at the same time a problem which concerned his art. Impressionism and Neo-Impressionism had been absorbed and left behind; and as far as Symbolism was concerned he stood alone. Inwardly, though not outwardly, he was more of a thorough-going Symbolist than Bernard, Gauguin, Denis and the others; the man who could so easily have joined in the revival of the symbols of Christ had mentally worked out the reality of things according to their nature as well as his own, and he wanted to go on depicting that reality.

196–99 One significant influence of the period at Auvers – though not a new discovery – was Puvis de Chavannes. Puvis, with his mural-like style and soft, light colours, neither followed nor turned his back on the Impressionists, but revived, with a nineteenth-century slant, something of the measured and timeless dignity of the great fresco-painters who preceded Raphael and Michelangelo. His openness to such an influence suggests the beginning of a change in his work, which he failed to bring to a conclusion, torn as he was between the violence and distortion of some of his landscapes and the resignation and consolation of the Gachet portrait.

As in a Shakespeare play, the final act brought the collapse of a family. Theo's delicate health deteriorated sharply within a month of the funeral, and in September he collapsed completely. He died in a Utrecht clinic on 25 January 1891. Hard pressed though they had always been, he and Jo had always had hopes for the future; Vincent's death was swiftly followed by the end of those hopes. In September 1890, Theo's employers appointed a successor.

170 Two Poplars on a Road Through the Hills, Oct. 1889
In the asylum at Saint-Rémy-de-Provence, Vincent was for the first time completely taken care of, but no longer had the freedom to eat (or not eat) as he chose, to drink, and to overwork, that he had had in the Maison Jaune. He submitted to the rules, and reluctantly consented to be kept indoors when a crisis was near. The immediate surroundings were also different. Nature – vineyards, olive trees, poplars, cypresses, hills, ravines – provided more frequent subjects. A painting like this has great tension in the main lines of the composition and in every detail of the mobile, baroque handling. The brush strokes never repeat themselves. He was reading a lot of Shakespeare, and thinking of the Greeks (Homer, Socrates). His emotional and reflective life remained at a high level even in the asylum. Listening to the summer music of the cicadas, 'dear to the good Socrates . . . here certainly they still sing in ancient Greek' (601).

Saint-Rémy

171 Olive Trees, Sept.–Nov. 1889
172 Undergrowth (Ivy), July 1889

173 *Pine Woods at Dusk*, Oct.–Dec. 1889
174 *Self-portrait*, Sept. 1889

These four works, of very high quality, all date from a phase of serious illness, after a crisis overtook him as he painted in the fields in July 1889. Between *Undergrowth*, probably the earliest in date, and *Olive Trees*, Vincent found his way to a direct transformation of the observed landscape into curving, moving lines that are sometimes outlines but mostly a fusion of brush strokes that convey both colour and line. He now went further than the Japanese had done: no question of a decorative line, but an inner process of instant obedience to the power of vision. Ivy had been a symbolic plant for Vincent since early in his life; it reappears in this period of ill-humour, fatigue and apathy. The *Pine Woods* has the biting incisive character of a wood-engraving; it was entirely painted in the painful atmosphere of a Mistral – something like his description: 'mournful pines . . . superb sky effects . . . sometimes red . . . sometimes of an extremely neutral tone, and again pale citron' (617). The *Self-portrait* (sometimes classed among the works painted at Auvers in 1890) shows a Vincent uncertain of any future, far from his own lucidity of mind, full of mistrust, tired to death.

The view from inside

175 Fountain in the Garden of the Hôpital van Gogh, Saint-Rémy, 1981
176 *Fountain in the Garden of the Hôpital Saint-Paul, Saint-Rémy*, May–June 1889

177 *Poppies in a Field*, Apr. 1890
178 *Wheatfield Behind the Hôpital Saint-Paul*, June–Sept., 1889

His environment was subjected, in every part and in every detail, to the full power of his penetrating gaze; he did not see as an Impressionist but always looked beneath the surface, the light, the form. His eye encounters the same objects as does the camera, but expresses the communication of his inner life with the perceived outer world (see also *168, 169*). *Poppies in a Field* has sometimes been ascribed to the Arles period, plausibly so, in view of its classic and harmonious composition; but the same might be said of the Auvers landscape with train and carriage (F760), only a few months later. Van Gogh could be unpredictable at times.

The reaper theme, one painted on the spot and two replicas, was born 'some days before my indisposition' (604). He saw in the reaper 'the image of death, in the sense that humanity might be the wheat he is reaping'. Rilke wrote: 'Van Gogh might lose his mental composure, but his work was still there, behind the composure; he could not fall out of *that*.'

212

185 Self-portrait, Sept 1889

The *Self-portrait* must be one of the two
mentioned in letters 604, 607, W14 (not
Auvers, nor Paris, nor the one he sent to
Theo). It came from the Gachet family
directly to the Louvre.

A longing for the North

Sketches often have the quality of an artist talking to himself. These sketches from Saint-Rémy represent moments when Vincent was overcome by a regressive longing for the North. The absent North and the present South create a weakening of contact with reality, a submission to the grip of the past. The past is represented by his first great master, Millet; but also by the lifelong dream of having a family, a centre. These sketches evoke Nuenen – the fireplace, the peasants – but also Madame Roulin of Arles with her baby. The diggers belong to Etten, to Nuenen, and to Saint-Rémy itself. The sketches represent the reality of the poor people on the roads, his own eternal, restless walking through the fields, whether at Courrières or at Arles. They have no faces, but their legs keep moving, never at a standstill. He longed to be away from Saint-Rémy, but where?

186 *Winter Landscape with Figures*, Jan.– Apr. 1890
187 *Peasant Family by the Fireside*, May 1890
188 *Night: the Watch (after Millet)*, Oct. 1889

189 *Study of Nine Peasants, Two Diggers,*
Two Men with Wheelbarrow, early 1890
190 *On the Road,* early 1890
191 *Hands; a Digger,* early 1890

Reinterpretations

It seems that, of the copies or paraphrases
from the works of other artists, mostly
painted at Saint-Rémy, some thirty-six
still exist. Novotny and Chetham have
studied this phenomenon thoroughly, and
found a number of rational explanations
for the origin of these works, although
something irrational remains unsaid.
Vincent's illness often kept him indoors;
he had no models; he loved to do works in
series, and was free to concentrate on
experimentation, the themes being fixed.
His original was always a monochrome
print. 'I improvise colour on it, not, you
understand, altogether myself, but
searching for memories of *their* pictures –
but the memory, "the vague consonance
of colours which are at least right-feeling"
– that is my own interpretation. . . . My
brush goes between my fingers as a bow
should on a violin, and absolutely for my
own pleasure' (609).

192 Rembrandt van Rijn.
*Raising of Lazarus, c.*1632
193 Eugène Delacroix.
*Christ on the Lake of
Genesareth, (The Bark of
Christ),* 1854

220

194 *Raising of Lazarus (after Rembrandt)*,
May 1890
195 *Pietà (after Delacroix)*, Sept. 1889

The choice of themes echoes old religious
affinities. *The Bark of Christ* was
remembered for its *terribilità* of colour
(533); but his account of the Delacroix
Pietà has more of the pathos of Van Gogh
in it than that of Delacroix: 'There is in it
the greyish white countenance, the lost,
vague look of a person exhausted by
anxiety and weeping and waking, rather in
the manner of *Germinie Lacerteux*' (W14). 'I
was very distressed,' he told Theo, but 'if
you could see me working, my brain so
clear and my fingers so sure . . . that I have
drawn that *Pietà* without a single
measurement' (630). The *Raising of
Lazarus* is an adaptation of a section of
Rembrandt's etching, replacing the central
figure of Christ, and some others, by the
sun, as if Vincent had been aware of
Rembrandt's suggestion of 'the evocative
power of light' (Karel Boon, *The Complete
Etchings of Rembrandt*, New York n.d.)

Hope

196 Pierre Puvis de Chavannes. *Hope* (second version), 1872
197 Pierre Puvis de Chavannes. *Inter artes et naturam*, 1890
198 *Sketch from a Letter to Willemien* (W22), 4/5 June 1890

Puvis de Chavannes was linked with a change in Van Gogh's conception of art, which had been manifest at Arles through references to antiquity, Petrarch, Dante and Giotto. As early as Nuenen, Puvis had caught his attention. On the way north from Provence in 1890 he saw *Inter artes et naturam* at the Paris Salon and sketched it in a letter to his sister. He had, he told her, witnessed 'a rebirth, total but benevolent, of all the things one should have believed in, should have wished for – a strange and happy meeting of very distant antiquities and crude modernity' (W22). In the superb portrait of Puvis' wife, Princess Cantacuzène, he saw 'a woman already old, but exactly as Michelet wrote, "there is no such thing as an old woman".' The Symbolist generation admired Puvis as an example of what modern painting could aspire to be: 'Perhaps some day everyone will have neurosis, St Vitus' Dance, or something else. But doesn't the antidote exist? . . . See *Hope*, by Puvis de Chavannes' (574).

199 Pierre Puvis de Chavannes. *Princess Maria Cantacuzène*, 1883
200 *Young Girl in White Against a Background of Wheat*, 2nd half June 1890

Auvers and Dr Gachet

201 Dr Gachet's house at Auvers-sur-Oise, 1981
202 *Dr Gachet's Garden*, May 1890
203 The Town Hall, Auvers, 1981
204 *Town Hall, Auvers*, July 1890

224

205 *Dr Paul Gachet*, June 1890

The portrait of Dr Gachet is the second of two versions (see F753). The expression, in both versions, is 'the grieving expression of our time' (643), and 'an expression of melancholy, which would look like a grimace to many who saw the canvas' (w23).

The harvest

The reapers of Nuenen had mostly been seen from the back or in profile. This frontal sketch proves how the grasp of movement dominates; curling lines unite figure, clouds and field. The background is not so much the sky as the plain itself, as an endless surface, imagined by Vincent in a great wealth of pale colour. In his landscapes of Auvers he deliberately adopted a new, elongated format. 'We are still far from the time when people will understand the curious relation between one fragment of nature and another, which all the same explain and enhance each other.' Every form in the horizontal picture is open, and the trees do not seem to be rooted in the earth but to be restless, animate figures. Repeated long horizontal lines comprise the main divisions; but all the forms converge irresistibly upon the horizon.

206 *The Plain of Auvers*, July 1890
207 *The Mower*, July 1890
208 *The Plain of Auvers*, July 1890

209 *Landscape at Auvers in the Rain*, July 1890

Last landscapes

Van Gogh's Auvers period lasted just sixty-nine days: enough for him to create at least fourteen paintings of very high quality, among over eighty items listed in the La Faille catalogue. Even if further research were to reduce the number of Auvers works, it would remain evident that Vincent's creative tension at this time was abnormally

210 *Thatched Sandstone Cottages at Chapenval,* July 1890

211 Daubigny's Garden, with Black Cat, June–July 1890

high. Those sixty-nine days are full of unanswered questions; even the dating of his letters is problematic. Art historians have written more about the duplicates of *Dr Paul Gachet* and of *Daubigny's Garden* than about other problems; it is, however, in the landscapes that Auvers witnessed crucial conflicts and changes of direction concerning pictorial space and colour. By contrast with Arles and Saint-Rémy, this unrest is not formulated in a distinctive 'Auvers style'. The works show a whirlwind succession of stylistic forms, from pseudo-classic to baroque. His capacity for ecstatic lucidity, his moments of communion with the stars, have disappeared.

212 Père Pilon's House, June 1890

The end

A few of the names of those who followed the coffin: Theo van Gogh, Paul Gachet, Père Tanguy, Emile Bernard, Charles Laval, Hirschig, Mademoiselle Mesdag, Ravoux, Andries Bonger, together with peasants and others from the locality.

When the family's tenure of Vincent's grave expired after fifteen years, Jo van Gogh–Bonger took another plot, in an extension of the cemetery, where the two brothers now lie side by side. Theo had survived his brother by less than six months.

216 The Church at Auvers, 3–8 June 1890
Vincent described this work entirely in terms of colour;
and if he had not mentioned 'sand with the pink glow of
sunshine on it' (w22), we should not be aware of any
natural source of light in the picture at all. He has conjured
up a pure cobalt blue, deep, but also dark as night; the roof
is violet-orange. The church is transfigured, visionary,
more spectral than real.

BIBLIOGRAPHICAL NOTE

THE LETTERS

Vincent van Gogh, *Brieven aan zijn broeder*, edited and with an introduction by Jo van Gogh-Bonger, Amsterdam 1914. Three volumes; includes all letters to Theo; letters written in French printed in French. First reprint, 1924, unchanged. Second reprint, 1952–54, includes letters to Van Rappard, Bernard and Willemien, and from Theo to Vincent, plus informative articles and notes.

The Complete Letters of Vincent van Gogh, Greenwich, Conn., and London 1958. Three volumes. Reprinted 1978.

Letters of Vincent van Gogh, 1886–1890, Amsterdam and London 1977. A facsimile edition covering only the Paris and subsequent periods, including letters to Theo, Willemien, his mother, Eugène Boch and J.J. Isaäcson.

Van Gogh door Van Gogh, edited by Jan Hulsker, Amsterdam 1973. Extracts from the letters, presented in the context of the works, and revised datings.

Lettres de Paul Gauguin à Emile Bernard, 1881–1891, Geneva 1954.

Letters to an Artist: from Vincent van Gogh to Anton Ridder van Rappard, 1881–1885, New York 1937. (Dutch edition Amsterdam 1937.)

Lettres de Vincent van Gogh à Emile Bernard, Paris 1911.

Vincent van Gogh, *Briefe an Emile Bernard und Gauguin*, Basle 1921.

CATALOGUES

J.B. de la Faille, *The Works of Vincent van Gogh*, revised, augmented and annotated by an Editorial Board, chairman A.M. Hammacher, members Jan van Gelder, W. Jos de Gruyter, Jan Hulsker, Ellen Joosten, Horst Gerson, Sturla Gudlaugson, Amsterdam 1970.

Paul Lecaldano, *Tutta la pittura di Van Gogh*, with an introduction by Paul Aletrino, Milan 1971. (French edition, *Tout van Gogh*, Paris 1971.) Basically a concise edition of the above.

Jan Hulsker, *The Complete Van Gogh: Paintings, Drawings, Sketches*, Oxford and New York 1980. (Dutch edition, *Van Gogh en zijn weg*, Amsterdam 1977, 1979.) This is a reworking of the La Faille catalogue; dates are revised, paintings and drawings are mixed, and the numbering is changed. Some documentation has been omitted. Dates in the present book are based on Dr Hulsker's research.

SPECIALIZED STUDIES

English period
Alan Bowness, 'Vincent in England', in exhibition catalogue 'Van Gogh', Hayward Gallery, London 1968–69.

Vincent van Gogh on England, compiled from his letters by Ir.Dr. V.W. van Gogh, Amsterdam 1968.

Dutch period
Walter van Beselaere, *De Hollandsche Periode (1880–1885) in het werk van Vincent van Gogh*, Antwerp and Amsterdam 1937. (French edition Antwerp and Amsterdam 1937.)

Carlo Derkert, 'Theory and Practice in Van Gogh's Dutch Painting', *Kunsthistorisk Tidskrift*, xv 3/4, 1946.

Marc Edo Tralbaut, *Vincent van Gogh in Drenthe*, Assen 1959.

Paul Nizon, Die Anfänge van Goghs: der Zeichnungsstil der holländischen Zeit, diss. Bonn 1960.

Griselda Pollock, Vincent van Gogh and the Hague School, diss. London 1972. This formed the basis of the exhibition, with a full introductory text, 'Vincent van Gogh in zijn Hollandse jaren', Rijksmuseum Vincent van Gogh, Amsterdam 1980–81. (English summary of text.) The accent is on the Dutch artists. Only five of the French artists, and none of the Belgian and English artists, in whom Vincent was interested at this time, are represented.

Belgian periods
Marc Edo Tralbaut, *Vincent van Gogh in zijn Antwerpse periode*, Amsterdam 1948.

'Van Gogh en Belgique', exhibition catalogue with introduction by A.M. Hammacher and full biographical notes on artists, 'Les Affinités de Vincent van Gogh', by Gisèle Ollinger-Zinque, Musée des Beaux-Arts, Mons 1980.

Paris period
Bogomila Welsh-Ovcharov, Vincent van Gogh: his Paris Period, diss. Utrecht, 1976. The first investigation of the only remaining poorly documented period in his life.

Arles, Saint-Rémy and Auvers periods
W. Scherfon and W.J. de Gruyter, *Vincent van Gogh's Great Period, Arles, Saint-Rémy and Auvers-sur-Oise*, Amsterdam 1937.

Charles Mauron, *Van Gogh au seuil de la Provence: Arles, de février à octobre 1888*, Saint-Rémy-de-Provence 1959. Mauron (1899–1966), pioneer of the psychoanalytical method in literary criticism (Mallarmé, Racine, Baudelaire), also concerned himself with visual art, and with Van Gogh in particular. His profound vision of Vincent in Arles, and his lecture 'Vincent et Théo van Gogh: une symbiose', together with his 'Notes sur la structure de l'inconscient chez Vincent van Gogh', in *Psyche* (1953), 75–78, have long influenced me more

than the work of any other critic.
(A.M.H.)

'Van Gogh et les peintres d'Auvers-sur-Oise', exhibition catalogue with texts by Germain Bazin and Paul Gachet *fils*, detailed catalogue by Albert Chatelet, note on Vincent's last self-portrait by Michel Florisoone, Orangerie des Tuileries, Paris 1954.

Stylistic and technical research

Carlo Derkert, 'Theory and Practice in Van Gogh's Dutch Painting', *Kunsthistorisk Tidskrift*, XV, 3/4 (1946).

Mark Buchmann, *Die Farbe bei Vincent van Gogh*, Zürich 1948.

A.M. Hammacher, *Les Grands Maîtres du dessin: van Gogh*, Milan 1953.

Douglas Cooper, *Drawings and Watercolours by Vincent van Gogh*, Basle 1954, New York 1955.

Kurt Badt, *Die Farbenlehre van Goghs*, Cologne 1961.

A.M. Hammacher, 'Van Gogh's Life in his Drawings', 'Van Gogh's Relationship with Space', in exhibition catalogue 'Van Gogh', Marlborough Fine Art, London 1962.

'Vincent van Gogh dessinateur', exhibition catalogue with essays by Ir.Dr. V.W. van Gogh and A.M. Hammacher, Institut néerlandais, Paris 1966.

Matthias Arnold, Duktus und Bildform bei van Gogh, diss. Heidelberg 1973. A rare analysis of Van Gogh's brush stroke.

Illnesses

A.J. Westerman Holsteyn, 'Die psychologische Entwicklung Vincent van Goghs', *Images*, X, 4 (1924).

A. Hutter, 'De vijf diagnoses van de ziekte van Vincent van Gogh', *Nederlandse Tijdschrift voor Geneeskunde*, 7 (1931).

Victor Doiteau and Edgar Leroy, *La Folie de Vincent van Gogh*, with preface by Paul Gachet, Paris 1928.

Ryuzaburo Shikiba, *Van Gogh, his Life and Psychosis*, Tokyo 1932.

J. Beer, Essai sur les rapports de l'art et de la maladie de Vincent van Gogh, diss. Strasbourg 1936.

Antonin Artaud, *Van Gogh – le suicidé de la société*, Paris 1947.

G. Kraus, *De verhouding van Theo en Vincent van Gogh*, Amsterdam 1954. (Earlier version, in English: 'The relation of Theo and Vincent van Gogh', in 'Vincent van Gogh en de psychiatrie', *Psychiatrische en Neurologische Bladen*, XLV [1941].)

Françoise Minkowska, *Van Gogh. Sa vie, sa maladie et son œuvre*, preface by Eugène Minkowski, Paris 1963. Although there have been criticisms of these studies, they constitute perhaps the closest psychoanalytical approach to Van Gogh, not clinically objective but personal, emotional, and with flashes of rare lucidity.

Marc Edo Tralbaut, 'Vincent van Gogh chez Aesculape – quelques apports nouveaux à la connaissance de la santé, la maladie et la mort du grand peintre', *Revue des lettres et des arts dans leurs rapports avec les sciences et la médecine* (Dec. 1957).

Marcel Heiman, 'Psychoanalytical Observations on the Last Paintings and Suicide of Vincent van Gogh', accompanied by critical observations by Arthur F. Valenstein and Anne Styles Wylie, *International Journal of Psychoanalysis*, 57 (1976), 71–79, 81–84.

Fernand Destaing, 'Le Soleil et l'orage ou la maladie de van Gogh', in his *La Souffrance et le génie*, Paris 1980. A recent reversion, with some revisions, to the epileptic diagnosis argued by Henri Gastaut in *Annales medico-psychologiques* (1956) and Jean Delay in *Congrès de médecins aliénistes et neurologues de France et de langue française*, Liège 1954.

Peter Gorsen, *Kunst und Krankheit: Metamorphosen der ästhetischen Einbildungskraft*, Frankfurt am Main 1980. A useful recent survey of the 'art and illness' issue in general.

Miscellaneous

C.S. Chatham, The Role of Vincent van Gogh's Copies in the Development of his Art, diss. Harvard 1960.

Fritz Novotny, 'Die Bilder van Goghs nach fremden Vorbildern', in *Festschrift Kurt Badt*, Berlin 1961.

Vincent: the Bulletin of the Rijksmuseum Vincent van Gogh (1970–76). A valuable source for points of detail concerning Vincent and his family. Unfortunately this quarterly closed after 16 numbers.

Bogomila Welsh-Ovcharov, *The Early Works of Charles Angrand and his Contact with Vincent van Gogh*, Utrecht and The Hague 1971.

'Les Sources de l'inspiration de van Gogh', exhibition catalogue with texts by Sadi de Gorter and Ir.Dr. V.W. van Gogh, Institut néerlandais, Paris 1972.

Mark Roskill, *Van Gogh, Gauguin and the Impressionist Circle*, London and Greenwich, Conn., 1976.

Evert van Uitert, 'Van Gogh in anticipation of Paul Gauguin', 'Van Gogh and Paul Gauguin in Competition', 'Vincent's Original Contribution', *Simiolus*, 10/11 (1978, 1979, 1980). Three fully documented studies.

'Vorstelijke boekbanden uit de Koninklijke Bibliotheek', exhibition catalogue with scholarly text by J. Storm van Leeuwen, Royal Library, The Hague 1978. Describes Vincent's grandfather Willem Carbentus as one of the most important nineteenth-century bookbinders in The Hague; the first to mark his work with a personal stamp (from 1816 on).

'Japanese Prints Collected by Vincent van Gogh', exhibition catalogue with essays by Willem van Gulik and Fred Orton and 352 entries, Rijksmuseum Vincent van Gogh, Amsterdam 1978.

Charles Michael Peglau, Image and Structure in Van Gogh's Later Paintings, diss. Pittsburgh 1979. Remarkable analysis of the problems of pictorial space, with references to literary descriptions of landscape (Flaubert, *Bouvard et Pécuchet*).

'Les Amis de van Gogh', exhibition catalogue, compiled and with an essay by A.M. Hammacher, Institut néerlandais, Paris 1960. Includes several of the Cloisonnist artists featured in the 1981 Toronto exhibition.

'Vincent van Gogh and the Birth of Cloisonism', exhibition catalogue compiled and with text by Bogomila Welsh-Ovcharov, Art Gallery of Toronto 1981. The exhibition, also shown in Amsterdam with a different arrangement in 1981, presented about a hundred masterpieces to illuminate the comparatively new art-historical issue of Cloisonnism, which in turn is closely allied to Japonism.

Linda Nochlin, 'Van Gogh, Renouard and the Weavers' Crisis in Lyon: the Status of a Social Issue in the Art of the Later Nineteenth Century', in *Art the Ape of Nature: Studies in Honour of H.W. Janson*, New York 1981. A welcome study of art and the impact of industrialization; omits only the importance to Van Gogh of Brontë's *Shirley* and the walk to Courrières.

LIST OF ILLUSTRATIONS

PLATES

All works of art listed without an artist's name are by Vincent van Gogh (1853–90). The medium, where not specified, is oil on canvas. Dimensions are given in centimetres and inches, height before width. References to the catalogue by J.B. de la Faille, *The Works of Vincent van Gogh*, revised edition, Amsterdam 1970, are given in parentheses thus (F827).

ABBREVIATIONS

NMVG: Collection National Museum Vincent van Gogh, Amsterdam (Rijksmuseum Vincent van Gogh).
SMKM: Collection State Museum Kröller-Müller, Otterlo, The Netherlands (Rijksmuseum Kröller-Müller).

1 Vincent van Gogh as a boy, 1866. NMVG.
2 Vincent's grandfather, Vincent van Gogh. NMVG.
3 Vincent's grandmother, Elisabeth Huberta Vrijdag. NMVG.
4 Town Hall of Zundert. NMVG.
5 Church of Zundert. NMVG.
6 Theodorus van Gogh (1822–85). NMVG.
7 Anna Cornelia van Gogh-Carbentus (1819–1907). NMVG.
8 The house where Vincent and Theo were born. NMVG.
9 Interior of Goupil & Cie, The Hague. NMVG.
10 Vincent van Gogh (1820–88). NMVG.
11 Rembrandt van Rijn (1606–69). *Burgomaster Jan Six*, 1647. Etching 24.5 × 19.1 (9⅝ × 7½). British Museum, London.
12 The Trippenhuis, Amsterdam. Photo Rijksmuseum, Amsterdam.
13 Henri de Braekeleer (1840–88). *Staalmeesterszaal, in the Trippenhuis*, 1883. Drawing 150 × 240 (59 × 94½). Rijksmuseum Stichting, Amsterdam.
14 August Jernberg (1826–96). *Nightwatch in the Trippenhuis*, 1895. 65 × 81 (25½ × 31¾). Malmö Museum.
15 Vincent van Gogh, *c.* 1872. NMVG.
16 Theo van Gogh, *c.* 1888–90. NMVG.
17 Emile Wauters (1846–1933). *Hugo van der Goes at the Red Monastery* (detail), 1872. 186 × 275 (73¼ × 108¼). Musées Royaux des Beaux-Arts de Belgique, Brussels. Photo ACL Brussels.
18 French School (formerly attrib. Philippe de Champaigne). *Woman in Mourning*, 17th c. 61 × 51 (24 × 20). Louvre, Paris. Photo Agraci.
19 Charles Bargue (d. 1883). *Cours de Dessin*, I 39. Edition Goupil. NMVG.
20 George Henry Boughton (1833–1905). *Early Puritans of New England Going to Worship Armed to Protect Themselves from Indians and Wild Beasts*, 1867. Engraving 29.5 × 50 (11¾ × 19⅝).

21 George Henry Boughton (1833–1905). *The Landing of the Pilgrim Fathers*, 1869. 78 × 103 (30¾ × 40½). Sheffield City Art Galleries.
22 George Henry Boughton (1833–1905). *Deserted*, 1859. From *The Christmas Art Annual*, 1904.
23 John Everett Millais (1829–96). *Chill October*, 1870. 140.9 × 186.7 (55½ × 73½). Private Collection, currently on loan to Perth Museum and Art Gallery.
24 John Everett Millais (1829–96). *The Lost Piece of Silver (The Lost Mite)*. Watercolour 14 × 10.6 (5½ × 4½). Courtesy of the Fogg Art Museum, Harvard University, Bequest – Grenville L. Winthrop.
25 Mathijs (Thijs) Maris (1839–1917). *Souvenir of Amsterdam*, 1871. 46.5 × 35 (18¼ × 13¾). Rijksmuseum, Amsterdam.
26 Rembrandt van Rijn (1606–69). *The Men of Emmaus*, 1848. Oil on wood 68 × 65 (26¾ × 25½). Louvre, Paris. Photo Agraci.
27 Jacob van Ruisdael (1628/9–82). *The Copse*. 68 × 82 (26¾ × 32¼). Louvre, Paris. Photo Agraci.
28 Adriaen van Ostade (1610–85). *Family Portrait*, 1654. Oil on wood 70 × 88 (27½ × 34¾). Louvre, Paris. Photo Agraci.
29 Jules Breton (1827–1906). *Blessing of the Harvest in Artois*, 1857. 32 × 130 (12½ × 51¼). Musée National, Compiègne.
30 Gustave Doré (1832–83). *Yard at Newgate Gaol*, 1872. Engraving 24.5 × 19.1 (9⅝ × 7½). NMVG.
31 Anonymous. *The Mineshaft (Rescue Team Going Down after a Firedamp Explosion)*. Engraving 33.9 × 24 (13¼ × 9½). NMVG.
32 Auguste Lançon (1836–87). *Men Shovelling Snow*, 1881. Engraving 15.9 × 23.7 (6¼ × 9¼). NMVG.
33 Hubert von Herkomer (1849–1914). *Sunday at Chelsea Hospital*, 1871. Engraving 34 × 26.2 (13½ × 10¼). NMVG.
34 Edwin Buckman (1841–1930). *People Waiting for Ration Tickets in Paris*, 1870. Engraving 17 × 24.8 (6¾ × 9¾). NMVG.
35 Luke Fildes (1844–1927). *Homeless and Hungry*, 1877. Engraving 31.6 × 40.3 (12½ × 15¾). NMVG.
36 Luke Fildes (1844–1927). *The Empty Chair, Gad's Hill, June 9th, 1870*. Engraving 30 × 49.8 (11¾ × 19½). NMVG.
37 Matthew White Ridley (1836–88). *Heads of the People: The Miner*, 1876. Engraving 32.8 × 25.1 (13 × 9¾). NMVG.
38 Ary Scheffer (1795–1858). *Christ on the Mount of Olives*, 1839. 140 × 98 (55¼ × 38½). Dordrechts Museum, Dordrecht.

39 Ary Scheffer (1795–1858). *Christus Consolator (Christ the Comforter)*, 1837. 68 × 90 (26¾ × 35½). Dordrechts Museum, Dordrecht.
40 Attributed to Rembrandt (1606–69). *Christ with Mary and Martha (The House at Bethany)*, *c.* 1650. Pen and sepia wash 18.4 × 26.2 (7¼ × 10¼). British Museum, London.
41 Marinewerf (dockyard commandant's house), Amsterdam, 1890. Photo Historisch Topografische Atlas, Gemeentelijke Archiefdienst, Amsterdam.
42 Vice-Admiral Johannes van Gogh. NMVG.
43 The Rev. Johannes P. Stricker. NMVG.
44 Oosterbegraafplaats, Oosterpark, Amsterdam. Photo Historisch Topografische Atlas, Gemeentelijke Archiefdienst, Amsterdam.
45 Marcasse (Pit 7), Wasmes. NMVG.
46 *Coal-heaver*, July–Aug. 1879. Chalk and pencil 49.5 × 27.5 (19½ × 10¾). SMKM (F827).
47 Vincent's psalter. Photo Jean-Pierre Landenberg.
48 *The Potato Eaters*, 1885. 82 × 114 (32¼ × 45). NMVG (F82).
49 Kee Vos-Stricker, 1879. NMVG.
50 *Corner of a Garden with an Arbour*, June 1881. Watercolour 44.5 × 56.5 (17½ × 22¼). SMKM (F902).
51 *Shacks*, 1881. Pen and ink 45.5 × 61 (18 × 24). Museum Boymans-van Beuningen, Rotterdam (F842).
52 *Old Peasant by the Fire*, Nov. 1881. Charcoal 56 × 45 (22 × 17¾). SMKM (F868).
53 *Worn Out*, 1881. Watercolour 23.5 × 31 (9¼ × 12¼). Foundation P. and N. de Boer, Amsterdam (F863).
54 *The Great Lady*, 1882. Pen and pencil 19 × 10.5 (7½ × 4¼). Letter to Theo. NMVG.
55 *Girl (Sien's Daughter with Shawl: Left Profile)*, Jan. 1883. Chalk and wash 43.5 × 25 (17¼ × 9¾). SMKM (F1007).
56 *Weeping Woman (Woman with her Head in her Hands, Seated on a Basket)*, 1883. Chalk 50.1 × 31.7 (19¾ × 12½). The Art Institute of Chicago, given in memory of Tiffany Blake (F1069).
57 *Sien with a Cigar, Sitting on the Ground by a Stove*, Apr. 1882. Pencil and chalk 45.5 × 56 (18 × 22). SMKM (F898).
58 Jules Breton (1827–1906). *The Harvest*, before 1885. 23 × 38 (9 × 15). Rijksmuseum H.W. Mesdag, The Hague.
59 Anton Mauve (1838–88). *Digging Potatoes*. Watercolour 33 × 44.5 (13 × 17½). Rijksmuseum-Stichting, Amsterdam.
60 Jean-François Millet (1814–75). *Fisherman's Wife*, *c.* 1849. 47.5 × 38.5 (18¾ × 15¼). Rijksmuseum H.W. Mesdag, The Hague.
61 Jacob Maris (1837–99). *Evening on the Dunes (Fisherman's Wife, Seated)*.

Watercolour 42 × 30 (16½ × 11¾). Rijksmuseum H.W. Mesdag, The Hague.

62 Jules Dupré (1811–89). *Evening* (exh. Hague Academy of Fine Arts, 1882). 46.5 × 56.6 (18¼ × 22¼). Rijksmuseum H.W. Mesdag, The Hague.

63 Charles-François Daubigny (1817–78). *Sunset at Villerville*, 1866. 55 × 100 (21¾ × 39¼). Rijksmuseum H.W. Mesdag, The Hague.

64 Anton Mauve (1838–88). *Sale of Wood*, c. 1881. Watercolour 33.5 × 50.5 (13¼ × 20). Rijksmuseum H.W. Mesdag, The Hague.

65 *Roofs seen from the Artist's Attic Window*, July 1882. Watercolour 39 × 55 (15¼ × 21¾). Private Collection (F943).

66 *Road at Loosduinen*, 1882. Chalk and pen 24 × 34 (9½ × 13½). NMVG (F1089).

67 *Gas Holders (The Gas Tanks of the Hague)*, Mar. 1882. Chalk and pencil 24 × 33.5 (9½ × 13¼). NMVG (F924).

68 *Factory in The Hague (Sterkman's Factory)*, Mar. 1882. Pencil and wash 24 × 33 (9½ × 13). Private Collection (F925).

69 *Entrance to the Pawnshop, The Hague*, Mar. 1882. Pencil and pen 24 × 34 (9½ × 13½). NMVG.

70 *Bridge at Nieuw Amsterdam (Drenthe)*, Nov. 1883. Watercolour 38.5 × 81 (15¼ × 32). Groninger Museum, Groningen (F1098).

71 *Vicarage Garden with Figures*, Oct.– Nov. 1885. Watercolour 38 × 49 (15 × 19¼). Private Collection (F1234).

72 *Work in the Fields*, Oct. 1883. Pencil and pen 31 × 37.5 (12¼ × 14¾). Courtesy, Museum of Fine Arts, Boston, gift of John Goelet (F1095).

73 *Avenue of Willows with Shepherd and Peasant Woman*, spring 1884. Pencil and pen 39.5 × 54.5 (15½ × 21½). NMVG (F1240).

74 *The Vicarage at Nuenen*, autumn 1885. 33 × 45 (13 × 17). NMVG (F182).

75 The vicarage at Nuenen. NMVG.

76 *Lane of Poplars at Nuenen*, autumn 1885. 78 × 97.5 (30¾ × 38½). Museum Boymans-van Beuningen, Rotterdam (F45).

77 *Coming out of Church in Nuenen*, Jan. 1884. 41 × 32 (16¼ × 12½). NMVG (F25).

78 Nuenen church. NMVG.

79 *Weaver, Facing Front*, July 1884. 47.5 × 61 (19 × 24). Museum Boymans-van Beuningen, Rotterdam (F27).

80 *Woman Spinning*, 1885. 41 × 32.5 (16¼ × 12¾). NMVG (F36).

81 Anton van Rappard (1858–92). *The Brickworks*, 1885. 24 × 44 (9½ × 17¼). Centraal Museum, Utrecht.

82 Constantin Meunier (1831–1905). *The Brickmakers*. Oil on panel 46 × 70 (18 × 27½). Musée Constantin Meunier, Ixelles/Bruxelles.

83 *Peasant Woman Stooping*, Aug. 1885. Chalk 52.5 × 43.5 (20¾ × 17¼). SMKM (F1269).

84 *The Reaper with Cap, Moving to the Right*, Aug. 1885. Chalk 43 × 55 (17 × 21¾). NMVG (F1317).

85 Anton van Rappard (1858–92). *Girl Holding a Brick Mould*, 1885. Pencil and charcoal 75.8 × 50 (30 × 19¾). Rijksprentenkabinet, Rijksmuseum, Amsterdam.

86 Anton Mauve (1838–88). *The Potato-digger*. Chalk 19 × 26.3 (7½ × 10¼). Rijksprentenkabinet, Rijksmuseum, Amsterdam.

87 Georg Hendrik Breitner (1857–1923). *Couple Walking*. 98 × 73 (38½ × 28¾). Present whereabouts unknown.

88 Frans Hals (c. 1580–1666) and Pieter Codde (1599–1678). *The Company of Captain Reynier Reael . . .* , 1633–36. 209 × 429 (82¼ × 169). Rijksmuseum, Amsterdam.

89 Rembrandt van Rijn (1606–69). *The Jewish Bride*, c. 1666. 121.5 × 166.5 (47¾ × 65½). Rijksmuseum, Amsterdam.

90 Jozef Israëls (1824–1911). *Alone in the World*, 1878. 39 × 90 (15¼ × 35½). Rijksmuseum, Amsterdam.

91 The *Maris Stella* window, Andrieskerk, Antwerp, 16th century. Photo de Schutter.

92 The house where Vincent lodged, in Beeldekenstraat (Rue des Images). NMVG.

93 Académie Royale des Beaux-Arts, Antwerp. NMVG.

94 Henri Leys (1815–69). *Het Steen, Antwerp*. 41 × 114 (16 × 45). Musée Royal des Beaux-Arts, Antwerp. Photo ACL Brussels.

95 *The Marketplace, Antwerp*, 18 Dec. 1885. Chalk 22.5 × 30 (8¾ × 11¾). NMVG (F1352).

96 Charles de Groux (1825–70). *Benedicite*, 1861. 80 × 154 (31½ × 60¾). Musées Royaux de Belgique, Brussels. Photo ACL Brussels.

97 Henri de Braekeleer (1840–88). *Baron Leys's Dining-room*, 1869. 67 × 84 (26½ × 33). Musée Royal des Beaux-Arts, Antwerp. Photo ACL Brussels.

98 Peter Paul Rubens (1577–1640). *St Theresa Saving Bernardo de Mendoza from Purgatory* (detail), c. 1638. Oil on wood 194 × 139 (76¼ × 54¾). Musée Royal des Beaux-Arts, Antwerp.

99 *Head of a Woman*, Dec. 1885. 35 × 24 (13¾ × 9½). NMVG (F206).

100 *Portrait of a Woman*, early Dec. 1885. Charcoal and chalk 50.6 × 39.4 (20 × 15½). NMVG (F1357).

101 Eugène Delacroix (1798–1863). *Study for the Panel 'War' on the ceiling of the Salon du Roi, Palais Bourbon*, 1833–38. Pen 21.6 × 41.3 (8½ × 16¼). Cabinet des dessins, Louvre, Paris.

102 *Women Dancing*, early Dec. 1885. Chalk 9.3 × 16.4 (3¾ × 6½). NMVG (F1350B).

103 *Female Nude*, Jan. 1886. Chalk 19.5 × 11 (7¾ × 4¼). NMVG (F1353).

104 Oko Kunisada II (1823–80). *Two Girls Bathing*, 1868. Colour woodblock 37.4 × 25.1 (14¾ × 10). NMVG.

105 *Skull with Burning Cigarette*, Dec. 1885. 32.5 × 24 (12¾ × 9½). NMVG (F212).

106 Félicien Rops (1833–98). *The Husband's Train; The Death of the Sinner*. Etching, pencil drawing at right of plate, 12.8 × 19 (5 × 7½). Musée Félicien Rops, Namur.

107 *Hanging Skeleton and Black Cat*, Dec. 1885–Jan. 1886. Pencil 10.5 × 6 (4¼ × 2¼). NMVG (F1361).

108 Rue Lepic, Montmartre, late 19th c. Photo L.L. Roger-Viollet.

109 Salon of the painter Fernand Cormon, Paris. Photo H. Roger-Viollet.

110 Jean-François Raffaelli (1850–1924). *View of Montmartre*. Etching 20.7 × 28.1 (8 × 11). NMVG.

111 John P. Russell (1858–1931). *Vincent van Gogh*, Nov. 1886. 60 × 45 (23½ × 17¾). NMVG.

112 Meyer de Haan (1852–95). *Theo van Gogh*, c. 1889. Crayon 20.8 × 14.3 (8¼ × 5¾). NMVG.

113 *Old Boots (A Pair of Boots)*, late 1886. 37.5 × 45.5 (14¾ × 18). NMVG (F255).

114 Henri de Toulouse-Lautrec (1864–1901). *Vincent van Gogh*, 1886. Pastel 53 × 44 (21¼ × 17¾). NMVG.

115 *Self-portrait with Easel*, early 1888. 65 × 50.5 (25½ × 20). NMVG (F522).

116 *Self-portrait with Grey Felt Hat*, summer 1887. 41 × 32 (16 × 12½). Stedelijk Museum, Amsterdam (F295).

117 *Self-portrait*, autumn 1887. 47 × 35 (18½ × 13¾). Louvre, Paris (F320). Photo Lauros-Giraudon.

118 Claude Monet (1840–1926). *Four Boats in Winter Quarters, Etretat*, 1885. 26 × 32 (10¼ × 12½). Courtesy of The Art Institute of Chicago, Charles H. and Mary F.S. Worcester Collection.

119 Louis Anquetin (1861–1932). *Avenue de Clichy*, 1887. 69 × 53 (27 × 21). Courtesy Wadsworth Atheneum, Hartford, Ella Gallup Sumner and Mary Catlin Sumner Collection.

120 Adolphe Monticelli (1824–86). *Vase of Flowers*, 1875–80. 51 × 39 (20 × 15¼). NMVG.

121 Paul Signac (1863–1935). *Still-life with Maupassant's Book 'Au Soleil'*, dated 1883. 32.5 × 46.5 (12¾ × 18¼). Nationalgalerie, Staatliche Museen, Preussischer Kulturbesitz, Berlin (West).

122 *Plaster Statuette*, 1886–87. 40.5 × 27 (16 × 10½). NMVG (F2169).

123 *Nude Woman on a Bed*, 1887. 59.5 × 73 (23½ × 28¾). Copyright, The Barnes Foundation, Merion Station, Pa., USA (F330).

124 *The Italian Woman, with Carnations (La Segatori)*, winter 1887–88. 81 × 60 (32 × 23½). Louvre, Paris. (F381). Photo Giraudon.

125 *Asnières: Bernard and Van Gogh*, early 1887. NMVG.

126 *Riverside Walk near Asnières*, early summer 1887. 49 × 66 (19¼ × 26). NMVG (F299).

127 *Factory near the Pont de Clichy, Asnières*, summer 1887. 46.5 × 54 (18¼ × 21¼). Copyright, The Barnes Foundation, Merion Station, Pa., USA. (F318).

128 Bridge at Asnières, late 19th century. Photo C.A.P. Roger-Viollet.

129 Emile Bernard (1868–1941). *Bridge at Asnières*, autumn 1887. 45.9 × 54.2 (18½ × 21¼). Collection, The Museum of Modern Art, New York, Grace Rainey Rogers Fund.

130 *Restaurant de la Sirène, Asnières*, early summer 1887. 57 × 68 (22½ × 26¾). Louvre, Paris (F313). Photo Giraudon.

131 *Bathing Place on the Seine, Asnières*, summer 1887. 19 × 27 (7½ × 10½). From the collection of Mr and Mrs Paul Mellon, Upperville, Virginia (F311).

132 *Factories at Asnières Seen from the Quai de Clichy*, summer 1887. 54 × 72 (21¼ × 28½). The St Louis Art Museum, Gift of Mrs Mark C. Steinberg (F317).

133 Utagawa Kuniyoshi (1797–1861). *Portrait of a Woman Viewing Flowers, with an Inset of Local Industry, Bitchu Province*, 1852. Colour woodblock 37.5 × 25.5 (14¾ × 10). NMVG.

134 Utagawa Hiroshige (1797–1858). *Plum Trees in Flower*, 1857. Colour woodblock 35 × 22 (13¾ × 8¾). NMVG.

135 Utagawa Hiroshige (1797–1858). *Shower on the Ohashi Bridge near Ataka*, 1857. Colour woodblock 33.8 × 21.8 (13¼ × 8½). NMVG.

136 *Flowering Plum Tree*, first half 1887. 55 × 46 (21¾ × 18). NMVG (F371).

137 *The Bridge in the Rain*, summer 1887. 73 × 54 (28¾ × 21¼). NMVG (F372).

138 *Japonaiserie: Oiran*, summer 1887. 105 × 61 (41¼ × 24). NMVG (F373).

139 *Père Tanguy*, autumn 1887. 65 × 51 (25½ × 20). Stavros S. Niarchos Collection (F364). Photo A.C. Cooper.

140 *Self-portrait*, Sept. 1888. 62 × 52 (24½ × 20½). Courtesy of the Fogg Art Museum, Harvard University, Bequest. Collection of Maurice Wertheim, Class of 1906. (F476).

141 *Harvest, La Crau, with Montmajour in the Background*, June 1888. 72.5 × 92 (28½ × 36¼). NMVG (F412).

142 *Boats with Men Unloading Sand*, Aug. 1888. 55 × 66 (21¾ × 26). Folkwang Museum, Essen (F499).

143 *The Poet's Garden: Sunshine in the Park*, Sept. 1888. 73 × 92 (28¾ × 36¼). Courtesy of The Art Institute of Chicago, Mr and Mrs Lewis L. Coburn Memorial Collection (F468).

144 *The Stevedores*, end Aug. 1888. 53.5 × 64 (21 × 25¼). Thyssen-Bornemisza Collection, Lugano-Castagnola (F438).

145 Sunflowers on the road from Arles to Tarascon, 1981. Photo Harold Chapman.

146 *The Road to Tarascon: Sky with Sun*, Aug. 1888. Ink on paper 24.5 × 32 (9½ × 12½). The Justin K. Thannhauser Collection, The Solomon R. Guggenheim Museum, New York (F1502a).

147 Paul Gauguin (1848–1903). *Vincent Painting Sunflowers*, autumn 1888. 73 × 92 (28¾ × 36¼). NMVG.

148 *Fourteen Sunflowers*, summer 1888. 93 × 73 (36½ × 28¼). National Gallery, London (F454).

149 *A Garden*, July 1888. Pen 49 × 61 (19¼ × 24). Oskar Reinhart Collection, Winterthur (F1455).

150 *Sailing Boats Coming Ashore*, 2nd half June 1888. Sepia drawing 24 × 32 (9½ × 12½). Musées Royaux des Beaux-Arts de Belgique, Brussels (F1430b).

151 *Street at Saintes-Maries-de-la-Mer*, 2nd half June 1888. Pen and ink 24 × 31 (9½ × 12½). Collection, The Museum of Modern Art, New York, Bequest of Abby Aldrich Rockefeller (F1435).

152 *Patience Escalier*, Aug. 1888. 69 × 56 (27¼ × 22). Stavros S. Niarchos Collection (F444). Photo A.C. Cooper.

153 *La Berceuse: Mme Augustine Roulin*, Jan. 1889. 92 × 73 (36¼ × 28¾). SMKM (F504).

154 *Joseph Roulin Seated at a Table*, Aug. 1888. 81 × 65 (32 × 25½). Museum of Fine Arts, Boston, gift of Robert Treat Paine II (F432).

155 *L'Arlésienne: Madame Ginoux*, Nov. 1888. 90 × 72 (35½ × 28¼). The Metropolitan Museum of Art, Bequest of Samuel A. Lewisohn, 1951, New York (F488).

156 *The Poet: Eugène Boch*, Sept. 1888. 60 × 45 (23½ × 17¾). Louvre, Paris (F462). Photo Giraudon.

157 Paul Gauguin (1848–1903). *Vineyard at Arles with Breton Women*, 1888. 75.5 × 92.5 (29 × 36½). Ordrupgaardsamlingen, Copenhagen.

158 *Memory of the Garden at Etten*, Nov. 1888. 73.5 × 92 (29 × 36½). Hermitage, Leningrad (F496).

159 *Gauguin's Chair, Candle and Books (The Empty Chair)*, Dec. 1888. 90.5 × 72 (35¾ × 28¼). NMVG (F499).

160 *Vincent's Chair with his Pipe and Tobacco Pouch*, Dec. 1888–Jan. 1889. 93 × 73.5 (36¼ × 28¾). National Gallery, London (F498).

161 The Maison Jaune, Place Lamartine, Arles. NMVG.

162 *Vincent's House on the Place Lamartine, Arles (The Yellow House)*, Sept. 1888. 76 × 94 (30 × 37). NMVG (F464).

163 *Vincent's Bedroom in the Maison Jaune*, Oct. 1888. 79 × 90 (28¼ × 35½). NMVG (F482).

164 *The Night Café*, Sept. 1888. 70 × 89 (27½ × 35). Yale University Art Gallery, Bequest of Stephen Carlton Clark, B.A. 1903 (F463).

165 *Self-portrait with Bandaged Ear*, Jan. 1889. 60 × 49 (23½ × 19¼). Home House Society Trustees, Courtauld Institute Galleries, London (F527).

166 *Still-life on Table, with Book, Pipe, Candle, Letter and Onions*, Jan. 1889. 50 × 64 (19¾ × 25¼). SMKM (F604).

167 *The Hospital Ward, Arles*, Apr.–Oct. 1889. 74 × 92 (29¼ × 36¼). Oskar Reinhart Collection, Winterthur (F646).

168 Courtyard of the Arles hospital, 1981. Photo Harold Chapman.

169 *Courtyard of the Arles Hospital*, Apr.–May 1889. Pen and pencil 45.5 × 59 (18 × 23¼). NMVG (F1467).

170 *Two Poplars on a Road Through the Hills*, Oct. 1889. 61 × 45.5 (24 × 18). The Cleveland Museum of Art, Bequest of Leonard C. Hanna, Jr. (F638).

171 *Olive Trees*, Sept.–Nov. 1889. 72.5 × 92 (28½ × 36¼). Private Collection (F712).

172 *Undergrowth (Ivy)*, July 1889. 74 × 92 (29¼ × 36¼). NMVG (F746).

173 *Pine Woods at Dusk*, Oct.–Dec. 1889. 92 × 73 (36¼ × 28¾). Rijksmuseum Kröller-Müller, Otterlo (F652).

174 *Self-portrait*, Sept. 1889. 51 × 45 (20 × 17¾). Nationalgalerie, Oslo. (F528).

175 Fountain in the garden of the Hôpital van Gogh, Saint-Rémy, 1981. Photo Harold Chapman.

176 *Fountain in the Garden of the Hôpital Saint-Paul, Saint-Rémy*, May–June 1889. Ink 48 × 45 (19 × 18). NMVG (F1531).

177 *Poppies in a Field*, Apr. 1890. 71 × 91 (28 × 35¾). Kunsthalle, Bremen (F581).

178 *Wheatfield Behind Hôpital Saint-Paul*, June–Sept. 1889. 72 × 92 (28¼ × 36¼). SMKM (F617).

179 *Enclosure Behind Hôpital Saint-Paul with Rising Sun*, Nov. 1889. Chalk and pen 47 × 62 (18½ × 24½). Staatliche Graphische Sammlung, Munich (F1552).

180 *Wheatfield with Peasant Bearing a Sheaf*, Oct. 1889. 73 × 92 (29 × 36¼). Indianapolis Museum of Art, Gift in memory of Daniel W. and Elizabeth C. Marmon (F641).

181 *Study of Arum Lilies*, Apr.–May 1890. Pen 31 × 41 (12¼ × 16¼). NMVG (F1613).

182 *Sower in the Rain*, Jan.–Apr. 1890. Pencil and chalk 23.5 × 31.5 (9¼ × 12½). Folkwang Museum, Essen (F1550).

183 *The Road-menders*, Dec. 1889. 73.5 × 92.5 (28 × 36½). The Phillips Collection, Washington DC. (F658).

184 Boulevard Mirabeau, Saint-Rémy-de-Provence. NMVG.

185 *Self-portrait*, Sept. 1889. 65 × 54 (25½ × 21¼). Louvre, Paris (F627). Photo Agraci.

186 *Winter Landscape with Figures*, Jan.–Apr. 1890. Pencil 24 × 32 (9½ × 12½). NMVG (F1592r).

187 *Peasant Family by the Fireside*, May 1890. Chalk. 23.5 × 32 (9½ × 12½). NMVG (F1608r).

188 *Night: the Watch (after Millet)*, Oct. 1889. 72.5 × 92 (28½ × 36¼). NMVG (F647).

189 *Study of Nine Peasants, Two Diggers, Two Figures with Wheelbarrows*, early 1890. Pencil 24 × 31.5 (9½ × 12½). NMVG (F1599r).

190 *On the Road*, early 1890. Pencil 24.5 × 25 (9½ × 9¾). NMVG (F1596v).

191 *Hands; a Digger*, early 1890. Chalk 23.5 × 32 (9¼ × 12¾). NMVG (F1608v).

192 Rembrandt van Rijn (1606–69). *Raising of Lazarus*, c. 1632. Etching 36.8 × 25.7 (14½ × 10). British Museum, London.

193 Eugène Delacroix (1798–1863). *Christ on the Lake of Genesareth*, 1854. 50 × 60 (20 × 24). Private Collection.

194 *Raising of Lazarus (after Rembrandt)*, May 1890. 48.5 × 63 (19 × 24¾). NMVG (F677).

195 *Pietà (after Delacroix)*, Sept. 1889. 73 × 60.5 (28¾ × 23¾). NMVG (F630).

196 Pierre Puvis de Chavannes (1824–98). *Hope* (second version), 1872. 70.7 × 82 (27¾ × 32¼). Louvre, Paris. Photo Giraudon.

197 Pierre Puvis de Chavannes (1824–98). *Inter artes et naturam*, 1890. 295 × 830 (116¼ × 326¾). Musée de Rouen.

198 *Sketch from a Letter to Willemien* (W22), 4/5 June 1890. Pen 6.5 × 17 (2½ × 6¾). NMVG.

199 Pierre Puvis de Chavannes (1824–98). *Princess Maria Cantacuzène*, 1883. 78 × 45 (30¾ × 18). Musée des Beaux-Arts, Lyon.

200 *Young Girl in White Against a Background of Wheat*, 2nd half June 1890. 66 × 45 (26 × 17¾). National Gallery of Art, Washington, Chester Dale Collection 1962 (F788).

INDEX